W9-CZU-839

MARKETING

MARKETING

Real People, Real Choices

FOURTH EDITION

Michael R. Solomon
AUBURN UNIVERSITY

Greg W. Marshall
ROLLINS COLLEGE

Elnora W. Stuart
THE AMERICAN UNIVERSITY IN CAIRO

PEARSON

Prentice Hall

Upper Saddle River, New Jersey 07458

Library of Congrees Cataloging-in-Publication Data

Solomon, Michael R.
    Marketing : real people, real choices / Michael R. Solomon, Greg W. Marshall, Elnora W. Stuart.—4th ed.
        p. cm.
    ISBN 0-13-144968-0
    1. Marketing—Vocational guidance. I. Marshall, Greg W. II. Stuart, Elnora W. III. Title.

HF5415.35.S65 2006.
S658.8'0023'73—dc22   2004025605

Editorial Director: Jeff Shelstad
Acquisition Editor: Katie Stevens
Assistant Editor: Melissa Pellerano
Editorial Assistant: Rebecca Lembo
Media Project Manager: Peter Snell
Executive Marketing Manager: Michelle O'Brien
Marketing Assistant: Joanna Sabella
Developmental Editor: Shannon LeMay-Finn
Senior Managing Editor (Production): Judy Leale
Production Editor: Cindy Durand
Permissions Coordinator: Charles Morris
Image Supervisor: Keri Jean Miksza
Production Manager: Arnold Vila

Buyer: Diane Peirano
Design Manager: Maria Lange
Art Director: Pat Smythe
Designer: John Romer
Illustrator: Steve Frim
Cover Illustration/Photo: Corbis
Photo Researcher: Melinda Alexander
Image Permission Coordinator: Nancy Seise
Manager, Print Production: Christy Mahon
Composition/Full-Service Project Management: GGS Book Services, Atlantic Highlands
Printer/Binder: Courier-Kendallville
Typeface: 10pt Garamond-Regular

Credits and acknowledgments borrowed from other sources and reproduced, with permission, in this textbook appear on the appropriate page within text or on the Notes or Credits pages at the end of the book.

Microsoft® and Windows® are registered trademarks of the Microsoft Corporation in the U.S.A. and other countries. Screen shots and icons reprinted with permission from the Microsoft Corporation. This book is not sponsored or endorsed by or affiliated with the Microsoft Corporation.

Copyright © 2006, 2003, 2000, and 1997 by Pearson Education, Inc., Upper Saddle River, New Jersey, 07458. Pearson Prentice Hall. All rights reserved. Printed in the United States of America. This publication is protected by Copyright and permission should be obtained from the publisher prior to any prohibited reproduction, storage in a retrieval system, or transmission in any form or by any means, electronic, mechanical, photocopying, recording, or likewise. For information regarding permission(s), write to: Rights and Permissions Department.

Pearson Prentice Hall™ is a trademark of Pearson Education, Inc.
Pearson® is a registered trademark of Pearson plc
Prentice Hall® is a registered trademark of Pearson Education, Inc.

Pearson Education LTD.
Pearson Education Singapore, Pte. Ltd
Pearson Education, Canada, Ltd
Pearson Education–Japan

Pearson Education Australia PTY, Limited
Pearson Education North Asia Ltd
Pearson Educación de Mexico, S.A. de C.V.
Pearson Education Malaysia, Pte. Ltd

1 0 9 8 7 6 5 4 3 2
ISBN 013-144968-0

To Gail, Amanda, Zachary, Alexandra, and Kelbie Rae—
my favorite market segment

—M.S.

To Patti and Justin

—G.M.

To Sonny, Patrick, Gabriela, and Marge

—E.S.

BRIEF CONTENTS

CONTENTS

PREFACE

Real People, Real Choices

Whether you're a student or an instructor, what's important to know about this introductory textbook is it's the only one that presents marketing from the perspective of the people who do marketing. In the pages ahead you'll meet **real** marketers—the people who are making marketing decisions at leading companies every day.

Before we describe this new edition, you tell us: What is marketing?

- **Definition 1:**

  Marketing is about memorizing a bunch of terms like zone pricing and merchant wholesaler.

- **Definition 2:**

  Marketing is about product, price, place, and promotion.

- **Definition 3:**

  Marketing is about the flesh-and-blood people who need to make tough decisions, about the best way to develop a new product, or about how to make a product so irresistible it flies off of store shelves.

We hope you chose Definition 3. We've been teaching and practicing marketing for a long time. And if there's one thing we've learned, it's that our discipline is fun, exciting, and—when communicated the right way—important. Sure, this book will give you all the terms you need to know to pass that final exam. But you'll also see how marketing can come alive when practiced by real people who make real choices. To us, marketing is about creating value—for customers, for companies, and for society as a whole.

This Book Is for You, the Student

This book is for students who want to be marketers as well as those who don't. If you fall into the first category, we'll teach you the basics so you can understand how marketers contribute to the creation of value. If you fall into the second category, maybe at the end of the term you'll change your mind and move into the first! Even if you don't, we're going to show you how the principles of marketing apply to many other fields—everything from the arts to accounting. And regardless of your reasons for taking this course, we've worked hard to make the material come alive by focusing on decision making. You won't just read about it—you'll do it.

Meet Real Marketers, Who Make Decisions

The "Real People, Real Choices" vignettes that weave through every chapter make this text unique. Each vignette highlights a marketer from a real company, and then asks you to consider a dilemma the marketer recently faced as well as three options the marketer had to choose from. At the beginning of the chapter, you're also asked to think about which option you'd choose, and why.

In the "Real People, Other Voices" feature, also in each chapter, students and professors from schools around the country discuss which of the three options they'd choose, and what they think the featured marketer should do to solve the marketing dilemma.

And—**new to this edition**—you'll find an "Across the Hall" feature, in which business professors who teach in subject areas other than marketing weigh in on the Real People, Real Choices vignettes and explain how marketing affects, and is affected by, disciplines such as human resources, logistics, and economics.

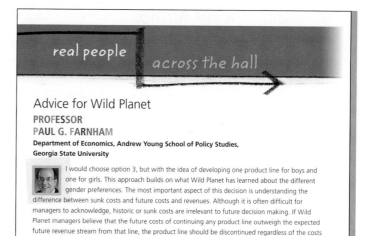

real people

across the hall

Advice for Wild Planet

PROFESSOR
PAUL G. FARNHAM
Department of Economics, Andrew Young School of Policy Studies, Georgia State University

I would choose option 3, but with the idea of developing one product line for boys and one for girls. This approach builds on what Wild Planet has learned about the different gender preferences. The most important aspect of this decision is understanding the difference between sunk costs and future costs and revenues. Although it is often difficult for managers to acknowledge, historic or sunk costs are irrelevant to future decision making. If Wild Planet managers believe that the future costs of continuing any product line outweigh the expected future revenue stream from that line, the product line should be discontinued regardless of the costs incurred in the past. However, if the best available evidence indicates that future revenues will be

real people, real choices
How It Worked Out at Monster

Jeff chose option 2. He sold The Monster Board to TMP Worldwide Inc., a recruitment advertising and Yellow Pages agency based in New York, NY. This company already had a vast global network of offices and client relationships as well as a local presence in most major cities in the United States and around the world. TMP added the resources that The Monster Board needed to provide career resources for its broad audience, which included everyone from interns to CEOs. Early in The Monster Board's history, the decision was made to focus the company's marketing efforts on the consumer. Jeff had the goal of creating a leading global brand, and the first step to accomplish that was reaching consumers and job seekers. This was the way to differentiate The Monster Board—now was the time to leverage it.

In January 1999, the company changed its name to "Monster.com" and launched a commercial, the award-winning "When I Grow Up," during the Super Bowl. The message conveyed in this spot truly resonated with job seekers across the nation, and they flocked to visit the site. About 2.2 million job searches were processed during a 24-hour period following the game—nearly a 450 percent increase from the 500,000 job searches prior to the Super Bowl. The humorous ad, regarded as one of the best Super Bowl commercials of all time, earned awards throughout the year, including *Advertising Age*'s "Best of Show," *Adweek*'s "Best Spot of the 90's," *Time*'s "Best Television of 1999," and *TV Guide*'s "Funniest Super Bowl Commercials of All Time."

Sure enough, the employers followed. By leading the online recruiting industry in job seeker traffic, employers posted jobs in droves on Monster because they knew that top talent from across the country was visiting the site. Since making the decision to market directly to job seekers/consumers first, Monster has been soaring, becoming the leading global online careers Web site and the ultimate destination to manage one's career or to find qualified candidates. What started as a small company with just a handful of employees has grown to include over 1,400 in 20 countries and is one of the few profitable public Internet companies today.

Finally, at the end of each chapter, you'll discover the marketer's "real choice" in a "How it Worked Out" feature.

Essentially, every chapter offers a situation, a variety of options, and then a resolution. No other introductory to marketing book is structured this way.

New Author

We are very pleased to have Greg W. Marshall, Ph.D., Professor of Marketing in the Crummer Graduate School of Business at Rollins College, Winter Park, Florida, join us as an author on the fourth edition. Professor Marshall's research interests in sales force selection, performance, and evaluation; adoption and successful use of technology by salespeople; sales force diversity; decision making by marketing managers; and intraorganizational relationships serve as a great complement to the author team and only strengthen this revision.

Real Marketing Topics and Events

This new edition reflects what's happening right now in the world of marketing. You'll start by learning the most recent definition of just what marketing is—the definition adopted by the American Marketing Association in 2004. You'll learn that marketing focuses on creating and transferring value from manufacturers to consumers, and ensuring that all parties in any marketing transaction are satisfied (making it more likely they'll continue to do business in the future). These steps include:

- Making Marketing Value Decisions (Part I)

- Understanding Consumers' Value Needs (Part II)

- Creating the Value Proposition (Part III)

- Communicating the Value Proposition (Part IV)

- Delivering the Value Proposition (Part V)

To keep you on top of the world of marketing, we've updated and expanded our coverage of countless marketing topics. Here's just a sample of what's new:

- New definition of marketing adopted by the American Marketing Association in 2004 (Chapter 1)

- Restructured and extended discussion of marketing as the creation of value—from the perspective of the consumer, the company, and society (Chapter 1)

- New CRM approach to marketing, including differential competency and lifetime value of the customer, value chains, and marketing ROI (Chapter 1)

- Tear-out marketing plan template tied to the book and fully executed in Appendix B (Chapter 2)

- Coverage of ethical business behavior and social responsibility reflecting lessons learned from Enron, Worldcom, and Parmalat (Chapter 3)

- New attention on utilizing data warehouses and data mining to acquire customers and build customer loyalty (Chapter 4)

- Coverage of current consumer trends such as the low-carb craze and new appeals to children (Chapter 4)

- Greater attention to not-for-profit organizations in business markets (Chapter 6)

- Emphasis on determining customer equity and focusing on high-value customers (Chapter 7)

- A more comprehensive look at branding, especially the importance of brand equity (Chapter 9)

- A revamped chapter that continues to focus not just on promotion but on the broader picture of integrated marketing communications (IMC) (Chapter 12)

- Enhanced and updated coverage of interactive marketing including a discussion of how marketers track and send customized messages (Chapter 12)

- Updated coverage of direct marketing including the Do Not Call registry (Chapter 13)

- Coverage of the worldwide growth of M-commerce, text messaging, and the hazards created for consumers by unscrupulous M-commerce marketers (Chapter 13)

- Increased attention to relationship selling as a driver of success with customers (Chapter 14)

- New discussion of the value chain concept as it relates to supply chain elements/activities (Chapter 15)

Fifteen of the Real People, Real Choices vignettes are new to this edition, featuring CEOs to brand managers. Here is just a sample of the people and companies featured:

- Jeff Taylor, CEO, Monster.com

- Steve Battista, Director of Brand Marketing, Under Armour

- Que Gaskins, VP of Global Marketing for RBK, Reebok

- Mario Polit, Manager of Marketing for Sedans, Infiniti Division, Nissan North America

- Robyn Eichenholz, Senior Brand Manager, Universal Theme Park

- Matt Ferguson, Vice President, Price/McNabb Integrated Communications

- Esther Ferre, Senior Account Supervisor, IBM

AN EASY-TO-FOLLOW MARKETING PLAN TEMPLATE

New to this edition is a pullout template of a marketing plan you can use as you make your way through the book. It provides a framework that will enable you to organize marketing concepts by chapter and create a solid marketing plan of your own.

AN EXCITING COMPANY TO FOLLOW: UNDER ARMOUR IN ACTION

To further illustrate how marketing is truly relevant to successfully running a business, this edition features a real company called Under Armour, which is making a big splash in the sports apparel industry. You'll be introduced to Under Armour in Chapter 2, where you'll learn how companies like UA make good strategic planning decisions in order to grow and prosper. Then, at the end of the book (Appendix A), you'll read a Q&A with Steve Battista, UA's marketing director, in which he answers key questions about strategic planning. Throughout the book you'll learn how companies like UA grapple with planning issues in the real world.

MEASURING THE VALUE OF MARKETING THROUGH "MARKETING METRICS"

MEASURING VALUE
marketing metrics

An Example of a Customer Service Scorecard

	Quarterly Scores 2003		
Item Text	**1st Qtr.**	**2nd Qtr.**	**3rd Qtr.**
Satisfaction with			
C1 Employee responsiveness	60%	65%	68%
C2 Product selection	60%	62%	63%
C3 Service quality	60%	62%	55%
C4 Cleanliness of facility	75%	80%	85%
C5 Knowledge of employees	62%	62%	58%
C6 Appearance of employees	60%	62%	63%
C7 Convenience of location	60%	65%	68%

Source: Adapted from C. F. Lundby and C. Racinowich, "The Missing Link," *Marketing Research*, winter 2003, 14–19, p. 18.

Just how do marketers add value to a company and can that value be quantified? More and more, businesses are demanding accountability, and marketers are responding by developing a variety of "scorecards" that show how specific marketing activities directly affect their company's ROI—return on investment. Throughout the book you'll find "Marketing Metrics" boxes that provide real-life examples of how marketers are calculating ROI based on their actions—and showing how marketing really matters.

LEARNING HOW TO MARKET YOURSELF: BRAND YOU

Have you ever considered that your employer is your customer? Employers have needs just like every other consumer. The *Brand You* supplement shows you step by step how to tune into employers' needs and market a brand called *You*.

You are a product. That may sound weird, but we often talk about ourselves and others in marketing terms. It is common for us to speak of "positioning" ourselves for job interviews, or to tell our friends not to "sell themselves short." You'll learn more about the most effective way to market yourself by following the advice provided in a dynamic and helpful "Brand You" handbook new to this edition. In it you'll find concrete advice you can use today that will help you to thrive in a competitive marketplace tomorrow. A teaser is located at the end of each chapter to illustrate how the marketing topics covered in that chapter relate to Brand You.

ALL END-OF-CHAPTER CASES ARE NEW TO THIS EDITION

Marketing in Action: Chapter 1 Case

Real Choices on *American Idol*

What musical genre will the show borrow from this week? Which contestants will perform the best? Most important, which performing hopeful will be sent home? Such questions are part of regular conversations among the millions of fans of the hit show *American Idol*, a reality television show on the FOX Network. After three seasons, *American Idol* is rivaled only by its reality show counterpart *Survivor* in terms of popularity and number of viewers on a weekly basis. However, when it comes to marketing the two shows, *American Idol* clearly is the winner in terms of the number and variety of different ways the show can be marketed.

From a product standpoint, *American Idol* is a phenomenon that stands alone among other reality shows in terms of its popularity. On a weekly basis, approximately 30 million viewers watch musical hopefuls vie for a chance at a recording contract. Almost 40 million viewers watched the final episode of *American Idol*'s second season, which represented a 33 percent increase over *American Idol*'s first season finale. In each weekly segment, contestants sing songs chosen from a specific song style in front of a live studio and television audience. After each contestant sings, the show's judges, who can be condescending, complimentary, and caustic all at the same time, provide feedback to the contestant about his or her performance, hairstyle, and clothing; basically, whatever they feel like commenting on. At the end of the show, audience members are given the opportunity to call in or text message a vote for their favorite performer. The following night, in another live show, America gets to find out which performer was "voted off." Because Americans' votes determine who leaves the show each week, *American Idol* ups the ante in terms of audience participation. *American Idol*'s format has resulted in a product that has been very popular in the 18- to 49-year-old age bracket of viewers—the age bracket most coveted by advertisers.

As a product, *American Idol* has given the FOX Network its highest ratings ever outside of sporting events like the Super Bowl. As a distribution outlet for the show, FOX has been able to reap the rewards of providing the place element of the marketing mix. Because of *American Idol*'s popularity, especially with an extremely desirable audience segment, the show appeals to advertisers wanting to reach that audience. The third season of *American Idol* resulted in the number of sponsors increasing from the three biggest sponsors of Coca-Cola, Ford, and AT&T Wireless to also include Subway, Old

Navy, and Clairol. In addition, FOX has been able to use advertising slots during *American Idol* to promote its other product offerings like *The OC*, *24*, and others. Another distribution outlet used by *American Idol*'s creators is the Web site. From the Web site, fans of the show can read the personal histories of contestants, send e-mails to contestants, and order merchandise and music videos. Each of these activities enhances audience participation in the show and its outcome. Promoters have also introduced a number of spin-off products, including *American Idol* clothing, fragrances, jewelry, video games, CDs, and even a concert tour.

Because of *American Idol*'s popularity and inherent strength as a product, its creators and producers are able to command a premium price for promoting sponsorship opportunities to other companies. For the current season, Coca-Cola, Ford, and AT&T Wireless are reportedly paying more than $20 million each for the opportunity to sponsor the show. For that investment, the companies are able to promote their products in innovative and interesting ways. For example, in addition to airing advertisements for Classic Coke and Vanilla Coke, Coca-Cola has designed the "Red Room," where contestants spend time before and after their performance with vending machines and furniture decorated in Coca-Cola graphics.

In another example of innovative promotions, *American Idol* viewers are exposed to the show's sponsors in minisegments integrated in with the show itself. For example, before cutting away to a commercial, the show often will highlight its contestants doing something associated with one of its sponsors' products. One week the segments will show the contestants driving a Ford to a fun destination while singing an upbeat song, while the next week the contestants will be shown making sandwiches and singing a song for customers at a local Subway. Such promotional tie-ins provide the impression of the show's contestants being actual users of the product—a very powerful message to the audience.

Given the show's success and its effective use of the marketing mix elements, there will undoubtedly be another season. However, *American Idol*'s popularity puts pressure on its creators and producers to capitalize on that popularity in new and innovative ways. How do marketers keep the show's use of the marketing mix fresh?

Things to Think About

1. What is the decision facing *American Idol* marketers?
2. What factors are important in understanding the decision situation?
3. What are the alternatives?
4. What decision(s) do you recommend?
5. What are some ways to implement your recommendation(s)?

Sources: Todd Wasserman, "Scent (and More) of an 'American Idol,'" *Adweek*, January 19, 2004, 8; Wayne Friedman and David Goetzl, "Fox Seeks $26 Million for New 'Idol,'" *Advertising Age*, October 14, 2002, 3, 57; and Steve McClellan, "Idol Moments Ahead for Advertisers," *Broadcasting & Cable*, January 5, 2004, 20.

SUPPLEMENTS

ANNOTATED INSTRUCTOR'S MEDIA EDITION (AIME)

Have you ever wanted to incorporate instructor media tools offered with a textbook but didn't know where to start or were simply too busy to spend hours planning your lectures? Here's your solution! In the instructor's edition of the textbook, we have inserted perforated outlines at the beginning of each chapter, with references to items in the following instructor supplements: Instructor's Manual, Test Item File, PowerPoint Presentation—Media Rich version, Video Library, and OneKey. Recognizing that your students have a variety of learning styles, we've selected highlights from these supplements to complement your lectures. Finally, the turnkey solution *you've* been waiting for!

INSTRUCTOR'S MANUAL

- **New feature:** "Outside Examples" offers instructors additional lecture material for each chapter. The examples may be a further development of a concept or company briefly mentioned in the chapter, or new material that helps to further develop a concept in the text.
- **New feature:** "Professors on the Go!" was created with the busy professor in mind. This feature serves to bring key material upfront in the manual, where an instructor who is short on time can take a quick look and find key points and assignments that he/she can incorporate into the lecture, without having to page through all the material provided for each chapter.
- Chapter overview and objectives, plus detailed lecture outlines—incorporating key terms from the text.
- Support for end-of-chapter material, along with additional student projects and assignments.

TEST ITEM FILE: BRAND NEW FOR YOU

- **Over 2,500 questions:** Each chapter consists of multiple choice, true/false, essay, and short-answer questions, with page references and difficulty level provided for each question.
- **New feature:** An entire section dedicated to application questions. These real-life situations take students beyond basic chapter concepts and vocabulary and ask them to apply their marketing skills.

TESTGEN EQ SOFTWARE

Prentice Hall's test generating software is all new for this edition. This supplement is available in two places: Download from the IRC Online (www.prenhall.com/solomon) or from the IRC on CD-ROM.

- PC/Mac compatible and preloaded with all of the Test Item File questions.
- Manually or randomly view test bank questions and drag-and-drop to create a test.
- Add or modify test bank questions using the built-in Question Editor.
- Print up to 25 variations of a single test and deliver the test on a local area network using the built-in QuizMaster feature.
- Free customer support is available at media.support@pearsoned.com or 1-800-6-PROFESSOR between 8:00 AM and 5:00 PM CST.

POWERPOINTS

When it comes to PowerPoints, Prentice Hall knows one size does not fit all. That's why *Marketing: Real People, Real Choices*, 4e, offers instructors more than one option.

- **PowerPoint BASIC:**

  This simple presentation includes only basic outlines and key points from each chapter. No animation or forms of rich media are integrated, which makes the total file size manageable and easier to share online or via email. BASIC was also designed for instructors who prefer to customize PowerPoints or who want to avoid having to strip out animation, embedded files, or other media rich features.

- **PowerPoint MEDIA RICH:**

  The MEDIA RICH alternative includes basic outlines and key points from each chapter, plus advertisements and art from the text, images from outside the text, discussion questions, Web links, and embedded video snippets from the accompanying video library. This is the best option if you want a complete presentation solution. Instructors can further customize this presentation using the image library featured on the IRC on CD-ROM.

- **PowerPoints for CLASSROOM RESPONSE SYSTEMS (CRS):**

  These text-specific Q&A-style slides are designed for classrooms using "clickers" or classroom response systems. Instructors who are interested in making CRS a part of their course should contact their Prentice Hall representative for details and a demonstration. CRS is a fun and easy way to make your classroom more interactive.

THE VIDEO LIBRARY

The video library features exciting and all-new segments. All segments are available online, on DVD, and on VHS. Instructors can also choose to have the DVD shrink-wrapped with this text at no additional cost for students. New segments include:

- American Express and the modern marketing environment
- The NFL and the importance of social responsibility
- Song Airlines and smart pricing strategies
- Eaton's approach to B2B issues, including buyer behavior
- Reebok's retailing and wholesaling policies
- Wild Planet's strategies in consumer markets
- AFLAC and its views on advertising and public relations
- Hasbro and its views on distribution channels and logistics management

You may download the Video Guide from the Instructor's Resource Center.

INSTRUCTOR'S RESOURCE CENTER (IRC)

● IRC—on CD-ROM:

One source for all of your supplement needs. New interface and searchable database makes sorting through and locating specific resources easier than ever before. Includes all the same supplements hosted at our IRC Online; however, the PowerPoint MEDIA RICH set is provided only on this CD-ROM due to its larger file size and embedded video clips. The CD-ROM also contains many images from the textbook, which you may incorporate into your lectures.

● IRC—ONLINE:

One destination for all of your supplement needs. The Prentice Hall catalog at www.prenhall.com/marketing is where instructors can access our complete array of teaching materials. Simply go to the catalog page for this text and click on the Instructor link to download the Instructor's Manual, Video Guide, Test Item File, TestGen EQ, PowerPoint slides (Basic and CRS only), and more.

NOTE: Prentice Hall manually checks every password request and verifies each individual's instructor status before issuing a password.

COMPANION WEBSITE

This FREE site offers students valuable resources. Two quizzes are offered per chapter. The Concept Check Quiz is to be administered prior to reviewing the chapter in order to assess the student's initial understanding. The Concept Challenge Quiz is to be administered after reviewing the chapter. Also featured is the text glossary, plus a link to the new Instructor's Resource Center.

ONEKEY

 OneKey means one site for all student premium resources and teaching resources. Visit www.prenhall.com/onekey.

For students:

- Additional quizzing and assessment resources, advertising exercises, marketing plan templates, and much more.

- Available for WebCT, Blackboard, and CourseCompass platforms.

- OneKey requires an access code, which can be shrink-wrapped free with new copies of this text. Please contact your local sales representative for the correct ISBN.

STUDY GUIDE

A one-of-a-kind companion for students. Includes detailed chapter outlines, student exercises plus exercises correlated to award-winning print advertisements. This guide serves as a great review tool in preparing for exams.

ADCRITIC.COM—SEE A TOUR AT WWW.PRENHALL.COM/MARKETING

- Prentice Hall and *AdAge's* AdCritic.com have partnered to bring current advertising commercials, news, commentaries, and more into marketing classrooms.

- Students can receive 16 weeks of access to an innovative AdCritic.com site at a deep discount Standalone access cards are not available, so instructors need to specify the value-package ISBN with their bookstores in advance. Contact your local Prentice Hall representative for ISBNs.

- Instructors who order this special value package for their students will receive 20 weeks of free access.

BRAND YOU HANDBOOK

Products aren't alone in benefiting from branding. People can benefit, too. Branding strategies help professionals get noticed and position them for exciting new career opportunities. New to this edition is a dynamic and helpful "Brand You" handbook that gives students concrete advice on how to thrive in a competitive marketplace and provides a hands-on approach to achieving career success. "Brand You" boxes appear throughout this textbook to help students plot their own branding strategies. This separate "Brand You" supplement can be packaged FREE with new copies of this text. Contact your Prentice Hall representative for the package ISBN.

ABOUT THE AUTHORS

Michael R. Solomon

MICHAEL R. SOLOMON, Ph.D. is the Human Sciences Professor of Consumer Behavior at Auburn University. Prior to joining Auburn in 1995, he was Chairman of the Department of Marketing in the School of Business at Rutgers University, New Brunswick, New Jersey. Professor Solomon's primary research interests include consumer behavior and lifestyle issues, branding strategy, the symbolic aspects of products, the psychology of fashion, decoration, and image, services marketing, and the development of visually-oriented online research methodologies. He currently sits on the Editorial Boards of the *Journal of Consumer Behaviour* and the *Journal of Retailing*, and he serves on the Board of Governors of the Academy of Marketing Science. In addition to other books, he is also the author of Prentice Hall's text *Consumer Behavior: Buying, Having, and Being,* which is widely used in universities throughout the world. Professor Solomon frequently appears on television and radio shows such as *The Today Show, Good Morning America, Channel One, The Wall Street Journal Radio Network,* and *National Public Radio* to comment on consumer behavior and marketing issues.

Greg W. Marshall

GREG W. MARSHALL, Ph.D. is Professor of Marketing in the Crummer Graduate School of Business at Rollins College, Winter Park, Florida. Prior to joining the Crummer School, he served on the faculties of Oklahoma State University, the University of South Florida, and Texas Christian University. Professor Marshall's primary research interests include sales force selection, performance, and evaluation; adoption and successful use of technology by salespeople; sales force diversity; decision making by marketing managers; and intraorganizational relationships. He currently serves on the Editorial Boards of the *Journal of the Academy of Marketing Science, Journal of Business Research,* and *Industrial Marketing Management* and he is Editor of the *Journal of Personal Selling & Sales Management.* Professor Marshall is Past-President of the American Marketing Association Academic Division and Past-President of the Society for Marketing Advances. His industry experience prior to entering academe includes product management, field sales management, and retail management positions with firms such as Warner-Lambert, the Mennen Company, and Target Corporation.

Elnora W. Stuart

ELNORA W. STUART, Ph.D., is Professor of Marketing and the BP Egypt Oil Professor of Management Studies at The American University in Cairo (AUC). Prior to joining AUC in 2000, she was Professor of Marketing at Winthrop University in Rock Hill, South Carolina and on the faculty of the University of South Carolina. She earned a B.A. degree in Theatre/Speech from the University of North Carolina at Greensboro and both a Master of Arts in Journalism and Mass Communication and a Ph.D. in Marketing from the University of South Carolina.

Professor Stuart's research has been published in major academic journals including the *Journal of Consumer Research, Journal of Advertising, Journal of Business Research,* and *Journal of Public Policy and Marketing.* For over 20 years she has served as a consultant for numerous businesses and not-for-profit organizations in the United States and in Egypt. Professor Stuart currently resides in Cairo, Egypt, and Hilton Head Island, South Carolina.

www.monster.com

real people, real choices

meet Jeff Taylor, a Decision Maker
at Monster

first job out of school   **career high(s)**

DJ.

Coming up with the idea
for Monster, graduating
from college at the age of
42, and speaking at my
own commencement.

WELCOME TO THE WORLD OF MARKETING: CREATING AND DELIVERING VALUE

Jeff Taylor is Founder and Chief Monster of Monster. The idea for Monster came to Jeff in a dream. As head of his own recruitment ad agency, he was focusing his business on big ideas for his high-tech clients. In 1993, a client said to him, "No more big ideas. I want a monster idea!" Soon afterward, Jeff says, "I woke up at 4:30 A.M. from a dream that I built a bulletin board system where people could look for jobs. In the dark, I wrote down on a pad next to my bed, 'The Monster Board.' " What started as a dream soon became Monster.com. Recognized as an innovator in both the Internet and career industries, Jeff has reinvented the way the world looks for employment. His "monster idea" is now the world's leading online career site, with local content and language sites in 20 countries and serving over 18 million unique visitors monthly.

Jeff has an undergraduate degree from the University of Massachusetts at Amherst, and holds an Honorary Doctorate from Bentley College. In March 2000, Jeff reached yet another notable milestone: he became the Blimp Water-Skiing World Champion.

Decision Time at Monster.Com

The Monster story began when Jeff Taylor was president of Adion, a niche recruitment-advertising agency he founded in 1989. At this time, 85 percent of companies were using newspapers for recruiting. But Jeff's high-tech clients were experiencing difficulty attracting candidates with technical skills by placing classified ads. Feeling pressure from his clients to offer innovative solutions to their staffing problems, Jeff decided to take a gamble on this new thing called the Internet. The Monster Board was born.

However, at that time, the Internet was not a mass medium, and there were few other commercial Web sites, so getting The Monster Board off the ground was a challenge. Many employers told Jeff his idea would not work because they would not associate themselves with a silly brand called "monster." While The Monster Board began to receive some traction through job postings from technology companies, growth was slow. It was tough to entice a significant number of clients to post jobs on the site, particularly those from nontechnology companies.

This created a real chicken-and-egg problem: For the site to work, Monster needed to have a healthy number of attractive employers as well as a high volume of qualified applicants who wanted to find one another. Jeff needed to come up with another way to market The Monster Board. He considered his options:

OPTION 1: Target marketing efforts towards employers; the job seekers will follow.

Since the Internet was still in its infancy, The Monster Board would have a tremendous opportunity to educate human resource managers about the benefits of online recruitment.

business hero/mentor	my mottos to live by	my management style	don't do this when interviewing with me
Richard Branson.	80 percent of life is showing up. The shortest distance between two points is a big idea.	Democratic and to be a good leader. I think it's important to step out in front of the organization and not be afraid to take risks, but also have the sense to step back and let people do their jobs.	Ask questions that are answered on the homepage.

objectives

1 Know who marketers are and where they work and understand marketing's role in the firm.

2 Define what marketing is and how it provides value to everyone involved in the marketing process.

3 Discuss the range of services and goods that are marketed.

4 Understand value from the perspectives of the customers, producers, and society.

5 Understand the basics of marketing planning and the marketing mix tools used in the marketing process.

6 Describe the evolution of the marketing concept.

Monster could show them how they could save time and money, and they would begin to post jobs on the site. Job seekers would follow suit later. On the other hand, the economy was beginning to heat up, and HR departments were short staffed. Would they risk their recruitment dollars on an unproven model? Could Monster convince them that they would reach the employees they needed in an online format?

OPTION 2: Target marketing efforts toward job seekers. The employers will follow.

Jeff's goal was to make The Monster Board a leading consumer brand. It seemed like the mushrooming popularity of the Internet (especially among techies who might be looking for jobs when not writing computer programs) would attract job seekers more than job recruiters. In addition, since it's free for job seekers to visit the site, they would be more likely to check out what The Monster Board had to offer. However, with few jobs posted on the site, would job seekers continue to return after their first visit? Consumers traditionally have low attention spans, and they often need a good reason to return to an Internet site.

OPTION 3: Build the product first. Save the marketing dollars until the concept began to catch on with both employers and job hunters.

After all, since the Internet was still in its infancy, saving money to hit the market with branding at just the right time could mean the company's financial survival. Was it too much of a risk to heavily invest in marketing early on, given the small number of people actually using the Internet? On the other hand, being first-to-market is essential. Building the right brand is the key to a company's success. There was a great opportunity for a new Internet company with an effective business model to invest in marketing-related initiatives in order to build the brand in the eyes of consumers and customers.

Now, put yourself in Jeff Taylor's shoes: Which option would you choose, and why?

Welcome to Brand You

You are a product. That may sound weird, but companies like Monster couldn't exist if you weren't. After all, you have "market value" as a person—you have qualities that set you apart from others and abilities other people want and need. After you finish this course, you'll have even more value because you'll know about the field of marketing and how this field relates to you both as a future businessperson and as a consumer. In addition to learning about how marketing influences each of us, you'll have a better understanding of what it means to be "Brand You."

Although it may seem strange to think about the marketing of people, in reality we often talk about ourselves and others in marketing terms. It is common for us to speak of "positioning" ourselves for job interviews or to tell our friends not to "sell themselves short." Some people who are cruising for potential mates even refer to themselves as "being on the market." In addition, many consumers hire personal image consultants to devise a "marketing strategy" for them, while others undergo plastic surgery or makeovers to improve their "product images." The desire to package and promote ourselves is the reason for personal goods and services markets ranging from cosmetics and exercise equipment to résumé specialists and dating agencies.[1] Throughout this book, you'll learn more about the most effective way to market *yourself* by following the advice we'll provide in a supplement called "Brand You."

So, the principles of marketing apply to people, just as they apply to peas, Porsches, and computer processors. Sure, there are differences in how we go about marketing each of these, but the general idea remains the same: Marketing is a fundamental part of our lives both as consumers and as players in the business world. We'll tell you why throughout this book. But first, we need to answer the basic questions of marketing: Who? Where? What? When? and Why? Let's start with Who and Where.

The Who and Where of Marketing

Marketers come from many different backgrounds. Although many have earned marketing degrees, others have backgrounds in areas such as engineering or agriculture. Retailers and fashion marketers may have training in merchandising or design. Advertising copywriters often have degrees in English. **E-marketers** who do business over the Internet may have studied computer science.

e-marketers
Marketers who use e-commerce in their strategies.

Marketers work in a variety of locations. They work in consumer goods companies such as Taco Bell or Nissan or at service companies like Monster.com. You'll see them in retail organizations like The Limited and at companies that manufacture products for other companies to use like DuPont. You'll see them in financial institutions such as Royal Bank and at advertising and public relations agencies such as PR 21.

And, although you may assume that the typical marketing job is in a large, consumer-oriented company such as IBM or Reebok, marketers work in other types of organizations too. There are many exciting marketing careers in companies that sell to other businesses. In small organizations, one person (perhaps the owner) may handle all the marketing responsibilities. In large organizations, marketers work on different aspects of the marketing strategy.

No matter where they work, all marketers are real people who make choices that affect themselves, their companies, and very often thousands or even millions of consumers. At the beginning of each chapter, we'll introduce you to marketing professionals like Jeff Taylor in a feature called "Real People, Real Choices." We'll tell you about a decision the marketer had to make and give you the possible options he or she considered. Then, at the end of each chapter, we'll tell you what option the marketer chose and why as well as what happened. Along the way, we'll share some other people's opinions about the featured marketer's decision in a box called "Real People, Other Voices."

Marketing's Role in the Firm

What role do marketers play in a firm? The importance assigned to marketing activities depends on the organization. Top management in some firms is very marketing oriented (especially when the chief executive officer comes from the marketing ranks), whereas in other companies marketing is an afterthought. Sometimes the company uses the term *marketing* when what it really means is *sales* or *advertising*. In some organizations, particularly small not-for-profit ones, there may not be anyone in the company specifically designated as "the marketing person."

In contrast, some firms realize that marketing applies to all aspects of the firm's activities. As a result, there has been a trend toward integrating marketing with other business functions (such as management and accounting) instead of setting it apart as a separate function. At several places in this book, we'll illustrate that marketers make decisions that affect other aspects of the business. To do this, we've asked professors from other business disciplines to weigh in on some of our "Real People, Real Choices" features by telling us how an executive in an area other than marketing (such as human resources) might approach the same decision from a different angle. You'll find their responses in boxes called "Across the Hall."

No matter what size the firm, a marketer's decisions affect—and are affected by—the firm's other operations. Marketing managers must work with financial and accounting officers to figure out whether products are profitable, to set marketing budgets, and to determine prices. They must work with people in manufacturing to be sure that products are produced on time and in the right

AVEENO® is a product that satisfies a need by providing blemish-free skin.

quantities. Marketers also must work with research-and-development specialists to create products that meet consumers' needs.

Okay, now that you've gotten a glimpse of who marketers are and where they work, it's time to dig into what marketing really *is*.

The Value of Marketing

Marketing. Lots of people talk about it, but what is it? When you ask people to define *marketing*, you get many answers. Some people say, "That's what happens when a pushy salesman tries to sell me something I don't want." Other people say, "Oh, that's simple—TV commercials." Students might answer, "That's a course I have to take before I can get my business degree." Each of these responses has a grain of truth in it, but the official definition of *marketing*, adopted by the American Marketing Association in late 2004, is as follows:

> **Marketing** is an organizational function and a set of processes for creating, communicating and delivering value to customers and for managing customer relationships in ways that benefit the organization and its stakeholders.[2]

The basic idea of this somewhat complicated definition is that marketing is all about delivering value to *everyone* who is affected by a transaction. Let's take a closer look at the different parts of this definition.

marketing
An organizational function and a set of processes for creating, communicating and delivering value to customers and for managing customer relationships in ways that benefit the organization and its stakeholders.

stakeholders
Buyers, sellers, investors in a company, community residents, and even citizens of the nations where goods and services are made or sold—in other words, any person or organization that has a "stake" in the outcomes.

consumer
The ultimate user of a good or service.

Marketing Is About Meeting Needs

One important part of our definition of *marketing* is that marketing is about meeting the needs of diverse stakeholders. The term **stakeholders** here refers to buyers, sellers, investors in a company, community residents, and even citizens of the nations where goods and services are made or sold—in other words, any person or organization that has a "stake" in the outcome. Thus, marketing is about satisfying everyone involved in the marketing process.

One important stakeholder is the consumer. A **consumer** is the ultimate user of a good or service. Consumers can be individuals or organizations, whether a company, government, sorority, or charity. We like to say that the consumer is king (or queen), but it's important not to lose sight of the fact that the seller also has needs—to make a profit, to remain in business, and even to take pride in selling the highest quality products possible. Products are sold to satisfy both consumers' and marketers' needs—it's a two-way street. When you strip away the big words, try this as a bumper sticker: *Marketers do it to satisfy needs.*

Most successful firms today practice the **marketing concept**. That is, marketers first identify consumer needs and then provide products that satisfy those needs, ensuring the firm's long-term profitability. A **need** is the difference between a consumer's actual state and some ideal or desired state. When the difference is big enough, the consumer is motivated to take action to satisfy the need. When you're hungry, you buy a snack. If you're not happy with your hair, you get a new hairstyle. When you need a job (or perhaps just get mad at your boss), you check out Monster.com.

Needs are related to physical functions (such as eating) or to psychological ones (such as wanting to look good). Levi Strauss & Company is one company that tries to meet the psychological needs of consumers to look good (as well as their basic need to be clothed). The company's research indicates that people wear Levi's jeans to say important things about themselves and their desired image. From time to time, the company even receives a beat-up, handed-down pair in the mail, with a letter from the owner requesting that the jeans be given a proper burial—that's a pretty "deep-seated" attachment to a pair of pants![3]

The specific way a need is satisfied depends on an individual's history, learning experiences, and cultural environment. A **want** is a desire for a particular product used to satisfy a need in specific ways that are culturally and socially influenced. For example, two classmates' stomachs rumble during a lunchtime lecture, and both need food. However, how each person satisfies this need might be quite different. The first student may be a health nut who fantasizes about gulping down a big handful of trail mix, while the second person may be enticed by a greasy cheeseburger and fries. The first student's want is trail mix, whereas the second student's want is fast food (and some antacid for dessert).

A product delivers a **benefit** when it satisfies a need or want. For marketers to be successful, they must develop products that provide one or more benefits that are important to consumers. The challenge is to identify what benefits people look for, then develop a product that delivers those benefits while also convincing consumers that their product is better than a competitor's product making the choice of which product to buy obvious. As management expert Peter Drucker writes, "The aim of marketing is to make selling superfluous."[4]

Everyone can want your product, but that doesn't ensure sales unless they have the means to obtain it. When you couple desire with the buying power or resources to satisfy a want, the result is **demand**. So, the potential customers for a snappy, red BMW convertible are the people who want the car *minus* those who can't afford to buy or lease one. A **market** consists of all the consumers who share a common need that can be satisfied by a specific product and who have the resources, willingness, and authority to make the purchase.

A **marketplace** used to be a location where buying and selling occurred face to face. In today's "wired" world, however, buyers and sellers might not even see each other. The modern marketplace may take the form of a glitzy shopping mall, a mail-order catalog, a television shopping network, an eBay auction, or an e-commerce Web site. In developing countries, the marketplace may be a street corner or an open-air market where people sell fruits and vegetables much as they did thousands of years ago.

Marketing Is About Creating Utility

Marketing activities play a major role in the creation of **utility**, which refers to the sum of the benefits we receive from using a product or service. By working to ensure that people have the type of product they want and where and when they want it, the marketing system makes our lives easier. Utility is what creates value. Marketing can provide several different kinds of utility in order to provide value to consumers:

- *Form utility* is the benefit marketing provides by transforming raw materials into finished products, as when a dress manufacturer combines silk, thread, and zippers to create a bridesmaid's gown.

- *Place utility* is the benefit marketing provides by making products available where customers want them. The most sophisticated evening gown sewn in New York's garment district is of little use to a bridesmaid in Kansas City if it isn't shipped to her in time.

- *Time utility* is the benefit marketing provides by storing products until they are needed. Some women rent their wedding gowns instead of buying them and wearing them only once (they hope!).

- *Possession utility* is the benefit marketing provides by allowing the consumer to own, use, and enjoy the product. The bridal store provides access to a range of styles and colors that would not be available to a woman outfitting a bridal party on her own.

marketing concept
A management orientation that focuses on identifying and satisfying consumer needs to ensure the organization's long-term profitability.

need
The recognition of any difference between a consumer's actual state and some ideal or desired state.

want
The desire to satisfy needs in specific ways that are culturally and socially influenced.

benefit
The outcome sought by a customer that motivates buying behavior—that satisfies a need or want.

demand
Customers' desire for products coupled with the resources to obtain them.

market
All the customers and potential customers who share a common need that can be satisfied by a specific product, who have the resources to exchange for it, who are willing to make the exchange, and who have the authority to make the exchange.

marketplace
Any location or medium used to conduct an exchange.

utility
The usefulness or benefit consumers receive from a product.

NEW Crest Whitestrips Premium
is clinically proven to remove up to
14 years of stain build-up in just
7 days – satisfaction guaranteed.**

©2004 P&G
OJAN03780

Crest Whitestrips provide a benefit many consumers want today: whiter teeth.

As we've seen, marketers provide utility in many ways. Now, let's see how customers "take delivery" of this added value.

Marketing Is About Exchange Relationships

At the heart of every marketing act—big or small—is something we refer to as an "exchange relationship." An **exchange** occurs when something is obtained for something else in return. The buyer receives an object, service, or idea that satisfies a need, and the seller receives something he or she feels is of equivalent value.

For an exchange to occur, at least two people or organizations must be willing to make a trade, and each must have something the other wants. Both parties must agree on the value of the exchange and how it will be carried out. Each party also must be free to accept or reject the other's terms for the exchange. Under these conditions, a gun-wielding robber's offer to "exchange" your money for your life does not constitute a valid exchange. In contrast, although someone may complain that a store's prices are "highway robbery," an exchange occurs if they still fork over the money to buy something there—even if they grumble about it for weeks to come.

To complicate things a bit more, everyone does not always agree on the terms of the exchange. Think for example about music piracy, which is a huge headache for music labels that claim they lose billions of dollars a year when consumers download songs without paying for them. On the other hand, a lot of people who engage in this practice don't feel that they

exchange
The process by which some transfer of value occurs between a buyer and a seller.

are participating in an unfair exchange that deprives manufacturers of the value of their products. They argue that music piracy is the fault of record companies that charge way too much for new songs. What do you think?

The debate over music downloading reminds us that an agreed-on transfer of value must occur for an exchange to take place. A politician can agree to work toward certain goals in exchange for your vote, or a minister can offer you salvation in return for your faith. Today, most exchanges occur as a monetary transaction in which currency (in the form of cash, check, or credit card) is surrendered in return for a good or a service.

What Can Be Marketed?

We are surrounded by marketers' creations in the form of advertisements, stores, and products competing for our attention and our dollars. Marketers filter much of what we learn about the world, such as when we see images of rich or beautiful people on television commercials or magazines. Ads show us how we should act and what we should own. Marketing's influence extends from "serious" goods and services such as health care to "fun" things such as extreme skateboarding and hip-hop music (though many people take these products as seriously as their health).

A marketplace can take many forms, such as a traditional bazaar or an upscale shopping mall.

Popular culture consists of the music, movies, sports, books, celebrities, and other forms of entertainment that the mass market consumes. The relationship between marketing and popular culture is a two-way street. The goods and services that are popular at any point in time often mirror changes in the larger society. Consider, for example, some U.S. products that reflected underlying cultural changes at the time they were introduced.

- The TV dinner signaled changes in family structure, such as a movement away from the traditional family dinner hour filled with conversation about the day's events.
- Cosmetics made of natural materials and not animal tested reflected social concerns about pollution and animal rights.
- Condoms marketed in pastel carrying cases intended for female buyers signaled changing attitudes toward sexual responsibility.

Marketing messages often communicate **myths**, stories containing symbolic elements that express the shared emotions and ideals of a culture.[5] Consider, for example, how McDonald's takes on mythical qualities. To some, the golden arches are virtually synonymous with American culture. They offer sanctuary to Americans in foreign lands who are grateful to know exactly what to expect once they enter. Basic struggles of good versus evil are played out in the fantasy world of McDonald's advertising, as when Ronald McDonald confounds the Hamburglar. McDonald's even runs Hamburger University, where fast-food majors learn how to make the perfect burger.

Is there any limit to what marketers can market? As we mentioned earlier, marketing applies to more than just canned peas or cola drinks. Some of the best marketers come from the ranks of services companies such as American Express or not-for-profit organizations such as Greenpeace. Politicians, athletes, and performers use marketing to their advantage (just think about that $30 T-shirt you may have bought at a baseball game or rock concert). Ideas such as political systems (democracy, totalitarianism), religion (Christianity, Islam), and art (realism, abstract) also compete for acceptance in a "marketplace." In this book, we'll refer to any good, service, or idea that can be marketed as a **product**, even though what is being sold may not take a physical form.

Consumer Goods and Services

Consumer goods are the tangible products that individual consumers purchase for personal or family use. **Services** are intangible products that we pay for and use but never own. Service transactions contribute on average more than 60 percent to the gross national product of all industrialized nations; as we'll see in Chapter 10, marketers need to understand the special challenges that arise when marketing an intangible service rather than a tangible good.[6]

popular culture
The music, movies, sports, books, celebrities, and other forms of entertainment consumed by the mass market.

myths
Stories containing symbolic elements that express the shared emotions and ideals of a culture.

product
A tangible good, service, idea, or some combination of these that satisfies consumer or business customer needs through the exchange process; a bundle of attributes including features, functions, benefits, and uses.

consumer goods
The goods purchased by individual consumers for personal or family use.

services
Intangible products that are exchanged directly from the producer to the customer.

Everyone's going low carb lately. We've been there since day one.

A friendly reminder from America's Peanut Farmers ^{SM}

One serving of dry roasted peanuts (30 grams) contains 12 grams of unsaturated fat and 2 grams of saturated fat, and 0 cholesterol.

Visit www.nationalpeanutboard.org for delicious recipes.

Successful marketers try to connect their products with trends in popular culture. The Peanut Board links its product to the current low-carb craze.

McDonald's is a familiar landmark to Americans (even when the menu is in a foreign language).

In both cases, though, keep in mind that the consumer is looking to obtain some underlying *value*, such as convenience, security, or status, from a marketing exchange. That value can come from a variety of competing goods and services, even those that don't resemble one another on the surface. For example, both a new CD and a ticket to a local concert may cost about the same, and each may provide the benefit of musical enjoyment, so consumers often have to choose among competing alternatives if they can't afford (or don't want) to buy them all.

Business-to-Business Goods and Services

Business-to-business marketing is the marketing of goods and services from one organization to another. Although we usually relate marketing to the thousands of consumer goods begging for our dollars every day, more goods are sold to businesses and other organizations than to consumers. These are called **industrial goods**; they are bought by organizations for further processing or for use in their business operations. For example, automakers buy tons of steel to use in the manufacturing process, and they buy computer systems to track manufacturing costs and other information essential to operations.

Similarly, there is a lot of buzz about **e-commerce** and the buying and selling of products—books, CDs, cars, and so forth—on the Internet. However, just like in the off-line world, much of the real online action is in the area of business-to-business marketing. The total value of goods and services purchased by businesses on the Web is estimated to increase from $282 billion in 2000 to $4.3 trillion by 2005. We'll talk more about business-to-business marketing in Chapter 6.

Not-for-Profit Marketing

As noted earlier, you don't have to be a businessperson to use marketing principles. Many **not-for-profit organizations**, including museums, zoos, and even churches, practice the marketing concept. Local governments are getting into the act as they adopt marketing techniques to create more effective taxpayer services and to attract new businesses and industries to their counties and cities. Even states are getting into the act: We've known for a long time that I ❤ NY, but in 2004, Kentucky and Oregon hired advertising agencies to develop statewide branding campaigns (the official state motto of Oregon is now "Oregon. We love dreamers.").[7] The intense competition for support of civic and charitable activities means that only those not-for-profits that meet the needs of their constituents and donors will survive.

watch us watch you

OREGON ZOO

Not-for-profit organizations like zoos need to market themselves too.

Idea, Place, and People Marketing

Marketing principles also get people to endorse ideas or to change their behaviors in positive ways. Many organizations work hard to convince consumers to use seat belts, not to litter our highways, to engage in safe sex, or to believe that one political system is preferable to another. In addition to ideas, places and people also are marketable. We are all familiar with tourism marketing that promotes exotic resorts like Club Med ("the antidote for civilization"). For many developing countries like Thailand, tourism may be the best opportunity available for economic growth.

You may have heard the expression, "Stars are made, not born." There's a lot of truth to that. Beyoncé Knowles may have a killer voice and Sammy Sosa may have a red-hot baseball bat, but talent alone doesn't make thousands or even millions of people buy CDs or stadium seats. Entertainment events do not just happen. People plan them. Whether a concert or a baseball game, the application of sound marketing principles helps ensure that patrons will continue to support the activity and buy tickets. Today, sports and the arts are hotbeds of activity for marketing. Many of the famous people you pay to see became famous with the help of shrewd marketing: They and their managers developed a "product" that they hoped would appeal to some segment of the population.

Indeed, some of the same principles that go into "creating" a celebrity apply to you. An entertainer—whether P. Diddy or Pavoratti—must "package" his or her talents, identify a target market that is likely to be interested, and work hard to gain exposure to these potential customers by appearing in the right musical venues. In the same way, everyday people "package" themselves by summing up their accomplishments on a résumé and distributing it at venues like Monster.com in order to attract potential buyers.

The Marketing of Value

So far, we've talked a lot about marketing delivering value to customers. But just what do we mean by that word? **Value** refers to the benefits a customer receives from buying a product or service. Marketing then communicates these benefits as the value proposition to the customer. The **value proposition** is a marketplace offering that fairly and accurately sums up the value that the customer will realize if he or she purchases the product or service. The challenge to the marketer is to create an attractive value proposition. A big part of this challenge is convincing customers that this value proposition is superior to others they might choose from competitors.

How do customers decide how much value they will get from a purchase? One way to look at value is to think of it simply as a ratio of benefits to costs. That is, customers "invest" their precious time and money to do business with a firm, and they expect a certain bundle of benefits in return. But here's the tricky part: *Value is in the eye of the beholder.* That means that something (or

business-to-business marketing
The marketing of those goods and services that business and organizational customers need to produce other goods and services, for resale or to support their operations.

industrial goods
Goods bought by individuals or organizations for further processing or for use in doing business.

e-commerce
The buying or selling of goods and services electronically, usually over the Internet.

not-for-profit organizations
Organizations with charitable, educational, community, and other public service goals that buy goods and services to support their functions and to attract and serve their members.

value
The benefits a customer receives from buying a product or service.

value proposition
A marketplace offering that fairly and accurately sums up the value that will be realized if the product or service is purchased.

What kind of people take blind kids mountain climbing?
The same ones who take paraplegics sailing and amputees horseback riding.

NATIONAL SPORTS CENTER FOR THE DISABLED

To participate, volunteer, or help financially, visit www.nscd.org.

Nonprofit organizations such as the National Sports Center for the Disabled regard value in terms of their ability to motivate, educate, or delight the public.

someone) may be worth a lot to one person but not to another. Your mother may believe that you are the greatest person on the planet, but a prospective employer may form a different conclusion. A big part of marketing is ensuring that the thing being exchanged is appreciated for the value it holds. Let's look at value from the different perspectives of the parties that are involved in an exchange: the customers, the producers, and society.

Value from the Customer's Perspective

Think about something you would like to buy, say a new pair of shoes. You have narrowed the choice down to several options. Your purchase decision no doubt will be affected by the ratio of costs versus benefits for each type of shoe. That is, in buying a pair of shoes, you consider the price (and other costs) along with all the other benefits (utilities) that each competing pair of shoes provides you.

As noted previously, the value proposition includes the whole bundle of benefits the firm promises to deliver, not just the benefits of the product itself. For example, although most people probably couldn't run faster or jump higher if they were wearing Nikes versus Reeboks, many die-hard loyalists swear by their favorite brand. These archrivals are largely marketed in terms of their images—meanings that have been carefully crafted with the help of legions of athletes, slickly produced commercials, and millions of dollars. When you buy a Nike "swoosh," you may be doing more than choosing shoes to wear to the mall—you may also be making a statement about the type of person you are or wish you were. In addition to providing comfort or letting you run faster, that statement also is part of the value the product delivers to you.

You can probably think of possessions you own with which you've "bonded" in some way—that is, their value to you goes beyond their function. Marketers who understand this know that in the long run, their value proposition will be successful if they manage to build a relationship between their product and the people who buy it.

Value from the Seller's Perspective

We've seen that marketing transactions produce value for buyers, but how do sellers experience value, and how do they decide whether a transaction is valuable? One answer is obvious: They determine whether the exchange is profitable to them. Has it made money for the company's management, its workers, and its shareholders?

That's a very important factor but not the only one. Just as value from the consumer's perspective can't be measured only in functional terms, value from the seller's perspective can take many forms. For example, in addition to making a buck or two, many firms measure value along other dimensions, such as prestige among rivals or pride in doing what they do well. Some firms by definition don't even care about making money, or they may not even be *allowed* to make money; nonprofits like Greenpeace, the Smithsonian Institution, or National Public Radio regard value in terms of their ability to motivate, educate, or delight the public.

Because value is such a complicated but important concept, now more than ever marketers are searching for new and better ways to accurately measure just what kind of value they are delivering, how this stacks up to the competition, and—as we'll see next—in some cases even whether the relationship they have with a customer possesses enough value for them to continue it.

CALCULATING THE VALUE OF A CUSTOMER Smart companies today understand that making money from a single transaction doesn't provide the kind of value they desire. Instead, their goal is to satisfy the customer over and over again so that they can build a long-term relationship rather than just having a "one-night stand."

As we'll see later in this chapter, in recent years many firms have transformed the way they do business and have begun to regard consumers as partners in the transaction rather than as passive "victims." That explains why it's becoming more common for companies to host events (sometimes called "brandfests") for their customers to thank them for their loyalty. In 2004, for example, the Ford Motor Company sponsored "The Great American Pony Drive II" in honor of devotees of its legendary Mustang. This party included a performace of the song "Mustang Sally" by Sir Mack Rice (who recorded the original version) as well as a preview of the 2005 next-generation Mustang.[8]

Ford's decision to reward Mustang owners with a party means the car company has learned an important secret: It often is more expensive to attract new customers than it is to retain current ones. While this notion has transformed the way many companies do business, in fact it doesn't always hold. In recent years, companies have been working harder to calculate the true value of their relationships with customers by asking, "How much is this customer really worth to us?" Firms recognize that it can be very costly in terms of both money and human effort to do whatever it takes to keep some customers loyal to the company. Very often these actions pay off, but there are cases when keeping a customer is a losing proposition.

This way of thinking is similar to how we may decide which friends are "worth keeping." You may do a lot of favors for two friends, only to discover that when you need something, one of them is always there for you, while the other is nowhere to be found. Over time, you may decide that maintaining a friendship with that second person just doesn't make sense. Similarly, a company may use a lot of its resources to appeal to two customers and find that one returns the favor by buying a lot of its products, while the other hardly buys anything at all. In the long run, the firm may decide to "fire" that second customer. Perhaps you once ordered something in a catalog, and you get that catalog in your mailbox every month. If you don't order anything for a certain period of time, you may no longer be sent the catalog. In the words of Donald Trump, "You're fired!"

Companies that calculate the **lifetime value of a customer** look at how much profit they expect to make from a particular customer, including each and every purchase he or she will make from them now and in the future. To calculate lifetime value, they estimate the amount the person will spend and then subtract what it will cost them to maintain this relationship.

PROVIDING VALUE TO STAKEHOLDERS BY CREATING A COMPETITIVE ADVANTAGE As noted earlier, all things equal, a firm creates value for its stakeholders when it convinces customers that they will acquire greater value by buying its products rather than those of competitors. How are companies able to accomplish this goal? The answer is that the underlying goal of all marketing strategies is to create a **competitive advantage** for the firm. A firm has a competitive advantage when it is able to outperform the competition, providing customers with a benefit the competition can't. A competitive advantage gives consumers a reason to choose one product over another again and again.

lifetime value of a customer
How much profit companies expect to make from a particular customer, including each and every purchase she will make from them now and in the future. To calculate lifetime value, companies estimate the amount the person will spend and then subtract what it will cost the company to maintain this relationship.

competitive advantage
The ability of a firm to outperform the competition, thereby providing customers with a benefit the competition can't.

distinctive competency
A superior capability of a firm in comparison to its direct competitors.

How does a firm go about creating a competitive advantage? The first step is to identify what it does really well. A **distinctive competency** is a firm's capability that is superior to that of its competition. For example, Coca-Cola's success in global markets—Coke commands 50 percent of the world's soft-drink business—is related to its distinctive competencies in distribution and marketing communications. Coke's distribution system got a jump on the competition during World War II. To enable U.S. soldiers fighting overseas to enjoy a five-cent Coke, the U.S. government assisted Coca-Cola in building 64 overseas bottling plants. Coke's skillful marketing communications program, a second distinctive competency, has contributed to its global success. In addition to its television commercials, Coke has blanketed less developed countries such as Tanzania with its print advertisements so that even people without televisions will think of Coke when they get thirsty.

differential benefit
Properties of products that set them apart from competitors' products by providing unique customer benefits.

The second step in developing a competitive advantage is to turn a distinctive competency into a **differential benefit**—one that is important to customers. Differential benefits set products apart from competitors' products by providing something unique that customers want. Differential benefits provide reasons for customers to pay a premium for a firm's products and exhibit a strong brand preference. For many years, loyal Apple computer users benefited from superior graphics capability compared to their PC-using counterparts. Later, when PC manufacturers caught up with this competitive advantage, Apple relied on its inventive product designers to create another differential benefit—futuristic looking computers in a multitude of colors. This competitive advantage even caused many loyal PC users to take a bite of the Apple.

Note that a differential benefit does not necessarily mean simply offering something different. For example, Mennen marketed a deodorant with a distinctive feature: It contained Vitamin D. Unfortunately, consumers did not see any reason to pay for the privilege of spraying a vitamin under their arms. Despite advertising claims, they saw no benefit, and the product failed. The moral: Effective product benefits must be both different from the competition and be wanted by customers. A firm that delivers these desired benefits provides value to its customers and to its other stakeholders.

ADDING VALUE THROUGH THE VALUE CHAIN Many different players—both within a firm and outside of it—need to work together to create and deliver value to customers. One approach to understanding the delivery of value and satisfaction is the **value chain**. Basically, this refers to a series of activities involved in designing, producing, marketing, delivering, and supporting any product. In addition to marketing activities, the value chain includes business functions such as human resource management and technology development.[9]

value chain
A series of activities involved in designing, producing, marketing, delivering, and supporting any product. Each link in the chain has the potential to either add or remove value from the product the customer eventually buys.

This concept reminds us that every product starts with raw materials that are of relatively limited value to the end customer. Each link in the chain has the potential to either add or remove value from the product the customer eventually buys. The successful firm is the one that can perform one or more of these activities better than other firms—this is its competitive advantage. The main activities of value chain members include the following:

- Bringing in materials to make the product (referred to as *inbound logistics*)
- Converting the materials into the final product (referred to as *operations*)
- Shipping out the final product (referred to as *outbound logistics*)
- Marketing the final product (where *marketing and sales* come into play)
- Servicing the product/customer (referred to as *service*)

For example, you buy a new Hewlett Packard (HP) PC at your local Circuit City store. Have you ever thought about all the people and steps involved in designing that product, manufacturing it, and delivering it to the store—not to mention other players that create brand advertising, conduct consumer research to figure out what people like or dislike about their computers, or even make the box it comes in or those little plastic peanuts that keep the unit from being damaged in shipment?

Figure 1.1 A Value Chain for Hewlett Packard

Inbound Logistics	Operations	Outbound Logistics	Marketing and Sales	Service
• Silicon producer • Microchip manufacturer • Software and video game manufacturers	• Consumer research • New product development team • Engineering and production	• Trucking companies • Wholesalers • Retailers	• Advertising • Sales force	• Computer technicians

As Figure 1.1 shows, all these companies (and more) belong to HP's value chain. This means that HP must make a lot of good decisions. What microchips will go into its computers? What games will be part of the package? What trucking companies, wholesalers, and retailers will deliver the computers to customers? What service will it provide to customers after the sale? And what marketing strategies will it use? In some cases, members of a value chain will work together to coordinate their activities in order to be more efficient (and thus create a competitive advantage). HP can also add value by choosing partners that provide a competitive advantage. For example, a supplier like Intel might develop a way to make a microprocessor even faster. In other cases, HP has relatively little control over the efficiency of its partners. For example, a spike in the cost of gasoline caused by political developments might increase the fees a trucking company charges to HP to deliver its computers to Circuit City. We'll discuss the value chain in more detail in Chapter 14.

This book is organized around the sequence of steps necessary to ensure that the appropriate value exchange occurs and that both parties to the transaction are satisfied—making it more likely they'll continue to do business in the future. These steps are shown in Figure 1.2.

Figure 1.2 Making and Delivering Value

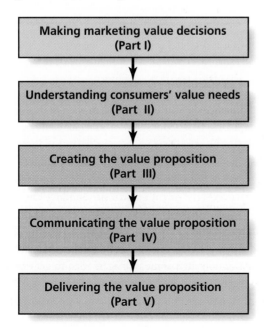

Making marketing value decisions
(Part I)

↓

Understanding consumers' value needs
(Part II)

↓

Creating the value proposition
(Part III)

↓

Communicating the value proposition
(Part IV)

↓

Delivering the value proposition
(Part V)

Advice for Monster.com

STUDENT
TCHOIA BROWN
University of Tulsa

I would choose option 3. Having a first-mover advantage is very important when coming out with a new product, but if you haven't spent time investing in the product and making sure it actually works, you're working against yourself. You're cluing your competition in to your idea and giving them time to figure out what you're doing wrong and how to do it better. Once the product has been solidified, I would recommend marketing it to job seekers. Since it was geared mostly to "techies" who could visit the site for free and who are looking for a job in a bad economy, they would be more likely to try anything to get a job, even if no one's done it before.

PROFESSOR
LINDA JANE COLEMAN
Salem State College

I would choose option 1, targeting the marketing efforts toward employers. Many times, marketing begins with education. Monster.com should use the time to build a strong foundation by educating human resource managers regarding this growing vehicle, to bring wants and needs together. The recruiters can't afford to overlook this innovative idea, and what follows is, "If you build it, they will come."

PROFESSOR
ROBERT J. STRASSHEIM
Mary Washington College

I would choose option 3, building the product first and saving the marketing dollars until the concept began to catch on. In order for Jeff Taylor and Monster.com to be a success, every effort should be made to save marketing dollars until a solid product is developed. While being first to market is important, it is even more important for a company to take a finalized product to market on its first try. A failed initial market entry could require the "retooling" of a product and thus a second (and more costly) market entry. Take AOL, for example. It was not first to market with its ISP concept—some companies beat AOL's entrance by several years. However, AOL did what most of them could not—deliver a sound product that consumers demanded. Monster.com should follow suit and develop a solid product before spending significant marketing dollars.

Value from Society's Perspective

Every company's activities influence the world around it, in ways both good and bad. Therefore, we must also consider how marketing transactions add or subtract value from society. In many ways, we are at the mercy of marketers because we trust them to sell us products that are safe and perform as promised. We also trust them to price and distribute these products fairly. As we'll discuss in Chapter 3, conflicts often arise in business when the pressure to succeed in the marketplace provokes dishonest business practices—the recent scandal surrounding Enron is a case in point.

Companies usually find that stressing ethics and social responsibility also is good business, at least in the long run. Some find out the hard way. For example, the Chrysler Corporation was accused of resetting the odometers of new cars that managers had actually driven prior to sale. The company admitted the practice only after some managers tried to get out of paying speeding tickets by claiming that their speedometers—and odometers—didn't work because the cables were disconnected.[10] These actions caused the company great embarrassment, and it took years of hard work to restore the public's trust.

In contrast, Procter & Gamble voluntarily withdrew its Rely tampons from the market following reports of women who had suffered toxic shock syndrome (TSS). Although scientists did not claim a causal link between Rely and TSS, the company agreed with the Food and Drug Administration to undertake extensive advertising notifying women of the symptoms of TSS and asking them to return their boxes of Rely for a refund. The company took a $75 million loss and sacrificed an unusually successful new product that had already captured about one-quarter of the billion-dollar sanitary product market.[11]

Whether intentionally or not, some marketers do violate their bond of trust with consumers, and unfortunately the "dark side" of marketing often is the subject of harsh criticism. In some cases, these violations are illegal, such as when a retailer adopts a "bait-and-switch" selling strategy, luring consumers into the store with promises of inexpensive products with the sole intent of getting them to switch to higher-priced goods.

In other cases, marketing practices have detrimental effects on society even though they are not actually illegal. Some alcohol and tobacco companies advertise in low-income neighborhoods where abuse of these products is a big problem. Others sponsor commercials depicting groups of people in an unfavorable light to get the attention of a target market. For example, many people complained that Coors beer's "Swedish bikini team" campaign demeaned women in order to appeal to men.

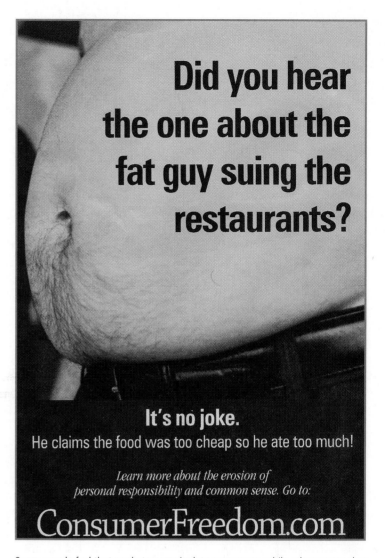

Some people feel that marketers manipulate consumers, while others argue that people should be held responsible for their own choices. This ad is critical of the current trend of lawsuits brought against fast-food companies by people who blame their health problems on the fast-food industry. What do you think?

Marketing as a Process

Our definition of marketing refers to *processes*. This means that marketing is not a one-shot operation. When it's done right, marketing is a decision process in which marketing managers determine the strategies that will help the firm meet its long-term objectives and then execute those strategies using the tools they have at their disposal. In this section, we'll look at how marketers go about the business of making decisions and planning their actions. We'll also take a brief look at the tools marketers have at their disposal as they execute their plans.

Marketing Planning

A big part of the marketing process is to engage in what is called *marketing planning* (more on this in the next chapter). The first phase of marketing planning is analyzing the marketing environment. This means understanding the firm's current strengths and weaknesses by assessing factors that might help or hinder the development and marketing of products. The analysis must also take into account the opportunities and threats the firm will encounter in the marketplace, such as the actions of competitors, cultural and technological changes, and the economy.

Firms (or individuals) engaging in marketing planning ask questions such as the following:

- What product benefits will our customers be looking for in three to five years?
- What capabilities does our firm have that set it apart from the competition?

THE **ADVANTAGE** IS **UNDENIABLE.**®

UNDER ARMOUR®, the original performance apparel, is made for every climate and condition. Our exclusive microfiber fabrics wick sweat from your skin, keeping you dry and light while allowing your body to adjust its temperature regardless of the elements. Wear HeatGear® when it's hot, ColdGear® when it's cold, and AllseasonGear® between the extremes. LooseGear®, the ultimate workout gear, delivers the benefits of HeatGear® in a relaxed fit. It's the perfect combination of performance and comfort.

UNDER ARMOUR®
PERFORMANCE APPAREL
1.888.4.ARMOUR • WWW.UNDERARMOUR.COM

Under Armour performance apparel is carefully laying plans to appeal to a wide variety of people who engage in physical activities. We'll see how they're doing this throughout the book.

marketing plan
A document that describes the marketing environment, outlines the marketing objectives and strategy, and identifies who will be responsible for carrying out each part of the marketing strategy.

mass market
All possible customers in a market, regardless of the differences in their specific needs and wants.

market segment
A distinct group of customers within a larger market who are similar to one another in some way and whose needs differ from other customers in the larger market.

- What additional customer groups might provide important market segments for us in the future?
- How will changes in technology affect our production process, our communication strategy, and our distribution strategy?
- What changes in social and cultural values are occurring that will impact our market in the next few years?
- How will consumers' awareness of environmental issues affect their attitudes toward our manufacturing facilities?
- What legal and regulatory issues may affect our business in both domestic and global markets?

Answers to these and other questions provide the foundation for developing an organization's **marketing plan**. The marketing plan is a document that describes the marketing environment, outlines the marketing objectives and strategy, and identifies who will be responsible for carrying out each part of the marketing strategy. Beginning in the next chapter, we'll introduce you to a dynamic company called Under Armour that started out small and is growing rapidly, largely because of the smart steps it has taken to develop and implement a sound marketing plan.

A major marketing decision for most organizations like Under Armour is which products to market to which consumers without turning off other consumers at the same time. Some firms choose to reach as many customers as possible by offering their goods or services to a **mass market**, which consists of all possible customers in a market regardless of the differences in their specific needs and wants. Marketing planning then becomes a matter of developing a basic product and a single strategy for reaching everyone.

Although this approach can be cost effective, the firm risks losing potential customers to competitors whose marketing plans are directed at meeting the needs of *specific* groups within the market. A **market segment** is a distinct group of customers within a larger market who are similar to one another in some way and whose needs differ from other customers in the larger market. Automakers such as Ford, General Motors, and BMW offer different automobiles for different market segments. Depending on its goals and resources, a firm may choose to focus on one segment. As we'll see in Chapter 7, the chosen market segment becomes the organization's **target market** toward which it directs its efforts. A product's **market position** is how the target market perceives the product in comparison to competitor's brands.

Marketing's Tools: The Marketing Mix

In determining the best way to present a good or service for consumers' consideration, marketers have many decisions to make, so they need many tools. The marketer's strategic toolbox is called the **marketing mix**, which consists of the tools that are used to create a desired response among a set of predefined consumers. These tools include the *product* itself, the *price* of the product, the *promotional* activities that introduce it to consumers, and the *place* where it is available. The elements of the marketing mix are commonly known as the Four Ps: product, price, promotion, and place. As Figure 1.3 shows, each P is a piece of the puzzle that must be combined with other pieces. Just as a radio DJ puts together a collection of separate songs (a musical mix) to create a certain mood, the idea of a mix in this context reminds us that no single marketing activity is sufficient to accomplish the organization's objectives.

Although we talk about the Four Ps as separate parts of a firm's marketing strategy, in reality, product, price, promotion, and place decisions are totally interdependent. Decisions about any single one of the four are affected by and affect every other marketing mix decision. For example, assume that a firm is introducing a superior quality product, one that is more expensive to produce than its existing line of products. The price the firm charges for this new product must cover these higher costs, but in addition the firm must create advertising and other promotional strategies to convey a top-quality image. At the same time, the price of the product must cover not only the costs of production but also the cost of advertising. Furthermore, the firm must include high-end retailers in its distribution strategy. The elements of the marketing mix therefore work hand in hand.

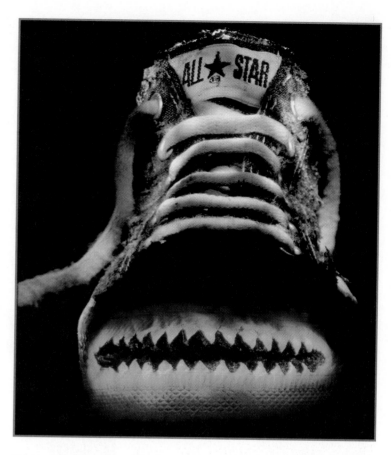

This Thai ad for Converse positions its All Stars as a sneaker for aggressive athletic performance.

We'll examine these components of the marketing mix in detail later in this book. For now, let's briefly look at each P to gain some insight into its meaning and role in the marketing mix.

PRODUCT We've already seen that the product is a good, a service, an idea, a place, a person—whatever is offered for sale in the exchange. This aspect of the marketing mix includes the design and packaging of a good, as well as its physical features and any associated services, such as free delivery. So we can see that the product is a combination of many different elements, all of which are important to the product's success. For example, when the British firm Virgin introduced Virgin Cola in the United States, the company attempted to make the product stand out from the competition through its distinctive packaging. Advertising that introduced the brand told customers about the curved squeezable bottles. "If all you got is Va Va, You got to get some Voom; It's in the curvy bottle, Yeah, Virgin Drinks' got Voom. . . . Virgin puts the Voom in you Va Va."[12] We're not quite sure what that means, but it does get your attention. Whether the focus is on the bottle or some other element, the product is an important part of the marketing mix. More about this in Part III when we talk about creating the value proposition.

PRICE Price is the assignment of value, or the amount the consumer must exchange to receive the offering. A price is often used as a way to increase consumers' interest in a product. This happens when an item is put on sale, but in other cases marketers try to sell a product with a higher price than people are used to if they want to communicate that it's high quality or cutting edge. For example, the new Adidas 1 computerized running shoe got a lot of attention in the media. Some of the fuss was that the shoe was billed as the first "smart shoe" because it contains a computer chip

target market
The market segments on which an organization focuses its marketing plan and toward which it directs its marketing efforts.

market position
The way in which the target market perceives the product in comparison to competitors' brands.

marketing mix
A combination of the product itself, the price of the product, the place where it is made available, and the activities that introduce it to consumers that creates a desired response among a set of predefined consumers.

price
The assignment of value, or the amount the consumer must exchange to receive the offering.

Figure 1.3 **The Marketing Mix**

What marketing is all about! The marketing mix is a combination of the Four Ps—product, price, place, and promotion—all used together to satisfy customer needs.

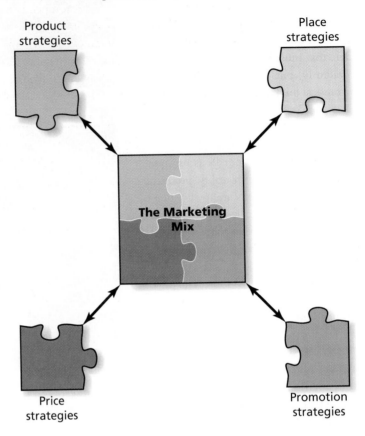

Product strategies

Place strategies

The Marketing Mix

Price strategies

Promotion strategies

that adapts its cushioning level to a runner's size and stride. But a lot of the press coverage also revolved around the hefty price tag of $250 per pair, which makes buying the shoe a status statement for the hard-core runner.[13] So, price is also an important part of creating the value proposition, and we'll return to this concept in Part III.

PROMOTION Promotion includes all the activities marketers undertake to inform consumers about their products and to encourage potential customers to buy these products. Promotions can take many forms, including personal selling, television advertising, store coupons, billboards, magazine ads, and publicity releases. All these actions are a part of communicating the value proposition—we'll go into more detail about these important issues in Part IV.

PLACE Place refers to the availability of the product to the customer at the desired time and location. As we'll see in Chapter 12, this P is related to a *channel of distribution*, which is the set of firms working together to get a product from a producer to a consumer. For clothing or electronics, this channel includes local retailers as well as other outlets, such as retail sites on the Web that strive to offer the right quantity of products in the right styles at the right time.

To achieve a competitive advantage over rivals in the minds of consumers, the marketer carefully blends the four Ps of the marketing mix. That is, a product is developed to meet the needs of the target market, as are its price, place, and promotion strategies. These strategies may vary from one country to another, and they may be injected with fresh ideas over time to maintain or change the product's position.

promotion
The coordination of a marketer's marketing communications efforts to influence attitudes or behavior; the coordination of efforts by a marketer to inform or persuade consumers or organizations about goods, services, or ideas.

place
The availability of the product to the customer at the desired time and location.

When Did Marketing Begin?
The Evolution of a Concept

Now that we have an idea of how the marketing process works, let's take a step back and see how this process worked (or didn't) in "the old days." Although it sounds like good old common sense to us, believe it or not the notion that businesses and other organizations succeed when they satisfy customers' needs actually is a pretty recent idea. Before the 1950s, marketing was basically a means of making production more efficient. Let's take a quick look at how the marketing discipline has developed. Table 1.1 tells us about some of the more recent events in this marketing history.

Table 1.1 Marketing Milestones

Year	Marketing Event
1955	Ray Kroc opens his first McDonald's.
1956	Lever Brothers launches Wisk, America's first liquid laundry detergent.
1957	Ford rolls out Edsel, loses more than $250 million in two years.
1959	Mattel introduces Barbie.
1960	The FDA approves Searle's Enovid as the first oral contraceptive.
1961	Procter & Gamble launches Pampers.
1962	Wal-Mart, Kmart, Target, and Woolco open their doors.
1963	The Pepsi Generation kicks off the cola wars.
1964	Blue Ribbon Sports (now known as Nike) ships its first shoes.
1965	Donald Fisher opens The Gap, a jeans-only store in San Francisco.
1971	Cigarette advertising is banned on radio and television.
1973	Federal Express begins overnight delivery services.
1976	Sol Prices opens first warehouse club store in San Diego.
1980	Ted Turner creates CNN.
1981	MTV begins.
1982	Gannett launches *USA Today*.
1983	Chrysler introduces minivans.
1984	Apple Computer introduces the Macintosh.
1985	New Coke is launched; Old Coke is brought back 79 days later.
1990	Saturn, GM's first new car division since 1919, rolls out its first car.
1993	Phillip Morris reduces price of Marlboros by 40 cents a pack and loses $13.4 billion in stock market value in one day.
1994	In largest switch in ad history, IBM yanks its business from scores of agencies worldwide and hands its entire account to Ogilvy & Mather.
1995	eBay goes online as an experimental auction service.
1997	McDonald's gives away Teenie Beanie Babies with Happy Meals. Consumer response is so overwhelming that McDonald's is forced to take out ads apologizing for its inability to meet demand. Nearly 100 million Happy Meals are sold during the promotion.[a]
1998	Germany's Daimler-Benz acquires America's Chrysler Corporation for more than $38 billion in stock to create a new global automaking giant called Daimler-Chrysler.[b]
2003	Amazon debuts its "Search Inside the Book" feature that allows you to search the full text of more than 33 million pages from over 120,000 printed books.
2004	Online sales in the United States top $100 billion.[c]

Source: Patricia Sellers, "To Avoid Trampling, Get Ahead of the Mass," *Fortune,* 1994, 201—2, except as noted.

[a]Tod Taylor, "The Beanie Factor," *Brandweek,* June 16, 1997, 22–27.
[b]Jennifer Laabs, "Daimler-Benz and Chrysler: A Merger of Global HR Proportions," *Workforce,* July 1998, 13.
[c]Keith Regan, "Report: Online Sales Top $100 Billion," *E-Commerce Times,* June 1, 2004, **www.ecommercetimes.com/story/34148.html.**

The Production Era

Many people say that Henry Ford's Model T changed America forever. Even from the start in 1908, when the "Tin Lizzie," or "flivver" as the T was known, sold for $825, Henry Ford continued to make improvements in production. By 1912, Ford got so efficient that the car sold for $575, a price even the Ford employees who *made* the car could afford.[14] As the price continued to drop, Ford sold even more flivvers. By 1921, The Model T Ford had 60 percent of the new car market. In 1924, the ten-millionth Model T rolled off the assembly line. The Model T story is perhaps the most well-known and most successful example of an organization that focuses on the most efficient production and distribution of products.

Ford's focus illustrates a **production orientation**, which works best in a seller's market when demand is greater than supply because it focuses on the most efficient ways to produce and distribute products. Essentially, consumers have to take whatever is available (there weren't a whole lot of other Tin Lizzies competing for drivers in the 1920s). Under these conditions, marketing plays a relatively insignificant role—the goods literally sell themselves because people have no other choices. Indeed, in the former Soviet Union, the centralized government set production quotas, and weary shoppers lined up (often for hours) to purchase whatever happened to be on a store's shelves at the time.

Firms that focus on a production orientation tend to view the market as a homogeneous group that will be satisfied with the basic function of a product. Sometimes this view is too narrow. For example, Procter & Gamble's Ivory soap has been in decline for some time because the company viewed the brand as plain old soap, not as a cleansing product that could provide other benefits as well. Ivory soap lost business to newer deodorant and "beauty" soaps containing cold cream that "cleaned up" in this market.[15]

After World War II, the peacetime economy boomed. Americans had plenty of money, and manufacturers used increased factory capacity created in wartime to turn out an abundance of civilian favorites. As this 1949 Ford ad indicates, suddenly people had a lot of choices, and a bounty of products awaited the returning GIs and their families.

production orientation
A management philosophy that emphasizes the most efficient ways to produce and distribute products.

The Selling Era

When product availability exceeds demand in a buyer's market, businesses may engage in the "hard sell" where salespeople aggressively push their wares. During the Great Depression in the 1930s, when money was scarce for most people, firms shifted their focus from a product orientation to moving their goods in any way they could.

This **selling orientation** means that management views marketing as a sales function, or a way to move products out of warehouses so that inventories don't pile up. The selling orientation gained in popularity after World War II. During the war, the United States dramatically increased its industrial capacity to manufacture tanks, combat boots, parachutes, and countless other wartime goods. After the war, this industrial capacity was converted to producing consumer goods.

selling orientation
A managerial view of marketing as a sales function, or a way to move products out of warehouses to reduce inventory.

Consumers eagerly bought all the things they couldn't get during the war years, but once these initial needs and wants were satisfied, they got more selective. The race for consumers' hearts and pocketbooks was on. The selling orientation prevailed well into the 1950s. But consumers as a rule don't like to be pushed, and the hard sell gave marketing a bad image.

Companies that still follow a selling orientation tend to be more successful at making one-time sales rather than building repeat business. This focus is most likely to be found among companies that sell *unsought goods*—products that people don't tend to buy without some prodding. For example, most of us aren't exactly "dying" to shop for cemetery plots, so some encouragement may be necessary to splurge on a final resting place.

Visitors to Reflect.com can customize their cosmetics order for their specific complexion and beauty needs—and their purchases even arrive in glitzy packages bearing their own name.

The Consumer Era

At Direct Tire Sales in Watertown, Massachusetts, customers discover an unusual sight: The customer lounge is clean, there is free coffee with fresh cream and croissants, employees wear ties, and the company will even pay your cab fare home if your car isn't ready on time. People don't mind paying 10 to 15 percent more for these extra services.[16] Direct Tire Sales has found that it pays to have a **consumer orientation** that satisfies customers' needs and wants.

As the world's most successful firms began to adopt a consumer orientation, marketers had a way to outdo the competition—and marketing's importance was also elevated in the firm. Marketers did research to understand the needs of different consumers, assisted in tailoring products to the needs of these various groups, and did an even better job of designing marketing messages than in the days of the selling orientation.

The marketing world was humming along nicely, but then inflation in the 1970s and recession in the 1980s took their toll on company profits. The marketing concept needed a boost. Firms had to do more than meet consumers' needs—they had to do this better than the competition and do it repeatedly. They increasingly concentrated on improving the quality of their products. By the early 1990s, an approach known as **Total Quality Management (TQM)** was widely followed in the marketing community. The TQM perspective takes many forms, but essentially it's a management effort to involve all employees from the assembly line onward in continuous product quality improvement. We'll learn more about this idea in Chapter 9.

The New Era

Over time, many forward-thinking organizations began to see their commitment to quality even more intensely than "just" satisfying consumers' needs during a single transaction. Instead, they began to focus on a **New Era orientation** that meant building long-term bonds with customers rather than merely selling them stuff today.

One outgrowth of this new way of thinking was the concept of **customer relationship management (CRM)**, which involves systematically tracking consumers' preferences and behaviors over time in order to tailor the value proposition as closely as possible to each individual's unique wants and needs (more on this in Chapters 7 and 12). With the advent of the Internet, a CRM approach got a lot easier to implement as more and more firms—like Monster.com—started to rely heavily on the Web to connect with consumers. The Internet provides the ultimate opportunity for implementation of the marketing concept because it allows a firm to personalize its messages and products to better meet the needs of each individual consumer.

consumer orientation
A management philosophy that focuses on ways to satisfy customers' needs and wants.

Total Quality Management (TQM)
A management effort to involve all employees from the assembly line onward in continuous product quality improvement.

New Era orientation
A management philosophy in which marketing means a devotion to excellence in designing and producing products that benefit the customer plus the firm's employees, shareholders, and communities.

customer relationship management (CRM)
A philosophy that sees marketing as a process of building long-term relationships with customers to keep them satisfied and to keep them coming back. A concept that involves systematically tracking consumers' preferences and behaviors over time in order to tailor the value proposition as closely as possible to each individual's unique wants and needs

100 ORIS YEARS

[Oris Limited Edition «Wings Around the World II, Voyage to the Ice with Polly Vacher».]

It Does Far More Than Tell The Time.

By buying Oris Limited Edition «Wings Around the World II – Voyage to the Ice», you will be supporting Polly Vacher's record-breaking attempt to fly solo around the world via the poles in a single engined aircraft. You will also help to raise funds for flying scholarships for the disabled. From the Wheelchair to the Cockpit is the name of the expedition – with Oris as the official watch partner, and with the legendary pilot's watch Oris Big Crown.

Support: Queen Noor of Jordan with a disabled pilot.

Record Flight: Polly Vacher in front of her single-engined Piper Dakota.

Pilot's Watch: The legendary Oris Big Crown featuring the «Wings Around the World» emblem. No. 654 7543 40 84, RRSP £ 545.–

Exclusive: The watch with maps of the two poles, a compass, a ruler, a pencil with eraser and sharpener.

ORIS
Swiss Made Watches
Since 1904

Tokyo, New York, Hong Kong, London, Paris, Milano, Sydney, Berlin, Genève, Bangkok, San Francisco, Taipei, Shanghai, Moscow. www.oris.ch
For further information and stockist details call 0800 214582, Fax 01204 704 155

Oris gives back to the community by donating money to disabled people who want to learn how to fly an airplane.

Although in recent years dot-com companies have taken a beating in the marketplace, many analysts believe that this is just a preliminary shakeout—the heyday of the Internet is yet to come. Indeed, some marketing analysts suggest that the Internet has created a *paradigm shift* for business, meaning that companies must adhere to a new model or pattern of how to profit in a wired world. They argue that we are moving toward an *attention economy*, where a company's success will be measured by its share of mind rather than share of market. This means that companies must find new and innovative ways to stand out from the crowd and become an integral part of consumers' lives rather than just being a dry company that makes and sells products. For example, major consumer packaged foods companies are drawing many more customers to their Web sites than in the past. More important, the sites are "sticky," meaning that they tend to keep visitors long enough to make a lasting impression on them and motivate people to keep coming back for more.

How are they doing this? Instead of following their old strategy of simply offering product information and recipes online, they now offer games, contests, and other promotions that transform their Web sites into less of a grocery store and more of a carnival. For example, about a third of the people who visit Kraft's Candy stand.com site, which promotes products like Lifesavers and Planters nuts, return to it again. They come back to play games like Nut Vendor, where the player assumes the role of a ballpark peanut hawker. Candystand, like other sites, gathers customers' e-mail addresses as they register for sweepstakes, then lures them back with offers of new recipes, games, and products.[17]

FOCUSING ON SOCIAL BENEFITS Another result of this new way of long-term thinking was the *social marketing concept*, which maintains that marketers must satisfy customers' needs in ways that also benefit society—and that also are profitable for the firm. This perspective is even more important since the terrorist attacks of 2001, which led many people and firms to reexamine their values and redouble their commitments to community and country.

As we'll see in Chapter 3, many big and small firms alike practice this philosophy. Their efforts include satisfying society's environmental and social needs for a cleaner, safer environment by developing recyclable packaging, adding extra safety features such as car air bags, voluntarily modifying a manufacturing process to reduce pollution, and sponsoring campaigns to address social problems.

Avon Products is one firm that believes social marketing is good for its customers and good for the company. For over 10 years, Avon has supported one and only one cause: breast cancer. Since the inception of the program in 1993, Avon has raised over $55 million for breast cancer programs through a variety of fund-raising channels. These efforts include Avon's "3-Day" event, a long-distance walking event in San Francisco, Boston, Atlanta, Chicago, Los Angeles, and New York.[18]

FOCUSING ON ACCOUNTABILITY   In addition to building long-term relationships and focusing on social responsibility, New Era firms place a much greater focus on *accountability*—measuring just how much value is created by marketing activities. This means that marketers at New Era firms ask hard questions about the true value of their efforts and their impact on the bottom line. These questions all boil down to the simple acronym of **ROI (Return on Investment)**. Marketers now realize that if they want to assess just how much value they are creating for the firm, they need to know exactly what they are spending and what the concrete results of their actions are.

However, assessing the value of marketing activities is not always easy. Many times marketing objectives are stated in vague phrases like "increase awareness of our product" or "encourage people to eat healthier snacks." These goals are important, but it is sometimes impossible for senior management at a firm to determine marketing's true impact. Because they are viewed as costs rather than investments, marketing activities often are among the first to get cut out of a firm's budget. In order to win continued support for what they do (and sometimes to keep their jobs), marketers in New Era firms do their best to prove to management that they are generating *measurable* value by aligning marketing activities with the firm's overall business objectives.[19]

How do they do this? Increasingly, marketers are developing scorecards that report (often in quantified terms) how the company or brand is actually doing in achieving various goals. We can think of a scorecard as a marketing department's report card. Scorecards tend to be short and to the point, and they often use charts and graphs to summarize information in an easy-to-read format. They might report "grades" on such factors as actual cost per sale, a comparison of Web downloads versus Web hits (i.e, the number of people who visit an e-commerce site compared to the number who actually buy something at the site), a measure of customers' satisfaction with a company's repair facilities, or perhaps even a percentage of consumers who respond to a mail piece that asks them to make a donation to a charity sponsored by the firm. Throughout this book, we'll be showing you examples of how marketers are trying to calculate ROI based on their actions in a box called "Marketing Metrics," like the one shown here.

An Example of a Customer Service Scorecard

Item Text	Quarterly Scores 2003		
	1st Qtr.	2nd Qtr.	3rd Qtr.
Satisfaction with			
C1 Employee responsiveness	60%	65%	68%
C2 Product selection	60%	62%	63%
C3 Service quality	60%	62%	55%
C4 Cleanliness of facility	75%	80%	85%
C5 Knowledge of employees	62%	62%	58%
C6 Appearance of employees	60%	62%	63%
C7 Convenience of location	60%	65%	68%

Source: Adapted from C. F. Lunbdy and C. Rasinowich, "The Missing Link," *Marketing Research*, winter 2003, 14–19, p. 18.

return on investment (ROI)
The direct financial impact of a firm's expenditure of a resource such as time or money.

real people, real choices
How It Worked Out at Monster.com

Jeff chose option 2. He sold The Monster Board to TMP Worldwide Inc., a recruitment advertising and Yellow Pages agency based in New York, NY. This company already had a vast global network of offices and client relationships as well as a local presence in most major cities in the United States and around the world. TMP added the resources that The Monster Board needed to provide career resources for its broad audience, which included everyone from interns to CEOs. Early in The Monster Board's history, the decision was made to focus the company's marketing efforts on the consumer. Jeff had the goal of creating a leading global brand, and the first step to accomplish that was reaching consumers and job seekers. This was the way to differentiate The Monster Board. The company already had an attention-grabbing name—now was the time to leverage it.

In January 1999, the company changed its name to "Monster.com" and launched a commercial, the award-winning "When I Grow Up," during the Super Bowl. The message conveyed in this spot truly resonated with job seekers across the nation, and they flocked to visit the site. About 2.2 million job searches were processed during a 24-hour period following the game—nearly a 450 percent increase from the 500,000 job searches prior to the Super Bowl. The humorous ad, regarded as one of the best Super Bowl commercials of all time, earned awards throughout the year, including *Advertising Age*'s "Best of Show," *Adweek*'s "Best Spot of the 90's," *Time*'s "Best Television of 1999," and *TV Guide*'s "Funniest Super Bowl Commercials of All Time."

Sure enough, the employers followed. By leading the online recruiting industry in job seeker traffic, employers posted jobs in droves on Monster because they knew that top talent from across the country was visiting the site. Since making the decision to market directly to job seekers/consumers first, Monster has been soaring, becoming the leading global online careers Web site and the ultimate destination to manage one's career or to find qualified candidates. What started as a small company with just a handful of employees has grown to include over 1,400 in 20 countries and is one of the few profitable public Internet companies today.

Have you ever considered that your employer is your customer? Employers have needs just like every other consumer. The *Brand You* supplement shows you step by step how to tune into employers' needs and market a brand called *You*. To learn more, go to Chapter 1.

CHAPTER SUMMARY

1. **Know who marketers are and where they work and understand marketing's role in the firm.** Marketers come from many different backgrounds and work in a variety of locations, from consumer goods companies to nonprofit organizations to financial institutions to advertising and public relations agencies. Marketing's role in the firm depends on the organization. Some firms are very marketing oriented, whereas others do not focus on marketing. However, marketing is being increasingly integrated with other business functions. Therefore, no matter what firm marketers work in, their decisions affect and are affected by the firm's other operations. Marketers must work together with other executives.

2. **Define what marketing is and how it provides value to everyone involved in the marketing process.** Marketing is an organizational function and a set of processes for creating, communicating, and delivering value to customers, and for managing customer relationships in ways that benefit the organization and its stakeholders. Therefore, marketing is all about delivering value to everyone who is affected by a transaction (stakeholders). Organizations that seek to ensure their long-term profitability by identifying and satisfying customers' needs and wants have adopted the marketing concept.

3. **Discuss the range of services and goods that are marketed.** Any good, service, or idea that can be marketed is a product, even though what is being sold may not take a physical form. Consumer goods are the tangible products that consumers purchase for personal or family use. Services are intangible products that we pay for and use but never own. Industrial goods are those goods sold to businesses and other organizations for further processing or for use in their business operations. Not-for-profit organizations, ideas, places, and people can also be marketed.

4. **Understand value from the perspectives of the customers, producers, and society.** Value is the benefits a customer receives from buying a product or service. Marketing communicates these benefits as the value proposition to the customer. For customers, the value proposition includes the whole bundle of benefits the product promises to deliver, not just the benefits of the product itself. Sellers determine value by assessing whether its transactions are profitable, whether it is providing value to stakeholders by creating a competitive advantage, and whether it is providing value through its value chain. Society receives value from marketing activities when producers and consumers engage in ethical, profitable, and environmentally friendly exchange relationships.

5. **Understand the basics of marketing planning and the marketing mix tools used in the marketing process.** The strategic process of marketing planning begins with an assessment of factors within the organization and in the external environment that could help or hinder the development and marketing of products. On the basis of this analysis, marketers set objectives and develop strategies. Many firms use a target marketing strategy in which they divide the overall market into segments and then target the most attractive one. Then they design the marketing mix to gain a competitive position in the target market. The marketing mix includes product, price, place, and promotion. The product is what satisfies customer needs. The price is the assigned value or amount to be exchanged for the product. The place or channel of distribution gets the product to the customer. Promotion is the organization's efforts to persuade customers to buy the product.

6. **Describe the evolution of the marketing concept.** Early in the 20th century, firms followed a production orientation in which they focused on the most efficient ways to produce and distribute products. Beginning in the 1930s, some firms adopted a selling orientation that encouraged salespeople to aggressively sell products to customers. In the 1950s, organizations adopted a consumer orientation that focused on customer satisfaction. This led to the development of the marketing concept. Today, many firms are moving toward a New Era orientation that includes not only a commitment to quality and value but also a concern for both economic and social profit.

KEY TERMS

CHAPTER REVIEW

MARKETING CONCEPTS: TESTING YOUR KNOWLEDGE

1. Where do marketers work, and what role does marketing have in the firm?

2. Briefly explain what marketing is.

3. Explain needs, wants, and demands. What is the role of marketing in each of these?

4. What is utility? How does marketing create different forms of utility?

5. Define the terms *consumer goods*, *services*, and *industrial goods*.

6. What does the lifetime value of the customer refer to, and how is it calculated?

7. What does it mean for a firm to have a competitive advantage? What gives a firm a competitive advantage?

8. What is involved in marketing planning?

9. List and describe the elements of the marketing mix.

10. Trace the evolution of the marketing concept.

MARKETING CONCEPTS: DISCUSSING CHOICES AND ISSUES

1. Have you ever pirated software? How about music? Is it ethical to give or receive software instead of paying for it? Does the answer depend on the person's motivation and/or if he or she could otherwise afford to buy the product?

2. The marketing concept focuses on the ability of marketing to satisfy customer needs. As a typical college student, how does marketing satisfy your needs? What areas of your life are affected by marketing? What areas of your life (if any) are not affected by marketing?

3. In both developed and developing countries, not all firms have implemented programs that follow the marketing concept. Can you think of firms that still operate with a pro-duction orientation? A selling orientation? What changes would you recommend for these firms?

4. Successful firms have a competitive advantage because they are able to identify distinctive competencies and use these to create differential benefits for their customers. Consider your business school or your university. What distinctive competencies does it have? What differential benefits does it provide for students? What is its competitive advantage? What are your ideas as to how your university could improve its competitive position? Write an outline of your ideas.

5. Ideally, each member of a value chain adds value to a product before someone buys it. Thinking about a music CD you might buy in a store, what kind of value does the music retailer add? How about the label that signs the artist? The public relations firm that arranges a tour by the artist to promote the new CD? The production company that shoots a music video to go along with the cut?

MARKETING PRACTICE: APPLYING WHAT YOU'VE LEARNED

1. An old friend of yours has been making and selling vitamin-fortified smoothies to acquaintances and friends of friends for some time. He is now thinking about opening a shop in a small college town, but he is worried about whether he'll have enough customers who want these smoothies to keep a business going. Knowing that you are a marketing student, he's asked you for some advice. What can you tell him about product, price, promotion, and place (distribution) strategies that will help him get his business off the ground?

2. Assume that you are employed by your city's chamber of commerce. One major focus of the chamber is to get industries to move to your city. As a former marketing student, you know that there are issues involving product, price, promotion, and place (distribution) that can attract busi-

ness. Next week you have an opportunity to speak to the members of the chamber, and your topic will be "Marketing a City." Develop an outline for that presentation.

3. As a marketing professional, you have been asked to write a short piece for a local business newsletter about the state of marketing today. You think the best way to address this topic is to review how the marketing concept has evolved and to discuss the New Era orientation. Write the short article you will submit to the editor of the newsletter.

4. As college students, you and your friends sometimes discuss the various courses you are taking. One of your friends says to you, "Marketing's not important. It's just dumb advertising." Another friend says, "Marketing doesn't really affect people's lives in any way." As a role-playing exercise, present your arguments against these statements to your class.

MARKETING MINIPROJECT: LEARNING BY DOING

The purpose of this miniproject is to develop an understanding of the importance of marketing to different organizations.

1. Working as a team with two or three other students in your class select an organization in your community that practices marketing. It may be a manufacturer, a service provider, a retailer, a not-for-profit organization—almost any organization will do. Then schedule a visit with someone within the organization who is involved in the market-

ing activities. Arrange for a short visit in which the person can give your group a tour of the facilities and explain the organization's marketing activities.

2. Divide the following list of topics among your team and ask each person to be responsible for developing a set of questions to ask during the interview to learn about the company's program:
   - What customer segments the company targets
   - How it determines needs and wants
   - What products it offers, including features, benefits, and goals for customer satisfaction
   - What its pricing strategies are, including any discounting policies it has
   - What promotional strategies it uses and what these emphasize to position the product(s)
   - How it distributes products and whether it has encountered any problems
   - How marketing planning is done and who does it
   - Whether social responsibility is part of the marketing program and, if so, in what ways

3. Develop a team report of your findings. In each section of the report, share what you learned that is new or surprising to you compared to what you expected.

4. Develop a team presentation for your class that summarizes your findings. Conclude your presentation with comments on what your team believes the company was doing that was particularly good and what was not quite so good.

REAL PEOPLE, REAL SURFERS: EXPLORING THE WEB

Monster.com is a company that is part of the e-marketing era. Visit Monster.com's Web site and visit the Web site of one or more of the company's competitors such as **www.hotjobs.com** or **www.headhunter.com**. Follow the links to find out as much as you can about the companies. Then on the basis of your experience, answer the following questions:

1. Which firm has the better Web site? What makes it better?

2. Do you think the firms are targeting specific market segments? If so, what market segments? What features of the Web site give you that idea?

3. Do you think there is anything about any of the Web sites that would make it more attractive than the others to employers?

4. What are your major criticisms of each of the Web sites? What would you do to improve each site?

MARKETING PLAN EXERCISE

A key to long-term business success lies in a firm's ability to offer value to customers through its product offerings. The task of communicating that value proposition rests largely with the company's marketers. A marketing plan not only must clarify the sources of value but also must specify how the value message gets out.

Pick a product or service you like—one that you believe has a strong value proposition.

1. Identify the specific source(s) of value. That is, what leads you to conclude the product or service offers value?

2. How is that value communicated?

3. What other sources of value might be developed for the product or service you identified? How might these new value-adding properties be communicated to customers?

Marketing in Action Case

Real Choices on *American Idol*

What musical genre will the show borrow from this week? Which contestants will perform the best? Most important, which performing hopeful will be sent home? Such questions are part of regular conversations among the millions of fans of the hit show *American Idol*, a reality television show on the FOX Network. After three seasons, *American Idol* is rivaled only by its reality show counterpart *Survivor* in terms of popularity and number of viewers on a weekly basis. However, when it comes to marketing the two shows, *American Idol* clearly is the winner in terms of the number and variety of different ways the show can be marketed.

From a product standpoint, *American Idol* is a phenomenon that stands alone among other reality shows in terms of its popularity. On a weekly basis, approximately 30 million viewers watch musical hopefuls vie for a chance at a recording contract. Almost 40 million viewers watched the final episode of *American Idol*'s second season, which represented a 33 percent increase over *American Idol*'s first season finale. In each weekly segment, contestants sing songs chosen from a specific song style in front of a live studio and television audience. After each contestant sings, the show's judges, who can be condescending, complimentary, and caustic all at the same time, provide feedback to the contestant about his or her performance, hairstyle, and clothing; basically, whatever they feel like commenting on. At the end of the show, audience members are given the opportunity to call in or text message a vote for their favorite performer. The following night, in another live show, America gets to find out which performer was "voted off." Because Americans' votes determine who leaves the show each week, *American Idol* ups the ante in terms of audience participation. *American Idol*'s format has resulted in a product that has been very popular in the 18- to 49-year-old age bracket of viewers—the age bracket most coveted by advertisers.

As a product, *American Idol* has given the FOX Network its highest ratings ever outside of sporting events like the Super Bowl. As a distribution outlet for the show, FOX has been able to reap the rewards of providing the place element of the marketing mix. Because of *American Idol*'s popularity, especially with an extremely desirable audience segment, the show appeals to advertisers wanting to reach that audience. The third season of *American Idol* resulted in the number of sponsors increasing from the three biggest sponsors of Coca-Cola, Ford, and AT&T Wireless to also include Subway, Old Navy, and Clairol. In addition, FOX has been able to use advertising slots during *American Idol* to promote its other product offerings like *The OC*, *24*, and others. Another distribution outlet used by *American Idol*'s creators is the Web site. From the Web site, fans of the show can read the personal histories of contestants, send e-mails to contestants, and order merchandise and music videos. Each of these activities enhances audience participation in the show and its outcome. Promoters have also introduced a number of spin-off products, including *American Idol* clothing, fragrances, jewelry, video games, CDs, and even a concert tour.

Because of *American Idol*'s popularity and inherent strength as a product, its creators and producers are able to command a premium price for promoting sponsorship opportunities to other companies. For the current season, Coca-Cola, Ford, and AT&T Wireless are reportedly paying more than $20 million each for the opportunity to sponsor the show. For that investment, the companies are able to promote their products in innovative and interesting ways. For example, in addition to airing advertisements for Classic Coke and Vanilla Coke, Coca-Cola has designed the "Red Room," where contestants spend time before and after their performance with vending machines and furniture decorated in Coca-Cola graphics.

In another example of innovative promotions, *American Idol* viewers are exposed to the show's sponsors in minisegments integrated in with the show itself. For example, before cutting away to a commercial, the show often will highlight its contestants doing something associated with one of its sponsors' products. One week the segments will show the contestants driving a Ford to a fun destination while singing an upbeat song, while the next week the contestants will be shown making sandwiches and singing a song for customers at a local Subway. Such promotional tie-ins provide the impression of the show's contestants being actual users of the product—a very powerful message to the audience.

Given the show's success and its effective use of the marketing mix elements, there will undoubtedly be another season. However, *American Idol*'s popularity puts pressure on its creators and producers to capitalize on that popularity in new and innovative ways. How do marketers keep the show's use of the marketing mix fresh?

Things to Think About

1. What is the decision facing *American Idol* marketers?
2. What factors are important in understanding the decision situation?
3. What are the alternatives?
4. What decision(s) do you recommend?
5. What are some ways to implement your recommendation(s)?

Sources: Todd Wasserman, "Scent (and More) of an 'American Idol,' " *Adweek*, January 19, 2004, 8; Wayne Friedman and David Goetzl, "Fox Seeks $26 Million for New 'Idol,' " *Advertising Age*, October 14, 2002, 3, 57; and Steve McClellan, "Idol Moments Ahead for Advertisers," *Broadcasting & Cable*, January 5, 2004, 20.

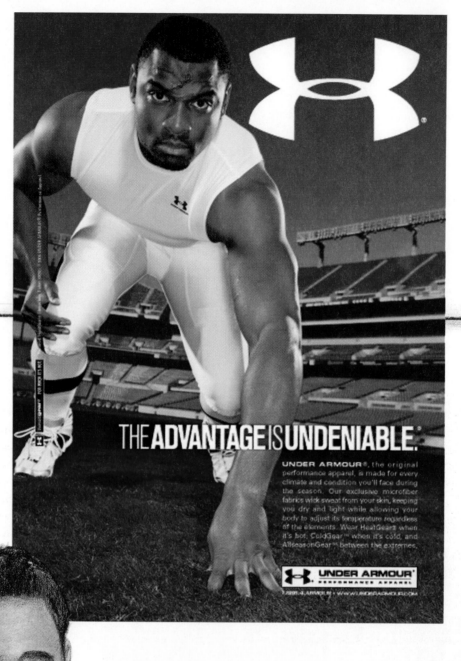

THE **ADVANTAGE** IS **UNDENIABLE.**

UNDER ARMOUR®, the original performance apparel, is made for every climate and condition you'll face during the season. Our exclusive microfiber fabrics wick sweat from your skin, keeping you dry and light while allowing your body to adjust its temperature regardless of the elements. Wear HeatGear® when it's hot, ColdGear™ when it's cold, and AllseasonGear™ between the extremes.

UNDER ARMOUR® PERFORMANCE APPAREL
1-888-4-ARMOUR • WWW.UNDERARMOUR.COM

www.underarmour.com

real people, real choices

meet Steve Battista, a Decision Maker at Under Armour, Inc.

first job out of school

Sportswriter.

what i do when i'm not working

That's family time, until everyone goes to sleep. Then I read or start writing copy for the next campaign.

STRATEGIC PLANNING AND THE MARKETING ENVIRONMENT: THE ADVANTAGE IS UNDENIABLE

Steve Battista is director of marketing at Under Armour, Inc. As the senior brand marketing executive reporting directly to founder and president Kevin Plank, Steve oversees all aspects of marketing, including the buying and placement strategy, public relations, merchandising, promotions, virtual marketing, and corporate communications. His campaigns have been highlighted in many newspapers and magazines, including *Brandweek*, the *Washington Post*, the *Wall Street Journal*, the *New York Times*, and the *Sports Business Journal*. Most recently, his team's television campaign, "We Must Protect This House," collected several industry awards, including the Addy for Best National Spot, while behind the scenes he struck an innovative deal with ESPN/ABC that resulted in landmark product placement on the football reality show *Playmakers*. In 2004, he won the American Business Award for Marketer of the Year.

Prior to joining Under Armour in 2000, Steve received a B.A. in English writing from Towson University and a Master's in writing from Johns Hopkins University.

Decision Time at Under Armour

Under Armour began with a T-shirt. But it wasn't just any T-shirt—it was a microfiber alternative to cotton that wouldn't retain perspiration and would dry almost immediately to keep athletes cool, dry, and light on the field. From that original T-shirt, Under Armour Performance Apparel has developed five gear lines to keep athletes substantially cooler (or warmer), not to mention two to three pounds lighter than the cotton standard, inspiring the company's slogan, "The Advantage Is Undeniable."

When Steve Battista went to work for Under Armour in 2000, the company had less than 20 employees—and no marketing department or marketing budget. The company has mushroomed dramatically since, to the point where in late 2003 *Inc.* magazine named it the second fastest growing company in the United States. Today it boasts more than 400 employees, two new national television commercial campaigns, an award-winning print and outdoor campaign, major sponsorships with networks like ESPN/ABC, and a widely popular and profitable Web site. Under Armour's war cry in its advertising—"Protect This House!"—is a familiar phrase to many consumers.

But is it possible to be *too* successful *too* quickly? With 90 new products being launched each year, senior management acknowledged the need to manage Under Armour's growth. For Steve and his department, that means being "protector of the brand"—making sure the company doesn't lose its focus or stray too far from its core brand mission. From a branding standpoint,

career high	business book i'm reading now	my hero	my management style
Having the "Protect This House" tagline adopted by the country and hearing it everywhere from ESPN's sports anchor Stuart Scott to the 70,000 screaming fans at a Ravens-Steelers game to the fifth graders playing basketball on the recess lot at my wife's school.	*Fashion Icon*, by Mike Toth.	Johnny Cash.	Player/manager.

objectives

1 Explain the strategic planning process.

2 Describe the steps in marketing planning.

3 Explain operational planning.

4 Discuss some of the important aspects of an organization's internal environment.

5 Explain why marketers scan an organization's external business environment.

Under Armour's complex technology has always been translated in a simple advertising message: wear HeatGear when it's hot, ColdGear when it's cold, AllSeasonGear in between.

But product extensions can be trickier because lifestyle trends in society are creating new opportunities to produce and sell many kinds of moisture-wicking performance apparel. And to stay on top of fabric technology and ahead of the growing list of competitors, the Apparel Design Team at Under Armour works many seasons (and often years) in advance. Thus, keeping all departments on point with the brand's mission is quite a challenge for Steve and his team.

In addition to collegiate and professional athletes, weekend warriors of all stripes can be enticed to forsake their sweat-soaked cotton T-shirts for the undeniable advantage of performance apparel that keeps them cool and dry on the playing fields or even in front of their television sets. Under Armour needed to figure out just what it wanted to be when it grew up. Steve considered his options:

OPTION 1: Position Under Armour apparel as a fashion brand.

Steve saw the possibility of white-hot growth in the fashion category, an easy way to get really big really quick. When your brand is hot and the public is hungry for your logo, it's tempting to fire out new advertising campaigns and tons of new products for the masses waiting to buy anything with your logo on it. On the other hand, Under Armour has always been about performance—a valuable tool for serious athletes rather than a status symbol for wannabes. In addition, most of Under Armour's products are worn under other clothing (like football jerseys), so they're primarily visible only in training sessions, warm-ups, and postgame interviews. And fashion is a fickle business—what's hot one year can be out the next. Steve and

the rest of senior management had to decide whether chasing this easy business and plastering the Under Armour logo on all kinds of products was worth the risk of stripping away the soul of the brand.

OPTION 2: Maintain Under Armour's focus on performance apparel to be worn exclusively by professional athletes.

This strategy would keep Under Armour in touch with its core customers and let the company continue to do what it did best. From a marketing and advertising standpoint, Steve felt that Under Armour's authenticity provided its main competitive advantage. On the other hand, new opportunities to expand into other areas such as clothing worn by hunters, fisherman, policemen, or even the military were very tempting, and Steve was afraid of pigeonholing the brand as being "only" for football players.

OPTION 3: Expand Under Armour outside its core customer base of team sports by developing a wider range of products targeted for other nonteam sports and for use by specific professions such as law enforcement and backing them with advertising in mainstream magazines and network television.

This strategy could result in much higher volume sales for Under Armour and grow brand awareness dramatically as shoppers started to see the Under Armour products outside the football field or baseball diamond. Steve's concern was that Under Armour would dilute the brand image with the core consumer (a man or woman into playing team sports) if products were made for and advertising was directed at runners, outdoorsman, hunters, skiers, and law enforcement officers.

Now, put yourself in Steve Battista's shoes: Which option would you choose, and why?

Business Planning: Seeing the Big Picture

Steve Battista understands that planning is everything. Just like Under Armour's slogan, for firms that plan well, "The Advantage Is Undeniable." Part of Steve's role as a planner is to help define his brand's distinctive identity and purpose. Careful planning enables a firm to speak in a clear voice in the marketplace so that customers understand what the firm is and what it has to offer that competitors don't—especially as it decides how to create value for customers, shareholders, employees, and society. We think this process is so important that we're launching into our exploration of marketing by starting with a discussion about what planners do and the questions they (both Under Armour and marketers in general) need to ask to be sure they keep their companies and products on course. Then, at the end of the book, we'll come full circle and see how Under Armour answers these questions to maintain its advantage.

Whether a firm is a well-established company like Hanes or Nike or a relative newcomer like Under Armour, planning for the future is a key to prosperity. Sure, it's true that a firm can be successful even if it makes some mistakes in planning. It's also true that some seat-of-the-pants businesses are successful. But without good planning for the future, firms will be less successful than they could be. In the worst-case scenario, a lack of planning can be fatal for both large and small businesses; and, of course, there are times when even the best planning cannot anticipate the future accurately. Still, just like a Boy Scout, it's always better to be prepared.

Business planning is an ongoing process of making decisions that guide the firm both in the short term and for the long haul. Planning identifies and builds on a firm's strengths, and it helps managers at all levels make informed decisions in a changing business environment. Planning means that an organization develops objectives before it takes action. In large firms like Sony and Kodak that operate in many markets, planning is a complex process involving many people from different areas of the company's operations. At a small business like Mac's Diner, however, planning is quite different. Mac himself is chief cook, occasional dishwasher, and the sole company planner. With midsize firms like Under Armour, the planning process falls somewhere in between, depending on the size of the firm and the complexity of its operations.

In this chapter, we'll look at the different steps in an organization's planning. First, we'll see how managers develop a **business plan** that includes the decisions that guide the entire organization or its business units. Then we'll examine the marketing planning process and the stages in that process that lead to the development and implementation of a **marketing plan**—a document that describes the marketing environment, outlines the marketing objectives and strategies, and identifies how the strategies will be implemented, monitored, and controlled. Finally, in the last part of the chapter, we'll take a more detailed look at the factors marketers must consider as they scan the marketing environment looking for information to help them make their decisions.

The Three Levels of Business Planning

We all know what planning is—we plan a vacation or a great Saturday night party. Some of us even plan how we're going to study and get our assignments completed. When businesses plan, the process is more complex. As shown in Figure 2.1, planning occurs at three levels: strategic, functional, and operational.

- **Strategic planning: Strategic planning** is the managerial decision process that matches the firm's resources (such as its financial assets and workforce) and capabilities (the things it is able to do well because of its expertise and experience) to its market opportunities for long-term growth. In a strategic plan, top management—usually the chief executive officer (CEO), president, and other top executives—define the firm's purpose and specify what the firm hopes to achieve over the next five or so years. For example, a firm's strategic plan may set an objective of increasing the firm's total revenues by 20 percent in the next five years. For large firms such as the Walt Disney Company that have a number of self-contained divisions or strategic business units (such as the theme park, movie, television network, and cruise line divisions), strategic planning occurs both at the overall corporate level (Disney headquarters planning for the whole corporation) and at the individual business unit level (at the theme park, movie studios, television networks, and cruise line level). We'll discuss these two levels later in the chapter.

business planning
An ongoing process of making decisions that guide the firm both in the short term and for the long haul.

business plan
A plan that includes the decisions that guide the entire organization.

marketing plan
A document that describes the marketing environment, outlines the marketing objectives and strategy, and identifies who will be responsible for carrying out each part of the marketing strategy.

strategic planning
A managerial decision process that matches an organization's resources and capabilities to its market opportunities for long-term growth and survival.

Figure 2.1   Planning at Different Management Levels

During planning, an organization determines its objectives and then develops courses of action to accomplish them. In larger firms, planning takes place at the strategic, functional, and operational levels.

What It Is	Strategic Planning	Functional Planning (In Marketing Department, called Marketing Planning)	Operational Planning
Who Does It	Planning done by top-level corporate management	Planning done by top functional-level management such as the firm's chief marketing officer (CMO)	Planning done by supervisory managers
What They Do	1. Define the mission 2. Evaluate the internal and external environment 3. Set organizational or SBU objectives 4. Establish the business portfolio (if applicable) 5. Develop growth strategies	1. Perform a situation analysis 2. Set marketing objectives 3. Develop marketing strategies 4. Implement marketing strategies 5. Monitor and control marketing strategies	1. Develop action plans to implement the marketing plan 2. Use marketing metrics to monitor how the plan is working

functional planning
A decision process that concentrates on developing detailed plans for strategies and tactics for the short term that support an organization's long-term strategic plan.

operational planning
A decision process that focuses on developing detailed plans for day-to-day activities that carry out an organization's functional plans.

- **Functional planning:** The next level of planning is **functional planning** (sometimes called "tactical planning"). This level gets its name because it is accomplished by the various functional areas of the firm, such as marketing, finance, and human resources. It is usually done by vice presidents or functional directors. The functional planning that is conducted in the marketing department is referred to as *marketing planning*. The person in charge of such planning may have the title of director of marketing, vice president of marketing, or chief marketing officer. Marketing planners like Steve Battista at Under Armour might set an objective to gain 40 percent of a particular market by successfully introducing three new products during the coming year. This objective would be part of a *functional area plan*. Functional planning typically includes both a broad five-year plan to support the firm's strategic plan and a detailed annual plan for the coming year.

- **Operational planning:** Still farther down the planning ladder are the first-line managers. In the marketing department, first-line managers include people such as sales managers, marketing communications managers, and marketing research managers. These managers are responsible for planning at a third level called **operational planning**. Operational plans focus on the day-to-day execution of the functional plans and include detailed annual, semiannual, or quarterly plans. Operational plans might show exactly how many units of a product a salesperson needs to sell per month or how many television commercials the firm will place on certain networks during a season. At the operational planning level for Under Armour, the marketing communications manager may develop plans to promote the new products to potential customers, while the sales manager may develop a quarterly plan for the company's sales force. Both of these activities are forms of operational planning.

Of course, marketing managers don't just sit in their offices dreaming up plans without any concern for the rest of the organization. Even though we've described each layer separately, all business planning is an integrated activity. This means that the organization's strategic, functional, and operational plans must work together for the benefit of the whole. So, planners at all levels must consider good principles of accounting, the value of the company to its stockholders, and the requirements for staffing and human resource management—that is, they must keep the "big picture" in mind even as they plan for their corner of the organization's world.

In short, the different functional- and operational-level planners within an organization have to make sure that their plans support the overall organization's mission and objectives and that they work well together. A marketing planner like Steve Battista at Under Armour can't go off and develop a successful plan for the marketing side of the firm without fully understanding how what he's doing fits with the overall organization's direction and resources. In the next sections, we'll further explore planning at each of these three levels: strategic, functional, and operational.

Strategic Planning: Driving a Firm's Success

Many large firms realize that relying on only one product can be risky, so they have become multi-product companies with self-contained divisions organized around products or brands. As mentioned earlier, firms such as Disney operate several distinctly different businesses. These self-contained divisions are called **strategic business units (SBUs)**—individual units representing different areas of business within the firm that are each different enough to have their own mission, business objectives, resources, managers, and competitors. As we pointed out earlier, Disney's SBUs include its theme parks, movie studios, television networks, and cruise line.

In firms with multiple SBUs, the first step in strategic planning is for top management to establish a mission for the entire corporation. Top managers then evaluate the internal and external environment of the business and set corporate-level objectives that guide decision making within each individual SBU. In small firms that are not large enough to have separate SBUs, strategic planning simply takes place at the overall firm level. Whether or not a firm has SBUs, the process of strategic planning is basically the same. Let's look at the planning steps in a bit more detail.

Step 1: Define the Mission

Theoretically, top management's first step in the strategic planning stage is to answer such questions as, What business are we in? What customers should we serve? How should we develop the firm's capabilities and focus its efforts? In many firms, the answers to questions such as these become the lead items in the organization's strategic plan. They become part of a **mission statement**—a formal document that describes the organization's overall purpose and what it hopes to achieve in terms of its customers, products, and resources. For example, the mission of Mothers Against Drunk Driving (MADD) is "to stop drunk driving, support the victims of this violent crime, and prevent underage drinking."[1] Under Armour's mission statement is to "find new technology and enhance the performance of every athlete and outdoorsman. Lighter. Faster. Stronger. Better."

The ideal mission statement is not too broad, too narrow, nor too shortsighted. Note that Under Armour's mission statement leaves no doubt about the focus of its business. A mission that is too broad will not provide adequate focus for the organization. It doesn't do much good to claim, "We are in the business of making high-quality products," as it's hard to find a firm that doesn't make this claim.

However, a mission statement that is too narrow may inhibit managers' ability to visualize possible growth opportunities. If, for example, a firm sees itself in terms of its product only, consumer trends or technology can make that product obsolete—and the firm is left with no future. If Xerox had continued to define its mission in terms of just producing copy machines instead of providing "document solutions," the shift to electronic documents would have left them in the dust the way the Model T Ford replaced the horse and buggy. And it's important to remember that the need for a clear mission statement applies to virtually any type of organization, even those like MADD, whose objective is to serve society rather than to sell goods or services.

strategic business units
Individual units within the firm that operate like separate businesses, with each having its own mission, business objectives, resources, managers, and competitors.

mission statement
A formal statement in an organization's strategic plan that describes the overall purpose of the organization and what it intends to achieve in terms of its customers, products, and resources.

Step 2: Evaluate the Internal and External Environment

The second step in strategic planning is to assess the firm's internal and external environments. This process is referred to as a *situation analysis, environmental analysis,* or sometimes a *business review.* The analysis includes a discussion of the firm's internal environment, which can identify a firm's strengths and weaknesses, as well as the external environment in which the firm does business so the firm can identify opportunities and threats.

internal environment
The controllable elements inside an organization, including its people, its facilities, and how it does things that influence the operations of the organization.

By **internal environment**, we mean all the controllable elements inside a firm that influence how well the firm operates. Internal strengths may lie in the firm's technologies. What is the firm able to do well that other firms would find difficult to duplicate? What patents does it hold? A firm's physical facilities can be an important strength or weakness, as can its level of financial stability, its relationships with suppliers, its corporate reputation, its ability to produce consistently high-quality products, and its ownership of strong brands in the marketplace.

Internal strengths and weaknesses often reside in the firm's employees—the firm's human and intellectual capital. What skills do the employees have? What kind of training have they had? Are they loyal to the firm? Do they feel a sense of ownership? Has the firm been able to attract top researchers and good decision makers? Southwest Airlines has always been very focused on hiring and developing employees who reflect the "Southwest Spirit" to customers. Anyone who has flown on Southwest can attest to the fact that the atmosphere is lively and fun, and flight attendants are likely to do all sorts of cute stunts (within the bounds of safety, of course) during the flight to promote a fun atmosphere. For Southwest, a real strength—one that's hard for the competition to crack—lies in this employee spirit.[2]

external environment
The uncontrollable elements outside an organization that may affect its performance either positively or negatively.

The **external environment** consists of elements outside the firm that may affect it either positively or negatively. The external environment includes consumers, government regulations, competitors, the overall economy, and trends in popular culture. Unlike elements of the internal environment that management can control to a large degree, these external factors are not controllable by the firm, and management must react to them.

Opportunities and threats can come from any part of the external environment. Sometimes trends or currently unserved customer needs provide opportunities for growth. On the other hand, if changing customer needs or buying patterns mean customers are turning away from a firm's products, it's a signal of possible danger or threats down the road. Like all airlines, Southwest has been impacted in recent years by enhanced security regulations, driven by the federal government through the Transportation Safety Administration. These regulations entail additional costs for the airlines that are not optional, and thus Southwest has no choice but to react to this demand from the external environment.

SWOT analysis
An analysis of an organization's strengths and weaknesses and the opportunities and threats in its external environment.

What is the outcome of an analysis of a firm's internal and external environments? Managers often synthesize the results of a situation analysis into a format called a **SWOT analysis**. A SWOT analysis allows managers to focus clearly on the meaningful strengths (S) and weaknesses (W) in the firm's internal environment and opportunities (O) and threats (T) coming from outside the firm (the external environment). A SWOT analysis enables a firm to develop strategies that make use of what the firm does best in seizing opportunities for growth while at the same time avoiding external threats that might hurt the firm's sales and profits. Table 2.1 shows an example of a sample SWOT analysis for Nokia.

Step 3: Set Organizational or SBU Objectives

After constructing a mission statement, top management translates that mission statement into organizational or SBU objectives. Organizational objectives are a direct outgrowth of the mission statement and broadly identify what the firm hopes to accomplish within the general time frame of the firm's long-range business plan. If the firm is big enough to have separate SBUs, each SBU will have its own objectives that are relevant to its operations.

To be effective, objectives need to be specific, measurable (so firms can tell whether they've met them or not), and attainable. Attainability is especially important—firms that

Table 2.1   A Suggested SWOT Analysis for Nokia

Strengths	• Nokia has a world-class research, design, and engineering team. • Nokia has global relationships with all major phone companies worldwide. • Nokia is rated as the world's fifth most valuable brand, ahead of Sony, Nike, and Mercedes-Benz. • Nokia's strong management team has come through many crises unscathed.
Weaknesses	• Nokia will likely be late in developing third-generation (Internet-enabled) phones.
Opportunities	• The world's biggest phone companies are willing to pay top dollar to offer its customers Nokia's snazzy phones. • There is a growing world market for cell phones, especially in developing countries such as China and India. • The cell phone market should reach 1 billion units per year by 2005.
Threats	• The European market for cellular phones with current technology is nearly saturated. • Nokia's key customers, Europe's telcos (telecommunications companies), are $125 billion in debt. • Nokia faces well-financed Japanese rivals.

Source: Adapted from Stephen Baker, John Shinal, and Irene M. Kunii, "Is Nokia's Star Dimming?," *Business Week*, January 22, 2001, 66–72.

establish "pie in the sky" objectives they can't realistically obtain can create frustration for their employees (who work hard but get no satisfaction of accomplishment) and other stakeholders in the firm, such as vendors and shareholders who are affected when the firm doesn't meet its objectives.

Objectives may relate to revenue and sales, profitability, the firm's standing in the market, return on investment, productivity, product development, customer relations and satisfaction, social responsibility, and so on. To ensure measurability, objectives are often stated in numerical terms. For example, a firm might have as an objective a 10 percent increase in profitability. It could reach this objective by increasing productivity, by reducing costs, or by selling off an unprofitable division. Or it might meet this 10 percent objective by developing new products, investing in new technologies, or entering a new market.

For many years, Proctor & Gamble (P&G) had an objective of having a number one brand in every product category in which it competed. This objective worked well, exemplified by brands such as Crest in the toothpaste category, Folgers in coffee, Pampers in diapers, and Head and Shoulders in shampoo. The objective was measurable in terms of the share of market of P&G's products versus those sold by competitors. However, in the long run, such an objective is very difficult to sustain because of competitive activity and ever-changing consumer tastes. Sure enough, over time, some P&G brands continued to hold a respectable market share, but they dropped from the number one position. Should P&G not sell in a product category simply because its brand is not number one? Management realized the answer to this question was clearly "no," and the objective morphed into one focused on profitability in each brand.

Step 4: Establish the Business Portfolio

For companies with several different SBUs, strategic planning includes making decisions about how to best allocate resources across these businesses to ensure growth for the total organization. As Figure 2.2 illustrates, each SBU has its own focus within the firm's overall strategic plan, and each has its own target market and strategies for reaching its objectives. Just like an independent

MEASURING VALUE
marketing metrics

A survey of leading marketing firms in five countries (United States, United Kingdom, France, Germany, and Japan) found that market share is the metric that is most likely to be reported to the company's board of directors. Other commonly used metrics include the following:

- Perceived product/service quality
- Customer loyalty/retention
- Customer/segment profitability
- Relative price

Across the five countries, German companies are the heaviest users of metrics and Japanese firms the lightest. Of the companies surveyed, 97 percent of German firms said they report their market share to their boards compared to 79 percent of American firms and only 57 percent of Japanese firms. Overall, firms that do business in multiple countries and those that have above-average marketing budgets are more likely to rely on metrics.

Source: Patrick Barwise and John U. Farley, "Which Marketing Metrics Are Used and Where?," *Working Paper Series*, Report No. 03-111 (Cambridge, Mass.: Marketing Science Institute, 2003).

Crest Whitening Expressions in Cinnamon Rush.
A whole new brushing experience that's like, oooh, ahhh. Also in kickin' flavors like Extreme Herbal Mint and Fresh Citrus Breeze. They'll whiten your teeth and blow your mind.

©2003 P&G   For a free mini tube, visit WhiteningExpressions.com

Crest toothpaste products are part of P&G's portfolio, which ranges from personal care products to coffee.

business, each SBU is a separate *profit center* within the larger corporation—that is, each SBU within the firm is responsible for its own costs, revenues, and profits.

Just as the collection of different stocks an investor owns is called a portfolio, the range of different businesses that a large firm operates is called its **business portfolio.** As with the GE example, these different businesses usually represent very different product lines, each of which operates with its own budget and management. Having a diversified business portfolio reduces the firm's dependence on one product line or one group of customers. For example, if travel suffers and Disney has a bad year in theme park attendance and cruises, its managers hope that the sales will be made up by stay-at-homers who go to Disney movies and watch Disney's television networks.

Portfolio analysis is a tool management uses to assess the potential of a firm's businesses portfolio. It helps management decide which of its current SBUs should receive more—or less—of the firm's resources, and which of its SBUs are most consistent with the firm's overall mission. Several models are available to assist management in the portfolio analysis process. Let's examine one popular model: the **BCG growth–market share matrix** developed by the Boston Consulting Group (BCG).

The BCG model focuses on determining the potential of a firm's existing successful SBUs to generate cash that the firm can then use to invest in other businesses. In the BCG matrix, shown in Figure 2.3 on page 42, the vertical axis represents the attractiveness of the market, the *market growth rate.* Even though Figure 2.3 shows "high" and "low" as measurements, marketers might ask whether the total market for the SBU's products is growing 10, 50, 100, or 200 percent annually.

The horizontal axis in Figure 2.3 shows the SBU's current strength in the market through its *relative market share.* Here, marketers might ask whether the SBUs share is 5, 25, or perhaps 75 percent of the current market. Combining the two axes creates four quadrants representing four different types of SBUs. Each quadrant of the BCG grid uses a symbol to designate business units that fall within a certain range for market growth rate and market share. Let's take a closer look at each cell in the grid:

• **Stars:** Stars are SBUs with products that have a dominant market share in high-growth markets. Because the SBU has a dominant share of the market, stars generate large revenues, but they also require large amounts of funding to keep up with production and promotion demands. Because the market has a large growth potential, managers design strategies to maximize market share in the face of increasing competition. The firm aims at getting the largest share of

Figure 2.2 Role of Strategic Business Units (SBUs)

Very large corporations are normally divided into self-contained divisions, or SBUs. SBUs represent different major areas of the overall firm's business. For example, General Electric has a jet engine division, a lighting division, an appliance division, and numerous other divisions. At GE as with most corporations, each SBU operates as an independent business with its own mission and objectives—and its own marketing strategy.

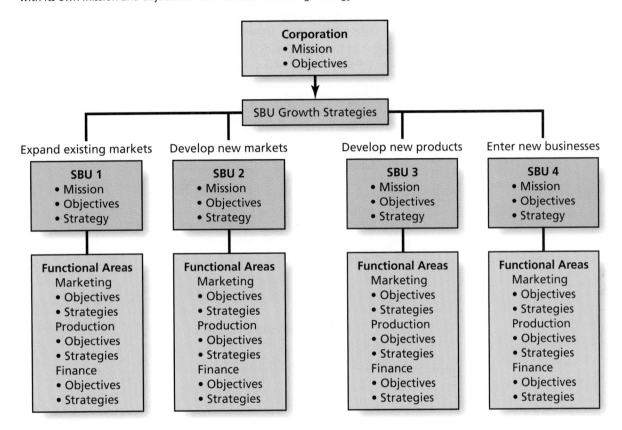

loyal customers so that the SBU will generate profits that can then be put into other parts of the company. For example, in recent years, Disney has viewed its movie brand for grown-ups, Touchstone Studios, as a star. Its strategy of investing in growing that brand is based on the huge market potential of adult moviegoers.

- **Cash cows:** Cash cows have a dominant market share in a low-growth potential market. Because there's not much opportunity for new companies, competitors don't often enter the market. At the same time, the SBU is well established and enjoys a high market share that the firm can sustain with minimal funding. Firms usually milk cash cows of their profits to fund the growth of other SBUs. Of course, if the firm's objective is to increase revenues, having too many cash cows with little or no growth potential can become a liability. For Disney, its Disney Pictures unit, which focuses on family films and animated features, fits into the cash cow category. In fact, Disney periodically recycles even its oldest animated films such as *Snow White* back into the theaters to delight another generation of fans.

- **Question marks:** Question marks—sometimes called *problem children*—are SBUs with low market shares in fast-growth markets. When a business unit is a question mark, it suggests that the firm has failed to compete successfully. Perhaps the SBU's products offer fewer benefits than competing products. Or maybe its prices are too high, its distributors are ineffective, or its advertising is too weak. The firm could pump more money into marketing the product and hope that market share will improve. But the firm may find itself "throwing good money after bad," gaining nothing but a negative cash flow and disappointment. For

business portfolio
The group of different products or brands owned by an organization and characterized by different income-generating and growth capabilities.

portfolio analysis
A management tool for evaluating a firm's business mix and assessing the potential of an organization's strategic business units.

BCG growth–market share matrix
A portfolio analysis model developed by the Boston Consulting Group that assesses the potential of successful products to generate cash that a firm can then use to invest in new products.

Figure 2.3   BCG Growth–Market Share Matrix

The Boston Consulting Group's (BCG) growth–market share matrix is one way a firm can examine its portfolio of different products or SBUs. By categorizing SBUs as stars, cash cows, question marks, or dogs, the matrix helps managers make good decisions about how the firm should grow.

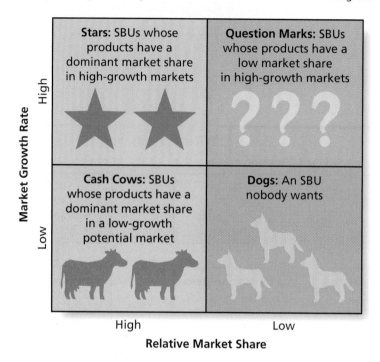

Stars: SBUs whose products have a dominant market share in high-growth markets

Question Marks: SBUs whose products have a low market share in high-growth markets

Cash Cows: SBUs whose products have a dominant market share in a low-growth potential market

Dogs: An SBU nobody wants

Market Growth Rate — High / Low

Relative Market Share — High / Low

Disney, its Disney Stores may be in the question mark category, as their performance compared to the overall specialty retail market has lagged in recent years.

- **Dogs:** Dogs have a small share of a slow-growth market. They are businesses that offer specialized products in limited markets that are not likely to grow quickly. When possible, large firms may sell off their dogs to smaller firms that may be able to nurture them—or they may take the SBU's products off the market. Disney, being very savvy strategic planners, does not appear to have any businesses that are currently in the dog house (so to speak).

Like Disney, Steve Battista at Under Armour may use the BCG matrix to evaluate his product lines to understand which ones are primarily cash generators and which are primarily cash users. This analysis will lead him to important decisions about where to invest for future growth of his business.

Step 5: Develop Growth Strategies

Although the BCG matrix helps managers decide which SBUs they should invest in for growth, it doesn't tell them much about *how* to make that growth happen. Should the growth of an SBU come from finding new customers, from developing new variations of the product, or from some other growth strategy? Part of the strategic planning at the SBU level entails evaluating growth strategies.

Marketers use the product–market growth matrix shown in Figure 2.4 to analyze different growth strategies. The vertical axis in Figure 2.4 represents opportunities for growth, either in existing markets or in new markets. The horizontal axis considers whether the firm would be better off putting its resources into existing products or if it should acquire new products. The matrix provides four different fundamental marketing strategies: market penetration, market development, product development, and diversification:

- **Market penetration strategies** seek to increase sales of existing products to existing markets such as current users, nonusers, and users of competing brands within a market. For exam-

market penetration strategies
Growth strategies designed to increase sales of existing products to current customers, nonusers, and users of competitive brands in served markets.

Figure 2.4 Role of Strategic Business Units

Product Emphasis

	Existing Products	New Products
Existing Markets	**Strategy = Market penetration** • Seek to increase sales of existing products to existing markets	**Strategy = Product development** • Create growth by selling new products in existing markets
New Markets	**Strategy = Market development** • Introduce existing products to new markets	**Strategy = Diversification** • Emphasize both new products and new markets to achieve growth

Market Emphasis (left axis label)

ple, Campbell's can advertise new uses for soup in lunches and dinners, encourage current customers to eat more soup, and prod nonusers to find reasons to buy soup. The firm might try to increase sales by cutting prices, improving distribution, or conducting promotions aimed at attracting users of competing soup brands.

- **Market development strategies** introduce existing products to new markets. This can mean reaching new customer segments within an existing geographic market, or it may mean expanding into new geographic areas. Adapting a local product to a broader market is a real challenge, but it can be done. For example, an entrepreneur in the Philippines is successfully selling a traditional working-class delicacy called *balut* to the middle class by developing a brand name, standardized outlets, and gourmet sauces to go with it. By the way, this dish is made from duck embryos that Filipino men like to slurp straight from the egg (feathers, beaks, and all) because they are reputed to enhance sexual stamina. The owner boasts, "Balut is the local Viagra, and we're repackaging it for a new generation."[3] Fries with that?

- **Product development strategies** create growth by selling new products in existing markets. Product development may mean that the firm improves a product's performance, or it may mean extending the firm's product line by developing new variations of the item. Take the humble Oreo cookie, which now appears in Oreo breakfast cereal, Oreo ice cream, and Oreo pudding crust, cake mix, frosting, brownies, and granola bars. Some marketing experts say Oreo is not just a cookie anymore, it's practically a flavor. This growth strategy of product development helped to more than double the sale of all things Oreo over the past decade.[4]

- **Diversification strategies** emphasize both new products and new markets to achieve growth. Feeling that it may be maxing out in the hamburger business, McDonald's is seeking to attract different customers with new products. In recent years, McDonald's has purchased several businesses in order to diversify, including Donatos Pizza, Aroma Café, Boston Market, and a controlling interest in Chipotle Mexican Grills.

For Steve Battista at Under Armour, using the product–market growth matrix can be a very important way to analyze where his future opportunities lie. Does he want to focus on growing current customers with their existing product line, taking share away from competitors and solidifying his position in his present market space? Or will he expand the product line, perhaps into new markets? These are fundamental issues in planning for future growth.

market development strategies
Growth strategies that introduce existing products to new markets.

product development strategies
Growth strategies that focus on selling new products in served markets.

diversification strategies
Growth strategies that emphasize both new products and new markets.

Advice for Under Armour

STUDENT
AMETHYST HOWELL
Tennessee State University

I would choose option 3 because it would increase the number of segments. The product will no longer be seen as one that is exclusively for professional athletes. If advertising campaigns effectively demonstrate possible uses and benefits of the product for different consumers, these segments can be tapped into. I don't believe that this option would dilute the brand image at all. In fact, I believe that this option would increase consumer awareness and the brand would be able to build a strong image as a product that does what it says and has a variety of uses. I think that Under Armour has the potential to become a reputable brand used by a variety of consumers who create a wide range of segments.

PROFESSOR
DAN ROBERTSON
Texas A&M University

I would choose option 3. The three options presented represent three different strategic alternatives. Option 1 is market development. Option 2 is a penetration strategy. Option 3 is product development. It is important to add that the choice of selecting an option occurs when Under Armour is experiencing extremely rapid sales and staff growth. To simultaneously try to cope with sales growth, hire, train and integrate new personnel and learn enough about admittedly "fickle" new markets where the firm has no experience or knowledge is a prescription for failure. Option 2 is the short-term safe bet but it continues their focus on one market segment. In the long-term, this is dangerous! Hence, option 3 appeals because it capitalizes on their strength—product development. It allows them to keep their core customer while simultaneously providing opportunities to "develop a wider range of products" built upon their strong existing base. I believe this provides Steve the best of both worlds while avoiding the risk inherent in options 1 and 2. In so doing, Under Armour will be following their own advertising theme— PROTECT THIS HOUSE!—by retaining their focus on their core customer base of team sports where they have mastered the two essential parts of marketing strategy—understanding their target market and developing a viable marketing mix for that market segment. The knowledge they gain by developing new products may lead them to additional success.

To review what we've learned, strategic planning includes developing the mission statement, assessing the internal and external environment (resulting in a SWOT analysis), setting objectives, establishing the business portfolio, and developing growth strategies. In the next section, we'll look at marketers' functional plans—marketing planning.

Functional Planning: From Strategic Planning to Marketing Planning

Up until now, we have focused on strategic plans. The strategic plan, however, does not provide details about how to reach the objectives that have been set. Strategic plans "talk the talk" but put the pressure on lower-level functional area managers (such as the marketing manager, production manager, finance manager, and so forth) to "walk the walk" by developing the functional plans—the nuts and bolts—to achieve organizational and SBU objectives. Thus, marketers develop functional plans (i.e., marketing plans)—the next step in planning as shown in Figure 2.1

The Four Ps of the marketing mix we discussed in Chapter 1 remind us that successful firms must have viable *products* at *prices* consumers are willing to pay, the means to get the products to the *place* consumers want to buy, and a way to *promote* the products to the right consumers. Making this happen requires a tremendous amount of planning by the marketer. The steps in this marketing planning process are quite similar to the steps at the strategic planning level. An important distinction between strategic planning and marketing planning, however, is that marketing professionals focus much of their planning efforts on issues related to the firm's product, its price, promotional approach, and distribution (place) methods. Let's look at the steps involved in the marketing planning process in a bit more detail.

Step 1: Perform a Situation Analysis

The first step in developing a marketing plan is for marketing managers to conduct an analysis of the *marketing* environment. To do this, managers build on the company's SWOT analysis by searching out information about the environment that specifically affects the marketing plan. For example, for Steve Batista at Under Armour to develop an effective marketing communications program, it's not enough for him to have a general understanding of the target market. He needs to know specifically what television shows potential customers watch, whether a coupon or a sweepstakes is most likely to make them buy, and whether they prefer buying their workout clothing in retail stores or on the Internet. Steve also must know how his competitors are communicating with customers so that he can plan effectively.

Step 2: Set Marketing Objectives

Once marketing managers have a thorough understanding of the marketing environment, the next step is to develop specific marketing objectives. How are marketing objectives different from corporate objectives? Generally, marketing objectives are more specific to the firm's brands, sizes, product features, and other marketing mix–related elements. Think of the connection between business objectives and marketing objectives this way: business objectives guide the entire firm's operations, while marketing objectives state what the marketing function must accomplish if the firm is ultimately to achieve its overall objectives. So for Steve Battista at Under Armour, setting marketing objectives means deciding what he wants to accomplish in terms of Under Armour's marketing mix–related elements, such as the development of new brands or specific sales figures.

Step 3: Develop Marketing Strategies

In the next stage of the marketing planning process, marketing managers develop their actual marketing strategies—that is, they make decisions about what activities they must accomplish to achieve the marketing objectives. Usually this means deciding which markets to target and actually developing the marketing mix strategies (product, price, promotion, and distribution) to support how the product is positioned in the market. At this stage, marketers must figure out how they want consumers to think of their product compared to competing products.

SELECTING A TARGET MARKET   The target market is the market segment selected because of the firm's belief that its offerings are most suited to winning those customers. The firm assesses the potential demand—the number of consumers it believes are willing and able to pay for its products—and decides it has the distinctive competencies that will create a competitive advantage in the marketplace among target consumers. Under Armour's mission statement provides insight about what business it is in. From this mission statement, Steve Battista should be able to derive several target markets for Under Armour's products, including the men's market, women's market,

Under Armour targets athletes of both sexes who are seeking moisture control when they play or work out.

youth market, and other markets that are driven by particular sports or fitness activities. (We'll tell you more about target markets in Chapter 7.)

DEVELOPING MARKETING MIX STRATEGIES
Marketing mix decisions identify how marketing will accomplish its objectives in the firm's target markets. As we'll see in later chapters, typically marketers tailor the marketing mix—product, price, promotion, and place—to implement a positioning strategy and thus meet the needs of *each* target market.

• **Product strategies:** Because the product is the most fundamental part of the marketing mix—firms simply can't make a profit without something to sell—carefully developed product strategies are essential to achieving marketing objectives. Product strategies include decisions such as product design, packaging, branding, support services (such as maintenance), if there will be variations of the product, and what product features will provide the unique benefits targeted customers want. For example, product planners for JetBlue decided to include in-seat video games and television as a key product feature during the flight. Their planes get you from point A to point B just as fast (or slow) as the other airlines—that is, the basic product is the same—but the flight seems shorter because there is more to do while you are in the air.

• **Pricing strategies:** In a nutshell, the pricing strategy determines what specific price a firm charges for a product. Of course, that price has to be one that customers are willing to pay. If not, all the other marketing efforts are futile. In addition to setting prices for the final consumer, pricing strategies usually establish prices that will be charged to wholesalers and retailers. As we'll see in Chapter 11, a firm's pricing strategies may be based on costs, demand, or the prices of competing products. Southwest Airlines, "the little airline that could," uses a pricing strategy to successfully target customers who could not previously afford air travel. Southwest does not compete solely on price. However, consumers do perceive Southwest as a low-priced airline compared to others, and the airline reinforces this theme regularly in its ads.[5]

• **Promotion strategies:** A promotion strategy is how marketers communicate product benefits and features to the target market. Marketers use promotion strategies to develop the product's message and the mix of advertising, sales promotion, public relations and publicity, direct marketing, and personal selling that will deliver the message. Many firms use all these elements to communicate their message to consumers. American Airlines strives to portray an image of quality and luxury for the serious business traveler. To do so, it combines television ads focused on that target with sales promotion in the form of the AAdvantage loyalty program, personal selling to companies and conventions to promote usage of American as the "official carrier" for the groups, direct marketing via mail and e-mail providing information to loyal users, and, its managers hope, positive publicity through word of mouth about the airline's good service and dependability.

Part of JetBlue's product strategy is to provide in-flight diversions to bored passengers.

- **Distribution strategies:** The distribution (or "place") strategy outlines how, when, and where the firm will make the product available to targeted customers. In developing a distribution strategy, marketers must decide whether to sell the product directly to the final customer or whether to sell through retailers and wholesalers. And the choice of which retailers should be involved depends on the product, pricing, and promotion decisions. For example, if the firm is producing a luxury good, it may wish to avoid being seen on the shelves of "discount stores" for fear that it will cheapen the brand image. In recent years, the airline industry has made major changes in its distribution strategy. For many years, most customers bought their airline tickets through travel agencies. Today, airlines are offering customers reduced prices for online purchase of "ticketless" flight reservations. For consumers, this is a win-win situation—they save money and have the convenience of scheduling the flight they want 24/7 through the Internet.

Step 4: Implement Marketing Strategies

Once the plan is developed, it's time to get to work and make it successful. Marketers spend much of their time managing the various elements of the marketing plan. For Under Armour, once Steve Battista and his group understand the marketing environment, determine the most appropriate objectives and strategies, and get their ideas organized and on paper in the formal plan, the rubber really hits the road. For Under Armour and all firms, how well they implement their plan is often what makes or breaks the success of the firm in the marketplace.

Step 5: Monitor and Control Marketing Strategies

Marketers must have some means to determine whether they are meeting their marketing objectives. Often called **control**, this process entails measuring actual performance, comparing this performance to the established marketing objectives, and then making adjustments to the strategies or objectives on the basis of this analysis. Maintaining control implies the need for strong *marketing metrics*, which, as we discussed in Chapter 1, are concrete measures of various aspects of marketing performance.

control
A process that entails measuring actual performance, comparing this performance to the established marketing objectives, and then making adjustments to the strategies or objectives on the basis of this analysis.

Steve Battista at Under Armour has to establish appropriate metrics related to his marketing objectives and then track those metrics in order to know how successful his marketing strategy is, as well as whether he needs to make changes in the strategy along the way. For example, what happens if Under Armour sets an objective to increase market share in the youth market by 10 percent in a given year but after the first quarter sales in this market are only even with the last year? The control process means that Steve and his crew would have to look carefully at why they are not meeting their objectives. Is it due to internal factors, external factors, or a combination of both? Steve would then have to either adjust the marketing plan's strategies (such as to increase advertising or implement product alterations) or adjust the marketing objective so that it reflects realistic goals.

Ultimately, this process gets documented into a formal written marketing plan. You'll find a template for a marketing plan in the foldout located at the end of this chapter. This will come in handy as you make your way through the book, as each chapter will give you information you can use to "fill in the blanks" of a marketing plan. By the time you're done, we hope that all these pieces will come together and you'll understand how real marketers make real choices.

As noted earlier, the marketing plan provides a complete road map for the firm to successfully market its products. In large firms, top management often requires such a written plan because putting the ideas on paper encourages marketing managers to formulate concrete objectives and strategies. In small entrepreneurial firms, a well-thought-out marketing plan is often a key factor in attracting investors who will help turn the firm's dreams into reality.

Operational Planning: Day-to-Day Execution of Marketing Plans

In the previous section, we discussed marketing planning—the process by which marketing planners perform a situation analysis, set marketing objectives, and develop, implement, monitor, and control marketing strategies. But talk is cheap: the best plan ever written is useless if it's not properly carried out. That's what operational plans are for. **Operational plans** focus on the day-to-day execution of the marketing plan, which is performed by the first-line supervisors we discussed earlier, such as sales managers, marketing communications managers, and marketing research managers. Operational plans generally cover a shorter period of time than either strategic plans or marketing plans—perhaps only one or two months—and they include detailed directions for the specific activities to be carried out, who will be responsible for them, and timelines for accomplishing the tasks.

Importantly, many of the important marketing metrics managers employ to gauge the success of plans actually get used at the operational planning level. Sales managers in many firms are charged with the responsibility of tracking a wide range of metrics related to the firm–customer relationship such as number of new customers, sales calls per month, customer turnover, and customer loyalty. The data are collected at the operational level, then sent to management for use in planning at the functional level and above.

operational plans
Plans that focus on the day-to-day execution of the marketing plan. Operational plans include detailed directions for the specific activities to be carried out, who will be responsible for them, and timelines for accomplishing the tasks.

Analyzing the Environment

Throughout the section on strategic planning at the business level and then again in our discussion of marketing planning, a central issue is gaining a good understanding of the environment in which the planning must take place. Now we'll take a look at how marketers understand the situation, or environment, in which the marketer's firm operates. First, we'll examine the elements of a firm's internal environment, which in the context of a SWOT analysis results in understanding key strengths and weaknesses within the company. We'll then move on to the many external factors of the environment that affect the marketing plan.

Internal Environment

Earlier in the chapter, we defined the internal environment as being the controllable elements inside an organization that influence how well the organization operates. As we mentioned earlier, internal strengths and weaknesses may lie in the firm's technologies, its physical facilities, its financial stability, its reputation, the quality of its products and services, and its employees. Ultimately, much of the internal environment of a firm is related to its corporate culture.

Corporate culture is made up of the values, norms, and beliefs that influence the behavior of everyone in the organization. Corporate culture may dictate whether new ideas are welcomed or discouraged, the importance of individual ethical behavior, and even the appropriate dress for work.

For many years, IBM was known as "the white shirt company" because of its unwritten rule that all employees must wear white shirts to look the part of an "IBMer." Fortunately, corporate cultures do evolve over time, and even radical changes such as blue shirts now are tolerated at "Big Blue." In contrast, Microsoft has always prided itself on having a more casual dress code, reflecting its roots as an entrepreneurial upstart (at least compared to IBM). If you visit Microsoft's headquarters in Redmond, Washington, you will notice everyone's informal attire right away. However, don't make the mistake of equating informal dress with low work productivity. Microsoft hasn't evolved into the corporate behemoth it is today by hiring slackers.

Some corporate cultures are more inclined to take risks than others. These firms value individuality and creativity, recognizing that nurturing these characteristics often leads to the creation of important competitive advantages. A risk-taking culture is especially important to the marketing function because firms must continually improve their products, their distribution channels, and their promotion programs to remain successful in a competitive environment. In firms with more traditional corporate cultures, getting managers to buy into a new way of doing things is like inviting the board of directors to go on a skydiving mission.

If a firm is totally focused on economic profit—increasing revenues and decreasing costs—management attitudes will be profit centered, often at the expense of employee morale. Firms that harbor a concern for employees, customers, and society, as well as shareholder profits, produce a corporate culture that is much more appealing for employees and other stakeholders in the business.

Fortune magazine publishes an annual list of the best companies to work for based on a variety of criteria, including company philosophy and practices, employee trust in management, pride in work and the company, and camaraderie. In 2004, the number one employer on *Fortune's* list was J.M. Smucker & Co. (yes, the jelly and jam manufacturer). Employees said the company treats them like family, with a corporate culture based on objectives including, "Listen with your full attention, look for the good in others, have a sense of humor, and say thank you for a job well done."[6]

Xerox is working to change the perception that it is a copier-only company.

corporate culture
The set of values, norms, and beliefs that influence the behavior of everyone in the organization.

External Environment

Planning does not happen in a vacuum. Planners must understand what is happening in the external environment that has an effect on their business. As noted earlier, the external environment consists of elements outside the organization that can affect it either positively or negatively. It includes such factors as the overall economy, competitors, technology, laws and regulations, and trends in society and popular culture. In order to stay successful, firms must keep up with what's happening in their external environment and respond to trends in ways that keep them competitive. Let's examine each of the key elements of the external environment.

The Economic Environment

business cycle
The overall patterns of change in the economy—including periods of prosperity, recession, depression, and recovery—that affect consumer and business purchasing power.

The state of the economy in which a firm does business is vital to the success of its marketing plans. The overall pattern of changes or fluctuations of an economy is called the **business cycle**. All economies go through cycles of prosperity (high levels of demand, employment, and income), recession (falling demand, employment, and income), and recovery (gradual improvement in production, lowering unemployment, and increasing income).

A severe recession is a *depression*, a period in which prices fall but there is little demand because few people have money to spend and many are out of work. *Inflation* occurs when prices and the cost of living rise while money loses its purchasing power because the cost of goods escalates. For example, between 1960 and 2004, prices increased over 5 percent per year so that an item worth $1.00 in 1960 would cost over $6.00 in 2004.[7] During inflationary periods, dollar incomes may increase, but real income—what the dollar will buy—decreases because goods and services cost more.

The business cycle is especially important to marketers because of its effect on customer purchase behavior. During times of prosperity, consumers buy more goods and services. Marketers are busy trying to grow the business and maintain inventory levels and even to develop new products to meet customers' willingness to spend. During periods of recession, consumers simply buy less. The challenge to most marketers is to maintain their firm's level of sales by convincing the customers who are buying to select the firm's product over the competition's. Of course, even recessions aren't bad for all businesses. Although it may be harder to sell luxury items, firms that make basic necessities are not likely to suffer significant losses.

It is important to note that when firms assess the economic environment, they evaluate all factors that influence consumer and business buying patterns, including the amount of confidence people have in the health of the economy. This "crystal ball" must be a global one because events in one country can impact the economic health of other countries. For instance, the economic impact of the terrorist attacks on the United States in September 2001 affected the fortunes of businesses around the world.

The Competitive Environment

A second important element of a firm's external environment is the competitive environment. For products ranging from toothpaste to sport-utility vehicles, firms must keep abreast of what the competition is doing so they can develop new product features, new pricing schedules, or new advertising to maintain or gain market share.

ANALYZING THE MARKET AND COMPETITION Before a firm can begin to develop strategies that will create a competitive advantage in the marketplace, it has to know who its competitors are and what they're doing. Marketing managers size up the competitors according to their strengths and weaknesses, monitor their marketing strategies, and try to predict their moves.

competitive intelligence
The process of gathering and analyzing publicly available information about rivals.

An increasing number of firms around the globe engage in **competitive intelligence (CI)** activities, the process of gathering and analyzing publicly available information about rivals. Most of the information that companies need to know about their competitors is available from rather mundane sources, including the news media, the Internet, and publicly available government documents such as building permits and patent grants. Successful CI means that a firm learns about a competitor's new products, its manufacturing, or the management styles of its executives. Then the firm uses this information to develop superior marketing strategies.[8]

COMPETITION IN THE MICROENVIRONMENT   To be successful in a competitive marketplace, marketers must have a clear understanding of exactly who their competition is. Competition in the microenvironment means the product alternatives from which members of a target market may choose. We can think of these choices at three different levels.

At a broad level, many marketers compete for consumers' **discretionary income**: the amount of money people have left after paying for necessities such as housing, utilities, food, and clothing. Few consumers are wealthy enough to buy anything and everything, so each of us is constantly faced with choices: whether to plow "leftover" money into a new MP3 player, donate it to charity, or turn over a new leaf and lose those extra pounds by investing in a healthy lifestyle. Thus, the first part of understanding who the competition is means understanding *all* the alternatives consumers consider for their discretionary income.

A second type of choice is **product competition**, in which competitors offering different products attempt to satisfy the same consumer's needs and wants. For example, if couch potatoes opt to clean up their acts, they may choose to buff up by joining a health club or they may purchase a Soloflex machine and pump iron at home.

The third type of choice is **brand competition**, in which competitors offering similar goods or services vie for consumer dollars. So, if our flabby friends decide to join a gym, they still must choose among competitors within this industry, such as Gold's Gym or the YMCA. Or they may forego the exercise thing altogether and count on the Atkins diet to work its magic by itself.

COMPETITION IN THE MACROENVIRONMENT   When we talk about examining competition in the macroenvironment, we mean that marketers need to understand the big picture—the overall structure of their industry. This structure can range from one firm having total control to numerous firms that compete on an even playing field. Four different structures describe differing amounts of competition. Let's review each structure, beginning with total control by one organization.

A **monopoly** exists when one seller controls a market. Because the seller is "the only game in town," it feels little pressure to keep prices low or to produce quality goods or services. In the old days, the U.S. Postal Service had a monopoly on the delivery of written documents, but the days of a snail-mail monopoly are over because the U.S. Postal Service now battles fax machines, e-mail, and couriers such as FedEx for market share.

In most U.S. industries today, the government attempts to limit monopolies by prosecuting firms for violations of antitrust legislation. Of course, these laws may generate controversy as powerful firms argue that they dominate a market simply because they provide a product most people want. This is at the heart of the ongoing controversy about Wal-Mart's domination of the retail business. The world's largest company (and getting bigger all the time) generates some amazing statistics, including the fact that 82 percent of U.S. households made a Wal-Mart purchase in 2002, and their sales are still growing.[9]

In an **oligopoly**, there are a relatively small number of sellers, each holding substantial market share, in a market with many buyers. Because there are few sellers in an oligopoly, each seller is very conscious of other sellers' actions. Oligopolies most often exist in industries requiring substantial investments in equipment or technology to produce a product—industries in which only a few competitors have the resources to enter the game. The airline industry is an oligopoly. It is pretty hard for an entrepreneur with little start-up cash to be successful entering the airline industry. Instead, a few large firms, such as American Airlines, Delta, and Southwest, dominate the market. Relatively smaller firms, such as JetBlue and Frontier, succeed by offering something special such as onboard entertainment, direct routes to underserved cities, or more leg room.

discretionary income
The portion of income people have left over after paying for necessities such as housing, utilities, food, and clothing.

product competition
When firms offering different products compete to satisfy the same consumer needs and wants.

brand competition
When firms offering similar goods or services compete on the basis of their brand's reputation or perceived benefits.

monopoly
A market situation in which one firm, the only supplier of a particular product, is able to control the price, quality, and supply of that product.

oligopoly
A market structure in which a relatively small number of sellers, each holding a substantial share of the market, compete in a market with many buyers.

monopolistic competition
A market structure in which many firms, each having slightly different products, offer unique consumer benefits.

perfect competition
A market structure in which many small sellers, all of whom offer similar products, are unable to have an impact on the quality, price, or supply of a product.

patent
Legal documentation granting an individual or firm exclusive rights to produce and sell a particular invention.

In **monopolistic competition**, there are many sellers who compete for buyers in a market. Each firm, however, offers a slightly different product, and each has only a small share of the market. In this type of market structure, many athletic shoes manufacturers, including Nike, New Balance, Reebok, and a host of others, vigorously compete with one another to offer consumers some unique benefit—even though you can get a computerized running shoe only from Adidas (at least for now).

Finally, **perfect competition** exists when there are many small sellers, each offering basically the same good or service. In such industries, no single firm has a significant impact on quality, price, or supply. Although true conditions of perfect competition are rare, agricultural markets in which there are many individual farmers each producing the same corn or jalapeño peppers come the closest. Even in the case of food commodities, though, there are opportunities for marketers to distinguish their offerings. Eggland's Best, Inc., for example, says it feeds its hens a high-quality, all-vegetarian diet, so the eggs they lay contain less cholesterol and six times more vitamin E than regular eggs.[10] Each egg is branded with a red "EB" seal. The company has scrambled the competition by creating an "egg-straordinary" difference where none existed before.

The Technological Environment

A third important element of a firm's external environment is the technological environment. Firms today see technology as an investment they can't afford *not* to make, as technology provides many firms with important competitive advantages. Many technological developments profoundly affect marketing activities. Toll-free telephone numbers, easy computer access to customer databases, and, of course, the Internet have made it possible for people to buy virtually anything they want (and even some things they don't want) without ever leaving their homes. And distribution has also improved because of automated inventory control afforded by such advancements as bar codes and computer light pens.

Changes in technology can dramatically transform an industry, as when transistors revolutionized consumer electronics. Successful marketers continuously scan the external business environment in search of ideas and trends to spark their own research efforts. They also monitor ongoing research projects in government and private organizations. When inventors feel they have come across something exciting, they usually want to protect their exclusive right to produce and sell the invention by applying for a patent. A **patent** is a legal document issued from a country's patent office that gives inventors—or individuals and firms—exclusive rights to produce and sell a particular invention in that country. Marketers monitor government patent applications to discover innovative products they can purchase from the inventor.

The Legal Environment

A fourth element of a firm's external environment is the legal environment, which refers to the local, state, national, and global laws and regulations that affect businesses. Legal and regulatory controls can be prime motivators for many business decisions. Laws in the United States governing business have two purposes.

Advancements in technology allow Maxell to eliminate the need for you to touch the adhesive side of a CD label by hand—and gets rid of bubbles and curling too.

Table 2.2 Overview of the Legal Environment

Law	Purpose
Sherman Antitrust Act (1890)	Developed to eliminate monopolies and to guarantee free competition. Prohibits exclusive territories (if they restrict competition), price fixing, and predatory pricing.
Food and Drug Act (1906)	Prohibits harmful practices in the production of food and drugs.
Clayton Act (1914)	Prohibits tying contracts, which require a dealer to take other products in the seller's line. Prohibits exclusive dealing if it restricts competition.
Federal Trade Commission Act (1914)	Created the Federal Trade Commission to monitor unfair practices.
Robinson-Patman Act (1936)	Prohibits price discrimination (offering different prices to competing wholesalers or retailers) unless cost justified.
Wheeler-Lea Amendment to FTC Act (1938)	Revised the FTC Act. Makes deceptive and misleading advertising illegal.
Lanham Trademark Act (1946)	Protects and regulates brand names and trademarks.
Fair Packaging and Labeling Act (1966)	Ensures that product packages are labeled honestly.
National Traffic and Motor Vehicle Safety Act (1966)	Sets automobile and tire safety standards.
Cigarette Labeling Act (1966)	Requires health warnings on cigarettes.
Child Protection Act (1966)	Bans dangerous products used by children.
Child Protection and Toy Safety Act (1969)	Sets standards for child-resistant packaging.
Consumer Credit Protection Act (1968) Fair Credit Reporting Act (1970)	Protects consumers by requiring full disclosure of credit and loan terms and rates. Regulates the use of consumer credit reporting.
Consumer Products Safety Commission Act (1972)	Created the Consumer Product Safety Commission to monitor and recall unsafe products. Sets product safety standards.
Magnuson-Moss Consumer Product Warranty Act (1975)	Regulates warranties.
Children's Television Act (1990)	Limits the amount of television commercials aired on children's programs.
Nutrition Labeling and Education Act (1990)	Requires that new food labeling requirements be set by the Food and Drug Administration.
National Do Not Call Registry (2003)	Established by the Federal Trade Commission to allow consumers to limit telemarketing calls they receive.

Some, such as the Sherman Antitrust Act and the Wheeler-Lea Act, make sure that businesses compete fairly with each other. Others, such as the Food and Drug Act and the Consumer Products Safety Commission Act, make sure that businesses don't take advantage of consumers. Although some businesspeople argue that excessive legislation only limits competition, others say that laws ultimately help firms by maintaining a level playing field for businesses and supporting troubled industries.

Table 2.2 lists some of the major federal laws that protect and preserve the rights of U.S. consumers and businesses. Federal and state governments have created a host of regulatory agencies—government bodies that monitor business activities and enforce laws. Table 2.3 lists some of the

Table 2.3 Regulatory Agencies and Responsibilities

Regulatory Agency	Responsibilities
Consumer Product Safety Commission (CPSC)	Protects the public from potentially hazardous products. Through regulation and testing programs, the CPSC helps firms make sure their products won't harm customers.
Environmental Protection Agency (EPA)	Develops and enforces regulations aimed at protecting the environment. Such regulations have a major impact on the materials and processes that manufacturers use in their products and thus on the ability of companies to develop products.
Federal Communications Commission (FCC)	Regulates telephone, radio, and television. FCC regulations directly affect the marketing activities of companies in the communications industries, and they have an indirect effect on all firms that use broadcast media for marketing communications.
Federal Trade Commission (FTC)	Enforces laws against deceptive advertising and product labeling regulations. Marketers must constantly keep abreast of changes in FTC regulations to avoid costly fines.
Food and Drug Administration (FDA)	Enforces laws and regulations on foods, drugs, cosmetics, and veterinary products. Marketers of pharmaceuticals, over-the-counter medicines, and a variety of other products must get FDA approval before they can introduce products to the market.
Interstate Commerce Commission (ICC)	Regulates interstate bus, truck, rail, and water operations. The ability of a firm to efficiently move products to its customers depends on ICC policies and regulations.

agencies whose actions affect marketing activities. We'll discuss issues related to the international legal environment in Chapter 3.

Sometimes firms learn the hard way that government watchdog activities can put a stop to their marketing plans. Warner-Lambert, the manufacturer of Listerine antiseptic, went on national television in the 1970s with advertising claims that its germ-killing properties help reduce the number and severity of the common cold. Unfortunately, the firm lacked data to substantiate the claim. The company stopped making this claim in its advertising only after it was forced to do so by the Federal Communications Commission and Federal Trade Commission. However, Warner-Lambert learned from its mistake, as a few years later it funded research with the American Dental Association that resulted in new claims (this time based on scientific evidence) that Listerine is effective against such gum and dental maladies as plaque and gingivitis. These claims continue to be a cornerstone of Listerine's advertising message to this day and have helped make it the number one selling mouthwash for over 20 years.

Socially responsible firms know that the best of all possible worlds is one where no government regulation is needed because firms work together to make sure everyone plays fairly. In fact, there are a number of nongovernmental organizations that serve as watchdogs on marketing activities. The most active of these is the National Advertising Division (NAD) of the Better Business Bureau. The NAD receives and investigates complaints from both consumers and other businesses about advertising. If the NAD investigation determines that a complaint is legitimate, the complaint is moved up to a National Advertising Review Board (NARB) panel that may make a recommendation to the offending advertiser to change or cease the advertising. As a voluntary, independent entity, the NARB has no power to enforce its recommendations to advertisers. Most

The Atkins diet and similar consumer trends toward healthier eating provide Planters a chance to tout the low-carb benefits of its peanuts.

advertisers, however, comply because they believe it is in the best interest of all advertisers to clean their own house rather than having the government step in and do it for them.

Another important arm of the Better Business Bureau is the Children's Advertising Review Unit (CARU). CARU was established in 1974 to help promote truthful, accurate, and socially responsible advertising for children. CARU reviews advertising directed to children under the age of 12 by systematically monitoring thousands of advertisements from print, broadcast, and online media.[11]

The Sociocultural Environment

Another element of a firm's external environment is the sociocultural environment. By the sociocultural environment, we mean the characteristics of the society, the people who live in that society, and the culture that reflects the values and beliefs of the society. We'll focus on these issues in detail in later chapters of the book. For now, just keep in mind that the first step toward understanding the characteristics of a society is to look at its **demographics**. These are statistics that measure observable aspects of a population, such as size, age, gender, ethnic group, income, education, occupation, and family structure. The information revealed in demographic studies is of great value to marketers in predicting the size of markets for many products, from home mortgages to brooms and can openers.

For example, one of the "biggest" cultural issues we are facing now is the spiraling rate of obesity. The Centers for Disease Control and Prevention estimates that 20 percent of American adults are obese, up from 12.5 percent in 1991. The consequences of this huge public health problem also trickle down to product decisions—which explains why some clothing manufacturers are branching out into larger sizes to satisfy consumer demand for clothes that fit and airlines are having to adjust their weight estimates in order to acccomodate heavier passengers. Ironically, this trend actually creates opportunities for businesses that cater to larger people, such as companies that make oversized coffins.[12]

Understanding consumers' attitudes, beliefs, and ways of doing things in different parts of the country or the world is especially important to firms when developing marketing strategy. These differences in values often explain why marketing efforts that are a big hit in one country can flop in another. For example, a hugely successful advertisement in Japan promoted breast cancer awareness by showing an attractive woman in a sundress drawing stares from men on the street as a voice-over says, "If only women paid as much attention to their breasts as men do." The same ad flopped in France because the use of humor to talk about a serious disease offended the French.[13]

demographics
Statistics that measure observable aspects of a population, including size, age, gender, ethnic group, income, education, occupation, and family structure.

To summarize what we've discussed in this chapter, business planning, a key element of a firm's success, occurs in several different stages. Strategic planning takes place at both the corporate and the SBU level in large firms and in a single stage in smaller businesses. Marketing planning, one of the functional planning areas, comes next. Operational planning ensures proper implementation and control of the marketing plan. In the next chapter, we'll see how firms practice ethical business behavior and social responsibility and look at the "big picture" of international marketing.

real people, real choices

How It Worked Out at Under Armour

Under Armour chose option #3, and the company started to investigate opportunities for expansion. But Steve knew that it was imperative to maintain quality and never waver from delivering on the Under Armour promise of guaranteeing performance, regardless of the product being sold. He put to paper what the company had been based on all along. Called the *Brand Endeavor,* the policy emphasized Under Armour's basic mission to act as a Universal Guarantee of Performance. This meant that the

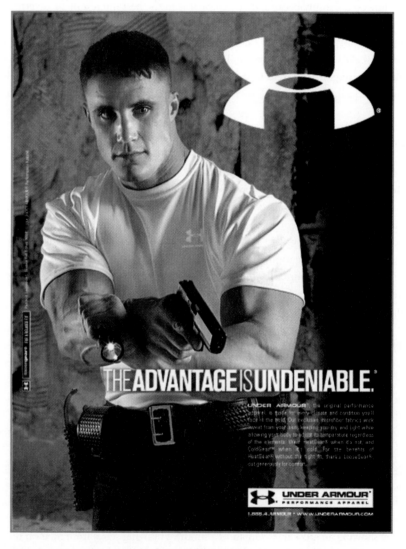

Part of Under Armour's growth strategy is to expand its product line to areas other than athletics, including law enforcement and military applications.

company would not use any fabrics that aren't performance based (i.e., moisture wicking). The objective was to maintain Under Armour's position among athletes as a high-quality product on the field while at the same time extending this brand promise to weekend warriors who might buy other products with the Under Armour logo on them.

The *Brand Endeavor* specified that any new product the company considered building must answer a series of proofs beginning with the primary question, Does it perform better than anything else in the market? If the answer is no, Under Armour doesn't pursue it. If the answer is yes, then it's a valid possibility for the brand.

Steve also found that the strong reputation Under Armour had built in the highest level of professional and collegiate sports earned credence in other markets, particularly with customers well versed in performance fabrics like those used in hunting, running, and skiing. Athletes who participated in these activities in the off-season took to wearing the gear on the slopes in the woods and on runs to further help authenticate Under Armour in these new markets. The same moisture-transport technology, and quite often the very same garments previously used only on the football gridiron, performed just as well in a variety of sports, activities, and jobs where the only option for so long had been cotton. Those trying Under Armour for the first time found that the advantage was indeed, truly undeniable.

How much do you know about the job market? How are jobs changing as we transition from an industrial economy to a knowledge-based economy? In Chapter 2 of *Brand You*, you'll learn how to spot new work opportunities in evolving trends.

CHAPTER SUMMARY

1. **Explain the strategic planning process.**   Strategic planning is the managerial decision process in which top management define the firm's purpose and specify what the firm hopes to achieve over the next five or so years. For large firms that have a number of self-contained business units, the first step in strategic planning is for top management to establish a mission for the entire corporation. Top managers then evaluate the internal and external environment of the business and set corporate-level objectives that guide decision making within each individual SBU. In small firms that are not large enough to have separate SBUs, strategic planning simply takes place at the overall firm level. For companies with several different SBUs, strategic planning also includes (1) making decisions about how to best allocate resources across these businesses to ensure growth for the total organization and (2) developing growth strategies.

2. **Describe the steps in marketing planning.**   Marketing planning is one type of functional planning. Marketing planning begins with an evaluation of the internal and external environments. Marketing managers then set marketing objectives usually related to the firm's brands, sizes, product features, and other marketing mix–related elements. Next, marketing managers select the target market(s) for the organization and decide what marketing mix strategies they will use. Product strategies include decisions about products and product characteristics that will appeal to the target market. Pricing strategies state the specific prices to be charged to channel members and final consumers. Promotion strategies include plans for advertising, sales promotion, public relations, publicity, personal selling, and direct marketing used to reach the target market. Distribution strategies outline how the product will be made available to targeted customers when and where they want it. Once the marketing strategies are developed,

they must be implemented. Control is the measurement of actual performance and comparison with planned performance. Maintaining control implies the need for concrete measures of marketing performance called *marketing metrics*.

3. **Explain operational planning.** Operational planning is done by first-line supervisors such as sales managers, marketing communication managers, and marketing research managers and focuses on the day-to-day execution of the marketing plan. Operational plans generally cover a shorter period of time and include detailed directions for the specific activities to be carried out, who will be responsible for them, and time lines for accomplishing the tasks.

4. **Discuss some of the important aspects of an organization's internal environment.** The internal environment includes the controllable elements inside an organization that influence how well the organization operates, including the firm's technologies, its physical facilities, its financial stability, its reputation, the quality of its products and services, and its employees. Ultimately, much of the internal environment of a firm is related to its corporate culture.

5. **Explain why marketers scan an organization's external business environment.** The external environment consists of elements outside the organization that can affect it either positively or negatively, including such factors as the overall economy, competition, technology, laws and regulations, and trends in society and popular culture. The business cycle (prosperity, recession, recovery, and depression) and inflation affect customer purchase behavior and business activities. In a firm's competitive environment, brand competition, product competition, and the more general competition for consumers' limited discretionary income affect the development of marketing strategies that give the firm a competitive advantage. Changes in the technological environment affect every aspect of marketing; thus, marketers must be knowledgeable about technological changes, often monitoring government and private research findings. The legal environment includes local, state, national, and global laws and regulations. The sociocultural environment relates to the characteristics of society including demographics. Understanding attitudes and beliefs in different parts of the world are especially important.

KEY TERMS

BCG growth–market share matrix, 40, 41
brand competition, 51
business cycle, 50
business plan, 35
business planning, 35
business portfolio, 40, 41
competitive intelligence, 50
control, 47
corporate culture, 49
demographics, 55
discretionary income, 51

diversification strategies, 43
external environment, 38
functional (tactical) planning, 36
internal environment, 38
market development strategies, 43
market penetration strategies, 42
marketing plan, 35
mission statement, 37
monopolistic competition, 52
monopoly, 51
oligopoly, 51

operational planning, 36
operational plans, 48
patent, 52
perfect competition, 52
portfolio analysis, 40, 41
product competition, 51
product development strategies, 43
strategic business units, 37
strategic planning, 35
SWOT analysis, 38

CHAPTER REVIEW

MARKETING CONCEPTS: TESTING YOUR KNOWLEDGE

1. What is strategic, functional, and operational planning? How does strategic planning differ at the corporate and the SBU levels?

2. What is a mission statement? What is a SWOT analysis? What role do these play in the planning process?

3. What is a strategic business unit (SBU)? How do firms use the Boston Consulting Group model for portfolio analysis in planning for their SBUs?

4. Describe the four business growth strategies: market penetration, product development, market development, and diversification.

5. Explain the steps in the marketing planning process.

The Marketing Plan

I. Situation Analysis
    a. Internal Environment

    b. External Environment

    c. SWOT Analysis

II. Marketing Objectives

III. Marketing Strategies
    a. Target Markets

    b. Positioning the Product

    c. Product Strategies

    d. Pricing Strategies

    e. Promotion Strategies

    f. Distribution Strategies

IV. Implementation Strategies
    a. Action Plans (for product, pricing, promotion, and distribution)
    b. Budgets
    c. Timing/schedules

V. Monitoring and Control Strategies
    a. Research
    b. Trend Analysis
    c. Marketing Audit

Questions Addressed in the Plan

> How does the marketing function support the company's mission, goals, and growth strategies?

> What has my company done in the past with its product? Pricing? Promotion? Distribution?

> What resources does my company have that make us unique? How has the company added value to it's offerings in the past?

> What is the overall domestic and global market for our product? How big is the market? Who buys our product?

> Who are our competitors? What are their marketing strategies?

> What is happening in the economic environment? The social and cultural environment? The regulatory environment? The technological environment?

> Based on my understanding of the internal and external environments, what are the key opportunities and threats for the marketing function?

> What does marketing need to accomplish to support the objectives of the firm?

> How do consumers and organizations go about buying, using, and disposing of products?

> What is the best way to divide our consumer and/or business markets?

> Which segments should we select to target?

> How will we position our product for our market(s)

> What is our core product? Actual product? Augmented product?

> What product line and/or product mix strategies should we use?

> How should we package and brand our product?

> What price should we charge for our product? What pricing tactics should we use?

> How do we develop a consistent message about our product?

> What advertising, public relations, and sales promotion activities should we use?

> What role should a sales force play in the marketing communications plan?

> How do we go about getting our product to consumers in the best way as we build customer relationships?

> What types of retailers should we work with to sell our product?

> How do we integrate these strategic elements to maximize the value we offer to our customers and other stakeholders?

> How do we make our marketing plan happen?

> What budget do we need to accomplish our marketing objectives?

> What is the timing for our marketing plan?

> How do we measure the actual performance of our marketing plan and compare it to our planned performance?

> How can we improve the marketing function overall?

Where You'll Find These Questions Discussed

Chapter 1: Welcome to the World of Marketing: Creating and Delivering Value

Chapter 3: Think Globally/Act Ethically

Chapter 4: Marketing Information and Research: Analyzing the Business Environment Off-Line and Online

Chapter 2: Strategic Planning and the Marketing Environment: The Advantage Is Undeniable

Chapter 3: Think Globally/Act Ethically

Chapter 4: Marketing Information and Research: Analyzing the Business Environment Off-Line and Online

Chapter 5: Consumer Behavior: How and Why People Buy

Chapter 6: Business-to-Business Markets: How and Why Organizations Buy

Chapter 7: Sharpening the Focus: Target Marketing Strategies and Customer Relationship Management

Chapter 8: Creating the Product

Chapter 9: Managing the Product

Chapter 10: Services and Other Intangibles: Marketing the Product That Isn't There

Chapter 11: Pricing the Product

Chapter 12: Connecting with the Customer: Integrated Marketing Communications and Interactive Marketing

Chapter 13: Advertising and Public Relations

Chapter 14: Sales Promotion, Personal Selling, and Sales Management

Chapter 15: Creating Value Through Supply Chain Management: Channels of Distribution, Logistics, and Wholesaling

Chapter 16: Retailing: Bricks and Clicks

Chapter 2: Strategic Planning and the Marketing Environment: The Advantage Is Undeniable

Appendix B: Sample Marketing Plan: S&S Smoothie Company

Chapter 2: Strategic Planning and the Marketing Environment: The Advantage Is Undeniable

Appendix B: Sample Marketing Plan: S&S Smoothie Company

6. How does operational planning support the marketing plan?

7. What are the elements of a formal marketing plan?

8. What is corporate culture? What are some ways that the corporate culture of one organization might differ from that of another? How does corporate culture affect marketing decision making?

9. Describe the business cycle. How does it influence marketing decisions?

10. Explain the types of competition marketers face: discretionary income competition, product competition, and brand competition. Why are all important to marketers?

11. What is a monopoly, an oligopoly, monopolistic competition, and pure competition? Why is an understanding of these important to marketers?

12. Describe the legal, technological, and sociocultural environments. Why do marketers need to understand these environments?

MARKETING CONCEPTS: DISCUSSING CHOICES AND ISSUES

1. The Boston Consulting Group matrix identifies products as stars, cash cows, question marks, and dogs. Do you think this is a useful way for organizations to examine their businesses? What are some examples of product lines that fit in each category?

2. In this chapter we talked about how firms do strategic, functional, and operational planning. Yet some firms are successful without formal planning. Do you think planning is essential to a firm's success? Can planning ever hurt an organization?

3. Most planning involves strategies for growth. But is growth always the right direction to pursue? Can you think of some organizations that should have contraction rather than expansion as their objective? Do you know of any organizations that have planned to get smaller rather than larger in order to be successful?

4. The technological environment has changed marketing in some important ways. What are some of these? What are your predictions for how technology will change marketing in the future?

5. Most marketers feel that fewer laws and less regulation of marketing is a desirable thing. What are the advantages and disadvantages of government controls of marketing? Are there any new laws about marketing you would recommend?

MARKETING PRACTICE: APPLYING WHAT YOU'VE LEARNED

1. Assume that you are the marketing director for a small firm that manufactures educational toys for children. Your boss, the company president, has decided to develop a mission statement. He's admitted that he doesn't know much about developing a mission statement and has asked that you help guide him in this process. Write a memo outlining what exactly a mission statement is, why firms develop such statements, how firms use mission statements, and your thoughts on what the firm's mission statement might be.

2. As a marketing student, you know that large firms often organize their operations into a number of strategic business units (SBUs). A university might develop a similar structure in which different academic schools or departments are seen as separate businesses. Working with a small group of four to six classmates, consider how your university might divide its total academic units into separate SBUs. What would be the problems with implementing such a plan? What would be the advantages and disadvantages for students and for faculty? Present your analysis of university SBUs to your class.

3. An important part of planning is a SWOT analysis, understanding an organization's strengths, weaknesses, opportunities, and threats. Choose a business in your community with which you are familiar. Develop a brief SWOT analysis for that business.

4. As an employee of a business consulting firm that specializes in helping people who want to start small businesses, you have been assigned a client who is interested in introducing a new concept in health clubs—one that offers its customers both the usual exercise and weight training opportunities and certain related types of medical assistance such as physical therapy, a weight loss physician, and diagnostic testing. As you begin thinking about the potential for success for this client, you realize that understanding the external environment for this business is essential. First, decide which environmental factors are most important to this client. Then choose one of these factors and use your library to identify the current and future trends in this area. Finally, in a role-playing situation, present all your recommendations to the client.

5. Assume that you have recently been employed by the marketing department of a firm that manufactures bicycles. Who are your competitors? Make a list of ways you might seek to gain competitive intelligence for your firm.

MARKETING MINIPROJECT: LEARNING BY DOING

The purpose of this miniproject is to gain an understanding of marketing planning through actual experience.

1. Select one of the following for your marketing planning project:
   - yourself (in your search for a career)
   - your university
   - a specific department in your university

2. Next, develop the following elements of the marketing planning process:
   - a mission statement
   - a SWOT analysis
   - objectives

- a description of the target market(s)
- a positioning strategy
- a brief outline of the marketing mix strategies—the product, pricing, distribution, and promotion strategies—that satisfy the objectives and address the target market.

3. Prepare a brief outline of a marketing plan using the template provided at the end of this chapter as a guide.

REAL PEOPLE, REAL SURFERS: EXPLORING THE WEB

Visit the home pages of one or more firms you are intersted in. Follow the links to find out about the company's products, pricing, distribution, and marketing communications strategies. Do a search of the Web for other information about the company. Based on your findings, answer the following questions:

1. What is the organization's business? What is the overall purpose of the organization? What does the organization hope to achieve?

2. What customers does the business want to serve?

3. What elements of the Web page specifically reflect the business of the organization? How is the Web page designed to attract the organization's customers?

4. Do you think the marketing strategies and other activities of the firm are consistent with its mission? Why do you feel this way?

5. Develop a report based on your findings and conclusions about the firm. Present your report to your class.

MARKETING PLAN EXERCISE

The airline industry has experienced a lot of turbulence in recent years that inhibits its ability to plan for the future. Pick your favorite airline and help it plan by doing the following:

1. See if you can locate its mission statement, then develop a few marketing objectives that you believe would nicely support it.

2. Identify some key external environmental factors that you believe the airline industry in general needs to pay attention to over the next couple of years as it does marketing planning. Try to come up with some factors across several of the categories of external issues we discussed in the chapter. Be sure to consider whether you believe each represents an opportunity or a threat to your selected airline and why.

3. Take a look at Figure 2.4, the product–market growth matrix, and the accompanying discussion. How might your chosen airline go about developing some strategies in each of the boxes: penetration, market development, product development, and diversification. (Hint: Remember that airlines are in the business of providing a service. Most likely the strategies you come up with will entail adding new or modified services in their targeted markets.)

Marketing in Action Case

Real Choices at McDonald's

The last quarter of 2002 and the first quarter of 2003 were tough ones for venerable fast-food icon McDonald's. In January 2003, the company reported its first quarterly loss in history, and boy was it a whopper at $343.8 million. In addition, McDonald's was coming to grips with numerous obstacles that could prevent it from returning to profitability. Those obstacles were (1) those that were threatening the company from the outside and (2) those that represented internal weaknesses. Understanding the effects of both external threats and internal weaknesses to its business and determining what, if anything, McDonald's could do about them would determine if the company, with its 13,000 U.S. and 18,000 international restaurants, continued to flounder or prosper in the years to come.

From an external environment standpoint, McDonald's faced many potential problems. First, McDonald's business was affected by the sudden and growing impact of low-carb diets. Diets like the South Beach diet and the Atkins diet both preached the benefits of consuming fewer carbohydrates in an effort to lose weight. In addition, many consumers were attempting to live more active and healthy lifestyles. Such trends were serious threats to McDonald's because its sandwich buns, french fries, and desserts were all loaded with carbohydrates and calories. Furthermore, not only were the buns bad for your health, but what's between those buns could be as well since mad cow disease had been found in the United States and Canada. Previously a European problem only, mad cow disease had now crossed the Atlantic and could become a threat to the North American beef supply.

Other external problems faced by McDonald's were from the legal and competitive arenas. McDonald's had recently been sued by two overweight teenagers who claimed that eating the company's food caused them to become obese. After the suit was thrown out of court, Congress passed a bill that protects the entire fast-food industry from such lawsuits in the future. Nonetheless, the publicity of the suit prompted one consumer to go on a 30-day binge of eating nothing but McDonald's food for breakfast, lunch, and dinner and film the experience for a documentary. The decline in the consumer's health during those 30 days was remarkable and caused McDonald's to defend the healthfulness of the food it serves once again.

From a competition standpoint, things were no better. McDonald's was confronted with competition not only from other fast-food burger chains but also from sandwich shops like Subway, Blimpie's, and others. Indeed, Subway had more restaurant locations in the United States than McDonald's. In addition, "fast casual" dining was becoming more popular. Such companies as Panera Bread and Cosi were leading the charge to appeal to older consumers who were no longer interested in eating McDonald's standard fare of burgers and fries. Moreover, in an effort to get customers to spend more time in their stores, some competitors were offering wireless Internet connections free of charge to customers who brought in their laptop computers. Such connections provide a distinctive advantage to restaurants because it allows businesspeople to check e-mail and continue working through their lunch period.

Add to these problems the anti-Americanism that exists in international markets and the challenge of appealing to a growing diverse population in the United States, and McDonald's clearly had its work cut out for it. In December 2002, McDonald's named Jim Cantalupo as CEO. Mr. Cantalupo took one look around the company and quickly realized that there were as many, if not more, problems inside the company as there were outside. During the late 1990s and early 2000s, McDonald's gained a reputation for providing poor service very slowly in an unclean restaurant setting. In fact, in industry surveys ranking customer satisfaction, McDonald's ranked last among all fast-food restaurants. In addition, the most recent new product introduction that was a success for McDonald's was Chicken McNuggets, which were introduced in 1983. Finally, Mr. Cantalupo was faced with a corporate culture that was designed around making money by renting store locations back to the restaurant operators rather than by selling its products. In other words, McDonald's was more of a real estate company than a fast-food company because most of its profits were the result of collecting rental payments and not from selling burgers, fries, and drinks. Such a culture explains why McDonald's always was more interested in adding new restaurant locations (nearly 1,700 per year over the previous decade) than improving customer service, food quality, and selection in its existing restaurants.

Mr. Cantalupo recognized this fundamental weakness and decided to switch the McDonald's business philosophy from building more stores to getting more people into the existing stores. Other changes made by the new CEO were to streamline operations by reducing the menu, thus making it easier for customers to place their orders, and reducing the number of keypad options on cash registers from 400 to 300. In addition, Mr. Cantalupo also reintroduced a restaurant grading system designed to measure each location in terms of the service provided. Such changes resulted in much-needed improvements, and those improvements brought back more customers. In the first quarter of 2004, McDonald's attracted nearly 2.3 million more customers per day to its restaurants compared to a year before, and profits increased too. But this was only a beginning. Whether the company would be able to devise other strategies that would address McDonald's numerous external and internal issues remained to be seen.

Things to Think About

1. What are the decisions facing McDonald's?
2. What factors are important in understanding the decision situation?
3. What are the alternatives?
4. What decision(s) do you recommend?
5. What are some ways to implement your recommendation(s)?

Sources: David Stires, "McDonald's Keeps Right on Cookin," *Fortune*, May 17, 2004, 174; A. O. Scott, "When All Those Big Macs Bite Back," *New York Times*, May 7, 2004; and David Grainger, "Can McDonald's Cook Again? The Great American Icon Ain't What It Used to Be," *Fortune*, April 14, 2003, 120–29.

Break the chain!

T-shirts, sweatshirts, and more...

* ✳ workers' cooperative—they own the company!
* ✳ unionized with UNITE!
* ✳ workers paid a living wage and benefits
* ✳ clean, healthy conditions
* ✳ organic and fashion styles available

Order now for your affinity group's next conference ✳ rally ✳ just because!

Bulk orders preferred. Single items for sale on website.

www.sweatx.net   ✳   toll-free 866.4SweatX   ✳   866.479.3289

www.sweatx.net

real people, real choices

meet Rick Roth, a Decision Maker
at SweatX

first job out of school

Counseling heroin addicts.

what i do when i'm not working

Working to free Tibet, going to punk shows, playing baseball, taking my kids to ice hockey, or drinking Guinness.

THINK GLOBALLY/ACT ETHICALLY

Rick Roth is the chief executive officer (CEO) of SweatX (**www.sweatx.net**), a company started by Ben Cohen of Ben & Jerry's ice cream fame that cuts and sews apparel in a unionized facility in Los Angeles. Rick graduated from Colgate University with a major in philosophy and religion in 1976. He also attended Franklin College in Switzerland and the Divinity School at Harvard University. Rick's leadership of SweatX builds on his many experiences as an entrepreneur and a social activist. Over the years, he's counseled heroin addicts, owned a construction business, played semipro basketball in Switzerland, worked as an aide at a mental hospital, and managed several outreach projects. He's also active in Amnesty International, Farm Aid, and Students for a Free Tibet.

Decision Time at SweatX

Many apparel companies have been criticized for manufacturing garments under "sweatshop" conditions, where underpaid (and often underage) workers toil long hours in substandard factories. In contrast, TeamX is a worker-owned, unionized apparel factory that manufactures SweatX brand garments. The mission of the SweatX brand is to produce quality clothing that is certified as being produced ethically—it's an anti-sweatshop brand. To

that end, TeamX workers receive reasonable wages and health and pension benefits and they have the protection of a union contract.

Rick Roth had been informally consulting for the company since late 2001, and in September 2003 he was asked to take over as CEO. In 2003, Rick's marketing plan for SweatX recommended that SweatX brand garments be manufactured at other unionized facilities in addition to the TeamX factory. These garments would then be sold through huge warehouses that have the technology to provide real-time inventory tracking, extensive customer service, and state-of-the-art credit departments. Using such modern warehouses would enable SweatX to stock hundreds of items in numerous colors, styles, and sizes and to provide superior customer service. For example, if a customer placed an order for 17 purple shirts and 35,000 gray shirts at 4 P.M. on a Monday, she would have the shirts delivered by the next morning. Such systems would also allow SweatX executives to find out to the piece how many shirts, hats, and jackets were in stock. Rick argued that distributing SweatX garments through these types of distribution warehouses would dramatically improve SweatX's efficiency and its ability to compete in the crowded market for imprintable sportswear (T-shirts and sweatshirts).

The consumers that SweatX is trying to reach can be described as "cultural creatives," a large and growing number of

career high	my hero	my motto to live by	my pet peeve
Being able to offer full health benefits to the workers and their families.	Muhammad Ali, His Holiness the Dalai Lama, Dorothy Day.	Leave the world a better place than you found it.	Racism.

1 Understand business ethics and why it is important for organizations to adhere to ethical business behavior.

2 Explain how marketers apply ethical business behavior to the marketing mix.

3 Describe how firms practice social responsibility.

4 Understand the big picture of international marketing: trade flows,

how firms define the scope of their markets, and how firms develop a competitive advantage in global marketing.

5 Explain how countries seek to protect local industries by establishing roadblocks to foreign companies and by bonding together into economic communities.

6 Understand how economic, political, legal, and cultural issues influence

global marketing strategies and outcomes.

7 Explain the strategies a firm can use to enter global markets.

8 Understand the arguments for standardization versus localization of marketing strategies in global markets and understand how elements of the marketing mix apply to foreign countries.

people who care deeply about issues such as human rights and protection of the environment—and who consider these issues when they decide where and what to buy. Rick's marketing plan initially targeted people who already were looking for union-made goods. With more money and more time, Rick felt that SweatX could target others who would want SweatX apparel once they understood the sweatshop issue.

Still, the question remained as to the best way to get SweatX products into the hands of these cultural creatives. Should the company focus on selling (1) directly to end users of bulk shirts (groups such as teams and small companies), (2) to middlemen (promotional products companies, specialty distributors, and so on), or (3) to distribution warehouses that supply these middlemen? A related issue was whether SweatX should produce only "blank" garments or provide the garments and also arrange the printing and embroidery on them. For Rick, it was tempting to include such embellishments because the profit margins would be better on garments that have printing on them than on blanks. However, these printing processes are complicated, and it wasn't clear to Rick that SweatX had the expertise to manage them. In fact, part of the company's earlier financial problems stemmed from the refusal by some clients to pay for an order in full because of botched print jobs. Clearly, if SweatX was to succeed in its social mission to put an end to sweatshops, the company had to get its act together. Rick considered his options:

OPTION 1: Market full-package deals to end users.

This option involves selling embellished (print, embroidered, or transfer) shirts to end users directly. For example, SweatX would sell 400 shirts with a logo printed on the front directly to a customer like Joe's Bar and Grill. SweatX had been selling such programs and had been subcontracting the embellishment in the past. This strategy would mean higher profit margins, and it

could also enhance the brand loyalty of end users who feel connected directly to the factory. On the other hand, it would be difficult to manage subcontracted custom printing and embroidery, and there would be less control over delivery times. In addition, SweatX would run the risk of angering trading partners who buy "blanks" from SweatX and who might view the company's actions as an attempt to steal some of their customers.

OPTION 2: Market only blank apparel to end users.

This option involves selling only blank garments to customers such as organizations that want to order shirts for their members. These customers would then have the shirts embellished themselves. This option would yield a higher price paid to SweatX than selling through distributors, and in addition end users would feel like they are "buying direct" from the factory, so their brand loyalty would be stronger. However, selling direct would require more extensive sales and marketing efforts. Furthermore, if SweatX chose to sell direct, most distributors would probably stop carrying its products.

OPTION 3: Market only to and through distributors.

In this scenario, end users wouldn't have the option of buying directly from SweatX but they would instead be directed to their local distributor for purchases. Middlemen such as printers would then order the blank shirts and either print them or have them printed elsewhere. This strategy would effectively make all these distributors sales agents for SweatX through their existing sales networks. Everyone could buy through this system, increasing the potential volume. On the other hand, this strategy would result in lower profit margins for SweatX than selling directly to organizations, and the company would not be able to build relationships with these individual customers.

Now, put yourself in Rick Roth's shoes: which option would you choose, and why?

Welcome to the New Era of Marketing

Change is in the wind. Marketers recognize that an increasingly competitive and truly global marketplace beckons them. Businesses seek new and improved ways to attract customers in that global marketplace. And savvy marketers like Rick Roth are more aware than ever that long-term profitability depends on making quality products while acting in an ethical and socially responsible manner. Anything less and consumers will run, not walk, into the arms of competitors. Aspiring tycoons, don't panic: Marketing still is concerned with the firm's bottom line, but now many managers also consider **social profit**, which is the net benefit both the firm and society receive from a firm's ethical practices and socially responsible behavior.[1]

Ben Cohen is an example of an entrepreneur who genuinely believes in social responsibility. His concern about sweatshop labor initially led him to start SweatX, and his concerns about the environment reflect the operating philosophy of another company he started, Ben & Jerry's. This successful ice cream maker is a good example of a firm that is concerned with more than just economic profit. Creating social profit is so important to the Vermont superpremium ice cream firm that part of its mission statement reads, "To operate the Company in a way that actively recognizes the central role that business plays in society by initiating innovative ways to improve the quality of life locally, nationally, and internationally."[2] That's why the firm donates some $1 million annually to the Ben & Jerry's Foundation, which awards grants to nonprofit organizations whose goals are aligned with Ben & Jerry's values.

We call efforts to do business right and do it well the New Era of Marketing. As we saw in Chapter 1, New Era firms create both economic and social profit through a commitment to ethical business behavior, social responsibility, and quality. In this chapter, we'll look at companies like SweatX that practice this philosophy. We'll focus on doing it right by talking about how firms practice ethical business behavior and social responsibility while producing quality goods and services they can be proud to sell. Then, in the second half of the chapter, we'll look at the "big picture" of international marketing and zero in on the opportunities and pitfalls of doing business in a world that seems to be getting smaller by the minute.

> **social profit**
> The benefit an organization and society receive from the organization's ethical practices, community service, efforts to promote cultural diversity, and concern for the natural environment.

Doing It Right: Ethical Behavior in the Marketplace

In the fall of 2001, Enron revealed a massive fraud. The energy company had hidden hundreds of millions of dollars of debt through unethical and illegal accounting practices with the assistance of the nationally renowned accounting firm Arthur Anderson. In 2002, when the giant telecommunications firm WorldCom collapsed into bankruptcy after revealing it had falsified its books by roughly $11 billion, the U.S. General Services Administration banned government contracts with the company, stating that WorldCom "lacked internal controls and business ethics."[3] And U.S. companies certainly don't hold a monopoly on questionable ethics. In late 2003, Italian dairy-foods giant Parmalat went into bankruptcy and its founder landed in jail when the company failed to account for at least 8 billion Euros (about $10 billion).[4]

The fallout from these and other cases raises the issue of how damaging unethical practices can be to society at large. Issues of accountability, corporate accounting practices, and government regulation fill the business press as the public and corporate world reassess what we define as ethical behavior.

Ethics are rules of conduct—how most people in a culture judge what is right and what is wrong. **Business ethics** are basic values that guide a firm's behavior. These values govern decisions managers make about what goes into their products, how they are advertised and sold, and how they are disposed of. Developing good business ethics is the first step toward creating social profit.

Of course, notions of right and wrong differ among organizations and cultures. Some businesses, for example, believe it is okay for salespeople to persuade customers to buy, even if it means giving them partly true or even false information, whereas other firms practice nothing less than

> **business ethics**
> Rules of conduct for an organization.

total honesty with customers. Because each culture has its own set of values, beliefs, and customs, ethical business behavior varies in different parts of the world.

Take bribery and extortion, for example. *Bribery* occurs when someone voluntarily offers payment to get an illegal advantage. *Extortion* occurs when payment is extracted under duress by someone in authority.[5] Bribes are given to speed up required work, to secure a contract, or to avoid having one canceled. Such payments are a way of life in many countries and seem much like giving a waiter a tip for good service. The Foreign Corrupt Practices Act of 1977 (FCPA), however, puts U.S. businesses at a disadvantage because it bars them from paying bribes to sell overseas.[6] It should be noted, however, that the FCPA does allow payments for " . . . routine governmental action . . . such as obtaining permits, licenses, or other official documents; processing governmental papers, such as visas and work orders; [and] providing police protection" but does not include " . . . any decision by a foreign official to award new business or to continue business with a particular party."[7] While some unethical activities are clearly illegal, others are not.

So how do business managers know what is expected of them? Many firms develop their own **codes of ethics**—written standards of behavior to which everyone in the organization must subscribe. These documents eliminate confusion about what the firm considers to be ethically acceptable behavior for employees. For example, the Dow Chemical Company's Code of Business Conduct (available through its Web site at **www.dow.com** in over 10 different languages) is based on Dow's stated corporate values of integrity, respect for people, unity, outside-in focus, agility, and innovation. The code deals with such issues as diversity, the environment, financial integrity, accurate company records, conflicts of interest, obligations to customers, competitors and regulators, and corporate social responsibility. It also includes policies to deal with issues such as bribery, political contributions, and equal employment opportunity.[8]

To help member firms adhere to ethical behavior in their marketing efforts, the American Marketing Association (AMA) developed its own code of ethics, as shown in Figure 3.1.[9]

The High Costs of Unethical Marketplace Behavior

Ethical business is good business. Today's marketers understand that unethical practices can wind up costing dearly in the long run. These actions hurt both financially and—as the companies we mentioned earlier found out the hard way—in terms of a firm's reputation.

Consumers also appreciate companies that practice ethical behavior, but sometimes we forget that ethics in the marketplace is a two-way street. For example, a retail security survey showed that U.S. retailers lose nearly $10 billion a year to shoplifting (so-called "five-finger discounts") and another $15 billion to employee theft.[10] Many retailers also lose sales to "retail borrowing," where the consumer purchases an item such as a party dress or an expensive business suit, wears it for a special occasion, and returns it the next day as if it had not been worn. Consumers ultimately pay for such practices when retailers and manufacturers raise prices to cover their losses. In fact, a family of four spends over $300 extra per year because of markups taken by stores to compensate for stolen or damaged merchandise. Although marketers work hard to prevent such behavior, they often must overlook dishonest customers in order to provide return policies and a pleasant retail shopping environment necessary to satisfy honest ones.

Consumerism: Fighting Back

Organized activities that bring about social and political change are not new to the American scene. Women's right to vote, child labor laws, the minimum wage, equal employment opportunity, and the ban on nuclear weapons testing all have resulted from social movements where citizens, public and private organizations, and businesses work to change society. **Consumerism** is the social movement directed toward protecting consumers from harmful business practices.

The modern consumerism movement began in the 1960s, when the publication of books—such as Rachel Carson's *Silent Spring*, which attacked the irresponsible use of pesticides, and Ralph Nader's *Unsafe at Any Speed*, which exposed safety defects in General Motors' Corvair automo-

codes of ethics
Written standards of behavior to which everyone in the organization must subscribe.

consumerism
A social movement that attempts to protect consumers from harmful business practices.

Figure 3.1   AMA Code of Ethics

The American Marketing Association helps its members adhere to ethical standards of business through its Code of Ethics.

Members of the American Marketing Association are committed to ethical, professional conduct. They have joined together in subscribing to this Code of Ethics embracing the following topics:

Responsibilities of the Marketer
Marketers must accept responsibility for the consequences of their activities and make every effort to ensure that their decisions, recommendations, and actions function to identify, serve, and satisfy all relevant publics: customers, organizations, and society.

Marketers' professional conduct must be guided by:
1. The basic rule of professional ethics: not knowingly to do harm;
2. The adherence to all applicable laws and regulations;
3. The accurate representation of their education, training and experience; and
4. The active support, practice, and promotion of this Code of Ethics.

Honesty and Fairness
Marketers shall uphold and advance the integrity, honor, and dignity of the marketing profession by:
1. Being honest in serving consumers, clients, employees, suppliers, distributors, and the public;
2. Not knowingly participating in conflict of interest without prior notice to all parties involved; and
3. Establishing equitable fee schedules including the payment or receipt of usual, customary, and/or legal compensation for marketing exchanges.

Rights and Duties of Parties in the Marketing Exchange Process
Participants in the marketing exchange process should be able to expect that:
1. Products and services offered are safe and fit for their intended uses;
2. Communications about offered products and services are not deceptive;
3. All parties intend to discharge their obligations, financial and otherwise, in good faith; and
4. Appropriate internal methods exist for equitable adjustment and/or redress of grievances concerning purchases.

It is understood that the above would include, but is not limited to, the following responsibilities of the marketer:
In the area of product development and management,
• disclosure of all substantial risks associated with product or service usage;
• identification of any product component substitution that might materially change the product or impact on the buyer's purchase decision;
• identification of extra-cost added features.

In the area of promotions,
• avoidance of false and misleading advertising;
• rejection of high pressure manipulations, or misleading sales tactics;
• avoidance of sales promotions that use deception or manipulation.

In the area of distribution,
• not manipulating the availability of a product for purpose of exploitation;
• not using coercion in the marketing channel;
• not exerting undue influence over the reseller's choice to handle a product.

In the area of pricing,
• not engaging in price fixing;
• not practicing predatory pricing;
• disclosing the full price associated with any purchase.

In the area of marketing research,
• prohibiting selling or fundraising under the guise of conducting research;
• maintaining research integrity by avoiding misrepresentation and omission of pertinent research data;
• treating outside clients and suppliers fairly.

Organizational Relationships
Marketers should be aware of how their behavior may influence or impact on the behavior of others in organizational relationships. They should not demand, encourage, or apply coercion to obtain unethical behavior in their relationships with others, such as employees, suppliers, or customers.
1. Apply confidentiality and anonymity in professional relationships with regard to privileged information;
2. Meet their obligations and responsibilities in contracts and mutual agreements in a timely manner;
3. Avoid taking the work of others, in whole, or in part, and represent this work as their own or directly benefit from it without compensation or consent of the originator or owner;
4. Avoid manipulation to take advantage of situations to maximize personal welfare in a way that unfairly deprives or damages the organization of others.

Any AMA member found to be in violation of any provision of this Code of Ethics may have his or her Association membership suspended or revoked.

Source: American Marketing Association.

biles—put pressure on businesses to mend their ways. Consumers organized to call for safer products and honest information—and to boycott companies that did not comply with their demands. Consumerism also prompted the establishment of government regulatory agencies and legislation such as the Cigarette Labeling Act of 1966 and the Child Protection and Safety Act of 1969.

Consumer Bill of Rights
The rights of consumers to be protected by the federal government.

In his 1961 inaugural speech, President John F. Kennedy outlined what became known as the **Consumer Bill of Rights**, which includes the following:

- **The right to be safe:** Products should not be dangerous when used as intended. Organizations such as the Consumer Products Safety Board and *Consumer Reports* magazine regularly announce products they find to be unsafe. Product safety was an important issue when a number of serious accidents, some fatal, were connected a few years ago to the sudden loss of tread on Firestone Wilderness AT tires installed as original equipment on Ford sport-utility vehicles. An engineering analysis conducted by the National Highway Traffic Safety Administration (NHTSA) found that the tires were defective, leading Firestone to recall over 10 million tires. The company stated that while it did not agree with the finding, it was recalling the tires to avoid a long confrontation with the NHTSA.[11]

- **The right to be informed:** Businesses should provide consumers with adequate information to make intelligent product choices. This right means that product information provided by advertising, packaging, and salespeople should be honest and complete.

- **The right to be heard:** Consumers should have the means to complain or express their displeasure in order to obtain redress or retribution from companies. Government agencies and industry self-regulatory groups should respond to every customer complaint.

- **The right to choose freely:** Consumers should be able to choose from a variety of products. No one business should be allowed to control the price, quality, or availability of goods and services.

Ethics in the Marketing Mix

As we've seen in previous chapters, marketing mix strategies are crucial to a firm's success in achieving its objectives. Marketing managers are responsible for determining the most ethical way to price, package, promote, and distribute their offerings to reach profit and market-share objectives. Let's see how ethical considerations can influence marketing mix decisions.

MAKING A PRODUCT SAFE   A key ethical decision concerns product safety. It can be tempting to cut costs on design, safety testing, and production to rush a new product to market. One infamous example is the case of the Ford Pinto, which was designed with an unprotected gas tank that exploded in rear-end crashes. Consumer watchdog Ralph Nader claimed that Ford had tested a safe fuel system as early as 1970 but had not installed it because doing so would increase production costs. In 1978, Ford recalled 1.5 million Pintos made between 1971 and 1976 to install two plastic shields to protect the cars' gas tanks in rear-end collisions—but not before the company had to pay $7 million to settle a rash of lawsuits.[12] More recently, horizontal window blinds have caused serious problems, with some of these products being recalled twice in the past decade because they caused the deaths of 130 infants and children.[13]

PRICING THE PRODUCT FAIRLY   The potential for unethical pricing strategies is so great that many shady pricing practices are illegal. Marketers in the United States face laws that prevent greedy firms from hurting consumers or other businesses with pricing practices that are deceptive, that are unfair, or that discriminate against some customers. A few years ago, the U.S. Federal Trade Commission (FTC) found personal computer manufacturer Gateway guilty of deceptive advertising when it made claims about a money-back guarantee with a full refund and on-site warranty service.[14] The FTC found that Gateway deducted the cost of shipping personal computers to consumers from the "full refund," a cost of approximately $62, and would not provide on-site service until Gateway diagnosed the problem over the phone and determined that the consumer could not make the needed repairs. Gateway settled with the FTC for $290,000. (We'll talk more about specific legal considerations in pricing in Chapter 11.)

New Era firms price their products fairly—and they have been known to cut their prices in times of need. Numerous stories of selfless acts abounded after the terrorist attacks on New York and Washington, D.C., on September 11, 2001. That morning, a Burger King near the World Trade Center immediately started handing out drinks to people running/walking by, a Starbucks gave free coffee to the rescue workers, and many restaurants in lower Manhattan donated hot meals to the rescue workers.

PROMOTING THE PRODUCT ETHICALLY   Marketing management's decisions on how to promote the firm's products are likely to draw the most criticism—and government regulation. To protect consumers from being misled, the FTC has specific rules regarding unfair or deceptive advertising.[15] Some deceptive ads make statements that can be proven false. For example, the FTC fined Volvo and its ad agency $150,000 each for an ad containing a "rigged" demonstration. The Volvo "Bear Food" ad campaign showed a monster truck running over a row of cars and crushing all but the Volvo station wagon. The Volvos, however, had been structurally reinforced, while the structural supports in some of the other cars had been cut.[16]

In addition to fining firms for deceptive advertising, the FTC also has the power to require firms to run **corrective advertising**, messages that clarify or qualify previous claims. For example, an FTC ruling required Warner-Lambert to state in corrective advertising that its Listerine mouthwash would "not help prevent colds or sore throats or lessen their severity"—a claim the company had been making for years.[17]

Other ads, although not illegal, create a biased impression of products with the use of **puffery**—claims of superiority that neither sponsors nor critics of the ads can prove are true or untrue. For example, Nivea bills itself as "the world's number 1 name in skin care," Neutrogena claims that its cream cleanser produces "the deepest feeling clean," and DuPont says that its Stainmaster Carpet is "a creation so remarkable, it's practically a miracle."

Does this mean that puffery is an unethical marketing practice? Not really. In fact, both advertisers and consumers generally accept puffery as a normal part of the advertising game. Although a little exaggeration may be reasonable, for New Era firms the goal is to create marketing communications that are both honest and that present their products in the most positive way possible. This approach works to the firm's advantage in the long run since it prevents consumers from becoming overly cynical about the claims it makes.

MAKING THE PRODUCT AVAILABLE TO CONSUMERS ETHICALLY   The steps companies take to make their products available to consumers also can create ethical dilemmas. For example, because their size gives them great bargaining power when negotiating with manufacturers, many large retail chains force manufacturers to pay a **slotting allowance**—a fee paid in exchange for agreeing to place the manufacturer's products on the retailer's valuable shelf space. Although the retailers claim that such fees pay the cost of adding products to their inventory, many manufacturers feel that slotting fees are more akin to highway robbery. Certainly, the practice prevents smaller manufacturers that cannot afford the slotting allowances from getting their products into the hands of consumers.

Doing It Right: A Focus on Social Responsibility

So far, we've learned how New Era firms gain social profit by practicing business ethics when making marketing mix decisions. The second part of social profit is **social responsibility**, a management philosophy in which organizations engage in activities that have a positive effect on society and promote the public good. These activities include promoting environmental stewardship, engaging in cause marketing, and promoting cultural diversity.

Firms that believe in social responsibility possess a value system that goes beyond the short-term bottom line. Instead, they consider the short- and long-term effects of decisions on the company, its employees, consumers, the community, and the world at large. Who are the current corporate leaders in social responsibility? *Business Ethics* magazine annually rates companies and lists the top 100 corporate citizens. In 2004, the top five companies were Fannie Mae, Proctor &

corrective advertising
Advertising that clarifies or qualifies previous deceptive advertising claims.

puffery
Claims made in advertising of product superiority that cannot be proven true or untrue.

slotting allowance
A fee paid by a manufacturer to a retailer in exchange for agreeing to place products on the retailer's shelves.

social responsibility
A management practice in which organizations seek to engage in activities that have a positive effect on society and promote the public good.

Powerful marketing communications can help to change people's attitudes and behaviors about environmental issues. This novel ad is sponsored by the Muir Heritage Land Trust, which works to save open spaces and support environmental education programs.

environmental stewardship
A position taken by an organization to protect or enhance the natural environment as it conducts its business activities.

green marketing
A marketing strategy that supports environmental stewardship by creating an environmentally founded differential benefit in the minds of consumers.

cause marketing
Marketing activities in which firms seek to have their corporate identity linked to a good cause through advertising, public service, and publicity.

Gamble, Intel Corporation, St. Paul Companies, and Green Mountain Coffee Roasters Inc.[18]

Serving the Environment

New Era firms assume a position of **environmental stewardship** when they make socially responsible business decisions that also protect the environment. Many firms preserve the environment by following a strategy called **green marketing**, which describes efforts to choose packages, product designs, and other aspects of the marketing mix that are earth friendly but still profitable. Green marketing practices can indeed result in black ink for a firm's bottom line. For example, Electrolux found that profits from its solar-powered lawn mowers, chain saws lubricated with vegetable oil, and water-conserving washing machines actually were 3.8 percent higher than the money made from the company's conventional products.[19] Here's how some other firms are "turning green":

- Stonyfield Farm is the nation's third-largest yogurt brand with the highest growth rate in the industry. At the same time, the company has received numerous awards for its waste reduction, energy efficiency, and environmental advocacy efforts. The company recycles most of its manufacturing solid waste, invests in green packaging research and carbon offsets to neutralize its manufacturing plant's contribution to global warming, uses its lids and packaging to promote environmental causes, donates 10 percent of its profits to environmental causes, and has converted 90 percent of its products to organic certification.[20]

- Boeing changed its factory lighting from incandescent to fluorescent. This saves 100,000 tons of carbon dioxide per year, which is one of the main contributors to global warming.[21]

- Office Depot offers its customers environmentally preferable products through "The Green Book," a catalog published for Office Depot's business customers that lists more than 1,000 products ranging from paper to machine supplies.[22]

Do New Era firms practice environmental stewardship because they're "righteous" or because they will benefit financially? The answer is a little of both. There are many business leaders who simply believe in doing the right thing, but most also need to see financial benefits from these decisions. Customers who are concerned about the future of the planet will buy green products even if the price is higher. But many marketers are wary of some environmental stewardship practices. For example, automobile manufacturers estimate that government fuel efficiency requirements will add as much as $1,000 to the cost of an automobile, an amount many consumers may be unwilling to pay.

Serving Society: Cause Marketing

Cause marketing is a strategy of joining forces with a not-for-profit organization to tackle a social problem. In the past, this practice usually meant running a short-term promotion and then donating profits to a charity. Marketing historians generally credit the American Express campaign to raise money for the renovation of the Statue of Liberty in 1983 as the beginning of this promotion-only form of cause marketing.[23]

The problem was that consumers often saw these programs as gimmicky and insincere—especially when there was no apparent connection between the company and the cause. The result was that sales increased during the promotion, but there were no long-term benefits to either the sponsoring firm or the cause it was trying to help. What to do?

Today, New Era firms have abandoned this one-shot approach and instead make a long-term commitment to tackle a social problem, such as illiteracy or child abuse. Indeed, in addition to being profitable, the main reason for SweatX's existence is to help stamp out sweatshop labor. New Era firms believe that sales of their products increase as a result of cause marketing activities. According to one survey of American adults, they are right: 84 percent said that cause marketing creates a positive image of a company, and 78 percent said they would be more likely to buy a product associated with an important cause.[24]

Avon's Breast Cancer Awareness Crusade is a well-known example of cause marketing. In 2002, the program reached its 10-year goal of raising $250 million. The money has been raised by more than 550,000 Avon employees, much of it through the sale of a variety of pink-ribbon products. The funds from the crusade are used to support programs in 50 countries around the world.[25]

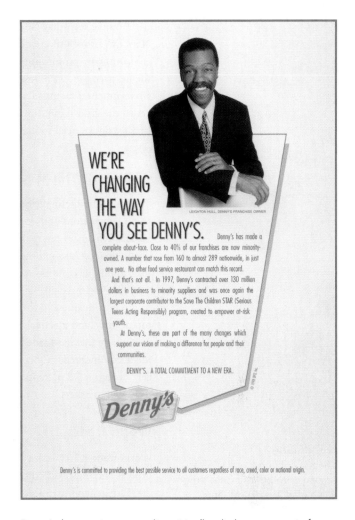

Denny's shows a strong commitment to diversity in every aspect of its business.

Serving the Community: Promoting Cultural Diversity

One day, two groups of hungry Secret Service agents walked into a Denny's restaurant. The all-white group said they got served right away. The other group, made up of African Americans, said they waited—and waited—and waited. The African American agents filed a lawsuit, charging unequal treatment of minorities at Denny's.[26] Although Denny's had written policies concerning equal and fair treatment of customers and employees, the lawsuit suggested the policies were ineffective. Negative press had a substantial effect on Denny's sales and on employee morale.[27]

Denny's found out that **cultural diversity** not only is the right thing to do but also is important to the financial health of the organization. Since then, Denny's has initiated a number of changes, including diversity training, recruiting practices that include minority universities, a redesigned performance appraisal system that evaluates managers on 10 core competencies including valuing and managing diversity, and an incentive program that ties 25 percent of senior management's bonuses to the number of women and minorities in their divisions.[28] As a result, since 1998, Denny's has been included every year in *Fortune* magazine's top Six Best Companies for Minorities, twice ranking number one.[29]

When a firm adopts cultural diversity programs, it makes sure that marketing policies and hiring practices give people an equal chance to work for the company and buy its products. TJX, parent company of off-price clothing retailers T.J. Maxx and Marshalls, has developed a national "Welfare-to-Work" program to help people who have been on welfare. With over 1,000 stores in 47 U.S. states, the company has hired over 30,000 former welfare recipients.[30]

This philosophy also extends to the disabled, a consumer market with a discretionary income of $176 billion. Smart marketers view the disabled as both customers and valued employees. Hertz, for example, offers cars that disabled people can drive at most Hertz rental locations, and the firm provides shuttle buses and vans equipped with lifts to transport these customers.[31]

cultural diversity
A management practice that actively seeks to include people of different sexes, races, ethnic groups, and religions in an organization's employees, customers, suppliers, and distribution channel partners.

We've seen that New Era firms create social profit by adhering to ethical business practices. New Era firms also create social profit when they practice social responsibility—protecting the environment, promoting diversity, and serving their communities through cause marketing. In the next section, we'll move from ethical considerations to global ones. We'll examine some of the environmental factors a marketer must consider before venturing out into another country and get to the crucial questions for marketers: How can we make our company global? What changes (if any) do we need to make to the marketing mix for our product to compete effectively?

Playing on a Global Stage

The global marketing game is exciting, the stakes are high—and it's easy to lose your shirt. Competition comes from both local and foreign firms, and differences in national laws, customs, and consumer preferences can make your head spin. The successful global business needs to set its sights on diverse markets around the world, but it needs to act locally by being willing to adapt business practices to unique conditions in other parts of the globe.

For example, in the mid-1990s, U.S. athletic shoe giant Nike had to adjust its global strategy to grow its business in foreign markets. The company made appealing to soccer fans worldwide a top priority, and it actively pursued new customers from France to Chile. This was a real change for a company that has made its mark in such "American" sports as basketball and football. Nike's president commented, "Once we set our sights on being a global company, we had to focus on soccer."[32] Figure 3.2 presents the major factors that marketers need to consider before making the leap to foreign markets.

World Trade

world trade
The flow of goods and services among different countries—the value of all the exports and imports of the world's nations.

World trade refers to the flow of goods and services among different countries—the value of all the exports and imports of the world's nations. World trade activity is steadily increasing year by year. In 2003, merchandise exports of all countries totaled $7.3 trillion, up 16 percent from 2002. Similarly, world exports of services totaled $1.8 trillion, up 12 percent. This growth was the largest in nearly

Figure 3.2   Decision Model for Entering Foreign Markets

Entering global markets involves a complex decision process. Marketers must fully understand market conditions and environmental factors in order to determine the best strategy for entering the market and to create a successful marketing mix.

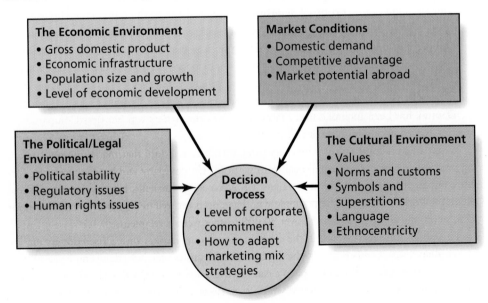

Figure 3.3 North America Trade Flows (in $billions)

Knowing who does business with whom is essential for overseas marketing strategies. As this figure shows, North America trades most heavily with Asia, western Europe, and Latin America.

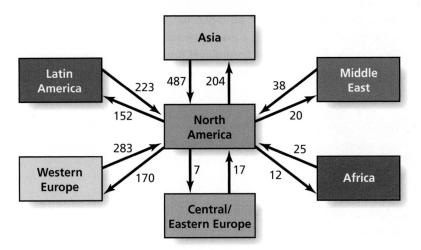

10 years and was the second year of growth since the world economy was sent into a tailspin by the September 2001 terrorist attacks on the United States.[33] Of course, not all countries participate equally in the trade flows among nations. Understanding the "big picture" of who does business with whom is important to marketers when they devise global trade strategies. Figure 3.3 shows the amount of merchandise traded by North America with its major partners around the world.

Having customers in far-reaching places is important, but it requires some flexibility since business must be done differently to adapt to local social and economic conditions. For example, firms engaged in global marketing must be able to accommodate the needs of trading partners when those foreign firms can't pay cash for the products they want to purchase. Believe it or not, the currency of as many as 70 percent of all countries is not convertible; it cannot be spent or exchanged outside the country's borders. In other countries, sufficient cash or credit is simply not available, so trading firms work out elaborate deals in which they trade (or *barter*) their products with each other or even supply goods in return for tax breaks from the local government. This **countertrade** accounts for about 25 percent of all world trade. For instance, PepsiCo has been selling its drinks in Russia for years in exchange for Stolichnaya vodka, which it then sells in the United States to those who want a different kind of refreshment break.[34]

countertrade
A type of trade in which goods are paid for with other items instead of with cash.

HOW "WORLDLY" CAN A COMPANY BE?   Not all companies that engage in world trade are alike. Take, for example, MTV, a very global company. Whether it's MTV Spain, MTV China, or MTV Brazil, teens (and some wannabe teens) are glued to the set every second of the day. While as much as 60 percent of its programming originates in the United States, the rest is produced in cooperation with local producers who create specialized products.

How do you gain a foothold in faraway places? The simplest and easiest way to enter the global marketplace is by *exporting*. Exporting firms expand sales by selling the same products they offer in their domestic markets to other countries. Firms that export generally use the same marketing strategies wherever they do business. For example, Harley-Davidson exports about a quarter of its choppers to avid bikers around the world. Bikers can buy the same Harley bike, helmet, and jacket in Tokyo and in Melbourne that they buy in Kansas City.

Multinational or global firms view the entire world as their markets. Some global firms adapt their basic strategies to local conditions, while others try to do the same thing everywhere. For example, whereas Kraft adds lemon, egg, or mustard to its mayonnaise to please different European palettes, Coca-Cola sells the same "Coke" everywhere. MTV, after having developed multiple MTV operations around the globe that meet country-specific music tastes, is now developing

As this French ad shows, MTV Europe tailors its messages to local markets.

born-global firms
Companies that try to sell their products in multiple countries from the moment they're created.

programming that can cross borders and even go global. One idea, a show titled "Famous Last Minutes," a parody about imagined rock stars' last minutes, was dreamed up in Germany but was then developed for a much larger market.[35]

The appeal of catering to a global market is so strong that it's even spawning a new breed of start-up companies called **born-global firms**.[36] These are companies that deliberately try to sell their products in multiple countries from the moment they're created rather than taking the usual path of developing business in their local market and then slowly expanding into other countries. For example, Logitech International is a Swiss company that quite possibly made your computer mouse. It has operational headquarters through its U.S. subsidiary in California and regional headquarters through local subsidiaries in Switzerland, Taiwan, and Hong Kong. The company has manufacturing facilities in Asia and offices in major cities in North America, Europe, and Asia. Logitech currently employs over 4,500 people worldwide. It's truly "born global."

MARKET CONDITIONS   Of course, not all firms can or should go global. The first step in deciding whether and how to go global is to examine some basic market conditions: domestic demand, the market potential abroad, and a firm's ability to have a competitive advantage in foreign markets.

Many times, a firm's decision to go global is based on conditions where domestic demand is declining while demand in foreign markets is growing. For example, the market for personal computers has leveled off in the United States, where more sales come from people replacing an old or obsolete machine than from those buying a new personal computer for the first time. In examining the market potential abroad for computers, however, the demand is much greater in some other parts of the world where consumers and businesses are only now beginning to tune into the power of the Web.

COMPETITIVE ADVANTAGE   In Chapter 1, we saw how firms seek to create competitive advantage, a means to outperform the competition. When competing in a global marketplace, this challenge is even greater because there are more players involved and typically some of these local firms have a "home-court advantage." It's kind of like soccer—increasing numbers of Americans play the game, but they are up against an ingrained tradition of soccer fanaticism in Europe and South America, where kids start dribbling a soccer ball when they start to walk.

Firms need to capitalize on their home country's assets and avoid competing in areas in which they are at a disadvantage. For example, German firms have trouble keeping production costs down because of the high wages, short workweeks, and long vacations that their skilled factory workers enjoy, so they compete better on high quality than on low price. Developing countries typically have a large labor force and low wages but relatively little in the way of highly trained workers or high-tech facilities, so they are better prospects for handmade crafts and low-cost manufacturing.

Some of the most significant U.S. exports are foods, industrial supplies, and services, including tourism and entertainment—industries in which consumers around the world value American products. The success of these industries shows that a firm's prospects for success depend not only on its own abilities but also on its home country's competitive advantage, barriers to trade, and memberships in economic communities.

Borders, Roadblocks, and Communities

Even the best of competitive advantages may not allow a firm to be successful in foreign markets if the opportunities for success are not available. We like to think of the world as one big, open marketplace where companies from every country are free to compete for business by meeting customers' needs better than the next guy. Although the world seems to be moving toward such an ideal of free trade, we're not quite there yet. Often a company's efforts to expand into foreign markets are hindered by roadblocks designed to favor local businesses over outsiders.[37]

PROTECTED TRADE In some cases, a government adopts a policy of **protectionism** in which it enforces rules on foreign firms designed to give home companies an advantage. Many governments set **import quotas** on foreign goods to reduce competition for their domestic industries. Quotas are limitations on the amount of a product allowed to enter or leave a country. Quotas can make goods more expensive to a country's citizens because the absence of cheaper foreign goods reduces pressure on domestic firms to lower prices. For example, in 2003, Russia put import quotas on meat products in order to protect its own meat production industry.[38]

An **embargo** is an extreme quota that prohibits specified foreign goods completely. Much to the distress of hard-core cigar smokers in the United States, the U.S. government prohibits the import of Cuban cigars, rum, and other products because of political differences with its island neighbor.

Governments also use **tariffs**, or taxes on imported goods, to give domestic competitors an advantage in the marketplace by making foreign competitors' goods more expensive than their own goods. For example, after the trade deficit with China reached $103 billion in 2002, the U.S. government proposed tariffs against some Chinese textiles and clothing.[39]

THE GERMAN WAY TO BRAKE.

Continental®
TYRES - ENGINEERED IN GERMANY

www.conti-online.com

Germany has a worldwide reputation for producing high-quality products. Continental Tire focuses on this to persuade consumers of the superior quality of their tires.

Established under the United Nations after World War II, the **General Agreement on Tariffs and Trade (GATT)** did a lot to reduce the problems that protectionism creates. This regulatory group is now known as the **World Trade Organization (WTO)**. The WTO was established during GATT's 1986–1994 Uruguay Round and effectively replaced GATT in 1995. During the 50-plus years of GATT/WTO, world trade exports increased by 6 percent annually. With nearly 150 members (and around 30 more negotiating membership now), the WTO member nations account for over 97 percent of world trade. The WTO's decisions are made by the entire membership, and all participating governments must ratify agreements.

Through a series of trade negotiations (known as *rounds*) that set standards for how much countries are allowed to favor their own goods and services, the WTO has become a global referee for trade.[40] The objective of the WTO is to "help trade flow smoothly, freely, fairly, and predictably." With over three-fourths of its membership being from the world's poorer countries, negotiations in recent years have focused on issues concerning these countries and GATT agreements giving special benefits to them.[41]

One important issue that the WTO tackles is protection of copyright and patent rights. This protection will help firms prevent pirated versions of their software, books, and music CDs from

protectionism
A policy adopted by a government to give domestic companies an advantage.

import quotas
Limitations set by a government on the amount of a product allowed to enter or leave a country.

embargo
A quota completely prohibiting specified goods from entering or leaving a country.

tariffs
Taxes on imported goods.

General Agreement on Tariffs and Trade (GATT)
International treaty to reduce import tax levels and trade restrictions.

World Trade Organization (WTO)
An organization that replaced GATT, the WTO sets trade rules for its member nations and mediates disputes between nations.

economic communities
Groups of countries that band together to promote trade among themselves and to make it easier for member nations to compete elsewhere.

European Union (EU)
Economic community that now includes most of Europe.

North American Free Trade Agreement (NAFTA)
The world's largest economic community composed of the United States, Canada, and Mexico.

being sold in other countries. This is a serious problem for U.S. companies, as their profits are eroded by illegal sales. According to a senior Microsoft executive based in Asia, "Piracy is clearly our number one competitor, and not only Microsoft's number one competitor but also a big impediment to the growth of the local software industry."[42]

Economic Communities

Groups of countries may also band together to promote trade among themselves and make it easier for member nations to compete elsewhere. These **economic communities** coordinate trade policies and ease restrictions on the flow of products and capital across their borders. Economic communities are important to marketers because they set policies in such areas as product content, package labeling, and advertising regulations that influence strategic decisions when doing business in these areas.

Table 3.1 illustrates the economic communities that have now been created around the world. South America has two groups: MERCOSUR and the Andean Community. Comesa includes 20 African countries, and the Asia-Pacific Economy Cooperation (APEC) includes 22 countries. The Association of Southeast Asian Nations (ASEAN) includes 10 nations, while the Central European Free Trade Agreement (CEFTA) and the South Asia Association for Regional Cooperation (SAPTA) include seven countries each.

The economic community in Europe is the **European Union (EU)**. In 1957, the Treaty of Paris created the European Union, which at that time consisted of six member countries—Belgium, France, Germany, Italy, Luxembourg, and the Netherlands. This community now includes 19 additional countries, 10 of which were admitted in 2004. The EU's membership represents about 450 million consumers, 300 million of whom use the same currency, the *Euro*.[43]

The **North American Free Trade Agreement (NAFTA)** is the world's largest economic community. Comprised of the United States, Canada, and Mexico, NAFTA became a unified trading bloc in 1994.[44] However, NAFTA is controversial. Some critics claim that it diverts jobs from the United States to Mexico, where cheaper labor rates prevail. Yet the agreement appears to be stimulating economic growth, as foreign investors pump money into North American markets.

An even larger American free trade zone might be in the making. Talks are expected to conclude in 2005 for development of the Free Trade Area of the Americas (FTAA). The FTAA, when in place, will include 34 countries in North, Central, and South America with a population of 800 million and combined output of $11 trillion.[45] Under the FTAA, firms in these 34 countries would operate in the "largest free-trade zone on the planet—a vast market marked by nonexistent or very low tariffs, streamlined customs regulations, and the gradual disappearance of quotas, subsidies, and other impediments to trade."[46]

The Global Marketing Environment

Now we've seen the "big picture" of world trade a firm must consider as it decides in which regions of the world it holds a competitive advantage. To complicate matters, companies that enter foreign markets need to consider how—and whether—to adapt to *local* conditions in a country or region. Environmental scanning of a foreign market is difficult because marketers usually aren't familiar with its economy, politics, laws, and culture. In this section, we'll see how economic, political, and cultural factors affect marketers' global strategies.

The Economic Environment

Countries vary in their level of economic development, and a firm thinking about marketing overseas needs to understand what its potential customers can afford. A maker of fine crystal will find it rough going in a country where few can afford its products.

Table 3.1 Major Economic Communities Around the World

Economic communities are organizations of countries that band together to promote trade among themselves and make it easier for member countries to trade elsewhere. Economic communities, only some of which are shown here, exist all around the globe, and the number continues to grow.

Community	Member Countries
The Andean Community www.comunidadandina.org	Bolivia, Colombia, Ecuador, Peru, Venezuela
APEC: Asia-Pacific Economy Cooperation www.apecsec.org	Australia, Brunei Darassalam, Canada, Chile, China, Hong Kong (China), Indonesia, Japan, Malaysia, Mexico, New Zealand, Papua New Guinea, Peru, Philippines, Republic of Korea, Russian Federation, Singapore, Taiwan (Chinese), Thailand, United States, Vietnam
ASEAN Association of Southeast Asian Nations www.aseansec.org	Brunei, Cambodia, Indonesia, Laos, Malaysia, Myanmar, Philippines, Singapore, Thailand, Vietnam
CEFTA Central European Free Trade Agreement www.cefta.org	Bulgaria, Czech Republic, Hungary, Poland, Romania, Slovak Republic, Slovenia
COMESA: Common Market for Eastern and Southern Africa[a] www.comesa.int	Angola, Burundi, Comoros, Democratic Republic of Congo, Djibouti, Egypt, Eritrea, Ethiopia, Kenya, Madagascar, Malawi, Mauritius, Namibia, Rwanda, Seychelles, Sudan, Swaziland, Uganda, Zambia, Zimbabwe
EU: European Union www.Europa.eu.int	Austria, Belgium, Cyprus, Czech Republic, Denmark, Estonia, Finland, France, Germany, Greece, Hungary, Ireland, Italy, Latvia, Lithuania, Luxembourg, Malta, Netherlands, Poland, Portugal, Slovakia, Slovenia, Spain, Sweden, United Kingdom
MERCOSUR www.mercosur.org	Argentina, Brazil, Paraguay, Uruguay
NAFTA: North American Free Trade Agreement www.nafta-sec-alena.org	Canada, Mexico, United States
SAPTA: South Asian Association for Regional Cooperation www.south-asia.com	Bangladesh, Bhutan, India, Maldives, Nepal, Pakistan, Sri Lanka

[a] Not included in the WTO International Trade Statistics 2003.

INDICATORS OF ECONOMIC HEALTH   One way to gauge the market potential for a product is to look at a country's economic health. The most commonly used measure of economic health of a country is the **gross domestic product (GDP)**, the total dollar value of goods and services a country produces within its borders in a year. A similar but less frequently used measure of economic health is the **gross national product (GNP)**, which measures the value of all goods and services produced by a country's individuals or organizations, whether located within the country's borders or not. Table 3.2 shows the GDP and other economic and demographic characteristics of a sampling of countries. In addition to total GDP, marketers may also compare countries on the basis of *per capita GDP*: the total GDP divided by the number of people in a country.

Still, such comparisons may not tell the whole story. Per capita GDP can be deceiving because the wealth of a country may be concentrated in the hands of a few. Furthermore, the costs of the same goods and services are much lower in some global markets. For example, goods and services valued at $30,000 in the United States would cost only $5,100 in Uganda.[47]

gross domestic product (GDP)
The total dollar value of goods and services produced by a nation within its borders in a year.

gross national product (GNP)
The value of all goods and services produced by a country's citizens or organizations, whether located within the country's borders or not.

Table 3.2 Comparisons of Several Countries on Economic and Demographic Characteristics

	Ecuador	China	Hungary	Spain	Japan	United States
Total GDP	$45.46 billion	$6.45 trillion	$139.7 billion	$885.5 billion	$3.567 trillion	$10.98 trillion
Per capita GDP	$3,300	$5,000	$13,900	$22,000	$28,000	$37,800
Percentage population below poverty level	65%	10%	8.6%	NA	NA	12%
Inflation rate	6.1%	1.2%	4.7%	2.6%	–0.3%	2.1%
Unemployment rate	9.8%	10%	6.1%	11.7%	5.3%	6.2%
Population	13,212,742	1,298,847,624	10,032,375	40,280,780	127,333,002	293,027,571
Birth rate per 1,000 population	23.18	12.98	9.77	10.11	9.56	14.13
Percentage population aged 0–14	33.9%	22.3%	16%	14.4%	14.3%	20.8%
Percentage population aged 15–64	61.2%	70.3%	69%	68%	66.7%	66.9%
Percentage population aged 65 and over	4.9%	7.5%	15%	17.6%	19%	12.4%

Source: Adapted from Central Intelligence Agency, *The World Factbook 2004,* accessed at **http://www.odci.gov/cia/publications/factbook.**

economic infrastructure
The quality of a country's distribution, financial, and communications systems.

Of course, GDP alone does not provide the information needed by marketers in deciding if a country's economic environment makes for an attractive market. Marketers also need to consider whether they can conduct "business as usual" in another country. The **economic infrastructure** is the quality of a country's distribution, financial, and communications systems. For example, Argentina boasts many modern conveniences, but its antiquated phone system is just starting to work properly after years of neglect by the government.

These are just some of the issues a marketer must think about when determining whether a country will be a good prospect. However, there are other economic conditions that marketers must understand as well, including the broader economic picture of a country, called its *level of economic development.*

LEVEL OF ECONOMIC DEVELOPMENT When marketers scout the world for opportunities, it helps if they consider a country's level of economic development to understand the needs of people who live there and the infrastructure conditions with which they must contend. Economists look past simple facts such as growth in GDP to decide this; they also look at what steps are being taken to reduce poverty, inequality, and unemployment. Economists describe the following three basic levels of development.

less developed country (LDC)
A country at the lowest stage of economic development.

standard of living
An indicator of the average quality and quantity of goods and services consumed in a country.

LESS DEVELOPED COUNTRIES A country at the lowest stage of economic development is a **less developed country (LDC)**. In most cases, its economic base is agricultural. Many nations in Africa and South Asia are considered LDCs. A country's **standard of living** is an indicator of the average quality and quantity of goods and services consumed by the country. In these countries, the standard of living is low, as are literacy levels. Opportunities to sell many products, especially luxury items such as diamonds and caviar, are minimal because most people don't have spending money. They grow what they need and barter for the rest. These countries are attractive markets for staples and inexpensive items. They may export important raw materials such as minerals or rubber to industrial nations.

developing countries
Countries in which the economy is shifting its emphasis from agriculture to industry.

DEVELOPING COUNTRIES When an economy shifts its emphasis from agriculture to industry, standards of living, education, and the use of technology rise. These countries are **developing countries**. In such locales, there may be a visible middle class, often largely composed of entrepreneurs working hard to run successful small businesses.

Because over three-fourths of the world's population lives in developing countries, the number of potential customers and the presence of a skilled labor force attract many firms to these areas.

People in developing countries are starting to integrate high-tech products like computers with traditional lifestyles, clothing, and other products.

Eastern Europe, with its more than 300 million consumers, is an important region that includes a number of developing countries. Similarly, the countries of Latin America are emerging from decades of state control, and their economies are opening to foreign business.[48] Finally, the Pacific Rim countries of China, South Korea, Malaysia, Indonesia, Thailand, Singapore, and Hong Kong are nicknamed the "Dragons of Asia" because of their tremendous economic growth. For example, in China, consumer spending on products such as cell phones is encouraging economic growth. Nokia Corporation estimates that more than 70 percent of Beijing residents and more than 60 percent of Shanghai residents have cell phone subscriptions.[49]

DEVELOPED COUNTRIES   A **developed country** boasts sophisticated marketing systems, strong private enterprise, and bountiful market potential for many goods and services. Such countries are economically advanced and they offer a wide range of opportunities for international marketers. The United States, the United Kingdom, Canada, France, Italy, Germany, and Japan are the most economically developed countries in the world.

developed country
A country that boasts sophisticated marketing systems, strong private enterprise, and bountiful market potential for many goods and services.

The Political and Legal Environment

When entering a foreign market, a firm must carefully weigh political and legal risks. A company's fortunes often are affected by political and legal issues that may be beyond its control.

POLITICAL ISSUES   Political actions taken by a government can drastically affect the business operations of outsiders. At the extreme, of course, it goes without saying that when two countries go to war, the business environment changes dramatically. When the United States engages in activities that some people overseas don't like, such as invading Afghanistan in 2001 and sending troops to Iraq a few years later, it's common for symbols of American culture like the Golden Arches to be the first target of demonstrations, vandalism, and in some cases destruction. Short of war, though, a country may impose **economic sanctions** that prohibit trade with another country (as the United States has done with several countries, including Cuba and North Korea), so access to some markets may be cut off.

economic sanctions
Trade prohibitions imposed by one country against another.

nationalization
A domestic government's takeover of a foreign company for its assets with some reimbursement, though often not for the full value.

expropriation
A domestic government's seizure of a foreign company's assets without any compensation.

In some situations, internal pressures may prompt the government to take over the operations of foreign companies doing business within its borders. It is called **nationalization** when the domestic government reimburses a foreign company (often not for the full value) for its assets after taking it over, and it is called **expropriation** when a domestic government seizes a foreign company's assets (and that firm is just out of luck). To keep track of the level of political stability or instability in foreign countries, firms often engage in formal or informal analyses of the potential political risk in various countries.

REGULATORY ISSUES Governments and economic communities impose numerous regulations about what products should be made of, how they should be made, and what can be said about them. For example, sometimes a company has no choice but to alter product content to comply with local laws. Heinz 57 Sauce tastes quite different in Europe simply because of different legal restrictions on preservatives and color additives.[50]

Other regulations are less focused on ensuring quality and more focused on ensuring that the host country gets a piece of the action. **Local content rules** are a form of protectionism stipulating that a certain proportion of a product must consist of components supplied by industries in the host country or economic community. For example, under NAFTA rules, cars built by Mercedes-Benz in Alabama must have 62.5 percent of their components made in North America to be able to enter Mexico and Canada duty free.[51] That helps explain why Japanese automakers such as Toyota have already beefed up their local presence by opening manufacturing plants in the United States and hiring local workers to run them.

HUMAN RIGHTS ISSUES Some governments and companies are vigilant about denying business opportunities to countries that mistreat their citizens. They are concerned about conducting trade with local firms that exploit their workers or that keep costs down by employing children or prisoners for slave wages. The Generalized System of Preferences is a set of regulations that allows developing countries to export goods duty free to the United States. The catch is that each country must constantly demonstrate that it is making progress toward improving the rights of its workers.[52]

On the other side of the coin, U.S. firms looking to expand their operations overseas often are enticed by the low wages they can pay to local workers. Although they provide needed jobs, some companies have been criticized for exploiting workers by paying wages that fall below local poverty levels, for damaging the environment, or for selling poorly made or unsafe items to consumers. For example, in May 2004, Gap Inc. conceded that working conditions were far from perfect at many of the 3,000 factories that make its clothing. The company also observed that the situation is even worse in many of the factories that don't earn its business—about 90 percent of foreign manufacturers who apply for a Gap contract fail the retailer's initial evaluation.[53]

Developed countries like Japan provide rich markets for a variety of products of global companies.

The Cultural Environment

After a firm clears the political and legal issues that can hamper entry into foreign markets, it still needs to understand and adapt to the customs, characteristics, and practices of its citizens. Basic beliefs about such cultural priorities as the role of family or proper relations between the sexes affect people's responses to products and promotional messages.

Today, many Western designers are finding enthusiastic buyers among Middle Eastern women. But they need to make certain adjustments. For example, Italian clothing manufacturer Missoni makes sure its collections include longer pants and skirts and evening gowns with light shawls to cover heads or bare shoulders. In addition, advertising options are more limited since companies can't use the erotic images they often rely on to push their clothes in the West. In the strict religious culture of Saudi Arabia, mannequins can't reveal a gender or human shape. At Saks Fifth Avenue's Riyadh store, models are headless and don't have fingers. Half of the two-level store is off-limits to men. In many stores, dressing rooms are larger than we're used to—customers often are accompanied by many family members.[54]

VALUES Every society has a set of **cultural values**, or deeply held beliefs about right and wrong ways to live, that it imparts to its members.[55] For example, cultures differ in their emphasis on collectivism and individualism. In **collectivist cultures**, such as those found in Venezuela, Pakistan, Taiwan, Thailand, Turkey, Greece, and Portugal, people tend to subordinate their personal goals to those of a stable community. In contrast, consumers in **individualist cultures**, such as the United States, Australia, Great Britain, Canada, and the Netherlands, tend to attach more importance to personal goals, and people are more likely to change memberships when the demands of the group become too costly.[56]

More than 8.2 million women in 50 countries read versions of *Cosmopolitan* in 28 different languages—even though, because of local norms about modesty, some of them have to hide the magazine from their husbands. Adapting the *Cosmo* credo of "Fun, Fearless Female" in all these places gets a bit tricky. Different cultures emphasize varying belief systems that define what it means to be female, feminine, or appealing—and what is considered appropriate to see in print on these matters. For example, in India and China, *Cosmo* is likely to have articles relating to sex replaced with stories about youthful dedication. Ironically, there isn't much down-and-dirty material in the Swedish edition either—but for the opposite reason; that is, the culture is so open about this topic that it doesn't grab readers' attention the way it would in the United States.[57]

NORMS AND CUSTOMS Values are general ideas about good and bad behaviors. From these values flow **norms**, or specific rules dictating what is right or wrong, acceptable or unacceptable. Some specific types of norms include the following:[58]

- A **custom** is a norm handed down from the past that controls basic behaviors, such as division of labor in a household.

- **Mores** are customs with a strong moral overtone. Mores often involve a *taboo*, or forbidden behavior, such as incest or cannibalism. Violation of mores often meets with strong punishment from other members of a society.

- **Conventions** are norms regarding the conduct of everyday life. These rules deal with the subtleties of consumer behavior, including the "correct" way to furnish one's house, wear one's clothes, host a dinner party, and so on.

All three types of norms may determine what behaviors are appropriate in different countries. For example, mores may tell us what kind of food is permissible to eat. A meal of dog may be taboo in the United States, whereas Hindus would shun a steak, and Muslims avoid pork products. A custom dictates the appropriate hour at which the meal should be served—many Europeans, Middle Easterners, and Latin Americans do not begin dinner until around 9:00 or later, and they are amused by American visitors whose stomachs are growling by 7:00. Conventions tell us how to eat

local content rules
A form of protectionism stipulating that a certain proportion of a product must consist of components supplied by industries in the host country.

cultural values
A society's deeply held beliefs about right and wrong ways to live.

collectivist cultures
Cultures in which people subordinate their personal goals to those of a stable community.

individualist cultures
Cultures in which people tend to attach more importance to personal goals than to those of the larger community.

norms
Specific rules dictating what is right or wrong, acceptable or unacceptable.

custom
A norm handed down from the past that controls basic behaviors.

mores
Customs with a strong moral overtone.

conventions
Norms regarding the conduct of everyday life.

Japanese culture is well known for its emphasis on the value of cleanliness. Tokyo bus drivers and cabdrivers wear white gloves while working.

the meal, including such details as the utensils, table etiquette, and even the appropriate apparel to be worn at dinnertime.

Aside from marketing the proper products in the proper ways, a global marketer must learn about the characteristics of people in different countries and adapt to local practices to avoid insulting local business partners. A vice president at Caterpillar, Inc., a company that exports over $3 billion in farm and industrial products per year, certainly demonstrated a willingness to understand unfamiliar customs. While toasting a new business relationship with a Saudi sheik, he was expected to eat what the Saudis regard as the choicest part of a lamb: its eyes. His reaction sums up what you sometimes must do to succeed in foreign cultures: "You just swallow hard and do it."[59]

Conflicting customs can be a problem when U.S. marketers try to conduct business in other countries where executives have different ideas about what is proper or expected. These difficulties even include body language; people in Latin countries tend to stand much closer to each other than do Americans, and they will be insulted if their counterpart tries to stand farther away. Understanding customs such as these can be the difference between a firm's success and failure on the global stage.

LANGUAGE Language barriers can be big obstacles to marketers breaking into foreign markets. These barriers affect product labeling and usage instructions, advertising, and personal selling. It's vital for marketers to work with local people who understand the subtleties of language to avoid the confusion that may result. For example, the meaning of a brand name—one of the most important signals a marketer can send about the character and quality of a product—can get mangled as it travels around the world. Local product names often raise eyebrows to visiting Americans who may be surprised to stumble on a Japanese coffee creamer called Creap or a Mexican bread named Bimbo.[60]

ETHNOCENTRISM Even if a firm succeeds in getting its products to a foreign market, there's no guarantee that local consumers will be interested. Sometimes a willingness to try products made elsewhere comes slowly. In marketing, the tendency to prefer products or people of one's own culture over those from other countries is called **ethnocentrism**. For example, the French tend to be a bit finicky about their cuisine, and they evaluate food products from other countries critically.

ethnocentrism
The tendency to prefer products or people of one's own culture.

Advice for SweatX

STUDENT
HYUN-JOO RACHEL LEE
Sejon-Syracuse Graduate School

I would choose option 1 because full-package apparel not only improves brand image but also gets more profit margins. These days, brand image directly affects the consumer's choice. Brand power is the best asset to a company. Compared with other options, option 1 is less risky and more profitable to the company. If they sell the blank apparel, in the long run, they can't improve their brand image.

PROFESSOR
CARLOS M. RODRIGUEZ
Delaware State University

I would choose option 3, marketing only to and through distributors. The rationale follows two imperatives: (1) Mr. Roth has to follow the mandate that derives from SweatX's mission: it is not ethical to promote consumption and purchases from sweatshops. In fact, it is SweatX's intent to slow down the demand of sweatshops production. (2) In order to be effective in this intent, SweatX has to generate a substantial sales unit volume increase for its own production. SweatX does not possess the capabilities to market full-package deals to end users and cannot afford to lose distribution penetration by marketing blank apparel to end users. Marketing only through distributors is challenging since lower profit margins are expected, which will slow increasing operation profits. However, this path will reinforce the relationship with distributors, which will bring more cooperation and collaboration to reach new sales goals, achieving volume in the short term and developing new product lines in the long run. Ethics and being consistent with the organization's beliefs has a cost. SweatX should be willing to pay for it and any other cost of opportunity involved.

PROFESSOR
SANDRA J. LAKIN
Hesser College

I would choose option 2 because, if successful, it is the best means of preserving the cultural identity of the SweatX brand. This choice, as the case suggests, would necessitate the need for a well-designed sales and marketing plan. Such a plan would require the hiring and training of sales and marketing professionals. It would be both expensive and time consuming and not without risk. Initially, sales would be lost as distributors refused to carry SweatX products. If, on the other hand, the plan succeeds, the result should be a loyal and expanding customer base, consisting of socially responsible organizations. The positive publicity, derived from such a strategy, should bode well for the future of the company.

However, the upscale British department store Marks & Spencer is making inroads in France selling English-style sandwiches like egg and watercress on whole wheat bread and ethnic dishes such as chicken *tikka masala* that are not popular in Paris. Young office workers view these as convenience foods, and they are less expensive than the traditional French loaf split down the middle and lathered with butter and ham or Camembert cheese.

American Krispy Kreme donuts are very popular at Harrods in London despite criticisms that they are contributing to increasing obesity in the United Kingdom.

In addition, ethnocentric consumers are likely to feel that it is ethically wrong to buy products from other countries because they want to support their domestic economy. Ethnocentric Americans, for example, are likely to agree with statements such as the following:

- Purchasing foreign-made products is un-American.
- The United States should place restrictions on all imports.
- American consumers who purchase products made in other countries are responsible for putting their fellow Americans out of work.[61]

Marketing campaigns stressing the desirability of "buying American" are more likely to appeal to this consumer segment.

I'D LIKE TO BUY THE WORLD A COKE: EXPORTING AMERICAN CULTURE One factor that makes it easy for some U.S. firms to go global is the special appeal American products have around the world. The laid-back American lifestyle (or at least the way it's portrayed on television) is desired by many consumers in other countries. That explains the popularity, for example, of homes being built in Argentina by Pulte Homes, the second-largest home builder in the United States. Pulte is exporting suburban American home models with names such as Stanford and Cambridge to Argentina, featuring the same floor plans, shingle roofs, and tiny lawns you might see in a typical U.S. community. Of course, some adjustments need to be made to make these homes compatible with the Argentinian lifestyle. In addition to amenities like whirlpool baths and granite countertops, these homes come with a bidet in the bathroom and a rear patio big enough to accommodate a big grill Argentinians use to cook their famous steak dish called a *parilla*.[62]

Of course, some American exports may be viewed negatively. Some Britons feel that Krispy Kreme donuts, now available at the famed Harrods department store in London, are just one more contribution to the increase in obesity in Britain.[63] To make matters worse, in recent years, widespread dissatisfaction with American foreign policy and environmental positions is fueling a greater tendency to criticize American products and people. Even revered American brands like Coca-Cola are being challenged by upstart local versions such as Mecca Cola in the Middle East and Cola Turka in Turkey.[64]

How "Global" Should a Global Marketing Strategy Be?

Going global is not a simple task. Even a popular television show may have to make "adjustments" as it travels across borders. Consider, for example, the incredibly popular show *American Idol,* which isn't really American at all—it originated in the United Kingdom. More than 100 million people around the globe tune into over 20 local versions of the *Idol* show, but sometimes the format has to be fine-tuned:[65]

- When a South African contestant was bluntly told to work on her clothes and her appearance, she broke down and told the judges she was too poor to afford nicer things. The station was swamped with calls from angry viewers who offered to donate clothing.
- The word "idol" has Hitler-like connotations for Germans, so in that country the show's title had to be changed to *Germany Seeks the Superstar.* Similarly, "idol" is sacrilegious in Arabic countries and can't be used.
- A riot broke out in Beirut when a Lebanese contestant was voted out in favor of a Jordanian woman—viewers accused the producers of fixing the show for political reasons.

As you can see, understanding all the economic, legal, and cultural differences around the world can be a daunting task. But if a firm decides to expand beyond its home country, it must make important decisions about how to structure its business and whether to adapt its product marketing strategy to accommodate local needs. First, the company must decide on the nature of its commitment, including whether it will partner with another firm or go it alone. Then it must make specific decisions about the marketing mix for a particular product or service. In this final section, we'll consider issues related to global strategy at these two levels: the company and the product.

Company-Level Decisions: Choosing a Market Entry Strategy

In 2003, General Electric (GE) was named the world's most respected company for the sixth straight year in a worldwide survey of chief executives conducted by the *Financial Times* and accounting firm PricewaterhouseCoopers.[66] Much of GE's success has come from its global operations.

GE made the decision to go global, and the company has never looked back. GE's strategy for shifting its "center of gravity" from the industrialized world of the United States to Asia and Latin America made it a local assembler of low-tech goods in some countries and a high-tech manufacturer of appliances and other products for export in others. GE tailors the type and extent of its commitment to local conditions in each market it chooses to enter.

Just like a romantic relationship, a firm deciding to go global must determine the level of commitment it is willing to make to operate in another country. This commitment can range from a casual involvement to a full-scale "marriage." At one extreme, the firm can simply export its products, while at the other it can directly invest in another country by buying a foreign subsidiary or opening its own stores. The decision about the extent of commitment entails a trade-off between control and risk. Direct involvement gives the firm more control over what happens in the country, but risk also increases if the operation is not successful.

Let's review four strategies representing increased levels of involvement: exporting, contractual arrangements, strategic alliances, and direct investment. These are summarized in Figure 3.4.

EXPORTING   If a firm chooses to export, it must decide whether it will attempt to sell its products on its own or rely on intermediaries to represent it in the target country. These representatives are specialists known as **export merchants** who understand the local market and can find buyers and negotiate terms.[67] An exporting strategy allows a firm to sell its products in global markets and cushions the firm against downturns in its domestic market. Because the exported products are made at home, the firm is able to maintain control over design and production decisions.[68]

Sometimes, exporting is the best way to be successful in a foreign market. Frontier Foods, Ltd, an Australian food-distributing company, has developed a thriving business importing cheese to China, where wealthy Chinese consumers are developing an unprecedented taste for cheese. Because there is so

export merchants
Intermediaries used by a firm to represent them in other countries.

Figure 3.4   Market Entry Strategies

Choosing a market entry strategy is a critical decision for companies that want to go global. Choosing whether to operate the new venture versus sharing responsibility with organizations in the local market involves a trade-off between control and risk.

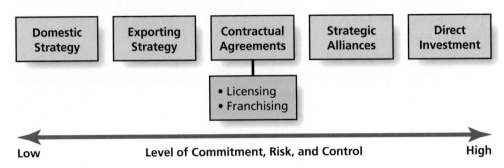

little open farmland in China for large herds of dairy cows, China can't produce enough milk to sustain a domestic cheese industry. Hence, it is easier to import cheese than to make it in China.[69]

CONTRACTUAL AGREEMENTS   The next level of commitment a firm can make to a foreign market is a contractual agreement with a company in that country to conduct some or all of its business there. These agreements can take several forms. Two of the most common are licensing and franchising.

In a **licensing** agreement, a firm (the licenser) gives another firm (the licensee) the right to produce and market its product in a specific country or region in return for royalties. Because the licensee produces the product in its home market, it can avoid many of the barriers-to-entry that the licenser would have encountered. However, the licenser also loses control over how the product is produced and marketed, so if the licensee does a poor job, the company's reputation may be tarnished.

Franchising is a form of licensing that gives the franchisee the right to adapt an entire way of doing business in the host country. Again, there is a risk to the parent company if the franchisee does not use the same quality ingredients or procedures, so firms monitor these operations carefully. More than 400 U.S. franchising companies, including 7-Eleven, Century 21, and Starbucks, operate about 40,000 outlets internationally. McDonald's, a major franchiser, has about 28,000 restaurants in 121 countries.[70] In India, where Hindus do not eat beef, all McDonald's have vegetarian and nonvegetarian burger-cooking lines and offer customers such vegetarian specialties as Pizza McPuff and McAloo Tikki (a spiced-potato burger).[71]

STRATEGIC ALLIANCE   Firms seeking an even deeper commitment to a foreign market develop a **strategic alliance** with one or more domestic firms in the target country. These relationships often take the form of a **joint venture**: a new entity owned by two or more firms is created to allow the partners to pool their resources for common goals. Strategic alliances also allow companies easy access to new markets, especially because these partnerships often bring with them preferential treatment in the partner's home country. We tend to think of the international automobile industry as fiercely competitive, but in reality many companies actually own pieces of each other. For example, General Motors has alliances with Fiat Auto SpA, Fuji Heavy Industries, Isuzu Motors, and Suzuki Motor Corp.[72]

DIRECT INVESTMENT   A deeper level of commitment occurs when a firm expands internationally by buying a business outright in the host country. Instead of starting from scratch in its quest to become multinational, direct investment allows a foreign firm to take advantage of a domestic company's political savvy and market position in the host country.

licensing (in foreign markets)
An agreement in which one firm gives another firm the right to produce and market its product in a specific country or region in return for royalties.

franchising
A form of licensing involving the right to adapt an entire system of doing business.

strategic alliance
Relationship developed between a firm seeking a deeper commitment to a foreign market and a domestic firm in the target country.

joint venture
A strategic alliance in which a new entity owned by two or more firms is created to allow the partners to pool their resources for common goals.

Aðdráttarafl

NÝR COROLLA - TILFINNINGIN ER GÓÐ. Þegar hönnuðir Toyota fengu það verkefni að hanna nýja kynslóð mest keypta bíls í heimi var markið sett hátt - að hefja orðið gæði í annað veldi. Aukið höfuð- og fótarými, einstaklega vel hannað innanrými og vandað efnisval eykur enn á þægindi ökumanns og farþega. Það er svo ekki til að minnka aðdráttaraflið að nýr Corolla er aflmeiri, eyðir minnu og rekstrarkostnaður hans er einn sá lægsti fyrir bifreiðar í þessum flokki. **www.corolla.is**

While markets for some Toyota models are limited to only one or a few countries, Toyota has selected its popular Corolla to be a true "world car" that is sold in all its markets from Egypt to Iceland.

Ownership gives a firm maximum freedom and control, and it also dodges import restrictions. For example, the United States bans the import of so-called Saturday night specials (cheap, short-barreled pistols), but it permits their sale. So, the Italian gun manufacturer Beretta got around this restriction by opening a manufacturing plant in Maryland.[73] But direct investment also carries greater risk. Firms that own businesses in foreign countries could suffer losses of their investment if economic conditions deteriorate or if political instability leads to nationalization or expropriation.

Product-Level Decisions: Choosing a Marketing Mix Strategy

In addition to "big picture" decisions about how a company will operate in other countries, there are many choices to be made regarding just how a product will be marketed in each place. The famous Four P's may need to be modified to suit local conditions. To what extent will the company need to adapt its marketing communications to the specific styles and tastes of each local market? Will the same product appeal to people there? Will it have to be priced differently? And, of course, how do we get the product in people's hands? Let's consider each of these questions in turn.

Standardization Versus Localization

When top management makes a company-level decision to expand internationally, the firm's marketers have to answer a crucial question: How necessary is it to develop a customized marketing mix for each country—a localization strategy? Gillette decided to offer the same products

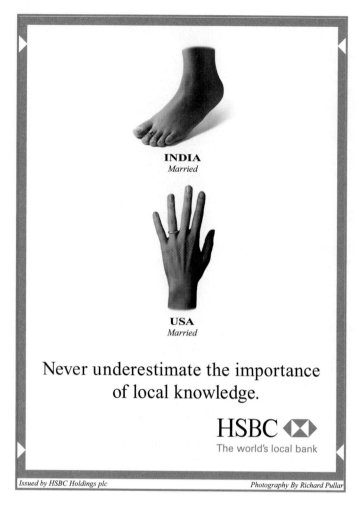

INDIA
Married

USA
Married

Never underestimate the importance
of local knowledge.

HSBC
The world's local bank

Issued by HSBC Holdings plc   Photography By Richard Pullar

Because norms and customs may differ greatly from one country to another, the decision to standardize or localize marketing strategies is not an easy one. This ad shows how HSBC has positioned itself as a global bank that understands and adapts to differences around the globe.

in all its markets—a standardization strategy. In contrast, Proctor & Gamble (P&G) adopted a localized strategy in Asia, where consumers like to experiment with different brands of shampoo. Most of P&G's shampoos sold in Asia are now packaged in single-use sachets to encourage people to try different kinds.[74]

So which is right? Advocates of standardization argue that the world has become so small with tastes so homogenized that basic needs and wants are the same everywhere.[75] A focus on the similarities among cultures certainly is appealing. After all, if a firm didn't have to make any changes to its marketing strategy to compete in foreign countries, it would realize large economies of scale because it could spread the costs of product development and promotional materials over many markets. Reebok, realizing this, created a new centralized product development center to develop shoe designs that can easily cross borders.[76] Widespread, consistent exposure also helps create a global brand by forging a strong, unified image all over the world—Coca-Cola signs are visible on billboards in London or on metal roofs deep in the forests of Thailand.

In contrast, those in favor of localization feel that the world is not *that* small and that products and promotional messages should be tailored to local environments. These marketers feel that each culture is unique and that each country has a *national character*—a distinctive set of behavioral and personality characteristics.[77] Snapple failed in Japan because consumers there didn't like the drink's cloudy appearance. Similarly, Frito-Lay Inc. stopped selling Ruffles potato chips (too salty for Japanese tastes) and Cheetos (the Japanese didn't appreciate having their fingers turn orange after eating a handful).[78]

PRODUCT DECISIONS A firm seeking to sell a product in a foreign market has three choices: sell the same product in the new market, modify it for that market, or develop a brand-new product to sell there. Let's take a closer look at each possibility:

- A *straight extension strategy* retains the same product for domestic and foreign markets. For generations, proper etiquette in Japan was for girls to bow and never raise their eyes to a man.[79] However, the new generation of Japanese women wants to look straight at you, showing their eyes and eyelashes. Japanese eyelashes are very short, so they have to be curled to show. To meet this need, L'Oreal introduced its Maybelline brand Wonder Curl that dramatically thickens and curls lashes as it is applied. The launch was such a success in Japan that local television news showed Japanese girls standing in line to buy the product.

- A *product adaptation strategy* recognizes that in many cases people in different cultures do have strong and different product preferences. Sometimes these differences can be subtle yet important. That explains why Kellogg had to remove the green "loops" from its Froot Loops cereal in European markets after research showed that Europeans felt they were too artificial looking. Americans like the green loops just fine.[80]

- A *product invention strategy* means a company develops a new product as it expands to foreign markets. For example, firms that wish to market household appliances in Japan where apartments are very small by Western standards must design and manufacture smaller prod-

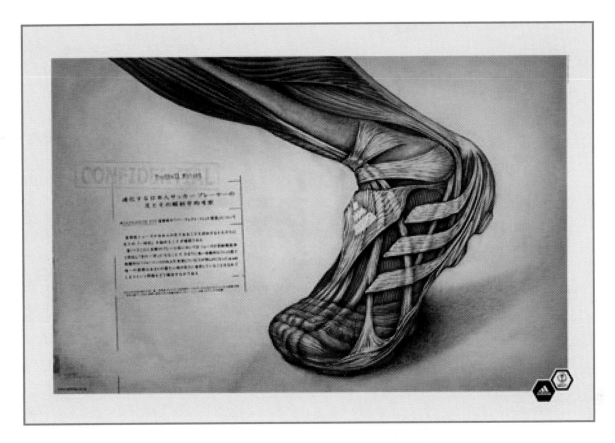

Global marketers like Adidas understand that in order to continue growing, they must develop products that appeal to consumers in other countries. This ad is for a pair of soccer shoes designed especially for the Japanese foot.

ucts. In some cases, a product invention strategy takes the form of *backward invention*. A firm may find it needs to offer a less complex product than it sells elsewhere, such as a manually operated sewing machine or a hand-powered clothes washer for people without access to a reliable source of electricity.

In some cases, marketers develop a product for an overseas market and then discover it could do well at home too. After tremendous success with its caramelized milk flavored *dulce de leche* ice cream in Buenos Aires, Häagen Dazs was able to duplicate that success among Latino consumers in the United States.

PROMOTION DECISIONS   Marketers must also decide whether it's necessary to change product promotions in a foreign market. Some firms endorse the idea that the same message will appeal to everyone around the world. The advertising director for the Unisys Corporation, a company that specializes in computers, explained the decision to launch a standardized global campaign: "Now they are seeing the same message, the same company, the same look wherever they go. That really stretches my advertising dollars."[81]

Unisys's decision to adopt a global message illustrates one key to the success of a standardized strategy: It is more likely to work if there are not unique cultural factors affecting the purchase—computer buyers tend to have more in common than, say, perfume buyers. This "one world, one message" promotional strategy also has a greater chance of success if the firm's target customers live in cosmopolitan, urban areas where they regularly see images from different countries.

PRICE DECISIONS   Costs associated with transportation, tariffs, differences in currency exchange rates, and even bribes paid to local officials often make the product more expensive for the company to make for foreign markets than in its home country.

We deliver to more countries than any other air express company. Come hell or high water.

Try us to New Orleans.

DHL is the world's leading express shipper because, for 34 years, we've delivered just about everywhere. And now that DHL has merged with Airborne, we offer that same dedicated service and customer support within the U.S. Give us a try. You'll see why DHL is the best new alternative for all your domestic shipping needs. Start at www.dhlairborne.com

WE MOVE THE WORLD ═══*DHL*═══

Companies like DHL need to adapt their practices to local conditions.

gray market goods
Items manufactured outside a country and then imported without the consent of the trademark holder.

dumping
A company tries to get a toehold in a foreign market by pricing its products lower than they are offered at home.

For example, Chrysler Corporation had a hard time offering its Jeep Cherokee to Japanese consumers at a competitive price. Chrysler priced the vehicle at about $19,000 when it left the plant in Toledo, Ohio. By the time it was sitting in a Tokyo showroom, the price had mushroomed to over $31,000. Chrysler fell victim to a number of factors, including the currency exchange rate, the cost of adapting the Jeep to comply with Japanese regulations, tariffs, and profits taken by local distributors.[82] To ease the financial burden of tariffs on companies that import goods, some countries have established *free trade zones*. These are designated areas where foreign companies can warehouse goods without paying taxes or customs duties until the goods are moved into the marketplace.

One danger of pricing too high is that competitors will find ways to offer their product at a lower price, even if this is done illegally. **Gray market goods** are items manufactured outside a country and then imported without the consent of the trademark holder. While gray market goods are not counterfeits, they may be different from authorized products in warranty coverage and compliance with local regulatory requirements.[83]

Another unethical and often illegal practice is **dumping**, in which a company prices its products lower than they are offered at home—often removing excess supply from home markets and keeping prices up there. In one case, Eastman Kodak accused Japanese rival Fuji Photo Film of selling color photographic paper in the United States for as little as a quarter of what it charges in Japan.[84]

DISTRIBUTION DECISIONS Getting the product to consumers in a remote location is half the battle. Thus, establishing a reliable distribution system is essential if a marketer is to succeed in a foreign market. Marketers used to dealing with a handful of large wholesalers or retailers may have to rely instead on thousands of small "mom-and-pop" stores or distributors, some of whom transport goods to remote rural areas on oxcarts or bicycles. In less developed countries, they may run into problems finding a way to package, refrigerate, or store goods for long periods of time.

Even the retailing giant Wal-Mart has occasionally stumbled at going global. When Wal-Mart attempted to ease its entry into the German market by buying local retailers, it underestimated the problems it would face in dealing with local distributors. When the chain tried to force the distributors to switch from supplying individual stores to utilizing Wal-Mart's new centralized warehouse system, they refused and left Wal-Mart with empty shelves. Now Wal-Mart is working hard to understand local business cultures and to work more closely with suppliers.[85]

real people, real choices
How It Worked Out at SweatX

Rick chose option 3. He decided to totally renounce selling directly. He felt that the only way to truly grow the business was to sell through big distributors who control 80 percent of the purchases. While part of Rick's motivation was profitability, he also felt that Sweat X's social mission to end sweatshops could be realized only by a large-scale effort that would change the apparel industry and serve as an example of how to produce and sell ethically.

Organizations like these that order promotional T-shirts from SweatX are doing good business but also advancing the cause of reducing the industry's reliance on sweatshop labor—this results in both economic and social profit.

Following the decision to only sell wholesale, SweatX set out to mend its relationships with its distributors. The total renunciation of embellishment was followed by a clear campaign to turn every direct inquiry over to the distributors. Hundreds of distributors might have literally hundreds of customers—too many for SweatX to handle on its own. And SweatX wanted to sell shirts to all of them.

The company now is focused on selling shirts to the largest distributors. There are 20 promotional products companies that control 70 percent of the union business. Marketing to those 20 is a relatively low-cost effort that basically involves exhibiting at a few select trade shows and custom producing marketing materials. These customers also don't need a great deal of convincing; they already are looking for a product like SweatX that is union made and of high quality. When they buy these items, they can have their cake and eat it too—they know that they are doing good business but also advancing the cause of reducing the industry's reliance on sweatshop labor.

Where you work is just as important as what you do. Chapter 3 in *Brand You* shows you how to find your niche in the global marketplace.

CHAPTER SUMMARY

1. **Understand business ethics and why it is important for organizations to adhere to ethical business behavior.** Ethics are rules of conduct and are how people judge whether a behavior is right or wrong. Business ethics are basic values that guide a firm's behavior. Some of these values are expressed in the Consumer Bill of Rights. Some firms communicate their ethical expectations of employees through a written code of ethics. Unethical behavior can cost a firm financially and damage its reputation.

2. **Explain how marketers apply ethical business behavior to the marketing mix.** Ethical marketing behavior means making products safe, pricing products fairly, promoting products honestly, focusing on product quality, and making the product available to consumers ethically.

3. **Describe how firms practice social responsibility.** Social responsibility means that firms act in ways that benefit the public, the community, and the natural environment. New Era marketers assume social responsibility through environmental stewardship, in which the firm's actions either improve or do not harm the natural environment, and cause marketing, which focuses on marketing strategies that promote the public good. New Era firms also practice social responsibility by promoting cultural diversity—that is, by including people of different races, ethnic groups, and religions as customers, suppliers, employees, and distribution channel members.

4. **Understand the big picture of international marketing: trade flows, how firms define the scope of their markets, and how firms develop a competitive advantage in global marketing.** The increasing amount of world trade, the flow of goods and services among countries, may take place through cash or credit payments or through countertrade. While some firms choose to remain domestic in scope, some become exporting firms, while others become multinational firms. A company's prospects for success in foreign markets are helped if it has a competitive advantage, which occurs when conditions in its home country make it easier to compete.

5. **Explain how countries seek to protect local industries by establishing roadblocks to foreign companies and by bonding together into economic communities.** Some governments adopt policies of protectionism with rules designed to give home companies an advantage. Such policies may include trade quotas, embargoes, or tariffs that increase the costs of foreign goods. The World Trade Organization works to reduce such protectionism and encourage free trade. Many countries have banded together to form economic communities to promote free trade.

6. **Understand how economic, political, legal, and cultural issues influence global marketing strategies and outcomes.** In evaluating potential foreign markets, firms may examine the economic health of a country using its gross domestic product, its economic infrastructure, and its level of economic development to classify it as less developed, developing, or developed. A country's political and legal environment includes the presence of economic sanctions and the prospects for nationalization or expropriation of foreign holdings, regulations such as local content rules, and labor and human rights regulations. Marketers also examine a country's cultural environment, that is, its values, norms and customs, symbols, superstitions, language, and ethnocentricity.

7. **Explain the strategies a firm can choose to enter global markets.** Different foreign market entry strategies represent varying levels of commitment for a firm. Exporting of goods entails little commitment but allows little control over how products are sold. Contractual agreements such as licensing or franchising allow greater control. With strategic alliances through joint ventures, commitment increases. Finally, the firm can choose to invest directly by buying an existing company or starting a foreign subsidiary in the host country.

8. **Understand the arguments for standardization versus localization of marketing strategies in global markets and understand how elements of the marketing mix apply to foreign countries.** Firms that operate in two or more countries can choose to standardize their marketing strategies by using the same approach in all countries or choose to localize by adopting different strategies for each market. The firm needs to decide whether to sell an existing product, change an existing product, or develop a new product. In many cases, the promotional strategy must be tailored to fit the needs of consumers in another country. The product may need to be priced differently, especially if income levels are not the same in the new market. Finally, different methods of distribution may be needed, especially in countries lacking a solid infrastructure that provides adequate transportation, communications, and storage facilities.

KEY TERMS

born-global firms, 74
business ethics, 65
cause marketing, 70
codes of ethics, 66
collectivist cultures, 81
Consumer Bill of Rights, 68
consumerism, 66
conventions, 81
corrective advertising, 69
countertrade, 73
cultural diversity, 71
cultural values, 81
custom, 81
developed country, 79
developing countries, 78

dumping, 90
economic communities, 76
economic infrastructure, 78
economic sanctions, 79
embargo, 75
environmental stewardship, 70
ethnocentrism, 82
European Union (EU), 76
export merchants, 85
expropriation, 80
franchising, 86
General Agreement on Tariffs and Trade (GATT), 75, 76
gray market goods, 90
green marketing, 70

gross domestic product (GDP), 77
gross national product (GNP), 77
import quotas, 75
individualist cultures, 81
joint venture, 86
less developed country (LDC), 78
licensing, 86
local content rules, 81
mores, 81
nationalization, 80
norms, 81
North American Free Trade Agreement (NAFTA), 76
protectionism, 75
puffery, 69

CHAPTER REVIEW

MARKETING CONCEPTS: TESTING YOUR KNOWLEDGE

1. What are business ethics? What are some ways that marketers practice ethical behavior in the marketing mix?

2. What is consumerism? What is the Consumer Bill of Rights?

3. What is social responsibility? What is cause marketing? How do marketers promote cultural diversity?

4. Describe the market conditions that influence a firm's decision to enter foreign markets.

5. What is protectionism? Explain import quotas, embargoes, and tariffs.

6. What are economic communities, and how have they changed global marketing opportunities?

7. Briefly describe the categories of economic development in less developed countries, developing countries, and developed countries.

8. What aspects of the political and legal environment influence a firm's decision to enter a foreign market? Why are human rights issues important to firms in their decisions to enter global markets?

9. What is the difference between collectivist and individualistic cultures? Why is an understanding of these two types of cultures important to marketers?

10. What is ethnocentricity? How does it affect a firm that seeks to enter a foreign market?

11. How is a firm's level of commitment related to its level of control in a foreign market? Describe the four levels of involvement that are options for a firm: exporting, contractual agreements, strategic alliances, and direct investment.

12. What are the arguments for standardization of marketing strategies in the global marketplace? What are the arguments for localization? What are some ways a firm can standardize or localize its marketing mix?

MARKETING CONCEPTS: DISCUSSING CHOICES AND ISSUES

1. Think about a company's cause marketing program with which you are familiar. Why do you think the firm chose the specific cause? Do you think the firm's customers became more loyal to the company because it sponsored the program? Why or why not?

2. Do you think U.S. firms should be allowed to use bribes to compete in countries where bribery is an accepted and legal form of doing business? Why or why not?

3. Some countries have been critical of the exporting of American culture by U.S. businesses. What about American culture might be objectionable? Can you think of some products that U.S. marketers export that can be objectionable to some foreign markets?

4. Trade regulations and protectionism are important political issues in the United States. What do you think are the positive and negative aspects of protectionist policies for U.S. firms? Do economic communities increase or decrease protectionism? More and larger economic communities are in the planning stages. What impact on world trade do you think these will have?

5. In recent years, terrorism and other types of violent activities around the globe have made the global marketplace seem very unsafe. How concerned should firms that have international operations be about such activities? Should they consider abandoning some of their global markets? How should firms weigh their concerns about terrorism against the need to help the economies of developing countries? Would avoiding countries such as those in the Middle East make good sense in terms of economic profit? What about in terms of social profit?

MARKETING PRACTICE: APPLYING WHAT YOU'VE LEARNED

1. Assume that you are employed in the marketing department of a medium-size firm in the dairy industry—a producer of cheeses and canned milk products. Your firm has recently been purchased, and the new owner is terribly concerned about social responsibility. As a member of the marketing department, you have been asked to put together a report on how this firm can become a more socially responsible organization. Develop your report for the new owner of the firm.

2. Assume that you have been hired by a firm that markets large household appliances in a global marketplace. You have been asked to develop a code of ethics for the company. Develop a draft of the code you would recommend.

3. Assume that your firm is interested in the global market potential for weight loss centers in the following countries: France, Russia, and Argentina.

   a. Prepare a summary of the demographic, economic, and cultural differences you expect to find in these countries.

   b. Tell how the differences might affect marketing strategies for weight loss centers.

4. Tide laundry detergent, Pizza Hut meals, and IBM computers are very different U.S. products that are marketed globally.

   a. Outline the reasons each of these companies might choose to:

1. standardize its product strategies or localize its product strategies
2. standardize its promotion strategies or localize its promotion strategies

b. Organize a debate in your class to argue the merits of the standardization perspective versus the localization perspective.

5. Although most large corporations have already made the decision to go global, many small to midsize firms are only now considering such a move. Consider a small firm that manufactures gas barbecue grills.

a. What type of market entry strategy (exporting, contractual agreement, strategic alliance, or direct investment) do you feel would be best for the firm? Why?

b. How would you recommend that the firm implement the strategy? That is, what type of product, price, promotion, and distribution strategies would you suggest? What role can the Internet play?

MARKETING MINIPROJECT: LEARNING BY DOING

The purpose of this miniproject is to begin to develop an understanding of a culture other than your own and how customer differences lead to changes in the ways marketing strategies and socially responsible decision making can be implemented in that culture.

1. As part of a small group, select a country you would like to know more about and a product you think could be successful in that market. As a first step, gather information about the country. Many campuses have international students from different countries. If possible, find a fellow student from the country and talk with him or her about the country. You will probably also wish to investigate other sources of information, such as books and magazines found in your library, or access information from the Web.

2. Prepare a summary of your findings that includes the following:

a. An overall description of the country, including such factors as its history, economy, religions, and so on, that might affect marketing of the product you have selected

b. A description of the cultural values and business ethics dominant in the country

c. The current status of this product in the country

d. Your recommendations for a product strategy (product design, packaging, brand name, price, and so on)

e. Your recommendations for promotional strategies

f. A discussion of the ethical and social responsibility issues present in the recommendations you have made

3. Present your findings and recommendations to the class.

REAL PEOPLE, REAL SURFERS: EXPLORING THE WEB

Assume that you are the director of marketing for a firm that manufactures small household appliances such as mixers, coffeemakers, toasters, and so forth. You are considering entering the market in _____ (the country you have selected). You recognize that businesses must carefully weigh opportunities for global marketing. Use the Internet to gather information that would be useful in your firm's decision. Although there are many governments, not-for-profit organizations, and businesses that have Web sites with information on international markets, the following sites may be useful to you:

- The U.S. Department of Commerce site on big emerging markets: **www.stat-usa.gov/itabems.html**
- I-Trade, a commercial site that also provides much free information of international trading: **www.i-trade.com**
- TradePort, a free site that provides a large number of links to country-specific Web sites: **www.tradeport.org**

Write a report that answers the following questions:

1. What are the physical characteristics of the country (geography, weather, natural resources, and so forth)?

2. Describe the economy of the country.

3. What is the country's investment climate?

4. What trade regulations will your firm face in entering the country?

5. What is the country's political climate? Are there obvious political risks?

6. Based on this information, what overall strategy do you recommend for your firm—exporting, a contractual agreement, a strategic alliance, or direct investment?

7. What are your specific recommendations for implementing the strategy?

As a final part of your report, describe the Internet sites you used to gather this information. Which sites were most useful and why?

MARKETING PLAN EXERCISE

1. Take a look at the American Marketing Association Code of Ethics. What role, if any, do issues related to ethics play in building a marketing plan? Which specific pieces of the marketing plan are most likely to involve ethical concerns? Give examples of what those concerns might be.

2. Should marketers include social marketing objectives into their plans? Why or why not? Are objectives related to such

social marketing initiatives as serving the environment, society, and the community consistent or inconsistent with serving customers and maximizing profits? Explain your thinking.

3. What are some important global marketing issues that one must be mindful of when developing a marketing plan? Why do these issues need to be considered separately from a firm's domestic plan?

Marketing in Action Case

Real Choices at Wal-Mart

With its ranking as the largest U.S. corporate enterprise, Wal-Mart is clearly a whopping success story. From its beginnings back in the early to mid 1960s in humble Bentonville, Arkansas, to its position atop the Fortune 500's list of the largest U.S. corporations, Wal-Mart has experienced a period of growth and success that is largely unprecedented among contemporary retailers. In fact, if Wal-Mart's sales of approximately $259 billion were ranked as its own country in terms of economic output, the company would rank 30th in the world, right behind Saudi Arabia. Clearly, Wal-Mart has figured out how to "do retail" in the United States. Its 3,550 stores in the United States are a testament to the company's operating philosophy and its ability to successfully execute the philosophy.

Wal-Mart's first entries into the international retail arena were very successful—mainly because those entries were into Canada and Mexico. When company founder Sam Walton died in 1992, Wal-Mart's international presence consisted of just two stores in Mexico City. Only 12 years later, the company has 640 stores in Mexico and roughly 240 in Canada. In both markets, Wal-Mart became the largest retailer in a very short time frame. However, further attempts at increasing its international business have not gone quite as well. Wal-Mart abandoned both Hong Kong and Indonesia after initial entry strategies were unsuccessful.

One of Wal-Mart's international expansions outside of the North American continent is in Germany. Because the company can't build stores in Germany, where it's impossible to obtain new licenses to sell food, Wal-Mart has entered the market by purchasing 21 stores from Wertkauf and 74 stores previously owned by Spar Handels. However, buying stores in Germany exposed the company's famous operating system to a number of legal and cultural differences that did not bode well for success. For example, Wal-Mart's U.S. policy of refunding price differences on any item sold for less at another store was illegal. In addition, there can be no 24-hour stores in Germany because the law doesn't allow it. Furthermore, in a country where there is a tradition of retail organizations providing lousy customer service, Wal-Mart had to drop its famous "10 Foot Rule," which in the United States requires any Wal-Mart employee standing within 10 feet of a customer to greet that customer. Instead, German employees are encouraged to simply "be nice" to the customers.

On the positive side, German customers who are used to "service with a snarl" are attracted by Wal-Mart's customer-focused culture and its "Everyday Low Price" (EDLP) philosophy. Employees like the more democratized work environment where employees are referred to as "associates" and have the information and power to make decisions. Furthermore, there are some important customer-pleasing improvements in the stores: fruit and vegetables displays have been rearranged, stores aisles are widened, stores are opening two hours earlier at 7 A.M., small red flags sticking out from the shelves indicate items that have been permanently marked down, customers can pay with debit and credit cards, and some stores are considering bagging customers' purchases for them.

Now Wal-Mart is attempting to enter Japan, the second-largest retail market in the world behind the United States. As in Germany, the company made a direct investment in Japan by purchasing a small percentage of ownership in the 400-store Seiyu chain. However, after two years of operations in Japan, Wal-Mart still seems to be struggling, as the most recent revenue numbers indicate a decline in revenues of 17 percent and an overall net loss of $65 million.

As with most Wal-Mart locations in the United States, Seiyu stores in Japan carry both groceries and general merchandise items. However, many of the stores require remodeling, and just a few have undergone the required transformation. In at least one store that has been remodeled, Wal-Mart has (1) put all of the grocery items on the first floor while moving the clothing and general merchandise to the second floor of the store, (2) made the fruit and vegetable displays more accessible and inviting, (3) installed greeters at the door to hand out shopping baskets and answer customer questions, (4) made the elevators big enough to hold shopping carts, and (5) radically increased the number of cash registers. The result of these changes is an overall sales increase of 17 percent with food sales increasing by 50 percent over the previous year.

Unfortunately, attempts to implement other Wal-Mart retail strategies have been less successful. When Wal-Mart replaced branded clothing with generics, prices were cut by 20 percent, but sales fell 10 percent. In Japan's distribution system, manufacturers will sell only through their traditional wholesalers and not directly to Wal-Mart. This means higher prices for Wal-Mart—and its customers. And there are other problems. Japanese customers can be difficult to please; many can tell whether a piece of fish has ever been frozen just by tasting it.

The challenge that Wal-Mart's international division faces is whether it will be possible to reproduce the retailer's previous successes in countries such as Mexico and Canada in Japan and, if so, what strategies will be essential to that success. How can Wal-Mart meet the needs of the more demanding Japanese consumer? How can it successfully implement its EDLP strategies while constrained by the Japanese distribution system? Indeed, the bigger question is how much of its operating philosophy—what makes Wal-Mart "Wal-Mart"—the company can transfer and successfully implement.

Things to Think About

1. What are the decisions facing Wal-Mart in Japan?
2. What factors are important in understanding the decision situation?
3. What are the alternatives?
4. What decision(s) do you recommend?
5. What are some ways to implement your recommendation(s)?

Sources: Bruce Upbin, "Wall-to-Wall Wal-Mart," *Forbes*, April, 12, 2004, 76–82; Benjamin Fulford, "Japan: The American Revolution," *Forbes*, April 12, 2004, 85; Janice Revell, "The Year of the Comeback," *Fortune*, April 5, 2004, 289–92; and Jeremy Kahn, "Wal-Mart Goes Shopping in Europe," *Fortune*, June 7, 1999, 105–12.

- The Difference Between a Good Bank and a Better Bank -

If your money would be better in another account, we'll call and tell you.

Annual Checking Account Reviews from RBC Centura. As life changes, so do your needs from a bank. That's why we look at your account annually just to make sure your money is in the right place. And if we discover there's a better checking account for you, we'll let you know. Especially if it'll save you some money. Stop by your local RBC Centura banking center, call 1-800-CENTURA or visit www.rbccentura.com.

RBC
Centura

**Building a better bank,
one customer at a time.™**

© 2003 RBC Centura Bank. Member FDIC.
™ Trademark of Royal Bank of Canada. RBC Centura is a trademark of Royal Bank of Canada.
™ "Building a better bank, one customer at a time." is a trademark of RBC Centura Banks, Inc.
RBC Centura is a trade name used by RBC Centura Bank.

www.rbccentura.com

real people, real choices
meet Cathy Burrows, a Decision
Maker at RBC Centura Bank

**first job out of
school**

**what i do when i'm
not working**

**File clerk at a collection
agency . . . because you
always need to know
what you never want to
do again . . . ever.**

**"Family networking"
because at the end of the
day it is family .that is
important.**

MARKETING INFORMATION AND RESEARCH: ANALYZING THE BUSINESS ENVIRONMENT OFFLINE AND ONLINE

Cathy Burrows is director of enterprise information and customer management support for RBC Centura Bank, which is based in Rocky Mount, North Carolina. Her responsibilities include developing and implementing enterprise information strategies to support business process standardization and customer relationship management (CRM) programs. Prior to joining RBC Centura in 2002, Cathy served as senior industry consultant for North American financial services for Teradata, a division of NCR. Her responsibilities included working with clients to implement CRM programs. Prior to working at Teradata, she was national manager of consumer markets with Royal Bank of Canada. She received a BA in sociology and business from the University of Toronto and an MBA in marketing and international business from York University in Toronto.

Decision Time at Royal Bank

RBC Financial Group is Canada's largest financial institution and the eighth largest in North America. The firm's personal and commercial (retail) banking division is called RBC Royal Bank, and it is made up of about 1,500 branches, 4,800 ATMs, and extensive point-of-sale and online channels. The bank had been evaluating the financial value of its substantial personal customer base since 1992 to determine which types of customers were the most "valuable" to the bank so that it could more effectively retain this customer base while also attracting additional customers who fit this profile.

To do this, Royal Bank used a profitability model based on "average" revenue/expenses for each financial product (loan, credit card, and so on) the bank sold. However, the model was not able to account fully for all transactions and activities associated with a particular customer's account. Cathy knew that in order to stay on top of each client's individual situation and maximize the services the bank would be able to offer, her team would have to change the way the bank collected and assessed information about its clients. Tracking simple averages wasn't good enough because this information did not provide enough detail to truly identify the most profitable customers. Instead, the team needed a research tool that would measure subtle changes and new trends in customer behavior, including transactions the customer initiated. In evaluating a new way to calculate profitability, the team had identified several types of data the bank would need to better track each customer's activities. These included such measures as where the customer did business with the bank (e.g., online or in a branch location), the interest rates they were paying for loans, and their credit scores (i.e., the rating that is assigned to a consumer based on his or her history of taking

business book i'm reading now	my hero	my motto to live by	my pet peeve
Michael Adams, *Fire and Ice: The United States and Canada and the Myth of Converging Values.*	Charlotte Whitton, first woman mayor of Ottawa. She said, "Whatever women do they must do twice as well as men to be thought half as good . . . luckily this is not difficult."	No regrets.	Lack of perspective and short-term focus at the expense of other opportunities.

objectives

1 Understand the role of the marketing information system and the marketing decision support system in marketing decision making.

2 Describe the marketing research process.

3 Understand the differences among exploratory, descriptive, and causal research and describe some research techniques available to marketers.

4 Describe the different types of data collection methods and types of consumer samples that researchers use.

5 Understand the growing use of online research.

out loans and repaying them). Cathy needed to come up with a better way to collect market research data on Royal Bank's customer base. She and the team considered their options:

OPTION 1: Develop a new market research tracking tool internally.

If Royal Bank developed its own system, the solution could be completely customized for its unique needs. And this tool might allow the bank to better manage currently unprofitable clients, which would give it a competitive advantage relative to competitors who simply "demarketed" (i.e., dropped) customers who were not profitable. But the bank did not necessarily have the competence internally to develop the software and analysis techniques to develop this new tool, and this strategy might require it to invest more in acquiring these resources than it was willing to do.

OPTION 2: Outsource the market research tracking to a service bureau that would be responsible for reporting its results to Royal Bank on a monthly basis.

This would eliminate the work Royal Bank would have to do internally, and the bank could take advantage of established marketing research industry practices that a service bureau

would follow. On the other hand, a bureau would provide very limited information regarding what made certain customers more profitable than others.

OPTION 3: Purchase software that could be customized to Royal Bank's specific market research needs and linked to its customer database.

This solution could be completely customized for Royal Bank's needs and allow the bank to take advantage of established industry experience while eliminating the need to develop software internally. However, the process of customizing the software would require a significant amount of effort by bank personnel. In addition, the new software program would have to be coordinated with the existing software system by trained specialists. And Cathy's team would have to develop a set of requirements and a process to evaluate at least three to five market vendors for the software, requiring time and effort.

Now, put yourself in Cathy Burrows's shoes: Which option would you choose, and why?

Knowledge Is Power

In Chapter 1, we talked about how marketing is a decision process in which marketing managers determine the strategies that will help the organization meet its long-term objectives. In Chapter 2, we said that successful planning means that managers make good decisions for guiding the organization. But how do marketers make good decisions? How do they go about developing marketing objectives, selecting a target market, positioning (or repositioning) their product, and developing product, price, promotion, and place strategies?

The answer is information. Information is the fuel that runs the marketing engine. To make good decisions, marketers must have information that is accurate, up to date, and relevant. As you'll see in Figure 4.1, we are now in Part II of the book, "Understanding Consumers' Needs." Part of the marketer's role in understanding these needs is to conduct marketing research in order to identify them. In this chapter, we will discuss some of the tools that marketers use to get that information. In the chapters that follow, we will look at consumer behavior, at how and why organizations buy, and then at how marketers sharpen their focus through target marketing strategies. But first, let's talk about the marketing information system.

The Marketing Information System

One of the ways in which firms collect information is through a **marketing information system (MIS)**. The MIS is a process that first determines what information marketing managers need and then gathers, sorts, analyzes, stores, and distributes relevant and timely marketing information to system users. As reflected in Figure 4.2, the MIS system includes three important components: (1) four types of data, (2) computer hardware and software to analyze that data and to create reports, and (3) information and the decision makers who use it.

Where exactly do all the data come from? As we mentioned, information to feed the system comes from four major sources: these are internal company data, marketing intelligence data on competition and other elements in the firm's business environment, information gathered through marketing research, and acquired databases.

The data are stored and accessed through computer hardware and software. Based on an understanding of managers' needs, MIS personnel generate a series of regular reports for various decision makers. For example, Frito-Lay's MIS generates daily sales data by product line and by region that its managers use to evaluate the market share of different Frito-Lay products compared to each other and to competing snack foods in each region where the company does business.[1]

Let's take a closer look at each of the four different data sources for the MIS.

Internal Company Data

The internal company data system uses information from within the company to produce reports on the results of sales and marketing activities. Internal company data include a firm's internal records of sales—information such as which customers buy which products in what quantities and at what intervals, what items are in stock and which ones are back-ordered because they are out of stock, when items were shipped to the customer, and what items have been returned because they are defective.

Often, an MIS allows salespeople and sales managers in the field to access internal records through a company intranet. An **intranet** is an internal corporate communications network that uses Internet technology to link company departments, employees, and databases. Intranets are secured so that only authorized employees have access. When the MIS is made available to sales-

marketing information system (MIS)
A process that first determines what information marketing managers need and then gathers, sorts, analyzes, stores, and distributes relevant and timely marketing information to system users.

intranet
An internal corporate communication network that uses Internet technology to link company departments, employees, and databases.

Figure 4.1 Making and Delivering Value

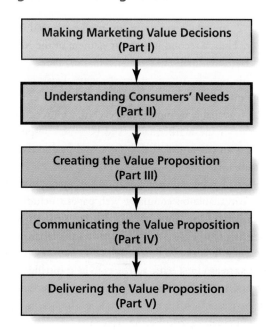

Making Marketing Value Decisions (Part I)
↓
Understanding Consumers' Needs (Part II)
↓
Creating the Value Proposition (Part III)
↓
Communicating the Value Proposition (Part IV)
↓
Delivering the Value Proposition (Part V)

Figure 4.2 The Marketing Information System

A firm's marketing information system (MIS) stores and analyzes data from a variety of sources and turns the data into information for useful marketing decision making.

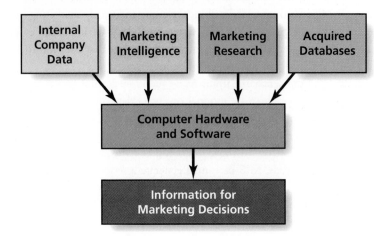

people and sales managers, they can better serve their customers by having immediate access to information on pricing, inventory levels, production schedules, shipping dates, and the customer's sales history. But equally important—because salespeople and sales managers are the ones in daily direct contact with customers—their reports are entered directly into the system via the company intranet. This means they can provide an important source of information on changes in sales patterns or new sales opportunities.

From the internal company data system, marketing managers can get daily or weekly sales data by brand or product line. They can also get monthly sales reports to measure progress toward sales goals and market share objectives. For example, managers and buyers at Wal-Mart's headquarters use up-to-the-minute sales information obtained from store cash registers around the country so they can detect problems with products, promotions, and even the firm's distribution system.

Marketing Intelligence

marketing intelligence system
A method by which marketers get information about everyday happenings in the marketing environment.

As we discussed in Chapter 2, to make good decisions, marketers need to have information about the marketing environment. Thus, a second important element of the MIS is the **marketing intelligence system**, a method by which marketers get information about everyday happenings in the marketing environment. Although the name *intelligence* may suggest cloak-and-dagger spy activities, in reality nearly all the information companies need about their environment—including the competitive environment—is available by monitoring everyday sources: newspapers, trade publications, or simple observations of the marketplace. And because salespeople are the ones "in the trenches" every day, talking with customers, distributors, and prospective customers, they too can provide valuable information.

In recent years, the Web has become a major source of marketing intelligence. Tremendous amounts of information are available on company Web pages (including those of competitors), through news sources from around the globe, through government reports, and on trade association sites. The ease of accessing and searching the Web and individual sites makes the Internet an attractive source of marketing intelligence.

Sometimes companies engage in specific activities to gain intelligence. For example, retailers often hire "mystery shoppers" to visit their stores (and those of their competitors) posing as customers to see how people are treated. (Imagine being paid to shop for a living!) Other information may come from speaking with organizational buyers about competing products, attending trade shows, or simply purchasing competitors' products.

Marketing managers may use marketing intelligence data to predict fluctuations in sales due to economic conditions, political issues, and events that heighten consumer awareness or to forecast the future so that they will be on top of developing trends. For example, knowledge of demographic trends such as a declining birthrate and an aging population prompted the Ford Motor Company to create a specialized division called Third Age Suit to design cars for older drivers. The average age of a Lincoln driver is 67. The Lincoln Town Car therefore features two sets of radio and air-conditioning controls, one on the dashboard and one on the steering wheel, because older drivers have trouble shifting attention from controls to the road.[2]

Indeed, some marketing researchers, known as *futurists*, specialize in predicting consumer trends to come. They try to forecast changes in lifestyles that will affect the wants and needs of customers in the coming years. Futurists try to imagine different **scenarios**, or possible future situations, that might occur and assign a level of probability to each.

A scenario can be shaped by a number of key outcomes. For example, deregulation laws could shape the future of the banking or telecommunications industries. In those cases, a futurist might develop different scenarios for different levels of deregulation, including forecasts assuming no deregulation, moderate deregulation, and complete deregulation. Each scenario allows marketers to consider the impact of different marketing strategies and to come up with plans based on which outcomes they consider are most likely to happen. No one can predict the future with certainty, but it's better to make an educated guess than no guess at all and be caught totally unprepared. Even something as seemingly simple as accurately predicting the price of a gallon of gasoline next year greatly impacts business success.

In a few cases, companies are enlisting consumers' help to predict the success or failure of different products. Visitors to the Hollywood Stock Exchange (**www.hsx.com**) use virtual dollars to "buy and sell" stocks—but in this case, the traders are avid moviegoers who trade soon-to-be released movies and bet on which will be hits or misses. Stocks start trading on the exchange as soon as a studio gives a green light to a project. Some studios find reactions to a movie stock very helpful in predicting box office receipts once film is released, so they monitor this "stock market" very closely.[3]

Of course, collecting marketing intelligence data is just the beginning. An effective MIS must include procedures to ensure that the marketing intelligence data are translated and combined with internal company data and other marketing data to create useful reports for marketing managers.

Marketing Research

A third type of data that is a part of a company MIS consists of information gathered through marketing research. **Marketing research** refers to the process of collecting, analyzing, and interpreting data about customers, competitors, and the business environment to improve marketing effectiveness. Although marketing intelligence data are collected continuously to keep managers abreast of happenings in the marketplace, marketing research is called for when unique information is needed for specific decisions. Whether their business is selling cool stuff to teens or coolant to factories, firms succeed by knowing what customers want, when they want it, where they want it—and what competing firms are doing about it. In other words, the better a firm is at obtaining valid marketing information, the more successful it will be. Therefore, virtually all companies rely on some form of marketing research, though the amount and type of research they conduct varies dramatically.

In general, marketing research data available in an MIS include *syndicated research reports* and *custom research reports*. **Syndicated research** is general research collected by firms on a regular basis that is then sold to many firms. The syndicated research firm Marketing Evaluations/TVQ Inc.

scenarios
Possible future situations that futurists use to assess the likely impact of alternative marketing strategies.

marketing research
The process of collecting, analyzing, and interpreting data about customers, competitors, and the business environment in order to improve marketing effectiveness.

syndicated research
Research by firms that collect data on a regular basis and sell the reports to multiple firms.

BEFORE OUR DESIGNERS CREATE A CAR THEY TALK TO OUTSIDE *EXPERTS.*

BUCKLE UP—TOGETHER WE CAN SAVE LIVES.

SEVERAL *times a year we invite people to come and brainstorm with Ford Motor Company designers and engineers. We talk about cars, sure. But often we talk about NON-CAR THINGS: computers, appliances, music, the environment, quality in very general terms. We know that to design cars and trucks with relevance and appeal, you have to LISTEN to your customers. It's part of the learning process that leads us to quality.*

· FORD · FORD TRUCKS · Ford · LINCOLN · MERCURY ·

QUALITY IS JOB 1.

Automakers such as Ford conduct extensive market research on consumers' car preferences.

custom research
Research conducted for a single firm to provide specific information its managers need.

reports on consumers' perceptions of over 1,700 performers such as Chris Rock and Lisa Kudrow for companies that are interested in using a performer in their advertising.[4] Other examples of syndicated research reports include Nielsen's television ratings and Arbitron's radio ratings. Simmons Market Research Bureau and Mediamark Research, Inc., are two syndicated research firms that combine information about consumers' buying behavior and their media usage with geographic and demographic characteristics.

As valuable as it may be, syndicated research doesn't provide all the answers to marketing questions because the information collected typically is broad but shallow; it gives good insights about general trends, such as who is watching what television shows or what brand of perfume is hot this year.

Often firms need to undertake custom marketing research. **Custom research** is research conducted for a single firm to provide answers to specific questions. This kind of research is especially helpful for firms when they need to know more about *why* certain trends have surfaced.

Some firms maintain an in-house research department that conducts studies on its behalf. Many firms, however, hire outside research companies that specialize in designing and conducting projects based on the needs of the client. These custom research reports are another kind of information that is included in the MIS.

Marketers may use marketing research to identify opportunities for new products, to promote existing ones, or to provide data about the quality of their products, who uses them, and how. Sometimes a company will even do research to counter a competitor's claim. For example, Procter & Gamble (P&G) challenged rival Revlon's claim that its ColorStay line of cosmetics won't rub off. P&G researchers wanted to answer a specific question—was ColorStay's claim true? That kind of question can't be answered by buying a syndicated report, so P&G commissioned 270 women to provide the specific information needed to support its case against Revlon. The women rubbed their cheeks against their shirts while wearing ColorStay and reported that, in fact, most of the shirts did get stained. But Revlon countered that P&G's test was flawed because the women may have been encouraged to rub too hard. They did their own test on 293 women who were told to use "the pressure they use when caressing someone else's face." This time the women found few stains. To avoid further controversy, Revlon now says that ColorStay won't rub off under "normal circumstances."[5] Aren't you relieved?

Acquired Databases

A large amount of information that can be useful in marketing decision making is available in the form of external databases. Firms may acquire databases from any number of sources. For example, some companies are willing to sell their customer database to noncompeting firms. Government databases, including the massive amounts of economic and demographic information compiled by the U.S. Census Bureau, are available at little or no cost. State and local governments may make information such as automobile license data available for a fee.

Recently, the use of such databases for marketing purposes has come under increased government scrutiny. Using the data for analyzing consumer trends and product planning is one thing—using it for outbound mailings and unsolicited phone calls and e-mails has evoked a backlash resulting in "do-not-call" lists and antispam laws. Maybe you have noticed that when you sign up for a credit card or have other occasion to give a seller your contact information, you receive an invitation to "opt out" of receiving promotional mailings from them or from others who may acquire your contact information from them later. By law, if you decide to opt out, companies cannot use your information for marketing purposes.

Marketing Decision Support Systems

As we have discussed, a firm's marketing information system generates regular reports for decision makers on what is going on in the internal and external environment. But sometimes these reports are inadequate. Different managers may want different information, and in some cases, the problem that must be addressed is too vague or unusual to be easily answered by the MIS process. As a result, many firms beef up their MIS with a **marketing decision support system (MDSS)**. An MDSS includes analysis and interactive software that allows marketing managers, even those who are not computer experts, to access MIS data and conduct their own analyses, often over the company intranet. Figure 4.3 shows the elements of an MDSS.

Typically, an MDSS includes sophisticated statistical and modeling software tools. Statistical software allows managers to examine complex relationships among factors in the marketplace. For example, a marketing manager who wants to know how consumers perceive her company's brand in relation to the competition's brand might use a sophisticated statistical technique called *multidimensional scaling* to create a "perceptual map," or a graphic presentation of the various brands in relationship to each other. You'll see an example of a perceptual map in Chapter 7.

Modeling software allows decision makers to examine possible or preconceived ideas about relationships in the data—to ask "what-if" questions. For example, media modeling software allows marketers to see what would happen if they made certain decisions about where to place their advertising. A manager may be able to use sales data and a model to find out how many consumers stay with his brand and how many switch, thus developing projections of market share over time. Table 4.1 presents some examples of the different marketing questions that an MIS and an MDSS might answer.

marketing decision support system (MDSS)
The data, analysis software, and interactive software that allow managers to conduct analyses and find the information they need.

Figure 4.3 The Marketing Decision Support System

Although an MIS provides many reports managers need for decision making, it doesn't answer all their information needs. The marketing decision support system (MDSS) is an enhancement to the MIS that makes it easy for marketing managers to access the MIS system and find answers to their questions.

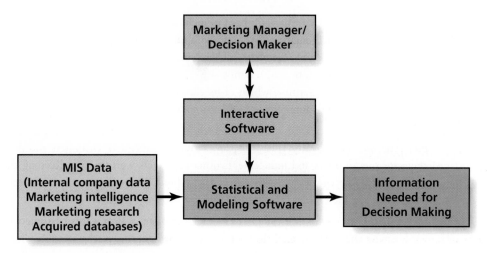

Table 4.1 Examples of Questions That Might Be Answered by an MIS and an MDSS

Questions Answered with an MIS	Questions Answered with an MDSS
What were our company sales of each product during the last month and the last year?	Have our sales declines simply reflected changes in overall industry sales, or is there some portion of the decline that cannot be explained by industry changes?
What changes are happening in sales in our industry, and what are the demographic characteristics of consumers whose purchase patterns are changing the most?	Are the same trends seen in our different product categories? Are the changes in consumer trends very similar among all our products? What are the demographic characteristics of consumers who seem to be the most and the least loyal?
What are the best media for reaching a large proportion of heavy, medium, or light users of our product?	If we change our media schedule by adding or deleting certain media buys, will we reach fewer users of our product?

Searching for Gold: Data Mining

As we have discussed, most MIS systems include internal customer transaction databases and many include acquired databases. Often these databases are extremely large. To take advantage of the massive amount of data now available, sophisticated analysis techniques called data mining are becoming a priority for many firms. **Data mining** is a process in which analysts sift through data (often measured in terabytes—much larger than kilobytes or even gigabytes) to identify unique patterns of behavior among different customer groups.

data mining
Sophisticated analysis techniques to take advantage of the massive amount of transaction information now available.

American Express, for example, uses data mining to understand shopping patterns. By mining the data, the company can identify customer segments whose shopping patterns indicate that they may respond to different types of offers. If its data show that some of its female cardholders buy a lot of clothes at Saks Fifth Avenue, American Express might offer these women a discount if they also buy shoes at the store and whip out their American Express card to pay for them.[6]

Data mining uses supercomputers that run sophisticated programs so that analysts can combine different databases to understand relationships among buying decisions, exposure to marketing messages, and in-store promotions. These operations are so complex that often companies need to build a *data warehouse* (sometimes costing more than $10 million) simply to store the data and process it.[7]

Data mining has four important applications for marketers:[8]

1. **Customer acquisition:** Many firms work hard to include demographic and other information about customers in their database. For example, a number of supermarkets offer weekly special price discounts for store "members." These stores' membership application forms require that customers indicate their age, family size, address, and so on. With this information, the supermarket can determine which of its current customers respond best to specific offers and then send the same offers to noncustomers who share the same demographic characteristics.

2. **Customer retention and loyalty:** The firm can identify big-spending customers and then target them for special offers and inducements other customers won't receive. Keeping the most profitable customers coming back is a great way to build business success because keeping good customers is less expensive then constantly finding new ones.[9]

3. **Customer abandonment:** Strange as it may sound, sometimes a firm wants customers to take their business elsewhere because they actually cost the firm too much to service them.

Today, this is popularly called "firing a customer." For example, a department store may use data mining to identify unprofitable customers—those who are not spending enough or who return most of what they buy. Data mining has allowed Federal Express to identify customers as "the good, the bad, and the ugly."[10] As a result, FedEx strategizes to keep the "good" consumers as profitable customers and make "bad" customers (those who cost the company more than they generate in revenues) more profitable by charging them higher shipping rates. For the "ugly" customers who spend very little, FedEx is saving money by no longer trying to attract their business.

4. **Market basket analysis:** Firms can develop focused promotional strategies based on their records of which customers have bought certain products. For example, the Fingerhut catalog company analyzes which of its 25 million customers have recently bought outdoor patio furniture and targets them to receive mailings about gas grills.

Ultimately, data mining gets translated into database marketing strategies—part of the firm's promotional strategy. We'll discuss database marketing in more detail in Chapter 12.

So far, we have looked at the MIS and the MDSS, the overall systems that provide the information marketers need to make good decisions. We've seen how the data included in the MIS and MDSS include internal company data, marketing intelligence data gathered by monitoring everyday sources, acquired databases, and information gathered to address specific marketing decisions through the marketing research process. In the rest of the chapter, we'll look at the steps that marketers must take when they conduct marketing research.

Steps in the Marketing Research Process

The collection and interpretation of strategic information is hardly a one-shot deal that managers engage in "just out of curiosity." Ideally, marketing research is an ongoing *process*, a series of steps marketers take to learn about the marketplace. Whether a company conducts the research itself or hires another firm to do it, the goal is the same: to help managers make informed marketing decisions. Figure 4.4 shows the steps in the research process, and we'll go over each of these now.

Step 1: Define the Research Problem

The first step in the marketing research process is to clearly understand what information managers need that the research is to provide. This step is referred to as *defining the research problem*. You should note that the word "problem" here does not necessarily refer to "something that is wrong" but instead to the overall questions for which the firm needs answers. Defining the problem has three components:

1. **Specifying the research objectives:** What questions will the research attempt to answer?

2. **Identifying the consumer population of interest:** What are the characteristics of the consumer groups of interest?

3. **Placing the problem in an environmental context:** What factors in the firm's internal and external business environment might be influencing the situation?

Providing the right kind of information for each of these pieces of the problem is not as simple as it seems. For example, suppose a luxury car manufacturer wants to find out why its sales have fallen off dramatically over the past year. The research objective could revolve around any number of possible questions: Is the firm's advertising failing to reach the right consumers? Is the right message being sent? Do the firm's cars have a particular feature (or lack of one) that is turning customers away? Is there a problem with the firm's reputation for providing quality service? Do consumers believe the price is right for the value they get? The particular objective chosen depends on a variety of factors, such as the feedback the firm is getting from its customers, the

Figure 4.4   Steps in the Marketing Research Process

The marketing research process includes a series of steps that begins with defining the problem or the information needed and that ends with the finished research report for managers.

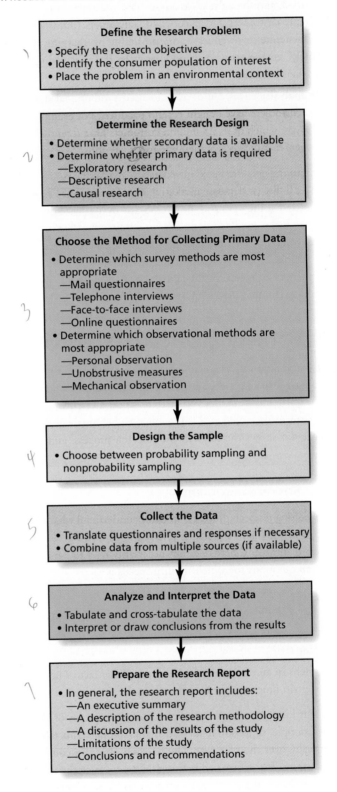

Define the Research Problem
- Specify the research objectives
- Identify the consumer population of interest
- Place the problem in an environmental context

Determine the Research Design
- Determine whether secondary data is available
- Determine whehter primary data is required
  —Exploratory research
  —Descriptive research
  —Causal research

Choose the Method for Collecting Primary Data
- Determine which survey methods are most appropriate
  —Mail questionnaires
  —Telephone interviews
  —Face-to-face interviews
  —Online questionnaires
- Determine which observational methods are most appropriate
  —Personal observation
  —Unobstrusive measures
  —Mechanical observation

Design the Sample
- Choose between probability sampling and nonprobability sampling

Collect the Data
- Translate questionnaires and responses if necessary
- Combine data from multiple sources (if available)

Analyze and Interpret the Data
- Tabulate and cross-tabulate the data
- Interpret or draw conclusions from the results

Prepare the Research Report
- In general, the research report includes:
  —An executive summary
  —A description of the research methodology
  —A discussion of the results of the study
  —Limitations of the study
  —Conclusions and recommendations

information it receives from the marketplace, and sometimes even the intuition of the people designing the research.

Often the focus of a research question is driven by feedback the firm gets from the marketplace that identifies a possible problem. For example, Mercedes-Benz continually monitors drivers' perceptions of its cars. When the company started getting reports from its dealers that people were viewing the cars as "arrogant" and "unapproachable," even to the point where they were reluctant to sit in showroom models, the company undertook a research project to better understand the reasons for this perception.

The research objective determines the consumer population that will be studied. In Mercedes' case, the research might focus on current owners to find out what they especially like about the car. Or the research might study nonowners to understand their lifestyles, what they look for in a luxury automobile, or their beliefs about the company itself that keep them from choosing the cars. Mercedes-Benz's research showed that although people rated its cars very highly on engineering quality and status, many were too intimidated by the elitist Mercedes image to consider buying one. Mercedes dealers reported that a common question from visitors to showrooms was, "May I actually *sit* in the car?" Based on these findings, Mercedes softened its image by projecting a slightly more down-to-earth image in its advertising.[11]

Mercedes-Benz tried to project a friendly, more approachable image by running ads such as this one featuring a cute rubber ducky sporting a Mercedes logo.

Placing the problem in the context of the firm's environment helps researchers structure the research, determine the specific types of questions to ask, and identify factors that will need to be taken into account when measuring results. Environmental conditions also matter. For example, when the economy is tight and sales of luxury cars are generally declining, the population to be studied might be narrowed down to a select group of consumers who are still willing and able to indulge in a luxury vehicle. Today, many consumers are moving away from status-conscious materialism and more toward functionality. In addition, as gasoline prices go up, drivers' sensitivity to miles per gallon translates even to luxury brands and huge sport-utility vehicles like the mighty Hummer. Thus, a research question might be to see how consumers react to different promotional strategies for luxury goods that go beyond simply "snob appeal."

Step 2: Determine the Research Design

Once marketers have isolated specific problems, the second step of the research process is to decide on a "plan of attack." This plan is the **research design**, which specifies exactly what information marketers will collect and what type of study they will do. Figure 4.5 summarizes many of the types of research designs in the researcher's arsenal. As you can see, research designs fall into two broad categories: secondary research and primary research. All marketing problems do not call for the same research techniques, and marketers solve many problems most effectively with a combination of techniques.

research design
A plan that specifies what information marketers will collect and what type of study they will do.

SECONDARY RESEARCH The very first question marketers must ask when determining their research design is whether the information required to make a decision already exists. For example, a coffee producer who needs to know the differences in coffee consumption among different demographic and geographic segments of the market may find that the information needed is already available from a study conducted by the National Coffee Association. Data that have been collected for some purpose other than the problem at hand are called **secondary data**.

Many marketers thrive on going out and collecting new, "fresh" data from consumers. However, if secondary data are available, it saves the firm time and money because the expense of

secondary data
Data that have been collected for some purpose other than the problem at hand.

Figure 4.5 Marketing Research Design

For some research problems, the secondary research may provide the information needed. At other times, one of the primary research methods may be needed.

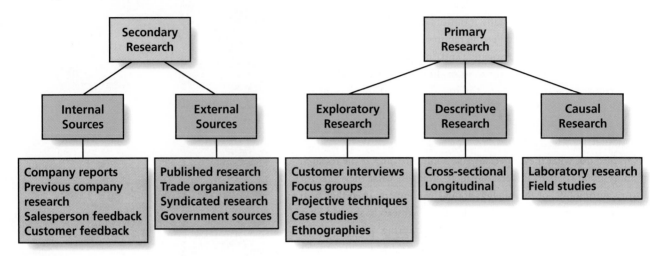

designing and implementing a study has already been incurred. Sometimes the data that marketers need may be "hiding" right under the organization's nose in the form of company reports; previous company research studies; feedback received from customers, salespeople, or stores; or even in the memories of longtime employees. More typically, though, researchers need to look elsewhere for secondary data. They may obtain reports published in the popular and business press, studies that private research organizations or government agencies conduct, and published research on the state of the industry from trade organizations.

For example, many companies subscribe to *Simmons Study of Media & Markets*, a national survey conducted semiannually by Simmons Market Research Bureau, the syndicated research firm mentioned earlier. Simmons publishes results that it then sells to marketers, advertising agencies, and publishers. This information is based on the self-reports of over 25,000 consumers who complete monthly logs detailing their purchases of products from aspirin to snow tires. Simmons data can give a brand manager a profile of who is using a product, identify heavy users, or even provide data on what magazines a target market reads. Marketers can also turn to the Internet for external information sources. Table 4.2 lists a number of Web sites helpful to marketers looking for secondary research topics.

primary data
Data from research conducted to help in making a specific decision.

PRIMARY RESEARCH   Of course, secondary research is not always the answer. When a company needs to make a specific decision, it often needs to conduct research to collect **primary data**, that is, information collected directly from respondents to specifically address the question at hand. Primary data include demographic and psychological information about customers and prospective customers, customers' attitudes and opinions about products and competing products, as well as their awareness or knowledge about a product and their beliefs about the people who use those products. In the next few sections, we'll talk briefly about the various designs useful in conducting primary research.

exploratory research
A technique that marketers use to generate insights for future, more rigorous studies.

EXPLORATORY RESEARCH   Marketers use **exploratory research** to generate topics for future, more rigorous studies to come up with ideas for new strategies and opportunities or perhaps just to get a better handle on a problem they are currently experiencing with a product. Because the studies are usually small scale and less costly than other techniques, marketers may use exploratory research to test their hunches about what's going on without too much risk.

Exploratory studies often involve in-depth probing of a few consumers who fit the profile of the "typical" customer. Researchers may interview consumers, salespeople, or other employees about products, services, ads, or stores. They may simply "hang out" and watch what people do

Table 4.2 Helpful Internet Sites for Marketing Research

URL	Description
www.findsvp.com	FindSVP provides access to a catalog of more than 300 industry reports.
www.census.gov	The U.S. Census Bureau publishes separate reports on specific industries (such as agriculture, construction, and mining) as well as on housing, population growth and distribution, and retail trade.
www.marketingtools.com	Marketing Tools is a site run by *American Demographics* magazine that lets users search for marketing books and articles.
www.marketingpower.com	The American Marketing Association provides many resources to its members on a variety of industry topics.
www.dialog.com	DIALOG sorts companies by location, size, and industry. The user can request telemarketing reports, preaddressed mailing labels, and company profiles.
www.lexis-nexis.com	LEXIS-NEXIS is a large database featuring information from such sources as Dun & Bradstreet, the *New York Times*, CNN, and National Public Radio transcripts.

when choosing among competing brands in a store aisle. Or they may locate places where the consumers of interest tend to be and ask questions in these settings. For example, some researchers find that members of Generation Y are too suspicious or skeptical in traditional research settings, so they may interview young people waiting in line to buy concert tickets or in clubs.[12] Some firms like Look-Look (**www.look-look.com**) send young "coolhunters" armed with video cameras to urban areas to interview people about the latest styles and trends.

Most exploratory research is referred to as *qualitative* in nature. That is, the results of the research project tend to be non-numeric and instead might be detailed verbal or visual information about consumers' attitudes, feelings, and buying behaviors in the form of words rather than in numbers. For example, when DuPont wanted to know how women felt about panty hose, marketers asked research participants to collect magazine clippings that expressed their emotions about the product.[13]

Exploratory research can take many forms. **Consumer interviews** are one-on-one discussions in which an individual shares his or her thoughts in person with a researcher. When Kimberly-Clark, maker of Huggies disposable diapers, was thinking about producing training pants, it sent researchers into women's homes and asked them to talk about their frustrations with toilet training.[14] Many women expressed feelings of failure and a horror at having to admit to other parents that their child was "still in diapers." Based on the research, Kimberly-Clark introduced Pull-Ups disposable training pants and sold $400 million worth per year before the competition caught up.

Intuit, the software company that produces personal finance software Turbo-Tax and Quicken, used personal interviews to better understand consumers' frustrations with installing and using its products. When customers told researchers that the software itself should "tell me how to do it," they took this advice literally and developed software that used computer audio to give verbal instructions. Intuit's probing went one step beyond interviews when its researchers left respondents microcassette recorders so that whenever they were having problems, they could simply push a button and tell the company of their frustration.[15]

The **focus group** is the technique marketing researchers use most often for collecting exploratory data. Focus groups typically consist of five to nine consumers who have been recruited because they share certain characteristics. These people sit together to discuss a product, ad, or

consumer interviews
One-on-one discussions between a consumer and a researcher.

focus group
A product-oriented discussion among a small group of consumers led by a trained moderator.

Seeing Inside The Mind Of Your Customer

To measure customers' true feelings about pantyhose, Du Pont asked women to assemble magazine clips that evoked their emotions about the product. The composite of clips at right, produced at the Harvard Business School, was used to improve marketing tactics.

Shopping for stockings can be confusing. This photo suggests the experience should be as easy as picking out fruit from an outdoor stand.

The spilled ice cream symbolizes the disappointment involved in buying an expensive pair of hose, only to have them run again after only two or three wearings.

These secretaries, hunched over their spartan desks, evoke the discomfort and frustration of having to wear stockings at work.

Joan Crawford represents glamour and sensuality. Her choice suggests that women really do like hose because they feel sexy.

SOURCE: SEEING THE VOICE OF THE CUSTOMER LAB

Exploratory research can be very useful in helping marketers understand how consumers feel about products. DuPont asked consumers to develop a collage to indicate how they feel about panty hose.

some other marketing topic introduced by a discussion leader. Focus group facilitation is a real art that requires discipline, patience, and a strong sense of when to sit back and listen and when to jump in and direct discussion. Typically, the leader video- or audiotapes these group discussions, which may be held at special interviewing facilities that allow for observation by the client, who watches from behind a one-way mirror.

In addition to getting insights from what the participants say about a product, a good moderator can sometimes learn by carefully observing other things such as body language. While conducting focus groups on bras, an analyst noted that small-chested women typically reacted with hostility when discussing the subject. The participants would unconsciously cover their chests with their arms as they spoke and complained that they were ignored by the fashion industry. To meet this overlooked need, the company introduced a line of A-cup bras called "A-OK" that depicted these women in a positive light.[16]

projective techniques
Tests that marketers use to explore people's underlying feelings about a product, especially appropriate when consumers are unable or unwilling to express their true reactions.

Many researchers use **projective techniques** to get at people's underlying feelings, especially when they think that people will be unable or unwilling to express their true reactions. A projective test asks the participant to respond to some object, often by telling a story about it. For example, Georgia-Pacific, the manufacturer of Brawny paper towels, was locked in a struggle with ScotTowels for the number two market position behind Bounty. The company decided to reexamine its brand identity, which was personified by a 60-foot character named Brawny who holds an ax. Managers were afraid that Brawny was too old-fashioned or that women were confused about why a man was selling paper towels in the first place. Researchers asked women in the focus groups questions such as, "What kind of woman would he go out with?" and "What is his home life like?" Then the researchers asked the women to imagine how he would act in different situations and even to guess what would happen if they were locked in an elevator with him for 20 minutes. Responses were reassuring—the women saw Brawny as a knight in shining armor who would get them out of the elevator—a good spokesman for a product that's supposed to be reliable and able to get the job done. Brawny kept his job and in fact has had two makeovers since he was originally introduced in 1975 to keep his look modern.[17]

The **case study** is a comprehensive examination of a particular firm or organization. In business-to-business marketing research in which the customers are other firms, for example, researchers may try to learn how one particular company makes its purchases. The goal is to identify the key decision makers, to learn what criteria they emphasize when choosing among suppliers, and perhaps to learn something about any conflicts and rivalries among these decision makers that may influence their choices.

An **ethnography** is a different kind of in-depth report. It is a technique borrowed from anthropologists who go to "live with the natives" for months or even years. This approach has been adapted by some marketing researchers who visit people's homes or participate in real-life consumer activities to get a handle on how they *really* use products. Imagine having a researcher follow you around while you shop and then while you use the products you bought to see what kind of consumer you are.

Of course, unlike anthropologists living with indigenous tribes, marketing researchers usually don't have months or years to devote to a project. Thus, they devise shortcuts to get the information they need. For example, when Nissan was preparing for the $60 million launch of its first full-size truck, the Titan, members of their ad agency (TBWA/Chiat/Day) were deployed to the field to understand the psyche of full-size truck owners. Team members hung out for several months in late 2002 at hunting expos, gun shows, Super Cross events, and even Montana fishing spots—places populated by the target consumers. Results from the observations, supported by results from focus groups and interviews, provided strong ammunition for Nissan to communicate its message of what the Titan can do. Ultimately, to portray a rough-and-tumble image the ads showed dirty Titans in action, sloshing through mud and driving up inclines.[18]

Delve is one of many companies specializing in qualitative research services.

Rise Above the Rest.

Qualitative research is all about seeing issues from a high level and using that information to make critical business decisions. At Delve, we have almost thirty years of experience and have a great perspective on helping you connect with your customers. Whether your project is in one city with one methodology or utilizing multiple field offices and multiple methodologies, we can help you understand the big picture.

Delve creates and fosters environments for dynamic dialogues between marketers and customers. Whether they be face-to-face, voice-to-voice or technology-based settings like the Web, we are committed to providing the best in the business.

Call your Delve representative today and we'll help you take the quality of your research to new heights!

Focus Groups
Pre-Recruits
Web Surveys
Telephone Interviews
Central Location Testing
Taste Tests
Interactive Voice Response

www.delve.com
800-325-3338

Appleton, WI   Dallas   Philadelphia
Atlanta   Kansas City   Phoenix
Chicago   Los Angeles   Seattle
Columbus   Minneapolis   St. Louis

Delve

DESCRIPTIVE RESEARCH We've seen that marketers have many tools in their arsenal, including focus groups and observational techniques, to help them better define a problem or opportunity. These are usually modest studies of a small number of people, enough to get some indication of what is going on but not enough for the marketer to feel confident about generalizing what he or she observes to the rest of the population.

The next step in marketing research, then, often is to conduct **descriptive research**, which probes systematically into the marketing problem and bases its conclusions on a large sample of participants. Descriptive research is typically expressed in quantitative terms—averages, percentages, or other statistics summarizing results from a large set of measurements. In such *quantitative* approaches to research, the project can be as simple as counting the number of Listerine bottles sold in a month in different regions of the country or as complex as statistical analyses of responses to a survey mailed to thousands of consumers. In each case, marketers conduct the descriptive research to answer a specific question in contrast to the "fishing expedition" that may occur in exploratory research.

case study
A comprehensive examination of a particular firm or organization.

ethnography
A detailed report based on observations of people in their own homes or communities.

descriptive research
A tool that probes more systematically into the problem and bases its conclusions on large numbers of observations.

cross-sectional design
A type of descriptive technique that involves the systematic collection of quantitative information.

longitudinal design
A technique that tracks the responses of the same sample of respondents over time.

Marketing researchers who employ descriptive techniques most often use a **cross-sectional design**. This approach usually involves the systematic collection of responses to a consumer survey instrument (a "questionnaire") from one or more samples of respondents at one point in time. The data may be collected on more than one occasion but generally not from the same pool of respondents.

In contrast to these one-shot studies, a **longitudinal design** tracks the responses of the same sample of respondents over time. Market researchers sometimes create *consumer panels* to get information; in this case a sample of respondents representative of a larger market agrees to provide information about purchases on a weekly or monthly basis. When 3M wanted to find out how it should market its Buf-Puf Sponge facial scrub pads, the company recruited a teen advisory board by running ads in *Seventeen, Sassy,* and *Teen.* 3M periodically consults these consumer panel members about their use of personal care products and their concerns about appearance.[19]

CAUSAL RESEARCH It's a fact that purchases of both diapers and beer peak between 5:00 P.M. and 7:00 P.M. Can we say that purchasing one of these products caused shoppers to purchase the other as well—and, if so, which caused which? Or is the answer simply that this happens to be the time that young fathers stop at the store on their way home from work to pick up some brew and Pampers?[20]

The descriptive techniques we've examined do a good job of providing valuable information about *what* is happening in the marketplace, but descriptive research, by its very nature, can only describe a marketplace phenomenon—it cannot tell us *why.* Sometimes marketers need to know if something they've done has brought about some change in behavior. For example, does placing one product next to another in a store mean that people will buy more of each? We can't answer this question through simple observation or description.

causal research
A technique that attempts to understand cause-and-effect relationships.

Causal research attempts to understand cause-and-effect relationships. Marketers use causal research techniques when they want to know if a change in something (e.g., placing cases of beer next to a diaper display) is responsible for a change in something else (e.g., a big increase in diaper sales). They call the factors that might cause such a change *independent variables* and the outcomes *dependent variables.* The independent variable(s) *cause* some change in the dependent variable(s). In our example, then, the beer display is an *independent variable,* and sales data for the diapers are a *dependent variable.* That is, the study would investigate whether an increase in diaper sales "depends" on the proximity of beer. Researchers can gather data and test the causal relationship statistically.

experiments
Techniques that test prespecified relationships among variables in a controlled environment.

To rule out alternative explanations, researchers must carefully design **experiments** that test prescribed relationships among variables in a controlled environment. Because this approach tries to eliminate competing explanations for the outcome, respondents may be brought to a laboratory so that the researcher can control precisely what respondents should see. For example, a study testing whether the placement of diapers in a grocery store influences the likelihood that male shoppers will buy them might bring a group of men into a testing facility and show them a "virtual store" on a computer screen. Researchers would ask the men to fill a grocery cart as they click through the "aisles." The experiment might vary the placement of the diapers—next to shelves of beer in one scenario, near paper goods in a different scenario. The objective is to see which placement gets the guys to put diapers into their carts.

Although a laboratory allows researchers to exert control over what test subjects see and do, marketers don't always have the luxury of conducting this kind of "pure" research. But it is possible to conduct *field studies* in the real world, as long as the researchers can control the independent variables.

For example, a diaper company might choose two grocery stores that have similar customer bases in terms of age, income, and so on. With the cooperation of the grocery store's management, the company might place its diaper display next to the beer in one store and next to the paper goods in the other and then record diaper purchases made by men over a two-week period. If a lot more diapers were bought by guys in the first store than in the second (and the company was sure that nothing else was different between the two stores, such as a dollar-off coupon for diapers being distributed in one store and not the other), the diaper manufacturer might conclude that the presence of beer in the background does indeed result in increased diaper sales.

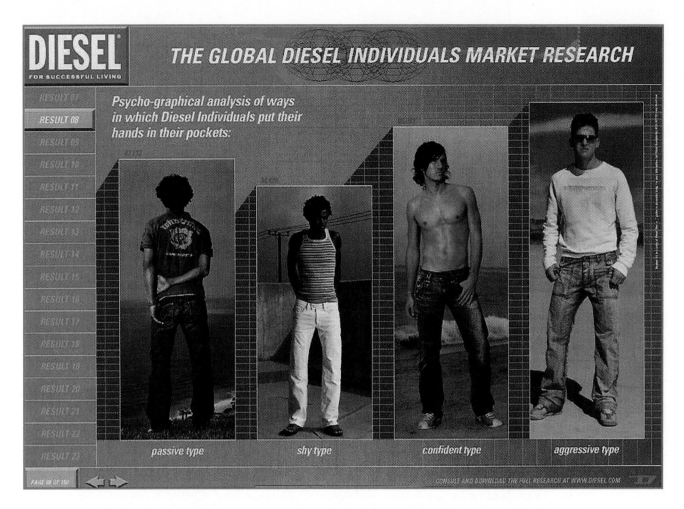

Trendy companies like Diesel jeans need to pay constant attention to the changing tastes of their customers, as this ad reminds us.

Step 3: Choose the Method for Collecting Primary Data

When the researcher decides to collect primary data, the next step in the marketing research process is to figure out just how to collect it. Primary data collection methods can be broadly described as either survey or observation. There are many ways to collect data, and new ones are being tried all the time. Today, a few marketing researchers are even turning to sophisticated brain scans to directly measure our brains' reactions to various advertisements or products. These "neuromarketers" hope to be able to tell companies how people will react to their brands by scanning consumers' brains rather than collecting data the old-fashioned way—by asking them.[21] These techniques are still in their infancy, so for now we'll still rely on other methods to collect primary data.

SURVEY METHODS Survey methods involve some kind of interview or other direct contact with respondents who answer questions. Questionnaires can be administered on the phone, in person, through the mail, or over the Internet. Table 4.3 provides a summary of the advantages and disadvantages of different methods for collecting data.

Questionnaires differ in their degree of structure. With a totally unstructured questionnaire, the researcher loosely determines the questions in advance. Questions may evolve from what the respondent says to previous questions. At the other extreme, the researcher uses a completely structured questionnaire. He or she asks every respondent the exact same questions and each participant responds to the same set of fixed choices. You have probably experienced this kind of questionnaire, where you might have had to respond to a statement by saying if you "strongly agree," "somewhat

Table 4.3 Advantages and Disadvantages of Data Collection Methods

Date Collection Method	Advantages	Disadvantages
Mail questionnaires	• Respondents feel anonymous • Low cost • Good for ongoing research	• May take a long time for questionnaires to be returned • Low rate of response, and many may not return questionnaires • Inflexible questionnaire • Length of questionnaire limited by respondent interest in the topic • Unclear whether respondents understand the questions • Unclear who is responding • No assurance that respondents are being honest
Telephone interviews	• Fast • High flexibility in questioning • Low cost • Limited interviewer bias	• Decreasing levels of respondent cooperation • Limited questionnaire length • High likelihood of respondent misunderstanding • Respondents cannot view materials • Cannot survey households without phones • Consumers screen calls with answering machines and caller ID • Do-not-call lists allow many research subjects to opt out of participation
Face-to-face interviews	• Flexibility of questioning • Can use long questionnaires • Can determine whether respondents have trouble understanding questions • Can use visuals or other materials	• High cost • Interviewer bias a problem • Take a lot of time
Online questionnaires	• Instantaneous data collection and analysis • Questioning very flexible • Low cost • No interviewer bias • Lack of geographic restrictions • Can use visuals or other materials	• Unclear who is responding • No assurance that respondents are being honest • Limited questionnaire length • Unable to determine whether respondent is understanding the question • Self-selected samples

agree," and so on. Moderately structured questionnaires ask each respondent the same questions, but the respondent is allowed to answer the questions in his or her own words.

Mail questionnaires are easy to administer and offer a high degree of anonymity to respondents. On the downside, because the questionnaire is printed and mailed, researchers have little flexibility in the types of questions they can ask and little control over the circumstances under which the respondent is answering them. Mail questionnaires also take a long time to get back to the company and are likely to have a much lower response rate than other types of data collection methods because people tend to ignore them.

Telephone interviews usually consist of a brief phone conversation in which an interviewer reads a short list of questions to the respondent. There are several problems with using telephone interviews as a data collection method. One problem with this method is that the growth of **telemarketing**, in which businesses sell directly to consumers over the phone, has eroded consumers' willingness to participate in phone surveys (especially during dinnertime!). In addition to aggravating people by barraging them with telephone sales messages, some unscrupulous telemarketers have "poisoned the well" for legitimate marketing researchers by hiding their pitches behind an illusion of doing research. They contact consumers under the pretense of doing a research study when, in fact, their real intent is to sell the respondent something or to solicit funds for some cause. The respondent also may not feel comfortable speaking directly to an interviewer, especially if the survey is about a sensitive subject. Of course, increasing numbers of people use voice mail and caller ID to screen calls, further reducing the response rate. And, as noted earlier, state and federal do-not-call lists allow many would-be research subjects to opt out of participation both in legitimate marketing research and unscrupulous telemarketing.[22]

telemarketing
The use of the telephone to sell directly to consumers and business customers.

In *face-to-face interviews*, a live interviewer asks questions of one respondent at a time. Although in "the old days" researchers often went door to door to ask questions, that's much less common today because of fears about security and because the large numbers of dual income families make it less likely to find people at home during the day. Typically, today's face-to-face interviews occur in a "mall intercept" study in which researchers recruit shoppers in malls or other public areas. You've probably seen this going on in your local mall where a smiling person holding a clipboard stops shoppers to see if they are willing to answer a few questions.

Mall intercepts offer good opportunities to get feedback about new package designs, styles, or even reactions to new foods or fragrances. However, because only certain groups of the population frequently shop at malls, a mall intercept study does not provide the researcher with a representative sample of the population (unless the population of interest is mall shoppers). In addition to being more expensive than mail or phone surveys, respondents may be reluctant to answer questions of a personal nature in a face-to-face context.

Online questionnaires are growing in popularity, but use of such questionnaires is not without concerns. Many questions linger about the quality of responses researchers will receive—particularly because (as with mail and phone interviews) no one can be really sure who is typing in the responses on the computer. In addition, it's uncertain whether savvy online consumers are truly representative of the general population.[23] However, these concerns are rapidly evaporating as research firms devise new ways to verify identities; present surveys in novel formats, including the use of images, sound, and animation; and recruit more diverse respondents.[24] More about this later in the chapter.

OBSERVATION METHODS   As we said earlier, the second major primary data collection method is observation. Observation is a type of data collection that uses a *passive instrument* in which the consumer's behaviors are simply recorded—often without his or her knowledge. Researchers do this through personal observation, unobtrusive measures, and mechanical observation.

When researchers use *personal observation*, they watch consumers in action to understand how they react to marketing activities. Advertising agency Ogilvy & Mather's research division sends researchers into homes with handheld video cameras to get pictures of how people use products and why.[25] The hours of footage are then condensed into a documentary-type video that helps marketers make decisions about future strategies.

A shopping mall in Texas became a laboratory for the workplace of the future when it put a "Connection Court" in the middle of the mall. In an observational project sponsored by the Internet Home Alliance, a group of mostly high-tech companies, including Cisco Systems, Microsoft, and IBM, workers installed chairs and couches; set up desks with laptops, flat-panel monitors, and printers; and hooked up a high-speed wireless Internet network. This space is free for use by people who want to work in a more casual—and public—setting. The motivation: to understand if and how people want to work outside their homes and offices. With the spread of wireless Internet by companies like McDonald's and Starbucks that are setting up networks to let their customers work, these companies are doing observational research to understand just how to structure the physical environment that will let them do that more comfortably.[26]

The "Connection Court" in a Texas shopping mall allows high-tech companies to observe how people work in a wireless environment.

Researchers use *unobtrusive measures* that measure traces of physical evidence that remain after some action has been taken when they suspect that people will probably alter their behavior if they know they are being observed. For example, instead of asking a person to report on the alcohol products currently in her home, the researcher might go to the house and perform a "pantry check" by actually counting the bottles in her liquor cabinet. Another option for collecting primary data is to sift through garbage, searching for clues about each family's consumption habits. The "garbologists" can tell, for example, which soft drink accompanied what kind of food. As one garbologist noted, "The people in this study don't know that we are studying their garbage so the information is totally objective."[27] Smelly, too!

Mechanical observation is a primary data collection method that relies on nonhuman devices to record behavior. For example, one well-known application of mechanical observation is A.C. Nielsen's use of "people meters," boxes attached to the television sets of selected viewers, to record patterns of television watching. Data obtained from these devices indicate who is watching which shows. These "television ratings" help the networks determine how much to charge advertisers for commercials and which shows to cancel or renew. Of course, many research firms are developing techniques to measure which Web sites are being visited and by whom (ever heard of "cookies"—the nonedible kind, that is?). As we'll see shortly, there are ways for companies to tell where you've traveled in virtual space, so be careful about the sites to which you surf!

DATA QUALITY: GARBAGE IN, GARBAGE OUT We've seen that a firm can collect data in many ways, including focus groups, ethnographic approaches, observational studies, and controlled experiments. But how much faith should marketing managers place in what they find out from the research?

All too often, marketers who have commissioned a study assume that because they have a massive report full of impressive-looking numbers and tables, they must have the "truth." Unfortunately, there are times when this "truth" is really just one person's interpretation of the facts. At other times, the data used to generate recommendations are flawed. As the expression goes, "Garbage in, garbage out!"[28] That is, bad data means bad managerial decisions. Typically, three factors influence the quality of research results—validity, reliability, and representativeness.

validity
The extent to which research actually measures what it was intended to measure.

VALIDITY **Validity** is the extent to which the research actually measures what it was intended to measure. This was part of the problem underlying the famous New Coke fiasco in the 1980s in which Coca-Cola underestimated people's loyalty to its flagship soft drink after it replaced "Old Coke" with a new, sweeter formula. In a blind taste test, the company assumed that testers' preferences for one anonymous cola over another was a valid measure of consumers' preferences for a cola brand. Coca-Cola found out the hard way that measuring taste only is not the same as measuring people's deep allegiances to their favorite soft drinks. After all, Coke is a brand that elicits strong consumer loyalty and is nothing short of a cultural icon. Tampering with the flavors was like assaulting Mom, home, and apple pie. Sales eventually recovered after the company brought back the old version as "Coca-Cola Classic."[29]

reliability
The extent to which research measurement techniques are free of errors.

RELIABILITY **Reliability** is the extent to which the research measurement techniques are free of errors. Sometimes, for example, the way a researcher asks a question creates error by biasing people's responses. Imagine that an attractive female interviewer working for Trojans condoms stopped male college students on campus and asked them if they used contraceptive products. Do you

Garbologists search for clues about consumption activities unobtrusively.

think their answers might change if they were asked the same questions on an anonymous survey they received in the mail? Most likely, their answers would be different because people are reluctant to disclose what they actually do when their responses are not anonymous. Researchers try to maximize reliability by thinking of several different ways to ask the same questions, by asking these questions on several occasions, or by using several analysts to interpret the responses. Thus, they can compare responses and look for consistency and stability.

Reliability is a problem when the researchers can't be sure the consumer population they're studying even understands the questions. For example, kids are difficult subjects for market researchers because they tend to be undependable reporters of their own behavior, they have poor recall, and they often do not understand abstract questions. In many cases, the children cannot explain why they prefer one item over another (or they're not willing to share these secrets with grown-ups).[30] For these reasons, researchers have had to be especially creative when designing studies on younger consumers. Figure 4.6 shows part of a *completion test* used to measure children's preferences for television programming.

REPRESENTATIVENESS **Representativeness** is the extent to which consumers in the study are similar to a larger group in which the organization has an interest. This criterion for evaluating research underscores the importance of **sampling**, the process of selecting respondents for a study. The issue then becomes how large or small the sample should be and how these people are chosen. We'll talk more about sampling in the next section.

Step 4: Design the Sample

Once the researcher has defined the problem, decided on a research design, and determined how to collect the data, the next step is to decide from whom to obtain the needed data. Of course, the researcher *could* collect the information from every single customer or prospective customer, but this would be extremely expensive and time consuming, if possible at all. Instead, researchers collect most of their data from a small proportion or *sample* of the population of interest. Based on the answers from this sample, researchers hope to generalize to the larger population. Whether such

representativeness
The extent to which consumers in a study are similar to a larger group in which the organization has an interest.

sampling
The process of selecting respondents who statistically represent a larger population of interest.

Figure 4.6 Completion Test

It can be especially difficult to get accurate information from children. Researchers often use visuals such as this Japanese completion test to encourage children to express their feelings. The test asked boys to write in the empty balloon what they think the boy in the drawing will answer when the girl asks, "What program do you want to watch next?"

inferences are accurate or inaccurate depends on the type and quality of the study sample. There are two main types of samples: probability and nonprobability samples.

PROBABILITY SAMPLING   With a **probability sample**, each member of the population has some known chance of being included in the sample. Using a probability sample ensures that the sample is representative of the population and that inferences about the population made from the sample are justified. For example, if a larger percentage of males than females in a probability sample say they prefer action movies to "chick flicks," one can infer with confidence that a larger percentage of males than females in the general population also would rather see a character get sliced and diced.

The most basic type of probability sample is a *simple random sample* in which every member of a population has a known and equal chance of being included in the study. For example, if we simply take the names of all 40 students in your class and put them in a hat and draw one out, each member of your class has a 1 in 40 chance of being included in the sample. In most studies, the population from which the sample will be drawn is too large for a hat, so marketers generate a random sample from a list of members of the population using a computer program.

Sometimes researchers use a *systematic sampling procedure* to select members of a population in which they select the *n*th member of a population after a random start. For example, if we want a sample of 10 members of your class, we might begin with the second person on the role and select every fourth name after that, that is, the 2nd, the 6th, the 10th, the 14th, and so on. Researchers know that studies that use systematic samples are just as accurate as with simple random samples. Unless a list of members of the population of interest is already in a computer data file, it's a lot simpler to create a systematic sample.

Yet another type of probability sample is a *stratified sample* in which a researcher divides the population into segments that are related to the study's topic. For example, imagine that you are interested in studying what movies are most liked by members of a population. You know from previous studies that men and women in the population differ in their attitudes toward different types of movies—men like action flicks and women like romances. To create a stratified sample,

probability sample
A sample in which each member of the population has some known chance of being included.

you would first divide the population into male and female segments. Then respondents from each of the two segments would be selected randomly in proportion to their percentage of the population. In this way, you have created a sample that is proportionate to the population on a characteristic that you know will make a difference in the study results.

NONPROBABILITY SAMPLING   Sometimes researchers do not believe the time and effort required to develop a probability sample are justified, perhaps because they need an answer quickly or they just want to get a general sense of how people feel about a topic. They may choose a **nonprobability sample**, which entails the use of personal judgment in selecting respondents—in some cases just asking whomever they can find. With a nonprobability sample, some members of the population have no chance at all of being included in the sample. Thus, there is no way to ensure that the sample is representative of the population. Results from nonprobability studies can be generally suggestive of what is going on in the real world but not necessarily definitive.

nonprobability sample
A sample in which personal judgment is used in selecting respondents.

A *convenience sample* is a nonprobability sample composed of individuals who just happen to be available when and where the data are being collected. For example, if you simply stand in front of the student union and ask students who walk by to complete your questionnaire, that would be a convenience sample.

In some cases, firms even use their own employees as a convenience sample or as "guinea pigs." When Gap Inc. was developing the concept for its chain of Old Navy stores, the company gave employees who fit the desired Old Navy customer profile $200 apiece. They set them loose on a shopping spree and then interviewed them about what they had bought so these products would be on Old Navy's shelves when the stores opened (nice work if you can get it!).[31]

Finally, researchers may also use a *quota sample* that includes the same proportion of individuals with certain characteristics as is found in the population. For example, if you are studying attitudes of students in your university, you might just go on campus and find freshmen, sophomores, juniors, and seniors in proportion to the number of members of each class in the university. The quota sample is much like the stratified sample except that with a quota sample, individual members of the sample are selected through personal judgment as they are in a convenience sample.

Step 5: Collect the Data

At this point, the researcher has determined the nature of the problem that needs to be addressed. He or she has decided on a research design that will specify how to investigate the problem and what kinds of information (data) will be needed. The researcher has also selected the data collection and sampling methods. Once these decisions have been made, the next task is to actually collect the data.

Although collecting data may seem like a simple process, researchers are well aware of its critical importance to the accuracy of research. When interviewers are involved, researchers know that the quality of research results is only as good as the poorest interviewer collecting the data. Careless interviewers may not read questions exactly as written, or they may not record respondent answers correctly. So marketers must train and supervise interviewers to make sure they follow the research procedures exactly as outlined. In this section, we'll talk about some of the problems in gathering data and some solutions.

GATHERING DATA IN FOREIGN COUNTRIES   Conducting market research around the world is big business for U.S. firms. Among the top 50 U.S. research firms, nearly 50 percent of revenues come from projects outside the United States.[32] However, market conditions and consumer preferences vary worldwide, and there are major differences in the sophistication of market research operations and the amount of data available to global marketers. For example, there are still large areas in Mexico where native Indian tribes speak languages other than Spanish, so researchers may bypass these groups in surveys.[33]

For these reasons and others, choosing an appropriate data collection method is difficult. In some countries, many people may not have phones, or low literacy rates may interfere with mail surveys. Local customs can be a problem as well. Offering money for interviews is rude in Latin American countries.[34] Saudi Arabia bans gatherings of four or more people except for family or religious events, and it's illegal to stop strangers on the street or knock on the door of someone's house.[35]

Cultural differences also affect responses to survey items. Both Danish and British consumers, for example, agree that it is important to eat breakfast, but the Danish sample may be thinking of fruit and yogurt while the British sample is thinking of toast and tea. Sometimes marketers can overcome these problems by involving local researchers in decisions about the research design.

Another problem with conducting marketing research in global markets is language. Sometimes translations just don't come out right. A sign at a Tokyo hotel once read, "You are invited to take advantage of the chambermaid," and a dry cleaner in Majorca urged passing customers to "drop your pants here for best results."[36] It is not uncommon for researchers to mistranslate questionnaires or for entire subcultures within a country to be excluded from research. In fact, this issue is becoming more and more prevalent inside the United States as non-English speakers increase as a percentage of the population.

To overcome language difficulties, researchers use a process called **back-translation**, which requires two steps. First, a native speaker translates the questionnaire into the language of the targeted respondents. Then this new version is translated back into the original language to ensure that the correct meanings survive the process. Even with precautions such as these, however, researchers must interpret data obtained from other cultures with care.

SINGLE-SOURCE DATA   One research issue that marketers have been trying to solve for years is knowing what impact each piece of their marketing mix is having on their total marketing strategy. Short of moving in with a family for a few months, marketers had no way to determine the effect of multiple promotional activities. Today, though, sophisticated technology allows researchers to gather data from actual store transactions that they can then trace to different components of the marketing mix.

The term **single-source data** refers to information that is integrated from large consumer panels comprised of people who agree to participate in ongoing research. In single-source systems, data on purchasing behavior and advertising exposure are measured for members of the consumer panel using electronic television meters, retail scanners, and split-cable technology in which different customers on a television cable system can be exposed to different ads. Because single-source systems can measure the impact of a number of different marketing activities in combination, they allow marketers to monitor the impact of many marketing communications on a particular customer group over time. For example, a firm that sells laundry detergent might use single-source systems to answer the following questions:

- Which consumer segments are more likely to be brand loyal, and which segments frequently switch brands of laundry detergent?
- Are coupons or price-off packs more likely to increase sales?
- Does increased advertising exposure influence brand switching?
- What is the total effect of increased advertising and the use of coupons?

A lot of single-source data come from checkout scanners in stores. In addition to speeding up your checkout time, those funny-looking little machines are storing a record of just how

back-translation
The process of translating material to a foreign language and then back to the original language.

single-source data
Information that is integrated from large consumer panels comprised of people who agree to participate in ongoing research.

Checkout scanners enable marketers to collect single-source data.

many bags of munchies you bought and what brands you chose. Combined with records from the store's other customers (and buyers at other locations), this is a potential pot of gold for firms willing to invest in the research needed to track all those millions of transactions. This technology is becoming so popular that up to 90 percent of apparel, electronics, and grocery purchases in the United States are scanned, and some companies are following up on the wealth of information sitting in their databases. For example, the grocery chain Safeway tracks the purchases of regular customers who show a Savings Club card when they get to the register. Every other week, these shoppers get a mail packet with coupons tailored to their individual purchases. So heavy users of hot dogs might be delighted to find cents-off coupons for mustard in their mailboxes.

Step 6: Analyze and Interpret the Data

Once marketing researchers have collected the data, what's next? It's like a spin on the old "if a tree falls in the woods" question: "If results exist but there's no one to interpret them, do they have a meaning?" Well, let's leave the philosophers out of it and just say that marketers would answer "no." Data need analysis for them to have meaning.

To understand the important role of data analysis, let's take a look at a hypothetical research example. In our example, a company that markets frozen foods wishes to better understand consumers' preference for varying levels of fat content in their diets. They have conducted a descriptive research study in which they collected primary data via telephone interviews. Because they recognize that gender is related to dietary preferences, they have used a stratified sample that includes 175 males and 175 females.

Typically, marketers first tabulate the data as shown in Table 4.4—that is, they arrange the data in a table or other summary form so they can get a broad picture of the overall responses. The data in this table show that 43 percent of the sample prefers a low-fat meal. In addition, there may be a desire to cross-classify or cross-tabulate the answers to questions by other variables.

Table 4.4   Examples of Data Tabulation and Cross-Tabulation Tables

Fat Content Preference
(number and percentages of responses)

Questionnaire Response	Number of Responses	Percentage of Responses
Do you prefer a meal with high fat content, medium fat content, or low fat content?		
High fat	21	6
Medium fat	179	51
Low fat	150	43
Total	350	100

Fat Content Preference by Gender
(number and percentages of responses)

Questionnaire	Number Females	Percentage of Females	Number Males	Percentage of Males	Total Number	Total Percentage
Do you prefer a meal with high fat content, medium fat content, or low fat content?						
High fat	4	2	17	10	21	6
Medium fat	68	39	111	64	179	51
Low fat	103	59	47	27	150	43
Total	175	100	175	100	350	100

Cross-tabulation means that the data are examined by subgroups, in this case males and females separately, to see how results vary between categories. The cross-tabulation in Table 4.4 shows that 59 percent of females versus only 27 percent of males prefer a meal with low-fat content. In addition, researchers may wish to apply additional statistical tests, which you'll learn about in subsequent courses (something to look forward to).

Based on the tabulation and cross-tabulations, the researcher must then interpret or draw conclusions from the results and make recommendations. For example, the study results shown in Table 4.4 may lead to the conclusion that females are more likely than males to be concerned about a low-fat diet. The researcher might then make a recommendation to a firm that it should target females in the introduction of a new line of low-fat foods.

Step 7: Prepare the Research Report

The final step in the marketing research process is to prepare a report of the research results. In general, a research report must clearly and concisely tell the readers—top management, clients, creative departments, and many others—what they need to know in a way that they can easily understand. In general, a research report will include these sections:

- An executive summary of the report that covers the high points of the total report
- An understandable description of the research methodology
- A complete discussion of the results of the study, including the tabulations, cross-tabulations, and additional statistical analyses
- Limitations of the study (no study is perfect)
- Conclusions drawn from the results and the recommendations for managerial action based on the results

Online Research

The growth of the Internet is rewriting some of the rules of the marketing research process. As more and more people have access to the Web, many companies are finding that the Internet is a superior way to collect data—it's fast, it's relatively cheap, and it lends itself well to forms of research from simple questionnaires to online focus groups. General Mills, for example, is a true believer in online research. The online research industry took in between $1 billion and $1.25 billion in 2002—roughly 20 percent of the total marketing research market.[37] Developments in online research are happening quickly, and it's worth taking some time at the end of this chapter to see how the trend is going.

The Web is revolutionizing the way many companies collect data and use the data to guide their marketing decisions. There are two major types of online research. One type is information gathered by tracking consumers while they are surfing. The second type is information gathered through questionnaires on Web sites, through e-mail, or from moderated focus groups conducted in chat rooms.

Online Tracking

The Internet offers an unprecedented ability to track consumers as they search for information. Marketers can better understand where people go to look when they want to learn about products and services—and which advertisements they stop to browse along the way. How can marketers do this? One way is by the use of cookies. Beware the Cookie Monster! **Cookies** are text files inserted by a Web site sponsor into a user's hard drive when the user connects with the site. Cookies remember details of a visit to a Web site, typically tracking which pages the user visits. Some sites request or require that visitors "register" on the site by answering questions about themselves and their likes and dislikes. In such cases, cookies also allow the site to access these details about the customer.

This technology allows Web sites to customize services, such as when Amazon.com recommends new books to users on the basis of what books they have ordered in the past. Most consumers have no idea that cookies allow Web sites to gather and store all this information. You can block cookies or curb them, although this can make life difficult if you are trying to log on to many sites, such as online newspapers or travel agencies that require this information to admit you.

WHO OWNS YOUR COOKIES? This information generated from tracking consumers' online journeys has become a product as well—companies sell these consumer data to other companies that are trying to target prospects. But consumers have become increasingly concerned about the sharing of these data. In a study of 10,000 Web users, 84 percent objected to the reselling of their information to

Why?

Because he thinks plaid is slimming. Because the chain makes him feel young again. Because he believes the world needs more purple.

You might not understand this guy. But you will.

Contact the Harris Interactive Qualitative Research Practice at **877.919.4765**. *We'll explore him together.*

To learn more, check out our free Online Demo at **www.harrisinteractive.com/qual**

*Harris*Interactive®
MARKET RESEARCH
The Harris Poll® PEOPLE

www.harrisinteractive.com Tel 877.919.4765
©2004, Harris Interactive Inc. All rights reserved. 36USC220506 EOE M/F/D/V 02.04

Marketing researchers carefully analyze data to better understand the profiles of different customer groups.

cookies
Text files inserted by a Web site sponsor into a Web surfer's hard drive that allow the site to track the surfer's moves.

Advice for RBC Centura Bank

STUDENT
ADEL SAKR
Auburn University

I would choose option 3, purchasing software that could be customized to Royal Bank's specific market research needs and linked to its customer database. This solution would result in long-term benefits for the bank. First, by purchasing software that could be customized to the bank's specific market research needs, the bank will not temporarily take advantage of the industry experience but will actually "own" it and control it. Furthermore, the software will be added to the bank's assets. Second, the efforts required by the bank's personnel to customize the new software can be included as part of a human resources training and development program. In this way, personnel's efforts can be valued, and they can also benefit professionally. Third, while different market vendors will be evaluated for the new software, the bank can continue to use the current profitability model based on "average" to evaluate its customers. In this way there will be no wasted time.

PROFESSOR
NANCY M. PUCCINELLI (UPTON)
Suffolk University

I would choose option 3. Purchasing customized software would enable Royal Bank to effectively gather the customer specific data needed to achieve their goal of assessing individual customer profitability. This option would allow them to benefit from existing market research insights, give them control over access to the data, and enable them to manage (as opposed to "demarket") unprofitable customers. While this option represents a significant investment of time and resources for Royal Bank, this investment makes good sense given the bank's size, the "largest financial institution in Canada," and "substantial personal customer base." Further, having data collection managed in-house and working with an experienced firm to streamline any customer interface should help prevent any customer privacy concerns. Should such concerns arise, Royal Bank might highlight how this technological investment will enable Royal Bank to better serve their customers. Considering this situation more broadly, as CRM systems increase in popularity, more and more organizations face dilemmas like that at Royal Bank. Development of such technology entails significant investment of time and money, and companies can find it difficult to identify the return on investment. Thus, when considering such an investment in market research, it is critical to consider the value of data to be yielded: (1) the quality of the data, (2) the research question the data answers, and (3) the link of the findings to the bottom line.

other companies. Although Internet users can delete cookie files manually or install anticookie software on their computers, there are many people who feel there is a need for privacy regulation and for cookie regulation in order to limit potential abuses.

To date, the Federal Trade Commission has relied on the Internet industry to develop and maintain its own standards instead of developing extensive privacy regulations, but many would like to see that situation changed. Privacy rights proponents advocate the following:

- Information about a consumer belongs to the consumer.
- Consumers should be made aware of information collection.
- Consumers should know how information about them will be used.
- Consumers should be able to refuse to allow information collection.
- Information about a consumer should never be sold or given to another party without the permission of the consumer.

COREMETRICS

OA 2004 LOGIN   CLIENT SUPPORT

→ SOLUTIONS   → TECHNOLOGY   → CLIENTS   → PARTNERS   → COMPANY

COUNT EVERY CLICK
MAKE EVERY CLICK COUNT

Coremetrics helps companies increase eBusiness profitability by
developing and acting upon a comprehensive understanding
of all online visitor and customer interactions.

→ LEARN MORE

COREMETRICS NAMED #1
BY FORRESTER RESEARCH

FORRESTER

Why Web Site Analytics Matter
Read the Full Report Here
→ GO

Coremetrics specializes in tracking the online behavior of all visitors to their clients' Web sites in order to help marketers understand how their current and potential customers interact with their Web site.

Online Testing, Questionnaires, and Focus Groups

The Internet offers a faster, less expensive alternative to traditional communication data collection methods. Here are some ways companies are using the Internet to get feedback from consumers:

- **New-product development:** Procter & Gamble spent more than five years testing products such as Febreze, Dryel, and Fit Fruit & Vegetable Wash the old-fashioned way before launching nationally. Using online tests, its Crest MultiCare Flex & Clean toothbrush was launched in less than a year. General Motors and Nissan are two automakers that now gather online consumer reactions to upcoming products. Such research allows manufacturers to learn what consumers want in future vehicles.[38]

- **Estimating market response:** A few cutting-edge companies are creating virtual worlds and using them to test consumers' responses to brands. Using "There-bucks," people who sign up to join the virtual community at There.com can choose to "buy" products like Levi's Type I jeans or Nike's high-end Zoom Celar shoes on the site. Companies can then analyze who chose to buy which brands and which activities they engaged in while on the site (e.g., do people who select the Levi's style tend to spend a lot of time socializing in There clubs that are available on the site?).[39]

- **Exploratory research:** Conducting focus groups online has mushroomed in popularity in recent years. For example, Procter & Gamble's Web site (**www.pg.com**) includes a Try & Buy New Products section that sells Proctor & Gamble products still being test-marketed and directs consumers to virtual, real-time focus groups.[40]

Of course, with online groups it is impossible to observe body language, facial expressions, and vocal inflection. But marketers continue to develop new ways to talk to consumers in virtual space, including software that allows online focus group participants to indicate nonverbal responses. For example, an online participant can register an expression of disgust by clicking on the command to "roll eyes."[41]

Many marketing research companies are running, not walking, to the Web to conduct studies for clients. Why? For one thing, replacing

Security

Security is MCI's wholly owned, seamless network, which offers end-to-end protection.

Security is MCI's award-winning Security Operations Center, delivering best-in-class defense against worms, viruses and other malicious intrusions.*

Security is MCI's proactive audit and analysis of over a million firewall log messages per day.

Security is secure with today's MCI.

MCI
www.mci.com

*Based on 2003 Security Technology Leadership Awards—The SANS Institute.

In focus groups and interviews about online shopping, consumers consistently rate security as their number one concern. MCI uses this knowledge to focus its message on the reliability of its product in blocking "worms, viruses, and other malicious intrusions."

ithinkinc.com

Just who really is answering your online survey?

With 7 years of online panel experience, we know our ithinkers

> Our panel was built one person at a time — Never through webmaster referral programs, co-registrations or mass web-site intercepts

> Respondent survey answers are validated against stored demographic information for consistency and accuracy

> Security, privacy and double opt-in best practices are strictly enforced

> Approximately 1.4 million US household members

> Survey programming and hosting also available for start-to-finish fielding solutions

[i.think_inc.]

www.ithinkinc.com   2811 McKinney Ave., Suite 218   Dallas, TX 75204   [214] 855-3777

Online research represents a large percentage of marketing research today.

traditional mail consumer panels with Internet panels allows marketers to collect the same amount of data in a weekend that used to take six to eight weeks. And consumers can complete surveys when it is convenient—even at 3 A.M. in their pajamas. There are other advantages: Large studies can be conducted at low cost. International borders are not a problem, either, since in many countries (e.g., in Scandinavia) Internet use is very high and it's easy to recruit respondents. Web-based interviews eliminate interviewer bias or errors in data entry.[42]

However, no data collection method is perfect, and online research is no exception—though many of the criticisms of online techniques also apply to off-line techniques. One potential problem is the representativeness of the respondents. Although the number of Internet users continues to grow, many segments of the consumer population, mainly the poor and elderly, do not have equal access to the Internet. In addition, in many studies (just as with mail surveys or mall intercepts) there is a *self-selection bias* in the sample in that respondents have agreed to receive invitations to take part in online studies, which means they tend to be the kind of people who like to participate in surveys. As with other kinds of research such as live focus groups, it's not unusual to encounter "professional respondents"—people who just enjoy taking part in studies (and getting paid for it). Online firms such as Harris Interactive, Survey Sampling, or Greenfield Online address this problem by monitoring their participants and regulating how often they are allowed to participate in different studies over a period of time.

There are other disadvantages of online research. Hackers can actually try to influence research results. Even more dangerous may be competitors who can learn about a firm's marketing plans, products, advertising, and so forth by intercepting information used in research. Despite the potential drawbacks, online research has a bright future. Indeed, it has the potential to take off even faster as a result of the 2001 terrorist attacks since many people are more hesitant to answer questions from strangers, drive to focus group facilities, or open mail surveys from sources they don't recognize.

real people, real choices
How It Worked Out at RBC Centura Bank

Cathy decided that the new CRM program required a tracking tool that could obtain detailed information about the bank's customers, so hiring a service bureau would not work. She still considered the possibility of developing her own tracking tool internally, while she also began a market review to identify companies that might provide software that could be customized to the bank's needs. She learned about a new application called *Value Analyzer* being developed by her former employer, NCR Teradata, to analyze customer profitability.

   Since RBC Royal Bank already used Teradata data warehousing capabilities to maintain its marketing and customer information database, Cathy thought that integrating data with the new application would be relatively easy. The *Value Analyzer* software was designed to combine all existing information on clients' activities, behaviors, and related transactions, accounts, and products. And the software would be regularly updated by the vendor, so the bank would not have to use internal resources for redevelopment.

After analyzing early results using the *Value Analyzer* software, the bank was able to identify much more clearly which of its offerings were valued by customers and which of its customers were the most attractive targets for gaining additional business. The cost and effort involved in developing a very sophisticated marketing research system that tracked costs and revenues linked to specific customers paid off royally for Royal Bank as it entered the new age of CRM.

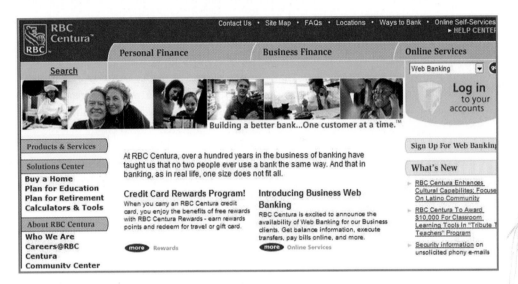

Royal Centura Bank offers many banking options to its customers, but now sophisticated marketing research techniques help the company to identify which specific services are likely to be most profitable for specific customers.

Do you know how to research careers to find one that matches your interests, values, and strengths? Once you've targeted a profession, do you know how to find the employers who need your skills? To learn how to find that dream job—or just get started on your career path, go to Chapter 4, in *Brand You*.

CHAPTER SUMMARY

1. **Understand the role of the marketing information system and the marketing decision support system in marketing decision making.** A marketing information system (MIS) is composed of internal data, marketing intelligence, marketing research data, acquired databases, and computer hardware and software. Firms use an MIS to gather, sort, analyze, store, and distribute information needed by managers for marketing decision making. The marketing decision support system (MDSS) allows managers to use analysis software and interactive software to access MIS data and to conduct analyses and find the information they need.

2. **Describe the marketing research process.** The research process begins by defining the problem and determining the research design or type of study. Next, researchers choose the data collection method, that is, whether there are secondary data available or if primary research with a communication study or through observation is necessary. Then researchers

determine what type of sample is to be used for the study and then collect the data. The final steps in the research are to analyze and interpret the data and prepare a research report.

3. **Understand the differences among exploratory, descriptive, and causal research and describe some research techniques available to marketers.** Exploratory research typically uses qualitative data collected by individual interviews, focus groups, or observational methods such as ethnography. Descriptive research includes cross-sectional and longitudinal studies. Causal research goes a step further by designing controlled experiments in order to understand cause-and-effect relationships between marketing independent variables, such as price changes, and dependent variables, such as sales.

4. **Describe the different types of data collection methods and types of samples that researchers use.** Researchers may choose to collect data using mail questionnaires, telephone interviews, face-to-face interviews, or online questionnaires. A study may utilize a probability sample such as a simple random or stratified sample in which inferences can be made to a population on the basis of sample results. Nonprobability sampling methods include a convenience sample and a quota sample. The research tries to ensure that the data are valid, reliable, and representative. Validity is the extent to which the research actually measures what it was intended to measure. Reliability is the extent to which the research measurement techniques are free of errors. Representativeness is the extent to which consumers in the study are similar to a larger group in which the organization has an interest.

5. **Understand the growing use of online research.** Marketers increasingly are using the Internet for online research. Online tracking uses cookies to record where consumers go on a Web site. Consumers have become increasingly concerned about privacy and how this information is used and made available to other Internet companies. The Internet also provides an attractive alternative to traditional communication data collection methods because of its speed and low cost. Many firms use the Internet to conduct online focus groups.

KEY TERMS

back-translation, 122
case study, 113
causal research, 114
consumer interviews, 111
cookies, 125
cross-sectional design, 114
custom research, 104
data mining, 106
descriptive research, 113
ethnography, 113
experiments, 114
exploratory research, 110

focus group, 111
intranet, 101
longitudinal design, 114
marketing decision support system (MDSS), 105
marketing information system (MIS), 101
marketing intelligence system, 102
marketing research, 103
nonprobability sample, 121
primary data, 110
probability sample, 120

projective techniques, 112
reliability, 118
representativeness, 119
research design, 109
sampling, 119
scenarios, 103
secondary data, 109
single-source data, 122
syndicated research, 103
telemarketing, 117
validity, 118

CHAPTER REVIEW

MARKETING CONCEPTS: TESTING YOUR KNOWLEDGE

1. What is a marketing information system (MIS)? What types of information are included in a marketing information system? How does a marketing decision support system (MDSS) allow marketers to easily get the information they need?

2. What is data mining? How is it used by marketers?

3. What are the steps in the marketing research process? Why is defining the problem to be researched so important to ultimate success with the research project?

4. What techniques are used to gather data in exploratory research? How can exploratory research be useful to marketers?

5. What are some advantages and disadvantages of telephone interviews, mail questionnaires, face-to-face interviews, and online interviews?

6. When considering data quality, what are the differences among validity, reliability, and representativeness? How do you know data have high levels of these characteristics?

7. How do probability and nonprobability samples differ? What are some types of probability samples? What are some types of nonprobability samples?

8. What is a cross-tabulation? How are cross-tabulations useful in analyzing and interpreting data?

9. What is a cookie? What ethical and privacy issues are related to cookies?

10. What important issues must researchers consider when planning to collect their data online?

MARKETING CONCEPTS: DISCUSSING CHOICES AND ISSUES

1. Some marketers attempt to disguise themselves as marketing researchers when their real intent is to sell something to the consumer. What is the impact of this practice on legitimate researchers? What do you think might be done about this practice?

2. Do you think marketers should be allowed to conduct market research with young children? Why or why not?

3. Are you willing to divulge personal information to marketing researchers? How much are you willing to tell, or where would you draw the line?

4. What is your overall attitude toward marketing research? Do you think it is a beneficial activity from a consumer's perspective? Or do you think it merely gives marketers new insights on how to convince consumers to buy something they really don't want or need?

5. Sometimes firms use data mining to identify and abandon customers who are not profitable because they don't spend enough to justify the service needed or because they return a large proportion of the items they buy. What do you think of such practices? Is it ethical for firms to prune out these customers?

6. Many consumers are concerned about online tracking studies and their privacy. Do consumers have the right to "own" data about themselves? Should governments limit the use of the Internet for data collection?

7. One unobtrusive measure mentioned in this chapter involved going through consumers' or competitors' garbage. Do you think marketers should have the right to do this? Is it ethical?

MARKETING PRACTICE: APPLYING WHAT YOU'VE LEARNED

1. Your firm is planning to begin marketing a consumer product in several global markets. You have been given the responsibility of developing plans for marketing research to

be conducted in South Africa, in Spain, and in China. In a role-playing situation, present the difficulties you expect to encounter, if any, in conducting research in each of these areas.

2. As an account executive with a marketing research firm, you are responsible for deciding on the type of research to be used in various studies conducted for your clients. For each of the following client questions, list your choices of research approaches.
   a. Will television or magazine advertising be more effective for a local bank to use in its marketing communication plan?
   b. Could a new package design for dry cereal do a better job at satisfying the needs of customers and, thus, increase sales?
   c. Are consumers more likely to buy brands that are labeled as environmentally friendly?
   d. How do female consumers determine if a particular perfume is right for them?
   e. What types of people read the local newspaper?
   f. How frequently do consumers switch brands of soft drinks?
   g. How will an increase in the price of a brand of laundry detergent affect sales?
   h. What are the effects of advertising and sales promotion in combination on sales of a brand of shampoo?

3. Your marketing research firm is planning to conduct surveys to gather information for a number of clients. Your boss has asked you and a few other new employees to do some preliminary work. He has asked each of you to choose three of the topics (from among those listed next) that will be included in the project and to prepare an analysis of the advantages and disadvantages of these communication methods of collecting data: mail questionnaires, telephone interviews, face-to-face interviews, and online questionnaires.
   a. The amount of sports nutrition drinks consumed in a city
   b. Why a local bank has been losing customers
   c. How heavily the company should invest in manufacturing and marketing home fax machines
   d. The amount of money being spent "over the state line" for lottery tickets
   e. What local doctors would like to see changed in the hospitals in the city
   f. Consumers' attitudes toward several sports celebrities

4. For each of the topics you selected in item 3, how might a more passive (observation) approach be used to support the communication methods employed?

MARKETING MINIPROJECT: LEARNING BY DOING

The purpose of this miniproject is to familiarize you with marketing research techniques and to help you apply these techniques to managerial decision making.

1. With a group of three other students in your class, select a small retail business or fast-food restaurant to use as a "client" for your project. (Be sure to get the manager's permission before conducting your research.) Then choose a topic from among the following possibilities to develop a study problem:

   - Employee–customer interactions
   - The busiest periods of customer activity
   - Customer perceptions of service
   - Customer likes and dislikes about offerings
   - Customer likes and dislikes about the environment in the place of business
   - The benefits customers perceive to be important
   - The age-groups that frequent the place of business
   - The buying habits of a particular age-group
   - How customer complaints are handled

2. Develop a plan for the research.
   a. Define the problem as you will study it
   b. Choose the type of research you will use
   c. Select the techniques you will use to gather data
   d. Develop the mode and format for data collection
3. Conduct the research.
4. Write a report (or develop a class presentation) that includes four parts.
   a. Introduction: a brief overview of the business and the problem studied
   b. Methodology: the type of research used, the techniques used to gather data (and why they were chosen), the instruments and procedures used, the number of respondents, duration of the study, and other details that would allow someone to replicate your study
   c. Results: a compilation of the results (perhaps in table form) and the conclusions drawn
   d. Recommendations: a list of recommendations for actions management might take based on the conclusions drawn from the study

REAL PEOPLE, REAL SURFERS: EXPLORING THE WEB

As discussed in this chapter, monitoring changes in demographics and other consumer trends is an important part of the marketing intelligence included in an MIS. Today, much of this information is gathered by government research and is available on the Internet.

The U.S. Census Bureau provides tabled data for cities and counties across the nations at its site, **www.census.gov**. The *Statistical Abstract of the United States* is available at **www.census.gov/prod/2/gen/96statab.96statab.html**. In addition, most states produce their own statistical abstract publications that are available on the Web. For example, the *New York Statistical Abstract* is available at **www.columbia.edu/cu/libraries/indiv/dsc/nys/html**, the *California Statistical Abstract* is at **www.dof.ca.gov/html/fs_data/stat-abs/sa_home.htm**, and the *South Carolina Statistical Abstract* is at **www.state.sc.us/drss/pop**.

You should be able to locate the statistical abstract for your state by using a search engine. Using both state data and U.S. Census data, develop a report on a city or county of your choice that answers these questions:

1. What is the total population of the city or county?
2. Describe the population of the area in terms of age, income, education, ethnic background, marital status, occupation, and housing.
3. How does the city or county compare to the demographic characteristics of the entire U.S. population?
4. What is your opinion of the different Web sites you used? How useful are they to marketers? How easy were they to navigate? Was there information that you wanted that was not available? Was there more or less information from the sites than you anticipated? Explain.

MARKETING PLAN EXERCISE

Select a company that produces a product that you use and with which you are familiar. For the company to make decisions about developing new products and attracting new customers, it must rely on marketing research. These decisions feed into the company's marketing plan. For the firm you selected:

1. Define one specific problem they could address through marketing research.
2. What type of research design do you recommend for addressing that problem, and why?
3. What is the most appropriate way to collect the data? Justify your choice.
4. How will you ensure high validity, reliability, and representativeness of the data?
5. Design an appropriate sampling plan.

Marketing in Action Case

Real Choices at Acxiom

Do you know where your information is being stored? Not just any information but *personal* information, like name, address, phone number, date of birth, social security number, credit card numbers and what you purchase with those credit cards, how much you paid for your car, and how much you still owe on it. The list goes on and on. We'll bet you had no idea this personal information is being collected and stored by a company in Little Rock, Arkansas, called Acxiom.

Acxiom is the world's largest processor of consumer data, collecting and analyzing more than *one billion* records a day. The companies providing Acxiom with this huge source of information include nine of the 10 largest credit card issuers, nearly all the major retail banks, insurance companies, and automakers. It seems that if you buy anything on credit or take out a loan of any kind, there is a digital file with your name on it in Acxiom's database. Indeed, search the "white pages" from **www.msn.com** for any person in the country, and you will find Acxiom's name at the bottom of the listing as the "source."

But what is it that Acxiom provides its clients that the clients cannot provide for themselves? First, Acxiom provides clients with the advantages of maintaining an internal data system without the hassles of doing it themselves. Second, as a source of marketing intelligence, Acxiom provides its clients with a means of accessing and manipulating its vast stores of information for insights on what is happening in the marketplace. By allowing this access, companies are able to engage in data mining; they use the results to implement customer retention programs with special offers and inducements for purchasing even more products or services. Third, Acxiom gives its clients the opportunity to conduct market analyses to determine which customers may be open to buying complementary products to what has already been purchased. Pretty powerful stuff.

Even though Acxiom's business provides a valuable service to its clients, there are still many problems associated with it. Obviously, in an industry where such personal information is being collected and stored digitally, data security is a concern. In fact, recently, investigators in Cincinnati found numerous compact discs containing the personal data of millions of Americans that someone obtained by hacking into Acxiom's database. Clearly, more needs to be done in terms of data security, but the question remains: How can Acxiom add security while still providing clients the access and data manipulation tools necessary to gain real insight from the information?

There are numerous ethical implications associated with having such sensitive personal information in a format convenient for hackers to access. In addition, there is the question of who really owns the data— Acxiom or their clients who give them the opportunity to collect and store it? If the data are not Acxiom's to sell, could they use those data as a product offering to the government? No doubt, as a company that relies on providing consumer research services and capabilities, Acxiom must make a decision about how it approaches these security problems. Otherwise, it will become more and more a target for government and consumer complaints, which no doubt will stifle its growth. How company executives decide these issues will determine the future of this company and perhaps the industry as a whole.

Things to Think About

1. What is the decision facing Acxiom?
2. What factors are important in understanding the decision situation?
3. What are the alternatives?
4. What decision(s) do you recommend?
5. What are some ways to implement your recommendation(s)?

Source: Richard Behar, "Never Heard of Acxiom? Chances Are It's Heard of You," *Fortune*, February 23, 2004, 140–48.

WILD PLANET

WELCOME TO WILD PLANET TOYS!

deutsch   español   français

WHAT'S NEW

Scope out new Spy Gear™ Shorts!
Only at Gapkids.com!
Read More...

Cool Down In The Sun!
Buy Wild Planet Summer & Water Toys Online!
Read More...

Meet the Aquapets!

SPY GEAR
VISIT SITE >

gls
Girls Living in Style
VISIT SITE >

Off THE MAP
Discover Your Own Adventure!
VISIT SITE >

OUTDOOR ANTICS!
VISIT SITE >

aquapets
VISIT SITE >

VISIT SITE >

www.wildplanet.com

real people, real choices

meet Daniel Grossman, a Decision Maker at Wild Planet

first job out of school	what i do when i am not working
Congressional aide to Congressman James Coyne in Washington, D.C.	Wrestle with my two sons.

CONSUMER BEHAVIOR: HOW AND WHY PEOPLE BUY

Daniel Grossman is the chief executive officer and founder of Wild Planet Toys. Prior to founding Wild Planet in 1993, Daniel was the director of international marketing for Aviva Sports. In that role, he was responsible for establishing Aviva's sales and marketing network with Mattel International and other distributors. Daniel earned a BA in Russian and East European studies from Yale University and an MBA from Stanford University. He also served seven years in the U.S. Foreign Service as a diplomat both overseas and at the Department of State. He has served on numerous nonprofit boards, including Stand for Children and the Toy Industry Association, where he serves currently as vice chair.

Decision Time at Wild Planet

Understanding kids and their needs lies at the core of Wild Planet's mission. Daniel Grossman founded the company with the goal of creating brands and products that parents would endorse but that kids would find cool. For the past 10 years, the company has marketed products worldwide that were either inspired by kids or invented by them. In 1999, for example, Wild Planet purchased Short Stack, a company started by a 10-year-old boy who had an idea for an underwater talking device called

Water Talkies. After Wild Planet acquired Short Stack, it continued to develop and sell more kid-invented water toys. Eventually, Wild Planet started to turns kids' ideas into toys in several categories, including room decor, spy gadgets, and exploration gear, always crediting and compensating the children for their inventions.

To be sure that Wild Planet makes products that kids really want, Daniel and his colleagues meet with kids in their homes, hoping that this more relaxed environment will encourage honesty and freedom of thought. During one such series of discussions, they intended to focus on recent toy purchases by 8- to 10-year-olds. However, they found that the kids focused less on specific products than they did on their rooms. In an age of insecurity and increasing homework, a child's room has become his or her castle (or at least the dungeon!). Wild Planet quickly learned that today's kids spend a lot of their free time in their rooms and that they are personalizing their living spaces to differentiate themselves from other kids and make a unique personal statement about who they are.

The lessons from these rounds of discussions led Wild Planet to develop a product line called Room Gear. These items would let kids decorate their rooms with cool gear and gadgets. The signature item in the line was invented by a 12-year-old girl who submitted an idea to Wild Planet's Kid Inventor Challenge

career high	my motto	what drives me	my management style
Playing a role in securing the release of political prisoners in the Soviet Union.	"Do unto others."	Pursuit of justice and love of kids.	Hire great people, plan together with them, then trust them.

1 Define consumer behavior and explain the reasons why consumers buy what they buy.

2 Explain the prepurchase, purchase, and postpurchase activities consumers engage in when making decisions.

3 Describe how internal factors influence consumers' decision-making processes.

4 Understand how situational factors at the time and place of purchase influence consumer behavior.

5 Describe how consumers' relationships with other people influence their decision-making processes.

6 Understand how the Internet offers consumers opportunities to participate in consumer-to-consumer marketing.

(a national program to encourage kids to think creatively and to invent toys). This girl's toy, called Talk Time, was an alarm clock that allowed the user to record a greeting that then became the alarm. As Daniel and his colleagues talked with boys and girls about this idea, their response was very positive. Wild Planet developed the Room Gear line to appeal to both genders and launched it in 2002.

The market reaction to the Room Gear line was mixed; while some items sold well, the line did not seem to be as popular with kids as the company had hoped. Wild Planet executives knew they had identified the right trends, but they realized that they may have intertwined two distinct trends that had sharply different gender appeals. While boys like to embellish their rooms with cool new gadgets, girls lean more toward decoration and personalization. Wild Planet's "Lights Off" toy, which gives the power to turn off any light switch remotely, had a strong appeal to boys because the toy has more of a utilitarian, show-off function. On the other hand, the company developed a door alarm called "Keep Out" that appealed more to girls because it helped them maintain their privacy. As Daniel thought about this, he considered his options regarding the future direction of the Room Gear line:

OPTION 1: Acknowledge that Wild Planet had missed the mark and drop the line.

After all, the failure rate for new consumer products is generally high, but even higher for toys. Bailing out now would help the company avoid throwing "good money after bad" by walking away from the sunk cost. Wild Planet would gain credibility from the trade by accepting its mistakes and moving on. Of course, a retreat now also would mean walking away from a significant investment. And the company would lose any chance of taking advantage of the trend toward products that allow kids to personalize their rooms.

OPTION 2: Retain the existing line concept and develop more products along the lines of those that were already selling.

By doing this, Wild Planet could continue to try to get some return on the substantial investment it had made in developing the Room Gear line, and the company could continue to explore whether the "space personalization" trend would "grow legs." On the other hand, it seemed likely that just doing more of the same wouldn't let Wild Planet take advantage of what Daniel still believed was a new and growing phenomenon.

OPTION 3: Reposition the line toward either boys or girls, keying off the insight that each gender approaches the "decoration" of their rooms very differently.

This course would let Wild Planet hedge its bets because the concept might hit with either boys or girls if not both. Still, this choice might mean throwing good money after bad since the line hadn't performed very well to date. And Wild Planet's trading partners might not be happy if the company continued to develop customizable kids' products that wound up sitting on store shelves.

Now, put yourself in Daniel Grossman's shoes: Which option would you choose, and why?

Decisions, Decisions

consumer behavior
The process involved when individuals or groups select, purchase, use, and dispose of goods, services, ideas, or experiences to satisfy their needs and desires.

Compelling new products, clever packaging, and creative advertising surround us, clamoring for our attention—and our money. But consumers don't all respond in the same way. Each of us is unique, with our own reasons for choosing one product over another. Recall that the focus of the marketing concept is to satisfy consumers' wants and needs. To do that, we need to understand what those wants and needs are.

Consumer behavior is the process individuals or groups go through to select, purchase, use, and dispose of goods, services, ideas, or experiences to satisfy their needs and desires.

Marketers recognize that consumer decision making is an ongoing process—it's more than what happens at the moment a consumer forks over the cash and in turn receives a good or service.

Let's look at an example of a consumer purchase—one you yourself probably make on a regular basis: dry cereal. While this may seem like a simple purchase, in reality there are quite a few steps in the process that cereal marketers need to understand. The first decision in the process is where to buy your cereal. If you eat a lot of cereal, you may choose to make a special trip to a warehouse-type retailer that sells super-duper size boxes rather than just pick up a box while at the local supermarket. Of course, if you get a yen for cereal in the middle of the night, you may dash to the local convenience store. Then there is the decision of the type of cereal. Do you eat only low-fat, high-fiber bran cereals, or do you go for the sugarcoated varieties with marshmallows? Of course, you may also like to have a variety of different cereals available to choose from.

Marketers also need to know how and when you consume their products. Do you eat cereal only for breakfast, or do you snack on it while sitting in front of the TV at night? And what about storing the product (if it lasts that long)? Do you have a kitchen pantry where you can store the supersize box, or is space an issue?

And there's more. Marketers also need to understand the many factors that influence each of these steps in the consumer behavior process—internal factors unique to each of us, situational factors at the time of purchase, and the social influences of people around us. In this chapter, we'll talk about how all these factors influence how and why consumers do what they do. But first we'll look at the types of decisions consumers make and the steps in the decision-making process.

Steps in the Consumer Decision Process

Traditionally, researchers have tried to understand how consumers make decisions by assuming that people carefully collect information about competing products, determine which products possess the characteristics or product attributes important to their needs, weigh the pluses and minuses of each alternative, and arrive at a satisfactory decision. But how accurate is this picture of the decision-making process?

Although it does seem that people do undergo these steps when making an important purchase (such as buying a new car), is it realistic to assume that they do this for everything they buy (like that box of cereal)? Researchers now realize that decision makers actually possess a set of approaches ranging from painstaking analysis to pure whim, depending on the importance of what is being bought and how much effort the person is willing to put into the decision.[1] They have found it convenient to think in terms of an "effort" continuum that is anchored on one end by *habitual decision making* (such as deciding to purchase a box of cereal) and at the other end by *extended problem solving* (such as deciding to purchase a new car).

When consumers make very important decisions—such as buying a new house or a car—they engage in extended problem solving and carefully go through the steps outlined in Figure 5.1—problem recognition, information search, evaluation of alternatives, product choice, and postpurchase evaluation.

With habitual decision making, however, consumers make little or no conscious effort. They don't search for information, and they don't compare alternatives. Rather, they make purchases automatically. You may, for example, simply throw the same brand of cereal in your shopping cart week after week without thinking about it. Figure 5.2 provides a summary of the differences between extended problem solving and habitual decision making.

Many decisions fall somewhere in the middle and are characterized by *limited problem solving*, which means that consumers do *some* work to make a decision but not a great deal. This is probably how you decide on a new pair of running shoes or a new calculator for math class. We

Figure 5.1 The Consumer Decision-Making Process

The consumer decision-making process involves a series of steps that is summarized here.

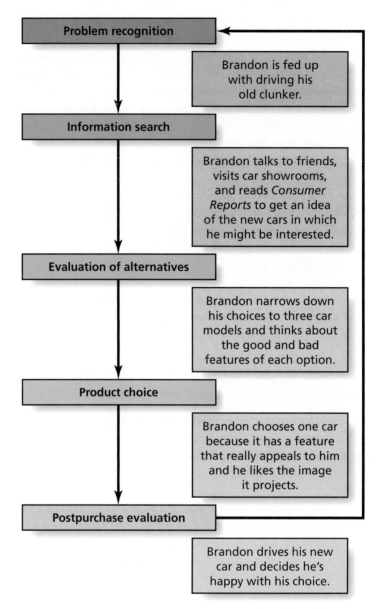

Problem recognition

Brandon is fed up with driving his old clunker.

Information search

Brandon talks to friends, visits car showrooms, and reads *Consumer Reports* to get an idea of the new cars in which he might be interested.

Evaluation of alternatives

Brandon narrows down his choices to three car models and thinks about the good and bad features of each option.

Product choice

Brandon chooses one car because it has a feature that really appeals to him and he likes the image it projects.

Postpurchase evaluation

Brandon drives his new car and decides he's happy with his choice.

---

often rely on simple "rules of thumb" instead of painstakingly learning all the ins and outs of every product alternative.

Just how much effort do we put into our buying decisions? The answer depends on our level of **involvement**—the importance of the perceived consequences of the purchase to the person. As a rule, we are more involved in the decision-making process for products that we think are risky in some way. **Perceived risk** may be present if the product is expensive or complex and hard to understand, such as a new computer or a sports car.

Perceived risk can also be a factor in product choice if choosing the wrong product results in embarrassment or social rejection. For example, a person who wears a pair of Doc Martens boots on a job interview may commit fashion suicide and jeopardize the job if the interviewer doesn't approve of this footwear.

When perceived risk is low, as in buying a box of cereal, the consumer feels low involvement in the decision-making process—she is not overly concerned about which option she

involvement
The relative importance of perceived consequences of the purchase to a consumer.

perceived risk
The belief that choice of a product has potentially negative consequences, either financial, physical, or social.

Figure 5.2 Extended Problem Solving versus Habitual Decision Making

	Extended Problem Solving	*Habitual Decision Making*
Product	New car	Box of cereal
Level of involvement	High (important decision)	Low (unimportant decision)
Perceived risk	High (expensive complex product)	Low (simple, low-cost product)
Information processing	Careful processing of information (search advertising, magazines, car dealers, Web sites)	Respond to environmental cues (store signage or displays)
Learning model	Cognitive learning (use insight and creativity to use information found in environment)	Behavioral learning (ad shows product in beautiful setting creating positive attitude)
Needed marketing actions	Provide information via advertising, salespeople, brochures, Web sites. Educate consumers to product benefits, risks of wrong decisions, etc.	Provide environmental cues at point of purchase such as product display

chooses because it is not especially important or risky. In low-involvement situations, the consumer's decision is often a response to environmental cues, such as when a person decides to try a new type of cereal because it's prominently displayed at the end of the grocery store aisle. Under these circumstances, managers must concentrate on how products are displayed at the time of purchase to influence the decision maker. For example, a cereal marketer may decide to spend extra money to be sure its cereal stands out at a store display or to change the packaging so consumers notice it.

For high-involvement purchases, such as buying a house or a car, the consumer is likely to carefully process all the available information and to have thought about the decision well before going to buy the item. The consequences of the purchase are important and risky, especially because a bad decision may result in significant financial losses, aggravation, or embarrassment. Most of us would not just walk into a real estate agent's office at lunchtime and casually plunk down a deposit on a new house. For high-involvement products, managers must start to reduce perceived risk by educating the consumer about why their product is the best choice well in advance of the time that the consumer is ready to make a decision.

To understand each of the steps in the decision-making process, in the next section we'll follow the fortunes of a consumer named Brandon, who, as shown in Figure 5.1, is in the market for a new car—a highly involving purchase decision, to say the least.

Step 1: Problem Recognition

Problem recognition occurs whenever a consumer sees a significant difference between her current state of affairs and some desired or ideal state. The consumer needs to solve a problem, which may be small or large, simple or complex. A woman whose 10-year-old Hyundai lives at the mechanic's shop has a problem, as does the man who thinks he'd have better luck getting dates if he traded his Hyundai for a new sports car. Brandon falls into the latter category—his old clunker runs okay, but he wants to sport some wheels that will get him admiring stares instead of laughs.

Do marketing decisions have a role in consumers' problem recognition? Although most problem recognition occurs spontaneously or when a true need arises, marketers can develop creative advertising messages that stimulate consumers to recognize that their current state—that old car—just doesn't equal their desired state—a shiny, new convertible. Figure 5.3 on page 141

problem recognition
The process that occurs whenever the consumer sees a significant difference between his or her current state of affairs and some desired or ideal state; this recognition initiates the decision-making process.

MAYBE THE BEST WAY TO HANDLE RISK
IS TO AVOID IT ALTOGETHER.

Business consumers may experience a high level of perceived risk for expensive items. Advertising such as this by Minolta for its copier seeks to reduce that risk.

information search
The process whereby a consumer searches for appropriate information to make a reasonable decision.

provides examples of marketers' responses to consumers' problem recognition and the other steps in the consumer decision-making process.

Step 2: Information Search

Once Brandon recognizes his problem (that he wants a newer car), he needs adequate information to resolve it. **Information search** is the step of the decision-making process in which the consumer checks his memory and surveys the environment to identify what options are out there that might solve his problem. Advertisements in newspapers, on TV or the radio, or even in the Yellow Pages or on the Internet often provide valuable guidance during this step. Brandon might rely on television ads about different cars, recommendations from his friends, and additional information he finds in *Consumer Reports*, at **www.caranddriver.com**, in brochures from car dealerships, or on the manufacturers' Web sites.

Increasingly, consumers are using Internet search engines, portals, or "shopping robots" to find information. Search engines, sites such as Google (**www.google.com**) and Excite (**www.excite.com**), help consumers locate useful information by searching millions of Web pages for key words and returning a list of sites that contain those key words. Shopping portals such as Yahoo! (**www.yahoo.com**) simplify searches by organizing information from many Web sites into topics or categories. Shopping robots, also called "shopbots," are software programs some Web sites use to find Internet retailers selling a particular product. The programs troll the Web for information and then "report" it back to the host site. Some of these sites also provide information on competitors' prices and ask customers to rate the retailers that they have listed on their site; this enables consumers to view both positive and negative feedback from other consumers.

The role of marketers during the information search step of the consumer decision-making process is to make the information consumers want and need about their product easily accessible. For example, marketers for automakers make sure information about their newest models is on the Web, is advertised frequently in magazines, radio, and TV, and, of course, is available in dealer showrooms.

Step 3: Evaluation of Alternatives

Once Brandon has identified his options, it's time to decide on a few true contenders. There are two components to this stage of the decision-making process. First, a consumer armed with information identifies a small number of products in which he is interested. Then he narrows down his choices by deciding which of all the possibilities are feasible and by comparing the pros and cons of each remaining option.

Brandon has always wanted a red Ferrari, but after allowing himself to daydream for a few minutes, he returns to reality and reluctantly admits that an Italian sports car is probably not in the cards for him right now. As he looks around, he decides that the cars he likes in his price range are the Saturn coupe, Ford Focus, and Honda Element. He's narrowed down his options by considering only affordable cars that come to mind or that his buddies suggest.

Now Brandon has to choose. It's time for him to look more systematically at each of the three possibilities and identify the important characteristics, or **evaluative criteria**, he will use to decide among them. The criteria may be power, comfort, price, the style of the car, or even safety. Keep in mind that marketers often play a role in educating consumers about *which* product characteristics they should use as evaluative criteria—usually, they will emphasize the dimensions in which their product excels. For example, ads for General Motors (GM) used cars stress how GM's 100-point inspection, warranty, roadside assistance, and satisfaction guarantee make buying a GM-certified used car a good decision. To make sure customers like Brandon come to the "right" conclusions in their evaluation of the alternatives, marketers must understand what criteria consumers use and

evaluative criteria
The dimensions used by consumers to compare competing product alternatives.

Figure 5.3 Marketers' Responses to Decision Process Stages

Stage in the Decision Process	Marketing Strategy	Example
Problem Recognition	Encourage consumers to see that existing state does not equal desired state	• TV commercials showing the excitement of owning a new car
Information Search	Provide information when and where consumers are likely to search	• Targeted advertising on TV programs with high target market viewership • Sales training that ensures knowledgeable salespeople • Make new car brochures available in dealer showrooms • Design exciting, easy-to-navigate, and informative Web sites
Evaluation of Alternatives	Understand the criteria consumers use in comparing brands and communicate own brand superiority	• Conduct research to identify most important evaluative criteria • Create advertising that includes reliable data on superiority of a brand (e.g., miles per gallon, safety, comfort)
Product Choice	Understand choice heuristics used by consumers and provide communication that encourages brand decision	• Advertise "Made in America" (country of origin) • Stress long history of the brand (brand loyalty)
Postpurchase Evaluation	Encourage accurate consumer expectations	• Provide honest advertising and sales presentations

which are more and which are less important. With this information, sales and advertising professionals can point out a brand's superiority on the most important criteria as they have defined them.

Step 4: Product Choice

After Brandon has examined his alternatives and gone on a few test drives, it's time to "put the pedal to the metal." Deciding on one product and acting on this choice is the next step in the decision-making process. After agonizing over his choice, Brandon decides that even though the Element and the Saturn have attractive qualities, the Focus has the affordability he needs and its carefree image is the way he wants others to think about him. All this thinking about cars is "driving" him crazy, and he's relieved to make a decision to buy the Focus and get on with his life.

How do consumers decide? Choices such as Brandon's often are complicated because it's hard to juggle all the product characteristics in your head. One car may offer better gas mileage, another is $2,000 cheaper, while another boasts a better safety record. How do we make sense of all these characteristics and arrive at a decision?

Consumers often rely on decision guidelines when weighing the claims that companies make. These **heuristics**, or rules, help simplify the decision-making process. One such heuristic is

heuristics
A mental rule of thumb that leads to a speedy decision by simplifying the process.

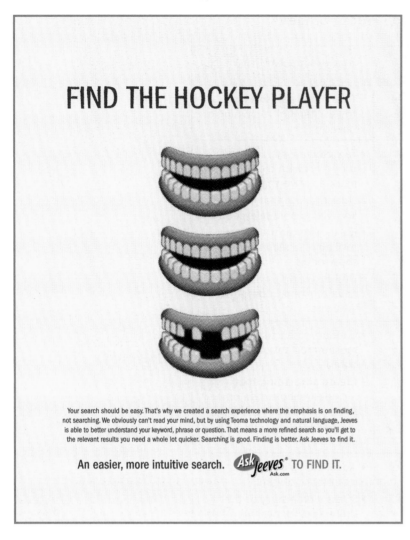

FIND THE HOCKEY PLAYER

Your search should be easy. That's why we created a search experience where the emphasis is on finding, not searching. We obviously can't read your mind, but by using Teoma technology and natural language, Jeeves is able to better understand your keyword, phrase or question. That means a more refined search so you'll get to the relevant results you need a whole lot quicker. Searching is good. Finding is better. Ask Jeeves to find it.

An easier, more intuitive search. **Ask Jeeves®** TO FIND IT.
Ask.com

Ask Jeeves is a popular search engine for Web surfers.

brand loyalty
A pattern of repeat product purchases, accompanied by an underlying positive attitude toward the brand, that is based on the belief that the brand makes products superior to its competition.

"price = quality," so many people willingly buy the more expensive brand because they assume that if it costs more, it *must* be better.

Perhaps the most common heuristic is **brand loyalty**, which assumes that people buy from the same company over and over because they believe that the company makes superior products. Consumers who have brand loyalties feel that it's not worth the effort to consider competing options. The creation of brand loyalty is a prized goal for marketers. People form preferences for a favorite brand and then may never change their minds in the course of a lifetime, making it extremely difficult for rivals to persuade them to switch. That explains why many companies are working harder to woo consumers early on—even when they're still toddlers. American Greetings, for example, is trying to rekindle interest in the Care Bears characters by providing a "Care Bears package," including posters, worksheets, and videos, to about 25,000 preschools. Each character (like Funshine Bear and Good Luck Bear) represents a different emotion, so the company is promoting the program as a way to teach kids about their feelings—and cement brand loyalty in the process.[2]

Still another heuristic is based on *country of origin*. We assume that a product has certain characteristics if it comes from a certain country. Our evaluations of cars are often strongly influenced by their countries of origin. Brandon assumed that the Japanese-made Honda would be a bit more reliable than the Ford or Saturn, so he factored that into his decision.

Sometimes a marketer wants to encourage a country association even when none exists. Anheuser-Busch, for example, recently introduced a new beer brand that it hopes customers will think of as an import—even though it's not. Anheuser World Select comes in a Heineken-style green bottle and a tagline that reads, "Ten Brewmasters. Four Continents. One Beer." The label on the neck of the bottle lists the home countries of the brewmasters involved in the beer's production, such as Japan, Ireland, Canada, and Spain, but the reality is that the beer is actually made in America.[3]

Step 5: Postpurchase Evaluation

In the last step of the decision-making process, the consumer evaluates just how good a choice it was. Everyone has experienced regret after making a purchase ("what *was* I thinking?"), and (hopefully) we have all been pleased with something we've bought. The evaluation of the product results in a level of **consumer satisfaction/dissatisfaction**, which is determined by the overall feelings, or attitude, a person has about a product after purchasing it.

Just how do consumers decide if they're satisfied with their purchases? One answer would be, "That's easy. The product is either wonderful or it isn't." However, it's a little more complicated than that. When we buy a product, we have some expectations of product quality. How well a

consumer satisfaction/ dissatisfaction
The overall feelings or attitude a person has about a product after purchasing it.

GOOD DECISION
Purchased GM Certified

BAD DECISION

SUSHI OYSTERS CLAMS

SUSHI & RAW BAR

GM Certified
USED VEHICLES

Buying a GM Certified Used Vehicle is always a good decision. They're from the GM brands you trust. Plus, each one gets a 110+ Point Inspection, a 3-Month/3,000-Mile Comprehensive Limited Warranty, 24-Hour GM Roadside Assistance and a 3-Day/150-Mile Satisfaction Guarantee. To learn more about GM Certified, call 1-888-999-7880 or check out over 75,000 GM Certified Used Vehicles at gmcertified.com.

CHEVROLET   PONTIAC   OLDSMOBILE   BUICK   GMC   THE RIGHT WAY. THE RIGHT CAR.

In this ad, GM attempts to persuade consumers that making the decision to buy a GM-certified used vehicle is a good decision.

product or service meets or exceeds these expectations determines customer satisfaction. In other words, consumers assess product quality by comparing what they have bought to a performance standard created by a mixture of information from marketing communications, informal information sources such as friends and family, and their own experience with the product category. That's why it's very important that marketers create *accurate* expectations of their product in advertising and other communications.

So, even though Brandon's new Focus is not exactly as powerful as a Ferrari, he's still happy with the car because he never *really* expected a fun little car to eat up the highway like a high-performance sports car costing 10 times as much. Brandon has "survived" the consumer decision-making process by recognizing a problem, conducting an information search to resolve it, identifying the (feasible) alternatives available, making a product choice, and then evaluating the quality of his decision.

Apart from understanding the mechanics of the consumer decision-making process, marketers also try to ascertain what influences in consumers' lives affect this process. There are three main categories: internal, situational, and social influences. In Brandon's case, for example, the evaluative criteria he used to compare cars and his feelings about each car were influenced by internal factors such as the connection he learned to make between a name like Saturn and an image of "slightly hip yet safe and solid," situational factors such as the way he was treated by the Ford salesperson, and social influences such as his prediction that his friends would be impressed when they saw him cruising down the road in his new wheels.

MEASURING VALUE
marketing metrics

The management consulting firm Booz Allen worked with a major auto manufacturer in Europe to pinpoint specific marketing activities that will bring customers into showrooms and give them strong incentives to buy cars. The firm developed a return-on-investment (ROI) approach that allows its client to tailor its efforts to specific objectives and correct weaknesses in what it calls the "purchase funnel," or the stages consumers undergo when they are considering buying a new car. The funnel opens with the consumer's awareness of the car, his or her consideration of the car, and his or her intent to purchase the car, and it ends with the actual transaction. The car company now looks at all its marketing campaigns at the end of each quarter to discern what worked in the funnel and what could work better. For example, if consumers are aware of a car but are not considering buying it, the firm can adjust its promotional strategy to focus on getting people to take that last step and decide to actually buy the car.

By looking more specifically at each step in the process, the company can identify what it needs to do in order to earn the customer's business. For example, it learned that once customers get into a showroom, they are more likely to buy if the dealer gives them incentives to defray the cost of ownership, such as two years' worth of free gas or free insurance for a period of time. Now that it uses these metrics, the company can say, "Last quarter we had 1,000 people go into showroom X each month. When we ran marketing campaign Y the following quarter, we saw 1,100 people go into the showroom, and those extra 100 people resulted in 20 additional sales."

Source: "When Art Meets Science: The Challenge of ROI Marketing," *Strategy + Business* (New York: Booz Allen Hamilton, Inc., December 17, 2003), 3.

perception
The process by which people select, organize, and interpret information from the outside world.

Figure 5.4 shows the influences in the decision-making process and emphasizes that all these factors work together to affect the ultimate choice each person makes. Let's consider how each of these three types of influences work, starting with internal factors.

Internal Influences on Consumer Decisions

Automakers know that one consumer's choice of the ideal car can be quite different from another's. You may think the ideal car is a sporty Ferrari, while your roommate dreams of a Jeep Wagoneer and your dad is set on owning a big Mercedes. Much of the cause of such differences can be attributed to the internal influences on consumer behavior—those things that cause each of us to interpret information about the outside world, including what car is the best, differently from one another. Let's see how internal factors relating to the way people absorb and interpret information influence the decision-making process.

Perception

Perception is the process by which people select, organize, and interpret information from the outside world. We receive information in the form of sensations, the immediate response of our sensory receptors—eyes, ears, nose, mouth, and fingers—to such basic stimuli as light, color, and sound. Our impressions about products often are based on their physical qualities. We try to make sense of the sensations we receive by interpreting them in light of our past experiences. For example, people associate the textures of fabrics and other surfaces with product qualities, and marketers are even exploring how touch can be used in packaging to arouse consumer interest. Some new plastic containers for household beauty items incorporate "soft touch" resins that provide a soft, friction-like resistance when held. Focus group members who tested one such package for Clairol's new Daily Defense shampoo described the sensations as "almost sexy" and were actually reluctant to let go of the containers![4] That's a powerful impact for a piece of plastic.

Consumers are bombarded with information on products—thousands of ads, in-store displays, special offers, opinions of their friends, and on and on. The perception process has implications for marketers because, as consumers absorb and make sense of the vast quantities of information competing for their attention, the odds are that any single message will get lost in the clutter. And, if they do notice it, there's no guarantee that the meaning they give it will be the same one the marketer intended. The issues that marketers need to understand during this process include exposure, attention, and interpretation:

- **Exposure:** The stimulus must be within range of people's sensory receptors to be noticed. For example, the lettering on a highway billboard must be big enough for a passing motorist to read easily, or the message will be lost. Many people believe that even messages they *can't* see will persuade them to buy advertised products. Claims about *subliminal advertising* of messages hidden in ice cubes (among other places) have been surfacing since the 1950s. A survey of American consumers found that almost two-thirds believe in the existence of subliminal advertising, and over one-half are convinced that this technique can get them to buy things they do not really want.[5] Even the Disney Corporation has been a victim of concerns about subliminal messages. The company recalled 3.4 million copies of its animated video *The Rescuers* because the film included a very brief image of a topless woman. (She appeared in two

Figure 5.4 Influences on Consumer Decision Making

A number of different factors in consumers' lives influence the consumer decision-making process. Marketers need to understand these influences and which ones are important in the purchase process to make effective marketing decisions.

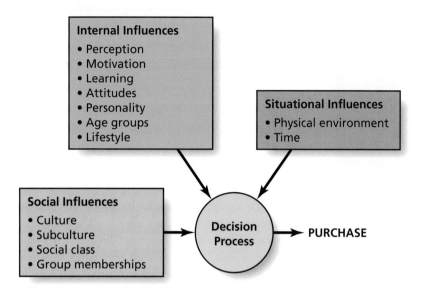

Internal Influences
- Perception
- Motivation
- Learning
- Attitudes
- Personality
- Age groups
- Lifestyle

Situational Influences
- Physical environment
- Time

Social Influences
- Culture
- Subculture
- Social class
- Group memberships

Decision Process → **PURCHASE**

frames of a 110,000-frame film, each for 1/30th of a second.) This picture was embedded as a prank in the master negative way back in 1977, but "the naked truth" surfaced only recently.[6] Despite an occasional joke like this, there is very little evidence to support the argument that this technique actually has any effect at all on our perceptions of products.

- **Attention:** As you drive down the highway, you pass hundreds of other cars. But to how many do you pay attention? *Attention* is the extent to which mental processing activity is devoted to a particular stimulus. Consumers are more likely to pay attention to messages that speak to their current needs. For example, you're far more likely to notice an ad for a fast-food restaurant when you're hungry, while smokers are more likely than nonsmokers to block out messages about the health hazards of smoking. And characteristics of the stimulus make a difference. For example, a TV ad that is unexpected or different from the norm is likely to attract viewers' attention. Yes, that's why advertisers create such crazy ads.

- **Interpretation:** Consumers assign meaning to the stimulus. This meaning is influenced by prior associations they have learned and assumptions they make. Extra Strength Maalox Whip Antacid flopped, even though a spray can is a pretty effective way to deliver this kind of tummy ache relief. But to consumers, aerosol whips mean dessert toppings, not medication.[7] If we don't interpret the product the way it was intended because of prior experiences, the best marketing ideas will be "waisted."

Motivation

Motivation is an internal state that drives us to satisfy needs. Once we activate a need, a state of tension exists that drives the consumer toward some goal that will reduce this tension by eliminating the need.

For example, think about Brandon and his old car. Brandon began to experience a gap between his present state (owning an old car) and a desired state (having a car that gets him noticed and is fun to drive). The need for a new car is activated, motivating Brandon to test different models, to talk with friends about different makes, and finally to buy a new car.

Psychologist Abraham Maslow developed an influential approach to motivation.[8] He formu-lated a **hierarchy of needs** that categorizes motives according to five levels of importance, the more

motivation
An internal state that drives us to satisfy needs by activating goal-oriented behavior.

hierarchy of needs
An approach that categorizes motives according to five levels of importance, the more basic needs being on the bottom of the hierarchy and the higher needs at the top.

Critics of subliminal perception claim that hidden messages lurk in ice cubes and elsewhere. This Pepsi ad borrows from that idea.

basic needs being on the bottom of the hierarchy and the higher needs at the top. The hierarchy suggests that before a person can meet needs in a given level, she must first meet the lower level's needs—somehow those hot new Seven jeans don't seem so enticing when you don't have enough money to buy food.

As illustrated in Figure 5.5, people start at the lowest level with basic needs for food and sleep and then progress to higher levels to satisfy more complex needs, such as the need to be accepted by others or to feel good about themselves. Ultimately, people can reach the highest-level needs, and they will be motivated to attain such goals as spiritual fulfillment. As the figure shows, if marketers understand the level of needs relevant to consumers in their target market, they can tailor their products and messages to them.

Learning

Learning is a change in behavior caused by information or experience. Learning about products can occur deliberately, as when we set out to gather information about different MP3 players before buying one brand. We also learn even when we are not trying. Consumers recognize many brand names and can hum many product jingles, for example, even for products they themselves do not use. Psychologists who study learning have advanced several theories to explain the learning process, and these perspectives are important because a major goal for marketers is to "teach" consumers to prefer their products. Let's briefly review the most important perspectives on how people learn.

learning
A relatively permanent change in behavior caused by acquired information or experience.

behavioral learning theories
Theories of learning that focus on how consumer behavior is changed by external events or stimuli.

classical conditioning
The learning that occurs when a stimulus eliciting a response is paired with another stimulus that initially does not elicit a response on its own but will cause a similar response over time because of its association with the first stimulus.

operant conditioning
Learning that occurs as the result of rewards or punishments.

BEHAVIORAL LEARNING **Behavioral learning theories** assume that learning takes place as the result of connections that form between events that we perceive. In one type of behavioral learning, **classical conditioning**, a person perceives two stimuli at about the same time. After a while, the person transfers his response from one stimulus to the other. For example, an ad shows a product and a breathtakingly beautiful scene so that (the marketer hopes) you will transfer the positive feelings you get from looking at the scene to the advertised product.

Another common form of behavioral learning is called **operant conditioning**, which occurs when people learn that their actions result in rewards or punishments. This feedback influences how they will respond in similar situations in the future. Just as a rat in a maze learns the route to a piece of cheese, consumers who receive a reward, such as a prize in the bottom of a box of cereal, will be more likely to buy that brand again. We don't like to think that marketers can train us like lab mice, but that kind of feedback does reward us for the behavior.

These learned associations in classical and operant conditioning also have a tendency to transfer to other similar things in a process called **stimulus generalization**. This means that the good or bad feelings associated with a product will "rub off" on other products that resemble it. For example, some marketers create *product line extensions* in which new products share the name of an established brand so that people's good feelings about the current product will transfer to the new one. Dole, which is associated with fruit, was able to introduce refrigerated juices and juice bars, while Sun Maid branched out from raisins to raisin bread.

COGNITIVE LEARNING In contrast to behavioral theories of learning, **cognitive learning theory** views people as problem solvers who do more than passively react to associations between stimuli. Supporters of this viewpoint stress the role of creativity and insight during the learning process. *Cognitive learning* occurs when consumers make a connection between ideas or by

Figure 5.5 Maslow's Hierarchy of Needs and Related Products

Abraham Maslow proposed a hierarchy of needs that categorizes motives. Savvy marketers know they need to understand the level of needs that motivates a consumer to buy a particular product or brand.

Higher-Level Needs

Hobbies, travel, education (U.S. Army—"Be all you can be.")

Self-Actualization
Self-fulfillment, enriching experiences

Cars, furniture, credit cards, stores, country clubs, liquors (Royal Salute Scotch—"What the rich give the wealthy.")

Ego Needs
Prestige, status, accomplishment

Clothing, grooming products, clubs, drinks (Pepsi—"You're in the Pepsi generation.")

Belongingness
Love, friendship, acceptance by others

Insurance, alarm systems, retirement investments (Allstate Insurance—"You're in good hands with Allstate.")

Safety
Security, shelter, protection

Medicines, staple items, generics (Quaker Oat Bran—"It's the right thing to do.")

Physiological
Water, sleep, food

Lower-Level Needs

---

observing things in their environment. *Observational learning* occurs when people watch the actions of others and note what happens to them as a result. They store these observations in memory and at some later point use the information to guide their own behavior. Marketers often use this process to create advertising and other messages that allow consumers to observe the benefits of using their products. Health clubs and manufacturers of exercise equipment feature well-muscled men and women using their products, while mouthwash makers show that fresh breath is the key to romance.

Now we've discussed how the three internal processes of perception, motivation, and learning influence how consumers absorb and interpret information. But the results of these processes—the interpretation the consumer gives to a marketing message—differ depending on unique consumer characteristics. Let's talk next about some of these characteristics: existing consumer attitudes, the personality of the consumer, and consumer age-groups.

Attitudes

An **attitude** is a lasting evaluation of a person, object, or issue.[9] Consumers have attitudes toward brands, such as whether McDonald's or Wendy's has the best hamburgers, as well as toward more general consumption-related behaviors, for example, whether high-fat foods including hamburgers are a no-no in a healthy diet.

A person's attitude has three components: affect, cognition, and behavior:

- *Affect* is the feeling component of attitudes. Affect refers to the overall emotional response a person has to a product. Affect (feeling) is usually dominant for expressive products such as perfume, in which simply whether or not and how much we like the product determines our attitude toward it.

- *Cognition*, the knowing component, is the beliefs or knowledge a person has about a product and its important characteristics. You may believe that a Mercedes is built better than most cars or that a Volvo is very safe. Cognition (knowing) is important for complex products, such as computers, where we may develop beliefs on the basis of technical information.

stimulus generalization
Behavior caused by a reaction to one stimulus occurs in the presence of other, similar stimuli.

cognitive learning theory
Theory of learning that stresses the importance of internal mental processes and that views people as problem solvers who actively use information from the world around them to master their environment.

attitude
A learned predisposition to respond favorably or unfavorably to stimuli on the basis of relatively enduring evaluations of people, objects, and issues.

Observational learning means we learn by observing the behavior or the experiences of others. In this ad, a guitar company wants to encourage observational learning by associating the Alvarez guitar with singer Ani DiFranco.

- *Behavior*, the doing component, involves a consumer's intention to do something, such as the intention to purchase or use a certain product. For products such as cereal, consumers act (purchase and try the product) on the basis of limited information and then form an evaluation of the product simply on the basis of how the product tastes or performs.

Depending on the nature of the product, one of these three components—feeling, knowing, or doing—will be the dominant influence in creating an attitude toward a product. Marketers often need to decide which part of an attitude is the most important driver of consumers' preferences. For example, Pepsi's advertising focus changed in 2003 from its typical emotional emphasis on celebrities, jingles, special effects, and music to an attempt to offer rational reasons to drink the beverage. The new campaign portrays the soft drink as the perfect accompaniment to foods and social situations like football games and dates.[10]

Personality

Personality is the set of unique psychological characteristics that consistently influences the way a person responds to situations in the environment. One adventure-seeking consumer may always be on the lookout for new experiences and cutting-edge products, while another is happiest in familiar surroundings, using the same brands over and over. For example, a research firm recently estimated that 12 percent of American adults are thrill seekers who like to break the rules and who are strongly attracted to extreme sports such as sky surfing or bungee jumping. This information led Isuzu to position its Rodeo sport-utility vehicle as a car that lets a driver break the rules. Advertising for the Rodeo showed kids jumping in mud puddles, running with scissors, and coloring outside the lines.[11]

personality
The psychological characteristics that consistently influence the way a person responds to situations in his or her environment.

PERSONALITY TRAITS For marketers, differences in personality traits such as thrill seeking underscore the potential value of considering personality when they are crafting their marketing strategies. The following are some specific personality traits relevant to marketing strategies:

- **Innovativeness:** The degree to which a person likes to try new things. Cutting-edge products such as radical new fashions might appeal to innovative women.

- **Materialism:** The amount of emphasis placed on owning products. Materialistic consumers focus on owning products simply for the sake of ownership.

- **Self-confidence:** The degree to which a person has a positive evaluation of her abilities, including the ability to make good decisions. People who don't have much self-confidence are good candidates for services like image consultants, who help clients select the right outfit for a job interview.

- **Sociability:** The degree to which a person enjoys social interaction. Sociable people might respond to entertainment-related products that claim to bring people together or make parties more fun.

- **Need for cognition:** The degree to which a person likes to think about things and expend the necessary effort to process brand information.[12]

THE SELF: ARE YOU WHAT YOU BUY? It makes sense to assume that consumers buy products that are extensions of their personalities. That's why marketers try to create *brand personalities* that will appeal to different types of people. For example, consider the different "personalities" invented by fragrance marketers: A brand with a "wholesome, girl-next-door" image such as Clinique's Happy would be hard to confuse with the sophisticated image of Christian Dior's Dolce Vita.

A person's **self-concept** is his attitude toward the self. The self-concept is composed of a mixture of beliefs about one's abilities and observations of one's own behavior and feelings (both positive and negative) about one's personal attributes, such as body type or facial features. The extent to which a person's self-concept is positive or negative can influence the products he buys and even the extent to which he fantasizes about changing his life.

Kenra, a marketer of hair and grooming products, recognized that many African American women have a poor self-concept because mainstream society tells them that only straight hair is beautiful.[13] A Kenra ad said to these women, "All your life, you've been told there's one kind of beautiful. And you're not it. Haven't we fought too hard for freedom to become slaves to fashion? Wear your hair any way you want." *Self-esteem advertising* attempts to stimulate positive feelings about the self.[14] This technique is also used in ads for Clairol ("You're not getting older, you're getting better"), Budweiser ("For all you do, this Bud's for you"), and L'Oréal ("Because you're worth it").

Age-Group

A person's age is another internal influence on purchasing behavior. Many of us feel we have more in common with those of our own age because we share

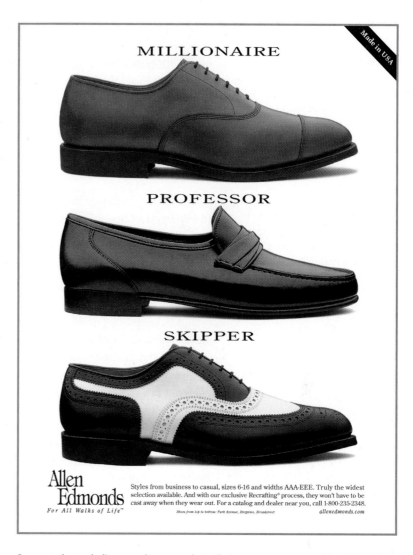

Some marketers believe we choose products that express our personalities. What do you think?

a common set of experiences and memories about cultural events, whether these involve World War II or the September 11 attacks.

Indeed, marketers of products from cookies to cars are banking on nostalgia to draw in customers, as people are attracted to products that remind them of past experiences. One trend is vacations that allow middle-age men to relive the madness of Spring Break from their college days. Myrtle Beach, South Carolina, boasts about a dozen bars that cater to aging party animals. They offer bikini contests, 75-cent draft beer, and hairy-chest competitions.[15] Wives and children not admitted.

Goods and services often appeal to a specific age-group. Although there are exceptions, it is safe to assume that most buyers of Lil' Kim's CDs are younger than those who buy Frank Sinatra discs. Thus, many marketing strategies appeal to the needs of such different age-groups as children, teenagers, the middle-aged, and the elderly.

Young people are among the most enthusiastic users of the Internet. In fact, teens spend over $1 billion online each year, so many firms are working hard to develop Web sites that will capture their interest. Iturf.com, a network of Web sites for teenagers, has the largest traffic numbers among teen-oriented sites. A subsidiary of Delia's (a catalog company that sells youth-oriented fashions), the site logs more than 1.5 million visitors per month.[16] What do teens do online? Approximately three out of four do research, and nearly two out of three use it for e-mail, while far fewer use the Internet for finding or buying products. For marketers, this means that the Internet may be a great way to get information about their goods and services to teens but not so good for sales.

self-concept
An individual's self-image that is composed of a mixture of beliefs, observations, and feelings about personal attributes.

family life cycle
A means of characterizing consumers within a family structure on the basis of different stages through which people pass as they grow older.

Marketers know that the process of change continues throughout consumers' lives. Interestingly, the purchase of goods and services may depend more on consumers' current position in the **family life cycle**—the stages through which family members pass as they grow older—than on chronological age. Singles (of any age) are more likely to spend money on expensive cars, entertainment, and recreation. Couples with small children purchase baby furniture, insurance, and a larger house, while older couples whose children have "left the nest" are more likely to buy a retirement home in Florida.

Lifestyles

lifestyle
The pattern of living that determines how people choose to spend their time, money, and energy and that reflects their values, tastes, and preferences.

A **lifestyle** is a pattern of living that determines how people choose to spend their time, money, and energy and that reflects their values, tastes, and preferences. Lifestyles are expressed in a person's preferences for activities such as sports, interests such as music, and opinions on politics and religion. Consumers often choose goods, services, and activities that are associated with a certain lifestyle. Brandon may drive a Ford Focus, hang out in Internet cafés, and go extreme skiing during Spring Break because he views these choices as part of a cool college student lifestyle.

Marketers often develop marketing strategies that recognize that people can be grouped into market segments based on similarities in lifestyle preferences.[17] For example, a growing emphasis on dieting and thinness is fueling a current lifestyle craze: low-carb mania. Food industry analysts say that a great number of people are now "carb aware," even carb-phobic, cutting out high-carb foods not as a way to lose weight but because of a general sense that carbohydrates are unhealthy. Analysts estimate that between 10 and 25 million Americans are on low-carb diets, and the industry expects that revenues from "Atkins-friendly" foods will reach $25 billion per year. Trends like this often prompt changes for companies—in this case, chains like Subway and T.G.I. Friday's have already hopped on the Atkins bandwagon, while McDonald's phased out its "supersize" portions that were the butt of criticism by those who claimed these whopping servings were contributing to the country's obesity problem.[18]

If lifestyles are so important, how do marketers identify them so that they can reach consumers who share preferences for products they associate with a certain lifestyle? Demographic characteristics, such as age and income, tell marketers *what* products people buy, but they don't reveal *why*. Two consumers can share the same demographic characteristics yet be different people—all 20-year-old male college students are hardly identical to one another. That's why it is often important to further profile consumers in terms of their passions and how they spend their leisure time.

For example, audio equipment manufacturer Pioneer Corp. recently focused on a select group of automobile hobbyists known as "Tuners"—typically single men in their late teens and early 20s with a yen for fast cars. These men come mostly from Latino and Asian communities, and most entered the car lovers' lifestyle by participating in illegal street racing late at night in the New York City and Los Angeles areas. Unlike other hot-rod enthusiasts, Tuners tinker with computer chips as well as carburetors and are always searching for specialized car parts. Pioneer created distinctive ads that ran in lifestyle-oriented media, such as magazines called *Import Tuner* and *Sport Compact Car*.[19] We'll look further at how marketers identify and find these kinds of specialized consumer groups in Chapter 7.

psychographics
The use of psychological, sociological, and anthropological factors to construct market segments.

To breathe life into demographic analyses, marketers turn to **psychographics**, which groups consumers according to psychological and behavioral similarities. One way to do this is to describe people in terms of their activities, interests, and opinions (known as AIOs). These AIOs are based on preferences for vacation destinations, club memberships, hobbies, political and social attitudes, tastes in food and fashion, and so on. Using data from large samples, marketers create profiles of customers who resemble each other in terms of their activities and patterns of product use.[20]

For example, marketers at the beginning of the walking shoe craze assumed that all recreational walkers were just burned-out joggers. Subsequent psychographic research that examined the AIOs of these walkers showed that there were actually several psychographic segments within the larger group who engaged in the activity for very different reasons, including walking for fun, walking to save money, and walking for exercise. This research resulted in the creation of walking shoes aimed at different segments, from Footjoy Walkers to Nike Healthwalkers.

Situational Influences on Consumer Decisions

We've seen that internal factors such as how people perceive marketing messages, their motivation to acquire products, and their unique personalities influence the decisions they make. In addition, when, where, and how consumers shop—what we call *situational influences*—shape their purchase choices. Some important situational cues are our physical surroundings and time pressures.

Marketers know that dimensions of the physical environment, including such factors as decor, smells, lighting, music, and even temperature, can significantly influence consumption. If you don't believe this, consider that one study found that pumping certain odors into a Las Vegas casino actually increased the amount of money patrons fed into slot machines.[21] Let's see how situational factors influence the consumer decision-making process.

WHY LEARN A FOREIGN LANGUAGE WHEN YOU'LL JUST SPEND THE WHOLE TRIP SPEECHLESS.

Just off the bow, enchanted landscapes reveal themselves in breathtaking ways—often spectacular, sometimes sublime, always unforgettable. This is the world as interpreted by Holland America. Where you'll sail in exquisite five-star comfort. With service so supremely intuitive, you may just find all your needs answered, without uttering so much as a word. CALL YOUR TRAVEL AGENT OR 1-877-SAIL HAL. EXT. 776 WWW.HOLLANDAMERICA.COM

Holland America

For products such as luxury cruises to exotic locales, marketers often target older consumers who are retired and have the time and money for expensive travel.

The Physical Environment

It's no secret that people's moods and behaviors are strongly influenced by their physical surroundings. Despite all their efforts to presell consumers through advertising, marketers know that the store environment influences many purchases. For example, consumers decide on about two out of every three of their supermarket product purchases in the aisles (so always eat *before* you go to the supermarket). The messages they receive at the time and their feelings about being in the store influence their decisions.[22]

Two dimensions, *arousal* and *pleasure*, determine whether a shopper will react positively or negatively to a store environment. In other words, the person's surroundings can be either dull or exciting (arousing) and either pleasant or unpleasant. Just because the environment is arousing doesn't necessarily mean it will be pleasant—we've all been in crowded, loud, hot stores that are anything but pleasant. Maintaining an upbeat feeling in a pleasant context is one factor behind the success of theme parks such as Disney World, which tries to provide consistent doses of carefully calculated stimulation to visitors.[23]

The importance of these surroundings explains why many retailers focus on packing as much entertainment as possible into their stores. For example, Bass Pro Shops, a chain of outdoor sports equipment stores, features giant aquariums, waterfalls, trout ponds, archery and rifle ranges, putting greens, and free classes in everything from ice fishing to conservation.[24] The Easy Everything café in London welcomes about 5,000 people every day, including Europe-crossing backpackers who can check their e-mail on the café's computers. This cyber-hangout is trying to increase traffic with computer game competitions, training seminars, and wine tastings.[25] Whether entertainment, e-mail, or information, providing surroundings that consumers want increases sales.

In-store displays are a marketing communication tool that attracts attention. Although most displays consist of simple racks that dispense the product or related coupons, some marketers use elaborate performances and scenery to display their products. And advertisers also are being more aggressive about hitting consumers with their messages, wherever they may be. *Place-based media* is a growing way to target consumers in nontraditional places. Today, messages can pop up in airports, doctors' offices, college cafeterias, and health clubs. Turner Broadcasting System began a number of place-based media ventures such as Checkout Channel for grocery stores and Airport Channel, and it even tested McDTV for McDonald's restaurants.[26] Although the Checkout Channel and McDTV didn't make it, the Airport Channel entertains bored passengers in many locales. A company called Privy Promotions and others like it even sell ad space on restroom walls in stadiums. According to the company's president, "It's a decided opportunity for an advertiser to reach a captive audience."[27] Guess so.

Time

In addition to the physical environment, time is another situational factor. Marketers know that the time of day, the season of the year, and how much time one has to make a purchase affect decision making. Time is one of consumers' most limited resources. We talk about "making time" or "spending time," and Americans are frequently reminded that "time is money."

Indeed, many consumers believe that they are more pressed for time than ever before.[28] This sense of *time poverty* makes consumers responsive to marketing innovations that allow them to save time, including such services as one-hour photo processing, drive-through lanes at fast-food restaurants, and ordering products on the Web.[29] A number of Web sites, including Apple's iTunes and even Wal-Mart, now offer consumers the speed and convenience of downloading music. These sites allow consumers to browse through thousands of titles, listen to selections, and order and pay for them—all without setting foot inside a store. This saves the customer time, plus the "store" is always open.

Social Influences on Consumer Decisions

Our discussion of consumer behavior so far has focused on factors that influence us as individuals, such as the way we learn about products. Although we are all individuals, we are also members of many groups that influence our buying decisions. Families, friends, and classmates often influence our decisions, as do larger groups with which we identify, such as ethnic groups and political parties. Now let's consider how social influences such as culture, social class, and influential friends and acquaintances affect the consumer decision-making process.

Culture

culture
The values, beliefs, customs, and tastes valued by a group of people.

Think of **culture** as a society's personality. It is the values, beliefs, customs, and tastes produced or practiced by a group of people. Although we often assume that what people in one culture think is desirable or appropriate will be appreciated in other cultures as well, that's far from the truth. The producers of the Middle Eastern version of the hit reality show *Big Brother* found that out when a male character kissed a female character on the cheek in the first few minutes of an

As consumers are exposed to more and more advertising, advertisers must work harder than ever to get their attention. Place-based media, in this case a message strategically put on a bathroom wall, offers a way to reach consumers when they are a "captive audience."

episode. In conservative Bahrain, the Persian Gulf island where the show was filmed, a social kiss between a young man and a young woman meeting for the first time suggested rampant moral depravity. In the wake of street protests, the show was pulled from the air.[30]

Thus, a consumer's culture influences his buying decisions. For example, cultures have their own *rituals*, such as weddings and funerals, that have specific activities and products associated with them. Although it may be customary for a funeral to be somber and reflective in most parts of the United States, in New Orleans the deceased is often given a grand farewell, complete with a graveside jazz band. As we saw in Chapter 3, very often these cultural expectations are so deeply ingrained that we don't realize how much they affect our consumer behavior.

As we also saw in Chapter 3, cultural values are deeply held beliefs about right and wrong ways to live.[31] For example, one culture might feel that being a unique individual is preferable to subordinating one's identity to a group, whereas another culture may emphasize the importance of the group over individuality. American cultural values include freedom, youthfulness, achievement, materialism, and activity. That's not to say, however, that values can't change. A recent study showed that both baby-boomer women (born between 1946 and 1964) and Generation X men (born between 1965 and 1976) and Generation Y men (born after 1976) are more likely to seek balance than to seek only material success[32] (see Table 5.1).

Marketers who understand a culture's values can tailor their product offerings accordingly. For example, cigarette brands Salem Pianissimo and Virginia Slims One, which emit less smoke than other brands, flopped in the United States yet sell well in Japan. Why? Because the Japanese culture values the welfare of others more than it values individual pleasure. The cigarettes that emit less smoke won't offend others (especially nonsmokers) quite as much, so the Japanese prefer to buy them. An industry executive observed, "Japanese are much more concerned about people around them. If you develop a product which helps them address these concerns, then you have a good chance of developing a hit product."[33]

Table 5.1 Ideas of Success Among Different Consumer Groups

Age Group	Definition of Success
Baby-Boomer Women (born 1946–1964)	• "Home life and being with friends and family are of the utmost importance. Work is just a monetary thing." • "I'm starting to demand a certain quality of relationships." • "More responsibility gives us more stress, and there's more confusion when we have more choices." • "I don't think about work as much as I used to. I just think about having more fun."
Generation X Men (born 1965–1976) and Generation Y Men (born after 1976)	• "The main goal is being at peace with myself. People come in and out of your life, but if you're at peace with yourself, that's the most important thing." • "I want to make sure that I have a job I enjoy, a personal life, and the opportunity to enjoy things outside of work. I want to have a mix of everything." • "The most important thing in my whole life, even if I don't become successful, is to be happy."

Source: Adapted from Becky Ebenkamp, "Chicks, Checks and Balances," *Brandweek,* February 12, 2001, 16.

Subcultures

subculture
A group within a society whose members share a distinctive set of beliefs, characteristics, or common experiences.

A **subculture** is a group coexisting with other groups in a larger culture whose members share a distinctive set of beliefs or characteristics. Each of us belongs to many subcultures. These subcultures could be religious groups, ethnic groups, or regional groups as well as those that form around music groups such as the Dave Matthews Band, media creations such as Trekkers (*Star Trek* fans), or leisure activities such as extreme sports. The hip-hop subculture has had enormous influence as many marketers relied on young trendsetters to help decide what brands were *off the hook* (good) and which were *wack* (bad). Sprite took on a hip-hop persona and went from seventh to fourth among the industry's top brands. The drink's brand manager noted, "Hip-hop epitomizes self-expression, which is the mantra of Sprite."[34]

For marketers, some of the most important subcultures are racial and ethnic groups because many consumers identify strongly with their heritage and are influenced by products that appeal to this aspect of their identities. Some racial differences in consumption preferences can be subtle but important. When Coffee-Mate discovered that African Americans are more likely than other ethnic groups to drink their coffee with sugar and cream, the company mounted a promotional blitz using black media and in return benefited from double-digit increases in sales volume and market share within this segment.[35]

Social Class

social class
The overall rank or social standing of groups of people within a society according to the value assigned to such factors as family background, education, occupation, and income.

Social class is the overall rank of people in a society. People who are within the same class work in similar occupations, have similar income levels, and usually share tastes in clothing, decorating styles, and leisure activities. These people also share many political and religious beliefs as well as ideas regarding valued activities and goals.

Many products and stores are designed to appeal to people in a specific social class.[36] Working-class consumers tend to evaluate products in more utilitarian terms, such as sturdiness or comfort, rather than style or fashion. They are less likely to experiment with new products or styles, such as modern furniture or colored appliances, because they tend to prefer predictability to novelty.[37] Marketers need to understand these differences and develop product and communication strategies that appeal to the different groups.

Luxury goods often serve as status symbols, visible markers that provide a way for people to flaunt their membership in higher social classes (or at least to make others believe they are members). The desire to accumulate these "badges of achievement" is evident in the popular bumper sticker "He who dies with the most toys wins." Marketers of high-end products often seek out rich people (or those who want others to think they are) to buy their brands. For example, Mercedes recently teamed up with designer Giorgio Armani to produce a line of products for the well-heeled, including a new car with sand-colored leather seats, jet-black dashboard, and brown leather steering wheel designed by Armani.[38]

However, it's important to note that over time, the importance of different status symbols rises and falls. For example, when James Dean was starring in the movie *Giant*, the Cadillac convertible was the ultimate status symbol car in America. Today, wealthy consumers who want to let the world know of their success are far more likely to choose a Mercedes or a Hummer. The "in" car five years from now is anyone's guess.

Group Memberships

Anyone who's ever "gone along with the crowd" knows that people act differently in groups than they do on their own. There are several reasons for this phenomenon. With more people in a group, it becomes less likely that any one member will be singled out for attention, and normal restraints on behavior may be reduced (think about the last wild party you attended). In many cases, group members show a greater willingness to consider riskier alternatives than they would if each member made the decision alone.[39]

Music crossovers like Enrique Iglesias are giving mainstream music a Hispanic flavor.

Since many of the things we buy are consumed in the presence of others, group behaviors are important to marketers. Sometimes group activities create new business opportunities. Consider, for example, the increasing popularity of tailgating during football games. Long a tradition at some college campuses, now many companies are figuring out that there's as much money if not more to be made outside the stadium as on the field. Coleman is selling grills designed just for tailgating as part of its RoadTrip line. A catalog called American Tailgater features tailgate flags, tailgate tents, and even a gas-powered margarita blender ($355). There are even tailgating training camps by Ragu (hosted by John Madden) and parking-lot contests by Jack Daniels. The National Football League itself says it sells $100 million per year of tailgating merchandise, including keg-shaped grills.[40]

A **reference group** is a set of people a consumer wants to please or imitate. Consumers "refer to" these groups in evaluating their behavior—what they wear, where they go, what brands they buy, and so on. Unlike a larger culture, the "group" can be composed of one person, such as your significant other, or someone you've never met, such as a statesman like Martin Luther King, a star like Gwyneth Paltrow, or a sophisticated man of the world like Austin Powers. The group can be small, such as your immediate family, or it could be a large organization, such as People for the Ethical Treatment of Animals.

reference group
An actual or imaginary individual or group that has a significant effect on an individual's evaluations, aspirations, or behavior.

Advice for Wild Planet

**PROFESSOR
PAUL G. FARNHAM**
**Department of Economics, Andrew Young School of Policy Studies,
Georgia State University**

I would choose option 3, but with the idea of developing one product line for boys and one for girls. This approach builds on what Wild Planet has learned about the different gender preferences. The most important aspect of this decision is understanding the difference between sunk costs and future costs and revenues. Although it is often difficult for managers to acknowledge, historic or sunk costs are irrelevant to future decision making. If Wild Planet managers believe that the future costs of continuing any product line outweigh the expected future revenue stream from that line, the product line should be discontinued regardless of the costs incurred in the past. However, if the best available evidence indicates that future revenues will be greater than future costs, the product line should continue. The Room Gear line appears to be an innovative concept that should catch on if Wild Planet managers can correctly target the gender issues.

Other economic issues that are missing from this discussion are the role of product prices and the reactions of major competitors. As an economic consultant to Wild Planet management, I would want to know the prices of the Room Gear products and how they are positioned relative to the competition. I would like evidence on how sensitive children (or their parents!) are to product prices and whether changes in prices would affect sales (the price elasticity of demand). The economic concept of demand examines the role of prices relative to all other factors also influencing consumer behavior. In addition, I would like to know more about the market environment in which Wild Planet operates. Are Wild Planet's strategies influenced by the moves of its major competitors? Does Wild Planet have any significant cost advantages relative to the competition that would give it a strategic edge? I would like Wild Planet to focus both on consumer/demand and production/cost issues as they evaluate their future strategies for the Room Gear products.

---

conformity
A change in beliefs or actions as a reaction to real or imagined group pressure.

Consumers often change their behavior to gain acceptance into a particular reference group. **Conformity** is at work when a person changes as a reaction to real or imagined group pressure. For example, a student getting dressed to go to a fraternity rush may choose to wear clothing similar to what he knows the brothers will be wearing so that he's accepted by the group.

Home shopping parties, as epitomized by the Tupperware party, capitalize on group pressures to boost sales. A company representative makes a sales presentation to a group of people who have gathered in the home of a friend or acquaintance. Participants model the behavior of others who can provide them with information about how to use certain products, especially because the home party is likely to be attended by a relatively homogeneous group (e.g., neighborhood homemakers). Pressures to conform may be particularly intense and may escalate as more group members begin to "cave in" (this process is sometimes termed the *bandwagon effect*). Even though Tupperware has moved into new sales venues, including a Web site (**www.tupperware.com**), the Home Shopping Network, and mall kiosks, it hopes the venerable shopping party remains a popular means of generating sales.[41]

Advice for Wild Planet

PROFESSOR
DAVID L. MOORE
LeMoyne College, and visiting professor, ESSEC, France

 I would choose option 2 because this product line seems to appeal to the motivational drives for both affiliation and differentiation. On the one hand, if Room Gear is considered acceptable by kids' friends, the drive for affiliation is satisfied. On the other hand, by personalizing the Room Gear that they choose, kids are differentiating themselves. In this way, kids derive meaning from both ads and consumption by actually creating themselves via their choices of Room Gear products. Developing a new product line can be quite expensive. Wild Planet has invested heavily in Room Gear, but they should not let sunk costs determine their decision. The only really relevant numbers should be potential future sales. Daniel Grossman seems reluctant to abandon this line, and I think he should go with his instinct to refine the Room Gear line rather than abandon it prematurely.

PROFESSOR
DIANE H. SAPPENFIELD
George Mason University

 I would choose option 2. The existing line concept is a good one, but the toy store channel of distribution, which I am assuming is being used, may be a weak one for finding and purchasing gear to make a teen's room unique. Pottery Barn Kids also found the gender issue to be important and has divided its stores down the middle, with girls' items on the left and boys' items on the right. Its catalog and Web site, which feature several customized items for a teen's room, are separated in a similar manner. Its model seems to be working. Would it be a possible channel of distribution for Wild Planet? My initial question when reading the case was how Wild Planet chose the teens they visited. I wonder if the interviewer could have encouraged the teens to elaborate on the reasons they chose various decorative items. Do the teens think Room Gear is "too young" for them? In reviewing a list of items in which young teens expressed interest for their rooms, the items cited were cell phones, e-mail, instant messaging, video game equipment, and portable video games. Perhaps Wild Planet should try positioning its Room Gear products to a younger age level, perhaps five to seven years of age. Some additional market research would be helpful.

PROFESSOR
JEFF MURRAY
University of Arkansas

 I would choose option 3, reposition the line toward boys and girls, keying off the insight that each gender approaches the decoration of their room differently. In marketing, there is truth to the old adage "nothing ventured, nothing gained." I don't think Wild Planet should give up yet. The company has already made a substantial investment in the Room Gear line, with some success; often, marketing strategies involve an iterative trial-and-error process that takes patience and some time to work through. The ethnographic technique is a great idea; when the informants have trouble articulating clearly exactly what their preferences are, these kinds of observations are really valuable. And Wild Planet admits that some of the items sold well. I think that they should continue their ethnographic work, paying attention to gender differences and maybe better linking the Room Gear line to other key trends in sports, music, fashion, and communication technology.

PROFESSOR
SUSAN GERINGER
California State University, Fresno

 I would choose option 3. Wild Planet has invested a good amount in their Room Gear line, although their initial venture did not succeed to their expectations. The lack of success appears to be directly associated with their lack of *correct* research. Although Wild Planet attempted to conduct consumer research, it is apparent that their endeavors did not include correct research methodology. It became evident that these consumers have varying preferences, primarily based on their gender. Daniel Grossman should now push for consumer behavior research focus groups that will glean the preferences of both boys and girls. Once this information is gathered, Wild Planet should develop the Room Gear line and position it with products aimed at boys, products aimed at girls, and products that cross gender lines. In summary, the Room Gear line was a viable concept, but the lack of correct consumer research caused a positioning problem, thus creating a product that did not sell to its potential.

Opinion Leaders

opinion leader

A person who is frequently able to influence others' attitudes or behaviors by virtue of his or her active interest and expertise in one or more product categories.

If, like Brandon, you are in the market for a new car, is there someone you know you would seek out for advice? Some individuals are particularly likely to influence others' product decisions. An **opinion leader** is a person who influences others' attitudes or behaviors because others perceive her as possessing expertise about the product.[42] Opinion leaders usually exhibit high levels of interest in the product category and may continuously update their knowledge by reading, talking with salespeople, and so on. Because of this involvement, opinion leaders are valuable information sources, and, unlike commercial endorsers who are paid to represent the interests of just one company, they have no ax to grind and can impart *both* positive and negative information about the product. In addition, opinion leaders often are among the first to buy new products, so they absorb much of the risk, reducing uncertainty for others who are not as courageous.

Today, many shrewd marketers appreciate the value of coaxing opinion leaders—and especially celebrities—to be seen using or wearing their products so that others will follow suit. For example, the founder of an upscale shoe company called Harry's Shoes Ltd. started to line up opinion leaders even before his first shoes were actually produced. He created a buzz by persuading actors like Denzel Washington and John Travolta to wear prototype versions to the Oscars. Of course, in this case it probably didn't hurt that the owner is a member of the family that also founded a few other organizations, including the Pittsburgh-based Mellon bank, Gulf Oil, Carnegie-Mellon University, and the investment bank Drexel Burnham and that he hung out with a lot of movie stars before going into the business.[43] Sometimes it's not what you know but who you know.

Sex Roles

sex roles

Society's expectations regarding the appropriate attitudes, behaviors, and appearance for men and women.

Some of the strongest pressures to conform come from our **sex roles**, society's expectations regarding the appropriate attitudes, behaviors, and appearance for men and women. These assumptions about the proper roles of men and women, flattering or not, are deeply ingrained in marketing communications.[44] For example, men are far less likely than women to see a doctor regularly, and 25 percent say they would delay seeking help as long as possible. Experts suggest that this may be because boys playing sports are taught to "ignore pain and not ask for help."[45]

Many products take on masculine or feminine attributes, and consumers often associate them with one gender or another.[46] For example, many women downplay their femininity at work by wearing masculine clothing such as pants suits. These women feel that feminine dress in the workplace hurts their chances of being promoted—that the corporate world still rewards men more than women. Pants suits, in this case, take on a masculine attribute.

Marketers play a part in teaching us how society expects us to act as men and women. As consumers, we see women and men portrayed differently in marketing communications and in products promoted to the two groups. And these influences teach us what the "proper" role of women or men is and, in addition, which products are appropriate for each gender. Some of these "*sex-typed*" products have come under fire from social groups. For example, feminists have criticized the Barbie doll for reinforcing unrealistic ideas about what women's bodies should look like—even though a newer version of the doll isn't quite as skinny and buxom. Other Barbie protests erupted when Mattel introduced a shopping-themed version called Cool Shoppin' Barbie. The doll comes with all the equipment kids need to pretend Barbie is shopping—including a Barbie-size MasterCard. When the card is pressed into the card scanner, her voice says, "Credit approved!" Although Mattel includes a warning about sticking to a budget, some critics fear the doll sends the wrong message to girls about the desirability of shopping.[47]

Consumer-to-Consumer E-Commerce

consumer-to-consumer (C2C) e-commerce

Communications and purchases that occur among individuals without directly involving the manufacturer or retailer.

Of course, not all consumer behavior is related to marketers offering goods and services to consumers. **Consumer-to-consumer (C2C) e-commerce** refers to online communications and purchases that occur among individuals without directly involving the manufacturer or retailer. EBay, the most famous of such sites, provides an opportunity for consumers (and an increasing number of small businesses) to sell everything from collectible comic books to a vintage trombone. In 2002, eBay ranked number eight in *Fortune*'s 100 fastest-growing companies list, had 28 million active users, and conducted nearly $15 billion of transactions. That's over $700 in deals done over eBay every second.[48]

Much of C2C e-commerce is far less sensational. It's more about groups of "netizens" around the world with similar interests united through the Internet by a shared passion. These virtual communities meet online and share their enthusiasm for a product, recording artist, art form, celebrity, and so on.[49] In fact, over 40 million people worldwide participate in such virtual communities. How many consumers actually visit these sites? The New York site for Craig's List alone had 950,000 page views in October 2003.[50]

Companies like Warner Bros. also are actively promoting virtual communities related to their products. The company noticed that many fans of Bugs Bunny, Batman, and the Tazmanian Devil were including images and sound clips on their personal Web pages and then selling ad space on those pages. Instead of suing its fans, Warner created an online community called ACME City that builds home pages for registered members.[51] Let's look at some specific types of virtual communities that are shaking up the ways businesses operate:

- **Multiuser dungeons:** Originally, these communities were environments where players of fantasy games met. Now they refer to any cyber environment in which people socially interact through role and game playing. Realizing that the average online player logs 17 hours per week, firms such as Sony, Microsoft, and Sega are building virtual worlds to get a piece of the action. Sony Online Entertainment's gaming Web site, the Station (**www.station.com**), has more than 12 million registered users, while Microsoft's Gaming Zone (**www.zone.com**) has a membership of some 29 million.[52] These virtual communities provide a communications medium with many possibilities for marketers since participants often render judgments on a variety of topics, such as hot new bands or movies, that can influence the opinions of other participants.

- **Chat rooms, rings, and lists:** These virtual communities include Internet relay chat, otherwise known as *chat rooms*. *Rings* are organizations of related home pages, and *lists* are groups of people on a single e-mail list who share information. For example, ICQ maintains rings devoted to many topics, such as music, electronics, genealogy, and so on.

A German ad for Schick razors challenges our sex role expectations (these are all men).

People visit thousands of online communities to put in their two cents about products, celebrities, media, and so on. At the Hollywood Stock Exchange site, movie buffs predict the success or failure of new releases by buying "stock" in upcoming pictures. The site is closely watched by studio executives.

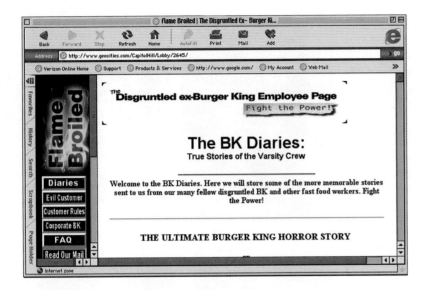

A former Burger King employee who was obviously unhappy about an experience with the company created this protest site. Because (almost) anyone can create a Web page for all to see, corporations have difficulty controlling the content of these sites.

- **Boards:** *Boards* are online communities organized around interest-specific electronic bulletin boards. Active members read and post messages sorted by date and subject. There are boards devoted to musical groups, movies, wine, cigars, cars, comic strips, and even fast-food restaurants.

- **Blogs:** The newest and fastest growing form of online community is the *weblog* or *blog*. A blog is simply a Web site where you write something on a regular basis. Visitors can read what you have written and comment on it. Blogs offer consumers the opportunity to dash off a few random thoughts, post them on a Web site, and read similar thoughts of others. The advantage of blogs over sites that offer Internet users free Web pages is that blogs allow users to upload a few sentences without going to the trouble of updating a traditional Web page.

- **Protest sites:** These sites let consumers "vent" by sharing negative experiences they have had with companies. Many of these sites have links you can find on **www.protest.com**: In some cases, these protest sites pose a public relations problem for companies, so companies try to eliminate them. Dunkin' Donuts bought a site from a disgruntled customer who created the Web page to complain after he could not get skim milk for his coffee.[53] And sometimes these sites spread untrue information about corporations. For example, rumors began spreading on the Internet that Procter & Gamble's Febreze cleaning product killed dogs. In a preemptive move to minimize problems before they started, Procter & Gamble registered numerous Web site names so that no one else could—including febrezekillspet.com, febrezesucks.com, and ihateprocterandgamble.com.[54] Procter & Gamble now maintains its own Web site dedicated to fighting rumors: **pg.com/rumor**.[55]

So what is the importance to marketers of all these different types of virtual communities? While there is no "one size fits all" way for marketers to make use of these virtual communities, clever marketers can look for opportunities to communicate with consumers online through these sites. Virtual communities are unique in that they do provide opportunities where, unlike traditional marketing communication venues, consumers are willing and eager to talk about a particular product. In addition, monitoring such sites will provide marketers with an important source of information for a firm—about its product, about consumer tastes, and about the competition.

real people, real choices
How It Worked Out at Wild Planet

Wild Planet selected option 3. Daniel and his team decided they would rather assume additional risk to achieve the higher upside than simply settle for mediocre sales. They directed the line toward girls, who have shown greater interest in decorating their rooms and in purchasing new items to do so. They renamed the line Girls Livin' in Style (GLS).

The GLS line features items such as the Dazzlin' Doorway, a version of a door curtain that allows you to program in a voice message that is triggered when someone enters your room. It also includes Mini Room Mates, miniature versions of a fan, a radio, and a lamp that are both decorative and functional. The line tested very well with girls during Wild Planet's research, and the company started to sell the line in the fall of 2004.

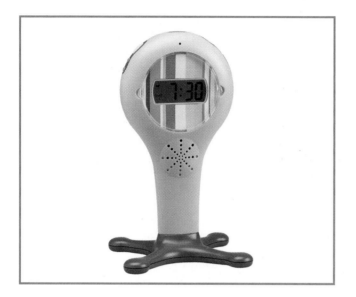

This is one of the items Wild Planet developed as part of its new Girls Livin' in Style product line.

Do you know what motivates an employer to "buy" a new hire? To learn how to identify employers' needs go to Chapter 5 in *Brand You*.

CHAPTER SUMMARY

1. **Define consumer behavior and explain the reasons why consumers buy what they buy.**
   Consumer behavior is the process individuals or groups go through to select, purchase, use, and dispose of goods, services, ideas, or experiences to satisfy their needs and desires. Consumer decisions differ greatly ranging from habitual, repeat (low-involvement) purchases to complex, extended problem-solving activities for important, risky (high-involvement) purchases.

2. **Explain the prepurchase, purchase, and postpurchase activities consumers engage in when making decisions.** When consumers make important purchasing decisions, they go through a set of five steps. First, they recognize there is a problem to be solved and search for information to make the best decision. They then evaluate a set of alternatives and judge them on the basis of various evaluative criteria. At this point, they are ready to make their purchasing decision. Following the purchase, consumers decide whether it matched their expectations.

3. **Describe how internal factors influence consumers' decision-making processes.** Several internal factors influence consumer decisions. Perception is how consumers select, organize, and interpret stimuli. Motivation is an internal state that drives consumers to satisfy needs. Learning is a change in behavior that results from information or experience. Behavioral learning results from external events, while cognitive learning refers to internal mental activity. An attitude is a lasting evaluation of a person, object, or issue and includes three components: affect, cognition, and behavior. Personality traits such as innovativeness, materialism, self-confidence, and sociability and the need for cognition may be used to develop market segments. Marketers seek to understand a consumer's self-concept in order to develop product attributes that match some aspect of the consumer's self-concept.

   The age of consumers and their lifestyle also are strongly related to consumption preferences. Marketers may use psychographics to group people according to activities, interests, and opinions that may explain reasons for purchasing products.

4. **Understand how situational factors at the time and place of purchase influence consumer behavior.** Situational influences include our physical surroundings and time pressures. Dimensions of the physical environment including decor, smells, lighting, music, and even temperature can influence consumption. The time of day, the season of the year, and how much time one has to make a purchase also affect decision making.

5. **Describe how consumers' relationships with other people influence their decision-making processes.** Consumers' overall preferences for products are determined by the culture in which they live and their membership in different subcultures. Social class, group memberships and opinion leaders are other types of social influences that affect consumer choices. A reference group is a set of people a consumer wants to please or imitate, and this affects the consumer's purchasing decisions. Purchases also often result from conformity to real or imagined group pressures. Another way social influence is felt is in the expectations of society regarding the proper roles for men and women. Such expectations have led to many sex-typed products.

6. **Understand how the Internet offers consumers opportunities to participate in consumer-to-consumer marketing.** Consumer-to-consumer (C2C) e-commerce includes marketing communication and purchases between individuals. C2C activities include virtual communities that allow consumers to do such things as share their enthusiasm or dislike for a product or company. Virtual communities and other C2C e-commerce activities provide both a source of information about the market and about competitors for marketers and an opportunity to communicate effectively with consumers.

KEY TERMS

attitude, 147
behavioral learning theories, 146
brand loyalty, 142
classical conditioning, 146
cognitive learning theory, 146, 147
conformity, 156
consumer behavior, 136
consumer satisfaction/dissatisfaction, 142
consumer-to-consumer (C2C)
   e-commerce, 158
culture, 152

evaluative criteria, 140
family life cycle, 150
heuristics, 141
hierarchy of needs, 145
information search, 140
involvement, 138
learning, 146
lifestyle, 150
motivation, 145
operant conditioning, 146
opinion leader, 158

perceived risk, 138
perception, 144
personality, 148
problem recognition, 139
psychographics, 150
reference group, 155
self-concept, 149
social class, 154
sex roles, 158
stimulus generalization, 146, 147
subculture, 154

CHAPTER REVIEW

MARKETING CONCEPTS: TESTING YOUR KNOWLEDGE

1. What is consumer behavior? Why is it important for marketers to understand consumer behavior?

2. Explain habitual decision making, limited problem solving, and extended problem solving. What is the role of perceived risk in the decision process?

3. What are the steps in the consumer decision process?

4. What is perception? Explain the parts of the perception process: exposure, attention, and interpretation. For marketers, what are the implications of each of these components?

5. What is motivation? What is the role of motivation in consumer behavior?

6. What is behavioral learning? What is cognitive learning? How is an understanding of behavioral and cognitive learning useful to marketers?

7. What are the three components of attitudes? What is personality? What are some personality traits that may influence consumer behavior?

8. Explain what is meant by lifestyle. What is the significance of family life cycle and lifestyle in understanding consumer behavior and purchasing decisions?

9. How do culture and subculture influence consumer behavior? What is the significance of social class to marketers?

10. What are reference groups, and how do they influence consumers? What are opinion leaders?

11. How does the physical environment influence consumer purchasing behavior?

12. What is consumer-to-consumer (C2C) e-commerce? What are virtual communities, and how are they related to consumer behavior?

MARKETING CONCEPTS: DISCUSSING CHOICES AND ISSUES

1. Demographic or cultural trends are important to marketers. What are some big trends that may affect the marketing of the following products?
   a. Housing
   b. Magazines
   c. Education
   d. Telecommunications
   e. Travel and tourism
   f. Automobiles

2. What are the core values of your culture? To which subcultures do you belong? What distinctive beliefs, characteristics, or experiences are a part of the subcultures?

3. Consumers often buy products because they feel pressure from reference groups to conform. Does conformity exert a positive or a negative influence on consumers? With what types of products is conformity more likely to occur?

4. The Internet provides a unique opportunity for consumers to communicate and make purchases from each other. What do you think the future of this C2C e-commerce is? How do you think it will affect traditional marketing firms?

5. Retailers often place impulse purchase items such as magazines and candy bars near the entrance to the store or near the checkout area. How would you describe the decision process for these products? Why are these locations effective?

6. In different cultures, perceptions about the proper roles for men and women, that is, sex roles, can vary greatly. What are some ways you think sex roles may differ in different countries, and what are the implications for marketers?

MARKETING PRACTICE: APPLYING WHAT YOU'VE LEARNED

1. Assume that you are an account executive with an advertising agency. Your current client is a firm that makes automobiles. You know that automobile purchases are often influenced by a variety of social or "other people" factors. Write a report that lists these social influences, explain why each is important, and outline how you might use these influences in developing an advertising campaign.

2. This chapter indicated that consumers go through a series of steps (from problem recognition to postpurchase evaluation) as they make purchases. Write a detailed report describing what you would do in each of these steps when deciding to purchase one of the following products:
   a. Mobile telephone
   b. A university
   c. A fast-food lunch

3. Using one of the products in question 2, what can marketers do to make sure that consumers going through each step in the consumer decision process move toward the purchase of their brand? Hint: Think about product, place, price, and promotion strategies.

4. Sometimes advertising or other marketing activities cause problem recognition to occur by showing consumers how much better off they would be with a new product or by pointing out problems with products they already own. For the following product categories, what are some ways marketers might try to stimulate problem recognition?
   a. Life insurance
   b. Mouthwash
   c. A new brand of laundry detergent
   d. An airline

5. Assume that you are a marketing manager for a firm that markets expensive watches. You are concerned about the effects of current consumer trends, including changing

ethnic populations, changing roles of men and women, increased concern for time and for the environment, and decreased emphasis on owning status goods. Others in your firm do not understand or care about these changes. They believe that the firm should continue to do business just as it always has. Develop a role-playing exercise with a classmate to discuss these two different points of view for your class. Each of you should be sure to include the importance of each of these trends to your firm and offer suggestions for marketing strategies to address these trends.

MARKETING MINIPROJECT: LEARNING BY DOING

The purpose of this miniproject is to increase your understanding of the roles of personal, social, and situational factors in consumer behavior.

1. With several other members of your class, select one of the following product categories (or some other product of your choice):

- Hairstyling
- Large appliances such as refrigerators or washing machines
- Children's clothing
- Banking
- Fine jewelry

2. Visit three stores or locations where the product may be purchased. (Try to select three that are very different from each other.) Observe and make notes on all the elements of each retail environment.

3. At each of the three locations, observe people purchasing the product. Make notes about their characteristics (e.g., age, race, gender, and so on), their social class, and their actions in the store in relation to the product.

4. Prepare a report for your class describing the situational variables and individual consumer differences between the three stores and how they relate to the purchase of the product.

5. Present your findings to your class.

REAL PEOPLE, REAL SURFERS: EXPLORING THE WEB

Visit two or three virtual communities such as the ones listed in this chapter's discussion of C2C e-commerce. Based on your experience, answer the following questions for each site you visit:

1. What is the overall reason for the site's existence?

2. What is your overall opinion of the site?

3. What type of consumer do you think would be attracted to the site?

4. How easy or difficult is it to navigate each site?

MARKETING PLAN EXERCISE

When developing a marketing plan, attention must be paid to consumer behavior—especially what motivates consumers to buy. This is because a substantial investment will be made, based on the marketing plan, in various approaches to influence consumers to purchase our products over those of competitors.

1. How does level of involvement by consumers with a product affect the way a marketing plan supports that product?

2. What can a marketer do to help ensure a more favorable postpurchase evaluation of a product? How might this be built into a marketing plan?

3. Consider the various social influences on consumer behavior discussed in this chapter. In planning for the future, how might knowledge of these factors' influence on your product or service impact your marketing plan?

Marketing in Action Case

Real Choices at Volkswagen

"How do I love thee? Let me count the ways. I love thee to the depth and breadth and height my soul can reach, when feeling out of sight." These are stirring words indeed from poet Elizabeth Barrett Browning. However, while such words may allow a young lover to capture the heart of his beloved, the question remains, Will they help sell automobiles? Volkswagen certainly hoped so as it introduced an ad campaign in the late summer of 2003 focused on linking love poems to key vehicles in the Volkswagen product line. Volkswagen launched the new ad campaign in Germany with a 20-page newspaper and magazine insert along with television advertisements. The print ads featured a love poem and a paragraph explaining the feelings the featured Volkswagen represented. For the VW Beetle, the ad contained a love poem from a student to his girlfriend and included a photo of the lower half of a VW Beetle in a field. Other poems are matched with Volkswagen's other products including the Passat, Touareg, Phaeton, Polo, Golf, Lupo, and Roadster. The primary theme of the campaign is "The love of the automobile."

Clearly, with this ad campaign Volkswagen is trying to tap into the emotional side of human behavior and take advantage of how consumer emotions impact decision making. The love affair between car owner and the car itself is well known. Many consumers have fond memories of their first or favorite car, and some would say that those memories result in a certain amount of affection being held for the car.

However, much car advertising focuses on how the car is "fun to drive" or how certain features make the automobile more safe or allow it to have more cargo area. Consequently, while consumers' thoughts of automobiles tend to evoke an image drawing on one's emotions, car advertising often focuses on product features and benefits. Joern Hinrichs, executive director of Volkswagen marketing, believes that while consumers relate to automobile brands for rational reasons such as quality and reliability, behind those values lie strong emotions. Thus, an advertising campaign linking a very strong emotion, love, to specific car brands and models essentially skips the step where the company appeals to one's practical side by emphasizing reliability and quality and goes right to those underlying emotions that Mr. Hinrichs believes are present.

Using love poems to sell automobiles is a risky proposition for Volkswagen. However, such a strategy may be effective for getting consumers thinking of purchasing a new automobile to include Volkswagen as one of their alternatives. Once the consumer includes a Volkswagen car in his set of choices, other decision criteria on which the company's cars perform particularly well, such as comfort, handling, performance, and reliability, may cause the consumer to choose a Volkswagen car over a competitor's car. In addition, linking love poems to certain cars may result in other factors influencing a consumer's decision about which car to buy. For example, love and friendship represent belongingness needs that all individuals experience. To the extent that a Volkswagen car, with its love poem association, can help satisfy those needs, consumers are more likely to consider the car when making a buying decision. Furthermore, an individual's self-concept can be a strong influence on buying behavior. As a result, if Volkswagen can instill the notion in consumers that one of their automobiles represents an extension of consumers' personalities, the ad campaign has the potential to result in greater sales for the company.

So, will linking love poems to automobiles help sell more cars? It seems that the evidence is somewhat mixed. In the United States, Volkswagen's overall sales for the first two months of 2004 were down 41.4 percent from the previous year. Such sales results prompted a new ad campaign in the United States. The new ads have the very down-to-earth goal of getting consumers to take a test drive, which, it is hoped, will lead to those consumers eventually buying the car. This ad campaign supports the American brand manager's belief that advertising must result in more cars being sold rather than just support a brand personality. However, Volkswagen is known for its off-beat advertising that is often described as cheeky, whimsical, and anything but hard sell. Which advertising strategy Volkswagen decides to pursue from here, the more practical "ads must sell cars" strategy or the more obscure "let's develop the brand image" strategy, remains to be seen.

Things to Think About

1. What is the decision facing Volkswagen?
2. What factors are important in understanding the decision situation?
3. What are the alternatives?
4. What decision(s) do you recommend?
5. What are some ways to implement your recommendation(s)?

Sources: Bill Brit, "Volkswagen Waxes Poetic to Stir up Emotions and Sales," *Advertising Age*, September 29, 2003, 8; Elizabeth Barrett Browning, "Sonnet XLIII," *Poetry Archives*, **www.emule.com/poetry/?page=poem&poem=216** (accessed May 25, 2004); and Karl Greenberg, "Far from Fahrvergnugen: Struggling VW Shifts Gears," *Brandweek*, April 26, 2004, 13.

nonporous   customizable   durable   seamless   heat-resistant

TRADITIONAL CHEF. DEVOUT MODERNIST. IS THERE A SURFACE   ENOUGH TO SATISFY BOTH?

DuPont™
CORIAN®
SOLID SURFACES

With a surface so durable it's backed by a ten-year warranty and a dazzling palette of over 100 colors, countertop works as beautifully as DuPont™ Corian®.
DuPont registered trademark for its solid surfaces. Only DuPont makes Corian®.

DUPONT
The miracles of science™

www.dupont.com

real people, real choices
meet Steve McCracken,
a Decision Maker at DuPont

**first job out of
college**

**a job-related mistake
i wish i hadn't made**

**Design engineer for a
nonwovens fabrics plant in
Tennessee for DuPont.**

**Major computer system
change.**

BUSINESS-TO-BUSINESS MARKETS: HOW AND WHY ORGANIZATIONS BUY

Steven McCracken became president of INVISTA in February 2002. Before that time, the company was called DuPont Textiles & Interiors, the division of DuPont that created such products as Lycra®, CoolMax®, and Stainmaster®. While with DuPont, Steve served as vice president and general manager. Steve graduated from Rose-Hulman Institute of Technology with a B.S. in mechanical engineering. He joined the company in 1975 as a field engineer in the engineering department assigned to nonwoven products. Since that time, he served in operations, finance, planning, marketing and business management positions within DuPont, in the United States and in Europe. While managing director of DuPont™ Lycra® in Europe, he oversaw unprecedented business growth and the building of a powerful consumer brand franchise. Then, during his five years as head of DuPont™ Corian® Surfaces worldwide, the business achieved record growth levels, based on innovation, segmentation and brand building. In 2004 he left INVISTA to become CEO of Owens-Illinois, one of the world's leading producers of glass and plastics packaging.

Decision Time at DuPont

More than thirty years ago, DuPont revolutionized the construction industry when it created the Corian® brand. This surface product can be cut, routed, drilled, sculpted, bent, or worked like a fine wood, and you can order it in a range of colors. DuPont developed an extensive product line made from its Corian surface. It sold the materials to companies that then used it to make high-end kitchen and bath countertop materials and sinks.

Despite its initial success, more recently, DuPont was running into a problem: The patent on Corian had expired, so competitors could copy the product. This segment of the construction products business was growing, but DuPont was losing its competitive edge. As a result, Corian had lost significant market share and was making very little money for the company.

DuPont's longstanding strategy had been to sell Corian through independent distributors that had exclusive territories. The distributors then sold to specialized fabricators, who in turn sold to kitchen dealers or commercial customers. All of these

my motto to live by	what drives me	my management style	my pet peeve
Growth is everything in nature.	Desire to grow, personally and professionally.	Open, casual, comfortable with conflict, involving, externally oriented, focused on the future.	Hallway politics.

objectives

1 Describe the general characteristics of business-to-business markets.

2 Explain the unique characteristics of business demand.

3 Describe how business or organizational markets are classified.

4 Explain the business buying situation and describe business buyers.

5 Explain the roles in the business buying center.

6 Understand the stages in the business buying decision process.

7 Understand the growing role of B2B e-commerce.

companies were authorized by DuPont to represent the product, and they offered a DuPont-backed warranty.

The firm focused on maintaining exclusive relationships with a few distributors. Meanwhile, other manufacturers began to build market share by developing relationships with larger retailers, builders, and major commercial accounts. As the race to sell high-end construction materials heated up, DuPont's marketing partners had lost faith in DuPont's commitment to the business. They were jumping ship to more aggressive and broad-based competitors. Within the company, however, DuPont's management regarded its Corian line as a mature business and limited its investment in new product development and marketing. The competition was taking advantage of this complacency to exploit the sleeping giant. Steve McCracken considered the best way to deal with this problem:

OPTION 1: Stay the course.

Hunker down and be satisfied with serving a small, high-end niche market by providing an exclusive group of distributors with well-designed (but relatively expensive) materials. This would be a pretty safe move, since DuPont still had good relationships with many of these partners and there would be no need to revamp the company's management team or marketing strategy. However, by settling for a low growth strategy, DuPont would wind up with significant excess manufacturing capacity and it would continue to lose market share. In addition, Steve

had to think about the effect on morale within the company if it continued to languish rather than to lead.

OPTION 2: Stay the course, but invest significantly more money on the Corian brand to reinforce its leadership position versus emerging look-alike competitors.

This option would be well-received by the current management and DuPont's remaining partners, who would be reassured of the company's commitment to the brand. Still, it meant a big up-front investment without any assurance of success—and DuPont would still be surrendering its leadership role in the larger market.

OPTION 3: Make a radical change by revamping Corian's strategy.

Go for growth in a growth category and take advantage of DuPont's current leadership position while this still existed. This more visionary option had the highest growth potential—but the biggest downside risk. It would mean substantial investments in developing new products, forging new relationships with new partners in different channels, adopting new mass-production techniques, and expansion to global markets. That would be very stimulating, but also very stressful for Corian's management. And, such a change ran the risk of alienating DuPont's traditional marketing partners who would lose the historical relationship they now enjoyed.

Now, put yourself in Steve McCracken's shoes: Which option would you choose, and why?

Business Markets: Buying and Selling When Stakes Are High

You might think most marketers spend their days dreaming up the best way to promote cutting-edge Web browsers or funky shoes. Not so. Many marketers know that the "real action" more likely lies in lead pipes, office supplies, safety shoes, group medical insurance, meat lockers, or home construction products that are sold to businesses and other organizations. In fact, some of the most interesting and lucrative jobs for young marketers are in industries you've never heard of because these businesses don't deal directly with consumers.

Like an end consumer, a business buyer makes decisions—but with an important difference: The purchase may be worth millions of dollars, and both the buyer and the seller have a lot at stake (maybe even their jobs). A consumer may decide to buy two or three T-shirts at one time, each emblazoned with a different design. Fortune 500 companies such as Exxon, Pepsi-Cola, and Texaco buy hundreds, even thousands, of employee uniforms embroidered with their corporate logos in a single order.

Consider these transactions: IBM makes computer network servers to sell to its business customers. Procter & Gamble contracts with several advertising agencies to promote its brands at home and around the globe. The Metropolitan Opera buys costumes, sets, and programs. Mac's Diner buys a case of canned peas from BJ's Wholesale Club. The U.S. government places an order for 3,000 new IBM computers.

All these exchanges have one thing in common: they're part of **business-to-business marketing**. This is the marketing of goods and services that businesses and other organizations buy for purposes other than personal consumption. Some firms resell these goods and services, so they are part of a channel of distribution, something we will discuss more in Chapters 15 and 16. Other firms use the goods and services they buy to produce still other goods and services that meet the needs of their customers or to support their own operations. These **business-to-business markets**, or **organizational markets**, include manufacturers, wholesalers, retailers, and a variety of other organizations, such as hospitals, universities, and government agencies.

To put the size and complexity of business markets into perspective, let's consider a single product—a pair of jeans. A consumer may browse through several racks of jeans and ultimately purchase a single pair, but the store at which the consumer shops has purchased many pairs of jeans in different sizes, styles, and brands from different manufacturers. Each of these manufacturers purchases fabrics, zippers, buttons, and thread from other manufacturers that in turn purchase the raw materials to make these components. In addition, all the firms in this chain need to purchase equipment, electricity, labor, computer systems, legal and accounting services, insurance, office supplies, packing materials, and countless other goods and services. Thus, even a single purchase of the latest style of Diesel jeans is the culmination of a series of buying and selling activities among many organizations—many people have been keeping busy while you're out shopping!

In this chapter, we'll look at the big picture of the business marketplace, a world in which the fortunes of business buyers and sellers can hang in the balance of a single transaction. Then we'll examine how marketers categorize businesses and other organizations to develop effective business marketing strategies. We'll look at business buying behavior and the business buying decision process. Finally, we'll talk about the important world of business-to-business e-commerce.

Some companies market products exclusively for other companies. WestLB arranges loans and provides other financial services for financial institutions and other corporate clients.

business-to-business marketing
The marketing of those goods and services that business and organizational customers need to produce other goods and services for resale or to support their operations.

business-to-business markets
The group of customers that include manufacturers, wholesalers, retailers, and other organizations.

organizational markets
Another name for business-to-business markets.

Characteristics That Make a Difference in Business Markets

In theory, the same basic marketing principles hold in both consumer and business markets—firms identify customer needs and develop a marketing mix to satisfy those needs. For example, take the company that made the desks and chairs in your classroom. Just like a firm that markets consumer goods, the classroom furniture company first must create an important competitive advantage for its target market of universities. Next the firm develops a marketing mix strategy beginning with a product—classroom furniture that will withstand years of use by thousands of students while providing a level of comfort required of a good learning environment (and you thought those hard-back chairs were intended just to keep you awake during class). The firm must offer the furniture at prices that universities will pay and that will allow the firm to make a reasonable profit. Then the firm must develop a sales force or other marketing communications strategy to make sure your university (and hundreds of others) consider—and hopefully choose—its products when it furnishes classrooms.

Although marketing to business customers does have a lot in common with consumer marketing, there are differences that make this basic process more complex.[1] Figure 6.1 provides a quick look at some of these differences. Let's review some now.

Multiple Buyers

In business markets, products often have to do more than satisfy an individual's needs. They must meet the requirements of everyone involved in the company's purchase decision. If you decide to buy a new chair for your room or apartment, you're the only one who has to be satisfied. For your classroom, the furniture must satisfy not only students but also faculty, administrators, campus planners, and the people at your school who actually do the purchasing. If your school is a state or other government institution, the furniture may also have to meet certain government-mandated engineering standards.

Number of Customers

Organizational customers are few and far between compared to end consumers. In the United States, there are about 100 million consumer households but less than half a million businesses and other organizations. Kodak's business division that markets sophisticated medical products to hospitals, health maintenance organizations, and other medical groups has a limited number of potential customers compared to its consumer film division. This means that business marketing strategies may be quite different from consumer markets. For example, in consumer markets Kodak may use TV advertising, but in its business markets a strong sales force is a far better means of promoting the product.

Size of Purchases

Business-to-business products can dwarf consumer purchases both in the quantity of items ordered and in the price of individual purchases. A company that rents uniforms to other businesses, for example, buys hundreds of large drums of laundry detergent each year to launder its uniforms. In contrast, even a hard-core soccer mom dealing with piles of dirty socks and shorts goes through a box of detergent only every few weeks. Organizations purchase many products, such as a highly sophisticated piece of manufacturing equipment or computer-based marketing information systems that can cost a million dollars or more. Recognizing such differences in the size of purchases allows marketers to develop effective marketing strategies. Although it makes perfect sense to use mass-media advertising to sell laundry detergent to consumers, selling thousands of dollars worth of laundry detergent or a million-dollar machine tool is best handled by a strong personal sales force. More on that in Chapter 14.

Geographic Concentration

Another difference between business markets and consumer markets is geographic concentration, meaning that many business customers are located in a small geographic area rather than being spread out across the country. Whether they live in the heart of New York City or in a

Figure 6.1 Differences Between Organizational and Consumer Markets

There are a number of major and minor differences between organizational and consumer markets. To be successful, marketers must understand these differences and develop strategies that can be effective with organizational customers.

Organizational Markets	Consumer Markets
• Purchases made for some purpose other than personal consumption	• Purchases for individual or household consumption
• Purchases made by someone other than the user of the product	• Purchases usually made by ultimate user of the product
• Decisions frequently made by several people	• Decisions usually made by individuals
• Purchases made according to precise technical specifications based on product expertise	• Purchases often based on brand reputation or personal recommendations with little or no product expertise
• Purchases made after careful weighing of alternatives	• Purchases frequently made on impulse
• Purchases based on rational criteria	• Purchases based on emotional responses to products or promotions
• Purchasers often engage in lengthy decision process	• Individual purchasers often make quick decisions
• Interdependencies between buyers and sellers; long-term relationships	• Buyers engage in limited-term or one-time-only relationships with many different sellers
• Purchases may involve competitive bidding, price negotiations, and complex financial arrangements	• Most purchases made at "list price" with cash or credit cards
• Products frequently purchased directly from producer	• Products usually purchased from someone other than producer of the product
• Purchases frequently involve high risk and high cost	• Most purchases are low risk and low cost
• Limited number of large buyers	• Many individual or household customers
• Buyers often geographically concentrated in certain areas	• Buyers generally dispersed throughout total population
• Products: often complex; classified based on how organizational customers use them	• Products: consumer goods and services for individual use
• Demand derived from demand for other goods and services, generally inelastic in the short run, subject to fluctuations, and may be joined to the demand for other goods and services	• Demand based on consumer needs and preferences, is generally price elastic, steady over time and independent of demand for other products
• Promotion emphasizes personal selling	• Promotion emphasizes advertising

small fishing village in Oregon, consumers buy and use toothpaste and televisions. Not so for business-to-business customers, who may be almost exclusively located in a single region of the country. Silicon Valley, for example, a 50-mile-long corridor along the California coast, is home to over 7,000 electronics and software companies because of its high concentration of skilled engineers and scientists.[2] For business-to-business marketers who wish to sell to these markets,

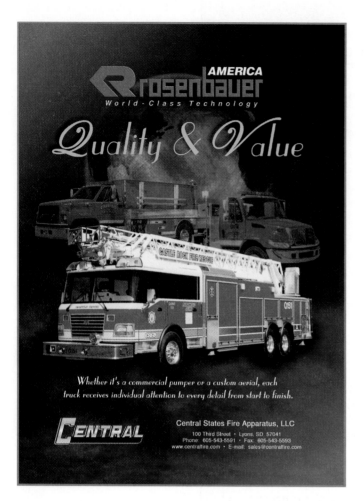

Sellers of firefighting equipment find a limited number of customers for their products.

AMERICA
Rosenbauer
World-Class Technology

Quality & Value

Whether it's a commercial pumper or a custom aerial, each truck receives individual attention to every detail from start to finish.

CENTRAL

Central States Fire Apparatus, LLC
100 Third Street • Lyons, SD 57041
Phone: 605-543-5591 • Fax: 605-543-5593
www.centralfire.com • E-mail: sales@centralfire.com

this means that they can concentrate their sales efforts and perhaps even locate distribution centers in a single geographic area.

Business-to-Business Demand

Demand in business markets differs from consumer demand. Most demand for business-to-business products is derived, inelastic, fluctuating, and joint. Understanding these differences in business-to-business demand is important for marketers in forecasting sales and in planning effective marketing strategies. Let's look at each of these concepts.

Derived Demand

Consumer demand is based on a direct connection between a need and the satisfaction of that need. But business customers don't purchase goods and services to satisfy their own needs. Business-to-business demand is **derived demand** because a business's demand for goods and services comes either directly or indirectly from consumers' demand.

Consider Figure 6.2. Demand for forestry products comes from the demand for pulp that makes paper used to make textbooks. The demand for textbooks comes from the demand for education (yes, that's the product you're buying—with the occasional party or football game thrown in as a bonus). As a result of derived demand, the success of one company may depend on another company in a different industry. The derived nature of business demand means that marketers must be constantly alert to changes in consumer trends that ultimately will have an effect on business-to-business sales.

derived demand
Demand for business or organizational products derived from demand for consumer goods or services.

inelastic demand
Demand in which changes in price have little or no effect on the amount demanded.

Inelastic Demand

Inelastic demand means that it usually doesn't matter if the price of a business-to-business product goes up or down—business customers still buy the same quantity. Demand in business-to-business markets is mostly inelastic because what is being sold is often just one of the many parts or materials that go into producing the consumer product. It is not unusual for a large increase in a business product's price to have little effect on the final consumer product's price.

For example, in 2004, you could buy a BMW Z4 Roadster 3.0i "loaded" with options for about $55,000.[3] To produce the car, BMW purchases thousands of different parts. If the price of tires, batteries, or stereos goes up or down, BMW will still buy enough to meet consumer demand for its cars. As you might imagine, increasing the price by $30 or $40 or even $100 won't change consumer demand for Beemers, so demand for parts remains the same (if you have to ask how much it costs, you can't afford it).

But business-to-business demand isn't always inelastic. Sometimes producing a consumer good or service relies on only one or a few materials or component parts. If the price of the part increases, demand may become elastic if the manufacturer of the consumer good passes the increase on to the consumer. Steel, for example, is a major component in automobiles. Automobile manufacturers will need to pay a lot more for steel should its price rise. An increase in the price of steel can drive up the price of automobiles so greatly that consumer demand for the automobiles drops, decreasing the demand for steel.

Figure 6.2 Derived Demand

Business-to-business demand is derived demand; that is, it is derived directly or indirectly from consumers' demand for another good or service. Some of the demand for forestry products is derived indirectly from the demand for education.

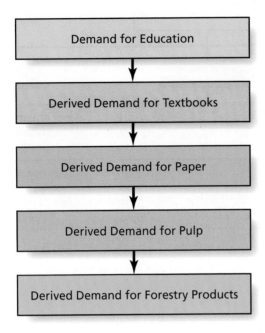

Fluctuating Demand

Business demand also is subject to greater fluctuations than is consumer demand. There are two reasons for this. First, even small changes in consumer demand can create large increases or decreases in business demand. Take, for example, air travel. Even a small increase in demand for air travel can cause airlines to order new equipment, creating a dramatic increase in demand for planes.

A product's life expectancy is another reason for fluctuating demand. Business customers tend to purchase certain products infrequently. Some types of large machinery may need to be replaced only every 10 or 20 years. Thus, demand for such products fluctuates—it may be very high one year when a lot of customers' machinery is wearing out but low the following year because everyone's old machinery is working fine. One solution for keeping production more constant is to use price reductions to encourage companies to order products *before* they actually need them.

Joint Demand

Joint demand occurs when two or more goods are necessary to create a product. For example, BMW needs tires, batteries, and spark plugs to make that Z4 roadster. If the supply of one of these parts decreases, BMW will be unable to manufacture as many automobiles, and so it will not buy as many of the other items either.

joint demand
Demand for two or more goods that are used together to create a product.

Types of Business-to-Business Markets

As we noted earlier, many firms buy products in business markets so they can produce other goods. Other business-to-business customers resell, rent, or lease goods and services. Still other customers, including governments and not-for-profit institutions such as the Red Cross or a local church, serve the public in some way. In this section, we'll look at the three major classes of business-to-business customers shown in Figure 6.3 (producers, resellers, and organizations). Then we'll look at how marketers classify specific industries.

Figure 6.3 The Business Marketplace

The business marketplace consists of three major categories of customers: producers, resellers, and organizations. Business-to-business marketers need to understand the different needs of these customers if they are to build successful relationships.

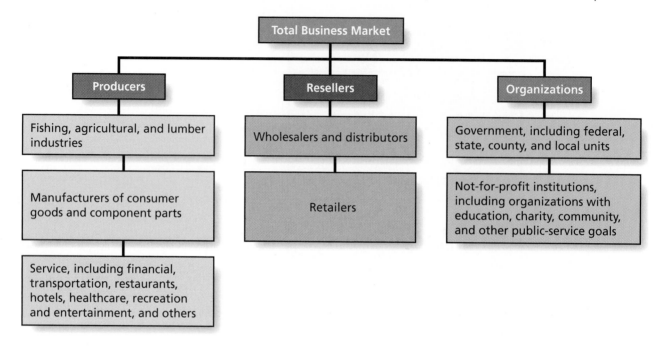

Producers

producers
The individuals or organizations that purchase products for use in the production of other goods and services.

Producers purchase products for the production of other goods and services that they in turn sell to make a profit. For this reason, they are customers for a vast number of products from raw materials to goods manufactured by still other producers. For example, DuPont buys resins and uses them to manufacture insulation material for sleeping bags. Dassault buys engines, high-tech navigation systems, passenger seats, and a host of other component parts to put into its planes. Luxury hotels buy linens, furniture, and food to produce the accommodations and meals their guests expect.

Resellers

resellers
The individuals or organizations that buy finished goods for the purpose of reselling, renting, or leasing to others to make a profit and to maintain their business operations.

Resellers buy finished goods for the purpose of reselling, renting, or leasing to other businesses. Although resellers do not actually produce goods, they do provide their customers with the time, place, and possession utility we talked about in Chapter 1 by making the goods available to consumers when and where they want them. For example, Wal-Mart buys toothpaste and peanuts and kids shoes and about a gazillion other products to sell in its 3,500-plus stores.

Organizations

government markets
The federal, state, county, and local governments that buy goods and services to carry out public objectives and to support their operations.

Governments and not-for-profit institutions are two types of organizations in the business market-place. **Government markets** make up the largest single business and organizational market in the United States. The U.S. Government market includes more than 3,000 county governments, 35,000 municipalities and townships, 28,000 special district governments, 50 states and the District of Columbia, plus the federal government. State and local government markets alone account for 15 percent of the U.S. gross national product.[4] And, of course, there are thousands more government customers around the globe.

Governments are just about the only customers for certain products—jet bombers, for example. But much of government expenditures are for more familiar and less expensive items. In

Speed. Power. Agility. The qualities that help a general — or a CEO — become a winner are the very qualities a Falcon 2000EX affords you. Small wonder our Falcon 2000-series jets have become the best selling large cabin planes among corporate and fractional owners. The 2000EX's ultra-spacious cabin is library-quiet. Its 3,800 nm range can take you from Paris to New York, Dubai to

London or São Paulo to Miami at .80 Mach — against headwinds — and a good deal faster on shorter flights. And perhaps best of all, you can enjoy all this capability and comfort at a surprisingly low cost of operation. So find out why a Falcon is the best designed, best built, best flying business jet in the world. Your charger awaits. www.falconjet.com

U.S. 201.541.4600 / France 33.1.47.11.82.32

DASSAULT FALCON
ENGINEERED WITH PASSION

The new Falcon 2000EX. From the family of best flying business jets in the world.

Dassault uses thousands of component parts to make corporate jets that are purchased by companies in order to transport their executives more efficiently (and in style).

one year, the government purchased more than five million bed sheets, nearly two million note pads, and 3.5 million paintbrushes.[5]

To inform possible vendors about purchases they are about to make, governments regularly make information on upcoming purchases available to potential bidders. The federal government provides information on business opportunities through its Web site at **www.FedBizOpps.gov**. All federal government buyers can post information directly to FedBizOpps.com via the Internet, and vendors can easily search, monitor, and retrieve opportunities at no cost.

Not-for-profit institutions are organizations with educational, community, and other public service goals, such as hospitals, churches, universities, museums, and charitable and cause-related organizations such as the Salvation Army and the Red Cross. These institutions tend to operate on low budgets. Because nonprofessional part-time buyers who have other duties often make purchases, these customers may rely on marketers to provide more advice and assistance before and after the sale.

North American Industry Classification System

In addition to looking at business-to-business markets within these three general categories, marketers identify their customers using the **North American Industry Classification System (NAICS)**. This is a numerical coding of industries developed by the United States, Canada, and Mexico. NAICS replaced the U.S. Standard Industrial Classification (SIC) system in 1997 so that the North American Free Trade Agreement (NAFTA) countries could compare economic and financial

not-for-profit institutions
The organizations with charitable, educational, community, and other public service goals that buy goods and services to support their functions and to attract and serve their members.

North American Industry Classification System (NAICS)
The numerical coding system that the United States, Canada, and Mexico use to classify firms into detailed categories according to their business activities.

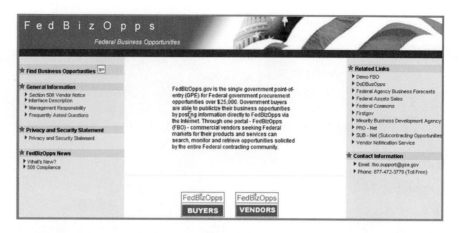

The federal government buys millions of dollars worth of goods and services each year. To find out about these purchases, marketers must check the Web site at **www.FedBizOpps.com**.

statistics.[6] The NAICS reports the number of firms, the total dollar amount of sales, the number of employees, and the growth rate for industries, all broken down by geographic region. Many firms use the NAICS to assess potential markets and to determine how well they are doing compared to their industry group (see Figure 6.4).

Firms may also use the NAICS to find new customers. A marketer might first determine the NAICS industry classifications of his current customers and then evaluate the sales potential of other firms occupying these categories. For example, a firm may determine that several large customers are in the wireless communication industry. To find new customers, the marketers could examine other firms in the same industrial group.

The Nature of Business Buying

So far we've talked about how business-to-business markets are different from consumer markets and about the different types of customers that make up business markets. In this section, we'll discuss some of the important characteristics of business buying. This is important because just like companies that

Figure 6.4 North American Industry Classification System (NAICS)

The North American Industrial Classification System (NAICS) identifies industries using a six-digit code that breaks the 20 sectors down into subsectors, industry groups, industries, and specific country industries.

		Frozen Fruit Example		*Cellular Telecommunications Example*
• Sector (two digits)	31–33	Manufacturing	51	Information
• Subsector (three digits)	311	Food Manufacturing	513	Broadcasting and Telecommunications
• Industry group (four digits)	3114	Fruit and Vegetable Preserving and Speciality Food Manufacturing	5133	Telecommunications
• Industry (five digits)	31141	Frozen Food Manufacturing	51332	Wireless Telecommunications Carriers (Except Satellite)
• U.S. Industry (six digits)	311311	Frozen Fruit, Juice, and Vegetable Manufacturing	513322	Cellular and Other Wireless Telecommunications

sell to end consumers, a successful business-to-business marketer needs to understand how his or her customers make decisions. Armed with this knowledge, the company is able to participate in the buyer's decision process from the start. Take a firm that sells equipment to hospitals. Understanding that physicians who practice at the hospital (rather than the employees who actually purchase medical supplies) often initiate new equipment purchases means that the firm's salespeople have to be sure that they establish solid relationships with doctors as well as with the hospital's buyers if they expect their products to be taken seriously.

The Buying Situation

Like end consumers, business buyers spend more time and effort on some purchases than on others. Devoting such effort to a purchase decision usually depends on the complexity of the product and how often the decision has to be made. A **buy class** framework identifies the degree of effort required of the firm's personnel to collect information and make a purchase decision. These classes, which apply to three different buying situations, are called straight rebuys, modified rebuys, and new-task buys.

STRAIGHT REBUY   A **straight rebuy** is the routine purchase of items that a business-to-business customer regularly needs. The buyer has purchased the same items many times before and routinely reorders them when supplies are low, often from the same suppliers. Reordering takes little time. Buyers typically maintain a list of approved vendors that have demonstrated their ability to meet the firm's criteria for pricing, quality, service, and delivery.

Because straight rebuys often contribute the "bread and butter" revenue a firm needs to maintain a steady stream of income, many business marketers go to great lengths to cultivate and maintain relationships with customers who submit reorders on a regular basis. Salespeople, for example, regularly call on these customers to personally handle orders and to see if there are additional products the customer needs. The goal is to be sure that the customer doesn't even think twice about just buying the same product every time he or she is running low. Rebuys keep a supplier's sales volume up and selling costs down.

MODIFIED REBUY   Alas, straight rebuy situations do not last forever. A **modified rebuy** occurs when a firm wants to shop around for suppliers with better prices, quality, or delivery times. This situation also can occur when the organization has new needs for products it already buys. A buyer who has purchased many office printers in the past, for example, may have to evaluate several lines of printers if the firm has a new need for office equipment.

Modified rebuys require more time and effort than straight rebuys. The buyer generally knows the purchase requirements and a few potential suppliers. Marketers know that modified rebuys can mean that some vendors get added to a buyer's approved supplier list while others may be dropped. Astute marketers routinely call on buyers to detect and define problems that can lead to winning or losing in such situations.

NEW-TASK BUY   A first-time purchase is a **new-task buy**. Uncertainty and risk characterize buying decisions in this classification, and they need the most effort because the buyer has no previous experience on which to base a decision.

By offering its customers the capability to send heavier shipments, DHL hopes that its business customers will routinely use the company for all its straight rebuy purchases.

buy class
One of three classifications of business buying situations that characterizes the degree of time and effort required to make a decision.

straight rebuy
A buying situation in which business buyers make routine purchases that require minimal decision making.

modified rebuy
A buying situation classification used by business buyers to categorize a previously made purchase that involves some change and that requires limited decision making.

new-task buy
A new business-to-business purchase that is complex or risky and that requires extensive decision making.

The purchase of office equipment is a modified rebuy for most business-to-business customers. Although companies have purchased printers and copiers before, Xerox now offers them a multitasking machine that prints, copies, e-mails, scans, and faxes.

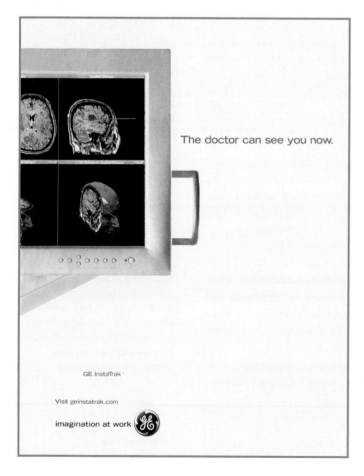

When companies like General Electric develop revolutionary new medical equipment, hospitals face a new-task buy.

Your university, for example, may decide (if it hasn't done so already) to go into the "distance learning" business, which is delivering courses to off-site students. Buying the equipment to set up classrooms with two-way video transmission is an expensive and complex new-task buy for a school. The buyer has to start from scratch to gather information on purchase specifications that may be highly technical and complex and require detailed input from others. In new-task buying situations, not only do buyers lack experience with the product, but they also are often unfamiliar with firms that supply the product. Supplier choice, then, is critical, and buyers gather much information about quality, pricing, delivery, and service from several potential suppliers.

A prospective customer's new-task buying situation represents both a challenge and an opportunity. Although a new-task buy can be significant in and of itself, many times the chosen supplier gains the added advantage of becoming an "in" supplier for more routine purchases that will follow.

A growing business that needs an advertising agency for the first time, for example, may seek exhaustive information from several firms before selecting one, but then it may continue to use the chosen agency's services for future projects without exploring other alternatives. Marketers know that to get the order in a new-buy situation, they must develop a close working relationship with the business buyer.

The Professional Buyer

Just as it is important for marketers of consumer goods and services to understand their customers, it is essential that business-to-business marketers understand who handles the buying for business customers. Trained professional buyers typically carry out buying in business-to-business markets. These people typically have titles such as purchasing agents, procurement officers, or directors of materials management.

While some consumers like to shop 'til they drop almost every day, most of us spend far less time roaming the aisles. However, professional purchasers do it all day, every day. These individuals focus on economic factors beyond the initial price of the product, including transportation and delivery charges, accessory products or supplies, maintenance, and other ongoing costs. They are responsible for selecting quality products and ensuring their timely delivery. They shop as if their jobs depended on it—and they do.

The Buying Center

Many times in business buying situations, several people work together to reach a decision. Depending on what they need to purchase, these participants may be production workers, supervisors, engineers, secretaries, shipping clerks, or financial officers. In a small organization, everyone may have a voice in the decision. The group of people in the organization who participate in

Advice for DuPont

PROFESSOR
ALKA VARMA CITRIN
College of Management, Georgia Institute of Technology

I would choose option 3. It is vital that DuPont capitalizes on its market position and brand recognition given the expanding market potential. Two important points need to be considered. First, DuPont should not allow the product life cycle stage to become a self-fulfilling prophecy. Since there is a clear demand for products with the benefits that Corian offers, DuPont should focus on rejuvenating the brand by investing in developing new uses and applications of Corian while simultaneously exploring new markets. This is particularly critical since its patent has expired and only continuous innovation both in the product and its applications can protect its market share from competition. Second, the exclusive relationships DuPont originally forged make sense only as long as the distribution partners help enhance market entry and positioning. The current market for Corian products appears to offer the potential both for high end, exclusive products and more mass market, quality product applications. Clearly, the existing distributing partners need to be "sold" on the profit potential which DuPont's new focus can offer.

PROFESSOR
EHSAN SALEK
Virginia Wesleyan College

I would choose option 3. Option 1 offers the status quo, and although it's a low-risk strategy, it results in further loss of market share and prestige for Dupont. Option 2, though better than option 1, is like fighting the old mature war with new ammunition. It will be exhausting to fight against well-heeled imitators who have established direct marketing relationships with major retail chains like Home Depot. Therefore, I recommend option 3, a radical change in strategy, involving new versions of Corian, with more marble-like shine to them, maybe a brand new product line with a new name. This strategy will require aggressive marketing and advertising and the establishment of more direct relationships with major distributors. Increasing sales and market share, which will employ the company's excess capacity, resulting in better cost efficiency and better margins, is the way to go.

---

the decision-making process is referred to as the **buying center**. Although this term may conjure up an image of offices buzzing with purchasing activity, a buying center is not a place at all. Instead, it is a cross-functional team of decision makers. Generally, the members of a buying center have some expertise or interest in the particular decision, and as a group they are able to make the best decision.

> **buying center**
> The group of people in an organization who participate in a purchasing decision.

Hospitals, for example, frequently make purchase decisions through a large buying center. When making a decision to purchase disposable oxygen masks, one or more physicians, the director of nursing, and purchasing agents may work together to determine quantities and select the best products and suppliers. A separate decision regarding the types of pharmaceutical supplies to stock might need a different cast of characters to advise the purchasing agent. Marketers must continually identify which employees in a firm take part in every purchase and develop relationships with them all.

Depending on the complexity of the purchase and the size of the buying center, a participant may assume one, several, or all of the six roles shown in Figure 6.5. Let's review them here:

- The *initiator* begins the buying process by first recognizing that the firm needs to make a purchase. A production employee, for example, may notice that a piece of equipment is not working properly and notify a supervisor. At other times, the initiator may suggest purchasing a new product because it will improve the firm's operations. Depending on the initiator's position in the organization and the type of purchase, the initiator may or may not influence the actual purchase decision. For marketers it's important to make sure that individuals who might initiate a purchase are aware of improved products they offer.

Figure 6.5 Roles in the Buying Center

A buying center is a group of individuals brought together for the purpose of making a purchasing decision. Marketers need to understand that the members of the buying center play a variety of different roles in the process.

Role	Potential Player	Responsibility
• Initiator	• Production employees, sales manager, almost anyone	• Recognizes that a purchase needs to be made
• User	• Production employees, secretaries, almost anyone	• Individual(s) who will ultimately use the product
• Gatekeeper	• Buyer/purchasing agent	• Controls flow of information to others in the organization
• Influencer	• Engineers, quality control experts, technical specialists, outside consultants	• Affects decision by giving advice and sharing expertise
• Decider	• Purchasing agent, managers, CEO	• Makes the final purchase decision
• Buyer	• Purchasing agent	• Executes the purchase decision

- The *user* is the member of the buying center who actually needs the product. The user's role in the buying center varies. For example, an administrative assistant may give his input on the features needed in a new copier that he will be "chained to" for several hours a day. Marketers need to inform users of their products' benefits, especially if the benefits outweigh those that competitors offer.

- The *gatekeeper* is the person who controls the flow of information to other members. Typically the gatekeeper is the purchasing agent who gathers information and materials from salespeople, schedules sales presentations, and controls suppliers' access to other participants in the buying process. For salespeople, developing and maintaining strong personal relationships with gatekeepers is critical to being able to offer their products to the buying center.

- An *influencer* affects the buying decision by dispensing advice or sharing expertise. By virtue of their expertise, engineers, quality control specialists, and other technical experts in the firm generally have a great deal of influence in purchasing equipment, materials, and component parts used in production. The influencers may or may not wind up using the product. Marketers need to identify key influencers in the buying center and work to persuade them of their product's superiority.

- The *decider* is the member of the buying center who makes the final decision. This person usually has the greatest power within the buying center; he or she often has power within the organization to authorize spending the company's money. For a routine purchase, the decider may be the purchasing agent. If the purchase is complex, a manager or chief executive officer (CEO) may be the decider. Quite obviously, the decider is key to a marketer's success and deserves a lot of attention in the selling process.

- The *buyer* is the person who has responsibility for executing the purchase. Although the buyer often has a role in identifying and evaluating alternative suppliers, this person's primary function is handling the details of the purchase. The buyer obtains competing bids, negotiates contracts, and arranges delivery dates and payment plans. Once a firm makes the purchase decision, marketers turn their attention to negotiating the details of the purchase with the buyer. Successful marketers are well aware that providing exemplary service in this stage of the purchase can be key to future sales.

The Business Buying Decision Process

We've seen there are a number of players in the business buying process, beginning with an initiator and ending with a buyer. To make matters even more challenging to marketers, members of the buying team go through several stages in the decision-making process. The business buying decision process, as Figure 6.6 shows, is a series of steps similar to those in the consumer decision process. To help understand these steps, let's say you've just started working at the Way Radical Skateboard Company and you've been assigned to be in the buying center for the purchase of new Web page design computer software, a new-task buy for your firm.

Step 1: Problem Recognition

As in consumer buying, the first step in the business buying decision process occurs when someone sees that a purchase can solve a problem. For straight rebuy purchases, this step may result because the firm has run out of paper, pens, or garbage bags. In these cases, the buyer places the order, and the decision-making process ends. Recognition of the need for modified rebuy purchases often comes from wanting to replace outdated existing equipment, from changes in technology, or from an ad, brochure, or some other marketing communication that offers the customer a better product or one at a lower price. Two events may occur in the problem recognition step. First, a request or requisition, usually written, is made. Depending on the complexity of the purchase, a buying center may be formed.

RUN EVERYTHING FASTER.

Only VERITAS software identifies the root cause of performance problems, from business applications all the way down to storage arrays. Software for Utility Computing. At veritas.com

VERITAS™

© 2004 VERITAS Software Corporation. All rights reserved. VERITAS and the VERITAS Logo are trademarks or registered trademarks of VERITAS Software Corporation or its affiliates in the U.S. and other countries. Other names may be trademarks of their respective owners.

Users are important members of the buying center for purchases like storage software.

The need for new-task purchases often occurs because the firm wants to enhance its operations in some way or when a smart salesperson tells the business customer about a new product that will increase the efficiency of the firm's operations or improve the firm's end products. In the case of Way Radical's new software purchase, your marketing department has previously had its Web page designed and maintained by an outside agency. The company has become dissatisfied with the outside supplier and has decided to move the design function in-house. Now new software is needed to create a truly Way Radical Web site.

Step 2: Information Search

In the second step of the decision process (for purchases other than straight rebuys), the buying center searches for information about products and suppliers. Members of the buying center may individually or collectively refer to reports in trade magazines and journals, seek advice from outside consultants, and pay close attention to marketing communications from different manufacturers and suppliers. As in consumer marketing, it's the job of marketers to make sure that information is available when and where business customers want it—by placing ads in trade magazines, by mailing brochures and other printed material to prospects, and by having a well-trained, enthusiastic sales force regularly calling on customers. For Way Radical's purchase, you may try to find

Figure 6.6 **Steps in the Business Buying Process**

The steps in the business buying decision process are the same as those in the consumer decision process. But for business purchases, each step may be far more complex and require more attention from marketers.

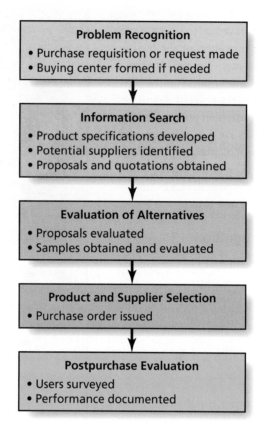

out what software your outside supplier has been using (if the supplier will tell you), you may talk to the information technology experts in your firm, or you may review ads and articles in trade magazines.

Indeed, there are thousands of specialized publications out there that cater to just about any industry you can think of, and each is bursting with information from competing companies that cater to a specific niche (who needs that fluffy romance novel at the beach—try leafing through the latest issue of *Chemical Processing* or *Meat and Poultry Magazine* instead).

Of course, sometimes business-to-business marketers try to get the information about their product into the hands of buyers by using less specialized media. Recently, Parker Hannifin, a company that makes products like hoses and valves, ran commercials on networks that engineers watch like the Learning Channel and the History Channel. In one spot, two men (presumably engineers) are checking out two gorgeous women sitting at the other end of a sushi bar. As one of the women sensuously uses chopsticks to dunk a piece of sushi in sauce and hoist it to her lips, one of the men says to his companion, "Do you see what I see?" His friend replies, "Oh yeah," as the picture cuts to a research lab where one of the guys demonstrates a robotic arm pulling a lobster out of a tank. The campaign's slogan is "Engineers see the world differently." We'll say.[7]

product specifications
A written description of the quality, size, weight, and so forth required of a product purchase.

DEVELOPING PRODUCT SPECIFICATIONS Business buyers often develop **product specifications**, that is, a written description of the quality, size, weight, color, features, quantity, training, warranty, service terms, and delivery requirements for the purchase. When the product needs are complex or technical, engineers and other experts are the key players in identifying specific product characteristics and determining whether standardized, off-the-shelf or customized, made-to-order goods and services will do. Although there is excellent Web design software available, for some computer applications custom-designed software is necessary.

IDENTIFYING POTENTIAL SUPPLIERS AND OBTAINING PROPOSALS   Once the product specifications are in hand, the next step may be to identify potential suppliers and obtain written or verbal proposals, or bids, from one or more of them. For standardized or branded products in which there are few if any differences in the products of different suppliers, this may be as simple as an informal request for pricing information, including discounts, shipping charges, and confirmation of delivery dates. At other times, the potential suppliers will receive a formal written request for proposal or request for quotation that requires detailed proposals or price quotations for supplying the product. For the Way Radical software, which is likely to be a standardized software package, you will probably just ask for general pricing information.

Step 3: Evaluation of Alternatives

In this stage of the business buying decision process, the buying center assesses the proposals. Total spending for goods and services can have a major impact on the firm's profitability, so all other things being equal, price is the primary consideration. Pricing evaluations must take into account discount policies for certain quantities, returned-goods policies, the cost of repair and maintenance services, terms of payment, and the cost of financing large purchases. For capital equipment, cost criteria also include the life expectancy of the purchase, the expected resale value, and disposal costs for the old equipment. In some cases, the buying center may negotiate with the preferred supplier to match the lowest bidder.

Although a bidder often is selected because it offers the lowest price, there are times when the buying decision is based on other factors. For example, American Express wins bids for its travel agency business by offering extra services other agencies don't typically offer, such as a corporate credit card and monthly reports that detail the company's total travel expenses.

The more complex and costly the purchase, the more time buyers spend searching for the best supplier—and the more marketers must do to win the order. In some cases, a company may even ask one or more of its current customers to participate in a *reference program* where they recommend products to others. For example, Siebel Systems regularly enlists about 350 corporate purchasers of its computer systems to explain to new prospects how their system works and why they chose Siebel's products. The payoff for customers? They can network with other existing customers to gain insights about how to better use the company's products—and as a Siebel executive observes, "We're able to make the customers heroes. . . . " by involving them in speaking engagements and articles in trade magazines—a win-win situation for everyone.[8]

Marketers often make formal presentations and product demonstrations to the buying center group. In the case of installations and large equipment, marketers sometimes arrange for buyers to speak with or even visit other customers to examine how the product performs. For less complex products, the buying firm may ask potential suppliers for samples of the products to try in order to evaluate alternatives. For the Way Radical Web site, your buying center may ask salespeople from various companies to demonstrate their software for your group so that you can compare the capabilities of different products.

Step 4: Product and Supplier Selection

Once buyers have assessed all proposals, it's time for the rubber to hit the road. The next step in the buying process is the purchase decision—the selection of the best product and supplier to meet the firm's needs. As noted earlier, although price is usually a factor, in firms that have adopted a Total Quality Management approach, the quality, reliability, and durability of materials and component parts are paramount. Reliability and durability rank especially high for equipment and systems that keep the firm's operations running smoothly without interruption. For some purchases, warranties, repair service, and regular maintenance after the sale are important. For Way Radical, the final decision may be based not only on the capabilities of the software itself but also on the technical support provided by the software company. What kind of support is available and at what cost to the company?

A supplier's ability to make on-time deliveries is the critical factor in the selection process for firms that have adopted an inventory management system called **just in time (JIT)**. JIT systems reduce stock to very low levels or even zero and ensure a constant inventory through deliveries just when needed. The advantage of JIT systems is the reduced cost of warehousing. For both manufacturers and resellers that use JIT systems, the choice of supplier may come down to one whose location is nearest. To win a large customer, a supplier may even have to be willing to set up production facilities close to the customer to guarantee JIT delivery.[9]

One of the most important decisions of a buyer is how many suppliers can best serve the firm's needs. Sometimes one supplier is more beneficial to the organization than multiple suppliers. **Single sourcing**, in which a buyer and seller work quite closely, is particularly important when a firm needs frequent deliveries or specialized products. But reliance on a single source means that the firm is at the mercy of the chosen supplier to deliver the needed goods or services without interruption.

Multiple sourcing means buying a product from several different suppliers. Under this system, suppliers are more likely to remain price competitive. And if one supplier has problems with delivery, the firm has others to fall back on. However, using one or a few suppliers rather than many has its advantages. A firm that buys from a single supplier becomes a large customer with a lot of clout when it comes to negotiating prices and contract terms. Having one or a few suppliers also lowers the firm's administrative costs because it has fewer invoices to pay, fewer contracts to negotiate, and fewer salespeople to see than if it used many sources.

Sometimes supplier selection is based on **reciprocity**, which means that a buyer and seller agree to be each other's customers by saying essentially, "I'll buy from you, and you buy from me." For example, a firm that supplies parts to a company that manufactures trucks would agree to buy trucks from only that firm.

The U.S. government frowns on reciprocal agreements and often determines that such agreements between large firms are illegal because they limit free competition—new suppliers simply don't have a chance against the preferred suppliers. Reciprocity between smaller firms, that is, firms that are not so large as to control a significant proportion of the business in their industry, is legal in the United States if it is voluntarily agreed to by both parties. In other countries, reciprocity is a practice that is common and even expected in business-to-business marketing.

Outsourcing occurs when firms obtain outside vendors to provide goods or services that might otherwise be supplied in-house. For example, Aramark provides a wide range of services for business and organizational customers—including uniforms for Wal-Mart, child care for the Pentagon, and even serving "mystery meat" in hundreds of university cafeterias.

Yet another type of buyer–seller partnership is **reverse marketing**. Instead of sellers trying to identify potential customers and then "pitching" their products, buyers try to find suppliers capable of producing specific needed products and then attempt to "sell" the idea to the suppliers. The seller aims to satisfy the buying firm's needs. Often large poultry producers practice reverse marketing. Perdue supplies baby chickens, chicken food, financing for chicken houses, medications, and everything else necessary for farmers to lay "golden eggs" for the company. The farmer is assured a market, and Perdue is guaranteed a supply of chickens.

Step 5: Postpurchase Evaluation

Just as consumers evaluate purchases, an organizational buyer assesses whether the performance of the product and the supplier is living up to expectations. The buyer surveys the users to determine their satisfaction with the product as well as with the installation, delivery, and service provided by the supplier. For producers of goods, this may relate to the level of satisfaction of the final consumer

just in time (JIT)
Inventory management and purchasing processes that manufacturers and resellers use to reduce inventory to very low levels and ensure that deliveries from suppliers arrive only when needed.

single sourcing
The business practice of buying a particular product from only one supplier.

multiple sourcing
The business practice of buying a particular product from many suppliers.

reciprocity
A trading partnership in which two firms agree to buy from one another.

outsourcing
The business buying process of obtaining outside vendors to provide goods or services that otherwise might be supplied in-house.

reverse marketing
A business practice in which a buyer firm attempts to identify suppliers who will produce products according to the buyer firm's specifications.

of the buying firm's product. Has demand for the producer's product increased, decreased, or stayed the same? By documenting and reviewing supplier performance, a firm decides whether to keep or drop the supplier. Many suppliers recognize the importance of conducting their own performance reviews on a regular basis. Measuring up to a customer's expectations can mean winning or losing a big account. Many a supplier has lost business because of a past history of late deliveries or poor equipment repairs and maintenance.

Business-to-Business E-Commerce

As we saw in our discussion of B2C e-commerce, the Internet has brought about massive changes in marketing—from the creation of new products to providing more effective and efficient marketing communications to the actual distribution of some products. And this is certainly true in business markets: **Business-to-business (B2B) e-commerce** refers to the Internet exchanges between two or more businesses or organizations. B2B e-commerce includes exchanges of information, products, services, and payments. It's not as glitzy as consumer e-commerce, but it sure has changed the way businesses operate. For example, in a typical year, General Electric and other firms like it save billions of dollars by buying supplies over the Internet. For sellers, too, e-commerce provides remarkable advantages. Boeing, for example, received orders for $100 million in spare parts in the first year its Web site was in operation.[10]

FANATICAL SUPPORT IS THE DIFFERENCE ™

Rackspace — Managed Hosting backed by Fanatical Support.™

Servers, data centers and bandwidth are not the key to hosting enterprise class Web sites and Web applications. At Rackspace, we believe hosting is a service, not just technology.

Fanatical Support is our philosophy, our credo. It reflects our desire to bring responsiveness and value to everything we do for our customers. You will experience Fanatical Support from the moment we answer the phone and you begin to interact with our employees.

Fanatical Support has made Rackspace the fastest-growing hosting company in the world. Call today to experience the difference with Fanatical Support at Rackspace.

Microsoft GOLD CERTIFIED Partner
Hosting Solutions Partner of the Year
Microsoft Honors Rackspace with "Hosting Solutions Partner of the Year"

rackspace MANAGED HOSTING
1.888.571.8961
or visit us at www.rackspace.com

The explosion in B2B e-commerce has created an entirely new industry composed of companies that manage other companies' data.

Using the Internet for e-commerce allows business marketers to link directly to suppliers, factories, distributors, and their customers, radically reducing the time necessary for order and delivery of goods, tracking sales, and getting feedback from customers. Forrester Research, an Internet research firm, projects that B2B sales growth will continue after reaching $2.7 trillion by 2004. Half of those transactions will take place through auctions, bids, and exchanges.[11]

In the simplest form of B2B e-commerce, the Internet provides an online catalog of products and services that businesses need. Companies find that their Internet site is important for delivering online technical support, product information, order status information, and customer service to corporate customers. Many companies, for example, save millions of dollars a year by replacing hard-copy manuals with electronic downloads. And, of course, B2B e-commerce has created some exciting opportunities for brand-new B2B service industries. Companies like RackSpace that host other companies e-commerce operations provide essential services for successful B2B e-commerce marketers.

Intranets, Extranets, and Private Exchanges

Although the Internet is the primary means of B2B e-commerce, many companies maintain intranets, which provide more secure means of conducting business. As we said in Chapter 4, an *intranet* is an internal corporate computer network that uses Internet technology to link company departments, employees, and databases. Intranets give access only to authorized employees. They allow companies to process internal transactions with greater control and consistency because of stricter security measures than those they can use on the entire Web. Businesses also use intranets for videoconferencing, distributing internal documents, communicating with geographically dispersed branches, and training employees.

business-to-business (B2B) e-commerce
Internet exchanges between two or more businesses or organizations.

The Web allows employees within a company and across companies to communicate and brainstorm in real time. Groove Networks is an innovative system that allows many people on a project to share ideas and submit sketches and text that can be viewed and modified by others on the team—or around the world.

extranet

A private, corporate computer network that links company departments, employees, and databases to suppliers, customers, and others outside the organization.

When a company allows certain suppliers, customers, and others outside the organization to access its intranet, the system is known as an **extranet**. A business customer who has been authorized to use a supplier's extranet can place orders online. Extranets can be especially useful for companies that need to have secure communications between the company and its dealers, distributors, and/or franchisees.

Tricon Restaurant International, parent company of Taco Bell, has found extranets a good way to communicate with franchisees.[12] Taco Bell had been spending hundreds of thousands of dollars per year sending informational update packages—everything from recipes to tie-ins to a popular ad campaign featuring a Spanish-speaking Chihuahua—to its 2,800 independent franchised restaurants around the world. Now thousands of documents are on Taco Bell's extranet where franchisees can wake up to new information every morning. Tricon plans to extend its extranet operations to its other two restaurant chains, Kentucky Fried Chicken and Pizza Hut.

As you can imagine, intranets and extranets are very cost efficient. Prudential Health Care's extranet allows its corporate customers to enroll new employees and check eligibility and claim status themselves. This saves Prudential money because fewer customer service personnel are needed, there are no packages of insurance forms to mail back and forth, and Prudential doesn't even have to input policyholder data into the company database.[13]

In addition to saving companies money, extranets allow business partners to collaborate on projects (such as product design) and to build relationships. Hewlett-Packard and Procter & Gamble swap marketing plans and review ad campaigns with their advertising agencies through extranets. This way they can exchange ideas quickly without having to spend money on travel and meetings. General Electric's extranet, called the Trading Process Network, also connects General Electric with large buyers such as Con Edison.[14]

private exchanges

Systems that link an invited group of suppliers and partners over the Web.

Some of the most interesting online activity in the B2B world is taking place on **private exchanges**. No, these aren't "adult sites"; they are systems that link a specially invited group of suppliers and partners over the Web. A private exchange allows companies to collaborate with suppliers they trust—without sharing sensitive information with others.

Wal-Mart, IBM, and Hewlett-Packard are among the giant firms already operating private exchanges. Many other companies are getting on board as well. For example, the director of inventory control for Ace Hardware can click his mouse and instantly get an up-to-the minute listing of the screwdrivers, hammers, and other products his suppliers have in stock. In addition, suppliers he has invited to participate in his private exchange (and *only* those suppliers) can submit bids when he sees that Ace stores are running low on hammers. In the "old days" before this process, it would take 7 to 10 days to purchase more hammers, and Ace's suppliers could only guess how many they should have on hand to supply the store chain at any given time. The system benefits everyone because Ace keeps tighter controls on its inventories, and its suppliers have a more accurate picture of the store's needs so they can get rid of unneeded inventory and streamline their costs.

Indeed, IBM estimates that it saved almost $400 million in 2000 by relying on a private exchange system. Small wonder that one research firm estimates that the world's biggest corporations will soon spend between $50 million and $100 million total to build private exchanges.[15] It all sounds great—perhaps too great. Is there a downside to B2B e-commerce? Let's see.

Security Issues

There are several security issues that impact B2B e-commerce. You may be concerned about someone obtaining your credit card number and charging even more to your account than you do, but companies have even greater worries. When hackers break into company sites, they can destroy company records and steal trade secrets. Both B2C and B2B e-commerce companies worry about *authentication* and ensuring that transactions are secure. This means making sure that only authorized individuals are allowed to access a site and place an order. Maintaining security also requires firms to keep the information transferred as part of a transaction, such as a credit card number, from criminals' hard drives.

Well-meaning employees also can create security problems. They can give out unauthorized access to company computer systems by being careless about keeping their passwords into the system a secret. For example, hackers can guess at obvious passwords—nicknames, birth dates, hobbies, or a spouse's name. To increase security of their Internet sites and transactions, most companies now have safeguards in place—firewalls and encryption devices, to name the two most common methods.

FIREWALLS A *firewall* is a combination of hardware and software that ensures that only authorized individuals gain entry into a computer system. The firewall monitors and controls all traffic between the Internet and the intranet to restrict access. Companies may even place additional firewalls within their intranet when they wish only designated employees to have access to certain parts of the system. Although firewalls can be fairly effective (even though none are totally foolproof), they require costly, constant monitoring.

ENCRYPTION *Encryption* means scrambling a message so that only another individual (or computer) that has the right "key" for deciphering it can unscramble it. Otherwise, it looks like gobbledygook. The message is inaccessible without the appropriate encryption software—kind of like a decoder ring you might find in a cereal box. Without encryption, it would be easy for unethical people to get your credit card number by creating a "sniffer" program that intercepts and reads messages. A sniffer finds messages with four blocks of four numbers, copies the data, and voila! someone else has your credit card number. Even with basic encryption software, hackers have been able to steal thousands of credit card numbers from companies including Creditcards.com, Western Union, and online music retailer CD Universe. In these cases, the hackers threatened to post the stolen credit card numbers online unless extortion money was paid.

Despite these and other measures, Web security for B2B marketers remains a serious problem. The threat to intranet and extranet usage goes beyond competitive espionage. The increasing sophistication of hackers and Internet criminals who create viruses and worms and other means of disrupting individual computers and entire company systems means that all organizations—and consumers—are vulnerable to attacks and must remain vigilant.

real people, real choices
How It Worked Out at DuPont

Steve and his colleagues decided to take a risk by choosing Option 3. After an initial internal struggle and a great deal of stress, DuPont's commitment to its revitalized Corian business became clear to its key trade partners. The company was able to become relevant in new channels, its new construction materials products were largely successful, operational ills were improved, and new applications and mass production technologies created a buzz in the industry.

Corian also launched an aggressive communications campaign to reinforce its new look. The company did regional TV advertising, complemented by national magazine placements.

Advertising featured active people using products made from Corian, and the company came up with the powerful tag line, "Created for Life." New products included more fashion-forward colors, new sink designs, new vanity top designs, and some new "do-it-yourself" kit products for home center distribution. The company also enlarged the scope of products to include shower surrounds,

furniture such as dining room table tops, and even in electronics. For example, Mitsubishi started to use Corian as a cabinetry component in its large-screen TVs. Corian became an element of differentiation for these manufacturers and helped DuPont's current customer base expand into new markets.

DuPont also helped its fabricators to go direct to large homebuilders like Pulte and Dell Webb. The company also made it easier for its network to develop relationships with major mass merchants like Home Depot without having to go through intermediate dealers as they had done traditionally. This gave the homebuilders a profit motivation to encourage their customers to upgrade their kitchens with Corian counters and other products, so these partners were more enthusiastic about featuring Corian displays in their design centers.

DuPont now has a whole new base of potential customers including home centers, plumbing wholesalers, and builders. As a result, the Corian brand is growing faster than you can say "kitchen renovation." And DuPont's historical channel partners are enjoying this success as well.

To learn the ins and outs of how employers select candidates, go to Chapter 6 in *Brand You*.

CHAPTER SUMMARY

1. **Describe the general characteristics of business-to-business markets.** Business-to-business markets include business or organizational customers that buy goods and services for purposes other than for personal consumption. Business customers are usually few in number, may be geographically concentrated, and often purchase higher-priced products in larger quantities.

2. **Explain the unique characteristics of business demand.** Business demand is derived from the demand for another good or service, is generally not affected by price increases or decreases, is subject to great fluctuations, and may be tied to the demand and availability of some other good.

3. **Describe how business or organizational markets are classified.** Business customers include producers, resellers, governments, and not-for-profit organizations. Producers purchase materials, parts, and various goods and services needed to produce other goods and services to be sold at a profit. Resellers purchase finished goods to resell at a profit as well as other goods and services to maintain their operations. Governments and other not-for-profit organizations purchase the goods and services necessary to fulfill their objectives. The North American Industry Classification System (NAICS), a numerical coding system developed by NAFTA countries, is a widely used classification system for business and organizational markets.

4. **Explain the business buying situation and describe business buyers.** The business buy class identifies the degree and effort required to make a business buying decision. Purchase situations can be straight rebuy, modified rebuy, and new-task buying. Business buying is usually handled by trained professional buyers.

5. **Explain the roles in the business buying center.** A buying center is a group of people who work together to make a buying decision.

    The roles in the buying center are (1) the initiator who recognizes the need for a purchase, (2) the user who will ultimately use the product, (3) the gatekeeper who controls the flow of information to others, (4) the influencer who shares advice and expertise, (5) the decider who makes the final decision, and (6) the buyer who executes the purchase.

6. **Understand the stages in the business buying decision process.** The stages in the business buying decision process are similar to but more complex than the steps in consumer decision making. These steps include problem recognition, information search during which buyers develop product specifications and obtain proposals from prospective sellers, evaluating the proposals, selecting a supplier, and formally evaluating the performance of the product and the supplier. A firm's purchasing options include single or multiple sourcing. In outsourcing, firms obtain outside vendors to provide goods or services that otherwise might be supplied in-house. Other business buying activities are reciprocity and reverse marketing.

7. **Understand the growing role of B2B e-commerce.** Business-to-business (B2B) e-commerce refers to Internet exchanges of information, products, services, or payments between two or more businesses or organizations and allows business marketers to link directly to suppliers, factories, distributors, and their customers. An intranet is a secure internal corporate network used to link company departments, employees, and databases. Extranets link a company with authorized suppliers, customers, or others outside the organization. Companies address security issues by using firewalls and encryption.

KEY TERMS

business-to-business (B2B) e-commerce, 185
business-to-business marketing, 169
business-to-business markets, 169
buy class, 177
buying center, 179
derived demand, 172
extranet, 186
government markets, 174
inelastic demand, 172

joint demand, 173
just in time (JIT), 184
modified rebuy, 177
multiple sourcing, 184
new-task buy, 177
North American Industry Classification System (NAICS), 175
not-for-profit institutions, 175
organizational markets, 169

outsourcing, 184
private exchanges, 186
producers, 174
product specifications, 182
reciprocity, 184
resellers, 174
reverse marketing, 184
single sourcing, 184
straight rebuy, 177

CHAPTER REVIEW

MARKETING CONCEPTS: TESTING YOUR KNOWLEDGE

1. How do business-to-business markets differ from consumer markets? How do these differences affect marketing strategies?

2. Explain the unique characteristics of business demand.

3. How are business-to-business markets generally classified? What is the NAICS?

4. Describe new-task buys, modified rebuys, and straight rebuys. What are some different marketing strategies called for by each?

5. What are the characteristics of business buyers?

6. What is a buying center? What are the roles of the various people in a buying center?

7. What are the stages in the business buying decision process? What happens in each stage?

8. How are the stages in the business buying decision process similar to the steps in the consumer buying process? How are they different?

9. What is single sourcing? Multiple sourcing? Outsourcing? Explain how reciprocity and reverse marketing operate in business-to-business markets.

10. Explain the role of B2B e-commerce in today's marketplace.

MARKETING CONCEPTS: DISCUSSING CHOICES AND ISSUES

1. E-commerce is dramatically changing the way business-to-business transactions take place. What are the advantages of B2B e-commerce to companies? To society? Are there any disadvantages of B2B e-commerce?

2. The practice of buying business products based on sealed competitive bids is popular among all types of business buyers. What are the advantages and disadvantages of this practice to buyers? What are the advantages and disadvantages to sellers? Should companies always give the business to the lowest bidder? Why or why not?

3. When firms implement a single sourcing policy in their buying, other possible suppliers do not have an opportunity. Is this ethical? What are the advantages to the company? What are the disadvantages?

4. Many critics of government say that strict engineering and other manufacturing requirements for products purchased by governments increase prices unreasonably and that taxpayers end up paying too much because of such policies. What are the advantages and disadvantages of such purchase restrictions? Should governments loosen restrictions on their purchases?

5. In the buying center, the gatekeeper controls information flow to others in the center. Thus, the gatekeeper determines which possible sellers are heard and which are not. Does the gatekeeper have too much power? What policies might be implemented to make sure that all possible sellers are treated fairly?

6. In the chapter, we discussed how Siebel Systems has a reference program where previous purchasers of products are encouraged to share their experiences with a product with potential new customers. What are the advantages and disadvantages of such a reference program for companies like Siebel Systems? For previous customers? For prospective customers? For competitor firms?

MARKETING PRACTICE:
APPLYING WHAT YOU'VE LEARNED

1. As a director of purchasing for a firm that manufactures motorcycles, you have been notified that the price of an important part used in the manufacture of the bikes has nearly doubled. You see your company having three choices: (1) buying the part and passing the cost on to the customer by increasing your price; (2) buying the part and absorbing the increase in cost, keeping the price of your bikes the same; and (3) buying a lower-priced part that will be of lower quality. Prepare a list of pros and cons for each alternative. Then explain your recommendation and justification for it.

2. Assume that you are the marketing manager for a small securities firm (a firm that sells stocks and bonds) whose customers are primarily businesses and other organizations. Your company has so far not made use of the Internet to provide information and service to its customers. You are considering whether this move is in the best interests of your firm. Write a memo outlining the pros and cons of e-commerce for your firm, the risks your firm would face, and your recommendations.

3. As a new director of materials management for a textile firm that manufactures sheets and towels, you are hoping to simplify the buying process where possible, thus reducing costs for the firm. You have first examined each purchase and classified it as a straight rebuy, a modified rebuy, or a new-task purchase. Your next job is to outline the procedures or

steps in the purchasing process for each type of purchase. Indicate the type of purchase and outline the steps that must be taken in the purchase of each of the following items:
a. Computer paper
b. Textile dyes for this year's fashion colors
c. New sewing robotics
d. New software to control the weaving processes

MARKETING MINIPROJECT:
LEARNING BY DOING

The purpose of this miniproject is to gain knowledge about one business-to-business market using the NAICS codes and other government information.

1. Select an industry of interest to you and use the NAICS information found on the Internet (**www.census.gov/pub/ epcd/www/naics.html**) or in your library.
   a. What are the codes for each of the following classifications?
      NAICS Sector (two digits)
      NAICS Subsector (three digits)
      NAICS Industry Group (four digits)
      NAICS Industry (five digits)
      U.S. Industry (six digits)
   b. What types of products are or are not included in this industry?

2. Locate the U.S. Industrial Outlook or Standard & Poor's Industry Surveys in your library to find the answers to the following:
   a. What was the value of industry shipments (sales) for the United States in the latest year reported?
   b. What were worldwide sales for the industry in the most recent year reported?

3. The U.S. Census Bureau publishes a number of economic censuses every five years covering years ending in the digits 2 and 7. These include the following publications: *Census of Retail Trade, Census of Wholesale Trade, Census of Service Industries, Census of Transportation, Census of Manufacturers, Census of Mineral Industries,* and *Census of Construction Industries.* Use the *Census of Manufacturers* to determine the value of shipments in your industry for the most recent year reported.

4. *Ward's Business Directory* provides useful industry-specific information. Use it to find the names and addresses of the top four public companies in the industry and their sales revenues.

5. Compact Disclosure provides information from company annual reports on CD-ROM. Use it to provide the following for the four companies listed in question 4:
   a. Income statements
   b. Net sales, gross profits, and income before tax

6. *The Statistical Abstract of the United States* provides information on the economic, demographic, social, and political structures of the United States. It provides data on the sales of products in consumer markets. Use it to complete the following:

a. Find a product in the consumer market that is produced by your industry (or is down the chain from your industry, e.g., automobiles from the steel industry).
b. Determine the sales of the consumer product category for the most recent year reported.

REAL PEOPLE, REAL SURFERS: EXPLORING THE WEB

DuPont isn't the only company that makes textiles like Corian. Visit DuPont's Corian Web site (**www.corian.com**). Then explore the Web sites of one or more other similar manufacturers. Some other products similar to Corian are Avonite (www.avonite.com), Swanstone (www.swanstone.com) and Zodiaq (www.zodiaq.com).

On the basis of your experience, answer the following questions:

1. What are DuPont/Corian's main competitors?

2. In general, how do the competitors' Web sites compare with DuPont/Corian's? Which are easier to navigate, and why? Which are more innovative and attractive, and why?

3. Evaluate each site from the perspective of a Home Depot manager. What feature in each site would be useful? What information is available that a Home Depot manager might need? Over all, which site do you feel would be most useful to the manager? Why?

MARKETING PLAN EXERCISE

As you have learned, business-to-business marketing, or marketing to organizational markets, is big business. A successful marketing plan—even one focused on products used by end-user consumers—must focus significant attention on getting those products into consumers' hands, usually through a retailer or some other source that involved a business-to-business market.

As an example, pick a product you often buy in the grocery store.

1. What key elements of the organizational market (the grocer) must the product's manufacturer plan for to market it successfully to the grocer?

2. How do the elements identified in question 1 differ from how it is marketed to you as an end user?

3. In the case of the product you selected, which market is most important (the grocer or you), and why?

Marketing in Action Case

Real Choices at Airbus

Does the world really need an airplane that will carry up to 555 passengers at once? The executives at Airbus Industrie, the airplane manufacturer located in Toulouse, France, hope that the answer to this question is a resounding yes.

Airbus is a company that began in 1970 with funding provided by owners from Germany, Spain, Britain, and France. It operates entirely in the business-to-business market as a producer of passenger airplanes. As such, the company is dependent on other companies, mostly airlines located throughout the world, to purchase its products.

To date, the company has been very effective at developing and building airplanes that compete successfully with its only world competitor, Boeing, which is headquartered in Chicago and has been in existence for almost 90 years. For example, Airbus's current product line features planes like the A320 and A330, which are configured to carry up to 150 and 200 passengers, respectively. These planes compete very effectively against planes of similar size produced by Boeing, such as the 737 and 777. In fact, for 2003, Airbus was on target to deliver 300 new planes, while Boeing was planning to deliver 280.

Until recently, Airbus had no plans to produce a plane that competed in the "jumbo" category—the category currently dominated by Boeing's 747. That situation will change in the spring of 2005 when Airbus's A380 airplane will be ready for its first test flight. The A380 is a complete double-decker plane, the first of its kind that will carry 35 percent more passengers than a Boeing 747. In addition, the plane is being designed to cost only 2.5 cents per seat-mile to operate. Such a low cost makes the A380 the least expensive plane to fly in the world. However, despite the size increase and low operating cost, Airbus has to ask whether there is a market for this larger plane and whether introducing the 380 is the right decision to make.

As noted earlier, Airbus operates in a business-to-business environment. This means the company must gauge the potential demand for the new products such as this "superjumbo" jet. Gauging an airline's demand for such a large plane is difficult because an airline's demand for new and larger planes is derived demand; that is, it depends on consumers' need for travel. As many airlines can attest, determining travel trends and habits by consumers has been anything but an exact science lately. Such factors as terrorism, memories of the September 11 attacks, war, global economic uncertainty, and SARS (a highly contagious flu-like illness that caused thousands of deaths around the world in 2003) all have contributed to reduced traveling by consumers. As a result, airlines around the world have lost nearly $30 billion since 2001, and many have cut back on plans to upgrade or expand their fleet of planes.

Another factor affecting the decision Airbus faces in the acceptance of this new plane is the selling effort that Airbus must put behind it. Purchasing a plane that costs nearly $280 million and lasts approximately 40 years will require a tremendous amount of study and research on the part of the potential customer airlines. Consequently, even though an airline may already be a customer of Airbus, the decision process to purchase the A380 will resemble more of a new-task purchase than a modified or straight rebuy.

In addition, the number of people involved in the purchase process for this plane will likely be rather large and could include people from the CEO level all the way down to flight attendants and maintenance personnel. As a result, identifying the right people with whom to discuss the merits of the A380 will be extremely important.

Finally, the size of the A380 requires Airbus executives to consider the potential that airports may not be large enough to handle the plane. Because of this factor, Airbus is working with 16 airports that will have to spend approximately $80 million each to get ready for the plane.

One advantage Airbus has when trying to sell the plane is that it knows who its customers are likely to be. Airlines flying large numbers of passengers on long routes, such as across the Pacific Ocean, are likely candidates. This means that Singapore Airlines, United, Northwest, British Airways, and Japan Airlines are the most likely initial customers. Other potential customers are freight haulers such as FedEx and UPS.

As an indicator of the potential success of the A380, the company already has booked 129 orders for the plane even though the first delivery will not happen until sometime in 2006. This number of orders represents more than half of what it will take for Airbus to break even on the plane. But is this enough to justify putting the 380 into full production? Despite this initial success, such a venture represents an enormous gamble by a company hoping to capitalize in a market that seems very uncertain in the existing environment.

Things to Think About

1. What is the decision facing Airbus?
2. What factors are important in understanding the decision situation?
3. What are the alternatives?
4. What decision(s) do you recommend?
5. What are some ways to implement your recommendation(s)?

Source: Alex Taylor III, "Lord of the Air: What's Left for Airbus after Overtaking Boeing in the Commercial Aircraft Market? Building a Really Big Plane," *Fortune,* November 10, 2003, 144–52.

www.reebok.com

real people, real choices

meet Que Gaskins, a Decision Maker at Reebok

career high

my heroes

Helping Allen Iverson get a lifetime deal with Reebok.

My parents.

SHARPENING THE FOCUS: TARGET MARKETING STRATEGIES AND CUSTOMER RELATIONSHIP MANAGEMENT

Que Gaskins is vice president of global marketing for RBK, a division of Reebok. He started at the shoe company in 1994 as business unit manager of basketball. He steadily advanced up the Reebok corporate ladder by becoming director of basketball, where he was responsible for all aspects of basketball marketing for Reebok, including advertising, public relations, product development, and grassroots marketing. Prior to being appointed to his present position, Que was the general manager of Allen Iverson Business, where he oversaw all aspects of marketing, advertising, promotions, public relations, apparel and footwear development, licensing, and international marketing for Reebok's Iverson business. He received his B.S. degree in the School of Business and Industry at Florida A&M University and an MBA from the J.L. Kellogg Graduate School of Management at Northwestern University.

Decision Time at Reebok

Reebok started off as a British brand that became known in the 1980s primarily for its aerobics shoes. However, while women were snapping these up, the company was not enticing many men to buy its products. At around the same time, Nike began to stake its claim as the brand for "Winners" by signing world-class athletes in virtually every sport to endorse its shoes. Reebok was slow to react to this challenge and saw its overall market share quickly decline. The company eventually tried a "follow the leader" approach by signing its own athletes, such as Shaquille O'Neill and Emmit Smith, but it was too late—Nike already "owned" its position in the market as being the shoe for champions. In particular, Michael Jordan cemented Nike's reputation as *the* brand to wear on the court, especially among teenage males.

Reebok needed a new strategy to effectively target the youth market, but how could it gain credibility and respect among young men? Enter Allen Iverson, a barely 6-foot, 160-pound bundle of energy, movement, and coolness. Iverson was a modern-day David among the Goliaths of the NBA, a player with whom kids could identify rather than idolize. Que and his colleagues at Reebok thought he could become the face of urban youth—young, rebellious, talented, loyal to friends and family, with an "I don't give a #$%@" attitude. The more adults hated Iverson and said he was bad news, the more youth around the world embraced him and accepted him as their own. He was the perfect counterpart to Michael Jordan. While "Air" Jordan took the game above the rim with his style and grace, Iverson brought hoops back down to earth with his unique "crossover" dribble. If the 1980s were about dunking and playing in the air, the late 1990s were about beating your man off the dribble. Over a

pet peeve	my motto to live by	what I do when I am not working	don't do this when interviewing with me
People who judge a book by its cover.	"Treat your first like it is your last and your last like it is your first."	Striving to be an all-star dad and husband and shopping and hunting for fashion.	Pretend to be something that you are not or take yourself too seriously.

objectives

1 Understand the need for market segmentation in today's business environment.

2 Know the different dimensions marketers use to segment consumer and business-to-business markets.

3 Explain how marketers evaluate and select potential market segments.

4 Explain how marketers develop a targeting strategy.

5 Understand how a firm develops and implements a positioning strategy.

6 Know how marketers practice customer relationship management to increase long-term success and profits.

period of six years, Reebok used Iverson to connect with youth and did a good job of changing its image from a brand worn by moms to their aerobics classes.

Still, Reebok languished in the number 2 position without a clear identity other than being the shoe that Allen Iverson wears. Their star endorser was a key asset but not strong enough to single-handedly win the hearts, minds, and dollars of youth culture. Despite its success with the Iverson endorsement, the Reebok brand overall still wasn't clicking with the young target market the company needed to attract. How could Que and Reebok's senior management capture the pulse of youth culture in the long run? Que considered his options:

OPTION 1: Mimic Nike's moves with Michael Jordan.

Invest the majority of Reebok's product development and marketing budgets into building a larger Allen Iverson brand that would include both core performance products and other brand extensions, such as casual lifestyle, cross training, and even other sports products like football cleats. Reebok has had tremendous success by playing on its Iverson connection, so why not continue to ride the wave? Its star endorser had an exclusive contract with Reebok, and he consistently ranks among the top three most recognizable athletes in the world. On the other hand, he appeals mostly to teenage males, so this strategy would leave a tremendous gap among female consumers. If Reebok is to become the brand of youth culture, it has to appeal to women as well. In addition, Iverson is moving into the back half of his career, so pinning the company's hopes onto his future performance might be risky.

OPTION 2: Build off of Reebok's success with Iverson while separating the brand from other performance sneaker brands like Nike.

To pull this off, Que would have to create a position for Reebok that would be unique and that the company would "own" globally. One possible focus was music; when Reebok researched the market, this emerged as one of the great influences on youth cul-

ture. Could Reebok branch out by somehow combining the forces of sports and music to speak to young people? After all, 80 percent of the shoes bought for a particular sport are never actually worn for that purpose, so maybe the key is to focus on lifestyle rather than athletics. On the other hand, Reebok has to ensure that it still is a credible brand for those who do want a shoe that delivers performance. And the youth market is always changing, so positioning the brand around a lifestyle and music could be risky since it would involve tracking a constantly moving target.

OPTION 3: Maintain the Iverson emphasis for basketball, and increase Reebok's marketing efforts to build credibility as the performance shoe of choice for the other two major global sports categories of soccer and track.

This strategy plays to the core competence and strengths of Reebok, and it doesn't involve a lot of risk. It would allow Reebok to develop complete product lines related to three major sports categories, and it would include apparel and accessories in addition to footwear. If Reebok can do this, the company will have a solid position as a true sports performance brand. On the other hand, this strategy would force Reebok to play on the same court with other performance sneaker brands, including Nike, Adidas, and New Balance. Nike was currently outspending Reebok almost 10 to 1 in dollars on endorsement opportunities for athletes, leagues, and schools. Reebok would have to be willing to outspend its competitors to make sure that its story got across to young people. This would get very expensive (especially since Reebok would have to secure endorsements from top athletes in each sport), and it also would be another follow-the-leader plan rather than staking out a unique leadership position. A spending war of this magnitude could be a no-win situation for Reebok.

Now, step into Que Gaskins' shoes: Which option would you choose, and why?

Selecting and Entering a Market

By now, we've heard over and over that the goal of the marketer is to create value and satisfy needs, but in our modern, complex society, it is naive to assume that everyone's needs are the same. Understanding people's needs is an even more complex task today because technological and cultural advances in modern society have created a condition of **market fragmentation**. This condition occurs when people's diverse interests and backgrounds divide them into numerous different groups with distinct needs and wants. Because of this diversity, the same good or service will not appeal to everyone.

Consider, for example, the effects of fragmentation in the health-and-fitness industry. Back in the days when Pritikin was a best-selling diet, health-conscious consumers thought that just cutting fat would yield a lean body and good health. Today's consumers, however, have a whole litany of diets from which to choose. There's the Atkins diet, Weight Watchers, Jenny Craig, Slim Fast, FitAmerica, and dozens of herbal remedies for people with weight problems. There are physicians who will even wire your jaw shut to keep you from gorging on treats and others who staple stomachs to create only a tiny capacity for food intake.

Marketers must balance the efficiency of mass marketing, serving the same items to everyone, with the effectiveness of offering each individual exactly what she wants. Mass marketing is certainly the most efficient plan. It costs much less to offer one product to everyone because that strategy eliminates the need for separate advertising campaigns and distinctive packages for each item. However, consumers see things differently; from their perspective, the best strategy would be to offer the perfect product for each individual. Unfortunately, that's often not realistic. Even Burger King's longtime motto, "Have It Your Way," was true only to a point: "Your way" is fine as long as you stay within the confines of familiar condiments such as mustard or ketchup. Don't dream of topping your burger with blue cheese or some other "exotic" ingredient.

Instead of trying to sell something to everyone, marketers select a **target marketing strategy** in which they divide the total market into different segments based on customer characteristics, select one or more segments, and develop products to meet the needs of those specific segments. The three-step process of segmentation, targeting, and positioning is illustrated in Figure 7.1, and it's what we're going to check out in this chapter. Let's start with the first step—segmentation.

Step 1: Segmentation

Segmentation is the process of dividing a larger market into smaller pieces based on one or more meaningful, shared characteristics. Segmentation is a way of life for marketers. The truth is that you can't please all the people all the time, so you need to take your best shot. Just how do marketers segment a population? How do they divide the whole pie into smaller slices they can "digest"? Segmenting the market is often necessary in both consumer and business-to-business markets. In each case, the marketer must decide on one or more useful **segmentation variables**, that is, dimensions that divide the total market into fairly homogeneous groups, each with different needs and preferences. In this section, we'll take a look at this process, beginning with the types of segmentation variables that marketers use to divide up end consumers.

Ways to Segment Consumer Markets

At one time, it was sufficient to divide the sports shoe market into athletes and nonathletes. But a walk through any sporting goods store today reveals that the athlete market has fragmented in many directions, as shoes designed for jogging, basketball, tennis, cycling, cross training, and even skateboarding beckon us from the aisles.

During the 1990s, obscure makers of athletic footwear geared to **Generation Y** (people born between 1977 and 1994), makers such as Vans, Airwalk, and DC, chalked up annual sales gains of 20 to 50 percent. Known to their peers as shredders, riders, or skaters, the kids who wear these shoes

market fragmentation
The creation of many consumer groups due to a diversity of distinct needs and wants in modern society.

target marketing strategy
Dividing the total market into different segments on the basis of customer characteristics, selecting one or more segments, and developing products to meet the needs of those specific segments.

segmentation
The process of dividing a larger market into smaller pieces based on one or more meaningful, shared characteristics.

segmentation variables
Dimensions that divide the total market into fairly homogeneous groups, each with different needs and preferences.

Generation Y
The group of consumers born between 1977 and 1994.

Figure 7.1 Steps in the Target Marketing Process

Target marketing strategy consists of three separate steps. Marketers first divide the market into meaningful segments, then select segments, and finally design a unique marketing mix for each segment.

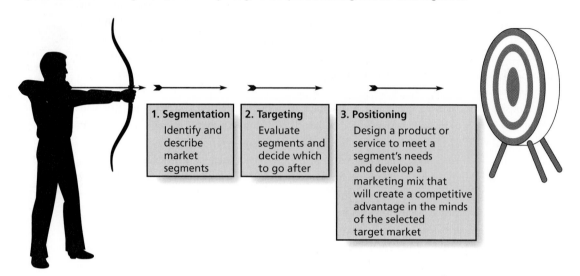

1. Segmentation
Identify and describe market segments

2. Targeting
Evaluate segments and decide which to go after

3. Positioning
Design a product or service to meet a segment's needs and develop a marketing mix that will create a competitive advantage in the minds of the selected target market

can be seen riding skateboards down the handrails of city parks. They coast downhill on snowboards. During mud season, they twist their bikes down slippery hills, and in summer they flip and glide on wakeboards pulled by powerboats. Over the next few years, marketers expect the skateboard and snowboard populations to double and wakeboarders to soar sixfold. That growth brings with it the potential to sell many new products in a market that barely existed a few years ago.

Several segmentation variables can slice up the market for all the shoe variations available today. First, not everyone is willing or able to drop $150 on the latest sneakers, so marketers consider income. Second, men may be more interested in basketball shoes while women snap up the latest aerobics styles, so marketers also consider gender. Because not all age-groups are going to be equally interested in buying specialized athletic shoes, the larger consumer "pie" can be sliced into smaller pieces in a number of ways, including demographic, psychological, and behavioral differences. Let's consider each variable in turn.

SEGMENTING BY DEMOGRAPHICS Demographics are measurable characteristics such as gender and age. Demographics are vital to identify the best potential customers for a good or service. These objective characteristics are usually easy to identify, and then it's just a matter of tailoring messages and products to relevant groups. IBM develops separate marketing messages to appeal to African American, Latino, Asian, Native American, disabled, gay and lesbian, and senior citizen groups. Each message uses copy and spokespeople likely to appeal to members of a specific segment. Ads for IBM's VoiceType software, which allows users to control the PC by voice, featured Curtis Mayfield, who was a Grammy Award–winning soul singer and a quadriplegic. The demographic dimensions that marketers usually look at are age, gender, family structure, income and social class, race and ethnicity, and geography (or where people live). Let's take a quick look at how marketers can use each of these dimensions to slice up the consumer pie.

AGE Consumers of different age-groups have different needs and wants. Members of a generation tend to share the same outlook and priorities. During the famous "cola wars" of the 1970s and 80s, Pepsi managed to convince a generation (the "Pepsi Generation") that its product reflected their core values of youth, idealism, and casting off old ways. By default, Coke became identified as their parents' drink.[1]

Children have become an attractive age segment for marketers. Although kids obviously have a lot to say about purchases of toys and games, they influence other family purchases as well. By one estimate, American children aged 4 to 12 have a say in family-related purchases of more than $130 billion a year.[2] Teens are also an attractive market segment. The 12-to-17 age group is growing nearly twice as fast as the general population—and teens spend an average of $3,000 per year.[3] Much of this money goes toward "feel-good" products: cosmetics, posters, and fast food—with the occasional nose ring thrown in as well. Because they are so interested in many different products and have the resources to obtain them, many marketers avidly court the teen market.[4] For example, veteran direct seller Avon is actively courting the lucrative teen and younger women market with the launch of its new line, "mark" (**www.meetmark.com**), in celebration of young women making their mark in the world today. This effort breaks away from Avon's traditional roots of appealing to an older, more conservative customer base to bring in both a new buyer and a potential seller for the company. And, of course, there are subgroups within the teen market with their own musical idols, distinctive styles, and so on.

As we said, Generation Y consists of those consumers born between the years 1977 and 1994. Sometimes referred to as the baby "boomlet," Generation Y is made up of the 71 million children of the baby boomers.[5] They are the first generation to grow up online and are more ethnically diverse than earlier generations. Generation Y is an attractive market for a host of consumer products because of its size

Young shredders are still a profitable market segment today.

(approximately 26 percent of the population) and because of its free-spending nature—as a group they spend about $200 billion annually. But Generation Y consumers are also hard to reach because they resist reading and increasingly turn the TV off. As a result, many marketers have had to develop other ways of reaching this generation, including online chat rooms, e-mail promotions, and some of the more unusual guerilla marketing techniques we'll talk about later in this book.

The group of consumers born between 1965 and 1976 consists of 46 million Americans sometimes known as **Generation X**, slackers, or busters (for the "baby bust" that followed the "baby boom"). Many of these people have a cynical attitude toward marketing—a chapter in a book called *Generation X* is "I am not a target market!"[6] As one 20-year-old Japanese Xer commented, "I don't like to be told what's trendy. I can make up my own mind."[7]

Generation X
The group of consumers born between 1965 and 1976.

Despite this tough reputation, members of Generation X, the oldest of whom are now entering their early 40s, have mellowed with age. One study revealed that Xers are already responsible for 70 percent of new start-up businesses in the United States. An industry expert observed, "Today's Gen Xer is both *values*-oriented and *value*-oriented. This generation is really about settling down."[8] Many people in this segment seem to be determined to have stable families after being latchkey children themselves. Seven out of 10 regularly save some portion of their income, a rate comparable to that of their parents. Xers tend to view the home as an expression of individuality rather than material success. More than half are involved in home improvement and repair projects.[9] So much for slackers.

Baby boomers, consumers born between 1946 and 1964 and who are now in their 40s, 50s, and (nearing) 60s, are an important segment to many marketers—if for no other reason than that there are so many of them who are making a lot of money. Boomers were the result of pent-up

baby boomers
The segment of people born between 1946 and 1964.

Copyright © 2003 Avon Products, Inc., All rights reserved. **mark**™ is a registered trademark. Read our Privacy Policy

Avon is betting big on the introduction of its new brand "mark," targeted to a younger consumer than traditional Avon-branded products.

desires on the part of their parents to start families after World War II interrupted their lives. Back in the 1950s and 60s, couples started having children younger and had more of them. The resulting glut of kids really changed the infrastructure of the country (more single family houses, more schools, migration to suburbs, and so on).

One aspect of boomers for marketers to always remember—they *never* age. At least, that's the way they look at it. Boomers are willing to invest a ton of money, time, and energy to maintain their youthful image. The show *Nip/Tuck* on FX chronicles the experiences of two cosmetic surgeons in Miami, baby boomers themselves, who crassly market their surgical fountain of youth to a seemingly endless stream of 50-somethings. Time Warner formed a separate unit to publish magazines, including *Health*, *Parenting*, and *Cooking Light*, that specifically address baby boomers' interests in staying young, healthy, and sane as they began to have kids of their own.

Another important aspect of boomers, a connection with the sociocultural trends discussed in Chapter 2, is that because there are so many of them, they are clogging the upward mobility pipeline in employment. Generation Xers and Yers complain that the boomers hold all the power and position. This trend has resulted in entrepreneurship becoming increasingly popular among the generations following boomers. Generation Xers and younger have no expectation of long-term employment with any one firm and are cynical about even ever receiving Social Security as a retirement benefit. These generations have had to very much make their own opportunities.

According to the 2000 census, there are 35 million Americans aged 65 or older—a 12 percent increase in this age segment since 1990.[10] Many consumers in their 60s and 70s are enjoying leisure time and continued good health. A key question is, What is a senior citizen? As we will see later in the chapter, perhaps it isn't age but rather lifestyle factors, including mobility, that best define this group. More and more marketers are offering products that have strong appeal to active lifestyle seniors. Even youth-oriented Walt Disney theme parks tempts seniors to come back to the park—with or without their grandchildren.

GENDER Many products, from fragrances to footwear, appeal to men or women either because of the nature of the product or because the marketer chose to appeal to one sex or the other. Segment-

Marketers know that baby boomers never age, at least in their own minds. The FX show *Nip/Tuck* shows how far some boomers will go to maintain a youthful appearance.

ing by sex starts at a very early age—even diapers come in pink for girls and blue for boys. As proof that consumers take these differences seriously, market researchers report that most parents refuse to put male infants in pink diapers.[11] In some cases, manufacturers develop parallel products to appeal to each sex. For example, male grooming products have traditionally been Gillette's priority since the company's founder introduced the safety razor in 1903. Today the company considers women a major market opportunity and continues to develop new shaving products for women.

One new segmentation buzzword you may have heard is **metrosexual**. A metrosexual is a man who is heterosexual, sensitive, educated, and an urban dweller who is in touch with his feminine side. Metrosexuals may have a standing appointment for a weekly manicure, have their hair done by a stylist instead of a barber, love to shop, like jewelry, and have a bathroom counter filled with male-targeted grooming products such as moisturizers. Physical appearance is very important, and one telltale sign you might be a metrosexual is a willingness to indulge yourself in order to get a lot of attention for your hair, clothes, or home. Okay guys, now go make an appointment for that facial![33]

metrosexual
A man who is heterosexual, sensitive, educated, and an urban dweller who is in touch with his feminine side.

FAMILY STRUCTURE   Because family needs and expenditures change over time, one way to segment consumers is to consider the stage of the family life cycle they occupy (see Chapter 5). Not surprisingly, consumers in different life cycle segments are unlikely to need the same products, or at least they may not need these things in the same quantities.[12] For example, Procter & Gamble introduced Folger's Singles for people who live alone and don't need to brew a full pot of coffee at a time.[13]

As families age and move into new life stages, different product categories ascend and descend in importance. Young bachelors and newlyweds are the most likely to exercise, to go to bars and movies, and to consume alcohol (in other words, party while you can). Older couples and bachelors are more likely to use maintenance services, and seniors are a prime market for resort condominiums and golf products. Marketers need to discern the family life cycle segment of their target consumers by examining purchase data by family life cycle group.

INCOME   The distribution of wealth is of great interest to marketers because it determines which groups have the greatest buying power. It should come as no surprise that many marketers yearn to capture the hearts and wallets of high-income consumers. Perhaps that explains a recent fashion trend featuring clothes made with real gold, including pinstriped suits selling from $10,000 to $20,000.[14] At the same time, other marketers target lower-income consumers, who make up about 40 percent of

LA REENCARNACION DE LAS ENSALADAS

Nace la nueva línea de ensaladas cocinadas a la parrilla de BURGER KING®. Pollo o camarón a la parrilla hacen que sean mucho más frescas.

La Bolsita a la parrilla de BURGER KING® le da vida a tu ensalada. Los ingredientes se mantienen calientes y tu ensalada fresca. Y por primera vez camarón a la parrilla calientito. Disfrútalas como tú más quieras. **A TU MANERA**℠

TM & © Burger King Brands, Inc. All rights reserved.

Hispanic consumers are a very attractive target for marketers.

the U.S. market (as defined by households with incomes of $25,000 or less). Discount stores such as Target and apparel retailers like Marshalls and Kohl's have done quite well by catering to this segment.

In the past, it was popular for marketers to consider social class segments, such as upper class, lower class, and the like. However, many consumers buy not according to where they may fall in that schema but rather according to the *image* they wish to portray. For example, readily available credit has facilitated many a sale of a BMW to a consumer who technically falls into the middle or lower class. Six years of making payments later, they finally "own" the car.

RACE AND ETHNICITY   A consumer's national origin is often a strong indicator of his preferences for specific magazines or TV shows, foods, apparel, and choice of leisure activities. Marketers need to be aware of these differences and sensitivities. Even overseas American restaurants must adapt to local customs. For example, in the Middle East, rules about the mixing of the sexes and the consumption of alcohol are quite strict. Chili's Grill & Bar is known simply as Chili's, and the chain offers a midnight buffet during Ramadan season, when Muslims are required to fast from dawn to dusk. McDonald's in Saudi Arabia offers separate dining areas for single men and women and children. Booths must have screens because women can't be seen eating meat.[15]

These cultural/religious issues also abound within the U.S. market, given our increasingly ethnically diverse culture. Burger King had to modify a commercial it aired on African American radio stations in which a coffeehouse poet reads an ode to a WHOPPER™ with bacon. In the original spot, the poet's name is Rasheed, and he uses a common Islamic greeting. The Council on American-Islamic Relations issued a press release noting that Islam prohibits the consumption of pork products. In the new version, the poet was introduced as Willie.[16]

African Americans, Hispanic Americans, and Asian Americans are the three fastest-growing ethnic groups in the United States. The Census Bureau projects that by the year 2050, non-Hispanic whites will make up only 50.1 percent of the population (compared to 74 percent in 1995) as these other groups grow.[17] Let's take a closer look at each ethnic segment.

African Americans account for about 12 percent of the U.S. population. This percentage has held steady for 20 years. A new generation of magazines has sprung up to meet the demands of this growing market, including *The Source* and *Vibe*.[18] There are even multicultural romance novels that feature African American heroes and heroines. The basic elements of a romance novel remain, but these books provide numerous references to African American culture, and the heroine is more likely to possess "curly brown locks" than "cascading blond hair."[19] Such books and magazines demonstrate the opportunities that await those who develop specialized products that connect with segments of consumers who share an ethnic or racial identity. The rap culture has migrated from the inner-city streets to hip-hop clubs, creating substantial opportunities for marketers to portray what started out as an urban street trend among the African American community to a broader cultural phenomenon appealing across ethnicities within the youth market.

Though their numbers are still relatively small, Asian Americans are the fastest-growing minority group in the United States. The Asian American population is projected to grow from 11.3 million in 2000 to 19.6 million in 2020.[20] Marketers in the United States are just beginning to recognize the potential of this segment, and some are beginning to adapt their products and messages to reach this group. WonderBra even launched a special line sized for a slimmer Asian body.[21]

The Hispanic American population is a sleeping giant, a segment that mainstream marketers largely ignored until recently. The Census Bureau projects that Hispanics have overtaken African Americans as the nation's largest minority group. In addition to its rapid growth, five other factors make the Hispanic segment attractive to marketers:

1. Hispanics tend to be brand loyal, especially to products made in their country of origin.[22]

2. They tend to be highly concentrated by national origin, which makes it easy to fine-tune the marketing mix to appeal to those who come from the same country. That's why some companies are trying to appeal to Mexican Americans, who make up about 60 percent of Hispanic Americans, by developing promotions celebrating Cinco de Mayo, a holiday commemorating Mexico's triumph over France in 1862. McDonald's once added fajitas to its regular menu during the holiday.[23]

3. This segment is young (the median age of Hispanic Americans is 23.6, compared with the U.S. average of 32), which is attractive to marketers because it is a great potential market for youth-oriented products such as cosmetics and music.

4. The average Hispanic household contains 3.5 people, compared to only 2.7 people for the rest of the United States. For this reason, Hispanic households spend 15 to 20 percent more of their disposable income than the national average on groceries and other household products.[24]

5. In general, Hispanic consumers are very receptive to relationship-building approaches to marketing and selling. As such, strong opportunities exist to build loyalty to brands and companies through emphasizing relationship aspects of the customer encounter.[25]

As with any ethnic group, appeals to Hispanic consumers need to take into account cultural differences. For example, the California Milk Processor Board discovered that its hugely successful "Got Milk?" campaign was not well received by Hispanics because biting, sarcastic humor is not part of the Hispanic culture. In addition, the notion of milk deprivation is not funny to a Hispanic mother because running out of milk means she has failed her family. To make matters worse, "Got Milk?" translates as "Are You Lactating?" in Spanish. So, new Spanish-language versions were changed to, "And you, have you given them enough milk today?" with tender scenes centered around cooking flan (a popular pudding) in the family kitchen.[26]

One of the most notable characteristics of the Hispanic market is its youth: Many of these consumers are "young biculturals" who bounce back and forth between hip-hop and *rock en Español*, blend Mexican rice with spaghetti sauce, and spread peanut butter and jelly on tortillas.[27] Latino youth are changing mainstream culture. By the year 2020, the Census Bureau estimates that the number of Hispanic teens will grow by 62 percent compared with 10 percent growth in teens overall. They are looking for spirituality, stronger family ties, and more color in their lives—three hallmarks of Latino culture. Music crossovers from the Latin charts to mainstream are leading the trend, including pop idol Enrique Iglesias.

One caution about the Hispanic market is that the term "Hispanic" itself is a misnomer. For example, Cuban Americans, Mexican Americans, and Puerto Ricans may share a common language, but their history, politics, and culture have many differences. Marketing to them as a homogeneous segment can be a big mistake.

GEOGRAPHY Recognizing that people's preferences often vary depending on where they live, many marketers tailor their offerings to appeal to different regions. Heileman Distilleries sells different brands of beer in different parts of the country, so drinkers in Texas buy the company's Lone Star brand, while those in Boston order Samuel Adams. As the company's marketing vice president once explained in an article, "The primary objective of being a regional brand is to make the consumer think that 'this product is mine.' . . . People tend to think positively about their hometowns, and a product strongly identified with this aura is likely to strike a responsive chord."[28]

When marketers want to segment regional markets even more precisely, they sometimes combine geography with demographics by using a technique called **geodemography**. A basic assumption of geodemography is that "birds of a feather flock together"—people who live near one another share similar characteristics. Sophisticated statistical techniques identify geographic areas that share the same preferences for household items, magazines, and other products. Through geodemography, marketers construct segments of households with a common pattern of preferences. This way the marketer can hone in on those customers who are most likely to be interested in its specific offerings, in some cases so precisely that families living on one block will be included in a segment while those on the next block will not.

Companies can even customize Web advertising by geocoding so that people who log on in different places will see ad banners for local businesses. For example, the Weather Channel (**www.weather.com**) can link localized ads to 1,300 U.S. weather-reporting stations, so a surfer can get both the local weather forecast and information about businesses in an area.[29]

One widely used geodemographic system is called PRIZM, a large database developed by Claritas, Inc. (**www.claritas.com**). This system classifies every U.S. ZIP code into one of 62 "clusters" based on analyses of demographics and lifestyles that define neighborhood types. The 62 clusters range from the highly affluent "Blue-Blood Estates" to the poor "Inner Cities" or "Hard Scrabble" neighborhoods. This system tells marketers which product categories and specific brands people in each cluster are likely to use. For example, Young Literati (see Table 7.1) are likely to plan for large purchases, take vitamins, use a discount broker, watch the Bravo channel, and read *GQ*, while Urban Gold Coast consumers are likely to attend the theater, use olive oil, bank online, and read *Self.* Armed with this knowledge, a marketer can identify precisely which ZIP codes will be the best prospects for a product while avoiding other nearby ZIP codes where residents aren't likely to be so interested. Go to the company's Web site, tell them your ZIP code, and they'll tell you which cluster you live in.

SEGMENTING BY PSYCHOGRAPHICS Demographic information is useful, but it does not always provide enough information to divide consumers into meaningful segments. Although we can use demographic variables to discover, for example, that the female college student segment uses perfume, we won't be able to tell whether certain college women prefer perfumes that express an image of, say, sexiness rather than athleticism. Psychographic data are useful to understand differences among consumers who may be statistically similar to one another but whose needs and wants vary.

For example, most of us are happy driving the speed limit (okay, a few miles over the limit) on the freeway, but some of us crave danger. For this psychographic segment, there is a variety of unique product offerings, including a tour of the sunken *Titanic* at 12,500 feet below the surface of the ocean or getting behind the wheel of a Formula One race car running at 120 miles per hour.[30]

Psychographics segment markets in terms of shared activities, interests, and opinions.[31] Psychographic segments usually include demographic information such as age or sex, but the richer descriptions that emerge go well beyond these characteristics. Web-based services such as geocities.com allow people to sort *themselves* into lifestyle communities based on specific, shared interests. These selections allow marketers to identify segments that want products and services that enable them to act on their passions, whether these passions include skiing or watching *Star Trek.*

Over the years, Harley-Davidson has done a great job of understanding buyers on the basis of psychographics. A Harley user's profile includes both thrill-seeking and affinity for a countercultural image (at least on weekends!). In fact, your doctor, banker, lawyer, or even marketing professor may be a member of HOG (the Harley Owners Group). However, demographics also come into play. Over the past decade, the age of the typical Harley buyer has risen to about 46, older than the motorcycle industry average of 38. But because the company knows the psychographics of its

geodemography
A segmentation technique that combines geography with demographics.

Table 7.1 Examples of PRIZM Clusters

Cluster Name	Demographics	Most Likely to	Neighborhood Examples
Urban Gold Coast	Elite urban singles Age-group: 45–64 Professional Average household income: $73,500	Attend the theater Use olive oil Bank online Watch *Mystery* Read *Self*	Marina Del Rey, CA Lincoln Park, IL Upper East Side, NY
Starter Families	Young, middle-class families Age-group: under 18, 25–34 Blue-collar/service occupations Average household income: $25,300	Belong to a book club Be boxing fans Use caller ID Watch *Nightline* Read *Bride's Magazine*	Woodland, CA Sioux Falls, SD Lowell, MA
Rural Industrial	Low-income, blue-collar families Age-group: under 18 Blue-collar/service occupations Average household income: $27,900	Be auto racing fans Belong to a fraternal order Have veterans' life insurance Watch TNN Read *Field and Stream*	Gas City, IN Wheeler, AR Worthington, KY
Young Literati	Upscale urban singles and couples Age-group: 25–44 Professional occupations Average household income: $63,400	Plan for large purchases Take vitamins Use a discount broker Watch *Bravo* Read *GQ*	Hermosa Beach, CA Diamond Heights, CA Edgewater, NJ
Inner Cities	Inner-city, single-parent families Age-group: under 18, 18–34 Blue-collar/service occupations Average household income: $16,500	Buy baby food Buy soul/R&B/black music Pay bills by phone Watch pay-per-view sports Read *National Enquirer*	Detroit, MI Hyde Park, IL Morningside, NY
Hispanic Mix	Urban Hispanic singles and families Age-group: under 18, 18–34 Blue-collar/service occupations Average household income: $19,000	Be pro basketball fans Use caller ID Use money orders Watch BET Read *Ebony*	Pico Heights, CA El Paso, TX Bronx, NY
New Ecotopia	Rural white- and blue-collar/farm families Age-group: 45+ White-collar/blue-collar/farming occupations Average household income: $39,000	Go cross-country skiing Own a dog Have a Keogh account Watch *Jeopardy* Read *Prevention*	Sutter Creek, CA East Chatham, NY Grafton, VT
Golden Ponds	Retirement town seniors Age-group: 65+ White-collar/blue-collar/service occupations Average household income: $28,300	Shop at Wal-Mart Go bowling Eat Grape-Nuts Watch QVC network Read *Golf*	Forest Ranch, CA Dollar Bay, MI Kure Beach, NC
Norma Rae-Ville	Young families, biracial mill town Age-group: under 18, 18–34 Blue-collar/service occupations Average household income: $20,500	Travel by bus Shop at Payless Shoes Buy Sears tires Watch *Oprah* Read *Seventeen*	Yazoo City, MS Americus, GA Salisbury, NC
Blue-chip Blues	Upscale blue-collar families Age-group: 35–64 White-collar/blue-collar occupations Average household income: $47,500	Shop online Belong to a religious club Drink Coke Watch *Days of Our Lives* Read *Car Craft*	Redford, MI Oakville, CT Barrington, NJ
Executive Suites	Upscale white-collar couples Age-group: 45–64 Professional occupations Average household income: $68,500	Belong to a health club Visit Japan/Asia Have an airline travel card Watch *Friends* Read *Entrepreneur*	Irving, CA Aurora, IL Mount Laurel, NJ

Source: Adapted from www.claritas.com.

Figure 7.2 VALS™

VALS™ uses psychological characteristics to segment the U.S. market into eight unique consumer groups.

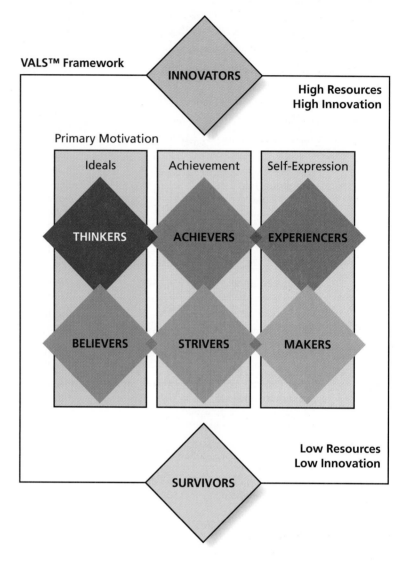

Source: **Courtesy of SRI Business Intelligence.**

target buyers, it isn't lulled into age stereotypes of safety and conservatism. Harley-Davidson knows that in spite of the older age demographic, its buyers are still a thrill-seeking bunch.

Although some advertising agencies and manufacturers develop their own psychographic techniques to classify consumers, other agencies subscribe to services that divide the entire U.S. population into segments and then sell pieces of this information to clients for specific strategic applications. The most well known of these systems is **VALS™ (Values and Lifestyles)**. The original VALS™ system was based on social values and lifestyles. Today, VALS™ is based on psychological traits that correlate with consumer behavior. VALS™ was developed by SRI Consulting Business Intelligence (**www.sric-bi.com**). You can easily go to their Web site and click on "VALS™ Survey" to complete a brief questionnaire for free to find out your own VALS™ type. VALS™ divides U.S. adults into eight groups that are determined both by primary motivation and by resources.

As Figure 7.2 shows, three primary consumer motivations are key to the system: ideals, achievement, and self-expression. Consumers who are motivated primarily by ideals are guided by knowledge and principles. Consumers who are motivated primarily by achievement look for products

VALS™ (Values and Lifestyles)
A psychographic system that divides the entire U.S. population into eight segments.

and services that demonstrate success to their peers. And consumers who are motivated primarily by self-expression desire social or physical activity, variety, and risk.

VALS™ helps match products and services to particular types of people. For example, VALS™ survey data show that 12 percent of American adults are Experiencers, who tend to be thrill seekers. VALS™ helped Isuzu market its Rodeo sport-utility vehicle by repositioning it to Experiencers, many of whom believe it is fun to break rules (in ways that do not endanger others). The company and its advertising agency repositioned the car as a vehicle that lets a driver break the rules by going off road. Isuzu created advertising to support this idea. One ad showed a kid jumping in mud puddles after his mother went to great lengths to keep him clean. Another ad showed a schoolchild with a mind of her own scribbling outside the lines after the teacher made a big deal about coloring carefully within the lines.[32] Isuzu sales increased significantly after this campaign.

The "Vals™ questionnaire" can be integrated into custom surveys to identify the VALS™ types of the respondents and to correlate their preference with their type. The VALS™ questionnaire is also integrated into syndicated surveys such as Mediamark Research Inc.'s (MRI's), *Survey of American Consumers*, with questions about hundreds of products, services, and media. GeoVALS™ estimates the percentages of the eight VALS™ types by zip code and block group for direct mail and site selection.

SEGMENTING BY BEHAVIOR   People may use the same product for different reasons, on different occasions, and in different amounts. So, in addition to demographics and psychographics, it is useful to study what consumers actually do with a product. **Behavioral segmentation** slices consumers on the basis of how they act toward, feel about, or use a product. Tropicana Essentials Healthy Heart, for example, targets consumers who want the health benefits of six added vitamins and no sodium added to their OJ.

One way to segment based on behavior is to divide the market into users and nonusers of a product. Users have acted to make a purchase, which is a *behavior*. Then marketers may attempt to reward current users or try to win over new ones. In addition to distinguishing between users and nonusers, current customers can further be segmented into groups of heavy, moderate, and light users.

Many marketers abide by a rule of thumb called the **80/20 rule**: 20 percent of purchasers account for 80 percent of the product's sales (this ratio is an approximation, not gospel). This means that it often makes more sense to focus on the smaller number of people who are really into a product rather than on the larger number who are just casual users. Kraft Foods began a $30 million campaign to remind its core users not to "skip the zip" after its research showed that indeed 20 percent of U.S. households account for 80 percent of the usage of Miracle Whip. Heavy users consume 17 pounds of Miracle Whip a year.[34]

Another way to segment a market based on behavior is to look at **usage occasions**, or when consumers use the product most. Many products are associated with specific occasions, whether time of day, holidays, business functions, or casual get-togethers. Businesses often divide up their markets according to when and how their offerings are in demand.

The palmOne and other PDAs are lifestyle-oriented products that provide many benefits for today's tech-savvy consumers.

behavioral segmentation
A technique that divides consumers into segments on the basis of how they act toward, feel about, or use a good or service.

80/20 rule
A marketing rule of thumb that 20 percent of purchasers account for 80 percent of a product's sales.

usage occasions
An indicator used in one type of market segmentation based on when consumers use a product most.

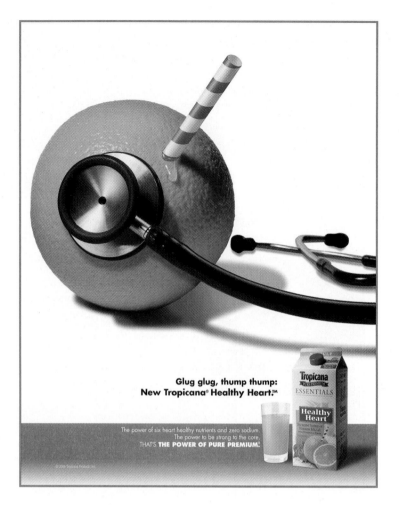

**Glug glug, thump thump:
New Tropicana® Healthy Heart.™**

The power of six heart healthy nutrients and zero sodium.
The power to be strong to the core,
THAT'S **THE POWER OF PURE PREMIUM.**

Tropicana Essentials Healthy Heart targets consumers who like orange juice and who also want extra vitamins and no sodium.

For example, consider how the Biltmore Estate in Asheville, North Carolina, went about increasing attendance during its annual Christmas celebration. Set on 8,000 acres and featuring four acres of lavishly decorated floor space under one roof, the Biltmore is the largest private home in America. Although 750,000 people visited the house annually, in the early 1990s attendance was starting to stagnate. Then the estate's marketers mixed things up by developing four separate strategies to target different types of visitors (e.g., heavy users such as those who have made a Christmas pilgrimage an annual family tradition versus light users who have visited only once). Each segment received a different invitation offering a customized package calculated to appeal to that segment. As a result, visits increased by 300 percent in one season, resulting in a Merry Christmas for the Biltmore.[35]

Segmenting Business-to-Business Markets

We've reviewed the segmentation variables marketers use to divide up the consumer pie, but how about all those business-to-business marketers out there? Segmentation also helps them slice up the pie of industrial customers. Though the specific variables may differ, the underlying logic of classifying the larger market into manageable pieces that share relevant characteristics is the same whether the product being sold is pesto or pesticides.

Organizational demographics also help a business-to-business marketer to understand the needs and characteristics of its potential customers. These classification dimensions include the size of the firms either in total sales or number of employees, the number of facilities, whether they are a domestic or a multinational company, policies on how they purchase, and the type of business they are in. Business-to-business markets may also be segmented on the basis of the production technology they use and whether the customer is a user or a nonuser of the product. DuPont's Apparel and Textile Science Division (the folks who bring you Lycra® and nylon) divides customers for its fibers (such as textile mills) into segments based on the types of products they make such as legwear (stockings), activewear, or home textiles.

Many industries use the North American Industry Classification System (NAICS) discussed in Chapter 6 to obtain information about the size and number of companies operating in a particular industry. Business-to-business marketers often consult information sources on the Web. For example, Hoovers Online (**www.hoovers.com**) provides subscribers with up-to-date information on private and public companies worldwide.

Step 2: Targeting

We've seen that the first step in developing a target marketing strategy is segmentation in which the firm divides the market into smaller groups that share certain characteristics. The next step is targeting in which marketers evaluate the attractiveness of each potential segment and decide which of these groups they will invest resources against to try to turn them into customers. The customer group or groups selected are the firm's **target market**. In this section, we'll review how marketers assess these customer groups, and we'll discuss selection strategies for effective targeting.

target market
A group or groups that a firm selects to turn into customers as a result of segmentation and targeting.

Advice for Reebok

STUDENT
KELLY BIRCHLER
University of Tulsa

I would choose option 2, build off of Reebok's success with Iverson while separating the brand from other brands like Nike. This allows Reebok to creatively position themselves in the athletic shoe market to the ever-changing youth. Reebok should market their shoes to a different primary target market than Nike to reach those teens who are more interested in the way the athletic shoe looks and the actual musicians wearing their products. Although the youth lifestyle is constantly changing, Reebok must evolve with their target markets; otherwise, the brand will lose loyal customers. Reebok must also reach their secondary target market of athletic youth who are attracted to their shoes mainly for the reputation of being a quality product.

ASSISTANT PROFESSOR
JOAN GIESE
Washington State University

I would choose option 3 (maintaining the Iverson emphasis for basketball and increasing marketing efforts to build credibility as the shoe of choice for soccer and track) with a complementary focus on style (modifying option 2). This approach is most consistent with Reebok's targeting objective of building credibility with the youth market in the long run. Reebok must capitalize on past successes and use its targeting strategy to appeal to both women and men. Achieving success with the youth market in the long run seems most likely if Reebok positions its products as meeting performance needs of athletes as well as style and comfort needs of the broader youth market. By adding other global sports (soccer and track), Reebok aligns its targeting strategy more closely with its global perspective and performance focus. However, to capture a large share of the youth market for the long run, Reebok must also appeal more broadly to young men and women with its unique emphasis on style. Although this is an expensive option, the payoff could be worth it.

PROFESSOR
ERIN WILKINSON
Johnson & Wales University

I would choose option 2. This option preserves the brand identity for Reebok sneakers generated by the Iverson campaign related to specific sports and performance but also targets the youth culture through lifestyle segmentation and music, creating differentiation. Music influences and binds the youth market, defining core values by shaping preferences, behaviors, and product decisions. We are talking about 50 million children and teenagers that form rock star crushes, download music on a daily basis, and spend the most for online and offline musical purchases of any age demographic. Reebok has spent 10 to 15 percent more for online advertising in the past few years, which could focus more on targeting this segment. With the strength of the youth music scene created by the Disney, MTV, Napster, and the underground music scene and the underground sneaker market, there are plenty of opportunities for Reebok. There are many underground music and sneaker sites that could be used to propagate interest in Reebok products. By positioning in the underground music and sneaker market, Reebok keeps it fresh for the youth in a constantly changing environment.

Evaluating Market Segments

Just because a marketer identifies a segment does not necessarily mean that it's a useful one to target. A viable target segment should satisfy the following requirements:

1. Are members of the segment similar to each other in their product needs and wants and, at the same time, different from consumers in other segments? Without real differences in consumer needs, firms might as well use a mass-marketing strategy. For example, it's a waste of

time to develop two separate lines of skin care products for working women and nonworking women if both segments have the same complaints about dry skin.

2. Can marketers measure the segment? Marketers must know something about the size and purchasing power of a potential segment before deciding if it is worth their efforts.

3. Is the segment large enough to be profitable now and in the future? For example, a graphic designer hoping to design Web pages for Barbie doll collectors must decide whether there are enough hard-core *aficionados* to make this business worthwhile and whether the trend will continue.

4. Can marketing communications reach the segment? It is easy to select television programs or magazines that will efficiently reach older consumers, consumers with certain levels of education, or residents of major cities because the media they prefer are easy to identify. It is unlikely, however, that marketing communications can reach only left-handed blondes with tattoos who listen to Jessica Simpson overdubbed in Mandarin Chinese.

5. Can the marketer adequately serve the needs of the segment? Does the firm have the expertise and resources to satisfy the segment better than the competition? Some years ago, Warner-Lambert made the mistake of trying to enter the pastry business by purchasing Entemann's Bakery. Entemann's sells high-end boxed cakes, cookies, pastries, and pies in supermarkets and is delivered to the grocer by route delivery trucks. Unfortunately, Warner-Lambert's expertise at selling Listerine mouthwash and Trident gum did not transfer to baked goods, and they soon lost a lot of dough on the deal.

Developing Segment Profiles

segment profile
A description of the "typical" customer in a segment.

Once a marketer has identified a set of usable segments, it is helpful to generate a profile of each to really understand segment members' needs and to look for business opportunities. This segment profile is a description of the "typical" customer in that segment. A **segment profile** might, for example, include customer demographics, location, lifestyle information, and a description of how frequently the customer buys the product.

When the R.J. Reynolds Company made plans to introduce a new brand of cigarettes called Dakota that would be targeted to women, it created a segment profile of a possible customer group it called the "Virile Female." The profile included these characteristics: Her favorite pastimes are cruising, partying, going to hot-rod shows and tractor pulls with her boyfriend, and watching evening soap operas. Her chief aspiration is to get married in her early 20s.[36] Anyone you know?

Choosing a Targeting Strategy

A basic targeting decision is how finely tuned the target should be: Should the company go after one large segment or focus on meeting the needs of one or more smaller segments? Let's look at four targeting strategies. Figure 7.3 summarizes these strategies.

undifferentiated targeting strategy
Appealing to a broad spectrum of people.

differentiated targeting strategy
Developing one or more products for each of several distinct customer groups and making sure these offerings are kept separate in the marketplace.

UNDIFFERENTIATED MARKETING A company such as Wal-Mart that selects an **undifferentiated targeting strategy** is appealing to a broad spectrum of people. If successful, this type of operation can be very efficient, especially because production, research, and promotion costs benefit from *economies of scale*—it's cheaper to develop one product or one advertising campaign than to choose several targets and create separate products or messages for each. But the company must be willing to bet that people have similar needs or that any differences among them will be so trivial that they will not matter so that the same product and message will appeal to many customers.

DIFFERENTIATED MARKETING A company that chooses a **differentiated targeting strategy** develops one or more products for each of several customer groups with different product needs. A differentiated strategy is called for when consumers are choosing among brands that are well

Figure 7.3 Choosing a Target Marketing Strategy

After the market is divided into meaningful segments, marketers must decide on a target marketing strategy. Should the company go after one total market, one or several market segments, or even target customers individually?

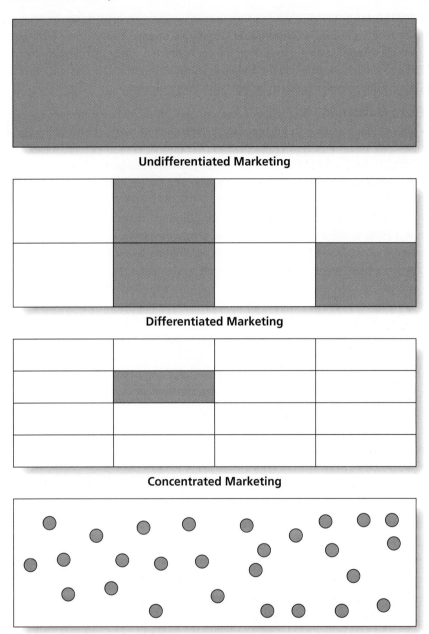

Undifferentiated Marketing

Differentiated Marketing

Concentrated Marketing

Customized Marketing

known in which each has a distinctive image in the marketplace and in which it's possible to identify one or more segments that have distinct needs for different types of products. The cosmetics giant L'Oréal follows this philosophy. The company has the resources to offer several product lines at a variety of prices. It targets the luxury market with such brands as Lancôme and Helena Rubinstein, while less expensive offerings such as Elseve and L'Oréal are targeted to large department stores and discounters.[37]

Differentiated marketing can also involve connecting one product with different segments by communicating differently to appeal to those segments. The milk industry runs its series of

"Got Milk?" ads using a variety of celebrities chosen for their appeal to different target consumers for milk purchases. Aerosmith's Steven Tyler appeals both to aging boomers who got into the band in the 1970s and Gen Yers who discovered the band in the 1990s with the Run DMC "Walk This Way" remake.

CONCENTRATED MARKETING   When a firm focuses its efforts on offering one or more products to a single segment, it is using a **concentrated targeting strategy**. A concentrated strategy is often useful for smaller firms that do not have the resources or the desire to be all things to all people. For example, the cosmetics company Hard Candy sells its funky line of nail polish and other products only to 20-something women (or to those who wish they still were).

CUSTOMIZED MARKETING   Ideally, marketers should be able to define segments so precisely that they can offer products and services that exactly meet the unique needs of each individual or firm. This level of concentration does occur (we hope) in the case of personal or professional services we get from doctors, lawyers, and hairstylists. A **custom marketing strategy** is common in industrial contexts in which a manufacturer often works with one or a few large clients and develops products and services that only these clients will use.

Of course, in most cases this level of segmentation is neither practical nor possible when mass-produced products such as computers or cars enter the picture. However, advances in computer technology, coupled with the new emphasis on building solid relationships with customers, have focused managers' attention on devising a new way to tailor specific products and the messages about them to individual customers. Thus, some forward-looking, consumer-oriented companies are moving toward mass customization in which they modify a basic good or service to meet the needs of an individual. Even a giant automaker such as Buick asks, "Can we build one for you?"

Dell uses **mass customization** in which it modifies a basic good or service to meet the needs of an individual.[38] Dell does this by offering customized computer products over the Internet at Dell.com. Users can create their own computers—everything from personal computers to networking systems.[39] We'll return to the issue of customization later in this chapter when we introduce the idea of customer relationship management.

Step 3: Positioning

The final stage of developing a target marketing strategy process is to provide consumers who belong to a targeted market segment with a good or service that meets their unique needs and expectations. **Positioning** means developing a marketing strategy aimed at influencing how a particular market segment perceives a good or service *in comparison* to the competition. Developing a positioning strategy entails gaining a clear understanding of the criteria target consumers use to evaluate competing products and then convincing them that your product will meet those needs. Of course, ultimately this positioning must be communicated to consumers.

Positioning can be done in many ways. Sometimes it's just a matter of making sure that cool people are seen using your product. That's exactly what BC Ethic did. This apparel manufacturer is known for repopularizing the style of retro, button-down bowling shirt worn by *Seinfeld*'s Kramer.[40] Instead of paying millions of dollars to hire a popular rock star for its ads, BC Ethic created shirts with customized, embroidered band logos and offered them free to nationally known music artists such as Barenaked Ladies, Cypress Hill, Sevendust, and Dick Dale. For some outdoor and print advertising, the company used the brand's color scheme—black and red—to develop stylized tinted likenesses of some of the groups and even created posters that became popular merchandising material for retailers including Nordstrom.

Developing a Positioning Strategy

The success of a target marketing strategy hinges on marketers' abilities to identify and select an appropriate market segment. Then marketers must devise a marketing mix that will effectively target the segment's members by positioning their products to appeal to that segment.

concentrated targeting strategy
Focusing a firm's efforts on offering one or more products to a single segment.

custom marketing strategy
An approach that tailors specific products and the messages about them to individual customers.

mass customization
An approach that modifies a basic good or service to meet the needs of an individual.

positioning
Developing a marketing strategy aimed at influencing how a particular market segment perceives a good or service in comparison to the competition.

A first step is to analyze the competitors' positions in the marketplace. To develop an effective positioning strategy, marketers must understand the current lay of the land. What competitors are out there, and how are they perceived by the target market? Aside from direct competitors in the product category, are there other products or services that provide the same benefits people are seeking (i.e., indirect competitors)?

Sometimes the indirect competition can be more important than the direct, especially if it represents an emerging consumer trend. For years, McDonald's developed positioning strategies based only on its direct competition, which it defined as other large fast-food hamburger chains (translation: Burger King and Wendy's). McDonald's failed to realize that consumers' needs for a quick, tasty, convenient meal was being fulfilled by a plethora of indirect competitors—from supermarket delis to frozen microwavable single-serving meals to call-ahead takeout from full-service restaurants like T.G.I. Friday's, Outback, and Chili's. Unfortunately, only recently has McDonald's begun to understand that it must react to this indirect competition by serving up a wider variety of adult-friendly food and shoring up lagging service.

The next task in developing a positioning strategy is to offer a good or service with a competitive advantage to provide a reason why consumers will perceive the product as better than the competition. If the company offers only a "me-too product," it can induce people to buy for a lower price. Other forms of competitive advantage include offering a superior image (Giorgio Armani), a unique product feature (Levi's 501 button-fly jeans), better service (Cadillac's roadside assistance program), or even better-qualified people (the legendary salespeople at Nordstrom's department stores).

BC Ethic positioned its shirts as "cool" by providing popular music groups with custom-designed shirts and then using the groups in its advertising.

Once a positioning strategy is set, marketers must finalize the marketing mix by putting all the pieces into place. The elements of the marketing mix must match the selected segment. This means that the good or service must deliver benefits that the segment values, such as convenience or status. Put another way, it must add value and satisfy consumer needs. Furthermore, marketers must price this offering at a level these consumers will pay, make the offering available at places consumers are likely to go, and correctly communicate the offering's benefits in locations where consumers are likely to take notice.

Finally, marketers must evaluate the target market's responses so they can modify strategies as needed. Over time, the firm may find that it needs to change which segments it targets or even redo a product's position to respond to marketplace changes. An example of such a makeover, a strategy called **repositioning**, is Charles Schwab, which used to be pegged primarily as a self-service stock brokerage. Competition in the budget broker business, especially from online brokers, prompted Schwab's repositioning to a full-line, full-service financial services firm. Think of it this way: there's not much value Schwab can add by being one of a dozen or more online providers of stock trades. In that environment, they are likely to be viewed as a commodity with no real differentiation. Schwab still has its no-frills products, but the real growth in sales and profits is expected to come from its expanded lines.

repositioning
Redoing a product's position to respond to marketplace changes.

Bringing a Product to Life: The Brand Personality

Brands are almost like people in that we can often describe them in terms of personality traits. We may use adjectives such as *cheap*, *elegant*, *sexy*, or *cool* when talking about a store, a perfume, a car, and so on. That's why a positioning strategy often tries to create a **brand personality** for a good or

brand personality
A distinctive image that captures a good's or service's character and benefits.

We often think of products as if they were people. In this Brazilian ad for engine oil, this product begs for help.

service—a distinctive image that captures its character and benefits. An advertisement for *Elle* magazine once said, "She is not a reply card. She is not a category. She is not shrink-wrapped. *Elle* is not a magazine. She is a woman."

Products as people? It seems funny to say, yet marketing researchers find that most consumers have no trouble describing what a product would be like "if it came to life." People often give clear, detailed descriptions, including what color hair the product would have, the type of house it would live in, and even whether it would be thin, overweight, or somewhere in between.[41] If you don't believe us, try doing this yourself.

Part of creating a brand personality is developing an identity for the product that the target market will prefer over competing brands. How do marketers determine where their product actually stands in the minds of consumers? One solution is to ask consumers what characteristics are important and how competing alternatives would rate on these attributes, too. Marketers use this information to construct a **perceptual map**, which is a vivid way to construct a picture of where products or brands are "located" in consumers' minds.

For example, suppose you wanted to construct a perceptual map of women's magazines as perceived by American women in their 20s to give you some guidance while developing an idea for a new magazine. After interviewing a sample of female readers, you might determine questions women ask when selecting a magazine: (1) Is it "traditional," that is, oriented toward family, home, or personal issues, or is it "fashion forward," oriented toward personal appearance and fashion? (2) Is it for "upscale" women who are older and established in their careers or for relatively "downscale" women who are younger and just starting out in their careers?

The perceptual map in Figure 7.4 illustrates how these ratings might look for certain major women's magazines. The map provides some guidance as to where your new women's magazine might be positioned. You might decide to compete directly with either the cluster of "service magazines" in the lower left or the traditional fashion magazines in the upper right. In this case, you would have to determine what benefits your new magazine might offer that these existing magazines do not. Condé Nast, for example, positioned *Allure* to compete against fashion magazines by going into more depth than others do on beauty issues, such as the mental, physical, and emotional dangers of cosmetic surgery.

perceptual map
A vivid way to construct a picture of where products or brands are "located" in consumers' minds.

Figure 7.4 **Perceptual Map**

Perceptual mapping allows marketers to identify consumers' perceptions of their brand in relation to the competition.

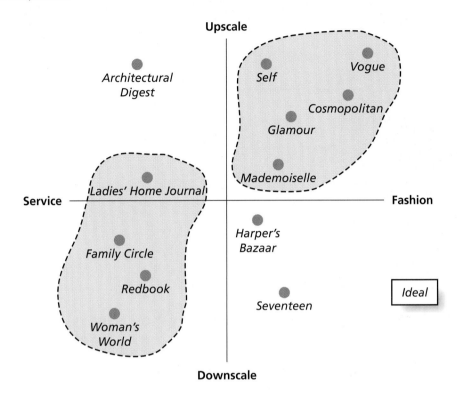

You might try to locate an unserved area in this map. There may be room for a magazine targeted to "cutting-edge" fashion for college-age women. An unserved segment is the "Holy Grail" for marketers: With luck, they can move quickly to capture a segment and define the standards of comparison for the category. This tactic has paid off for Chrysler, which first identified the minivan market, and Liz Claiborne, which pioneered the concept of comfortable, "user-friendly" clothing for working women. In the magazine category, perhaps *Marie Claire* comes closest to this position.

Creating a positioning strategy is the last step in the target marketing process. We can summarize this sequence of events by looking at the strategy developed by the SoBe Beverage Company, a small drink manufacturer based in Connecticut. The company segmented the market in terms of age and psychographics and then targeted a segment of 18- to 35-year-olds whose profiles indicated they were into "New Age" beverages that would give them a feeling of energy without unhealthy additives. SoBe created XTC, a drink inspired by "herbal ecstasy" cocktails of extracts and amino acids popular at "raves" featuring all-night gyrations to techno music. As an industry executive noted, this strategy provides a unique position for the elixir: "People are taking something that provides a four-times-removed high without having to get arrested or wrecking their bodies. It carries the image of being a little further out there without carrying the risk."[42]

Customer Relationship Management: Toward a Segment of One

We've talked about identifying a unique group of consumers and developing products specifically to meet their needs. And we talked about how marketers can build products to meet the needs of individual consumers with mass customization. Today many highly successful marketing firms embrace **customer relationship management (CRM)** programs that allow companies to talk to

customer relationship management (CRM)
A philosophy that sees marketing as a process of building long-term relationships with customers to keep them satisfied and to keep them coming back.

Brand personalities often are reflected in logos. This clothing ad from Chile pits a shark against the more familiar crocodile—with bloody results.

individual customers and adjust elements of their marketing programs in light of how each customer reacts to elements of the marketing mix.[43] The CRM trend facilitates one-to-one marketing, a term popularized in the writings of Don Peppers and Martha Rogers.[44]

Peppers and Rogers have identified four steps in one-to-one marketing.[45] The first step is to identify customers and get to know them in as much detail as possible. Next, marketers need to differentiate these customers in terms of both their needs and their value to the company. Third, marketers must interact with customers and find ways to improve cost efficiency and the effectiveness of the interaction. Finally, marketers need to customize some aspect of the products or services they offer to each customer. This means treating each customer differently based on what has been learned through customer interactions. Table 7.2 suggests some activities for implementing these four steps. Successful one-to-one marketing is dependent on CRM.

Peppers and Rogers define CRM as "managing customer relationships. If I'm managing customer relationships, it means I'm treating different customers differently, across all enterprises. . . . The relationship develops a context over time, it drives a change in behavior . . . [this] means that I have to change my behavior as an enterprise based on a customer."[46] A CRM strategy allows a company to identify its best customers, stay on top of their needs, and increase their satisfaction.

Is CRM for all companies? Should producers of consumer goods that target the entire market adopt CRM strategies? Of course, CRM seems to make more sense for firms such as business-to-business companies and consumer products companies that have a limited number of customers. But, as we'll see in the next section, even soft-drink and automobile companies have used CRM to build customer relationships and brand loyalty.

Table 7.2 Four Steps of One-to-One Marketing

Step	Suggested Activities
Identify	Collect and enter names and additional information about your customers. Verify and update, deleting outdated information.
Differentiate	Identify top customers. Determine which customers cost the company money. Find higher-value customers who have complained about your product or service more than once. Find customers who buy only one or two products from your company but a lot from other companies. Rank customers into A, B, and C categories based on their value to your company.
Interact	Call the top three people in the top 5 percent of dealers, distributors, and retailers that carry your product and make sure they're happy. Call your own company and ask questions; see how hard it is to get through and get answers. Call your competitors and compare their customer service with yours. Use incoming calls as selling opportunities. Initiate more dialogue with valuable customers. Improve complaint handling.
Customize	Find out what your customers want. Personalize your direct mail. Ask customers how and how often they want to hear from you. Ask your top 10 customers what you can do differently to improve your product or service. Involve top management in customer relations.

Source: Adapted from Don Peppers, Martha Rogers, and Bob Dorf, "Is Your Company Ready for One-to-One Marketing?," *Harvard Business Review*, January–February 1999, 151–160.

CRM: A New Perspective on an Old Problem

CRM is about communicating with customers and about customers being able to communicate with a company one to one. CRM systems are applications that, through computers, CRM computer software, databases, and often the Internet, capture information at each *touch point* (or interaction) between customers and companies to allow for overall better customer care. They include everything from Web sites that let you check on the status of a bill or package to *call centers* that solicit your business. When you log on to the Federal Express Web site to track a lost package, that's part of a CRM system. When you get a phone message from the dentist reminding you about that filling appointment tomorrow, that's CRM. And when you get a call from the car dealer asking how you like your new vehicle, that's also CRM. In a nutshell, CRM helps firms communicate with and serve customers by better understanding their needs. Remember how in Chapter 4 we said information is the fuel that runs the marketing engine? CRM is how much of that customer information is managed and acted on.

To fully appreciate the value of a CRM strategy, consider the experience of financial services firms such as Salomon Smith Barney and Fidelity Investments, both of which have embraced CRM. In general, an investment banker needs to manage accounts as well as open new ones—often 30 to 50 per month. Just opening the account can take 45 minutes, not a satisfying process for the banker or for the customer. But with an automated CRM system, the banker can open an account, issue a welcome letter, and produce an arbitration agreement in 10 minutes. She can create a unique marketing campaign for each client based on that person's life cycle—including such variables as when a person opened an account, his annual income, family situation, desired retirement age, and so on. The marketer can generate a happy anniversary letter to clients (to commemorate

Siebel Systems is the largest and most famous vendor of CRM solutions. Siebel's Web site is a terrific source of information about CRM and includes an outstanding tutorial you can walk through to better understand how implementing a CRM system can enhance your business.

when they became customers of the firm, not when they got married) and include an invitation to update their investment objectives. These firms have found that this level of individualized attention results in a much higher rate of customer retention and satisfaction, so CRM creates a win-win situation for everyone.[47]

That success helps explain why CRM has become a driving philosophy in many successful firms. Industry sources estimate that in 2005 companies will spend $14 billion to purchase sophisticated software that will let them build these electronic bridges.[48] Even the Internal Revenue Service (IRS) bought a CRM software system worth more than $10 million. The system allows taxpayers to obtain tax records and other information around the clock. An agency spokesman commented that this purchase is part of the IRS's ongoing effort to become more customer friendly and will allow many disgruntled taxpayers to receive quick (and, it is hoped, accurate) answers automatically rather than sitting on the phone for hours.[49]

The airline industry, rocked by financial problems the past few years, is also concerned about customer relations and has invested heavily in CRM systems. These systems help flyers by automating crucial information and reducing phone call volume—and in the process those nasty "holds" we're all accustomed to.[50] CRM also helps identify flying patterns, favored destinations, and loyal users so that extra perks (upgrades, tailored special offers, and so on) can be sent their way.

In addition to mollifying angry customers, marketers can also use CRM systems to keep better track of enthusiastic ones. For example, Sprite staged a "Rocket Cash" sweepstakes promotion by sending out legions of marketing representatives with handheld touch-screen devices. They hung out at concerts and on street corners and enticed young people to enter the sweepstakes by tapping their names, e-mail addresses, and birthdays into the devices on the spot. Every evening, data were uploaded to Sprite's Web site, and entrants were kept informed by e-mail of their status in the sweepstakes. In return, Sprite wound up with a list of consumers with whom it could communicate in the future.[51]

CRM is also a more efficient way to serve new customers who may have been overlooked by prior marketing efforts. Many experts are excited about this possibility. Consider this: Although African Americans have $447 billion in purchasing power, the average African American household receives only one catalog per week during the holiday season as compared with 10 catalogs per Caucasian household per week. Similarly, the average Hispanic household ($350 billion in purchasing power) gets 20 pieces of direct mail annually compared to 300 pieces for non-Hispanic households. That explains why some companies are working hard to compile lists of ethnic households and develop new relationships in the race to make "new friends."[52]

Perhaps the most important aspect of CRM is that it presents a new way of looking at how to effectively compete in the marketplace. This begins with looking at customers as partners. CRM proponents suggest that the traditional relationship between customers and marketers is an adversarial one where marketers try to sell their products to customers and customers seek to avoid buying.[53] The customer relationship perspective sees customers as partners, with each partner learning from the other every time they interact. Successful firms compete by establishing relationships with individual customers on a one-to-one basis through dialogue and feedback. What does *this* customer really want? That's one-to-one marketing.

And, of course, when we say customers, we don't just mean end consumers—CRM is widely used to strengthen business-to-business relationships as well. To understand the importance of this kind of thinking, consider the experience of Dow, a giant corporation that sells $30 billion worth of chemicals, plastics, and agricultural products each year in more than 170 countries. Although Dow uses cutting-edge manufacturing technology every day, until recently it had literally no centralized mechanism to keep track of its many customers.

Eventually, Dow launched a major effort to install a company-wide CRM system that would be a central repository for customer information and would allow its customers to interact with Dow more efficiently—letting them access information automatically without having to deal with a large corporate bureaucracy. The result? A Web-based interface called MyAccount@Dow that lets customers log on (with a secure password, of course), enter new orders, check on the status of old orders, pay invoices electronically, and collaborate with others throughout the system. As a result, Dow lowered its customer support costs by $15 million and is taking electronic orders of $100 million per month.[54]

Characteristics of CRM

In addition to having a different mind-set, companies that successfully practice CRM have different goals, use different measures of success, and look at customers in some different ways. So, CRM marketers look at their share of the customer, at the lifetime value of a customer, at customer equity, and at focusing on high-value customers.

SHARE OF CUSTOMER   Historically, marketers have measured success in a product category by their share of market. For example, if there are 100 million pairs of athletic shoes sold each year, a firm that sells 10 million of them has a 10 percent market share. If the shoemaker's marketing objective is to increase market share, it may lower the price of its shoes, increase its advertising, or offer customers a free basketball with every pair of shoes purchased. Such tactics may increase sales in the short run but, unfortunately, may not do much for the long-term success of the shoemaker. In fact, such tactics may actually *decrease* the value of the brand by cheapening its image with giveaways.

Because it is always easier and less expensive to keep an existing customer than to get a new customer, CRM firms focus on increasing their **share of customer**, not share of market. Let's say that a consumer buys six pairs of shoes a year—two pairs from each of three different

MEASURING VALUE
marketing metrics

Many firms today look at their relationships with customers as a financial asset. A firm's goal always is to bring in a high return on the investment made in a customer relationship and to maximize the value of customer equity. For this reason, it is very important for the firm to invest in the *right* customers. Loyalty plays a big role here. Loyal customers are more likely to deliver a greater financial return to the company because they tend to pay higher prices for the same products and services. Loyal customers also engage in more positive word of mouth. In this way, they help the firm acquire even more customers. One approach to identifying "best customers" is fairly simple, but it requires firms to maintain a database that includes a history of past purchases.[55] Using such a database, the firm can perform analyses to answer the following questions in order to create a marketing metric that will identify "best customers":

- Recency of purchase: How long has it been since the customer last placed an order?
- Frequency of purchase: How often does this customer buy a product/service?
- Monetary value of purchase: How much does the customer spend on a typical transaction?

share of customer
The percentage of an individual customer's purchase of a product that is a single brand.

manufacturers. Let's assume one shoemaker has a CRM system that allows it to send letters to its current customers inviting them to receive a special price discount or a gift if they buy more of the firm's shoes during the year. If the firm can get the consumer to buy three or four or perhaps all six pairs from it, it has increased its share of customer. And that may not be too difficult because the customer already buys and supposedly likes the firm's shoes. Without the CRM system, the shoe company would probably use traditional advertising to increase sales, which would be far more costly than the customer-only direct-mail campaign. So the company can increase sales and profits at a much lower cost than it would spend to get one, two, or three new customers.

lifetime value of a customer
The potential profit generated by a single customer's purchase of a firm's products over the customer's lifetime.

LIFETIME VALUE OF THE CUSTOMER   As you'll recall from Chapter 1, the **lifetime value of a customer** is the potential profit generated by a single customer's purchase of a firm's products over the customer's lifetime. With CRM, a customer's lifetime value is identified and is the true goal, not an individual transaction. It just makes sense that a firm's profitability and long-term success are going to be far greater if it develops long-term relationships with its customers so that those customers buy from it again and again. Costs will be far higher and profits lower if each customer purchase is a first-time sale.

How do marketers calculate the lifetime value of a customer? They first estimate a customer's future purchases across all products from the firm over the next 20 or 30 years. The goal is to try to figure out what profit the company could make from the customer in the future. For example, an auto dealer might calculate the lifetime value of a single customer by first calculating the total revenue that could be generated by the customer over his lifetime: the number of automobiles he would buy times their average price, plus the service the dealership would provide over the years, and even possibly the income from auto loan financing. The lifetime value of the customer would be the total profit generated by the revenue stream.

customer equity
The financial value of a customer relationship throughout the lifetime of the relationship.

CUSTOMER EQUITY   Today an increasing number of companies are considering their relationships with customers as financial assets. Such firms measure success by calculating the value of their **customer equity**—the financial value of customer relationships throughout the lifetime of the relationships.[56] To do this, firms compare the investments they make in acquiring customers, retaining customers, and relationship enhancement with the financial return on those investments. The goal is to reap a high return on the investments made in customer relationships and maximize the value of a firm's customer equity.

A GREATER FOCUS ON HIGH-VALUE CUSTOMERS   Using a CRM approach, customers must be prioritized and communication customized accordingly. For example, any banker will tell you that not all customers are equal—when it comes to profitability. So banks use CRM systems to generate a profile of each customer based on factors such as value, risk, attrition, and interest in buying new financial products. This automated system helps the bank decide which current or potential customers it will target with certain communications or how much effort to expend on retaining a person's account—all the while cutting its costs by as much as a third.[57] It just makes sense to use different types of communication contacts based on the value of each individual customer. For example, personal selling (the most expensive form of marketing communication per contact) may constitute 75 percent of all contacts with high-volume customers, while direct mail or telemarketing is more often the best way to contact low-volume customers.

real people, real choices
How It Worked Out at Reebok

Que chose option 2. In 2002, Reebok created a new category called Rbk that fuses sports with youth lifestyle and entertainment. The goal of Rbk is to own the streets around the world and the mind share of youth globally by fusing music, fashion, style, and sports. It represents the sharp edge of the Reebok brand. Through Rbk, Reebok is able to speak directly and clearly to youth through its cool positioning as

"The Sounds and Rhythms of Sports." This platform enables Reebok to drive global growth by being experts on youth culture, developing relevant product collections, and creating marketing surprises that connect to the desired audience.

Zigzagging away from the competition, the company signed hip-hop artists along with NBA stars to promote its products. Rbk now is home to the Allen Iverson collection, the Above the Rim collection (Barron Davis, Steve Francis, Kenyon Martin, and Jason Richardson), the G-Unit collection (50 Cent), the S. Carter collection (Jay-Z), the Icecream collection (Pharrell Williams of The Neptunes), and others to come.

The Iverson collection continues to grow and is the biggest Rbk line. However, the new additions of the S. Carter and G-Unit collections have improved Reebok's distribution, positioning, and shelf space in stores. It has strengthened the connection among youth consumers by allowing the brand to use respected icons of hip-hop, such as Jay-Z, 50 Cent, and Pharrell.

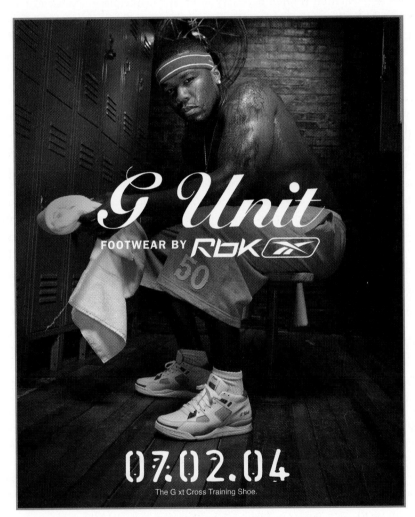

Rapper 50 Cent promotes Rbk's G-Unit shoe collection.

This target marketing strategy has given Reebok the ability to broaden its appeal beyond just sports performance. The risky strategy paid off for the company; earnings and sales have grown by double digits since the Rbk division was created. Reebok will always be known as the sports performance and lifestyle brand that gave rappers their first signature shoes. Rbk is "The Sounds and Rhythms of Sports."

Some time during your job search, you may be tempted to say, "I'm willing to do anything." Savvy job hunters know it's important to target the employers who need your skills. Learn how in Chapter 7 of *Brand You*.

CHAPTER SUMMARY

1. **Understand the need for market segmentation in today's business environment.** Market segmentation is often necessary in today's marketplace because of market fragmentation, that is, the splintering of a mass society into diverse groups due to technological and cultural differences. Most marketers can't realistically do a good job of meeting the needs of everyone, so it is more efficient to divide the larger pie into slices in which members of a segment share some important characteristics and tend to exhibit the same needs and preferences.

2. **Know the different dimensions marketers use to segment consumer and business-to-business markets.** Marketers frequently find it useful to segment consumer markets on the basis of demographic characteristics, including age, gender, family life cycle, social class, race or ethnic identity, and place of residence. A second dimension, psychographics, uses measures of psychological and social characteristics to identify people with shared preferences or traits. Consumer markets may also be segmented on the basis of how consumers behave toward the product, for example, their brand loyalty, usage rates (heavy, moderate, or light), and usage occasions. Business-to-business markets are often segmented on the basis of industrial demographics, type of business based on the North American Industry Classification (NAICS) codes, and geographic location.

3. **Explain how marketers evaluate and select potential market segments.** To choose one or more segments to target, marketers examine each segment and evaluate its potential for success as a target market. Meaningful segments have wants that are different from those in other segments, can be identified, can be reached with a unique marketing mix, will respond to unique marketing communications, are large enough to be profitable, have future growth potential, and possess needs that the organization can satisfy better than the competition.

4. **Explain how marketers develop a targeting strategy.** After the different segments have been identified, the market potential of each segment is estimated. The relative attractiveness of segments also influences the firm's selection of an overall marketing strategy. The firm may choose an undifferentiated, differentiated, concentrated, or custom strategy based on the company's characteristics and the nature of the market.

5. **Understand how a firm develops and implements a positioning strategy.** After the target market(s) and the overall strategy have been selected, marketers must determine how they wish the brand to be perceived by consumers relative to the competition; that is, should the brand be positioned like, against, or away from the competition? Through positioning, a brand personality is developed. Brand positions may be compared using such research techniques as perceptual mapping. In developing and implementing the positioning strategy, firms analyze the competitors' positions, determine the competitive advantage offered by their product, tailor the marketing mix in accordance with the positioning strategy, and evaluate responses to the marketing mix selected. Marketers must continually monitor changes in the market that might indicate a need to reposition the product.

6. **Know how marketers practice customer relationship management to increase long-term success and profits.** Companies using customer relationship management (CRM) programs establish relationships and differentiate their behavior toward individual customers on a one-to-one basis through dialogue and feedback. Success is often measured one customer at a time using the concepts of share of customer, lifetime value of the customer, and customer equity. In CRM strategies, customers are prioritized according to their value to the firm, and communication is customized accordingly.

KEY TERMS

baby boomers, 199
behavioral segmentation, 207
brand personality, 213
concentrated targeting strategy, 212
custom marketing strategy, 212
customer relationship management (CRM), 215
customer equity, 220
differentiated targeting strategy, 210
80/20 rule, 207

Generation X, 199
Generation Y, 197
geodemography, 204
lifetime value of a customer, 220
market fragmentation, 197
mass customization, 212
metrosexual, 201
perceptual map, 214
positioning, 212
repositioning, 213

segment profile, 210
segmentation, 197
segmentation variables, 197
share of customer, 219
target market, 208
target marketing strategy, 197
undifferentiated targeting strategy, 210
usage occasions, 207
VALS™ (Values and Lifestyles), 206

CHAPTER REVIEW

MARKETING CONCEPTS: TESTING YOUR KNOWLEDGE

1. What is market segmentation, and why is it an important strategy in today's marketplace?

2. List and explain the major demographic characteristics frequently used in segmenting consumer markets.

3. Explain consumer psychographic segmentation.

4. What is behavioral segmentation?

5. What are some of the ways marketers segment industrial markets?

6. List the criteria used for determining whether a segment may be a good candidate for targeting.

7. Explain undifferentiated, differentiated, concentrated, and customized marketing strategies. What is mass customization?

8. What is product positioning? Describe the three approaches that marketers use to create product positions.

9. What is CRM? How do firms practice CRM?

10. Explain the concepts of share of customer, lifetime value of a customer, and customer equity.

MARKETING CONCEPTS: DISCUSSING CHOICES AND ISSUES

1. Some critics of marketing have suggested that market segmentation and target marketing lead to an unnecessary proliferation of product choices that wastes valuable resources. These critics suggest that if marketers didn't create so many different product choices, there would be more resources to feed the hungry and house the homeless and provide for the needs of people around the globe. Are the results of segmentation and target marketing harmful or beneficial to society as a whole? Should these criticisms be of concern to firms?

2. One of the criteria for a usable market segment is its size. This chapter suggested that to be usable, a segment must be large enough to be profitable now and in the future and that some very small segments get ignored because they can never be profitable. So how large should a segment be? How do you think a firm should go about determining if a segment is profitable? Have technological advances made it possible for smaller segments to be profitable? Do firms ever have a moral or ethical obligation to develop products for small, unprofitable segments?

3. Some firms have been criticized for targeting unwholesome products to certain segments of the market—the aged, ethnic minorities, the disabled, and others. What other groups deserve special concern? Should a firm use different criteria in targeting such groups? Should the government oversee and control such marketing activities?

4. Customer relationship management (CRM) focuses on share of customer, lifetime value of the customer, customer equity, and high-value customers. What do you think are some problems with replacing earlier concepts such as share of market with these concepts?

MARKETING PRACTICE: APPLYING WHAT YOU'VE LEARNED

1. Assume that you have been hired to develop a marketing plan for a small regional beer brewery. In the past, the brewery has simply produced and sold a single beer brand to the

entire market—a mass-marketing strategy. As you begin your work for the firm, you feel that the firm could be more successful if it developed a target marketing strategy. The owner of the firm, however, is not convinced. Write a memo to the owner outlining the following:

a. The basic reasons for target marketing

b. The specific advantages of a target marketing strategy for the brewery

2. As the marketing director for a company that is planning to enter the business-to-business market for photocopy machines, you are attempting to develop an overall marketing strategy. You have considered the possibility of using mass-marketing, concentrated marketing, differentiated marketing, and custom marketing strategies.

a. Write a report explaining what each type of strategy would mean for your marketing plan in terms of product, price, promotion, and distribution channel.

b. Evaluate the desirability of each type of strategy.

c. What are your final recommendations for the best type of strategy?

3. As an account executive for a marketing consulting firm, your newest client is a university—your university. You have been asked to develop a positioning strategy for the university. With a group of classmates, develop an outline of your ideas, including the following:

a. Who are your competitors?

b. What are the competitors' positions?

c. What target markets are most attractive to the university?

d. How will you position the university for those segments relative to the competition? Present the results to your class.

4. Assume that you have been hired as marketing manager for a chain of retail bookstores. You feel that the firm should develop a CRM strategy. Outline the steps you would take in developing that strategy.

MARKETING MINIPROJECT: LEARNING BY DOING

This miniproject will help you to develop a better understanding of how target marketing decisions are made. The project focuses on the market for women's beauty care products.

1. Gather ideas about different dimensions useful for segmenting the women's beauty products market. You may use your own ideas, but you probably will also want to examine advertising and other marketing communications developed by different beauty care brands.

2. Based on the dimensions for market segmentation that you have identified, develop a questionnaire and conduct a survey of consumers. You will have to decide which questions should be asked and which consumers should be surveyed.

3. Analyze the data from your research and identify the different potential segments.

4. Develop segment profiles that describe each potential segment.

5. Generate several ideas for how the marketing strategy might be different for each segment based on the profiles. Develop a presentation (or write a report) outlining your ideas, your research, your findings, and your marketing strategy recommendations.

REAL PEOPLE, REAL SURFERS: EXPLORING THE WEB

In this chapter, we learned about VALS2™, a popular market segmentation system developed by SRI International. Visit the SRI Web site (**www.sric-bi.com**). When you follow the VALS links, you will discover that SRI has also developed at least two other segmentation systems: GeoVALS and Japan-VALS. Follow the links to find out the following:

1. How has VALS2 been used by various SRI clients?

2. Describe Geo-VALS and Japan-VALS. What are some ways these segmentation systems might be used by organizations?

3. What is your opinion of the VALS2 Web site? Whom do you think SRI is targeting with its site? Do you think the site is an effective way to promote its product to potential customers? What suggestions do you have for improving the Web site? Write a report of your findings.

MARKETING PLAN EXERCISE

Check out a Web site for a company that manufacturers a product that you like and are familiar with. Pay special attention to the company's product lines and how it describes its products and product uses. Select one particular product and answer the following questions:

1. What market segmentation approaches do you believe are most relevant for your chosen product given the type of product it is? Why do you recommend these over other possible approaches?

2. Describe the top three target markets for the product you selected. What makes these particular targets so attractive?

3. From your review of the Web site as well as your knowledge of the product, write out a positioning statement for the product. Keep it to a few sentences; start out with "Product X is positioned as . . . "

4. In what ways could CRM help the company conduct successful target marketing and positioning of the product?

Marketing in Action Case

Real Choices at JetBlue

Why would anyone want to start a new airline in today's economic and competitive environment? The airline industry is notorious for its high operating costs, contentious labor issues, and high needs for capital to purchase airplanes. In addition, since November 2000, the five largest airlines in the country have lost a combined $20 billion.

Nonetheless, into this adverse situation entered David Neeleman and the airline he started named JetBlue. JetBlue operates in the low-fare category of the airline industry, competing with such airlines as Southwest, Frontier, and AirTran. However, unlike these other low-fare airlines, JetBlue is not a "no-frills" airline. JetBlue offers its passengers such amenities as leather seats, live satellite TV, and more passenger legroom. The airline also flies its planes from point to point, which means it doesn't use the "hub and spoke system" favored by companies like American Airlines, Delta, and United, which fly nearly all their routes through "hubs" like Dallas–Fort Worth, Atlanta, and Chicago. Jet Blue avoids these clogged hub airports, which, combined with its lower-cost structure, has allowed the company to realize one of the highest gross profit percentages in the industry.

Operating in a point-to-point system has also allowed JetBlue to be very selective when picking the geographic markets where it wants to compete. Currently, the airline provides service to only 22 cities. As a result, in terms of target markets, JetBlue is less extended geographically and can do a better job of providing quality service to its customers in its limited market.

In addition, over half of all airline passengers being recreational passengers and about a third being business passengers, JetBlue must consider behavioral segmentation variables, such as usage occasions, when segmenting its potential markets. For example, business travelers enjoy comfort as well as airlines that take off and land on time, making JetBlue's extra legroom and industry-leading, on-time departures and arrivals very important to that market segment. On the other hand, families and recreational passengers might consider entertainment to be a more important feature. In this case, JetBlue provides 24 channels of satellite TV. Finally, segmenting on the basis of demographics, such as income, is important to JetBlue because it is a low-fare airline.

Is the sky the limit for JetBlue's success? Not if the competition has a say in it. United and Delta have started their own low-fare airlines (United's "Ted" and Delta's "Song") and are offering service in JetBlue's markets. These carriers are betting their future on providing a level of service and amenities equal to JetBlue's but with a more extensive route system. Could turbulence be on the horizon for JetBlue and its aggressive growth pace? Possibly.

Regardless of how JetBlue decides to proceed from here, one thing is certain about its future. If the company is to continue on its growth path, choosing the right markets, targeting the right customers to serve, and establishing the right positioning for the airline with those customers will be extremely important.

Things to Think About

1. What is the decision facing JetBlue?
2. What factors are important in understanding this decision situation?
3. What are the alternatives?
4. What decision(s) do you recommend?
5. What are some ways to implement your recommendation(s)?

Sources: Andy Serwer, "Naked Ambition in the Air," *Fortune*, December 8, 2003, 231–32; Jennifer Comiteau, "David Neeleman on the Spot," *Adweek*, December 22–29, 2003, 16; Mike Bierne, "Are These the Little Airlines That Could?" *Brandweek*, March 29, 2004, 30–36; Perry Flint, "It's a Blue World After All," *Air Transport World*, June 2003, 36–41; and Wendy Zellner, "Is JetBlue's Flight Plan Flawed?," *Business Week*, February 16, 2004, 72–75.

Always an
Impressive Lineup

BLACK&DECKER®

Since 1910

real people, real choices

meet Eleni Rossides, a Decision
Maker at Black & Decker®

www.blackanddecker.com

first job out of school	what i do when i'm not working
Professional tennis player.	Spend time with my family.

CREATING THE PRODUCT

Eleni Rossides is senior manager of business development in the Black & Decker® Consumer Group of The Black & Decker Corporation, a leading manufacturer of power tools, outdoor power equipment, and household cleaning equipment. After attending Stanford University on a tennis scholarship, she graduated with a degree in communications and then competed on the women's professional tennis tour. In 2001, she received her MBA from Northwestern University, where she did a marketing internship at Johnson & Johnson. After graduating, she accepted a consulting position at McKinsey and Co. Since coming to Black & Decker in 2003, her responsibilities have included developing market research/marketing strategy for all the company's businesses.

Decision Time at Black & Decker

Black & Decker sells a line of household cleaning products that includes the DustBuster® cordless vacuum, the SteamBuster® wet/dry vacuum, and the ScumBuster® cordless wet scrubber. The ScumBuster can be used to clean many surfaces, such as tub and shower walls, barbecue grills, dishes, and even car exteriors. It has been popular for almost a decade because of its uniqueness and the lack of similar products available to consumers. Over time, however, the ScumBuster had started to take a back seat as Black & Decker focused its efforts on promoting newer products. In addition, competitors finally started to enter the market with similar devices that also boasted other features, such as a power-operated brush.

If Black & Decker was going to continue to be a leader in this category, the company needed to develop a new and improved ScumBuster—but preferably one that would not cost much more at retail to enable Black & Decker to maintain its profit margin on this product. In order to do that, Eleni and her colleagues needed to learn more about who was buying the ScumBuster so that Black & Decker would know how best to promote and package the product. They also wondered which specific features people would find most valuable if Black & Decker decided to redo the product's design. In focus groups, for example, people said it was important to get their cleaning jobs done faster. They were enthusiastic about ideas for new features, such as a liquid dispenser that included a reservoir to hold a cleaning solution that would make the ScumBuster a more convenient all-in-one system.

Eleni knew that it is risky to base important decisions on the comments of a few people in focus groups. She decided to commission a survey of ScumBuster users in order to learn more about what they liked or disliked about the product and which

business book i'm reading now	**what drives me**	**don't do this when interviewing with me**	**my pet peeve**
Don't Make Me Think by Stephen Krug.	To improve.	Be unprepared.	Untrustworthy people.

objectives

1 **Explain the layers of a product.**

2 **Describe the classifications of products.**

3 **Explain the importance of new products.**

4 **Describe how firms develop new products.**

5 **Explain the process of product adoption and the diffusion of innovations.**

features they might like to see added to it. Working with Mind/Share, a marketing research firm that specializes in Internet-based surveys, Eleni and her colleagues designed a survey in 2003. Along with product manager Christina Hamilton, she recruited 355 registered ScumBuster owners to respond to questions from their home computers. They answered questions about their cleaning needs, their reasons for buying the ScumBuster, their favorite accessories (such as a scrubbing pad, an area brush, or a shampoo brush), and how they typically used the ScumBuster (e.g., in a shower or tub, on a grill, or to clean the inside of a car). The owners also were given a list of benefits such as run time, ease of changing accessories, and rotation speed. They were asked to tell Black & Decker how important each was to them and also how satisfied they were with their ScumBuster product on each of these dimensions. In addition, they were given a list of features that might be added (such as variable speed control, an extension handle, and disposable batteries). They were asked to say which (if any) they would most like to see on a ScumBuster.

Survey participants told Black & Decker that power was the most important reason leading to their choice of the Scum-Buster over competitors. They also recommended additional improvements to the product, including variable speed, a contouring head, an extendable handle, and a power scrub with a liquid cleaner. But it wasn't clear that they were necessarily willing to pay a lot more for these extra features. The survey found that one of the main reasons for choosing the Scum/Buster was price/value. Furthermore, many of the users reported that they rarely or never used some of the accessories that came with the ScumBuster they currently owned. Based on the feedback she got from this survey, Black & Decker had the following options:

OPTION 1: Don't fix it if it ain't broke.

Keep the ScumBuster as it is. Although the initial allure of the product had worn off, Black & Decker continued to sell Scum-Busters without spending a lot to promote them. Survey respondents said that overall they were quite satisfied with the product. The product development team could focus its attention on creating new devices to meet other household needs. On the other hand, it wasn't clear how long the ScumBuster would continue to "rest on its laurels" now that competing brands were starting to challenge its dominance in the category. Eventually, Black & Decker would not sell enough ScumBusters to justify their place on store shelves, and it would have to walk away from the business.

OPTION 2: Emphasize value for your money.

The survey showed that by far the ScumBuster's primary use was to clean shower tubs and walls. Therefore, Black & Decker could remove all the accessories except those that are used for tub and tile cleaning and in the process lower the price of the appliance. This price/value strategy might enable Black & Decker to accelerate sales of a stripped-down, task-focused ScumBuster. And the survey showed that about 15 percent of respondents received the product as a gift, so having a more reasonable offering might encourage others to give ScumBusters as gifts also. On the other hand, people did seem to like the ScumBuster's versatility (even if they didn't always take advantage of its other potential uses). If Black & Decker focused only on tub/shower applications, the company might leave the market wide open to competitors that offered cleaning solutions for other areas such as kitchen counters or car detailing.

OPTION 3: Ramp up the ScumBuster's features.

Give consumers what they said they wanted to make their cleaning chores easier and faster: variable speed, new attachments for hard-to-reach places, and an onboard liquid cleaning system. This would allow Black & Decker to introduce a new "loaded" version of its product to meet the competition and give the company a reason to promote it more heavily. Of course, Black & Decker ran the risk of "preaching to the converted" since its research showed that most people were already reasonably happy with the current version.

Now, put yourself in Eleni Rossides's shoes: Which option would you choose?

Build a Better Mousetrap

"Build a better mousetrap and the world will beat a path to your door." Although we've all heard that adage, the truth is that just because a product is better is no guarantee it will succeed. For decades, the Woodstream Company built wooden mousetraps. Then the company decided to build a better one. Woodstream's product development people researched eating, crawling, and resting habits of mice. They built prototypes of different mousetraps to come up with the best possible design and tested them in homes. Then the company unveiled the sleek-looking "Little Champ," a black plastic miniature inverted bathtub with a hole. When the mouse went in and ate the bait, a spring snapped upward, and the mouse was history.[1]

Sounds like a great new product (if you're not a mouse), but the Little Champ failed. Woodstream studied mouse habits, *not* consumer preferences. The company later discovered that husbands set the trap at night, but wives were left in the morning to dispose of the trap holding the dead mouse. Unfortunately, wives thought the Little Champ looked too expensive to throw away, so they felt they should empty the trap for reuse. This was a task most women weren't willing to do—they wanted a trap they could happily throw away.

Woodstream's *failure* in the "rat race" underscores the importance of creating products that provide benefits that people seek. It also tells us that any number of products, from low-tech cheese to high-tech traps, potentially deliver these benefits. In this case, cheese and a shoe box could trap a mouse as well as a high-tech trap. So we need to take a close look at how products successfully trap consumers' dollars.

As defined in Chapter 1, a product is anything tangible or intangible that, through the exchange process, satisfies consumer or business customer needs. Products can be physical goods, services, ideas, people, or places. A good may be a pack of cookies, a digital camera, a house, a fancy new computer, or a pair of stone-washed jeans. A **good** is a tangible product, something that we can see, touch, smell, hear, taste, or possess. In contrast, intangible products—services, ideas, people, places—are products that we can't always see, touch, taste, smell, or possess. We'll talk more about intangible products in Chapter 10.

good
A tangible product that we can see, touch, smell, hear, or taste.

Marketers think of the product as more than just a *thing* that comes in a package. They view a product as a *bundle* of attributes that includes the packaging, brand name, benefits, and supporting features in addition to a physical good. As you see in Figure 8.1, we are now in Part III of this book, "Creating the Value Proposition." A large part of the marketer's role is creating the value proposition to develop and market products appropriately. In this chapter, we'll first examine what a product is and see how marketers classify consumer and business-to-business products. Then we'll go on to look at new products, how marketers develop new products, and how markets accept them. In the chapters that follow, we'll look at issues such as managing and pricing products and services.

Figure 8.1 Making and Delivering Value

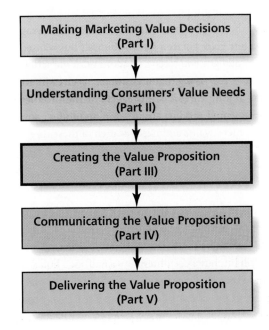

Figure 8.2 Layers of the Product

A product is everything a customer receives—the basic benefits, the physical product and its packaging, and the "extras" that come with the product.

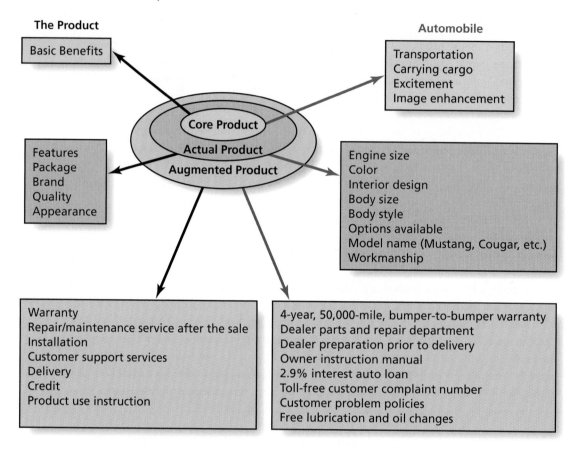

The Product

Basic Benefits

Features
Package
Brand
Quality
Appearance

Core Product
Actual Product
Augmented Product

Warranty
Repair/maintenance service after the sale
Installation
Customer support services
Delivery
Credit
Product use instruction

Automobile

Transportation
Carrying cargo
Excitement
Image enhancement

Engine size
Color
Interior design
Body size
Body style
Options available
Model name (Mustang, Cougar, etc.)
Workmanship

4-year, 50,000-mile, bumper-to-bumper warranty
Dealer parts and repair department
Dealer preparation prior to delivery
Owner instruction manual
2.9% interest auto loan
Toll-free customer complaint number
Customer problem policies
Free lubrication and oil changes

Layers of the Product Concept

No doubt you've heard someone say, "It's the thought, not the gift that counts." This means that the gift is a sign or symbol that the gift giver has remembered you. When we evaluate a gift we may consider the following: Was the gift presented with a flourish? Was it wrapped in special paper? Was it obviously something the gift giver got as a gift for himself but wanted to pass on to me? These dimensions are a part of the total gift you receive in addition to the actual goodie sitting in the box.

Like a gift, a product is *everything* that a customer receives in an exchange. As Figure 8.2 shows, we can distinguish among three distinct layers of the product—the core product, the actual product, and the augmented product. In developing product strategies, marketers need to consider how to satisfy customers' wants and needs at each of these three levels. Let's consider each layer in turn.

The Core Product

The core product consists of all the benefits the product will provide for consumers or business customers. As noted in Chapter 1, a benefit is an outcome that the customer receives from owning or using a product. Wise old marketers (and some young ones, too) will tell you, "A marketer may make and sell a half-inch drill bit, but a customer buys a half-inch hole." This timeworn saying tells us that people are buying the core product, in this case, the ability to make a hole. If a new product such as a laser comes along that provides that outcome in a better way or more cheaply, the drill bit

Table 8.1 Product Testing

Product	Testing Procedure	Benefit
Louis Vuitton Handbags	A mechanical arm lifts a handbag, loaded with an eight-pound weight, 1.5 feet off the floor, and then drops it over and over again, for four days.	An attractive yet durable handbag
Chrysler Cars	Cars face gale-force, blizzard conditions (snow included). If the car passes that test, it is subjected to simulated desert heat the next day.	Reliable transportation even under the worst weather conditions
Sherwin Williams Paint	40,000 panels, painted with both Sherwin Williams and competitors' paints, are subjected to the weather for up to 15 years (the length of the warranty on some paint).	A house paint that remains attractive throughout the warranty period
Apple Computers	To simulate real-life conditions, computers are drenched with soda, smeared with mayonnaise, and baked in ovens (to mimic the trunk of a car in the summer heat).	Computing power that is impervious to normal wear and tear—and more
Mattel's Barbie	Quality testers yank and pull Barbie's hair and limbs to make sure she can withstand the strong hands and teeth of five-year-olds. They pour sand on her and bake her in simulated sunlight. Only Barbies that pass the tensile strength, UV, heat, and saliva tests are accepted.	A toy that is both fun and safe for children
Shaw Industries Carpet Products	Workers pace up and down rows of carpet samples eight hours a day. One worker reads three books a week and has lost 40 pounds in three years as a carpet walker.	Carpeting that is attractive and durable after years of wear
Otis Elevators	Elevator components are strapped to a vibrating "shaker table," then subjected to heat reaching 400 degrees Fahrenheit and as cold as −150 degrees Fahrenheit.	An elevator that provides a smooth, safe ride and can withstand extreme conditions (such as a lightning strike)
Procter & Gamble Hair Care Products	P&G pays over $1,000 for mannequin heads with realistic hair for testing new hair care products. Each of P&G's 15 "heads" has a name. When the hair begins to get thin, the "head" is retired.	Attractive, healthy hair

Sources: Otis Research Center, "Shaking, Baking and Proving Technology," August 27, 2003; **http://home.fuse.net/mllwyd/barbie_misc.html**; Faye Rice, "Secrets of Product Testing," *Fortune*, November 28, 1994, 166–72; **www.utc.com/press/highlights/2003-08-27_tower.htm**; and Carol Matlack, "The Vuitton Machine," *Business Week*, March 22, 2004, 98–102.

maker has a problem. The moral of this story? Marketing is about supplying benefits, not products. Table 8.1 illustrates how some marketers rigorously test their products "in action" to be sure they deliver the benefits they promise.

Many products actually provide multiple benefits. For example, the primary benefit of a car is transportation—all cars (in good repair) provide the ability to travel from point A to point B. But products also provide *customized benefits*—benefits customers receive because manufacturers have added "bells and whistles" to win customers. Different drivers seek different customized benefits in a car. Some want economical transportation; others want a top-of-the-line, all-terrain vehicle; and still others look for a hot car that will be the envy of their friends.

The Actual Product

The second level of the product, the *actual product*, is the physical good or the delivered service that supplies the desired benefit. For example, when you buy a washing machine, the core product is the ability to get clothes clean, but the actual product is a large, square, metal apparatus. When you get a medical exam, the core product is maintaining your health, but the actual product is a lot of annoying poking and prodding. The actual product also includes the unique features of the product, such as its appearance or styling, the package, and the brand name. Canon makes a wide range of different cameras from inexpensive, disposable cameras to expensive digital models that do everything but take the photo for you—all offering the same core benefit of recording a person or event on film or in a digital format.

The Augmented Product

Finally, marketers offer customers an *augmented product*—the actual product plus other supporting features such as a warranty, credit, delivery, installation, and repair service after the sale. Marketers know that adding these supporting features to a product is an effective way for a company to stand out from the crowd.

For example, Netflix provides rental of DVDs (the actual product) to customers who want access to movies (the core product). Netflix successfully competes with video/DVD rental stores by letting customers rent an unlimited number of DVDs, with three movies out at a time, for a monthly subscription fee of around $20. Unlike renting from a video store, customers can keep the movies as long as they want with no late fees. Customers pay no shipping fees in either direction, and they can choose from 20,000 titles—a much more extensive collection than what the largest movie-rental stores can offer. Netflix also offers a movie recommendation service based on each customer's rating of previous movies. Netflix augmented product (free shipping, no time limits, extensive selection, and targeted recommendation) has paid off for the company, which will reach $1 billion in revenues by 2005. Stockholders have also done well: the stock price grew 400 percent in 2003.[2]

Classifying Products

So far, we've learned that a product may be a tangible good or an intangible service or idea and that there are different layers to the product. Now we'll build on that idea by looking at how products differ from one another. Marketers classify products into categories because the categories represent differences in how consumers and business customers feel about products and how they purchase different products. Such an understanding helps marketers develop new products and a marketing mix that satisfies customer needs. Figure 8.3 summarizes these categories.

Generally, products are either *consumer products* or *business-to-business products*, although sometimes the same products—such as toilet paper, vacuum cleaners, and lightbulbs—are bought by consumers and businesses. Of course, as we saw in Chapters 5 and 6, customers differ in how they make the purchase decision depending on whether the decision maker is a consumer or a business purchaser. Let's first consider differences in consumer products based on how long the product will last and on how the consumer shops for the product. Then we will discuss the general types of business-to-business products.

Figure 8.3   Classification of Products

Marketers classify products as a means of better understanding how consumers make purchase decisions. The goal is to do a better job of satisfying customers than the competition.

Consumer Products

Classified by how long they last
Durable: products that provide a benefit over a long period
- Example: Refrigerator

Nondurable: products that provide a benefit over a short time
- Example: Toothpaste

Classified by how consumers buy them
Convenience Products: products that are frequently purchased with little effort
- Examples: Staples (milk)
            Impulse Products (candy bars)
            Emergency Products (drain opener)

Shopping Products: products that are selected with considerable time and effort
- Examples: Attribute-based (shoes)
            Price-based (water heater)

Specialty Products: products that have unique characteristics to the buyer
- Examples: Favorite restaurant, Rolex watch

Unsought Products: products that consumers have little interest in until need
                       arises
- Example: Retirement plans

Business-to-Business Products

Classified by how organizational customers use them
Equipment
- Examples: Capital Equipment (buildings)
            Accessory Equipment (computer terminals)

Maintenance, Repair, and Operating (MRO) Products
- Examples: Maintenance Products (lightbulbs, mops)
            Repair Products (nuts, bolts)
            Operating Supplies (paper, oil)

Raw Materials
- Example: Iron ore

Processed Materials
- Example: Sheets of steel

Specialized Services
- Example: Legal services

Component Parts
- Example: Car water pump

Consumers spend a lot of time and energy in making the decision to buy a computer monitor but very little to grab a package of soup at the supermarket.

Consumer Product Classes Defined by How Long a Product Lasts

Marketers classify consumer goods as durable or nondurable depending on how long the product lasts. You expect a refrigerator to last many years, but a gallon of milk will last only a week or so until it turns into a science project. **Durable goods** are consumer products that provide benefits over a period of months, years, or even decades, such as cars, furniture, and appliances. In contrast, **nondurable goods**, such as newspapers and food, are consumed in the short term.

Durable goods are more likely to be purchased under conditions of high involvement (as we discussed in Chapter 5), while purchases of nondurable goods are more likely to be low-involvement decisions. When consumers buy a computer or a house, they will spend a lot of time and energy on the decision process. When they offer these products, marketers need to understand consumers' desires for different product benefits and the importance of warranties, service, and customer support. So they must be sure that consumers can find the information they need. One way to do this is by providing a Frequently Asked Questions (FAQ) section on a company Web site.

Consumers usually don't "sweat the details" so much when choosing among nondurable goods. There is little if any search for information or deliberation. Sometimes this means that consumers buy whatever brand is available and reasonably priced. In other instances, the purchase of non-durable goods is based largely on past experience. Because a certain brand has performed satisfactorily in the past, customers see no reason to consider other brands and choose the same one out of habit. For example, some consumers buy that familiar orange box of Tide laundry detergent again and again. In such cases, marketers can probably be less concerned with developing new-product features to attract customers and should focus more on pricing and distribution strategies.

durable goods
Consumer products that provide benefits over a long period of time, such as cars, furniture, and appliances.

nondurable goods
Consumer products that provide benefits for a short time because they are consumed (such as food) or are no longer useful (such as newspapers).

convenience product
A consumer good or service that is usually low priced, widely available, and purchased frequently with a minimum of comparison and effort.

Consumer Product Classes Defined by How Consumers Buy the Product

Marketers also classify products based on where and how consumers buy the product. Both goods and services can be thought of as *convenience products, shopping products, specialty products,* or *unsought products*. In Chapter 5, you will recall that we talked about how consumer decisions differ in terms of effort from habitual decision making to limited problem solving to extended problem solving. Classifying products based on how consumers buy them is tied to these differences in consumer decision making. By understanding how consumers buy products, marketers have a clearer vision of the buying process and can develop effective marketing strategies.

CONVENIENCE PRODUCTS A **convenience product** typically is a nondurable good or service that consumers purchase frequently with a minimum of comparison and effort. As the name implies, consumers expect these products to be handy and will buy whatever brands are easy to obtain. In general, convenience products are low priced and widely available. You can buy a gallon of milk or a loaf of bread at grocery stores, at convenience stores, and even at many service stations. Consumers generally know all they need or want to know about a convenience product, devote little effort to purchases, and willingly accept alternative brands if their preferred brand is not available in a convenient location. Most convenience products purchases are the results of habitual consumer decision making. What's the most important thing for marketers of convenience products? You guessed it—make sure the product is in stores where it's convenient for customers.

But all convenience product purchases aren't alike. You may stop by a local market on your way home from school or work to pick up that gallon of milk because milk is something you always keep in the refrigerator. As long as you're there, why not grab a candy bar for the drive home? Later that night, you dash out to buy something to unclog your kitchen drain—also a convenience product. Marketers classify convenience products as staples, impulse products, and emergency products.

Staples such as milk, bread, and gasoline are basic or necessary items that are available almost everywhere. Most consumers don't perceive big differences among brands. When selling staples, marketers must offer customers a product that consistently meets their expectations for quality and make sure it is available at a price comparable to the competition's prices.

Consider this situation: You are standing in the checkout line at the supermarket and notice a copy of *People* magazine featuring a photo of Beyoncé with a provocative headline. You've got to check out that article! This magazine is an *impulse product*— something people often buy on the spur of the moment. With an impulse product, marketers have two challenges: to create a product or package design that is enticing, that "reaches out and grabs the customer," and to make sure their product is highly visible, for example, by securing prime end-aisle or checkout lane space.

Emergency products are those products we purchase when we're in dire need. Bandages, umbrellas, and something to unclog the bathroom sink are examples of emergency products. Because we need the product badly and immediately, price and sometimes product quality may be irrelevant to our decision to purchase. If you're caught out in a sudden downpour, any umbrella at any price may do.

What are the challenges to marketers of emergency products? As with any other product, emergency products are most successful when they meet customer needs—you won't sell a drain cleaner that doesn't unclog a drain more than once. And emergency products need to be offered in the sizes customers want. If you cut your finger in the mall, you don't want to buy a box of 100 bandages—you want a box of 5 or 10. Of course, making emergency products available when and where an emergency is likely to occur is the real key to success.

See Sally run.

See Sally fall.

See Sally heal faster.

Amazing gel strips clinically proven to heal faster than ordinary bandages

BAND-AID® Brand Advanced Healing stays on better so you heal faster. Revolutionary gel strips are specially designed to stay on for days to better protect your cuts and scrapes from water, dirt and germs. They act like an instant scab, sealing in your body's natural fluids, so you heal faster. And now, there's also Advanced Healing Finger-Care for your knuckles and fingers.

BAND-AID® the better healing brand

Cut your finger? A blister on your foot? A BAND-AID® Brand Adhesive Bandage is an emergency product you expect to find whenever and wherever you need it.

SHOPPING PRODUCTS In contrast to convenience products, a **shopping product** is a good or service for which consumers will spend time and effort gathering information on price, product attributes, and product quality. They are likely to compare alternatives before making a purchase. The purchase of shopping products is typically a limited problem-solving decision. Often consumers have little prior knowledge about these products. Because they gather new information for each purchase occasion, consumers are only moderately brand loyal and will switch whenever a different brand offers new or better benefits. They may visit several stores and devote considerable effort to comparing products.

Laptop computers are a good example of a shopping product because they offer an ever-expanding array of new features and functions. There are trade-offs and decisions to make about the price, speed, screen size, weight, and battery life. Consumers may ask, "Does it have an internal DVD drive to play my movies?" "How much does it weigh?" "How long is the battery life?" "Does

shopping product
A good or service for which consumers spend considerable time and effort gathering information and comparing alternatives before making a purchase.

The third-generation AIBO ERS-7 is a specialty product that looks for its toys and communicates with its owner. Sony says the entertainment robot has six emotions and seven instincts programmed into its brain. The more you interact with it, the more it learns. AIBO learns to recognize your face and voice, performs tricks, and sulks when ignored—and you don't have to feed it.

it have built-in Wi-Fi wireless networking?[3] Designing successful shopping products means making sure they have the attributes that customers want. And it helps to design product packaging that points out those features consumers need to know about in order to make the right decisions.

Some shopping products have different characteristics. For these *attribute-based shopping products*, such as a new party dress or a pair of designer jeans, consumers spend time and energy finding the best possible product selection. At other times, when choices available in the marketplace are just about the same, products are considered shopping products because of differences in price. For these *price-based shopping products*, determined shoppers will visit numerous stores in hopes of saving an additional $10 or $20.

In business-to-consumer e-commerce, shopping is easier when consumers use "shopbots" or "intelligent agents," which are computer programs that find sites selling a particular product. Some of these programs also provide information on competitors' prices, and they may even ask customers to rate the various e-businesses that they have listed on their site so consumers have recommendations from other consumers on which sellers are good and which are less than desirable. It should be noted, however, that some sites do not wish to compete on price and don't give bots access to their listings.

specialty product
A good or service that has unique characteristics and is important to the buyer and for which the buyer will devote significant effort to acquire.

SPECIALTY PRODUCTS Who would pay $1,800 for a robot dog? Apparently a lot of people—Sony's AIBOs learn to do many things that real live dogs can do, and you don't need a pooper-scooper. Despite their hefty price tag, the robots quickly sold out when they were introduced in 1999. Now, the third-generation AIBO ERS-7 does even more, including looking for toys and communicating with its owner. The AIBO is a good example of a **specialty product**, as are a Big Bertha golf club and a Rolex watch. Specialty products have unique characteristics that are important to buyers at any price. Even the mundane product category of water can have a specialty product: VOSS water has sleek packaging that makes it stand out from other bottled waters. Extracted from an aquifer that was buried under snow and ice for centuries in Norway, VOSS markets its water as the purest in the world.

Consumers usually know a good deal about specialty products and are loyal to specific brands. Generally, a specialty product is an extended problem-solving purchase that requires a lot of effort to choose. That means that firms selling these kinds of products need to create marketing strategies that make their product stand apart from the rest. For example, advertising for a specialty product such as a big-screen TV may talk about the brand's unique characteristics, attempting to convince prospective customers that savvy shoppers won't accept a substitute for the "real thing."

unsought products
Goods or services for which a consumer has little awareness or interest until the product or a need for the product is brought to his or her attention.

UNSOUGHT PRODUCTS A fourth category of consumer products is the unsought product. **Unsought products** are goods or services (other than convenience products) for which a consumer has little awareness or interest until a need arises. For college graduates with their first "real" jobs, retirement plans and disability insurance are unsought products. It requires a good deal of advertising or personal selling to interest people in unsought products—just ask any life insurance salesperson. Marketers are challenged to find convincing ways to interest consumers in unsought products. One solution may be to make pricing more attractive; for example, reluctant consumers may be more willing to buy an unsought product for "only pennies a day" than if they have to think about their yearly or lifetime cash outlay.

Business-to-Business Products

Although consumers purchase products for their own use, as we saw in Chapter 6, organizational customers purchase products to use in the production of other goods and services or to facilitate the organization's operation. Marketers classify business-to-business products based on how organizational customers use them. As with consumer products, when marketers know how their business customers use a product, they are better able to design products and craft the entire marketing mix.

Equipment refers to the products an organization uses in its daily operations. Heavy equipment, sometimes called *installations* or *capital equipment*, includes items such as buildings and robotics used to assemble automobiles. Installations are big-ticket items and last for a number of years. Computers, photocopy machines, and water fountains are examples of *light* or *accessory equipment*; they are portable, cost less, and have a shorter life span than capital equipment. Equipment marketing strategies usually emphasize personal selling and may mean custom-designing products to meet an industrial customer's specific needs.

Maintenance, repair, and operating (MRO) products are goods that a business customer consumes in a relatively short time. *Maintenance products* include lightbulbs, mops, cleaning supplies, and the like. *Repair products* are such items as nuts, bolts, washers, and small tools. *Operating supplies* include computer paper and oil to keep machinery running smoothly. Although some firms use a sales force to promote MRO products, others rely on catalog sales, the Internet, and telemarketing to keep prices as low as possible.

Raw materials are products of the fishing, lumber, agricultural, and mining industries that organizational customers purchase to use in their finished products. For example, a food company may transform soybeans into tofu, and a steel manufacturer changes iron ore into large sheets of steel used by other firms to build automobiles, washing machines, and lawn mowers.

Processed materials are produced when firms transform raw materials from their original state. Organizations purchase processed materials that become a part of the products they make. A builder uses treated lumber to add a deck onto a house, and a company that creates aluminum soda cans for 7-Up buys aluminum ingots for this purpose. Some business customers purchase **specialized services** from outside suppliers. Specialized services may be technical, such as equipment repair, or nontechnical, such as market research and legal services. These services are essential to the operation of an organization but are not part of the production of a product.

Component parts are manufactured goods or subassemblies of finished items that organizations need to complete their own products. For example, a computer manufacturer needs silicon chips to make a computer, and an automobile manufacturer needs batteries, tires, and fuel injectors. As with processed materials, marketing strategies for component parts usually involve nurturing relationships with customer firms and on-time delivery of a product that meets the buyer's specifications.

To review, we now understand what a product is. We also know how marketers classify consumer products based on how long they last and how they are purchased, and we've seen how they classify business-to-business products according to how they are used. In the next section we'll learn about the marketing of new products, or innovations.

It's "New and Improved!" Understanding Innovations

"New and improved!" What exactly do we mean when we use the term *new product*? The Federal Trade Commission says (1) that a product must be entirely new or changed significantly to be called new and (2) that a product may be called new for only six months.

That definition is fine from a legal perspective. From a marketing standpoint, though, a new product or an **innovation** is anything that customers *perceive* as new and different. Innovations may be a cutting-edge style such as tongue piercings, a fad such as Razor scooters, a new communications

equipment
Expensive goods that an organization uses in its daily operations that last for a long time.

maintenance, repair, and operating (MRO) products
Goods that a business customer consumes in a relatively short time.

raw materials
Products of the fishing, lumber, agricultural, and mining industries that organizational customers purchase to use in their finished products.

processed materials
Products created when firms transform raw materials from their original state.

specialized services
Services purchased from outside suppliers that are essential to the operation of an organization but are not part of the production of a product.

component parts
Manufactured goods or subassemblies of finished items that organizations need to complete their own products.

innovation
A product that consumers perceive to be new and different from existing products.

technology such as WiMAX, or a new product such as personal digital assistants. It may be a completely new product that provides benefits never available before, such as personal computers when they were first introduced, or it may simply be an existing product with a new style, in a different color, or with some new feature. If an innovation is successful, it spreads throughout the population. First, it is bought and used by only a few people, and then more and more consumers adopt it.

The Importance of Understanding Innovations

Understanding innovations can be critical to the success of firms for at least two reasons. First, technology is advancing at a dizzying pace. Products are introduced and become obsolete faster than ever before. In many industries, firms are busy developing another new-and-better product before the last new-and-better product even hits store shelves. Nowhere is this more obvious than with personal computers, for which a steady change in technology makes consumers want a bigger, faster machine before the dust even settles on the old one. Another reason why understanding new products is important is the high cost of developing new products and the even higher cost of new products that fail. In the pharmaceutical industry, the cost of bringing each new drug to market is in the hundreds of millions.[4] Even the most successful firms can't afford many product failures with that kind of price tag.

Marketers must understand what it takes to develop a new product successfully. They must do their homework and learn what it is about existing products consumers find less than satisfactory and exactly what it will take to do a better job satisfying customer needs. Savvy marketers know they'll waste a ton of investment money if they don't.

Finally, new-product development is an important contribution to society. We would never suggest that everything new is good, but many new products, some of which are listed in Table 8.2, allow us to live longer, happier lives of better quality than before. Although there are some who disagree, most of us feel that our lives are better because of telephones, televisions, CD players, microwave ovens, and computers—except, of course, when these items break down.

New medical products help to keep us from breaking down: In the near future, doctors will be able to replace or assist almost every part of the body with bionic products such as replacement spinal discs, insulin pumps that mimic a natural pancreas in diabetes patients by automatically testing blood-glucose levels, microdetectors implanted into retinas allowing patients with retinal damage to see light, and bionic ears that allow the deaf to hear.[5] Truly useful new products benefit the users and the companies that make them.

Types of Innovations

Innovations differ in their degree of newness, and this helps to determine how quickly the products will be adopted by a target market. Because innovations that are more novel require greater effort and more changes in behavior, they are slower to spread throughout a population than new products that are similar to what is already available.

Marketers classify innovations into three categories based on their degree of newness: continuous innovations, dynamically continuous innovations, and discontinuous innovations. However, it is better to think of these three types as ranges along a continuum that goes from a very small change to a totally new product. The three types of innovations are based on the amount of disruption or change they bring to people's lives. For example, when the first automobiles were produced, they caused tremendous changes in the lives of people who were used to getting places under "horse power." While a more recent innovation like GPS systems that feed us driving directions by satellite are undoubtedly cool, in a relative sense we have to make fewer changes in our lives to adapt to them (other than not having to ask a stranger when you're lost).

CONTINUOUS INNOVATIONS A **continuous innovation** is a modification to an existing product, such as when Cheerios introduced Honey Nut and Frosted versions of its cereal. This type of modification can set one brand apart from its competitors. For example, Volvo cars are known for their safety, and Volvo comes out with a steady stream of safety-related innovations. Volvo was the

continuous innovation
A modification of an existing product that sets one brand apart from its competitors.

Table 8.2 Innovations That Have Changed Our Lives

Products that have changed how we play

1900	Kodak Brownie camera
1948	Polaroid camera
1976	JVC video recorder
1982	Philips/Sony CD player
1995	DVD player

Products that have changed how we work

1959	Xerox photocopier
1966	Xerox fax machine
1971	Intel microprocessor
1980	3M Post-It Notes
1984	Apple Macintosh
1998	Blackberry PDA

Products that have changed how we travel

1908	Ford Model T
1936	DC-3
1950s	Skateboard
1957	Boeing 707
2001	Segway Human Transporter
2003	Toyota Prius hybrid car

Products that have changed our health and grooming

1921	Johnson & Johnson Band-Aid
1928	Penicillin
1931	Tampax tampon
1960	Searle birth control pill
2003	Crest Whitestrips

Products that have changed our homes

1907	Vacuum cleaner
1918	Frigidaire refrigerator
1928	Home air conditioner
1967	Amana microwave oven
2003	TMIO Internet-accessible refrigerated oven

Products that have changed the way we communicate

1921	RCA radio
1935	RCA television
1991	World Wide Web
2003	Treo cell phone/PDA/camera

Products that have changed our clothing

1913	Zipper
1914	Bra
1939	Nylons
1954	Velcro
1961	Procter & Gamble Pampers

Sources: Adapted from Christine Chen and Tim Carvell, "Products of the Century," *Fortune,* November 22, 1999, 133–36; "Best of What's Next," *Popular Science,* November 13, 2003; **http://inventors.about.com/library/inventors/bldvd.htm; www.time.com/time/2003/inventions/list.html**; Thomas Hoffman, "Segway's Tech Plans Look Down the Road to Growth," *Computerworld,* January 26, 2004, 4; Louis E. Frenzel, "The BlackBerry Reaps the Fruits of Innovation," *Electronic Design,* March 29, 2004, 41(5); David Stires, "Rx for Investors," *Fortune,* May 3, 2004, 158; and "Procter & Gamble," *Drug Store News,* January 19, 2004, 57.

Each of these national brands is standing next to its legal knockoff.

first car to offer full front and side air bags, and all its 2004 models come with an extensive menu of air bags, including Inflatable Curtain head-protection air bags for front and rear passengers, side air bags for front passengers, and the usual dual-stage front air bags. Additional crash protection for the 2004 Volvo V40 comes from whiplash-reducing front seats and seatbelt pretensioners.[6]

The consumer doesn't have to learn anything new to use a continuous innovation. From a marketing perspective, this means that it is far easier to convince consumers to adopt this kind of new product. For example, Samsung's line of flat-screen monitors doesn't require computer users to change their behavior. We all know what a computer monitor is and how it works. The flat-screen continuous innovation simply gives users the added benefits of taking up less space and being easier on the eyes.

How different does a new product have to be from existing products? We've all heard that "imitation is the sincerest form of flattery," but decisions regarding how much (if at all) one's product should resemble those of competitors often are a centerpiece of marketing strategy. Sometimes marketers feel that the best strategy is to follow the competition. For example, the packaging of "me-too" or look-alike products can create instant market success because consumers assume that similar packaging means similar products.

A **knockoff** is a new product that copies, with slight modification, the design of an original product. Firms deliberately create knockoffs of clothing, jewelry, or other items, often with the intent to sell to a larger or different market. For example, companies may copy the *haute couture* clothing styles of top designers and sell them at lower prices to the mass market. It is difficult to legally protect a design (as opposed to a technological invention) because it can be argued that even a very slight change—different buttons or a slightly wider collar on a dress or shirt—means the knockoff is not an exact copy.

DYNAMICALLY CONTINUOUS INNOVATIONS   A **dynamically continuous innovation** is a pronounced modification to an existing product that requires a modest amount of learning or change in behavior to use it. The history of audio equipment is a series of dynamically continuous innovations. For many years, consumers enjoyed listening to their favorite Frank Sinatra songs on record players. Then in the 1960s, that same music became available on a continuous-play eight-track tape (requiring the purchase of an eight-track tape player, of course). Then came cassette tapes (oops, now a cassette player is needed). In the 1980s, consumers could hear Metallica songs digitally mastered on compact discs (that, of course, required the purchase of a new CD player).

knockoff
A new product that copies with slight modification the design of an original product.

dynamically continuous innovation
A change in an existing product that requires a moderate amount of learning or behavior change.

In the 1990s, recording technology moved one more step forward with MP3 technology, allowing music fans to download music from the Internet or to exchange electronic copies of the music with other fans. Mobile MP3 players hit the scene in 1998, letting music fans download their favorite tunes into a portable player. In November 2001, Apple Computer introduced the iPod, a pocket-sized mobile player with a hard disk built in. With the iPod, music fans could take 1,000 songs with them wherever they went. By 2004, iPods could hold 10,000 songs.[7] Music fans can go to Web sites like Musicmatch.com to download songs legally and to get suggestions for new music they might enjoy. Even though each of these changes required learning how to operate new equipment, consumers were willing to buy the new products because of the improvements in music reproduction, the core product benefit. Hopefully the music will continue to improve, too.

One of the most talked-about changes in the future of the digital world is convergence. Convergence has already begun providing consumers with a host of new products that may be classified as dynamically continuous innovations. **Convergence** means the coming together of two or more technologies to create new systems that provide greater benefit than the original technologies alone. For example, phone, organizer, and camera all come together in the Handspring Treo. The Treo is a wireless personal digital assistant (PDA) that synchs with your computer so that you can have your calendar, contacts, and to-do list wherever you go. The palm-sized PDA has a keyboard so you can send e-mail or text messages or surf the Web. The built-in phone lets you chat (by ear, earbud, or speakerphone), and the integrated camera lets you snap a photo and e-mail it to a friend instantly.[8]

convergence
The coming together of two or more technologies to create a new system with greater benefits than its parts.

DISCONTINUOUS INNOVATIONS   A **discontinuous innovation** creates major changes in the way we live. To use a discontinuous innovation, consumers must engage in a great amount of learning because no similar product has ever been on the market. Major inventions such as the airplane, the car, and the television have radically changed modern lifestyles. Another discontinuous innovation, the personal computer, changed the way we shop and allowed more people to work from home or anywhere else.

discontinuous innovation
A totally new product that creates major changes in the way we live.

Understanding the degree of newness of innovations helps marketers develop effective marketing strategies. For example, if marketers know that consumers may resist adopting a new and radically different product, they may offer a free product trial or place heavier emphasis on a personal selling strategy to convince consumers that the new product offers benefits worth the hassle. Business-to-business marketers often provide in-service training for employees of their customers who invest in new products.

Developing New Products

Building on our knowledge of different types of innovations, we'll now turn our attention to how firms go about developing new products. Product development doesn't simply mean creating totally new products never before on the market. Of course, a lot of companies do that, but for many other firms, product development is a continuous process of looking for ways to make an existing product better or finding just the right shade of purple for this year's new pants styles. No product category is immune to this process—even a "boring" product like a toilet is constantly being improved on by enterprising companies. Consider, for example, the Neorest toilet recently introduced in the United States by Toto, a Japanese firm. For a "mere" $5,000 you get a toilet (along with a 48-page instruction manual) with a lid that automatically opens as you approach and closes as you leave, a heated seat, a temperature-controlled water spray and blow dryer, a catalytic air deodorizer, and even a "white noise" control to mask sounds.[9]

For several reasons, new-product development is increasingly important to firms. First, technology is changing at an ever-increasing rate so that products are developed, get adopted, and then are replaced by better products faster and faster. In addition, competition in our global marketplace makes it essential for firms to continuously offer new choices for consumers if they are to compete

Lonnie Johnson walked into the slick conference room of the Larami Corporation; smiled mischievously; opened his pink, battered Samsonite suitcase; and took out a gizmo that looked a bit like a phaser gun from *Star Trek*. Holding this combination of a handheld pump apparatus, PVC tubing, Plexiglas, and plastic soda bottles, Lonnie aimed—and fired! A giant stream of water shot across the room. A year later, the Super Soaker became the most successful water gun in U.S. retail history.

idea generation
The first step of product development in which marketers brainstorm for products that provide customer benefits and are compatible with the company mission.

product concept development and screening
The second step of product development in which marketers test product ideas for technical and commercial success.

with companies all around the world rather than just down the street. Firms need to stay on top of current developments in popular culture, religion, politics, and so on to develop products that are consistent with consumers' mind-sets. Sometimes new hit products are based on careful research, but in many cases being at the right place at the right time doesn't hurt. For example, Hasbro developed a new version of its G.I. Joe toy as a search-and-rescue firefighter prior to the September 11, 2001 attacks, and renewed respect for firefighters lit the fire under sales the following Christmas.[10] Unfortunately, most new-product introductions need a bit more than good timing to score big in the marketplace.

Indeed, if anything, successful new-product introductions are becoming more and more difficult. First, the costs of research and development are often so huge that firms must limit the number of new products in development. Because products are outdated faster than ever, firms have less time to recover their research-and-development costs. And with so many products competing for limited shelf space, retailers often charge manufacturers exorbitant fees to stock a new product, increasing manufacturers' costs even more.[11] Firms must reduce the time it takes to get good products to market and increase the speed of adoption to quickly recover these costs. New-product development generally occurs in seven phases as shown in Figure 8.4.

Phase 1: Idea Generation

In the first phase of product development, **idea generation**, marketers use a variety of sources to come up with great new-product ideas that provide customer benefits and that are compatible with the company mission. Sometimes ideas come from customers. Ideas also come from salespeople, service providers, and others who have direct customer contact. And some companies encourage their designers to "think outside the box" by exposing them to new ideas, people, and places. Nike sends its creative teams on cultural field trips it calls "Deep Dives" so they can understand a range of consumer experiences, from studying American car culture to inner-city hip-hop music to origami (the Japanese art of paper folding).[12]

Often firms use marketing research activities such as focus groups in their search for new-product ideas. For example, a company such as Cable News Network (CNN) that is interested in developing new channels might hold focus group discussions to get ideas about types of programs not currently available.

Phase 2: Product Concept Development and Screening

The second phase in developing new products is **product concept development and screening**. Although ideas for products initially come from a variety of sources, it is up to marketers to expand these ideas into more complete product concepts. Product concepts describe what features the product should have and the benefits those features will provide for consumers.

When screening, marketers and researchers examine the chances that the product concept might achieve technical and commercial success, weeding out concepts that have little chance of success. Estimating *technical success* is assessing whether the new product is technologically feasible—is it possible to build this product? Estimating *commercial success* is deciding whether anyone is likely to buy the product. The marketing graveyard is piled high with products that sounded interesting but that failed to catch on, including jalapeño soda, aerosol mustard, and edible deodorant.[13]

The achievement of technical success but not commercial success confounded Burger King when the chain invested heavily to develop a new french fry.[14] This innovation was a potato stick coated with a layer of starch to make it crunchier and keep the heat in to stay fresh longer. Burger

Figure 8.4 Phases in New Product Development.

Phases in Development	Outcome
• Idea generation	Identify product ideas that will provide important customer benefits compatible with company mission.
• Product concept development and screening	Expand product ideas into more complete product concepts and estimate the potential commercial success of product concepts.
• Marketing strategy development	Develop preliminary plan for target markets, pricing, distribution and promotion.
• Business analysis	Estimate potential for profit. What is the potential demand, what expenditures will be required, and what is the cost of marketing the product?
• Technical development	Design the product and the manufacturing and production process.
• Test marketing	Develop evidence of potential success in the real market.
• Commercialization	Implement full-scale marketing plan.

King created 19 pages of specifications for its new item, including a requirement that there must be an audible crunch present for seven or more chews. The $70 million rollout of the new product included a "Free Fryday" when 15 million orders of fries were given to customers free, advertising on the Super Bowl, and official proclamations by the governors of three states.

Unfortunately, the new fry was a "whopper" of a product failure. Burger King blamed the product failure on inconsistent cooking by franchisees and a poor potato crop, but a more likely explanation is that consumers simply did not like the fry as well as those they might find at certain (golden) archrivals. Just because it's new doesn't always make it better.

Phase 3: Marketing Strategy Development

The third phase in new-product development is to develop a marketing strategy that can be used to introduce the product to the marketplace. This means that marketers must identify the target market, estimate its size, and determine how the product can be positioned to effectively address the target market's needs. And, of course, marketing strategy development includes planning for pricing, distribution, and promotion expenditures both for the introduction of the new product and for the long run.

Phase 4: Business Analysis

Once a product concept passes the screening stage, the next phase is to conduct a **business analysis**. Even though marketers have evidence that there is a market for the product, they still must find out if the product can be a profitable contribution to the organization's product mix. How much potential demand is there for the product? Does the firm have the resources that will be required for successful development and introduction of the product?

Larger firms typically develop new products in-house in their own laboratories, but in some cases even they prefer to scout out new ideas from entrepreneurs and just buy the technology. For example, Procter & Gamble's successful SpinBrush (that works on batteries and sells for about one-tenth of the cost of electric toothbrushes) was developed by four entrepreneurs and then acquired by Procter & Gamble.[15]

business analysis
The step in the product development process in which marketers assess a product's commercial viability.

Advice for Black & Decker

STUDENT
TRACY RICKMAN
University of Memphis

I would choose option 1—leave well enough alone and focus on new product development. Although strong growth in sales has diminished (as competitors have entered the market with similar products), the ScumBuster's sales have continued without a lot of promotion. Customers are satisfied with the current performance of the ScumBuster and choose it over competitors' products because of the power it offers and the perceived price/value. Although the current accessories are rarely used by the consumer, they are already developed and should remain a part of the bundling, as versatility adds to perceived value. The survey and focus group revealed an interest in upgrades and accessories to the product, but because price/value was cited as the main reason for purchasing the brand, there is no indication that the consumer would be willing to pay for them. As the product approaches the maturity/decline cusp, there is not enough market growth potential to justify revamping a product that is currently satisfying the market. The product should be managed carefully—controlling costs and monitoring profitability.

PROFESSOR
TED ATKINSON
Eastern Oregon University; CEO, Athic Enterprises Inc.

I would choose Option 3, ramp up the ScumBuster's features. The small tool market is very competitive and in order to lead the competition, Black and Decker (B&D) must push the performance and features of its ScumBuster to the next level. Resting on the reputation of the original ScumBuster would be a fatal mistake in the small tool market. Using the Boston Consulting Group Model (BCG), the original ScumBuster would be classified as a Cash Cow in the late maturity stage of its life cycle. Even though the customer survey indicates an adequate level of satisfaction, the respondents indicated a desire for upgraded features. The next generation of ScumBuster would initially fall into the Question Mark Category (BCG), but should quickly move to a Rising Star (BCG) status if marketed correctly. To expand their market share, B&D should "ramp" the features and introduce the "Super ScumBuster". During the introduction stage, the original ScumBuster would continue to be offered and support for replacement parts should be available. Current customers would have a choice of the original or the super model. The marketing focus for the "Super ScumBuster should be directed toward the Baby Boomer and Generation X market segment. This group has a greater disposable income and is willing to pay a premium for superior products with multiple features and power to spare. If B&D fails to move quickly on this opportunity, I predict they will lose market share to an aggressive competitor willing to move to the next level of performance.

The business analysis for a new product begins with assessing how the new product will fit into the firm's total product mix. Will the new product increase sales, or will it simply cannibalize sales of existing products? Are there possible synergies between the new product and the company's existing offerings that may improve visibility and the image of both? And what are the marketing costs likely to be?

Phase 5: Technical Development

technical development
The step in the product development process in which a new product is refined and perfected by company engineers and the like.

If it survives the scrutiny of a business analysis, a new-product concept then undergoes **technical development** in which a firm's engineers work with marketers in refining the design and production process. For example, when McDonald's recognized the need to bulk up its breakfast menu by adding something sweeter than its Egg McMuffin, the company's executive chef had to scramble to

New products often need to be rigorously tested before they are released. This ad from Hong Kong tells us that these jeans have been "tested on humans."

develop a pancake offering that could be eaten while driving. He first considered a pancake shaped like a muffin, but he decided this would be too confusing to customers—and besides, how could he add in the all-important syrup? Fortunately, one of the company's suppliers had just developed a technology that crystallizes syrup—just stir crystals into the batter, and the syrup will seep through the entire pancake once it's heated. McDonald's did a lot of laboratory work to adapt this process so the syrup would melt uniformly and produce what the industry calls the correct "mouth feel." Enter the McGriddle, a sausage and egg sandwich served between two pancakes instead of bread.[16]

Typically, a company's research-and-development department will develop one or more physical versions or **prototypes** of the product. These prototypes may be evaluated by prospective customers—the better a firm understands how customers will react to a new product, the better its chances of commercial success.

Those involved in the technical development process must determine which parts of a finished good the company will make and which ones will be bought from other suppliers. If goods are to be manufactured, the company may have to buy new production equipment or modify existing machinery. Someone has to develop work instructions for employees and train them to produce the product. In developing service processes, technical development includes such decisions as which activities will occur within sight of customers and whether parts of the service can be automated to make delivery more efficient.

Technical development sometimes requires application for a patent. Because patents legally prevent competitors from producing or selling the invention, a patent may reduce or eliminate competition

prototypes
Test versions of a proposed product.

DON'T THROW GOOD MONEY AT A BAD IDEA.

Before you launch your new product, see if anyone wants it.

Pretest your new concept—online—with the company that pioneered marketing research on the Internet. Our panel of more than one million consumers from all across the Internet, the largest of its kind, includes exactly the people you want to reach.

Join the Research Revolution!™ Contact the world's most experienced Internet marketing research company for studies online, on time, on target and on budget.

www.greenfield.com 888.291.9997

Greenfield *Online*
Leading the Research Revolution®

New online technologies let marketers test consumer reactions to product ideas faster and more cheaply than ever before.

in a market for many years, allowing a firm "breathing room" to recoup investments in technical development.

Phase 6: Test Marketing

The next phase of new-product development includes **test marketing**. This means the firm tries out the complete marketing plan—the distribution, advertising, and sales promotion—but in a small geographic area that is similar to the larger market it hopes to enter.

There are both pluses and minuses to test marketing. On the negative side, test marketing is extremely expensive. It can cost over a million dollars to conduct a test market even in a single city. A test market also gives the competition a free look at the new product, its introductory price, and the intended promotional strategy—and an opportunity to get to the market first with a competing product. On the positive side, by offering a new product in a limited area of the market, marketers can evaluate and improve the marketing program. Sometimes test marketing uncovers a need to improve the product itself. At other times, test marketing indicates product failure, allowing the firm to save millions of dollars by "pulling the plug."[17]

For years, Listerine manufacturer Warner-Lambert wanted to introduce a mint-flavored version of the product to compete with Procter & Gamble's Scope (the product was originally introduced under the brand Listermint). Unfortunately, every time Warner-Lambert tried to run a test market, P&G found out and poured substantial extra advertising and coupons for Scope into the cities in which the test market was conducted. This had the effect of thwarting the usefulness of the test market results on

test marketing
Testing the complete marketing plan in a small geographic area that is similar to the larger market the firm hopes to enter.

Warner-Lambert's market planning for the nationwide introduction of Listermint. In fact, because P&G's aggressive response to the test market actually increased Scope's market share in the test cities, there was no way to determine how well Listermint would actually do. As a result, Listermint was eventually introduced nationally and achieved only marginal success.

Because of the problems with test marketing, marketers sometimes conduct *simulated test marketing* that imitates the introduction of a product into the marketplace using special computer software as we saw in Chapter 4. These simulations allow the company to see the likely impact of price cuts and new packaging—or even to determine where in the store the product should be placed to maximize sales. The process entails gathering basic research data on consumer perceptions of the product concept, the physical product, the advertising, and other promotional activity. The test market simulation model uses that information to predict the product's success much less expensively (and more discreetly) than a traditional test market. As this simulated test market technology improves, traditional test markets may become a thing of the past.

Phase 7: Commercialization

commercialization
The final step in the product development process in which a new product is launched into the market.

The last phase in new-product development is **commercialization**. This means the launching of a new product, and it requires full-scale production, distribution, advertising, sales promotion—the works. For this reason, commercialization of a new product cannot happen overnight. A launch requires planning and careful preparation. Marketers must implement trade promotion plans that offer special incentives to encourage dealers, retailers, or other members of the channel to stock the

Highlights

- Available in FreshBurst®. Also available in Cool Mint and Cinnamon flavors.
- Dissolves instantly, releasing the powerful germ killing ingredients found in Listerine® Antiseptic.
- Discreet, works quickly, and you can use it anytime/anywhere.
- Sugar free, no calories.
- Kills 99.9% of odor-causing bacteria in 30 seconds!
- Gives you a Clean Mouth Feeling®.
- Sugar-free, alcohol-free, with no calories.
- Available sizes for Listerine PocketPaks® oral care strips: 24 (single pack), 48 (two pack), 72 (3 pack), 120 (5 pack) and Club Warehouse 144 strips (6 pack) and 240 strips (10 pack).

The Listerine Pocket Pak is a recent new product that gives consumers a new, portable way to freshen their breath.

new product so that customers will find it on store shelves the very first time they look. They must also develop consumer promotions such as coupons. Marketers may arrange to have point-of-purchase displays designed, built, and delivered to retail outlets. If the new product is especially complex, customer service employees must receive extensive training and preparation.

As launch time nears, preparations gain a sense of urgency—like countdown to blastoff at NASA. Sales managers explain special incentive programs to salespeople. Soon the media announce to prospective customers why they should buy and where they can find the new product. All elements of the marketing program—ideally—come into play like a carefully planned liftoff of the space shuttle.

And there is always a huge element of risk in a new product launch—even for products that seem like a sure thing. For example, the makers of FluMist, a flu vaccine that is given through a spray in the nose rather than an often painful shot in the arm, predicted they would sell 4 million to 6 million doses when the product came on the market in 2003—a not unreasonable forecast since 60 million to 90 million Americans get a flu shot each year. Despite spending $25 million on advertising to tout the new product, only about 100,000 doses were sold—probably because the product was priced far higher than a flu shot, and the Food and Drug Administration approved the product only for healthy people aged 5 to 49. Unfortunately, the majority of people who get flu shots are over 50 or have other health problems like asthma or diabetes that make them more likely to die from the flu.[18]

Adoption and Diffusion Processes

In the previous section, we talked about the steps marketers take to develop new products from generating ideas to launch. Moving on, we'll look at what happens after that new product hits the market—how an innovation spreads throughout a population.

A painting is not a work of art until someone views it. A song is not music until someone sings it. In the same way, new products do not satisfy customer wants and needs until the customer uses them. **Product adoption** is the process by which a consumer or business customer begins to buy and use a new good, service, or idea.

product adoption
The process by which a consumer or business customer begins to buy and use a new good, service, or idea.

diffusion

The process by which the use of a product spreads throughout a population.

The term **diffusion** describes how the use of a product spreads throughout a population. One way to understand how this process works is to think about a new product like a computer virus that spreads from a few computers to infect many or a cold or some other disease that gets spread to large numbers of people like an epidemic (though hopefully with more positive consequences). A brand like Hush Puppies, for example, might just slog around—sometimes for years and years. It's initially bought by a small number of people, but change happens in a hurry when the process reaches the moment of critical mass. This moment of truth is sometimes called the *tipping point*. For example, Sharp introduced the first low-price fax in 1984 and sold about 80,000 in that year. There was a slow climb in the number of users for the next three years. Then, suddenly, in 1987 enough people had faxes that it made sense for everyone to have one—Sharp sold a million units that year.[19]

After months or even years spent developing a new product, the real challenge to firms is getting consumers to buy and use the product and to do so quickly to recover the costs of product development and launch. To accomplish this, marketers must understand the product adoption process. In the next section, we'll discuss the stages in this process. We'll also see how consumers and businesses differ in their eagerness to adopt new products and how the characteristics of a product affect its adoption (or "infection") rate.

Stages in a Customer's Adoption of a New Product

Whether the innovation is better film technology or a better mousetrap, individuals and organizations pass through six stages in the adoption process. Figure 8.5 shows how a person goes from being unaware of an innovation through the stages of awareness, interest, evaluation, trial, adoption, and confirmation. At every stage, people drop out of the process, so the proportion of consumers who wind up using the innovation on a consistent basis is a fraction of those who are exposed to it.

AWARENESS Learning that the innovation exists is the first step in the adoption process. To make consumers *aware* of a new product, marketers may conduct a massive advertising campaign, called a media blitz. For example, Microsoft launched a massive $500 million marketing campaign when it introduced the Xbox, promoting the new product through in-store merchandising, retailer

Figure 8.5 Adoption Pyramid

Consumers pass through six stages in the adoption of a new product—from being unaware of an innovation to becoming loyal adopters. The right marketing strategies at each stage help ensure a successful adoption.

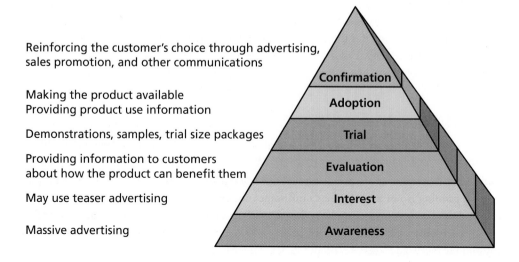

Reinforcing the customer's choice through advertising, sales promotion, and other communications — **Confirmation**

Making the product available
Providing product use information — **Adoption**

Demonstrations, samples, trial size packages — **Trial**

Providing information to customers about how the product can benefit them — **Evaluation**

May use teaser advertising — **Interest**

Massive advertising — **Awareness**

Marketers often build interest for a product or service by showing how it will benefit customers. This Hong Kong ad for a spa and salon boasts "dramatic transformations daily."

incentives, events, and sponsorships in addition to traditional advertising.[20] At this point, some consumers will say, "So there's a new gaming console out there. So what?" and they will fall by the wayside, out of the adoption process. But this strategy works for new products when consumers see a new product as something they want and need and just can't live without.

INTEREST   For some of the people who become aware of a new product, a second stage in the adoption process is *interest*. By interest, we mean that a prospective adopter begins to see how a new product might satisfy an existing or newly realized need. Interest also means that consumers look for and are open to information about the innovation. For example, a few intrepid organic food companies are trying to entice high school kids to give up their beloved chips, soda, and candy by placing vending machines in schools that dispense items like soy milk, yogurt, and carrots with spinach dip.[21] Marketers often design teaser advertisements that give prospective customers just enough information about the new product to make them curious and to stimulate their interest. Despite marketers' best efforts, though, some consumers drop out of the process at this point.

EVALUATION   In the *evaluation* stage, a prospect weighs the costs and benefits of the new product. On the one hand, for complex, risky, or expensive products, people think about the innovation a great deal before trying it. For example, a firm will carefully evaluate spending hundreds of thousands of dollars on manufacturing robotics prior to purchase. Marketers for such products help prospective customers see how such products can benefit them.

Your body is a temple. Even if you do let cupcakes in once in a while.

Silk soymilk stimulated the adoption process by distributing free samples of its product to American consumers who were not familiar with milk that doesn't come from cows.

impulse purchase
A purchase made without any planning or search effort.

But little evaluation may occur with an impulse purchase. An **impulse purchase** is a purchase made without any planning or search effort. As an example, consumers may do very little thinking before buying a virtual pet such as the Tamagotchi (Japanese for "cute little egg"). For these products, marketers design the product to be eye-catching and appealing to get consumers to notice the product quickly. Tamagotchis certainly grabbed attention of consumers—40 million of them bought the virtual pets. Toymaker Bandai Co. came out with a second generation of Tamagotchis in 2004, this time offering pets that can communicate with other Tamagotchis via infrared ports. Now the pets can make friends, "marry" other Tamagotchis, and even give birth.[22]

Some potential adopters will evaluate an innovation positively enough to move on to the next stage. Those who do not think the new product will provide adequate benefits drop out.

TRIAL The next stage in the adoption process, *trial*, means the potential adopters will actually experience or use the product for the first time. Often marketers stimulate trial by providing opportunities for consumers to sample the product. White Wave Inc., the maker of Silk soymilk, gave away free samples of its product to get consumers to try the first refrigerated soymilk sold in America. Since Silk's introduction, 11 percent of American households have purchased Silk soymilk.[23] Similarly, lawn care company John Deere offers a test drive program for its 100 series tractors. Consumers can go to Home Depot or John Deere dealerships and try driving through an obstacle course with simulated lawn hazards.[24]

Based on the trial experience, some potential buyers move on to adoption of the new product. Sometimes prospective customers will not adopt a new product because it costs too much. This was the case with onboard navigation systems in cars. Consumers could try out the system in rental cars from Hertz and Avis, but the initial price of $2,000 put off prospective customers. By 2004, with prices in the $799 range, more consumers were buying the units for their own cars.[25]

ADOPTION In the *adoption* stage, a prospect chooses a product. If the product is a consumer or business-to-business good, this means buying the product and learning how to use and maintain it. If the product is an idea, this means that the individual agrees with the new idea.

Does this mean that all individuals or organizations that first choose an innovation are permanent customers? That's a mistake many firms make. Some potential customers, even after initial adoption, do not go on to the final stage of confirmation. Marketers need to provide follow-up contacts and communications with adopters to ensure they are satisfied and remain loyal to the new product over time.

CONFIRMATION After adopting an innovation, a customer weighs expected versus actual benefits and costs. Favorable experiences contribute to new customers becoming loyal adopters, as their initially positive opinions result in *confirmation*. Of course, nothing lasts forever—even loyal customers may decide that a new product is not meeting expectations and reject it. Some marketers feel that *reselling* the customer in the confirmation stage is important. They provide advertisements, sales presentations, and other communications to reinforce a customer's choice.

Figure 8.6 Categories of Adopters

Because consumers differ in how willing they are to buy and try a new product, it often takes months or years for an innovation to be adopted by most of the population.

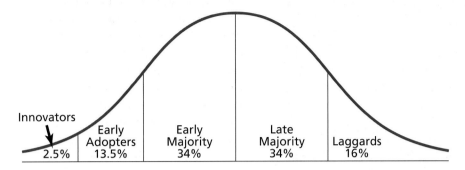

The Diffusion of Innovations

Diffusion describes how the use of a product spreads throughout a population. Of course, marketers would prefer that their entire target market would immediately adopt a new product, but this is not the case. Consumers and business customers differ in how eager or willing they are to try something new, lengthening the diffusion process by months or even years. Based on adopters' roles in the diffusion process, experts have classified them into five categories.

ADOPTER CATEGORIES   Some people like to try new products. Others are so reluctant you'd think they're afraid of anything new. As Figure 8.6 shows, there are five categories of adopters: innovators, early adopters, early majority, late majority, and laggards.[26] To understand how the adopter categories differ, we'll study the adoption of one specific technology, Wi-Fi (wireless fidelity).

Innovators are roughly the first 2.5 percent of adopters. This segment is extremely adventurous and willing to take risks with new products. Innovators are typically well educated, younger, better off financially than others in the population, and worldly. Innovators who were into new technology knew all about Wi-Fi before other people were aware of the concept. Because innovators pride themselves on trying new products, they purchased laptops with Wi-Fi cards way back in 1999, when the first computer company, Apple Computer, introduced them in its laptops.

Early adopters, approximately 13.5 percent of adopters, buy product innovations early in the diffusion process but not as early as innovators. Unlike innovators, early adopters have greater concern for social acceptance. Typically, they are heavy media users and often are heavy users of a new-product category. Others in the population often look to early adopters for their opinions on various topics, making early adopters key to a new product's success. For this reason, marketers often target them in developing advertising and other communications efforts. Columnists who write about personal technology for popular magazines like *Time* were testing Wi-Fi in mid-2000. They experienced some early adopter problems (like PCs crashing when setting up a wireless network at home) but touted the benefits of wireless connectivity. Road warriors adopted the technology as Wi-Fi access spread into airports and hotels. Intel, maker of the Centrino mobile platform, launched a major campaign with Condé Nast's *Traveler* magazine, offering a location guide to T-Mobile hotspots nationwide.

The **early majority**, roughly 34 percent of adopters, avoid being either first or last to try an innovation. They are typically middle-class consumers and are deliberate and cautious. Early majority consumers have slightly above-average education and income levels. When the early majority adopts a product, it is no longer considered new or different—it is, in essence, already established. By 2002, Wi-Fi access was available in over 500 Starbucks cafés, and monthly subscription prices were dropping rapidly (from $30 to $9.95 per month).

Late majority adopters, about 34 percent of the population, are older, more conservative, and typically have lower-than-average levels of education and income. The late majority adopters avoid trying a new product until it is no longer risky. By that time, the product has become an economic

innovators
The first segment (roughly 2.5 percent) of a population to adopt a new product.

early adopters
Those who adopt an innovation early in the diffusion process but after the innovators.

early majority
Those whose adoption of a new product signals a general acceptance of the innovation.

late majority
The adopters who are willing to try new products when there is little or no risk associated with the purchase, when the purchase becomes an economic necessity, or when there is social pressure to purchase.

Table 8.3 Adoption Rate Factors

A variety of product factors cause adoption of the innovation by consumers to be faster or slower. Understanding these factors means marketers can develop strategies to encourage people to try a new product.

Product Factors Affecting Rate of Adoption	Product Rated High on Factor	Product Rated Low on Factor	Rating of Wi-Fi on the Factors
Relative advantage	Faster	Slower	Low until lifestyles changed
Compatibility	Faster	Slower	Low—required new PC card and base station
Complexity	Slower	Faster	Early setups were complex
Trialability	Faster	Slower	Low until infrastructure was established
Observability	Faster	Slower	Moderately low: wireless is invisible

necessity or there is pressure from peer groups to adopt. By 2004, Wi-Fi capability was bundled into almost all laptops. Wi-Fi capability was available in mainstream venues like McDonald's restaurants and sports stadiums. Towns like Santa Clara, California, were considering blanket Wi-Fi coverage throughout the entire town through WiMax technology.[27]

laggards
The last consumers to adopt an innovation.

Laggards, about 16 percent of adopters, are the last in a population to adopt a new product. Laggards are typically lower in social class than other adopter categories and are bound by tradition. By the time laggards adopt a product, it may already be superseded by other innovations.

By understanding these adopter categories, marketers are able to better develop strategies that will speed the diffusion or widespread use of their products. For example, early in the diffusion process, marketers may put greater emphasis on advertising in special-interest magazines to attract innovators and early adopters. Later they may lower the product's price or come out with lower-priced models with fewer "bells and whistles" to attract the late majority. We will talk more about strategies for new and existing products in the next chapter.

PRODUCT FACTORS AFFECTING THE RATE OF ADOPTION Not all products are successful. Crystal Pepsi, Premier smokeless cigarettes, the Betamax video player, the Ford Edsel automobile, and Snif-T-Panties (women's underwear that smelled like bananas, popcorn, whiskey, or pizza) all litter the marketing graveyard.[28] The reason for such product failures is very simple—consumers did not perceive that they satisfied a need better than competitive products on the market.

If you could predict which new products will succeed and which will fail, you'd quickly be in high demand as a consultant by companies worldwide. That's because companies make large investments in new products, but failures are all too frequent. Experts suggest that between one-third and one-half of all new products fail. As you might expect, there is much research devoted to making us smarter about new-product successes and failures.

Researchers have identified five characteristics of innovations that affect the rate of adoption: relative advantage, compatibility, complexity, trialability, and observability.[29] Whether a new product has each of these characteristics affects the speed of diffusion. It may take years for a new product to become widely adopted. Examining these five factors shown in Table 8.3 helps explain both why the new product was not adopted during its early years and why adoption sped up later.

Relative advantage is the degree to which a consumer perceives that a new product provides superior benefits. In the case of the microwave oven, consumers in the 1960s did not feel that the product provided important benefits that would improve their lives. But by the late 1970s, that perception had changed because more women had entered the workforce. The 1960s woman had all day to prepare the evening meal, so she didn't have a need for the microwave. But in the 1970s, when many women left home for work at 8:00 A.M. and returned home at 6:00 P.M., an appliance that would "magically" defrost a frozen chicken and cook it in 30 minutes provided a genuine advantage.

Compatibility is the extent to which a new product is consistent with existing cultural values, customs, and practices. Did consumers see the microwave oven as being compatible with existing ways of doing things? Hardly. Cooking on paper plates? If you put a paper plate in a conventional oven, you'll likely get a visit from the fire department. By anticipating compatibility issues early in the new-product development stage, marketing strategies can address such problems in planning communications programs, or there may be opportunities for altering product designs to overcome some consumer objections.

Complexity is the degree to which consumers find a new product or its use difficult to understand. Many microwave users today haven't a clue about how a microwave oven cooks food. But when the product was introduced, consumers asked and marketers answered—microwaves cause molecules to move and rub together, creating friction, which produces heat. Voilà! Cooked pot roast. But that explanation was complex and confusing for the homemaker of the Ozzie and Harriet days.

Trialability is the ease of sampling a new product and its benefits. Marketers took a very important step in the 1970s to speed up adoption of the microwave oven—product trial. Just about every store that sold microwaves invited shoppers to visit the store and sample an entire meal cooked in the microwave.

Observability is how visible a new product and its benefits are to others who might adopt it. The ideal innovation is easy to see. For example, scooters such as the Razor became the hippest way to get around as soon as one preteen saw his friends flying by. The microwave was moderately observable. Only close friends and acquaintances who visited someone's home could see whether she owned a microwave.

SKIN THE WORLD'S THINNEST WATCH swatch**planet**.com

SwatchPlanet.com hopes that consumers will believe that wearing Swatch's new ultrathin watch provides a relative advantage over their existing timepieces.

Organizational Differences Affect Adoption

Just as there are differences among consumers in their eagerness to adopt new products, businesses and other organizations are not alike in their willingness to buy and use new industrial products.[30] New or smaller companies may be more nimble and able to jump onto emerging trends. Those that do often are rewarded with higher sales (though, of course, the risks are higher, too). For example, Samsung recognized early on that color screens on cell phones were going to be in demand by consumers, while some other companies were slower to pick up on this trend (that originated in Asia). Now, all the big cell phone manufacturers are trying to update their models more rapidly to keep up with new competitors including Chinese companies like Ningo Bird that replace some of their phones every six months.[31]

Firms that welcome product innovations are likely to be younger companies in highly technical industries with younger managers and entrepreneurial corporate cultures. Early adopter firms

Firms are more likely to accept a new product if they perceive the improvement to be large in relation to the investment they will have to make. Due to its versatility and cost efficiencies, the U.S. Army adopted the John Deere Gator™ Utility Vehicle to replace some of its more expensive Humvees.   (Photo courtesy of Deere & Company, Moline, IL)

are likely to be market-share leaders that adopt new innovations and try new ways of doing things to maintain their leadership. Firms that adopt new products only when they recognize they must innovate to keep up are in the early majority. Late majority firms tend to be oriented toward the status quo and often have large financial investments in existing production technology. Laggard firms are probably already losing money.

Business-to-business products, like consumer products, also may possess characteristics that will increase their likelihood of adoption. Organizations are likely to adopt an innovation that helps them increase gross margins and profits. It is unlikely that firms would have adopted new products like voice mail unless they provided a way to increase profits by reducing labor costs. Organizational innovations are attractive when they are consistent with a firm's ways of doing business.

Cost is also a factor in the new products firms will adopt. Firms are more likely to accept a new product if they perceive the improvement to be large in relation to the investment they will have to make. This was the case when the U.S. Army adopted the John Deere Gator. At under $10,000, or about an eighth of the price of a Humvee, the Gator is an inexpensive off-road utility vehicle that's just right for rescuing wounded soldiers from foxholes. Although the Gator won't replace the Humvee altogether, the military is able to buy fewer of the expensive Humvees and save big taxpayer bucks.[32]

real people, real choices
How it Worked Out at Black & Decker

Black & Decker chose option 3. Black & Decker's product development team designed a new ScumBuster that sports an onboard cleaner for ready-to-go scrubbing that will help consumers to get the job done faster. The company responded to survey respondents' desires for variable speed control by including the option of selecting either high or low speeds, depending on the application.

And it developed a new set of attachments, including one that enables the cleaning pads to contour with the curves of a tub or sink. The new-and-improved ScumBuster launched during the 2004 Christmas season, and Eleni and her colleagues at Black & Decker are hoping it will "clean up" in the next few years.

If you are the product, how can you identify your benefits so employers will hire you? To learn how to communicate your value to employers—your customers—go to Chapter 8 in the *Brand You* supplement.

CHAPTER SUMMARY

1. **Explain the layers of a product.**   A product may be anything tangible or intangible that satisfies consumer or business-to-business customer needs. Products include goods, services, ideas, people, and places. The core product is the basic product category benefits and customized benefit(s) the product provides. The actual product is the physical good or delivered service including the packaging and brand name. The augmented product includes both the actual product and any supplementary services, such as warranty, credit, delivery, installation, and so on.

2. **Describe the classifications of products.**   Marketers generally classify goods and services as either consumer or business-to-business products. They further classify consumer products according to how long they last and by how they are purchased. Durable goods provide benefits for months or years, whereas nondurable goods are used up quickly or are useful for only a short time. Consumers purchase convenience products frequently with little effort.

Customers carefully gather information and compare different brands on their attributes and prices before buying shopping products. Specialty products have unique characteristics that are important to the buyer. Customers have little interest in unsought products until a need arises. Business products are for commercial uses by organizations. Marketers classify business products according to how they are used, for example, equipment; maintenance, repair, and operating (MRO) products; raw and processed materials; component parts; and business services.

3. **Explain the importance of new products.** Innovations are anything consumers perceive to be new. Understanding new products is important to companies because of the fast pace of technological advancement, the high cost to companies for developing new products, and the contributions to society that new products can make. Marketers classify innovations by their degree of newness. A continuous innovation is a modification of an existing product, a dynamically continuous innovation provides a greater change in a product, and a discontinuous innovation is a new product that creates major changes in people's lives.

4. **Describe how firms develop new products.** In new-product development, marketers first generate product ideas from which product concepts are first developed and then screened. Next they develop a marketing strategy and conduct a business analysis to estimate the profitability of the new product. Technical development includes planning how the product will be manufactured and may mean obtaining a patent. Next, the effectiveness of the new product may be assessed in an actual or a simulated test market. Finally, the product is launched, and the entire marketing plan is implemented.

5. **Explain the process of product adoption and the diffusion of innovations.** Product adoption is the process by which an individual begins to buy and use a new product, whereas the diffusion of innovations is how a new product spreads throughout a population. The stages in the adoption process are awareness, interest, trial, adoption, and confirmation. To better understand the diffusion process, marketers classify consumers according to their readiness to adopt new products as innovators, early adopters, early majority, late majority, and laggards.

Five product characteristics that have an important effect on how quickly (or if) a new product will be adopted by consumers are relative advantage, compatibility, product complexity, trialability, and observability. Similar to individual consumers, organizations differ in their readiness to adopt new products based on characteristics of the organization, its management, and characteristics of the innovation.

KEY TERMS

CHAPTER REVIEW

MARKETING CONCEPTS: TESTING YOUR KNOWLEDGE

1. What is the difference between the core product, the actual product, and the augmented product?

2. What is the difference between a durable good and a non-durable good? Provide examples of each.

3. What are the main differences among convenience, shopping, and specialty products?

4. What is an unsought product? How do marketers make such products attractive to consumers?

5. What types of products are bought and sold in business-to-business markets?

6. What is a new product? Why is understanding new products so important to marketers?

7. What are the types of innovations?

8. List and explain the steps in developing new products.

9. What is a test market? What are some pros and cons of doing test markets?

10. List and explain the categories of adopters.

MARKETING CONCEPTS: DISCUSSING CHOICES AND ISSUES

1. Technology is moving at an ever-increasing speed, and this means that new products enter and leave the market faster than ever. What are some products you think technology might be able to develop in the future that you would like? Do you think these products could add to a company's profits?

2. In this chapter, we talked about the core product, the actual product, and the augmented product. Does this mean that marketers are simply trying to make products that are really the same seem different? When marketers understand these three layers of the product and develop products with this concept in mind, what are the benefits to consumers? What are the hazards of this type of thinking?

3. Discontinuous innovations are totally new products—something seldom seen in the marketplace. What are some examples of discontinuous innovations introduced in the past 50 years? Why are there so few discontinuous innovations? What do you think the future holds for new products?

4. In this chapter, we explained that knockoffs are slightly modified copies of original product designs. Should knockoffs be illegal? Who is hurt by knockoffs? Is the marketing of knockoffs good or bad for consumers in the short run? In the long run?

5. It is not necessarily true that all new products benefit consumers or society. What are some new products that have made our lives better? What are some new products that have actually been harmful to consumers or to society?

Should there be a way to monitor new products that are introduced to the marketplace?

MARKETING PRACTICE: APPLYING WHAT YOU'VE LEARNED

1. Assume that you are the director of marketing for a major producer of mobile (cellular) phones. Your company has just developed a new mobile phone that is also a digital camera and an Internet communication device. Consumers can use the phone to take digital photos and e-mail them to their friends. As opposed to phones that do nothing but make telephone calls, this product could be classified as a dynamically continuous innovation. What recommendations do you have for marketing the new phone that would address the problems of convincing consumers to adopt such an innovation?

2. Assume that you are employed in the marketing department of the firm that is producing the world's first practical, battery-powered automobile. In developing this product, you realize that it is important to provide a core product, an actual product, and an augmented product that meets the needs of customers. Develop an outline of how your firm might provide these three product layers in the battery-powered car.

3. Firms go to great lengths to develop new-product ideas. Sometimes new ideas come from brainstorming in which groups of individuals get together and try to think of as many different, novel, creative—and hopefully profitable—ideas for a new product as possible. With a group of other students, participate in brainstorming for new-product ideas for one of the following (or some other product of your choice):
   a. An exercise machine
   b. A cell phone
   c. A new type of university

   Then, with your class, screen one or more of the ideas for possible further product development.

4. As a member of a new-product team with your company, you are working to develop an electric car jack that would make changing tires for a car easier. You are considering conducting a test market for this new product. Outline the pros and cons for test-marketing this product. What are your recommendations?

MARKETING MINIPROJECT: LEARNING BY DOING

What product characteristics do consumers think are important in a new product? What types of service components do they demand? Most important, how do marketers know how to develop successful new products? This miniproject is designed to let you make some of these decisions.

1. Create (in your mind) a new-product item that might be of interest to college students such as yourself. Develop a written description and possibly a drawing of this new product.

2. Show this new-product description to a number of your fellow students who might be users of the product. Ask them to tell you what they think of the product. Some of the questions you might ask them are the following:

   a. What is your overall opinion of the new product?

   b. What basic benefits would you expect to receive from the product?

   c. What about the physical characteristics of the product? What do you like? Dislike? What would you add? Delete? Change?

   d. What do you like (or would you like) in the way of product packaging?

   e. What sort of services would you expect to receive with the product?

   f. Do you think you would try the product? How could marketers influence you to buy the product?

3. Develop a report based on what you found. Include your recommendations for changes in the product and your feelings about the potential success of the new product.

REAL PEOPLE, REAL SURFERS: EXPLORING THE WEB

Go to the Black & Decker Web site (**www.blackanddecker.com**). Check out the information on the ScumBuster as well as a few other Black & Decker products that interest you. Then spend a few minutes perusing the "How To" center.

1. Pick any Black & Decker product and describe the core product, the actual product, and the augmented product.

2. In your opinion, is Black & Decker engaged in product innovation? What clues from the Web site lead you to this conclusion?

3. What do you think of Black & Decker's "How To" center? Did you find the information there relevant and useful? Was it easy to navigate?

4. Why would a company such as Black & Decker include a "How To" center on its Web site instead of just focusing on the products themselves?

MARKETING PLAN EXERCISE

Go to the Procter & Gamble Web site (**www.pg.com**) and click on "Products" at the top of the page. Next, find and click on "Oral Care" and then click on "Crest." Look over the information about Crest products, then answer these questions that Procter & Gamble must answer when doing marketing planning for the Crest product line:

1. Crest has several product innovations listed, including SpinBrush, Whitestrips, and Night Effects. How would you "classify" each of these products based on the discussion in the chapter? What leads you to classify each as you do?

2. What type of innovation do you consider each of these three products? Why?

3. Pick any one of the three products and consider the process Procter & Gamble likely went through when initially developing it. Give an example of how each of the steps in Figure 8.4, "Phases in New Product Development," might have been utilized for that product.

4. For the same product you selected in item 3, what stage in the adoption process do you believe that product currently occupies with most consumers? What leads you to this conclusion? Why is knowledge of the adoption process important in marketing planning?

Marketing in Action Case

Real Choices at VOSS Water

Creating a new product is challenging in any industry but even more so when that product is one consumers take for granted and can get for little or no cost. The people working at VOSS Water, a producer of bottled water located in Norway, faced just this situation. VOSS executives had an even bigger problem because they were trying to figure out how to convince people to pay up to $12 a bottle for the water when they dined in finer restaurants in the United States. The key question for the company was, What *is* the product? Is it just water—or something else? VOSS bet it was something else.

In the product development process, VOSS executives realized that ordinary water is a consumer, nondurable product that most consumers consider a commodity. Therefore, a high-quality, prestigious image had to be built around VOSS to entice customers to pay a premium price. Developing such an image meant that the producers of VOSS water had to carefully plan not only its core product offering but especially its actual and augmented product offerings.

For the actual product offering, the features that VOSS water provides are a result of the *source* of the water: a "virgin aquifer" that is protected from the air by both rock and layers of ice in the "untouched wilderness" of central Norway (are you thirsty yet?). In addition, the water is said to be naturally pure, low in sodium, and free of other minerals. As a result, VOSS says no other water on the planet can match its quality level and clean taste. Another part of the actual product that sets VOSS water apart is its packaging. VOSS designed the bottle's shape to enhance the desired image of prestige, high quality, and purity. A visit to the company's Web site (**www.vosswater.com**) is enough to convince anyone that the bottle is "stimulating" in terms of its sexiness and visual appeal.

From an augmented product standpoint, VOSS will have to provide a high level of service to the companies that distribute the product. These include such services as (1) training on how to handle and sell the product, (2) market studies on the type of customers to target with the product, and (3) providing credit to distributors so they can purchase an adequate amount of the product.

In addition to developing a superior product, VOSS has begun to reach important adopters who can influence the tastes of the mainstream market. The company is developing a celebrity following, and it hopes these high-profile early adopters will persuade a lot of other consumers to try the water.

However, although VOSS has spent much time developing the product, the company still faces obstacles in terms of getting consumers to adopt the product. For one, what is the relative advantage offered by VOSS water? Water is water, isn't it? Can one brand of water be so much better than others that it would command such a premium price?

Also, how can VOSS encourage more people to try the product? There are many factors that influence a person to adopt a new product, and VOSS seems sorely lacking in all of them. The level of awareness for VOSS among the vast majority of consumers is extremely low or nonexistent, and without awareness it is very difficult for people to become interested in the product and seek it out to conduct an evaluation. Despite the fact that some celebrities drink VOSS, they will have to become more visible in their consumption of the product before usage will really begin to accelerate.

Finally, just how does someone try out a product like water? Very few, if any, companies provide taste tests for the water they sell. Consequently, the challenges for VOSS to increase consumption of its water in the United States are great and not easy to overcome. However, if VOSS succeeds in its quest, the company will be rewarded with a flood of success.

Things to Think About

1. What are the decisions facing VOSS?
2. What factors are important in understanding the decision situation?
3. What are the alternatives?
4. What decision(s) do you recommend?
5. What are some ways to implement your recommendation(s)?

Sources: Bill Hensel Jr., "A Crystalline Niche in Importing," *Houston Chronicle*, April 7, 2004, Business section, 1; Wesley Morris and Amy Graves, "Food Hits Make Up for Ruby Room Misses," *Boston Globe*, June 6, 2004, Living, C2; and VOSS Water, *General,***www.vosswater.com/general/html** (accessed June 3, 2004).

CHOOSE YOUR SICK DAYS WISELY.

NISSAN XTERRA
1-877-XTERRA7   xterra1.com

www.nissan.com

real people, real choices

meet Mario A. Polit, a Decision Maker at Nissan North America, Inc.

what I do when I'm not working

Enjoy the company of friends and family, tennis, alpine skiing, and building and flying radio-controlled sailplanes.

career high

Leading a team in crafting the marketing strategy for the Xterra.

MANAGING THE PRODUCT

Mario Polit is senior manager of marketing for Sedans, Infiniti Division, at Nissan North America, Inc. He received a B.S. in business management from the University of Tampa and a Master's in international management from the American Graduate School of International Management.

Decision Time at Nissan North America, Inc.

In 1998, Nissan North America began preparations for the launch of the Nissan Xterra, its new sport-utility vehicle (SUV). The product concept and positioning were all set, but there was considerable debate on the best way to communicate the image of this vehicle to potential buyers. But first, a little background.

The Xterra would be an entirely new product in the Nissan lineup, and it would be the second SUV model, following the more upscale Nissan Pathfinder. To the company, the Xterra represented an opportunity to connect with a new group of consumers who were not passionate about any Nissan products.

Critical to the debate was Xterra's position in the SUV market, which industry feedback indicated was beginning to split off into two groups: (1) minicar/minivan–based SUVs (industry insiders called these vehicles "posers" or "pretenders") and (2) full-size and luxury SUVs. Mario and his colleagues on Nissan North America's product planning team saw an emerging opportunity for a truck-based SUV with a "back to basics" approach. Xterra's product concept focused on an "authentic and affordable" SUV, a functional, tough, and rugged piece of "gear" based on Nissan's Frontier pickup truck. By leveraging the Frontier's platform, the model would offer authenticity, affordability, and hardiness rather than luxury amenities. Product features would include a roof rack with gear basket, a first-aid kit, water-resistant seat covers, and an interior bike rack—all for the outdoor enthusiast.

Challenged with managing the marketing strategy for both the Pathfinder and the Xterra, Mario set out to differentiate the two vehicles' positioning in all marketing communications. The Pathfinder had been positioned as "premium equipment." The Xterra was positioned as "tough (and affordable) gear that helps you attack life."

heroes

My father and mother.

motto

The definition of luck: when preparation meets opportunity.

management style

Instead of allowing employees the "freedom to fail," I believe in encouraging the "freedom to succeed." Challenging people to maximize their effectiveness is my ultimate goal.

don't do this when interviewing with me

Don't wait for me to extract everything that may be relevant. Tell me why you're a good fit for the job and how you can take it to a new level.

objectives

1 Explain the different product objectives and strategies a firm may choose.

2 Explain how firms manage products throughout the product life cycle.

3 Discuss how branding creates product identity and describe different types of branding strategies.

4 Explain the roles packaging and labeling play in developing effective product strategies.

5 Describe how organizations are structured for new and existing product management.

Mario aimed the launch at two types of drivers: (1) true outdoor enthusiasts and (2) those who want to be outdoor enthusiasts. Targeting these two groups called for a unique creative and media approach. The marketing team needed to decide the best way to introduce the Xterra to the market in order to connect with both true outdoor types and "weekend warriors." Mario pondered several options:

OPTION 1: Pursue a targeted, integrated media and creative strategy.

Such a strategy would almost ensure that Nissan would reach the targeted consumer with the right message, it would be more cost effective, and it would clearly differentiate Xterra from Pathfinder. However, a campaign of this kind would be risky. Targeted "edgy" imagery could alienate some SUV consumers. Nissan would be placing all its "eggs in one basket," which would not be the case in a diversified, broad-based strategy. A strategy this targeted was relatively untested and unproven for Nissan.

OPTION 2: Pursue a wide-reaching media and creative strategy to launch Xterra.

Nissan had taken this tack before with very good results. However, Nissan could risk alienating the target consumer. If positioned as a mass-market SUV, Xterra faced the risk of compromising its authenticity and credibility with hard-core enthusiasts and might result in a cannibalizing of Pathfinder sales. Also, such an approach would certainly be more costly than a targeted campaign.

OPTION 3: Use the strategy laid out in option 1 but also offer consumers popular options and/or accessory equipment, such as a leather interior.

This strategy would likely broaden the appeal of Xterra to the large segment of consumers with SUVs that were so equipped. However, this might damage the Xterra's rugged image that was so critical to the target consumer audience. It would also narrow the product and price differentiation with Pathfinder.

Now, join the decision team at Nissan North America: Which option would you choose, and why?

Product Planning: Taking the Next Step

In 2004, Adidas introduced the Adidas 1, the first running shoe with an embedded microchip that adjusts the cushion of the shoe as you jog. A sensor in the heel measures the force you're exerting as you walk or run. The microchip (with the processing power of an early Palm Pilot) extrapolates information about your stride and running surface and then sends a signal to the cushioning element. The result is more cushion when you're pounding the pavement and less when you're strolling across the lawn. "This is the first intelligent shoe ever," said Erich Stamminger, global marketing director for Adidas. "It senses, understands and adapts."[1]

Will the Adidas 1 succeed? A lot depends on how this innovative product is marketed and managed. What makes one product fail and another succeed? It's worth repeating what we said in Chapter 2: Firms that plan well succeed. Product planning plays a big role in the firm's *tactical marketing plans*. The strategies outlined in the product plan spell out how the firm expects to develop a product that will meet marketing objectives.

Today successful product management is more important than ever. As more and more competitors enter the global marketplace and as technology moves forward at an ever-increasing pace, products are created, grow, reach maturity, and decline at faster and faster speeds. This means that good product decisions are more critical than ever. Marketers just don't have the time to try one thing, find out it doesn't work, and then try something else.

Figure 9.1 Steps in Managing Products

Effective product strategies come from a series of orderly steps.

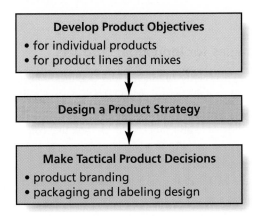

In Chapter 8, we talked about what a product really is and about how new products are developed and introduced into the marketplace. In this chapter, we'll finish the product part of the story by seeing how companies manage products and examine the steps in product planning, as Figure 9.1 outlines. These steps include developing product objectives and the strategies required to successfully market products as they evolve from "new kids on the block" to tried-and-true favorites. Next, we'll discuss branding and packaging, two of the more important tactical decisions product planners make. Finally, we'll examine how firms organize for effective product management. Let's start by seeing how firms develop product-related objectives.

Using Product Objectives to Decide on a Product Strategy

When marketers develop product strategies, they make decisions about product benefits, features, styling, branding, labeling, and packaging. But what do they want to accomplish? Clearly stated product objectives provide focus and direction. Product objectives should support the broader marketing objectives of the business unit in addition to supporting the overall mission of the firm. For example, the objectives of the firm may focus on return on investment. Marketing objectives then may concentrate on market share and/or the unit or dollar sales volume necessary to attain that return on investment. Product objectives need to specify how product decisions will contribute to reaching a desired market share or level of sales.

To be effective, product-related objectives must be measurable, clear, and unambiguous— and feasible. Also, they must indicate a specific time frame. Consider, for example, how a frozen entrée manufacturer might state its product objectives:

- "In the upcoming fiscal year, modify the product's fat content to satisfy consumers' health concerns."

- "Introduce three new items this quarter to the product line to take advantage of increased consumer interest in Mexican foods."

- "During the coming fiscal year, improve the chicken entrées to the extent that consumers will rate them better tasting than the competition."

Planners must keep in touch with their customers so that their objectives accurately respond to customer needs. An up-to-date knowledge of competitive product innovations also is important in developing product objectives.

Above all, product objectives should consider the *long-term implications* of product decisions. Planners who sacrifice the long-term health of the firm to reach short-term sales or financial goals may be on a risky course. Product planners may focus on one or more individual products at a time, or they may look at a group of product offerings as a whole. In this section, we'll briefly examine both these approaches. We'll also look at one important product objective: product quality.

Objectives and Strategies for Individual Products

How do you launch a new car that's only 142 inches long and makes people laugh when they see it? BMW did it by emphasizing the small size and poking fun at the car itself. The launch of the MINI Cooper included bolting the MINI onto a Ford Excursion with a sign "What are you doing for fun this weekend?" Full-size MINIs were also mocked up to look like coin-operated kiddie rides you find outside grocery stores with a sign "Rides $16,850. Quarters only." The advertising generated buzz among the 20- to 34-year-old target market.

As a smaller brand, the MINI didn't have the advertising budget for TV commercials—in fact, it was the first launch of a new car without TV advertising. Instead, the MINI launched with print, outdoor, and Web ads. The aim wasn't a heavy car launch but more of a "discovery process." Ads promoted "motoring" instead of driving, and magazine inserts included MINI-shaped air fresheners and pullout games. *Wired* magazine ran a cardboard foldout of the MINI suggesting readers assemble and drive it around their desks making "putt-putt" noises. *Playboy* came up with the idea of a six-page MINI "centerfold" complete with the car's vital statistics and hobbies. By the end of the year, the MINI was the second most memorable new product of the year, following the heavily advertised Vanilla Coke.[2]

Some product strategies, such as that for the new MINI Cooper, focus on a single new product. Strategies for individual products may be quite different for new products, for regional products, and for mature products. For new products, not surprisingly, the objectives relate to successful introduction. After a firm has experienced success with a product in a local or regional market, it may decide to introduce it nationally. Coors, for example, started out as a regional beer sold only in Colorado. It didn't move east of the Mississippi until 1981 and took another decade to move into all 50 states.

With a relatively tiny advertising budget for a new car model, the marketers of the MINI Cooper had to be very creative.

For mature products like Doritos, product objectives may focus on breathing new life into a product while holding on to the traditional brand personality. For Doritos, this means introducing a host of new flavors—guacamole, salsa verde, cooler ranch—as well as bite-size snacks called Rollitos and lower-fat versions like Nacho Cheesier Baked! Doritos. Doritos have been around since 1966 but continue to try to stay fresh with new flavors, shapes, and formulations that match popular trends.

Objectives and Strategies for Multiple Products

Although a small firm might make a go of focusing on one product, a larger firm often markets a set of related products. This means that strategic decisions affect two or more products simultaneously. The firm must think in terms of its entire portfolio of products. As Figure 9.2 shows, product planning means developing *product line* and *product mix* strategies encompassing multiple offerings. Figure 9.3 illustrates how this works for Procter & Gamble.

PRODUCT LINE STRATEGIES A **product line** is a firm's total product offering designed to satisfy a single need or desire of a group of target customers. For example, Procter & Gamble's line of cleaning products includes three different liquid dish detergent brands: Dawn stresses grease-cutting power, Ivory emphasizes mildness, and Joy is for people who want shiny dishes. To do an even better job of meeting varying consumer needs, each of the three brands comes in more than one formulation. For example, in addition to regular Dawn, there is an antibacterial Dawn and Dawn Special Care that promises to be easy on hands. The number of separate items within the same category determines the *length* of the product line.

A large number of variations in a product line is described as a *full line* that targets many customer segments to boost sales potential. A *limited-line strategy* with fewer product variations can improve the firm's image if it is perceived as a specialist with a clear, specific position in the market.

Figure 9.2 Objectives for Single and Multiple Products

Product objectives provide focus and direction for product strategies. Objectives can focus on a single product or a group of products.

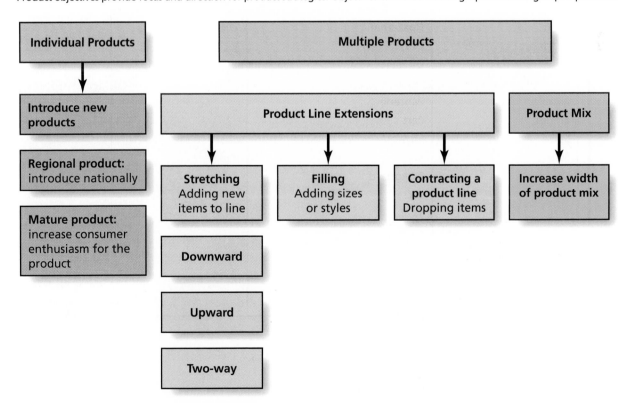

Figure 9.3 Product Line Length and Product Mix Width

A product line is a firm's total offerings that satisfy one need, whereas the product mix includes all the products that a firm offers. Here we see the entire length of Procter & Gamble's product lien as well as the entire width of its product mix.

Width of Product Mix

Length of Product Line

Fabric and Home Care	Beauty Care	Health Care/Baby and Family Care	Snacks and Beverages
Ace Laundry and Bleach	Ausonia	Actonel	Folgers
Alomatik	Aussie	Asacol	Millstone
Ariel	Camay	Bounty	Pringles
Bold	Clairol's Herbal Essences	Charmin	Punica
Bonux	Cover Girl	Codi	Sunny Delight
Bounce	Evax	Crest	Torengos
Cascade	Giorgio	Didronel	
Cheer	Head & Shoulders	Dodot	
Dash	Hugo Boss	Eukanuba	
Dawn	Infasil	Fixodent	
Daz	Infusion 23	Iams	
Downy	Ivory Personal Care	Kandoo	
Dryel	Lacoste	Luvs	
Era	Laura Biagiotti	Macrobid	
Fairy	Lines Feminine Care	Metamucil	
Febreze	Max Factor	Pampers	
Flash	Mum Always Whisper	Pepto-Bismol	
Gain	Muse	Puffs	
Hi Wash	Natural Instincts and Hydrience	PUR	
Ivory Dish	Naturella	Scope	
Joy	Nice'n Easy	Tempo	
Lang	Noxzema	ThermaCare	
Lenor	Olay	Vicks	
Maestro Limpio	Old Spice		
Mr. Clean/Proper	Orkid		
Myth	Pantene		
Rindex	Pert		
Salvo	Physique		
Swiffer	Rejoice		
Tide	Safeguard		
Viakal	Secret		
Vizir	SK-II		
	Sure		
	Tampax		
	Vidal Sassoon		
	Wash&Go		
	Zest		

Rolls-Royce Motor Cars, for example, makes expensive, handcrafted cars built to each customer's exact specifications and for decades has maintained a unique position in the automobile industry. The only three Rolls-Royce models are the Silver Seraph, the Corniche, and the Park Ward.[3]

Organizations may decide to extend their product line by adding more brands or models when they develop product strategies. For example, Patagonia, Gap, and Lands' End extended their reach by adding children's clothing. When a firm stretches its product line, it must decide which is the best direction to go. If a firm's current product line includes middle and lower-end items, an *upward line stretch* adds new items—higher priced and claiming more quality, bells and whistles, and so on. Hyundai decided it could tap the market for bigger, more luxurious cars, and so it introduced its XG 300, a car as big as Toyota's Avalon and larger than Nissan's Maxima but selling for thousands of dollars less.[4]

Conversely, a *downward line stretch* augments a line by adding items at the lower end. Here the firm must take care not to blur the images of its higher-priced, upper-end offerings. Rolex, for example, may not want to run the risk of cheapening its image with a new watch line to compete with lower-priced watches.

In some cases, a firm may decide that it is targeting too small a market. In this case, the product strategy may call for a *two-way stretch* that adds products at both the upper and lower ends. Marriott Hotels, for example, added Fairfield Inns and Courtyard at the lower end and Marriott Marquis Hotels and J.W. Marriott at the upper end to round out its product line.

A *filling-out strategy* may mean adding sizes or styles not previously available in a product category. Nabisco did this by introducing "bite-size" versions of its popular Oreo and Nutter Butter cookies.[5] In other cases, the best strategy may be to *contract* a product line, particularly when some of the items are not profitable. For example, Heinz scrapped its "Bite Me" brand of frozen pizza snacks because of poor sales. The product, targeted at teens, failed to meet company expectations and was withdrawn.[6]

We've seen that there are many ways a firm can modify its product line to meet the competition or take advantage of new opportunities. To further explore these strategic decisions, let's return to dish detergents. What does Procter & Gamble do if the objective is to increase market share? One possibility would be to expand its line of liquid dish detergents. If the line extension meets a perceived consumer need currently not being addressed, this would be a good strategic objective.

But whenever a product line or a product family is extended, there is risk of **cannibalization**, which occurs when sales of an existing brand are eaten up by the new item as the firm's current customers switch to the new product. That may explain why Procter & Gamble met consumer demands for an antibacterial dish liquid by creating new versions of existing brands Joy and Dawn.

AN ASSORTMENT OF COPIERS

When it comes to copying solutions tailored to fit your business, Toshiba thought of everything. Choose from a family of affordable, state-of-the-art copiers: the expandable e-STUDIO16 for small workgroups, the powerful e-STUDIO35 for medium-size businesses, and the FC-22i for affordable, high quality color. All fit nicely in digital network environments to keep you and your company connected. How sweet is that? To learn more about our complete line of copiers, fax machines and printers, visit copiers.toshiba.com or call 1-800-GO-TOSHIBA.

©2002 Toshiba America Business Solutions, Inc. Electronic Imaging Division. All rights reserved.

TOSHIBA
Don't copy. Lead.

A product line consists of an assortment of different products tailored to different consumers' needs.

product line
A firm's total product offering designed to satisfy a single need or desire of target customers.

cannibalization
The loss of sales of an existing brand when a new item in a product line or product family is introduced.

Fuji's "family" of cameras.

product mix
The total set of all products a firm offers for sale.

Kansei engineering
A Japanese philosophy that translates customers' feelings into design elements.

total quality management (TQM)
A management philosophy that focuses on satisfying customers through empowering employees to be an active part of continuous quality improvement.

PRODUCT MIX STRATEGIES   Product planning can go beyond a single product item or a product line to entire groups of products. A firm's **product mix** is its entire range of products. For example, in addition to a deep line of shaving products, Gillette offers toiletries such as Dry Idea and Right Guard deodorant, Paper Mate and Flair writing instruments, Oral B toothbrushes, Braun oral care products, Duracell batteries, and Cricket cigarette lighters.

In developing a product mix strategy, planners usually consider the *width of the product mix*, that is, the number of different product lines produced by the firm. By developing several different product lines, firms can reduce the risk associated with putting all their eggs in one or too few baskets. Normally, firms develop a mix of product lines that have some things in common, be it distribution channels or manufacturing facilities.

Nike's entry into the golf equipment market is an example of a successful product mix expansion strategy.[7] When golf star Tiger Woods began using Nike's Tour Accuracy balls, its market share increased from 0.9 to 3.9 percent. Cashing in on this success, Nike continued the strategy with Tiger Woods golf clubs retailing for $850.

Quality as a Product Objective

Product objectives often focus on product quality, the overall ability of the product to satisfy customers' expectations. Quality is tied to how customers *think* a product will perform and not necessarily to some technological level of perfection. Product quality objectives coincide with marketing objectives for higher sales and market share and to the firm's objectives for increased profits.

In some cases, quality means fanatical attention to detail and also getting extensive input from actual users of a product as it's being developed or refined—this is known as integrating the *voice of the consumer* into product design. The Japanese take this idea a step further with a practice that they call **Kansei engineering**, a philosophy that translates customers' feelings into design elements. In one application of this practice, the designers of the Mazda Miata focused on young drivers who saw the car as an extension of their body, a sensation they call "horse and rider as one." After extensive research, they discovered that making the stick shift exactly 9.5 centimeters long conveys the optimal feeling of sportiness and control.[8]

TOTAL QUALITY MANAGEMENT   In 1980, just when the economies of Germany and Japan were finally rebuilt from World War II and were threatening American markets, an NBC documentary on quality titled *If Japan Can Do It, Why Can't We?* demonstrated to the American public—and to American CEOs—the poor quality of American products.[9] So began the TQM revolution in American industry.

As noted in Chapter 1, many firms with a quality focus have adopted the principles and practices of **total quality management (TQM)**, a philosophy that calls for company-wide dedication to the development, maintenance, and continuous improvement of all aspects of the company's operations. Indeed, many of the world's most admired, successful companies—firms such as Nordstrom, 3M, and Coca-Cola—have adopted a total quality focus.

Product quality is one way that marketing can add value to customers. However, TQM as an approach to doing business is far more sophisticated and impactful than simply paying attention to product quality. TQM firms promote the attitude among employees that everybody working there has customers—even employees who never interact with customers outside the firm. In such cases, that employees' customers are internal customers, other employees with whom he or she interacts to do the job. In this way, TQM seeks to ensure customer satisfaction by involving all employees, regardless of their function, in efforts to continually improve quality. For example, TQM firms encourage employees, even the lowest-paid factory workers, to suggest ways to improve products— and then reward employees for good ideas.

But how do you know when you've attained your goal of quality? Other than increased sales and profits, a few key award programs recognize firms that are doing the job well. For example, in 1987, the U.S. Congress established the Malcolm Baldrige National Quality Award to recognize excellence in U.S. firms. Major purposes for the award are "helping to stimulate American companies to improve quality and productivity for the pride of recognition while obtaining a competitive edge through increased profits" and "recognizing the achievements of those companies that improve the quality of their goods and services."[10] Table 9.1 shows recent winners of the Baldrige Award.

Of course, recognition of the benefits of TQM programs is not limited to the United States. Around the world, many companies look to the uniform standards of the International Organization for Standardization (ISO) for quality guidelines. This Geneva-based organization developed a set of criteria in 1987 to improve and standardize product quality in Europe. The broad set of guidelines, known as **ISO 9000**, sets established voluntary standards for quality management.[11] Quality management is what the organization does to ensure that its products conform to the customer's requirements. In 1996, the ISO developed **ISO 14000** standards, which concentrate on "environmental management," meaning the organization works to minimize any harmful effects it may have on the environment.[12] Because members of the European Union and other European countries prefer suppliers with ISO 9000 certification, U.S. companies must comply with these standards to be competitive overseas.

One way that companies can improve quality is by using the "Six Sigma" methodology. The term *Six Sigma* comes from the statistical term "sigma," which is a standard deviation from the mean. Six Sigma, therefore, refers to six standard deviations from a normal distribution curve. In practical terms, that translates to no more than 3.4 defects per million—getting it right 99.9997 percent of the time. To achieve that level of quality requires a very rigorous approach, and that's what Six Sigma offers. The methodology involves a five-step process (define, measure, analyze, improve, and control). Employees are trained in the methodology and, like in karate, progress toward "black belt" status on successfully completing all the levels of training. Employees can use Six Sigma processes to remove defects from services, not just products. (A "defect" means failing to meet customer expectations.) For example, hospitals can use Six Sigma processes to reduce medical errors, and airlines can use Six Sigma to improve flight scheduling.

ADDING A DOSE OF QUALITY TO THE MARKETING MIX   Marketing people research the level of quality consumers want and need in their products and what price they are willing to pay for them. The price-versus-quality decision is a major aspect of providing value to consumers. Marketing also has to *inform* consumers about product quality through its marketing communications.

But keeping on top of what customers want is just the beginning. Firms also have to deliver a (customer-perceived) quality product at the right place and at the right price. Instead of being satisfied with doing things the same way year after year, marketers must continuously seek ways to improve product, place, price, and promotion. Let's see how quality concerns affect the marketing mix:

- **Product:** One way firms can offer quality for their customers is by improving their customer service support. For example, Whirlpool has been steadily improving the repair ser-

ISO 9000
Criteria developed by the International Organization for Standardization to regulate product quality in Europe.

ISO 14000
Standards of the International Organization for Standardization concerned with "environmental management" aimed at minimizing harmful effects on the environment.

Table 9.1 2003 Malcolm Baldrige Award Winners

To receive the prestigious Malcolm Baldrige Quality Award, companies must demonstrate excellence in seven areas: strategic planning, leadership, information and analysis, customer and market focus, human resources focus, process management, and business results. Winners come from five general categories: service, manufacturing, education, health care, and small business. To read why these companies won, visit the National Institute of Standards and Technology's Web site at http://www.nist.gov/public_affairs/releases/2003baldrigewinners.htm.

Award Category	Company
Manufacturing	Medrad, Inc.
Service	Boeing Aerospace Support and Caterpillar Financial Services Corp.
Small business	Stoner, Inc.
Education	Community Consolidated School District 15, Palatine, Illinois
Health care	Baptist Hospital, Inc., Pensacola, Florida and Saint Luke's Hospital of Kansas City

vices it offers on its appliances. In the past, if your washing machine broke down, you'd call Whirlpool, they'd refer you to a service center, and you'd call the service center and try to schedule a repair time. Today, technology lets Whirlpool's customer service reps view the schedules of all its repair technicians in your area and then schedule a repair time that suits your schedule—all during the first phone call. Whirlpool also offers an online service that lets customers schedule service themselves, without even talking with a rep. The easier it is for customers to interact with the company and get results, the more satisfied they will be.[13]

- **Place:** TorPharm, the largest generic pharmaceutical manufacturer in Canada, involved its suppliers in its efforts to improve on-time delivery to customers. First, TorPharm developed purchasing and delivery strategies to ensure that more than 99 percent of the time the right quantities of raw materials arrived from suppliers when expected. Then TorPharm worked with its customers, namely U.S. pharmacies, to improve its on-time delivery rate of products from as low as 60 to 95 percent or better.[14]

- **Price:** Hewlett-Packard (HP) is lowering costs and improving service to customers at the same time. HP developed a "sure supply" technology that is embedded into its printer cartridges. The technology has a sensor that detects when the ink supply is low, and the networked printer automatically orders a new cartridge. By building an automated cartridges-supply service into the printer, HP reduces its own costs (e.g., for processing a customer's phone order) as well as those of its customers.[15]

- **Promotion:** Today's marketing firms realize that customers want information when they need it, not when it's convenient for the marketer. The Gap exemplifies this philosophy. At Gap's Old Navy stores, salespeople wear headsets so they can quickly get information to answer customers' questions.

DIMENSIONS OF PRODUCT QUALITY But what exactly *is* quality? As we discussed in earlier chapters, quality has many meanings (see Figure 9.4). In some cases, product quality means durability; for example, athletic shoes shouldn't develop holes after their owner shoots hoops for a few weeks. Reliability also is an important aspect of product quality—just ask Maytag and its lonely repairman. For many customers, a product's versatility and its ability to satisfy their needs are central to product quality.

Figure 9.4 Product Quality

Some product objectives focus on quality or the ability of a product to satisfy customer expectations—no matter what those expectations are.

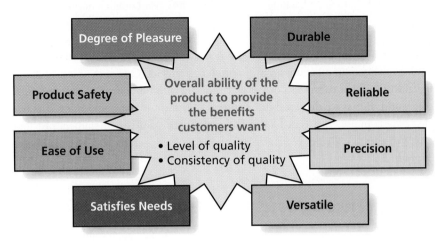

For other products, quality means a high degree of precision; for example, high-tech audio equipment promises clearer music reproduction with less distortion. Quality, especially in business-to-business products, is also related to ease of use, maintenance, and repair. Yet another crucial dimension of quality is product safety. Finally, the quality of products such as a painting, a movie, or even a wedding gown relates to the degree of aesthetic pleasure they provide. Of course, evaluations of aesthetic quality differ dramatically among people: To one person, quality TV may mean *Masterpiece Theater*, while to another it's MTV's *Jackass*.

Marketing planners often focus product objectives on one or both of two key aspects of quality: level and consistency. Customers often determine the *level of quality* of a product by comparison with other brands in the same product category. A handcrafted Rolls-Royce boasts higher quality than an assembly-line Ford Mustang, but this may be irrelevant to a Mustang buyer inclined to compare it to a MINI Cooper and not an elite luxury car.

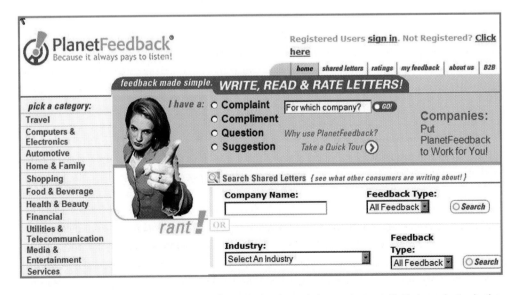

Planet Feedback encourages consumers to tell companies about their experiences with their products—both good and bad.

Consistency of quality means that customers experience the same level of quality in a product time after time, bringing repeat business and free word-of-mouth advertising or buzz. Consistent quality is also one of the major benefits of adopting TQM practices. Consumer perceptions can change overnight when quality is lacking. Ask anybody who's ever bought a new car that turned out to be a lemon.

THE IMPACT OF E-COMMERCE ON QUALITY AS A PRODUCT OBJECTIVE The Internet has made product quality even more important in product strategies. One of the most exciting aspects of the digital world is that consumers can interact directly with other people—around the block or around the world. But as we discussed in Chapter 6, this form of communication cuts both ways since it lets people praise what they like and slam what they don't to an audience of thousands. Numerous Web sites like Planet Feedback let consumers "vent" about bad experiences they have had with products.

Marketing Throughout the Product Life Cycle

product life cycle
A concept that explains how products go through four distinct stages from birth to death: introduction, growth, maturity, and decline.

Many products have very long lives, while others are "here today, gone tomorrow." The **product life cycle** is a useful way to explain how product features change over the life of a product. In Chapter 8, we talked about how marketers go about introducing new products, but the launch is only the beginning. Product marketing strategies must evolve and change as they continue through the product life cycle.

This concept relates to either a product category or, less frequently, to a specific brand. Some individual brands may have short life expectancies even though the product lives on in other successful brands. Who can remember the Nash car or Evening in Paris perfume? Other brands seem almost immortal. For example, Coca-Cola has been the number one cola brand for 118 years, General Electric has been the number one lightbulb brand for 102 years, and Kleenex has been the number one tissue brand for 80 years. It wasn't that these products were necessarily the first in their category, but they were the first to establish the brand in the consumer's mind.[16]

The Introduction Stage

introduction stage
The first stage of the product life cycle in which slow growth follows the introduction of a new product in the marketplace.

Like people, products are born, they "grow up" (well, most people grow up anyway), and eventually they die. We can divide the life of a product into four separate stages. The first stage, shown in Figure 9.5, is the **introduction stage**. Here customers get the first chance to purchase the good or service. During this early stage, a single company usually produces the product. If it clicks and is profitable, competitors will follow with their own versions.

During the introduction stage, the goal is to get first-time buyers to try the product. Sales (hopefully) increase at a steady but slow pace. As is also evident in Figure 9.5, the company usually does not make a profit during this stage. Why? Two reasons: Research-and-development (R&D) costs and heavy spending for advertising and promotional efforts cut into revenue.

During the introduction stage, pricing may be high to recover the R&D costs (demand permitting) or low to attract large numbers of consumers (see Figure 9.6). For example, the suggested retail price of the Adidas 1 smart shoe described at the beginning of this chapter is $250, more than double that of a nondigital shoe. The price is designed to appeal to consumers who are willing to pay for the most advanced running shoes. The high cost helps Adidas recover its R&D costs.

How long does the introduction stage last? As we saw in Chapter 8's Wi-Fi example, it can be quite long. A number of factors come into play, including marketplace acceptance and the producer's willingness to support its product during start-up.

Not all products make it past the introduction stage. For a new product to be successful, consumers must first know about it. Then they must believe that it is something they want or need. Marketing during this stage often focuses on informing consumers about the product, how to use it, and its promised benefits. However, nearly 40 percent of all new products fail.[17]

Figure 9.5   The Product Life Cycle

The product life cycle helps marketers understand how a product changes over its lifetime and suggests how marketing strategies should be modified accordingly.

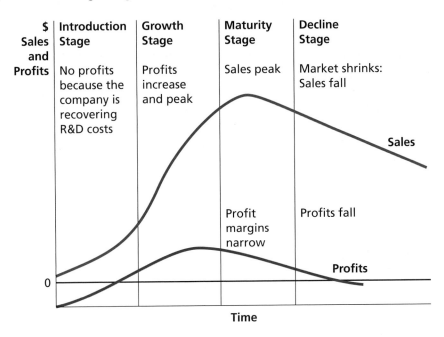

Figure 9.6   Marketing Mix Strategies Through the Product Life Cycle

Marketing mix strategies—the Four Ps—change as a product moves through the life cycle.

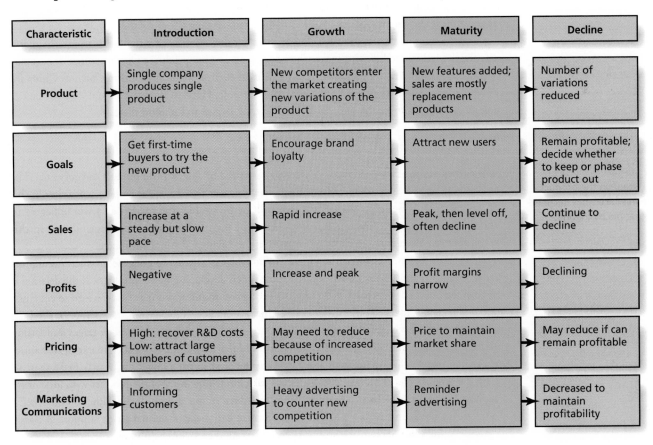

The Growth Stage

growth stage
The second stage in the product life cycle during which the product is accepted and sales rapidly increase.

In the **growth stage**, sales increase rapidly while profits increase and peak. Marketing's goal here is to encourage brand loyalty by convincing the market that this brand is superior to others. In this stage, marketing strategies may include the introduction of product variations to attract market segments and increase market share. The cell phone is an example of a product that is still in its growth stage as worldwide sales continue to increase.

When competitors appear, marketers must use heavy advertising and other types of promotion. Price competition may develop, driving profits down. Some firms may seek to capture a particular segment of the market by positioning their product to appeal to a certain group. And, if pricing has initially been set high, it may be reduced to meet the increasing competition.

The Maturity Stage

maturity stage
The third and longest stage in the product life cycle in which sales peak and profit margins narrow.

The **maturity stage** of the product life cycle is usually the longest. Sales peak and then begin to level off and even decline while profit margins narrow. Competition grows intense when remaining competitors fight for their share of a shrinking pie. Price reductions and reminder advertising may be used to maintain market share. Because most customers have already accepted the product, sales are often to replace a "worn-out" item or to take advantage of product improvements. For example, almost everyone owns a TV, which means a large share of sales are replacements. During the maturity stage, firms will try to sell their product through as many outlets as possible because availability is crucial in a competitive market. Consumers will not go far to find one particular brand if satisfactory alternatives are close at hand.

To remain competitive and maintain market share during the maturity stage, firms may tinker with the marketing mix. Competitors may add new "bells and whistles," as when producers of potato chips and other snack foods modify their products. When consumers became concerned about carbohydrates, Frito-Lay introduced new lines of low-carb chips like the Tostitos Edge low-carb tortilla chips. Unilever likewise rolled out 18 new low-carb products, rejuvenating venerable brands like Ragu spaghetti sauce and Wishbone salad dressing.[18]

Attracting new users of the product can be another strategy that marketers use in the maturity stage. Market development means introducing an existing product to a market that doesn't currently use it. Many U.S. firms are finding new markets in developing countries such as China for products whose domestic sales are stagnant. For example, Harvard Business School Press is marketing its case studies in China now, as the case method begins to catch on there.[19]

The Decline Stage

decline stage
The final stage in the product life cycle in which sales decrease as customer needs change.

The **decline stage** of the product life cycle is characterized by a decrease in product category sales. The reason may be obsolescence forced by new technology—where do you see a new typewriter in this computer age? Although a single firm may still be profitable, the market as a whole begins to shrink, profits decline, there are fewer variations of the product, and suppliers pull out. In this stage, there are usually many competitors, with none having a distinct advantage.

A firm's major product decision in the decline stage is whether to keep the product. An unprofitable product drains resources that could be better used developing newer products. If the decision is to keep the product, advertising and other marketing communications may be decreased to cut costs, and prices may be reduced if the product can remain profitable. If the decision is to drop the product, elimination may be handled in two ways: phase it out by cutting production in stages and letting existing stocks run out or simply drop the product immediately. If the established market leader anticipates that there will be some residual demand for the product for a long time, it may make sense to keep the product on the market. The idea is to sell a limited quantity of the product with little or no support from sales, merchandising, advertising, and distribution and just let it "wither on the vine."

Some products have been able to hang in there with little or no marketing support. A classic example is the Pilot Stapler, which has been on the market for over 70 years. Despite sleeker and

Advice for Nissan North America, Inc.

ASSISTANT PROFESSOR
BRIAN LARSON
Widener University

I would choose option 1, pursuing a targeted, integrated media and creative strategy. This option seems to best demonstrate not only well-defined efforts to position the Xterra but also the most consideration for Xterra's distinct contribution to the entire Nissan product line. As with any new product introduction, it will take time for consumers to develop an understanding of and attachment to the Xterra. While you risk alienating some SUV consumers with a targeted and "edgy" campaign, the gain would be a more clearly differentiated product (not your father's Pathfinder). This option minimizes the risk of cannibalizing existing Pathfinder sales and maximizes the potential to create a clear image of what the new Xterra is. Moreover, a clearly defined Xterra would strengthen Nissan's SUV line by offering prospective SUV consumers a new alternative within Nissan. This might serve to draw new consumers "not passionate about Nissan." It might additionally satisfy the needs of outdoor (and wannabe outdoor) enthusiasts who hold positive attitudes toward the auto manufacturer but who previously had no choice of SUV within the Nissan family.

LECTURER
MICHAEL MUNRO
Florida International University

I would recommend option 1. Xterra is a product aimed specifically at a young outdoor enthusiast segment. Promoting this product is best done through efficient media and distinctive creative execution suited to the identified outdoor enthusiasts and "weekend warriors." Nissan should not be concerned with customers preferring a large luxury SUV with ample creature comforts or those looking for minicars or minivans but focus instead on functional performance and power. Media and creative executions should not be directed to a broader base, nor should the accessory packages (e.g., leather seats), because such a move would be inconsistent with Xterra's rugged image and would defuse the core character and weaken its brand equity. Further, the other considered strategies would threaten cannibalization of Nissan's Pathfinder brand.

less costly competitors, the Pilot sustains its reputation as *the* heavy-duty stapler for a small but loyal group of fans still very "attached" to it.[20]

Oil of Olay has been a steady performer for over 50 years. The pink moisturizer was first developed during World War II for Britain's Royal Air Force as a lotion to treat burns. In 1962, another company bought it and started to market it as a "beauty fluid." Procter & Gamble acquired that company in 1985 and reinvigorated it by pumping a lot of advertising dollars into it. In the early 1990s, P&G started to launch line extensions built around the Oil of Olay name. The company also began revamping the product's image to make it more appealing to women. P&G figured out that they are grossed out by the word "oil" because they equate it with greasy. Now the $500 million line of skin-care products and cosmetics is known simply as Olay.[21] New Olay line extensions include Olay Moisturinse In-Shower Body Lotion and Olay Daily Facials Intensives Clear Skin Lathering Cloths. P&G also started advertising Olay on MTV to attract the 18-to-35 demographic.[22]

Creating Product Identity: Branding Decisions

Successful marketers keep close tabs on their products' life cycle status, and they plan accordingly. Equally important, though, is giving that product an identity like Skippy Peanut Butter is doing with its Skippy Snack Bars. That's where branding comes in. The brand personality connotes pure,

Consumers recognize brand logos with just a single letter—from A to Z. How many can you recognize?

unadulterated fun, and the launch of the new snack bars features TV commercials with the animated Nutshells, a band of musical elephants.[23] How important is branding? Well, of the more than 17,000 new products or line extensions introduced each year, 25 percent are new brands. About $127.5 billion per year is spent on introducing these new brands—that's $7.5 million per brand on average.

We said earlier that nearly 40 percent of all new products fail, but for new brands the failure rate is even higher—up to 80 to 90 percent.[24] Branding is an extremely important (and expensive) element of product strategies. In this section, we'll examine what a brand is and how certain laws protect brands. Then we'll discuss the importance of branding and how firms make branding decisions.

What's in a Name (or a Symbol)?

How do you identify your favorite brand? By its name? By the logo (how the name appears)? By the packaging? By some graphic image or symbol, such as Nike's swoosh? A **brand** is a name, a term, a symbol, or any other unique element of a product that identifies one firm's product(s) and sets it apart from the competition. Consumers easily recognize the Coca-Cola logo, the Jolly Green Giant (a *trade character*), and the triangular red Nabisco logo (a *brand mark*) in the corner of the box. Branding provides the recognition factor products need to succeed in regional, national, and international markets.

CHOOSING A BRAND NAME, BRAND MARK, OR TRADE CHARACTER There are several important considerations in selecting a brand name, brand mark, or trade character. First, it must have a positive connotation and be memorable. Consider Toro's experience when it introduced a lightweight snow thrower called the "Snow Pup." Sales were disappointing because "pup" conveyed a small, cuddly animal—not a desirable image for a snow thrower. Renamed the "Snow Master," its sales went up markedly.[25]

A brand name is probably the most used and most recognized form of branding. Kool-Aid and Jell-O are two of the first words kids learn. Smart marketers use brand names to maintain relationships with consumers "from the cradle to the grave." For example, Jell-O now markets low-carb versions of its gelatin dessert to appeal to carb-counting adults.[26]

A good brand name may position a product by conveying a certain image or personality (Ford Mustang) or by describing how it works (Drano). Brand names such as Caress and Shield help position these different brands of bath soap by saying different things about the benefits they promise. The Nissan Xterra combines the word *terrain* with the letter *X*, which is associated by many young people with extreme sports to give the brand name a cutting-edge, off-road feel.

How does a firm select a good brand name? Good brand designers say there are four "easy" tests: *easy to say, easy to spell, easy to read, and easy to remember* like P&G's Tide, Cheer, Dash, Bold, Gain, Downy, and Ivory Snow. And the name should also "fit" four ways: *fit the target market, fit the product's benefits, fit the customer's culture,* and *fit legal requirements.*

When it comes to graphics for a brand symbol, name, or logo, the rule is that it must be recognizable and memorable. No matter how small or how large, the triangular Nabisco logo in the corner of the box is a familiar sight. And it should have visual impact. That means that from across a store or when you are quickly flipping the pages in a magazine, the brand will catch your attention. Some successful marketers enhance brand recognition by creating a trade character such as the Pillsbury Dough Boy.

TRADEMARKS A **trademark** is the legal term for a brand name, brand mark, or trade character. The symbol for legal registration in the United States is a capital "R" in a circle: ®. Marketers register trademarks to make their use by competitors illegal. Because trademark protection applies only in individual countries where the brand has been registered, unauthorized use of marks on counterfeit products is a huge headache for many companies.

brand
A name, a term, a symbol, or any other unique element of a product that identifies one firm's product(s) and sets them apart from the competition.

trademark
The legal term for a brand name, brand mark, or trade character; trademarks legally registered by a government obtain protection for exclusive use in that country.

It is possible for a firm to have protection for a brand even if it has not legally registered it. In the United States, *common-law protection* exists if the firm has used the name and established it over a period of time (sort of like a common-law marriage). Although a registered trademark prevents others from using it on a similar product, it may not bar its use for a product in a completely different type of business. Consider the range of "Quaker" brands: Quaker Oats (cereals), Quaker Funds (mutual funds), Quaker State (motor oil), Quaker Bonnet (gift food baskets), and Quaker Safety Products Corporation (firemen's clothing).

The Importance of Branding

A brand is more than the product—the best brands build an emotional connection with the consumer. Strong brands don't just meet rational needs, they create an emotional reaction. Think about the most popular diaper brands—they're Pampers and Luvs, not AbsorbancyMaster. The names evoke the joys of parenting, not utility of the diaper. Marketers spend huge amounts of money on new-product development, advertising, and promotion to develop strong brands. If it works, this investment creates **brand equity**, which is a brand's value to its organization. If we look at how customers feel about products, we can identify different levels of loyalty or lack thereof. At the lowest level, customers really have no loyalty to a brand and will change brands for any reason, often jumping ship if they find something else at a lower price. At the other extreme, some brands command fierce devotion, and loyal users will go without rather than buy a competing brand.

Figure 9.7 shows one way to think about these escalating levels of attachment to a brand. At the lowest level of the "brand equity pyramid," consumers are aware of a brand's existence. Moving up the pyramid, they might look at the brand in terms of what it literally does for them or how it performs relative to competitors. Going up still farther, they may think more deeply about the product and form beliefs and emotional reactions to it. The truly successful brands, however, are those that make the long climb to the top of the pyramid—they "bond" with their customers so

brand equity
The value of a brand to an organization.

Figure 9.7 The Brand Equity Pyramid

The brand equity pyramid shows one way to think about escalating levels of attachment to a brand.

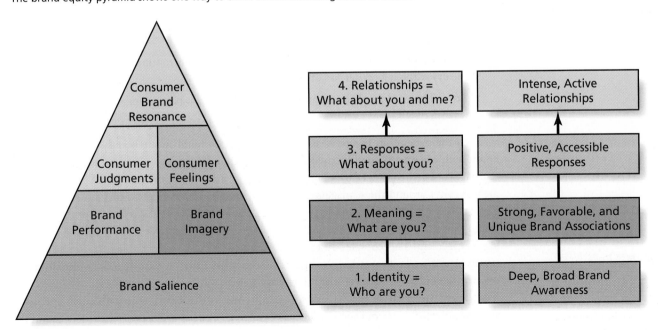

Source: Kevin Lane Keller, *Building Customer-Based Brand Equity: A Blueprint for Creating Strong Brands*, Working Paper Series, Report 01-107 (Cambridge, Mass.: Marketing Science Institute, 2001), 7.

Table 9.2   Dimensions of Brand Meaning

Dimension	Example
Brand identification markers	Coca-Cola's red and white colors, the Nike swoosh logo, Harley-Davidson's characteristic sound
Product attribute and benefit associations	Starbucks as good coffee; BMW as the ultimate driving machine
Gender	WWF, Harley-Davidson, Marlboro and masculinity; Laura Ashley and femininity
Social class	Mercedes and the old-guard elite; Jell-O and the lower-middle class
Age	Skechers, Nokia, and teen America
Reference group	Dockers and the casual workforce; Williams-Sonoma and the serious cook
Life stage	Dewar's and the coming of age; Parent's Soup and new mothers
Lifestyles and taste subcultures	BMW and the yuppie; Vans and the skateboard culture
Place	Coke and America; Ben & Jerry's and rural Vermont
Time and decade	Betty Crocker and the 1950s; VW and the 1960s countercultural revolution
Trends	Pottery Barn and cocooning; Starbucks and small indulgences
Traditions and rituals	Häagen-Dazs ice cream and the pampering of self

Source: Adapted from Susan Fournier, Michael R. Solomon, Basil G. Englis, and Jeff Green, "How Brands Mean: Resonance as a Mediator of the Brand Meaning—Brand Strength Connection," unpublished manuscript, March 2004.

that people feel they have a real relationship with the product. Here are some of the types of relationships a person might have with a product:

- **Self-concept attachment:** The product helps establish the user's identity. (For example, do you feel more like yourself in Ralph Lauren or Sean John clothing?)

- **Nostalgic attachment:** The product serves as a link with a past self. (Does eating the inside of an Oreo cookie remind you of childhood?)

- **Interdependence:** The product is a part of the user's daily routine. (Could you get through the day without a Starbucks coffee?)

- **Love:** The product elicits emotional bonds of warmth, passion, or other strong emotion. (Hershey's Kiss, anyone?)[27]

As the pyramid in Figure 9.7 shows us, the way to build strong brands is to build strong bonds with customers—bonds based on meaning. Brand meaning encompasses the beliefs and associations that a consumer has about the brand. In many ways, the practice of brand management revolves around the management of meanings. Brand marketers craft meanings for their brands. Advertising agencies, package designers, name consultants, logo developers, and public relations firms are just some of the collaborators in a global industry devoted to the task of meaning management. This complex and synergistic system is based on one simple but critical truth: strong brands are built on strong meanings. The corollary: brands die when their meanings lose value in consumers' worlds. Table 9.2 shows some of the dimensions of brand meaning.

Brand equity means that a brand enjoys customer loyalty, perceived quality, and brand name awareness. For a firm, brand equity provides a competitive advantage because it gives the brand the power to capture and hold on to a larger share of the market and to sell at prices with higher profit margins. For example, among pianos, the Steinway name has such brand equity that its market share among concert pianists is 95 percent.[28]

What makes a brand successful? Here is a list of 10 characteristics of the world's top brands:[29]

1. The brand excels at delivering the benefits customers truly desire.

2. The brand stays relevant.

3. The pricing strategy is based on consumers' perceptions of value.

4. The brand is properly positioned.

5. The brand is consistent.

6. The brand portfolio and hierarchy make sense.

7. The brand makes use of and coordinates a full repertoire of marketing activities to build equity.

8. The brand's managers understand what the brand means to consumers.

9. The brand is given proper support, and that support is sustained over the long run.

10. The company monitors sources of brand equity.

Products with strong brand equity provide enticing opportunities. A firm may leverage a brand's equity with **brand extensions**, new products sold with the same brand name. For example, a few years ago, Alka-Seltzer came out with a product to treat hangovers. A commercial for the extension features a young man (the new product's target market) in bed—he has a flashback to the wild events of the night before, and a voice-over asks, "Wish you could undo what you did last night?"[30]

Alka-Seltzer has created brand extensions for specific problems, including drinking one too many.

Because of the existing brand equity, the firm is able to sell the brand extension at a higher price than if it had given it a new brand, and the brand extension will attract new customers immediately. Of course, if the brand extension does not live up to the quality or attractiveness of the original brand, brand equity will suffer, as will brand loyalty and sales.

brand extensions
A new product sold with the same brand name as a strong existing brand.

Branding Strategies

Because brands are important to a marketing program's success, branding strategies are a major part of product decision making. Marketers have to determine whether to create individual or family brands, national or store brands, or cobrands—it's not that easy.

INDIVIDUAL BRANDS VERSUS FAMILY BRANDS   Part of developing a branding strategy is deciding whether to use a separate, unique brand for each product item—an *individual brand strategy*—or market multiple items under the same brand name—a **family brand** or *umbrella brand* strategy. Individual brands may do a better job of communicating clearly and concisely what the consumer can expect from the product. The decision of whether to use an individual or family branding strategy often depends on characteristics of the product and whether the company's overall product strategy calls for introduction of a single, unique product or for the development of a group of similar products. For example, Atkins Nutritionals Inc.'s Atkins name establishes that the products are

family brand
A brand that a group of individual products or individual brands share.

Brand equity is the value of a product with a particular brand name compared to the value of a product without the brand name. Many corporations, marketing research firms, and ad agencies have devised various measures of brand equity because this is an important way to assess if a branding strategy has been successful. For example, Harris Interactive conducts its EquiTrend® study twice a year to measure the brand equity of over 1,000 brands. The company interviews over 25,000 consumers to determine how they feel about competing brands.[31] For example, in a 2003 survey, the following were the most highly rated brands across all categories: (1) Smithsonian Institution, (2) Craftsman Tools, (3) Crayola Crayons and Markers, (4) Bose, and (5) Hershey's Kisses.[32]

If consumers have strong, positive feelings about a brand and are willing to pay extra in order to choose it over others, you are in marketing heaven. Each of the following approaches to measuring brand equity has some good points and some bad points:

1. *Customer mind-set metrics* focus on consumer awareness, attitudes, and loyalty toward a brand. However, these metrics are based on consumer surveys and don't usually provide a single objective measure that can be used to assign a financial value to the brand.
2. *Product-market outcomes metrics* focus on the ability of a brand to charge a higher price than the one charged by an unbranded equivalent. This usually involves asking consumers how much more they would be willing to pay for a certain brand compared to others. These measures often rely on hypothetical judgments and can be complicated to use.
3. *Financial market metrics* consider the purchase price of a brand if it is sold or acquired. They may also include subjective judgments about the future stock price of the brand.

More recently, a team of marketing professors proposed a simpler measure that they claim reliably tracks the value of a brand over time. Their *revenue premium* metric compares the revenue a brand generates with the revenue generated by a similar private-label product (that doesn't have any brand identification). In this case, brand equity is just the difference in revenue (net price times volume) between a branded good and a corresponding private label.[33]

national or manufacturer brands
Brands that the manufacturer of the product owns.

private-label brands
Brands that are owned and sold by a certain retailer or distributor.

for consumers who are trying to maintain an Atkins diet and minimize consumption of carbohydrates. Under the Atkins umbrella brand are individual brands like Endulge, Advantage, and Morning Start.

NATIONAL AND STORE BRANDS Retailers today often are in the driver's seat when it comes to deciding what brands to stock and push. In addition to choosing from producers' brands, called **national or manufacturer brands**, retailers decide whether to offer their own versions. **Private-label brands**, also called store brands, are the retail store's or chain's exclusive trade name. Wal-Mart, for example, sells store brand Sam's Cola and Sam's cookies along with national brands such as Coke and Oreos. Store brands are gaining in popularity for many value-conscious shoppers. Retailers continue to develop new ones, and some are adding services to the mix: Safeway even offers its own private-label banking to shoppers wishing to apply for a loan while buying their lemons and limes.[34]

Retailers choose a private-label branding strategy because they generally make more profit on these than on national brands. Loblaws, Canada's largest supermarket chain, developed its own President's Choice "premium quality" private-label brand. Loblaws sells over 4,000 food items under the President's Choice label, from cookies to beef, olive oil, curtains, and kitchen utensils. Sales of President Choice items run from 30 to 40 percent of store volumes. Under the private label, Loblaws can introduce new products at high quality but lower prices than brand names. It can also keep entire categories profitable by its mix of pricing options. Competitors that sell only national brands can cut prices on those brands, but that hurts their overall profitability. Loblaws can bring prices down on national brands but still make money on its private-label products.[35]

Discount retailers such as Target have used private-label clothing to lure millions of customers away from more upscale department stores. Target's Linden Hill brand has become a significant force without any advertising.[36] In an attempt to regain some of this market, many department stores have followed the discount retailers by beefing up their own private-label offerings.

GENERIC BRANDS An alternative to either national or store branding is generic branding, which is basically no branding. Generic branded products are typically packaged in white with black lettering that name only the product itself (e.g., "green beans"). Generic branding is one strategy to meet customers' demand for the lowest prices on standard products such as dog food or paper towels. Generic brands were first popularized during the inflationary period of the 1980s, when consumers became especially price conscious because of rising prices. However, today generic brands account for very little of consumer spending.

LICENSING Some firms choose to use **licensing** to brand their products. In these cases, a licensing agreement means that one firm sells another firm the right to use a legally protected brand name for a specific purpose and for a specific period of time. Firms choose a licensing strategy for a variety of reasons. Licensing can provide instant recognition and consumer interest in a new product, and licensing may be important to positioning a product for a certain target market. For example, bourbon

The phenomenal success of the Harry Potter books and the movie have made it a hot property. Characters popped up all over in numerous licensed products.

maker Jack Daniels licensed its name to T.G.I. Friday's for use on menu items. The menu partnership was so successful that Friday's went on to license the Atkins name to create low-carb menu items.[37]

Much better known, however, is the licensing of entertainment names, such as when movie producers license their properties to manufacturers of a seemingly infinite number of products. Each time the blockbuster Harry Potter movies hit the screens, a plethora of Potter products packed the stores. In addition to toys and games, you can buy Harry Potter candy, clothing, all manner of back-to-school items, home items, and even wands and cauldrons.

COBRANDING Frito-Lay sells K.C. Masterpiece–flavored potato chips, and Post sells Oreo O's cereal. Strange marriages? No, these are examples of **cobranding**. This branding strategy benefits both partners when combining the two brands provides more recognition power than either enjoy alone. For example, Panasonic markets a line of digital cameras that use Leica lenses. Leica lenses are legendary for their superb image quality. Panasonic is known for its consumer electronics. Combining the best in traditional camera optics with a household name in consumer electronics helps both brands.[38]

A new and fast-growing variation on cobranding is **ingredient branding**, in which branded materials become "component parts" of other branded products.[39] Consumers, for example, can buy Breyer's Ice Cream with Reese's Peanut Butter Cups or M&M's candies or Twix cookies or Snickers bars. Van De Camp's Fish & Dips come with Heinz ketchup dipping cups. The ultimate cobranding in a single package may be an Oscar Meyer Lunchables Mega Pack, which has up to five brands in a single package. Its Pizza Stix pack, for example, comes with Tombstone pizza sauce, Kraft cheese, a Capri Sun Splash Cooler, and a 3 Musketeers bar.

The practice of ingredient branding has two main benefits. First, it attracts customers to the host brand because the ingredient brand is familiar and has a strong brand reputation for quality. Second, the ingredient brand's firm can sell more of its product, not to mention the additional revenues it gets from the licensing arrangement.[40]

licensing
An agreement in which one firm sells another firm the right to use a brand name for a specific purpose and for a specific period of time.

cobranding
An agreement between two brands to work together in marketing a new product.

ingredient branding
A form of cobranding in which branded materials are used as ingredients or component parts of other branded products.

Creating Product Identity: Packaging and Labeling Decisions

So far, we've talked about how marketers create product identity with branding. In this section, we'll learn that packaging and labeling decisions also are important in creating product identity.

How do you know if the soda you are drinking is "regular" or "caffeine free"? How do you keep your low-fat grated cheese fresh after you have used some of it? Why do you always leave your bottle of Glow perfume out on your dresser so everyone can see it? The answer to all these questions is effective packaging and labeling. In this section, we will talk about the strategic functions of packaging and some of the legal issues of package labeling.

Packaging Functions

package
The covering or container for a product that provides product protection, facilitates product use and storage, and supplies important marketing communication.

A **package** is the covering or container for a product, but it's also a lot more. Marketers who want to create great packaging that meets and exceeds consumers' needs and that creates a competitive advantage must understand all the things a package does for a product. Figure 9.8 shows how packaging serves a number of different functions.

First, packaging protects the product. For example, packaging for computers, TV sets, and stereos protects the units from damage during shipping, storage, and shelf life. Cereal, potato chips, or packs of grated cheese wouldn't be edible for long if packaging didn't provide protection from moisture, dust, odors, and insects. The chicken broth in Figure 9.8 is protected (before opening) from spoilage by a multilayered, soft box. In addition to protecting the product, effective packaging makes it easy for consumers to handle and store the product.

Over and above these utilitarian functions, the package plays an important role in communicating brand personality. Effective product packaging uses colors, words, shapes, designs, and pictures to provide brand and name identification for the product. In addition, packaging provides specific information consumers want and need, such as information about the specific variety, flavor or fragrance, directions for use, suggestions for alternative uses (e.g., recipes), product warnings, and product ingredients. Packaging may also include warranty information and a toll-free telephone number for customer service.

In an effort to make its packaging more user friendly, Ben & Jerry's Ice Cream redesigned its package.[41] Because the top is the first thing customers see in a coffin-type freezer, the photo of Ben and Jerry on the carton lid was replaced with text identifying the flavor. Other changes included a more upscale look of a black-on-gold color scheme and enticing realistic watercolors of the product's ingredients.

Universal Product Code (UPC)
The set of black bars or lines printed on the side or bottom of most items sold in grocery stores and other mass-merchandising outlets. The UPC, readable by scanners, creates a national system of product identification.

A final communication element is the **Universal Product Code (UPC)**, which is the set of black bars or lines printed on the side or bottom of most items sold in grocery stores and other mass-merchandising outlets. The UPC is a national system of product identification. Each product has a unique 10-digit number assigned to it. These numbers supply specific information about the type of item (grocery item, meat, produce, drugs, or a discount coupon), the manufacturer (a five-digit code), and the specific product (another five-digit code). At checkout counters, electronic scanners read the UPC bars and automatically transmit data to a computer controlling the cash register, allowing retailers to track sales and control inventory.

Designing Effective Packaging

Designing effective packaging involves a multitude of different decisions. Should the package have a zip-lock closing, have an easy-to-pour spout, be compact for easy storage, be short and fat so it won't fall over, or be tall and skinny so it won't take up much shelf space?

Planners must consider the packaging of other brands in the same product category. For example, dry cereal usually comes in tall rectangular boxes. Quaker, however, has introduced a line of cereal packaged in reclosable plastic bags. Quaker offers its cereals at prices that are 25 to 35 per-

Figure 9.8 Functions of Packaging

Great packaging provides a covering for a product, and it also creates a competitive advantage for the brand.

cent less than well-known brands packaged in boxes. Not all customers are willing to accept a radical change in packaging, and retailers may be reluctant to adjust their shelf space to accommodate such packages.

In addition to functional benefits, the choice of packaging material has aesthetic and environmental considerations. Enclosing a fine liqueur in a velvet or silk bag may enhance its image. A fine perfume packaged in a beautifully designed glass bottle means consumers are buying not only the fragrance but an attractive dressing table accessory as well.

Firms seeking to act in a socially responsible manner also consider the environmental impact of packaging. Shiny gold or silver packaging transmits an image of quality and opulence, but certain metallic inks are not biodegradable and are harmful to the environment. Some firms are developing innovative *green packaging* that is less harmful to the environment than other materials. Of course, there is no guarantee that consumers will accept such packaging. They didn't take to plastic pouch refills for certain spray bottle products even though the pouches may take up less space in landfills than the bottles do. They didn't like pouring the refill into their old spray bottles. Still, customers have accepted smaller packages of concentrated products such as laundry detergent, dishwashing liquid, and fabric softener.

What about the shape: Square? Round? Triangular? Hourglass? How about an old-fashioned apothecary that consumers can reuse as an attractive storage container? What color should it be? White to communicate purity? Yellow because it reminds people of lemon freshness? Brown because the flavor is chocolate? Sometimes these decisions trace back to irrelevant personal factors. The familiar Campbell's Soup label is red and white because a company executive many years ago liked the football uniforms at Cornell University!

Cheers!
There's big news for big and little sippers.

Great new designs. Great new colors.
They're the new Playtex® Sipster™Cups.
Available in your choice of spouts – one
designed for littler sippers. One for bigger
ones. And each our break-proof, spill-proof
best. Now that's something to cheer about.

Trademarks of Playtex Products, Inc.
©2004

Playtex®

FIRST SIPSTER•**SIPSTER**•SPARKLIN' SIPSTER•INSULATOR•BIG SIPSTER

In many cases, the package is part of the product's story.

Finally, what graphic information should the package show? Should there be a picture of the product on the package? Should cans of green beans always show a picture of green beans? Should there be a picture of the results of using the product, such as beautiful hair? Should there be a picture of the product in use, perhaps a box of crackers showing crackers with delicious-looking toppings arranged on a silver tray? Should there be a recipe or coupon on the back? Of course, all these decisions rest on a marketer's understanding of consumers, ingenuity, and perhaps a little creative luck.

Labeling Regulations

The Federal Fair Packaging and Labeling Act of 1966 controls package communications and labeling in the United States. This law aims at making labels more helpful to consumers by providing useful information. More recently, the requirements of the Nutrition Labeling and Education Act of 1990 have forced food marketers to make sweeping changes in how they label products. Since August 18, 1994, the U.S. Food and Drug Administration (FDA) has required most foods sold in the United States to have labels telling, among other things, how much fat, saturated fat, cholesterol, calories, carbohydrates, protein, and vitamins are in each serving of the product. These regulations are forcing marketers to be more accurate than before in describing their products. Juice makers, for example, must state how much of their product is real juice rather than sugar and water.

Starting on January 1, 2006, the FDA will also require that all food labels list the amount of trans fats in the food, directly under the line for saturated fat content. The new labeling reflects scientific evidence showing that consumption of trans fat, saturated fat, and dietary cholesterol raises "bad" cholesterol levels that increase the risk of coronary heart disease. The new information is the first significant change on the Nutrition Facts panel since it was established.[42]

Organizing for Effective Product Management

Of course, firms don't create great packaging, brands, or products—people do. Like all elements of the marketing mix, the effectiveness of product strategies depends on marketing managers. In this section, we'll talk about how firms organize for the management of existing products and for the development of new products.

Management of Existing Products

In small firms, the marketing function is usually handled by a single marketing manager responsible for new-product planning, advertising, working with the company's few sales representatives, marketing research, and just about everything else. But in larger firms such as Nissan, there are a number of managers like Mario A. Polit responsible for different brands, product categories, or markets. Depending on the organization, product management may include brand managers, product category managers, and market managers. Let's take a look at how each operates.

BRAND MANAGERS   Sometimes a firm has different brands within a single product category. For example, General Foods produces quite a few different brands of coffee, including Brim, Maxim, Maxwell House, International Coffees, Sanka, and Yuban. In such cases, each brand may have its own **brand manager.**

Procter & Gamble brand managers once acted independently and were responsible for coordinating all marketing activities for a brand: positioning, identifying target markets, research, distribution, sales promotion, packaging, and evaluating the success of these decisions. Today P&G's brand managers function more like team leaders. They still are responsible for positioning of brands and developing brand equity, but they are likely to work with sales, finance, and logistics staff members as a part of customer business teams working with major retail accounts.[43]

The brand management system is not without its own problems, however. Acting independently, brand managers may fight for increases in short-term sales for their own brand. They may push too hard with coupons, cents-off packages, or other price incentives to a point at which customers will refuse to buy the product without them. That can hurt long-term profitability.

PRODUCT CATEGORY MANAGERS   Some larger firms have such diverse product offerings that there is a need for extensive coordination. Take Eastman Kodak. Best known for its cameras, film, and other photography supplies, it also markets X-ray film and equipment, printers, motion picture film, and batteries.

In such cases, organizing for product management may include **product category managers** who coordinate the mix of product lines within the more general product category and who consider the addition of new-product lines. In recent years, both Procter & Gamble and Lever Brothers have consolidated brands under product category managers who are responsible for profit (or losses) within the category.[44]

MARKET MANAGERS   Some firms have developed a **market manager** structure in which different managers focus on specific customer groups rather than on the products the company makes. This type of organization can be useful when firms offer a variety of products that serve the needs of a wide range of customers. Take, for example, Raytheon, a company that specializes in consumer electronics products, special-mission aircraft, and business aviation. Raytheon sells some products directly to consumer markets, others to manufacturers, and still others to the government.[45]

Organizing for New-Product Development

Because launching new products is so important, the management of this process is a serious matter. In some instances, one person handles new-product development, but within larger organizations, new-product development almost always needs many people. One person, however, may be assigned the role of new-product manager. Often individuals who are assigned to manage new-product development are especially creative people with entrepreneurial skills.

The challenge in large companies is to get specialists in different areas to work together in **venture teams.** These teams focus exclusively on the new-product development effort. Sometimes the venture team is located away from traditional company offices, usually in a remote location called a "skunk works." This colorful term originated with the Skonk Works, an illicit distillery in the comic strip "Li'l Abner." Because illicit distilleries were bootleg operations, typically located in an isolated area with minimal formal oversight, the term has been adopted in organizational settings to refer to a usually small and often isolated department or facility that functions with minimal supervision.[46]

brand manager
An individual who is responsible for developing and implementing the marketing plan for a single brand.

product category managers
Individuals who are responsible for developing and implementing the marketing plan for all the brands and products within a product category.

market manager
An individual who is responsible for developing and implementing the marketing plans for products sold to a particular customer group.

venture teams
Groups of people within an organization who work together focusing exclusively on the development of a new product.

How it Worked Out at Nissan North America, Inc.

Mario and the Xterra team chose option 1, the targeted creative and media campaign. It was hypothesized all along that crafting communication efforts that were specifically targeted to the "pure" outdoor enthusiasts and their lifestyle would not only clearly speak to the target but would resonate with other consumers outside the target who viewed the Xterra as empowering them to own a piece of the outdoor enthusiasts' lifestyle. The campaign entailed significant prelaunch and launch marketing activities, many of which were a first for an automotive brand.

Nissan parked Xterras at trail heads, surfing beaches, ski resorts, coffeehouses, and night spots to gain exposure among target consumers and to generate word-of-mouth "buzz." The company also sponsored the Xterra America Tour, a series of three off-road triathlons that included swimming, off-road biking, and off-road running and culminated in the Xterra Championship in Hawaii, aired on ESPN and CBS.

Nissan also established a unique Xterra Web site several months prior to launch where consumers could get advance incremental Xterra product information and register as "handraisers" (defined as those consumers who entered the Xterra database by providing their e-mail/mail addresses to be "kept

This ad for the Xterra was distributed prior to launch to build awareness and interest. It establishes the strategic positioning of the vehicle as a "no frills" SUV and is targeted to outdoors enthusiasts who participate actively in such sports as biking, mountain climbing, and kayaking.

in the loop" on updated product/launch information). And, finally, Nissan placed teaser ads with response cards in outdoors lifestyle–oriented printed media. After the launch, Nissan used television, print, and radio ads to market the product as well as outdoor venues, such as billboards and bus shelters. The prelaunch and launch campaigns were extremely targeted and focused, and the launch budget was relatively small, approximately two-thirds of what Jeep spends to support the established Cherokee model and about 5 percent of total SUV marketing dollars.

The result: Xterra launched very successfully. Sales were 133.8 percent of projections, and Nissan's SUV share more than doubled, from 4.3 to 8.9 percent. The positioning strategy was also successful because there was no apparent cannibalization of Pathfinder sales. Xterra has continued to sustain its sales volume, market share, and profitability despite competitive launches of the Toyota RAV 4, Ford Escape, Mazda Tribute, and Jeep Liberty. Annual sales are currently exceeding 80,000 units. And in model year 2002, Xterra received a considerable facelift and turbocharged engine. Marketing support and positioning have been sustained, building Xterra and Nissan brand equity with consumers. At launch, Mario was aware of at least 25 Xterra Web sites created by outdoor enthusiasts, and there are, at last count, 15 Xterra owners clubs in the United States. Nissan reaped the benefits of a well-integrated plan and "turbocharged" product launch.

How can you translate academics, internships, and work experience into skills that matter to employers? How does communicating your value sustain your career? To learn more, go to Chapter 9 in the *Brand You* supplement.

CHAPTER SUMMARY

1. **Explain the different product objectives and strategies a firm may choose.** Objectives for individual products may be related to introducing a new product, expanding the market of a regional product, or rejuvenating a mature product. For multiple products, firms may decide on a full- or a limited-line strategy. Often companies decide to extend their product line with an upward, downward, or two-way stretch or with a filling-out strategy, or they may decide to contract a product line. Firms that have multiple product lines may choose a wide product mix with many different lines or a narrow one with few. Product quality objectives refer to the durability, reliability, degree of precision, ease of use and repair, or degree of aesthetic pleasure.

2. **Explain how firms manage products throughout the product life cycle.** The product life cycle explains how products go through four stages from birth to death. During the introduction stage, marketers seek to get buyers to try the product and may use high prices to recover research and development costs. During the growth stage, characterized by rapidly increasing sales, marketers may introduce new-product variations. In the maturity stage, sales peak and level off. Marketers respond by adding desirable new-product features or with market development strategies. During the decline stage, firms must decide whether to phase a product out slowly, to drop it immediately, or, if there is residual demand, to keep the product.

3. **Discuss how branding creates product identity and describe different types of branding strategies.** A brand is a name, term, symbol, or other unique element of a product used to identify a firm's product. A brand should be selected that has a positive connotation and is recognizable and memorable. Brand names need to be easy to say, spell, read, and remember

and should fit the target market, the product's benefits, the customer's culture, and legal requirements. To protect a brand legally, marketers obtain trademark protection. Brands are important because they help maintain customer loyalty and because brand equity or value means a firm is able to attract new customers. Firms may develop individual brand strategies or market multiple items with a family or umbrella brand strategy. National or manufacturer brands are owned and sold by producers, whereas private-label or store brands carry the retail or chain store's trade name. Licensing means a firm sells another firm the right to use its brand name. In cobranding strategies, two brands form a partnership in marketing a new product.

4. **Explain the roles packaging and labeling play in developing effective product strategies.** Packaging is the covering or container for a product and serves to protect a product and to allow for easy use and storage of the product. The colors, words, shapes, designs, pictures, and materials used in package design communicate a product's identity, benefits, and other important product information. Package designers must consider cost, product protection, and communication in creating a package that is functional, aesthetically pleasing, and not harmful to the environment. Product labeling in the United States is controlled by a number of federal laws aimed at making package labels more helpful to consumers.

5. **Describe how organizations are structured for new and existing product management.** To successfully manage existing products, the marketing organization may include brand managers, product category managers, and market managers. Large firms, however, often give new-product responsibilities to new-product managers or to venture teams, groups of specialists from different areas who work together for a single new product.

KEY TERMS

brand, 276
brand equity, 277
brand extensions, 279
brand manager, 285
cannibalization, 267
cobranding, 281
decline stage, 274
family brand, 279
growth stage, 274
ingredient branding, 281

introduction stage, 272
ISO 14000, 269
ISO 9000, 269
Kansei engineering, 268
licensing, 280, 281
market manager, 285
maturity stage, 274
national or manufacturer brands, 280
package , 282
private-label brands, 280

product category managers, 285
product life cycle, 272
product line, 267
product mix, 268
total quality management (TQM), 268
trademark, 276
Universal Product Code (UPC), 282
venture teams, 285

CHAPTER REVIEW

MARKETING CONCEPTS: TESTING YOUR KNOWLEDGE

1. What are some reasons a firm might determine it should expand a product line? What are some reasons for contracting a product line? Why do many firms have a product mix strategy?

2. Why is quality such an important product strategy objective? What are the dimensions of product quality? How has e-commerce affected the need for quality product objectives?

3. Explain the product life cycle concept. What are the stages of the product life cycle?

4. How are products managed during the different stages of the product life cycle?

5. What is a brand? What are the characteristics of a good brand name? How do firms protect their brands?

6. What is a national brand? A store brand? Individual and family brands?

7. What does it mean to license a brand? What is cobranding?

8. What are the functions of packaging? What are some important elements of effective package design?

9. What should marketers know about package labeling?

10. Describe some of the different ways firms organize the marketing function to manage existing products. What are the ways firms organize for the development of new products?

MARKETING CONCEPTS: DISCUSSING CHOICES AND ISSUES

1. Brand equity means that a brand enjoys customer loyalty, perceived quality, and brand name awareness. What brands are you personally loyal to? What is it about the product that creates brand loyalty and, thus, brand equity?

2. Quality is an important product objective, but quality can mean different things for different products, such as durability, precision, aesthetic appeal, and so on. What does quality mean for the following products?
   a. Automobile
   b. Pizza
   c. Running shoes
   d. Hair dryer
   e. Deodorant
   f. College education

3. Many times firms take advantage of their popular, well-known brands by developing brand extensions because they know that the brand equity of the original or parent brand will be transferred to the new product. If a new product is of poor quality, it can damage the reputation of the parent brand while a new product that is of superior quality can enhance the parent brand's reputation. What are some examples of brand extensions that have damaged and that have enhanced the parent brand equity?

4. Sometimes marketers seem to stick with the same packaging ideas year after year regardless of whether they are the best possible design. Following is a list of products. For each one, discuss what, if any, problems you have with the package of the brand you use. Then think of ways the package could be improved. Why do you think marketers don't change the old packaging? What would be the results if they adopted your package ideas?
   a. Dry cereal
   b. Laundry detergent
   c. Frozen orange juice
   d. Gallon of milk
   e. Potato chips
   f. Loaf of bread

MARKETING PRACTICE: APPLYING WHAT YOU'VE LEARNED

1. The Internet allows consumers to interact directly with other people so they can praise products they like and slam those they don't. With several of your classmates, conduct a brief survey of students and of older consumers. Find out if consumers complain to each other about poor product quality. Have they ever used a Web site to express their displeasure over product quality? Make a report to your class.

2. You may think of your college or university as an organization that offers a line of different educational products. Assume that you have been hired as a marketing consultant by your university to examine and make recommendations for extending its product line. Develop alternatives that the university might consider:
   a. Upward line stretch
   b. Downward line stretch
   c. Two-way stretch
   d. Filling-out strategy

   Describe how each might be accomplished. Evaluate each alternative.

3. Assume that you are the vice president of marketing for a firm that markets a large number of specialty food items (gourmet sauces, marinades, relishes, and so on). Your firm is interested in improving its marketing management structure. You are considering several alternatives: a brand manager structure, having product line managers, or focusing on market managers. Outline the advantages and disadvantages of each type of organization. What is your recommendation?

4. Assume that you are working in the marketing department of a major manufacturer of athletic shoes. Your firm is introducing a new product, a line of disposable sports clothing. You wonder if it would be better to market the line of clothing with a new brand name or use the family brand name that has already gained popularity with your existing products. Make a list of the advantages and disadvantages of each strategy. Develop your recommendation.

5. Assume that you have been recently hired by Kellogg, the cereal manufacturer. You have been asked to work on a plan for redesigning the packaging for Kellogg's cereals. In a role-playing situation, present the following report to your marketing superior:
   a. Discussion of the problems or complaints customers have with current packaging
   b. Several different package alternatives
   c. Your recommendations for changing packaging or for keeping the packaging the same

MARKETING MINIPROJECT: LEARNING BY DOING

In any supermarket in any town, you will surely find examples of all the different types of brands discussed in this chapter: individual brands, family brands, national brands, store brands, and cobranded and licensed products. This miniproject is designed to give you a better understanding of branding as it exists in the marketplace.

1. Go to a typical supermarket in your community.
2. Select two product categories of interest to you: ice cream, cereal, laundry detergent, soup, paper products, and so on.
3. Make a list of the brands available in each product category. Identify what type of brand each is. Count the number of shelf facings (the number of product items at the front of each shelf) for each brand.

4. Arrange to talk with the store manager at a time that is convenient with him or her. Ask the manager to discuss the following:
   a. How the store decides which brands to carry
   b. Whether the store is more likely to carry a new brand that is an individual brand versus a family brand
   c. What causes a store to drop a brand
   d. The profitability of store brands versus national brands
   e. Other aspects of branding that the store manager sees as important from a retail perspective
5. Present a report to your class on what you learned about the brands in your two product categories.

REAL PEOPLE, REAL SURFERS: EXPLORING THE WEB

As we discussed in this chapter and in Chapter 8, companies protect their products by obtaining patents and legal protection for their brands with trademarks. The U.S. Patent and Trademark Office issues both of these forms of protection. Visit the Patent Office Web site at **www.uspto.gov**. Use the Internet site to answer the following questions.

1. What is a patent? What can be patented?
2. Who may apply for a patent? Can foreign individuals or companies obtain a U.S. patent? Explain.
3. What happens if someone infringes on a patent?
4. What does the term *patent pending* mean?

5. What is a trademark? What is a service mark?
6. Who may file a trademark application? Do firms have to register a trademark? Explain.
7. What do the symbols TM, SM, and ® mean?
8. What are the benefits of federal trademark registration?
9. What are common-law rights regarding trademarks?
10. How long does a trademark registration last? How long does a patent last?
11. How would you evaluate the Patent and Trademark Office Web site? Was it easy to navigate? Was it useful? What recommendations do you have for improving the Web site?

MARKETING PLAN EXERCISE

Dr. Pepper is an interesting brand with a long history (the history is worth reading—go to **www.drpepper.com**, then click on "About Us" and then "Our Story"). Suffice it to say, it is the oldest soft-drink brand in the United States. Assume for a moment that Cadbury Schweppes, the London-based firm that owns Dr. Pepper, is doing some marketing planning involving this brand.

1. What are some product line strategies you might suggest that Dr. Pepper consider?
2. How important is TQM and product quality in general to a brand like Dr. Pepper? How do these issues play into their marketing plan?

3. Take a look at the different Dr. Pepper products portrayed on their Web site. Where does each fall on the product life cycle? What leads you to conclude this?
4. What realistic opportunities do you believe exist for brand extensions for Dr. Pepper? Explain how they might go about introducing each to the market.
5. Does Dr. Pepper have high brand equity? What evidence do you have for your answer? What can Dr. Pepper do to enhance their brand equity, given the 800-pound gorillas they compete against (Coke and Pepsi)?

Marketing in Action Case

Real Choices at Samsung

How does a company go in less than six years from a financially strapped, perennial "also-ran" with a reputation for producing cheap, me-too products to one that produces some of the most highly sought-after products in its industry and wins product design awards? Well, if you are Samsung Electronics, you do it by cranking up the product innovation process to develop and introduce hundreds of new products based on the latest technology available and getting those products to market before any of your competitors. The Samsung of today is producing premium priced, feature-jammed products and has become one of the most-watched competitors by rivals Sony, Panasonic, and Mitsubishi.

Samsung manufactures products in three primary areas of electronic component manufacturing: audio, data, and imaging. These products include televisions, cell phones, digital music players, personal digital assistants (PDAs), DVD players, camcorders, camera phones, phone/PDA combinations, complete home theater systems—the list goes on and on. In each of these product categories, Samsung provides many different models, thus extending the company's product length. In addition to developing new products for the marketplace, Samsung has executed an upward line stretch strategy with its products. Instead of selling at discount stores, Samsung products are now sold at stores like Best Buy, Circuit City, and Sears.

In addition, the company has vastly upgraded the quality of its products and has begun to include more features desired by consumers. That upgrade has resulted in their products commanding premium prices. For example, in the highly competitive cell phone arena, Samsung phones, on average, command a 24 percent price premium over those of its closest competitor, Nokia. Furthermore, among the market for large, high-definition, flat-panel TVs, those selling for $3,000 or above, Samsung is the best-selling brand. The company's products have been featured in hit movies such as *The Matrix: Reloaded*, and its business partners include many well-respected companies such as Dell and Microsoft. Clearly, Samsung's product strategy has been executed very well to this point.

Despite Samsung's recent success, it will have to determine how to maintain its growth in an industry where stalwarts like Sony, Mitsubishi, and Toshiba have faltered. The product life cycle in this industry is extremely short, and many companies have had trouble keeping up in the past. Even though Samsung has reduced its new product development time from 14 months to 5 months and refreshes its product line every 9 months, that still may not be fast enough. Samsung may want to consider expanding its product line downward and go back to offering lower-quality and lower-priced goods to sell in stores like Wal-Mart and Target. Many consumers purchase electronic equipment in these stores, so why shouldn't Samsung provide a product line that can be sold profitably to discount store retailers? However, the downward line stretch strategy could have serious consequences on the brand equity that Samsung has worked so hard to develop over the past several years. Clearly, Samsung company executives have many options for how to move forward, and the choices these executives will have to make in the future are anything but obvious.

Things to Think About

1. What is the decision facing Samsung?
2. What factors are important in understanding this decision situation?
3. What are the alternatives?
4. What decision(s) do you recommend?
5. What are some ways to implement your recommendation(s)?

Source: Cliff Edwards, Moon Ihlwan, and Pete Engardio, "The Samsung Way," *Business Week*, June 16, 2003, 56–64.

www.universalstudios.com

UNIVERSAL STUDIOS®

MARDI GRAS

SHAKE IT, GROOVE IT AND JUST PLAIN MOVE IT!

The Party kicks off in the Yard at 6:00 pm.

TONIGHT ONLY -
2 additional jumbo screens
for concert viewing.

See Mardi Gras map on other side for details.

The following attractions will stay open until 10 pm tonight!
E.T. Adventure® • Earthquake®-The Big One • Shrek 4-D™
Jimmy Neutron's Nicktoon Blast™ • Twister...Ride It Out®

real people, real choices

meet Robyn Eichenholz,
a Decision Maker at one of
Universal's Theme Parks in Orlando

first job out of school	career high
Sales assistant at COOL 105.9FM, the Oldies station.	Being assigned the "crown jewel" event at Universal Orlando: Halloween Horror Nights® and attaining record-breaking results for the company.

SERVICES AND OTHER INTANGIBLES: MARKETING THE PRODUCT THAT ISN'T THERE

Robyn Eichenholz is senior brand manager at Universal Orlando® in Orlando, Florida. She graduated in 1993 from the University of Florida with a B.S. in advertising. Her first job was as a sales assistant at a local radio station, where she worked her way up to account executive. Before joining Universal, Robyn also was employed at an advertising agency in Orlando as well as at Walt Disney World, where she worked in the Direct Marketing and Travel Industry Marketing departments.

Robyn started at Universal Orlando in 1997, where she watched the organization grow from having one theme park to a resort destination with two theme parks, an entertainment complex, and three on-site hotels. During her tenure at Universal, she has worked in Travel Industry Marketing, Advertising, Annual Pass, Sales Development, and Brand Marketing. In November 2003, she was promoted to senior brand manager of Universal's Islands of Adventure®. In her current position, she is responsible for maximizing attendance and earnings at the theme parks (both Universal Studios and Islands of Adventure) by developing and promoting special events and ensuring that the brand vision is recognized and aligned in communication pieces.

Decision Time at Universal Studios

One of Robyn's responsibilities is to supervise added value or special ticket events in the parks. These usually are special productions related to a holiday like Halloween or Christmas. Some of the events are included when guests buy a regular admission ticket to the theme park. Other events require a separate ticket. One of the added value events is called Mardi Gras. This is modeled after a Mardi Gras experience in New Orleans, complete with an opening concert, a Mardi Gras parade with authentic floats from New Orleans, and a final concert. Guests can enjoy the park all day and then party at Mardi Gras in the evening.

In 2004, Universal Studios held its Mardi Gras on seven consecutive Saturdays starting in February. The last concert was slated to feature a performance by Donna Summer. Soon after the Mardi Gras nights got under way, the buzz about this concert started to grow. The singer had not been in concert for a while, and Robyn knew that Summer's music was very appealing to the park's annual pass-holder base. Many of these customers were sure to be attracted to such a concert.

my motto to live by	my management style	don't do this when interviewing with me	my pet peeve
Good things come to good people.	Collaborative.	Not know the product or have a typo on your résumé.	Typos/poor-quality work.

Guests don't need to purchase tickets specifically for the Mardi Gras event since admission is included in a regular ticket. While Robyn guessed there would be a large turnout for the last Mardi Gras celebration when Donna Summer would be appearing, she had no data on which to base a reliable forecast of attendance. The guest experience is very important to the park's management, and they monitor people's satisfaction with each and every event very carefully. If the park was going to see record-breaking attendance, accommodations would have to be made to ensure that guests had a good experience. It would be important to anticipate the expected attendance and do as much advance planning as possible if special arrangements were needed. Since Robyn was the project leader, it was her job to coordinate with other departments (such as Operations) to decide how to plan for the Donna Summer concert.

Robyn considered her options:

OPTION 1: Don't make any special plans for the event.

The initial buzz about the concert was positive, and the park was used to handling large numbers of people every day. While Robyn considered adding A-frame or LED signage on the roads and within the parks, adding viewing screens, changing the parade route, and moving food and beverage carts to better accommodate the guests, these arrangements would cost money and might not be necessary. On the other hand, if larger-than-expected numbers of people started to flood the park the night of the concert, it would be too late to make special arrangements. In addition, a lack of planning might result in a less positive experience for guests who had to put up with heavy traffic and long lines for concessions and restrooms. Robyn knew that one bad experience often is enough to make a guest decide not to return to a theme park.

OPTION 2: Create a plan to accommodate extremely large crowds both in the entry to the parking garages and roads to Universal and within the park.

By thinking through possible scenarios, all departments involved (Operations, Entertainment, Revenue Operations, and Marketing) could better plan for crowding. Guests could have a better experience and more fun. But these adjustments would require additional unbudgeted expenses. If attendance was lower than expected, this money would be wasted and Universal Studios might lose revenue. Robyn's job was to help make money for Universal Studios, not lose it.

OPTION 3: Publicize the big expected turnout in advance to let guests know that the event might be exceptionally crowded.

This strategy would let the park manage guests' expectations and therefore discourage people who do not like overly crowded events from attending. In addition, guests who did choose to come would know that they had to arrive at the park early in order to get a good spot, meaning fewer frustrated fans. On the other hand, this idea was risky because if people read in the newspaper that the event was likely to be really crowded, it was possible that a lot of people wouldn't show up. Robyn thought about the old expression to describe why a restaurant was empty: "Nobody goes there anymore; it's too crowded." She was afraid the plan might work *too* well and she would be faced with an empty park on the night of the big concert.

Now, put yourself in Robyn Eichenholz's shoes: Which option would you choose, and why?

Marketing What Isn't There

Instead of something tangible like toothpaste or a new car, the product that Universal Theme Park is selling is an experience. Robyn Eichenholz understands the challenges of marketing what people can't touch. As a senior brand manager, she realizes that a customer's decision to visit a theme park for a concert or other special event is based on a number of different considerations. And if the experience isn't a good one, future sales just won't happen. That's why it's important to successfully meet challenges the first time.

These same challenges apply to other types of consumer experiences. For example, what do a Coldplay concert, a college education, and a football game have in common? Like the Mardi Gras night at Universal, each is a product that combines experiences with physical goods to create an event that the buyer consumes. You can't have a concert without instruments, a college education without textbooks (Thursday night parties don't count), or a pigskin showdown without the pigskin. But these tangibles are secondary to the primary product, which is some act that, in these cases, produces enjoyment, knowledge, or excitement.

This chapter will consider some of the challenges and opportunities facing marketers such as Robyn Eichenholz, whose primary offerings are **intangibles**. Intangibles are services and other experience-based products that cannot be touched. The marketer whose job it is to build and sell a better football, automobile, or MP3 player—all tangibles—must deal with different issues than someone who wants to sell tickets to a football game, limousine service to the airport, or a hot new rock star. In the first part of this chapter, we'll discuss services, a type of intangible that also happens to be the fastest-growing sector in our economy. As we'll see, all services are intangible, but not all intangibles are services. Then we'll move into other types of intangibles.

intangibles
Experience-based products that cannot be touched.

Does Marketing Work for Intangibles?

Does marketing work only for companies that sell laundry detergent and automobiles, or does it apply to many types of "products," including politicians, the arts, and the places we live and visit? We might look to the Boston Symphony Orchestra (BSO) for an answer. Beginning in 1998, the BSO began an integrated marketing program designed to attract younger audiences.[1] Marketing research found that whereas older audiences were avid readers of magazines and books, younger audiences preferred the Internet and electronic media, so BSO's new marketing campaign included broadcast commercials, taxi-top ads (to promote a specific concert date or performance), customized Internet infomercials, and e-mail. The result? BSO increased sales from $16.7 million in 1997 to over $19 million in 2002. Yes, marketing does work for intangibles.

Even an intangible such as electric power, normally thought of as a commodity, is now branded and marketed directly to consumers. In an increasing number of states, customers are allowed to pick an electricity supplier from several competitors as deregulation of the industry continues. The first national energy brand was EnergyOne, introduced in 1995 by UtiliCorp United. Cinergy Corp. of Cincinnati paid $6 million to gain brand exposure by renaming the city's Riverfront Stadium to Cinergy Field.[2] Energy company Enron, at the time the seventh-largest firm in the United States, paid to have a stadium in Houston named after it. Unfortunately, the energy giant's subsequent bankruptcy scandal prompted the Astros to pay Enron $2.1 million in 2002 to buy back the naming rights to the stadium. The Enron name had to be removed from all brochures, the stadium Web site, and all publicity photos of the Astros team.[3] (The only consolation is that the firm's demise may have been the fault of the accountants, the chief executive officer [CEO], and the former CEO but not the marketers.)

Sound marketing concepts don't apply only to companies looking to make a buck or two. Indeed, not-for-profit organizations, including charities, zoos, museums, and youth organizations, increasingly are thinking about branding and image building. The not-for-profit sector consists of 546,000 organizations with 9.7 million employees, so competition for customers and donors is fierce. These organizations have to come up with new marketing strategies all the time. When Goodwill wanted to increase donations to its clothing bins, it redesigned its smiling face logo and added a new headline, "Helping Create a Better Community." Clothing donations increased by 10 percent after the change.[4]

Still, some producers of intangibles have been slow to accept the idea that what they do *should* be marketed. Many people who work in health care, the legal profession, or the arts resist the notion that the quality of what they produce and the demand for their services are affected by the same market forces driving the fortunes of paper producers, food canners, or even power utilities. Do you agree?

Let's take a quick look at how some basic marketing concepts would apply to an artistic product. Suppose a local theater company wanted to increase attendance at its performances.

New York feeds all of us in its own way. Now it's time for us to help City Harvest feed the hungry of New York.

WILL WORK FOR FOOD

When you support City Harvest, your dollars help rescue and deliver food for working families, seniors and children. In the past year alone, New York's hunger rate increased dramatically, with 1 of every 5 people unsure of their next meal. So make a financial donation to City Harvest today.

To donate by credit card, call 1 800 77-HARVEST

CITY HARVEST

Many not-for-profit organizations, including charities, know that marketing is key to their success.

Remembering the basics of developing a strategic plan (Chapter 2), here are some marketing actions the organization might take to realize its goals:[5]

- The organization could develop a *mission statement,* such as "We seek to be the premier provider of quality theater in the region."

- A *SWOT analysis* could include an assessment of the organization's strengths and weaknesses and the environmental threats and opportunities. The arts marketer is, after all, competing for the consumer's discretionary dollar against other theater groups. The marketer is also up against other forms of entertainment the consumer might choose instead of going to a play at all, from attending an Outkast concert to a Tom Cruise movie to a pro wrestling match.

- The theater company should use information obtained in the SWOT analysis to develop a number of concrete measurable *objectives,* such as to "increase the number of season ticket holders by 20 percent over the next two years."

- Next, the organization must develop marketing strategies. For example, it must consider which *target markets* it wishes to attract. If audience levels for its plays have been fairly stable for several years, it should consider developing new markets for its performances. This might lead to product modifications as some opera companies do when they project English translations above the stage to draw new patrons who are unfamiliar with opera's foreign tongues.

As you can see, by using some marketing savvy and a strategic plan, an organization such as a theater can better reach its goals. More important, service organizations can be sure they are successfully meeting the needs of their "customers."

What Is a Service?

As we've said, marketing can help sell all kinds of intangibles, from theater performances to ideas about birth control. But first, let's take a look at services, an important type of intangible.

services
Intangible products that are exchanged directly from the producer to the customer.

Services are acts, efforts, or performances exchanged from producer to user without ownership rights. Like other intangibles, a service satisfies needs by providing pleasure, information, or convenience. In 2004, service industry jobs accounted for 83 percent of all employment in the United States[6] and over 67 percent of the gross domestic product (GDP).[7] If you pursue a marketing career, it's likely that you will work in some aspect of services marketing. Got your interest?

Of course, the service industry includes services provided for consumers, such as dry cleaning and a great rock concert. But it also includes a vast number of services provided for organizations. Some of the more commonly used business services include vehicle leasing, computer technology services, insurance, security, legal advice, food services, consulting, cleaning, and maintenance. In addition, businesses also purchase some of the same services as consumers, such as electricity, telephone service, and gas.

The market for business services has grown rapidly because it is often more cost effective for organizations to hire outside firms that specialize in these services than to try to hire a workforce and handle the service themselves. In other instances, firms buy business services because they do not have the expertise necessary to provide the service.

Characteristics of Services

Services come in many forms, from those done to you, such as a massage or a teeth cleaning, to those done to something you own, such as having your DVD player repaired or getting a new paint job on your classic 1965 Mustang. Regardless of whether they affect our bodies or our possessions, all services share four characteristics: intangibility, perishability, inseparability, and variability. Table 10.1 shows how marketers can address the unique issues related to these characteristics of services that don't pop up when they deal with tangible goods.

INTANGIBILITY Service **intangibility** is the characteristic of a service that means customers can't see, touch, or smell good service. Unlike the purchase of a tangible good, services cannot be inspected or handled before the purchase is made. This makes many services much more difficult for consumers to evaluate. Although it may be easy to evaluate your new haircut, it is far less easy to determine whether the dental hygienist has done a great job cleaning your teeth.

Because they're buying something that isn't there, customers look for reassuring signs before purchasing, and marketers must ensure that these signs are readily available. That's why marketers seek to overcome the problem of intangibility by providing physical cues to reassure the buyer. These cues might be the "look" of the facility, its furnishings, logo, stationery, business cards, the appearance of its employees, and well-designed advertising and Web sites, just to name a few.

PERISHABILITY Service **perishability** refers to the characteristic of a service that makes it impossible to store for later sale or consumption—it's a case of use it or lose it. When rooms go unoccupied at a ski resort, there is no way to make up for the lost opportunity to rent them for the weekend. Marketers try to avoid these problems by using the marketing mix to encourage demand for the service during slack times. One option is to reduce prices to increase demand for otherwise unsold services. Airlines do this by offering more lower-priced seats in the final weeks before a

intangibility
The characteristic of a service that means customers can't see, touch, or smell good service.

perishability
The characteristic of a service that makes it impossible to store for later sale or consumption.

Table 10.1	Marketing Strategies for Different Service Characteristics
Characteristic	**Marketing Response**
Intangibility	Provide tangibility through physical appearance of the facility
	Furnishings
	Employee uniforms
	Logo
	Web sites
	Advertising
Perishability	Adjust pricing to influence demand
	Adjust services to match demand (capacity management)
Variability	Institute total quality management programs
	Offer service guarantees
	Conduct gap analysis to identify gaps in quality
Inseparability	Train employees on successful service encounters
	Explore means for disintermediation

capacity management
The process by which organizations adjust their offerings in an attempt to match demand.

flight. TV stations offer advertisers low-priced airtime at the last minute. We'll talk more about these pricing tactics in Chapter 11.

Capacity management is the process by which organizations adjust their services in an attempt to match demand. Capacity management may mean adjusting the product, or it may mean adjusting the price. In the summer, for example, the Winter Park Ski Resort in Colorado combats its perishability problem by opening its lifts to mountain bikers who tear down the sunny slopes.[8] Rental car companies offer discounts on days of the week when business travel is light, and many hotels offer special weekend packages to increase weekend occupancy rates.

Even movie theaters are starting to catch on to the idea of encouraging greater usage of their facilities during weeknights when they often show films to a few people at a time: When Prince started his "Musicology" tour in the spring of 2004, the cheapest concert ticket was $49.50. But fans who wanted a version of "Prince Lite" attended the concert as it was simulcast in a chain of movie theaters where tickets went for $15.00. One-night-only broadcasts of performances by top acts like Linkin Park, Beyoncé, and Gloria Estefan are in the works.[9]

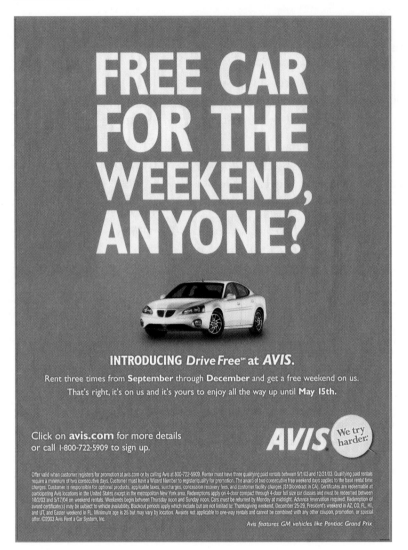

FREE CAR FOR THE WEEKEND, ANYONE?

INTRODUCING *Drive Free*℠ at **AVIS**.

Rent three times from **September** through **December** and get a free weekend on us. That's right, it's on us and it's yours to enjoy all the way up until **May 15th**.

Click on **avis.com** for more details or call 1-800-722-5909 to sign up.

AVIS We try harder®

Offer valid when customer registers for promotion at avis.com or by calling Avis at 800-722-5909. Renter must have three qualifying paid rentals between 9/1/03 and 12/31/03. Qualifying paid rentals require a minimum of two consecutive days. Customer must have a Wizard Number to register/qualify for promotion. The award of two consecutive free weekend days applies to the base rental time charges. Customer is responsible for optional products, applicable taxes, surcharges, concession recovery fees, and customer facility charges ($10/contract in CA). Certificates are redeemable at participating Avis locations in the United States except in the metropolitan New York area. Redemptions apply on 4-door compact through 4-door full size car classes and must be redeemed between 10/2/03 and 5/17/04 on weekend rentals. Weekends begin between Thursday noon and Sunday noon. Cars must be returned by Monday at midnight. Advance reservation required. Redemption of award certificate(s) may be subject to vehicle availability. Blackout periods apply which include but are not limited to: Thanksgiving weekend, December 25-29, President's weekend in AZ, CO, FL, HI, and UT, and Easter weekend in FL. Minimum age is 25 but may vary by location. Awards not applicable to one-way rentals and cannot be combined with any other coupon, promotion, or special offer. ©2003 Avis Rent a Car System, Inc.

Avis features GM vehicles like Pontiac Grand Prix

One way to counter the effects of perishability is to develop strategies that make use of excess capacity during low-demand periods. Avis, for example, offers free weekends (when demand for rental cars is lowest) to increase sales among its high-usage customers.

VARIABILITY An NFL quarterback may be "hot" one Sunday and ice cold the next, and the same is true for most services. Service **variability** is the characteristic of a service that means that even the same service performed by the same individual for the same customer can vary. This means that there may be inevitable differences in a service provider's performances over time. It's rare when you get *exactly* the same cut from a hairstylist.

It is difficult to standardize services because service providers and customers vary. Think about your experiences in your college classes. A school can standardize its offerings to some degree—course catalogs, course content, and classrooms are fairly controllable. Professors, however, vary in their training, life experiences, and personalities, so there is little hope of being able to make teaching uniform (not that this would

variability
The characteristic of a service that means that even the same service performed by the same individual for the same customer can vary.

necessarily be desirable anyway). And because students with different backgrounds and interests vary in their needs, the lecture that one finds fascinating might put another to sleep (trust us on this). The same is true for customers of organizational services. Differences in the quality of individual security guards or cleaning personnel mean variability in how these services get delivered.

In fact, we don't necessarily *want* standardization when we purchase a service. Most of us want a hairstyle that fits our face and personality and a personal trainer who will address our unique physical training needs. Businesses like McDonald's, Wendy's, and Burger King want unique advertising campaigns. Because of the nature of the tasks performed in services, customers often appreciate the firm that customizes its service for each individual (as Burger King used to promise, "Have it your way . . . ").

One solution to the problem of variability is to institute total quality management (TQM) programs for continuous improvement of service quality. As you learned in Chapter 1, TQM is a management effort to involve all employees from the assembly line onward in continuous product quality improvement. In addition to instituting TQM programs, offering service guarantees assures consumers that if service quality fails, they will be compensated. We'll talk later in the chapter about how service marketers can provide greater quality and consistency in service delivery through gap analysis and employee empowerment.

inseparability
The characteristic of a service that means that it is impossible to separate the production of a service from the consumption of that service.

INSEPARABILITY **Inseparability** is the characteristic of a service meaning that it is impossible to separate the production of a service from the consumption of that service. Although a firm can manufacture goods prior to sale, a service can take place only at the time the service provider performs an act on either the customer or the customer's possession. It's hard to take notes on a lecture when the professor doesn't show. In some cases, of course, the service can be sold prior to delivery, such as a ticket to a Red Sox game months before attending the event.

Still, the expertise, skill, and personality of a provider or the quality of a firm's employees, facilities, and equipment cannot be detached from the offering itself. The central role played by employees in making or breaking a service underscores the importance of the **service encounter**, or the interaction between the customer and the service provider.[10] The most expertly cooked meal is just plain mush if a surly or incompetent waiter brings it to the table. We'll talk more about the importance of service providers later in this chapter.

To minimize the potentially negative effects of bad service encounters and to save on labor costs, some service businesses are experimenting with **disintermediation**, which eliminates the need for customers to interact with people at all. Examples include self-service gas tanks and bank ATM machines. Even salad and dessert bars reduce reliance on a waiter or waitress. Although some consumers resist dealing with machines, pumping their own gas, or fixing their own salad, most prefer the speed and efficiency provided by disintermediation. The remaining consumers who want a Caesar salad prepared table-side or a fill-up that includes an oil check and a clean windshield provide marketing opportunities for full-service restaurants and the few gas stations that still provide these higher levels of service—usually at a higher price.

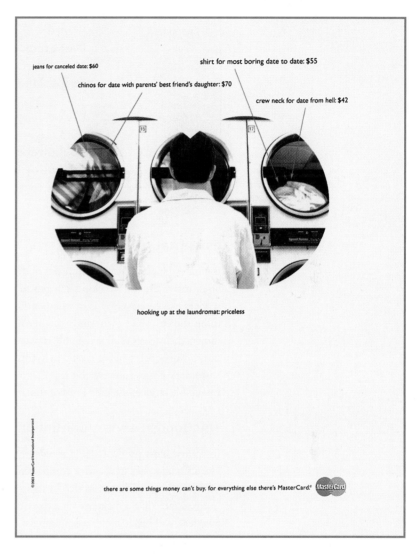

jeans for canceled date: $60

shirt for most boring date to date: $55

chinos for date with parents' best friend's daughter: $70

crew neck for date from hell: $42

hooking up at the laundromat: priceless

there are some things money can't buy. for everything else there's MasterCard.® MasterCard

Mastercard emphasizes the tangible benefits of its product, while recognizing that other outcomes are intangible or "priceless."

service encounter
The actual interaction between the customer and the service provider.

disintermediation
Eliminating the interaction between customers and salespeople so as to minimize negative service encounters.

The Internet has provided opportunities for disintermediation, especially in the financial services area. Banking customers can access their accounts, transfer funds from one account to another, and pay their bills with the click of a mouse. Many busy consumers can check out mortgage interest rates and even apply for a loan at their convenience—a much better option than taking an afternoon off from work to sit in a mortgage company office. Online brokerage services are increasingly popular as many consumers seek to handle their investments themselves, thus eliminating the commission a full-service brokerage firm would charge.

Figure 10.1 Classification of Services by Inputs and Tangibility

Services can be classified according to whether the customer or his or her possessions are the recipient of the service and as to whether the service itself consists of tangible or intangible elements.

	Tangible Services	*Intangible Services*
Customer	Hair cut	College education
	Plastic surgery	A religious service
	Manicure	A TV program
	Personal trainer	A flower arranging course
		Marriage counseling
Possessions	Dry cleaning	Banking
	Auto repair	Accounting services
	Housecleaning	Insurance
	Package delivery	Home security service

Classification of Services

By understanding the characteristics of different types of services and just which type of service they offer, marketers can develop strategies to ramp up customer satisfaction. As shown in Figure 10.1, services may be classified as to whether the service is performed directly on the customer or on something the customer owns and whether the service consists of tangible or intangible actions. Customers themselves receive tangible services to their bodies—a haircut or a heart transplant. The education (we hope!) you are receiving in this course is an intangible service directed at the consumer. A customer's possessions are the recipient of such tangible services as the repair of a favorite carpet. Intangible services directed at a consumer's possessions include insurance and home security.

The Goods/Services Continuum

In reality, most products are a *combination* of goods and services. The purchase of a "pure good" like a Cadillac still has service components, such as bringing it to the dealer for maintenance work or using its new OnStar service to figure out how to find the dealer's location. The purchase of a "pure service" like a makeover at a department store has product components, for example, lotions, powders, and lipsticks the cosmetologist uses to create the "new you."

The service continuum in Figure 10.2 shows that some products are dominated by either tangible or intangible elements, such as salt versus teaching, whereas others tend to include a mixture of goods and services, such as flying in an airplane. A product's placement on this continuum gives some guidance as to which marketing issues are most likely to be relevant. As the product approaches the tangible pole of this continuum, there is fairly little emphasis on service. The physical product itself is the focal point, and people will choose one option over others because of the product's function or image.

But as the product gets near the intangible pole, the issues we've discussed such as intangibility and inseparability play a key role in shaping the service experience. In the middle of the continuum, both goods and services contribute substantially to the quality of the product because these products rely on people to satisfactorily operate equipment that will in turn deliver quality service. Let's consider each of these three positions as we move from products dominated by tangibles to those dominated by intangibles.

GOODS-DOMINATED PRODUCTS Many tangible products are accompanied by supporting services, even if this means only that the company maintains a toll-free telephone line for questions or provides a 30-day warranty against defects. Today, with an increasingly competitive global market-

Figure 10.2 The Service Continuum

Products vary in their level of tangibility. Salt is a tangible product, teaching is an intangible product, and the products offered by fast-food restaurants include both tangible and intangible elements.

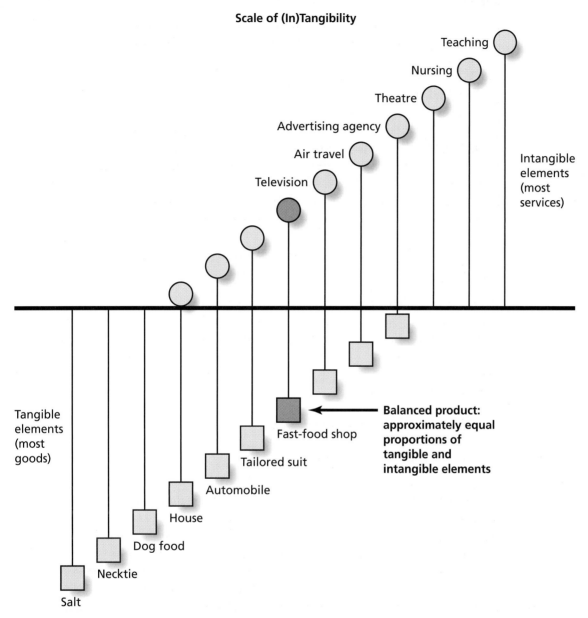

Scale of (In)Tangibility

Teaching

Nursing

Theatre

Advertising agency

Air travel

Television

Intangible elements (most services)

Tangible elements (most goods)

Fast-food shop

← **Balanced product: approximately equal proportions of tangible and intangible elements**

Tailored suit

Automobile

House

Dog food

Necktie

Salt

Source: Adapted from G. Lynn Shostack, "How to Design a Service," *European Journal of Marketing* 16, no. 1 (1982): 52.

place, providing services is more important than ever for those who sell tangible products. Automobile, home appliance, and electronics firms can realize a major competitive advantage when they provide customers with service that is better than that provided by the competition. Services may be even more important for marketers of business-to-business tangibles. Business customers often will not even consider buying from manufacturers who don't provide services like employee training and equipment maintenance. For example, hospitals that buy lifesaving patient care and monitoring equipment costing hundreds of thousands of dollars demand not only in-service training of their nursing and technician personnel, but also regular maintenance of the equipment if needed and quick response to breakdowns.

EQUIPMENT- OR FACILITY-BASED SERVICES   As we see in Figure 10.2, some products include a mixture of tangible and intangible elements. While a restaurant is a balanced product because it includes the preparation and delivery of the food to your table plus the food itself, the tangible elements of the service are less evident for other products. Many hospitals and hotels fall in the middle of the continuum not because customers take a tangible good away from the service encounter but because these organizations rely on expensive equipment or facilities to deliver a product. Facility-driven services, such as automatic car washes, amusement parks, museums, movie theaters, health clubs, tanning salons, and zoos, must be concerned with the following three factors:[11]

- **Operational factors:** Clear signs and other guidelines must show customers how to use the service. In particular, firms need to minimize waiting times. Marketers have developed a number of tricks to give impatient customers the illusion that they aren't waiting too long. One hotel chain, responding to complaints about the long wait for elevators, installed mirrors in the lobby: People tended to check themselves out until the elevators arrived, and lo and behold, protests decreased.[12] Burger King's research showed that multiple lines create stress in customers—especially if one moves faster than the others—so it shifted to single lines in which customers at the head of the line order at the next available register. Now if supermarkets would only do the same!

- **Locational factors:** These are especially important for frequently purchased services, such as dry cleaning or retail banking, that are obtained at a fixed spot. When you select a bank, a restaurant, or a health club, its location often factors into your decision. Marketers of these services make sure their service sites are convenient and in neighborhoods that are attractive to prospective customers.

- **Environmental factors:** Service managers who operate a storefront service requiring people to come to their location realize they must create an attractive environment to lure customers. That's why NFL stadiums are upgrading their facilities by offering plush "sky boxes" to well-heeled patrons and a better assortment of food and merchandise to the rest of us. One trend is for such services to adopt a more retail-like philosophy, borrowing techniques from clothing stores or restaurants to create a pleasant environment as part of their marketing strategy. Banks, for example, are creating signature looks for their branches through the use of lighting, color, and art.

PEOPLE-BASED SERVICES   At the intangible end of the continuum are people-based services. Take the Great American Backrub store in Manhattan, for example. To experience this service (no appointment necessary), customers sit in a specially designed chair and for $7.95 get a massage that lasts exactly eight minutes. The owner of the store explained, "To get Americans to buy massages, I realized you had to solve three problems. You had to come up with something that was quick, inexpensive, and most important, you had to find a way to do it without asking people to take their clothes off."[13] In effect, the Great American Backrub has created a competitive advantage by providing a benefit consumers want.

Because people have less and less time to get things done, the importance of people-based services is increasing. Self-improvement services such as those offered by wardrobe consultants and personal trainers are becoming increasingly popular, and in some cities even professional dog walkers do a brisk business. Many of us hire someone to do our legal work, repair our cars and appliances, or do our tax returns.

core service
The basic benefit of having a service performed.

augmented services
The core service plus additional services provided to enhance value.

Core and Augmented Services

When we buy a service, we may in fact be buying a *set* of services. The **core service** is a benefit that a customer gets from the service. For example, when your car breaks down, repairing the problem is a core service you seek from an auto dealer or a garage. In most cases, though, the core service alone just isn't enough. To attract customers, a service firm often tries to offer **augmented services**, which are additional service offerings that differentiate the firm from the competition. When the auto dealership provides pickup and delivery of your car, a free wash job, or a customer lounge with donuts and coffee, it gains your loyalty as a customer.

Think about the core service you buy with an airline ticket: transportation. Yet airlines rarely stress the basic benefit of arriving safely at your destination (other than making you wait in long lines to get through security checks). Instead, they emphasize augmented services such as frequent-flyer miles, speedy check-in, laptop connections, and in-flight movies. In addition, augmented services may be necessary to deliver the core service. In the case of air travel, airports have added attractions to encourage travelers to fly to one site rather than another.[14] Here are some augmented services now available at airports around the world:

- London Gatwick: Internet café, Planet Hollywood restaurant, personal shopper services
- Amsterdam Schiphol: casino, airport television station, sauna, dry cleaner, grocery store
- Frankfurt International: supermarket, disco, sex shop
- Singapore Changi: fitness center, karaoke lounge, putting green

And what about your college education? With increased competition for students, universities are finding that their augmented products must provide a variety of amenities such as the University of Houston's $53 million wellness center that features a five-story climbing wall, hot tubs, waterfalls, and pool slides. At the University of Wisconsin, Oshkosh, students can get massages, pedicures, and manicures, while Washington State University has the largest Jacuzzi on the West Coast—it holds 53 people. And Ohio State University is spending $140 million to build a 657,000-square-foot complex that will feature kayaks and canoes, indoor batting cages, rope courses, and a climbing wall that 50 students can scale simultaneously.[15]

Security is a critical issue these days. Especially for high-profile leaders and dignitaries. No one understands this better than Mark Jones, Founder and CEO of a security-consulting firm. Mark is a man who earned the title of 'go-to guy' by being entrusted to jump from 13,000 feet with a former U.S. President. A man responsible for meeting different heads of state while serving as a Senior Aide to the 14th Chairman of the Joint Chiefs of Staff. Someone who started out as a cook but quickly learned to convert one challenging task after another into opportunity. A Master Sergeant from the U.S. Army Rangers who, day after day, brought honor to three simple words, "Complete the mission."

SENSE OF MISSION
– MARK "RANGER" JONES
UNITED STATES ARMY 1986-2003

The qualities you acquire while in the Military are qualities that stay with you forever.™

TODAY'S MILITARY
See it for what it really is.℠
1.866.VIEW NOW
www.todaysmilitary.com
Active • Guard • Reserve

Despite all of the high-tech equipment, at the end of the day the military is a people-based service that depends on well-trained soldiers to carry out its objectives.

Services on the Internet

From DVD rentals to fine restaurant cuisine, anything that can be delivered can be sold on the Web. In some cities, Web site companies will arrange to have your dry cleaning picked up, your family photos developed, or your shoes repaired.[16] Here are some of the newest and most popular Web services:

- **Banking and brokerages:** Cyberbanking customers can check their statements, pay bills, transfer money, and balance their accounts 24/7 whether they're at home or traveling around the globe. Some banks offer online customers higher interest rates on deposits, lower rates on loans, and free electronic bill payment. Online discount brokerage houses such as Etrade.com offer lower fees for stock purchases, and some sites allow traders to track their portfolios online.

A college's core service may be education, but students often are attracted by augmented services, including recreation facilities like those offered at the University of Houston.

- **Software:** Siebel Systems, Inc., a maker of customer management software, is one of the first firms in what experts predict will be a trend toward software sold to corporations and paid for on a monthly basis or on a rental basis and delivered via the Internet.[17]

- **Music:** After years of struggling with illegal downloading, music merchants including Apple, Dell, Sony, Wal-Mart, Coca-Cola (in Europe) and a new and improved Napster are selling (legal) tracks via the Internet. These online music firms have introduced a number of innovations, including cheaper downloads, better-quality files, and the opportunity for consumers to share songs and listen to them before paying.[18]

- **Travel:** Internet airline, travel, and tourism sites now command a large portion of the travel business for both business customers and individual consumers. With Priceline.com, consumers bid on the price they want to pay for airline tickets, hotel rooms, and other travel products. Many believe traditional travel agencies eventually will disappear.

- **Dating sites:** Dating services have now hit the Internet. In fact, EHarmony.com has even received a patent for its system of identifying people who are likely to have a successful relationship. EHarmony develops personality profiles from clients' answers to more than 430 online questions. Couples are then paired only when EHarmony's "marital satisfaction index" indicates 95 percent confidence that they are compatible.[19]

- **Career-related sites:** Employment agencies and recruiting firms such as Monster.com (remember Chapter 1) provide important job services and a less expensive way for applicants and employers to advertise their availability.

- **Distance learning:** Columbia, Stanford, Chicago, Carnegie Mellon, and the London School of Economics have teamed up to create Unext.com, a new Internet university.[20] Meanwhile, the University of Phoenix, the biggest player in online college programs, enrolls more than 186,000 students in 91 countries (most of whom have never even visited Phoenix).[21]

- **Medical care:** An increasing number of physicians are available to patients through e-mail. Nearly 40 percent of all physicians now have some kind of Web presence, and 25 percent of them use e-mail to communicate with patients.[22]

To stay in the game, marketers of such services need to think seriously about developing an Internet presence as well. Effective Internet sites not only allow customers to access the services online but also provide information for those customers who still want a personal contact. Because customers seek access to Internet-based services for convenience, marketers must make sure Internet sites are fast, simple, continuously updated, and easy to navigate.

The Service Encounter

Earlier we said that the service encounter occurs when the customer comes into contact with the organization—which usually means interacting with one or more employees who represent that organization. Despite all the attention (and money) paid to creating an attractive facility and delivering a quality product, this contact is "the moment of truth"—the employee often determines whether the customer will come away with a positive or a negative impression of the service. Our interactions with service providers can range from the most superficial, such as buying a movie ticket, to telling a psychiatrist (or bartender) our most intimate secrets. In each case, though, the quality of the service encounter can play a big role in determining how we feel about the service we receive.

The service encounter has several dimensions of importance to marketers.[23] First, there is the social contact dimension—one person interacting with another person. The physical dimension is also important—customers often pay close attention to the environment where the service is delivered and where the consumer and the service provider interact.

Music downloading, both the illegal kind and the legal version offered by the reincarnated Napster, is one of the most popular Internet services.

SOCIAL ELEMENTS OF THE SERVICE ENCOUNTER: EMPLOYEES AND CUSTOMERS Because services are intimately tied to company employees who deliver the service, the quality of a service is only as good as its poorest employee. The employee represents the organization; his actions, words, physical appearance, courtesy, and professionalism—or a lack of it—reflect the values of the organization. Customers entrust themselves and/or their possessions into the care of the employee, so it is important that employees look at the encounter from the customer's perspective.

The customer also plays a part in ensuring that a quality experience will result from a service encounter. When you visit a doctor, the quality of the health care you receive depends not only on the physician's competence but also on your ability to accurately and clearly communicate the problems you are experiencing. The business customer must provide accurate information to her accounting firm. And even the best personal trainer is not going to make the desired improvements in a client's body condition if the client refuses to stay on the exercise and diet regimen prescribed for him. At times, being a good customer means controlling your temper when

At the new Kowloon Shangri-La much has changed, but the important things remain the same.

The award-winning Kowloon Shangri-La invites you to experience a new level of opulence in our beautifully renovated harbour-front hotel. The famous Lobby and Lobby Lounge are now more magnificent than ever. All 700 guestrooms and suites have been tastefully refurbished, and exciting new restaurant concepts have been introduced. But beneath it all, our soul remains the same, with breathtaking harbour views and legendary Shangri-La service from warm, caring people.

Kowloon Shangri-La, Hong Kong Tel:(852) 2721 2111, Fax:(852) 2723 8686, E-mail: ksl@shangri-la.com
For reservations, please call USA & Canada toll-free 1 800 942 5050, your travel consultant or book on-line at www.shangri-la.com

AUSTRALIA • MAINLAND CHINA • HONG KONG SAR • FIJI ISLANDS • INDONESIA • MALAYSIA
MYANMAR • PHILIPPINES • SINGAPORE • TAIWAN • THAILAND • UNITED ARAB EMIRATES

Kowloon Shangri-La
HONG KONG

Upscale hotels like the Kowloon Hong Kong feature elaborate servicescapes to underscore their claims to luxury and careful attention to guests' needs.

servicescape
The actual physical facility where the service is performed, delivered, and consumed.

the encounter is worse than expected. Increasing incidents of "customer rage" are being reported, including the following:

- **Checkout counter rage:** A woman who barged into the express lane with more than 12 items had half her nose bitten off by a fellow shopper.
- **Pub rage:** A man who was refused service at closing time repeatedly smashed his tractor into a bar.
- **ATM rage:** When a bank machine ate a man's ATM card, he stuck it with a utility knife and threw a second knife at a cashier.[24]

So marketers beware: customers do fight back.

PHYSICAL ELEMENTS OF THE SERVICE EN-COUNTER: SERVICESCAPES AND OTHER TANGI-BLES As we noted earlier in the chapter, because services are intangible, marketers focus attention on providing *physical evidence* of the service they deliver. An important part of this physical evidence is the **servicescape**, the environment in which the service is delivered and where the firm and the customer interact. Servicescapes include facility exteriors—such elements as the exterior design of the facility, the signage, parking, and even the landscaping. They also include interior elements, such as the design of the office or store, equipment, colors, air quality, temperature, and smells. For hotels, restaurants, banks, airlines, and even schools, the servicescape is quite elaborate. For other services, such as an express mail drop-off, a dry cleaner, or an ATM machine, the servicescape can be very simple.

Marketers know that carefully designed servicescapes can have a positive influence on customers' purchase decisions, their evaluations of service quality, and their ultimate satisfaction with the service. Thus, for a service such as a pro baseball game, much planning goes into designing not only the actual playing field but also the exterior design and entrances of the ballpark, landscaping, seating, restrooms, concession stands, and ticketing area. Similarly, marketers pay close attention to the design of other tangibles that facilitate the performance of the service or provide communications. For the baseball fan, these include the signs that direct fans to the ballpark, the game tickets, the programs, and the uniforms worn by the team and by the hundreds of ballpark employees who help in the delivery of the service.

Providing Quality Service

If a service experience isn't positive, it can turn into a *disservice* with nasty consequences. Quality service ensures that customers are satisfied with what they have paid for. However, satisfaction is relative because the service recipient compares the current experience to some prior set of expectations. That's what makes delivering quality service tricky. What may seem like excellent service to one customer may be mediocre to another person "spoiled" by earlier encounters with an exceptional service provider. So, marketers must identify customer expectations and then work hard to exceed them. That's just what JetBlue has done with expectations of a low-fare airline. JetBlue gives customers a friendly cabin crew, roomy overhead bins, live satellite TV at every leather seat, and even pay-per-view movies.[25] Compare this to a more typical airline, and you'll see why JetBlue's extras exceed customer expectations.

Of course, meeting or exceeding expectations is not always so easy. These expectations can be influenced by stories people hear from friends and acquaintances, and they are not always realistic in the first place.[26] In some cases, there is little marketers can do to soothe ruffled feathers. Exaggerated customer expectations, such as providing a level of personal service impossible for a large company to accomplish, account for about 75 percent of the complaints reported by service businesses. However, providing customers with logical explanations for service failures and compensating them in some way can substantially reduce dissatisfaction.[27]

Dimensions of Service Quality

Because services are inseparable in that they are not produced until the time they are consumed, it is difficult to make a prepurchase evaluation of quality. Most service businesses cannot offer a free trial. Because services are variable, it is hard to predict consistency of quality and there is little or no opportunity for comparison shopping. The selection process for services is somewhat different than for goods, especially for services that are highly intangible, such as those on the right end of the continuum in Figure 10.2.[28] Service marketers have to come up with creative ways to illustrate the benefits their service will provide.

Search qualities are the characteristics of a product that the consumer can examine prior to purchase. These include color, style, price, fit, smell, and texture. Tangible goods, of course, are more likely to have these characteristics, so services need to build them in by paying attention to such details as the style of flight attendants' uniforms or the decor of a hotel room. The "Service Experience Blueprint™," shown in Figure 10.3, illustrates how one design firm tried to build in such cues for a grocery chain. The company planned an upgraded, freshly painted parking lot that

search qualities
Product characteristics that the consumer can examine prior to purchase.

Figure 10.3   Service Experience Blueprint

Firms often build in cues their customers can easily see because service quality is often difficult to determine. Grocery stores such as this one often use a variety of cues to convince consumers of superior quality.

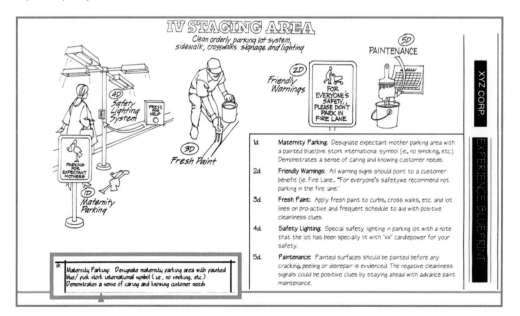

Source: Lewis P. Carbone and Stephan H. Haeckel, "Engineering Customer Experiences," *Marketing Management* 3 (winter 1994), reprint, exhibit 4.

included a special preferred parking space for expectant mothers (complete with a stork logo) to signal that the company cares.[29] Attention to detail makes a difference.

experience qualities
Product characteristics that customers can determine during or after consumption.

Experience qualities are product characteristics that customers can determine during or after consumption. For example, we can't really predict how good a vacation we'll have until we have it, so marketers need to reassure customers *before* the fact that they are in for a positive experience. A travel agency may invest in a slick presentation complete with alluring images of a tropical resort and perhaps even supply enthusiastic recommendations from other clients who had a positive experience at the same location.

credence qualities
Product characteristics that are difficult to evaluate even after they have been experienced.

Credence qualities are attributes we find difficult to evaluate even *after* we've experienced them. For example, most of us don't have the expertise to know if our doctor's diagnosis is correct.[30] Evaluations here are difficult, and to a great extent the client must trust the service provider. That is why tangible clues of professionalism, such as diplomas or an organized office, count toward purchase satisfaction.

Measuring Service Quality

Because the customer's experience of a service is crucial to determining future patronage, service marketers feel that measuring positive and negative service experiences is the "Holy Grail" for the services industry. Indeed, one-third of the business of marketing research firms is now devoted to measuring customer satisfaction *after* the sale.[31]

Marketers can gather consumer responses in a variety of ways (see Chapter 4). For example, some companies hire "mystery shoppers" to check on hotels and airlines and report back. These shoppers usually work for a research firm, although some airlines reportedly recruit "spies" from the ranks of their most frequent flyers. Some firms also locate "lost customers" (former patrons) so they can find out what turned them off and correct the problem.

gap analysis
A marketing research methodology that measures the difference between a customer's expectation of a service quality and what actually occurred.

GAP ANALYSIS Gap analysis (no, nothing to do with a Gap clothing store) is a measurement tool that gauges the difference between a customer's expectation of service quality and what actually occurred. By identifying specific places in the service system where there is a wide gap between what is expected and what is received, services marketers can get a handle on what needs improvement. Some major gaps include the following:[32]

- **Gap between consumer expectations and management perceptions:** A major quality gap can occur when the firm's managers don't understand what its customers' expectations are in the first place. Many service organizations have an operations orientation rather than a customer orientation. For example, a bank may close its branches at midday to balance transactions because that's more efficient for the bank, even though it's not convenient for customers who want to do their banking during their lunch hour.

- **Gap between management perception and quality standards set by the firm:** Quality suffers when a firm fails to establish a quality control program. Successful service firms, such as American Express and McDonald's, develop written quality goals. American Express found that customers complained most about its responsiveness, accuracy, and timeliness. The company established 180 specific goals to correct these problems, and it now monitors how fast employees answer phones in an effort to be more responsive.

- **Gap between established quality standards and service delivery:** One of the biggest threats to service quality is poor employee performance. When employees do not deliver the service at the level specified by the company, quality suffers. Teamwork is crucial to service success. Unfortunately, many companies don't clearly specify what they expect of employees. Merrill Lynch addressed this problem by assembling its operations personnel into quality groups of 8 to 15 employees each to clarify its expectations for how the workers should interact with clients.

- **Gap between service quality standards and consumer expectations:** Sometimes a firm makes exaggerated promises or does not accurately describe its service to customers. When the Holiday Inn hotel chain developed an advertising campaign based on the promise that guests would receive "No Surprises," many operations personnel opposed the idea, saying that *no* service organization, no matter how good, can anticipate every single thing that can go wrong. Sure enough, the campaign was unsuccessful. A services firm is better off communicating exactly what the customer can expect and what will happen if the company doesn't deliver on its promises.

- **Gap between expected service and perceived service:** Sometimes consumers misperceive the quality of the service. Thus, even when communications accurately describe what service quality is provided and can be expected, consumers are less than satisfied. Some diners at fine restaurants are so demanding that even their own mothers couldn't anticipate their every desire.

MEASURING VALUE
marketing metrics

A consulting firm called Market Metrix Inc. developed a metric called the Marketing Metrix Hospitality Index (MMHI) to measure customer satisfaction with hotel, airline, and car rental companies based on 35,000 in-depth consumer interviews. The MMHI contains 135 hotel brands, 25 airlines, and 11 car rental companies. Subscribers to the quarterly report can measure their company's stand-alone performance and also benchmark their ratings against those of competitors and highly ranked companies within and across the other hospitality industries. In 2003, the top-rated hospitality services were Four Seasons Hotels, Jet Blue Airways, and Enterprise Rent-A-Car. Also that year, the metric began to include measures of customer satisfaction with Web sites offering online hotel reservations—Yahoo! Travel placed first.[35]

THE CRITICAL INCIDENT TECHNIQUE The **critical incident technique** is another way to measure service quality.[33] The company collects and closely analyzes very specific customer complaints. It can then identify *critical incidents*—specific contacts between consumers and service providers that are most likely to result in dissatisfaction.

Some critical incidents happen when the expectations of customers cannot be met by the service organization. For example, it is impossible to satisfy a passenger who says to a flight attendant, "Come sit with me. I don't like to fly alone." In other cases, though, the firm is capable of meeting these expectations but fails to do so. For example, the customer might complain to a flight attendant, "My seat won't recline."[34] A potentially dissatisfied customer can be turned into a happy one if the problem is addressed or perhaps even if the customer is told why the problem can't be solved at this time. Customers tend to be fairly forgiving if they are given a reasonable explanation for the problem.

critical incident technique
A method for measuring service quality in which marketers use customer complaints to identify critical incidents—specific face-to-face contacts between consumer and service providers that cause problems and lead to dissatisfaction.

Strategies for Developing and Managing Services

We've seen that quality is the goal of every successful service organization. What can the firm do to maximize the likelihood that a customer will choose its service and become a loyal customer?

With services differing from goods in so many ways, decision makers struggle to market something that isn't there. However, many of the same strategic issues apply. For example, Table 10.2 illustrates how three different types of service organizations can devise marketing strategies.

Of course, sometimes service quality does fail. Some failures, such as when your dry cleaner places glaring red spots on your new white sweater, are easy to see at the time the service is performed. Others, such as when the dry cleaner shrinks your sweater, are less obvious and are recognized only at a later time when you're running late and get a "surprise."

But no matter when or how the failure is discovered, the important thing is that the firm takes fast action to resolve the problem. Quick action means that the problem won't occur again (hopefully) and that the customer's complaint will be satisfactorily resolved. The key is speed; research shows that customers whose complaints are resolved quickly are far more likely to buy from the same company again than when complaints take longer to be resolved.[36]

To make sure that service failures are at a minimum and that recovery is fast, managers should first understand the service and the potential places where failures are most likely to occur and then make plans ahead of time to recover.[37] That's why the process of identifying critical incidents can be so important. In addition, employees should be trained to listen for complaints and be empowered to take appropriate actions immediately. For example, Marriott allows employees to spend up to $2,500 to compensate guests for certain inconveniences.[38]

Table 10.2 Marketing Strategies for Service Organizations

	Dry Cleaner	City Opera Company	A State University
Marketing objective	Increase total revenues by 20 percent within one year by increasing business of existing customers and obtaining new customers	Increase to 1,000 the number of season memberships to opera productions within two years	Increase applications to undergraduate and graduate programs by 10 percent for the coming academic year
Target markets	Young and middle-aged professionals living within a five-mile radius of the business	Clients who attend single performances but do not purchase season memberships	Primary market: prospective undergraduate and graduate students who are residents of the state
		Other local residents who enjoy opera but do not normally attend local opera performances	Secondary market: prospective undergraduate and graduate students living in other states and in foreign countries
Benefits offered	Excellent and safe cleaning of clothes in 24 hours or less	Experiencing professional quality opera performances while helping ensure the future of the local opera company	High-quality education in a student-centered campus environment
Strategy	Provide an incentive offer to existing customers such as one suit cleaned for free after 10 suits cleaned at regular price	Write letters to former membership holders and patrons of single performances encouraging them to purchase new season memberships	Increase number of recruiting visits to local high schools; arrange a special day of events for high school counselors to visit campus
	Use newspaper advertising to communicate a limited time discount offer to all customers	Arrange for opera company personnel and performers to be guests for local television and radio talk shows	Send letters to alumni encouraging them to recommend the university to prospective students they know

The Future of Services

As we look into the future, we recognize that the importance of service industries as part of the U.S. and global economies will continue to grow. In particular, there are several trends that are important to consider. These trends will provide both opportunities and challenges for the marketers of services down the road (that means you). In the future, we can expect services we can't even imagine yet. Of course, they will also provide many new and exciting job opportunities for future marketers.

- **Changing demographics:** As populations age, service industries that meet the needs of older consumers will see dramatic growth. Companies offering recreational opportunities, health care, and living assistance for seniors will be in demand.

- **Globalization:** The globalization of business will increase the need for logistics and distribution services to move products around the world (we'll talk more about these in Chapter 15) and for accounting and legal services that facilitate these global exchanges. In addition, global deregulation will affect the delivery of services by banks, brokerages, insurance, and other financial service industries because globalization means greater competition. For example, many patients now are going to countries like Thailand and India, where common surgical procedures may cost less than half what they would in the United States. Meanwhile, hospitals back home often look more like luxury spas, offering such amenities as adjoining quarters for family members, choice of different ethnic cuisines, and in-room Internet access.[39] In the hotel industry, demand for luxury properties is growing around the world. Hyatt International recently expanded its five-star hotels in Tokyo, Hong Kong, and Paris, and the company is planning an aggressive building campaign of luxury hotels in mainland China, where it expects to have as many as 24 properties within a decade.[40]

Advice for One of Universal's Theme Parks in Orlando

STUDENT
LAURA BORDEN
Cornell University

I would choose option 2, creating a plan to accommodate large crowds in the entry to the parking garages and roads to Universal as well as within the park. In gauging attendance from the previous weekends and the publicity surrounding the highly anticipated appearance of Donna Summer, Robyn should plan to accommodate larger-than-usual crowds rather than deal with the potential repercussions of appearing unprepared and unorganized. This would negatively reflect on the park's image and possibly hurt future attendance. She can come to this conclusion by considering the audience's characteristics. Say, for example, the typical Donna Summer fan/Universal Studios visitor falls into an age-group and type of lifestyle that is more likely to avoid highly crowded, uncomfortable concert situations and prefers cleanly organized events that can accommodate the whole family. If Robyn does not plan for the situation, this will likely discourage people from visiting again. If the team opts to publicize a large turnout, it may also deter this type of audience member from attending the event altogether. Research should be conducted to determine these characteristics so that every possibility can be accounted for. In order to make up for the added expense of choosing this option, the team should escalate their promotions efforts, particularly by reaching out with "free" publicity through local and national media outlets and partnering with local businesses. Finally, Robyn should keep in mind that by properly promoting the event and preparing to have as well an executed event as possible, the park can hope to make up for the costs through increased admission ticket sales.

PROFESSOR
JANICE M. KARLEN
LaGuardia Community College/City University of New York

I would choose option 2 because having a fun experience in a safe environment is at the heart of guest satisfaction. Long lines and traffic jams would result in visitor frustration, disappointment, and even anger. Universal Studios is a large organization that should consistently be viewing special events as a means for bringing in guests for that day as well as encouraging them to return for future events. In addition, an enjoyable experience at the Mardi Gras concert would result in positive "word of mouth," which may contribute to increased attendance at Universal Studios by new visitors. If the attendance was lower than expected, it should be viewed as an investment in the future rather than a waste.

- **Technological advances:** Changing technology will provide opportunities for growth and innovation in global service industries such as telecommunications, health care, banking, and Internet services. And we can also expect technological advances to provide opportunities for services that we haven't even thought of yet but that will dramatically change and improve the lives of consumers. We're already seeing a small industry of consultants who make a nice living by simply showing people how to program their VCRs or set up their home theaters—with new advances there will always be "clueless" customers who need help keeping up with progress!

Meanwhile, the Internet is becoming an increasingly important way to market some charities. Internet news media vehicles provide an opportunity for charities to inform potential donors of a need and to request donations and charity Web sites provide an easy

The health insurance is
FOR HER
Many of the benefits are
FOR YOU

You love your pet. You want her to get the best care when she gets sick or hurt. With VPI Pet Insurance, you can be sure of it. As the nation's largest and oldest provider of health insurance for pets, VPI offers affordable coverage for emergency and major medical care, plus routine procedures like spaying/neutering and vaccinations. We even help cover prescriptions and lab fees. What's more, you can go to the veterinarian of your choice. Which leads us to the biggest benefit of all: peace of mind. For an instant quote, visit petinsurance.com or call 800-USA-PETS (800-872-7387).

*Enroll Today
its Easy and Affordable*
petinsurance.com
800-USA-PETS

VPI PET insurance

Services such as health insurance for pets that were once unimaginable are now a very real—and fast-growing—part of our culture as companion pets increasingly become thought of as family members and veterinary care has become both more sophisticated and costly.

uncomplicated way for donors to contribute as much or as little as they want 24 hours a day. The American Red Cross raised nearly $140,000 for Turkey's earthquake victims in one day, and Catholic Relief Services raised $350,000 from 2,000 donors for Kosovar refugees in only two weeks.[41]

- **Shift to flow of information:** In many ways, we have become in information society as both organizations and individuals have experienced a dramatic increase in the importance of obtaining, manipulating, reporting, and using information. The availability, flow, and access of information is becoming increasingly critical to the success of organizations. These changes will provide greater opportunities for database services, artificial intelligence systems, communications systems, and other services that facilitate the storage and transfer of knowledge.

Marketing People, Places, and Ideas

By now, you understand that services are intangibles that marketers work hard to sell. But as we said earlier, services are not the only intangibles that organizations need to market. Intangibles such as people, places, and ideas often need to be "sold" by someone and "bought" by someone else. Let's consider how marketing is relevant to each of these.

Marketing People

As we saw in Chapter 1, people are products, too. If you don't believe that, you've never been on a job interview or spent a Saturday night in a singles bar. Many of us find it distasteful to equate people with products. In reality, though, a sizable number of people hire personal image consultants to devise a marketing strategy for them, and others undergo plastic surgery, physical conditioning, or cosmetic makeovers to improve their "market position" or "sell" themselves to potential employers, friends, or lovers.[42] Let's briefly touch on a few prominent categories of people marketing.

Politicians are created and marketed by sophisticated consultants who "package" candidates and compete for "market share" of votes. This perspective can be traced back to the 1952 and 1956 presidential campaigns of Dwight Eisenhower, when advertising executive Rosser Reeves repackaged the bland but amiable army general by inventing jingles and slogans such as "I like Ike" and contrived man-on-the-street interviews to improve the candidate's market position.[43] For better or worse, Reeves's strategies revolutionized the political landscape as people realized that the same selling tactics used to sell soap could sell candidates. Today, the basic idea remains the same even though the techniques are different. For example, in 2004, Democratic presidential candidate Howard Dean almost staged a major upset by orchestrating an Internet campaign to energize young supporters around the country.

From actors and musicians to athletes and supermodels, the famous and near-famous jockey for market position in popular culture. Celebrities are carefully packaged by agents who connive to get them exposure on TV, starring roles in movies, recording contracts, or product endorsements.[44] Like other products, celebrities even rename themselves to craft a "brand identity" using the same

Figure 10.4 Strategies to Sell a Celebrity

There is more than one approach to selling an intangible—even for selling a celebrity. Successful marketing has to determine the best approach to take for each product.

Marketing Approach	Implementation
Pure Selling Approach	*Agent presents a client*
	to record companies
	to movie studios
	to TV production companies
	to talk show hosts
	to advertising agencies
	to talent scouts
Product Improvement Approach	*Client is modified*
	New name
	New image
	Voice lessons
	Dancing lessons
	Plastic surgery
	New back-up band
	New music genre
Market Fulfillment Approach	*Agent looks for market opening*
	Identify unmet need
	Develop a new product (band, singer) to the specifications of consumer wants

Superstar Beyoncé is one of the latest celebrities to extend her "brand identity" by branching out to other areas. In addition to her singing career, she has starred in films and is a spokeswoman for various products, including Pepsi and the Tommy Hilfiger perfume True Star.

strategies marketers use to ensure that their products make an impression on consumers, including memorability (Evel Knievel), suitability (fashion designer Oscar Renta reverted to his old family name of de la Renta because it sounded more elegant), and distinctiveness (Steveland Morris Hardaway became Stevie Wonder).

In addition to these branding efforts, there are other strategies marketers use to "sell" a celebrity as shown in Figure 10.4.[45] These include (1) the *pure selling approach,* in which an agent presents a client's qualifications to potential "buyers" until he finds one who is willing to act as an intermediary; (2) the *product improvement approach,* in which the agent works with the client to modify certain characteristics that will increase market value; and (3) the *market fulfillment approach,* in which the agent scans the market to identify unmet needs. After identifying a need, the agent then finds a person or a group that meets a set of minimum qualifications and develops a new "product."

Marketing Places

place marketing
Marketing activities that seek to attract new businesses, residents, or visitors to a town, state, country, or some other site.

Place marketing strategies regard a city, state, country, or other locale as a brand and attempt to position this location so that consumers choose to visit. Because of the huge amount of money associated with tourism, the competition to attract visitors is fierce. There are about 1,600 visitors' bureaus in the United States alone that try to brand their locations. In addition, almost every town or city has an economic development office charged with luring new businesses or residents. For example, after the 2001 attack on the World Trade Center, New York City unveiled a new tourism advertising campaign that November with the slogan "The New York Miracle: Be a Part of It." The campaign included

Many cities, states, and countries recognize that by using effective marketing strategies, they can increase vital tourism revenues and attract business investment needed for growth.

six 30-second TV commercials and some of New York's biggest celebrities such as Woody Allen and Robert DeNiro.[46]

Marketing Ideas

You can see people. You can stand in a city. So how do you market something you can't see, smell, or feel? **Idea marketing** is about gaining market share for a concept, philosophy, belief, or issue. Even religious organizations market ideas about faith and desirable behavior by adopting secular marketing techniques to attract young people. Some evangelists use the power of television to convey their messages. So-called "megachurches" are huge steel and glass structures, with acres of parking and slickly produced services complete with live bands and professional dancers to draw huge audiences. Some even offer aerobics, bowling alleys, and multimedia Bible classes inspired by MTV to attract "customers" turned off by traditional approaches to religion.[47]

In 2003, Home Depot's 40 Arizona stores participated with the Arizona Department of Water Resources and the cities of Phoenix, Mesa, and Scottsdale in a $1.8 million "Water—Use It Wisely" campaign. For this cause marketing program, a local marketing firm developed a multimedia package centered around "100 Ways in 30 Days to Save Water." To encourage a change in behavior, Home Depot ran in-store workshops on water conservation, arranged for television appearances by its employees to demonstrate water conservation, and created in-store signage to advertise relevant products for each of the 100 tips.[48]

The marketing of ideas, however, can be even more difficult than marketing goods and services. Consumers often do not perceive that the *value* received from wearing seat belts or recycling garbage or even not driving while drinking is worth the *cost*—the extra effort necessary. Governments and other organizations use marketing strategies, often with only limited success, to sell ideas that will save the lives of millions of unwilling consumers or that will save our planet.

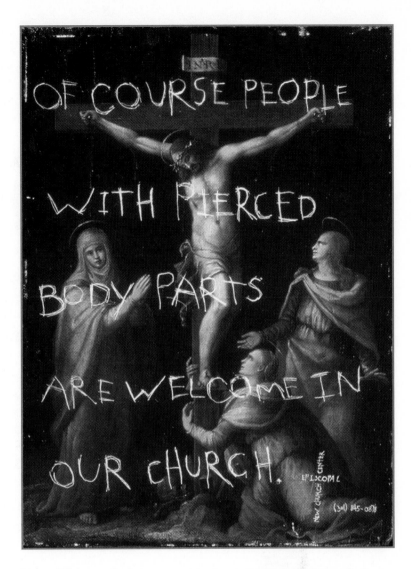

Many religious organizations use a variety of marketing strategies to grow their organizations.

idea marketing
Marketing activities that seek to gain market share for a concept, philosophy, belief, or issue by using elements of the marketing mix to create or change a target market's attitude or behavior.

real people, real choices
How it Worked Out at One of Universal's Theme Parks in Orlando

The team selected a combination of options 2 and 3 to alleviate crowding concerns and enhance the guest experience. They changed the parade route and added two viewing screens away from the concert stage to provide concert viewing in an open space (versus the stage area). Some of the food and beverage locations were moved to accommodate the changes. They also created a flyer that featured the new parade route and recommended viewing areas (that tended to have less people) for

both the parade and the concert. They distributed these flyers to each guest entering through the turnstiles in the front of the park.

Attendance at the Donna Summer concert was high, as expected. Fortunately, the advance planning ensured that guests had a fun experience despite the additional people who attended. In addition to enjoying themselves in the concert area, the guests partied in the streets and had a great evening. Robyn's risk of investing in additional accommodations for the event paid off both for those who got to see the singer and for the park's management.

Do you want to be an entrepreneur, free agent, or consultant? If so, you really need a brand. Learn tips from the pros in Chapter 10 of the *Brand You* supplement.

CHAPTER SUMMARY

1. **Describe the four characteristics of services.** Services are products that are intangible and that are exchanged directly from producer to customer without ownership rights. Generally, services are acts that accomplish some goal and may be directed either toward people or toward an object. Both consumer services and business-to-business services are important parts of the economy. Important service characteristics include (1) intangibility (they cannot be seen, touched, or smelled), (2) perishability (they cannot be stored), (3) variability (they are never exactly the same from time to time), and (4) inseparability from the producer (most services are produced, sold, and consumed at the same time).

2. **Understand how services differ from goods.** In reality, most products are a combination of goods and services. Some services are goods dominant (i.e., tangible products are marketed with supporting services). Some are equipment- or facility-based (i.e., elaborate equipment or facilities are required for creation of the service). Other services are people-based (i.e., people are actually a part of the service marketed). Like goods, services include both a core service or the basic benefit received and augmented services, including innovative features and convenience of service delivery.

3. **Explain how marketers create and measure service quality.** The customer's perception of service quality is related to prior expectations. Because services are intangible, evaluation of service quality is more difficult, and customers often look for cues to help them decide whether they received satisfactory service. Gap analysis measures the difference between customer expectations of service quality and what actually occurred. Using the critical incident technique, service firms can identify the specific contacts between customers and service providers that create dissatisfaction.

4. **Explain marketing strategies for services.** As with strategies for marketing physical goods, service strategies include targeting segments of service customers and positioning the service to differentiate it from competitors' offerings. This can be done by emphasizing such dimensions as tangibles (including employee appearance, design of facilities, and company logos), responsiveness, empathy, and assurance. Internet marketing is often an effective way to market a service because it's an easy way for consumers to compare core and augmented services.

5. **Explain the marketing of people, places, and ideas.** Managers follow the steps for marketing planning when marketing other intangibles as well. People, especially politicians and celebrities, are often packaged and promoted. Place marketing aims to create or change the market position of a particular locale, whether a city, state, country, resort, or institution. Idea marketing (gaining market share for a concept, philosophy, belief, or issue) seeks to create or change a target market's attitude or behavior. Marketing is used by religious organizations and to promote important causes. Marketing of ideas may be especially difficult, as consumers may not see the value to be worth the cost.

KEY TERMS

augmented services, 302

capacity management, 298

core service, 302

credence qualities, 308

critical incident technique, 309

disintermediation, 299

experience qualities, 308

gap analysis, 308

idea marketing, 315

inseparability, 299

intangibility, 297

intangibles, 295

perishability, 297

place marketing, 313

search qualities, 307

service encounter, 299

services, 296

servicescape, 306

variability, 298

CHAPTER REVIEW

MARKETING CONCEPTS: TESTING YOUR KNOWLEDGE

1. What are intangibles? How do basic marketing concepts apply to the marketing of intangibles?

2. What is a service? What are the important characteristics of services that make them different from goods?

3. What is the goods/services continuum? What are good-dominated services, equipment- or facility-based services, and people-based services?

4. What are core and augmented services? How do marketers increase market share with augmented services?

5. What are the physical and social elements of the service encounter?

6. Describe some popular means of marketing of services on the Internet.

7. What dimensions do consumers and business customers use to evaluate service quality? How do marketers work to create service quality?

8. How do marketers measure service quality?

9. What are some ideas about the future of services?

10. What do we mean by marketing people? Marketing places? Marketing ideas?

MARKETING CONCEPTS: DISCUSSING CHOICES AND ISSUES

1. Sometimes service quality may not meet customers' expectations. What problems have you experienced with quality in the delivery of the following services?

   a. A restaurant meal

   b. An airline flight

   c. Automobile repairs

   d. Your college education

   What do you think is the reason for the poor quality?

2. Internet dating services, while becoming very popular, may present some dangers for those who use their services. Who do you think uses Internet dating services? What if anything should dating services do to protect their clients?

3. There has been a lot of criticism about the way politicians have been marketed in recent years. What are some of the ways marketing has helped our political process? What are some ways the marketing of politicians might have an adverse effect on our government?

4. Many not-for-profit and religious organizations have found that they can be more successful by marketing their ideas. What are some ways that these organizations market them-selves that are similar to and different from the marketing by for-profit businesses?

5. Many developed countries including the United States have in recent decades become primarily service economies; that is, there is relatively little manufacturing of goods, and most people in the economy are employed by service industries. Why do you think this has occurred? In what ways is this trend a good and/or a bad thing for a country? Do you think this trend will continue?

MARKETING PRACTICE: APPLYING WHAT YOU'VE LEARNED

1. Because of increased competition in its community, you have been hired as a marketing consultant by a local bank. You know that the characteristics of services (intangibility, perishability, and so on) create unique marketing challenges. You also know that these challenges can be met with creative marketing strategies. Outline the challenges for marketing the bank created by each of the four characteristics of services. List your ideas for what might be done to meet each of these challenges.

2. Assume that you are a physician. You are opening a new family practice clinic in your community. You feel that you have the best chance of being successful if you can create a product that is superior to that offered by competing businesses. Put together a list of ways in which you can augment the basic service offering to develop a better product. List the advantages and disadvantages of each.

3. You are currently a customer for a college education, a very expensive service product. You know that a service organization can create a competitive advantage by focusing on how the service is delivered after it has been purchased—making sure the service is efficiently and comfortably delivered to the customer. Develop a list of recommendations for your school for improving the delivery of its service. Consider both classroom and nonclassroom aspects of the educational product.

4. Assume that you work for a marketing firm that has been asked to develop a marketing plan for a new up-and-coming rock band. Prepare an outline for your marketing plan. First, list the special problems and challenges associated with marketing people rather than a physical product. Then outline your ideas for product, price, and promotion strategies.

5. Answer the questions in question 4 for your hometown.

6. Assume that you have been recently hired by your city government to head up a program to create 100 percent compliance with recycling regulations. Develop a presentation

for the city council in which you will outline the problems in "selling" recycling. Develop an outline for the presentation. Be sure to focus on each of the four Ps.

MARKETING MINIPROJECT: LEARNING BY DOING

1. Select a service that you will purchase in the next week or so.
2. As you experience the service, record the details of every aspect, including the following:
   a. People
   b. Physical facilities
   c. Location
   d. Waiting time
   e. Hours
   f. Transaction
   g. Other customers
   h. Tangible aspects
   i. Search qualities
   j. Credence qualities
3. Recommend improvements to the service encounter.

REAL PEOPLE, REAL SURFERS: EXPLORING THE WEB

Theme and entertainment parks like Universal Studios fall in the middle of the goods/services continuum—half goods and half services. To be successful in this highly competitive market, these parks must carefully develop targeting and positioning strategies. Visit the Web sites of the three top theme park organizations. Disneyland (**http://disneyland.disney.go.com**), Six Flags parks (**www.sixflags.com**), and Universal's Orlando Theme Park (**http://themeparks.universalstudios.com**). Thoroughly investigate each site.

1. How is the Web site designed to appeal to each theme park organization's target market?
2. How does each park position its product? How is this positioning communicated through the Web site?
3. What changes or improvements would you recommend for each Web site?

MARKETING PLAN EXERCISE

Organizations that market services face special challenges because services are intangible. One way they address the challenges created by intangibility is by designing an effective servicescape, that is, the environment where the service is delivered and where the firm and the customer interact.

1. Select a service that you are familiar with, such as a bank, an airline, or even your university.

2. Describe the weaknesses that might be in a SWOT analysis for the business that occur because of the intangibility of the service.
3. Develop strategies for creating a servicescape that will be a positive influence on customers' purchase decision, their evaluations of the service quality, and their ultimate satisfaction with the service.

Marketing in Action Case

Real Choices at XM Satellite Radio

What do two satellites, one named *Rock* and the other named *Roll,* traveling in geostationary orbit 22,500 miles above the equator have to do with one of the hottest, fastest-growing new services in America today?

It just so happens that both of those satellites, costing $200 million apiece, broadcast radio signals to subscribers of XM Satellite Radio. Similar to satellite TV, satellite radio is a relatively new equipment-based service that beams radio signals from its broadcast center to the satellites, which then go to the subscribers. XM Radio provides 101 different satellite radio stations to over 1.4 million customers throughout the United States at a cost of $10 per month.

In addition to the $10-per-month subscription fee, XM subscribers pay up to $200 for a satellite radio receiver. Depending on the type of receiver, XM radio can be enjoyed in a subscriber's car, truck, boat, home, or place of work. With approximately 200 million cars and light trucks, 4 million boats, 3 million heavy trucks, and 100 million households in the United States, the potential market for satellite radio is huge.

Two main competitive advantages are provided by satellite radio that make it preferable over other radio options. One advantage is that the radio signal broadcast is of consistent high quality and contains no static. As a result, there is no variability in the quality of service provided, and the stations always come across loud and clear regardless of the listener's location. Indeed, with satellite radio, you could drive across the United States and pick up the same station everywhere. Because of the consistency in signal quality, airlines such as JetBlue and AirTran have begun offering XM radio services on their flights.

The second main competitive advantage provided by XM is the variety of programming offered. With 101 channels, there is literally something for everyone. From classic rock to top 40, Radio Disney, dedicated musical genre stations (classical, reggae, jazz, and so on), sports broadcasts, and a variety of talk shows, the list of augmented service offerings seems endless.

In addition, unlike regular broadcast AM and FM stations, XM satellite stations try not to play any songs more than once per day, and all the stations are broadcast commercial free. Consequently, once a subscriber decides on a music station to listen to, he or she is assured of hearing a wide variety of songs and artists in the chosen genre. As a result of XM's service offerings and their effective targeting and positioning strategies, the company has developed relationships with GM, Honda, Acura, and Toyota to provide factory-installed satellite radio in many of their automobile offerings.

Despite XM's initial success, many troubles still exist. One of those problems is the cost, in terms of promotions and incentives offered, that the company pays to acquire new customers. Each new customer costs XM approximately $74 to acquire. At a subscription fee of $10 per month, each new customer must remain a subscriber for 7.5 months before the company breaks even. Such incentives eat away at the operating margins XM could be earning if the cost of acquiring new customers were less.

In addition, analysts have estimated that the company needs 7.5 million customers and $1 billion in revenue to cover its capital and interest costs. Achieving such revenue goals will be difficult since the company does no advertising on its various stations and thus cannot collect advertising revenues. Furthermore, *Rock* and *Roll,* the two satellites providing the service, are degrading at a much faster rate than anticipated. As a result, XM will have to spend around $400 million to replace these satellites sooner than they expected. This cost will most likely delay XM's progress to profitability and require still more subscribers to offset the additional expense.

Like many new businesses, XM must decide whether the existing marketing strategy is going to work for the long term. Will the $10-per-month subscription fee be adequate to cover all the costs of doing business and give owners a profit, or will other sources of revenue be necessary? Might customers be willing to pay more for XM broadcasts? Another alternative XM might consider is to follow the business model of traditional radio and sell advertising to generate the revenues necessary to survive. This might be a risky decision, however, if customers don't feel XM's program variety and quality of transmission are enough to keep them tuned in. Needless to say, the challenges for XM Satellite Radio in the early stages of this fledgling industry are huge, and the company will require adept management of its service offering before it can realize any profits in the future.

Things to Think About

1. What is the decision facing XM Satellite Radio?
2. What factors are important in understanding this decision situation?
3. What are the alternatives?
4. What decision(s) do you recommend?
5. What are some ways to implement your recommendation(s)?

Sources: Catherine Yang, Diane Brady, Adam Aston, and Steve Rosenbush, "This Is the Dawning of the Age of—XM?" *Business Week,* July 7, 2003, 90–92, and Justin Martin, "Radio Heads," *Fortune Small Business,* February 14, 2004,**www.fortune.com/fortune/print/0,15935,576478,00.html** (accessed June 2, 2004).

THINK OUTSIDE THE BUN™

TACO BELL®

www.tacobell.com

real people, real choices

*meet Danielle Blugrind,
a Decision Maker at Taco Bell*

what i do when i'm not working

I'm a mom to a wonderful Kindergarten-age daughter! And I can't get enough of reading.

career high

Every day is a new one! There is always something to look forward to.

PRICING THE PRODUCT

Danielle Blugrind is director of consumer and brand insights for Taco Bell Corporation. After she received her B.A. from the University of California, Irvine, in 1989, she earned an MBA in marketing at Claremont Graduate School. Her first job out of the MBA program was as an analyst in the Consumer Research department of Mattel Toys. At first, she worked on research for sports toys, activity toys, and action figures. Then she was promoted to senior analyst working on the Barbie brand, and she spent the next six years on Barbie for girls and Barbie Collectibles before working her way up to senior manager. At her current job at Taco Bell, Danielle oversees all research related to overall brand and advertising strategy, value products, late night, multibranding, beverages, promotions and combos.

Decision Time at Taco Bell

Back in the 1990s, Taco Bell realized that a major barrier to broadening its reach and sales was the fact that many consumers found the food there to be too expensive. To combat this problem, the company developed a 59-79-99¢ Value Menu. Taco Bell's sales shot through the roof as consumers responded positively to the price-based approach. However, after several years, the competition began to offer similar alternatives (such as the McDonald's Value Meals), so Taco Bell no longer "owned" a value position in the industry as it had in the mid-1990s. In response, the company tried to refocus its strategy and move away from a value emphasis—a decision that wound up hurting the company.

Fast-forward to the year 2000. Taco Bell knows that value is here to stay in the fast-food industry, but it has abandoned its 59-79-99¢ menu and needs a new direction. The firm test-marketed several value menus and ideas, but nothing really generated a much-needed boost in sales. Danielle and her colleagues were forced to step back and think hard about what value means to its customers and how the chain could deliver the food people wanted at the price they wanted. Danielle knew that as competitors began to claim they were providing greater value, Taco Bell needed to break through the cluttered value landscape that is fast food and "think outside the bun."

The company looked at numerous alternatives, including new products, new ways to price its menu, and new product combinations. A pricing strategy began to take shape. Many of Taco Bell's competitors continued to focus on the 99¢ price point, which is virtually synonymous with value in the fast-food world. Although it was tempting for Taco Bell to follow suit by adding items to the menu for 99¢, most of the company's products could not feasibly be offered at such a low price. And Taco

business book i'm reading now — I'm rereading *The Sweet Spot* by Lisa Fortini Campbell.

don't do this when interviewing with me — Never act nervous! Don't try to sell me on what a big Taco Bell fan you are. And don't try to tell me you don't have a single question about the job or the company.

my management style — Too hands-on, at times! Let's say it is evolving into a better demonstration of my belief in people and their abilities.

my motto to live by — There is always a bright side.

1 Explain the importance of pricing and how prices can take both monetary and nonmonetary forms.

2 Understand the pricing objectives that marketers typically have in planning pricing strategies.

3 Describe how marketers use costs, demands, and revenue to make pricing decisions.

4 Understand some of the environmental factors that affect pricing strategies.

5 Understand key pricing strategies.

6 Explain pricing tactics for single and multiple products and for pricing on the Internet.

7 Understand the opportunities for Internet pricing strategies.

8 Describe the psychological, legal, and ethical aspects of pricing.

Bell wanted to show that it was different from other fast-food restaurants—this wouldn't happen if it used the same pricing strategy as everyone else.

Danielle and her team began to test other pricing options, including the idea of pricing all menu items the same. She knew from other research that the "value threshold" for Taco Bell's menu items was $1.29; this represents the highest possible price that consumers might still consider to be a value for some items. In total, the company tested eight different price configurations that it determined would make financial sense; these included four options where each menu item was priced the same and would cost either 99¢, $1.09, $1.19, or $1.29 as well as four other mixed price options. These are the eight combinations they tested:

	99¢ Menu	$1.09 Menu	$1.19 Menu	$1.29 Menu	Mixed Price #1	Mixed Price #2	Mixed Price #3	Mixed Price #4
Burrito #1	99¢	$1.09	$1.19	$1.29	$1.29	$1.29	99¢	$1.29
Burrito #2	99¢	$1.09	$1.19	$1.29	$1.19	$1.19	$1.29	$1.29
Burrito #3	99¢	$1.09	$1.19	$1.29	$1.29	$1.29	$1.29	$1.29
Taco #1	99¢	$1.09	$1.19	$1.29	99¢	$1.09	99¢	99¢
Taco #2	99¢	$1.09	$1.19	$1.29	99¢	99¢	99¢	99¢
Nachos	99¢	$1.09	$1.19	$1.29	99¢	99¢	$1.19	99¢
Specialty item	99¢	$1.09	$1.19	$1.29	$1.19	$1.19	$1.29	$1.29

Based on the results from the concept testing of the eight different menus, Danielle identified three possible ways to proceed:

OPTION 1: Price the entire menu at $1.29.

This would make things simple for the company, and it would be easy for consumers to understand. This option would also offer the most potential profit per item. But the challenge would be to convince people that these $1.29 items were all truly a "value" in a world where competitors offered many items for 99¢. This problem surfaced in Taco Bell's research; consumers rated the $1.29 menu the lowest of the eight menus it tested.

OPTION 2: Price items at 99¢ and $1.29 (Mixed Price Menu #4).

Purchase intent and overall liking were much stronger than for the $1.29 Menu. The pricing structure was still pretty simple since any item would cost either 99¢ or $1.29. Not surprisingly, though, consumers didn't rate a menu that included some $1.29 items as high as one that included only 99¢ items.

OPTION 3: Price items at 99¢, $1.19, and $1.29 (Mixed Price Menu #1).

Danielle's research showed that purchase intent, overall liking, and ratings of uniqueness were all strong for this menu. On the downside, the pricing structure was more complex. If customers were to accept it, they would have to be made to understand why there are three price points on a value menu and why certain items cost more than others.

Now, put yourself in Danielle Blugrind's shoes: Which option would you choose, and why?

"Yes, But What Does It Cost?"

As Danielle Blugrind discovered, the question of what to charge for a product is a central part of marketing decision making. In this chapter, we'll tackle the basic question, What is price? We'll also see how marketers begin to determine pricing strategies by developing pricing objectives and by looking at the role of demand, costs, revenues, and the environment in the pricing decision process. Then we'll explore how the pricing decision process leads to specific pricing strategies and tactics.

Monetary and Nonmonetary Prices

"If you have to ask how much it is, you can't afford it!" We've all heard that, but how often do you buy something without asking the price? If price weren't an issue, we'd all drive dream cars, take trips to exotic places, and live like royalty. In the real world, though, most of us need to consider a product's price before we buy it.

Price is the value that customers give up or exchange to obtain a desired product. Payment may be in the form of money, goods, services, favors, votes, or anything else that has *value* to the other party. As we explained in Chapter 1, marketing is the process that creates exchanges of things of value. We usually think of this exchange as people trading money for a good or a service. But in some marketplace practices, price can mean exchanges of nonmonetary value as well. Long before societies minted coins, people exchanged one good or service for another. This practice still occurs today. For example, someone who owns a home at a mountain ski resort may exchange a weekend stay for car repair or dental work. No money changes hands, but there is an exchange of value.

Other nonmonetary costs often are important to marketers. What is the cost of wearing seat belts? What is it worth to people to camp out in a clean national park? It is also important to consider an *opportunity cost*, or the value of something that is given up to obtain something else. For example, the cost of going to college includes more than tuition—it also includes the income that the student could have earned by working instead of going to classes (no, we're not trying to make you feel guilty). And what about a public service campaign designed to reduce alcohol-related accidents? The cost is a designated driver, a taxi fare—or simply not drinking. The value is reducing the risk of having a serious or possibly fatal accident. Unfortunately, too many people feel the chance of having an accident is so slim that the cost of abstaining from drinking is too high.

How important are good pricing decisions? Even during the best of economic times, most consumers rank "reasonable price," a price that makes the product affordable and that appears to be fair, as the most important consideration in a purchase and one that counts the most when they decide where to shop.[1] The plight of U.S. airlines is a good example of how bad pricing decisions can hurt an entire industry. From about 1982 to 1992, the airline industry engaged in a fierce price war, lowering the per-mile fare nearly 25 percent (accounting for inflation of the dollar) while costs such as labor and fuel more than doubled.[2] As a result, from 1990 to 1992, the airlines lost over $10 billion—more than they had earned since the start of commercial air travel. Of course, things haven't gotten much better for airlines today. In 2001–2002, the industry lost a record $30 billion, much of this loss driven by the terrorist attacks of September 11, 2001.[3]

price
The value that customers give up or exchange to obtain a desired product.

Developing Pricing Objectives

As shown in Figure 11.1, the first step in price planning is *developing pricing objectives*. Pricing objectives must support the broader objectives of the firm (such as maximizing shareholder value) as well as its overall marketing objectives (such as increasing market share). Table 11.1 provides examples of different types of pricing objectives, which we'll discuss next.

If you're going to drink and drive tonight, don't forget to kiss your mother goodbye.

A message from the Reader's Digest Foundation   MADD. Mothers Against Drunk Driving

Selling sobriety behind the wheel: Sometimes intangible costs are too high.

Figure 11.1   Steps in Price Planning

Successful price planning includes a series of orderly steps beginning with setting pricing objectives.

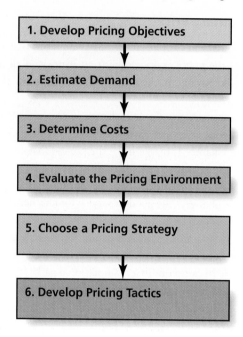

1. Develop Pricing Objectives

2. Estimate Demand

3. Determine Costs

4. Evaluate the Pricing Environment

5. Choose a Pricing Strategy

6. Develop Pricing Tactics

Sales or Market Share Objectives

Often the objective of a pricing strategy is to maximize sales (either in dollars or in units) or to increase market share. Does setting a price intended to increase unit sales or market share, one that focuses on sales objectives, simply mean pricing the product lower than the competition? Sometimes this is the case. Long-distance telephone companies such as MCI, Sprint, and AT&T relentlessly make rate adjustments to keep them ahead in the "telephone wars" (and they pay for numerous commercials to promote these changes). But lowering prices is not always necessary to increase market share. If a company's product has a competitive advantage, keeping the price at the same level as other firms may satisfy sales objectives (see Table 11.1).

Profit Objectives

As we discussed in Chapter 2, often a firm's overall objectives relate to a certain level of profit. When pricing strategies are determined by profit objectives, the focus is on a target level of profit growth or a desired net profit margin. A profit objective is important to firms that see profit as what motivates shareholders and bankers to invest in a company.

Although profits are an important consideration in the pricing of all goods and services, they are critical when the product is a fad. Fad products have a short market life, making a profit objective essential to allow the firm to recover its investment in a short period of time. In such cases, the firm must harvest profits before customers lose interest and move on to the next pet rock or hula hoop.

Competitive Effect Objectives

Competitive effect objectives mean that the pricing plan is intended to have a certain effect on the marketing efforts of the competition. Sometimes a firm may deliberately seek to preempt or reduce the effectiveness of one or more competitors. That's what happened when new low-fare airline JetBlue entered Delta's hub Atlanta market with flights from Atlanta to Los Angeles. Delta slashed its fares to respond to the new competitor, forcing JetBlue to abandon the Atlanta market.[4]

Table 11.1 Pricing Objectives

Type of Objective	Example
Sales or market share	Institute pricing strategy changes to support a 5 percent increase in sales.
Profit	During the first six months, set a price to yield a target profit of $200,000.
	Or
	Set prices to allow for an 8 percent profit margin on all goods sold.
Competitive effect	Alter pricing strategy during first quarter of the year to increase sales during competitor's introduction of new product.
	Or
	Maintain low end pricing policies to discourage new competitors from entering the market.
Customer satisfaction	Simplify pricing structure to simplify decision process for customers.
	Or
	Alter price levels to match customer expectations.
Image enhancement	Alter pricing policies to reflect the increased emphasis on the product's quality image.

Customer Satisfaction Objectives

Many quality-focused firms believe that profits result from making customer satisfaction the primary objective. These firms believe that by focusing solely on short-term profits, a company loses sight of keeping customers for the long term. Recognizing that many people hate to buy new cars because they feel the dealers are untrustworthy hucksters, Saturn started a trend with its value pricing strategy where customers get one price and one price only—no haggling, no negotiation, no "deals." Customers can even go to Saturn's Web site to get detailed price information without needing a salesperson. This objective is not only satisfying customers but also generating a new breed of car salespeople who use low-pressure sales tactics and promise customer satisfaction and long-term service.

Image Enhancement Objectives

Consumers often use price to make inferences about the quality of a product. In fact, marketers know that price is often an important means of communicating not only quality but also image to prospective customers. The image enhancement function of pricing is particularly important with **prestige products** (or luxury products), which have a high price and appeal to status-conscious consumers. Most of us would agree that the high price tag on a Rolex watch or a Rolls-Royce car, although representing the higher costs of producing the product, is vital to shaping an image of an extraordinary product with ownership limited to wealthy consumers.

Purex's pricing objectives focus on the competition. The number-two-selling detergent sets its price lower than the best-selling brand.

IT'S NOT YOUR SHOES.
IT'S NOT YOUR CAR.
IT'S NOT YOUR MUSIC.

IT'S YOUR WATCH THAT
TELLS MOST ABOUT WHO YOU ARE.

ARCTURA   THE WORLD'S ONLY KINETIC CHRONOGRAPH.
KINETIC   POWERED BY THE MOVEMENT OF YOUR BODY.
Chronograph   NEVER NEEDS A BATTERY.

SEIKO

SeikoUSA.com

AVAILABLE AT MARSHALL FIELD'S

People often are willing to pay a premium price for a luxury product like a watch because they believe (rightly or wrongly) that it makes a statement about their own worth.

prestige products
Products that have a high price and that appeal to status-conscious consumers.

Estimating Demand: How Demand Influences Pricing

The second step in price planning is to estimate demand. Demand refers to customers' desires for a product: How much of a product are they willing to buy as the price of the product goes up or down? Obviously, marketers should know the answer to this question before setting prices. Therefore, one of the earliest steps that marketers take in price planning is to estimate demand for their products.

Demand Curves

The effect of price on the quantity demanded of a product is often illustrated on a graph using a demand curve. The demand curve (which can be a curved or straight line) shows the quantity of a product that customers will buy in a market during a period of time at various prices if all other factors remain the same.

Figure 11.2 shows demand curves for normal and prestige products. The vertical axis for the demand curve represents the different prices that a firm might charge for a product (P). The horizontal axis shows the number of units or quantity (Q) of the product demanded. The demand curve for most goods (shown on the left side of Figure 11.2) slopes downward and to the right. As the price of the product goes up (P_1 to P_2), the number of units that customers are willing to buy goes down (Q_1 to Q_2). If prices decrease, customers will buy more. This is known as the *law of demand*. For example, if the price of bananas goes up, customers will probably buy fewer of them. And if the price really gets high, customers will eat their cereal without bananas.

Although this type of price–quantity relationship is typical, there are exceptions. There are situations in which (otherwise sane) people desire a product more as it *increases* in price. For prestige products such as luxury cars or jewelry, an increase in price may actually result in an *increase* in the quantity demanded because consumers see the products as more valuable. In such cases, the demand curve slopes upward. If the price decreases, consumers perceive the product to be less desirable, and demand may decrease. The right-hand side of Figure 11.2 shows the "backward-bending" demand curve associated with prestige products.

Still, the higher-price/higher-demand relationship has its limits. If the firm increases the price too much, making the product unaffordable for all but a few buyers, demand will begin to decrease, as shown by the backward direction taken by the top portion of the backward-bending curve.

SHIFTS IN DEMAND   The demand curves we've shown assume that all factors other than price stay the same. But what if they don't? What if the product is improved? What happens when there is a glitzy new advertising campaign that turns a product into a "must-have" for a lot of people? What if a stealthy photographer catches Russell Crowe using the product at home? Any of these things could cause an *upward shift* of the demand curve. An upward shift in the demand curve means that at any given price, demand is greater than before the shift occurs.

Figure 11.2 Demand Curves for Normal and Prestige Products

For normal products, there is an inverse relationship between price and demand. For prestige products, demand will increase—to a point—as price increases or will decrease as price decreases.

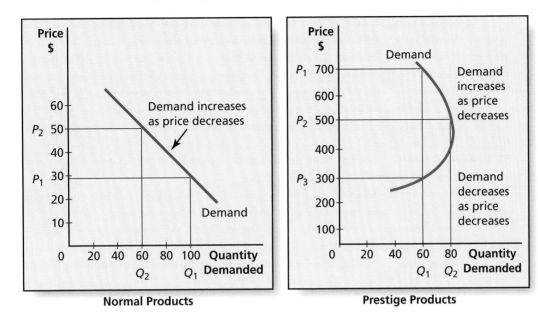

Normal Products   Prestige Products

Figure 11.3 shows the upward shift of the demand curve as it moves from D_1 to D_2. At D_1, before the shift occurs, customers will be willing to purchase the quantity Q_1 (or 80 units in Figure 11.3) at the given price, P (or $60 in Figure 11.3). For example, customers at a particular store may buy 80 barbecue grills at $60 a grill. But then the store runs a huge advertising campaign, featuring Queen Latifah on her patio using the barbecue grill. The demand curve shifts from D_1 to D_2. (The store keeps the price at $60.) Take a look at how the quantity demanded has changed to Q_2. In our example, the store is now selling 200 barbecue grills at $60 per grill. From a marketing standpoint, this shift is the best of all worlds. Without lowering prices, the company can sell more of its product. As a result, total revenues go up, and unless the new promotion costs as much as the increase in revenues it triggers, so do profits.

Figure 11.3 Shift in Demand Curve

Changes in the environment or in company efforts can cause a shift in the demand curve. A great advertising campaign, for example, can shift the demand curve upward.

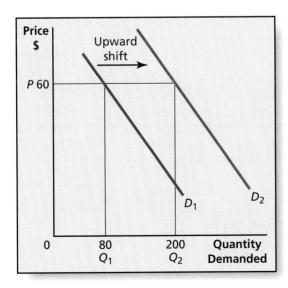

Of course, demand curves may also shift downward. That's what has happened with the demand for first-class airline seats. As companies and families become more concerned about costs, fewer customers buy first-class seats. In response, airlines are adding some first-class tickets that are 50 to 70 percent off the standard rate.[5]

In the real world, factors other than the price and marketing activities influence demand. If it rains, the demand for umbrellas increases and the demand for tee times on a golf course is a wash. As we noted earlier, demand for airline tickets decreased drastically after September 11, 2001. Because the airlines bought less jet fuel in reaction to this slowdown, gas prices fell at service stations around the country. In addition, the development of new products may influence demand for old ones. Even though some firms may still produce phonographs, the introduction of cassette tapes, CDs, and MP3s has all but eliminated the demand for new vinyl records and turntables to play them on.

ESTIMATING DEMAND Understanding and estimating demand is extremely important for marketers. For one, a firm's production scheduling is based on anticipated demand that must be estimated well in advance of when products are brought to market. In addition, all marketing planning and budgeting must be based on reasonably accurate estimates of potential sales.

So how do marketers reasonably estimate potential sales? Marketers predict total demand first by identifying the number of buyers or potential buyers for their product and then multiplying that estimate times the average amount each member of the target market is likely to purchase. Table 11.2 shows how a small business, such as a start-up pizza restaurant, estimates demand in markets it expects to reach. For example, the pizza entrepreneur may estimate that there are 180,000 consumer households in his market who would be willing to buy his pizza and that each household would purchase an average of six pizzas a year. The total annual demand is 1,080,000 pizzas (hold the anchovies on at least one of those, please).

Once the marketer estimates total demand, the next step is to predict what the company's market share is likely to be. The company's estimated demand is then its share of the whole (estimated) pie. In our pizza example, the entrepreneur may feel that he can gain 3 percent of this market, or about 2,700 pizzas per month—not bad for a new start-up business. Of course, such projections need to take into consideration other factors that might affect demand, such as new competitors entering the market, the state of the economy, and changing consumer tastes like a sudden demand for low-carb take-out food.

The Price Elasticity of Demand

In addition to understanding the relationship between price and demand, marketers also need to know how sensitive customers are to *changes* in price. In particular, it is critical to understand whether a change in price will have a large or a small impact on demand. How much can a firm increase or decrease its price before seeing a marked change in sales? If the price of a pizza goes up $1, will people switch to subs and burgers? What would happen if the pizza went up $2? Or even $5?

Table 11.2   Estimating Demand for Pizza

Number of families in market	180,000
Average number of pizzas per family per year	6
Total annual market demand	1,080,000
Company's predicted share of the total market	3%
Estimated annual company demand	32,400 pizzas
Estimated monthly company demand	2,700
Estimated weekly company demand	675

Price elasticity of demand is a measure of the sensitivity of customers to changes in price: If the price changes by 10 percent, what will be the percentage change in demand for the product? The word *elasticity* indicates that changes in price usually cause demand to stretch or retract like a rubber band. Price elasticity of demand is calculated as follows:

$$\text{Price elasticity of demand} = \frac{\text{percentage change in quantity demanded}}{\text{percentage change in price}}$$

Sometimes customers are very sensitive to changes in prices, and a change in price results in a substantial change in the quantity demanded. In such instances, we have a case of **elastic demand**. In other situations, we describe a change in price that has little or no effect on the quantity that consumers are willing to buy as **inelastic demand**.

For example, using the formula, suppose the pizza maker finds (from experience or from marketing research) that lowering the price of his pizza 10 percent (from $10 per pizza to $9) will cause a 15 percent increase in demand. He would calculate the price elasticity of demand as 15 divided by 10. The price elasticity of demand would be 1.5. If the price elasticity of demand is greater than 1, demand is elastic; that is, consumers respond to the price decrease by demanding more. Or, if the price increases, consumers will demand less. Figure 11.4 shows these calculations.

As Figure 11.5 illustrates, when demand is elastic, changes in price and in total revenues (total sales) work in opposite directions. If the price is increased, revenues decrease. If the price is decreased, total revenues increase. With elastic demand, the demand curve shown in Figure 11.5 is

price elasticity of demand
The percentage change in unit sales that results from a percentage change in price.

elastic demand
Demand in which changes in price have large effects on the amount demanded.

inelastic demand
Demand in which changes in price have little or no effect on the amount demanded.

Figure 11.4   Price Elasticity of Demand

Elastic demand

Price changes from $10 to $9.

$10 − 9 = $1

1/10 = 10% change in price

Demand changes from 2,700 per month to 3,100 per month

$$\begin{array}{r} 3{,}100 \\ -\,2{,}700 \\ \hline \end{array}$$

Increase   400 pizzas

Percentage increase   400/2,700 = .148 ~ 15% change in demand

$$\text{Price elasticity of demand} = \frac{\text{percentage change in quantity demanded}}{\text{percentage change in price}}$$

$$\text{Price elasticity of demand} = \frac{15\%}{10\%} = 1.5$$

Inelastic demand

Price changes from $10 to $9.

$10 − 9 = $1

1/10 = 10% change in price

Demand changes from 2,700 per month to 2,835 per month

$$\begin{array}{r} 2{,}835 \\ -\,2{,}700 \\ \hline \end{array}$$

Increase   135 pizzas

Percentage increase   135/2,700 = 0.05 ~ 5% change in demand

$$\text{Price elasticity of demand} = \frac{\text{percentage change in quantity demanded}}{\text{percentage change in price}}$$

$$\text{Price elasticity of demand} = \frac{5\%}{10\%} = 0.5$$

Figure 11.5 Price Elastic and Inelastic Demand Curves

Price elasticity of demand represents how demand responds to changes in prices. If there is little change in demand, then demand is said to be price inelastic. If there is a large change in demand, demand is price elastic.

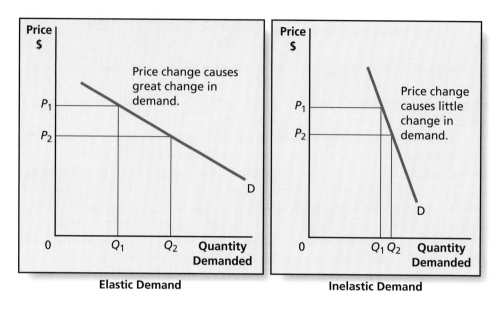

Elastic Demand   **Inelastic Demand**

more horizontal. With an elasticity of demand of 1.5, a decrease in price will increase the pizza maker's total sales.

As we noted earlier, in some instances, demand is *inelastic* so that a change in price results in little or no change in demand. For example, if the 10 percent decrease in the price of pizza resulted only in a 5 percent increase in pizza sales, then the price elasticity of demand calculated would be 5 divided by 10, which is 0.5 (less than 1), and our pizza maker faces inelastic demand. When demand is inelastic, price and revenue changes are in the same direction; that is, increases in price result in increases in total revenue, while decreases in price result in decreases in total revenue. With inelastic demand, the demand curve shown in Figure 11.5 becomes more vertical. Generally, the demand for necessities such as food and telephone service is inelastic. Even large price increases do not cause us to buy less food or to give up our telephone (though we may switch to a lower-priced alternative).

If demand is price inelastic, can marketers keep raising prices so that revenues and profits will grow larger and larger? And what if demand is elastic? Does it mean that marketers can never raise prices? The answer to these questions is no. Elasticity of demand for a product often differs for different price levels and with different percentages of change.

As a general rule, pizza makers and other companies can determine the *actual* price elasticity only after they have tested a pricing decision and calculated the resulting demand. Only then will they know whether a specific price change will increase or decrease revenues. To estimate what demand is likely to be at different prices for new or existing products, marketers often do research.

One approach is to conduct a study in which consumers tell marketers how much of a product they would be willing to buy at different prices. For example, researchers might ask participants if they would rent more movies if the price were reduced from $4 to $3 or how many bags of their favorite chocolate chip cookies they would buy at $3, $4, or $5. At other times, researchers conduct *field studies* in which they vary the price of a product in different stores and measure how much is actually purchased at the different price levels.

Other factors can affect price elasticity and sales. Consider the availability of *substitute* goods or services. If a product has a close substitute, its demand will be elastic; that is, a change in price will result in a change in demand, as consumers move to buy the substitute product. For example,

Coke and Pepsi may be considered close substitutes by all but the most die-hard cola fans. If the price of Pepsi goes up, many people will buy Coke instead. Marketers of products with close substitutes are less likely to compete on price, recognizing that doing so could result in less profit as consumers switch from one brand to another.

Changes in prices of other products also affect the demand for an item, a phenomenon called **cross-elasticity of demand**. When products are substitutes for each other, an increase in the price of one will increase the demand for the other. For example, if the price of bananas goes up, consumers may instead buy more strawberries, blueberries, or apples. However, when products are complements—that is, when one product is essential to the use of a second—an increase in the price of one decreases the demand for the second. For example, if the price of gasoline goes up, consumers may drive less, and thus demand for tires will decrease.

Determining Costs

Estimating demand helps marketers develop possible prices to charge for a product. It tells them how much they think they'll be able to sell at different prices. Knowing this brings them to the third step in determining a product's price: making sure the price will cover costs. Before marketers can determine price, they must understand the relationship of cost, demand, and revenue for their product. In this next section, we'll talk about different types of costs that marketers must consider in pricing. Then we'll show two types of analyses that marketers use in making pricing decisions.

The gasoline/electric hybrid Prius. It drives efficiently even when you don't. It combines a super-efficient gas engine with an advanced electric motor that never needs to be plugged in. It idles less, so it wastes less energy. It even comes with available GPS navigation. All of which makes Prius a more intelligent way to drive. So you can concentrate on other things.

GET THE FEELING. TOYOTA.
toyota.com/prius

52/45 MPG°   PRIUS | genius

°All figures based on 2001 EPA estimates. City/hwy MPG. Actual results may vary. SULEV-certified for California and some Northeastern states. ULEV-certified for the rest of the country. For more information, please see www.arb.ca.gov. ©2001 Toyota Motor Sales, U.S.A., Inc.

In the short run, the demand for gasoline is inelastic. In the long term, though, introduction of hybrid automobiles such as the Prius that run on gas and electricity may change that.

Types of Costs

It's obvious that the cost of producing a product plays a big role in deciding what to charge for it. If a firm prices a product lower than the cost to produce it, it doesn't take a rocket scientist to figure out that the firm will lose money. Before looking at how costs influence pricing decisions, it is necessary to understand the different types of costs that firms incur.

VARIABLE COSTS   First, in producing a product, a firm incurs **variable costs,** the per-unit costs of production that will fluctuate depending on how many units or individual products a firm produces. For example, if it takes 25 cents' worth of nails—a variable cost—to build one bookcase, it will take 50 cents' worth for two, 75 cents' worth for three, and so on. For the production of bookcases, variable costs would also include the cost of lumber and paint, and there would also be the cost of factory workers.

Figure 11.6 shows some examples of the variable cost per unit or average variable cost and the total variable costs at different levels of production (for producing 100, 200, and 500 bookcases). If the firm produces 100 bookcases, the average variable cost per unit is $50, and the total

cross-elasticity of demand
When changes in the price of one product affect the demand for another item.

variable costs
The costs of production (raw and processed materials, parts, and labor) that are tied to and vary depending on the number of units produced.

Figure 11.6 Variable Costs at Different Levels of Production

Variable Costs for Producing 100 Bookcases		Variable Costs for Producing 200 Bookcases		Variable Costs for Producing 500 Bookcases	
Wood	$13.25	Wood	$13.25	Wood	$9.40
Nails	0.25	Nails	0.25	Nails	0.20
Paint	0.50	Paint	0.50	Paint	0.40
Labor (3 hours × $12.00 per hr)	$36.00	Labor (3 hours × $12.00 per hr)	$36.00	Labor (2½ hours × $12.00 per hr)	$30.00
Cost per unit	$50.00	Cost per unit	$50.00	Cost per unit	$40.00
Multiply by number of units	100	Multiply by number of units	200	Multiply by number of units	500
Cost for 100 units:	$5,000	Cost for 200 units:	$10,000	Cost for 500 units:	$20,000

One bookcase = one unit.

variable cost is $5,000 ($50 × 100). If production is doubled to 200 units, the total variable cost now is $10,000 ($50 × 200).

In reality, calculating variable costs is usually more complex than what we've shown here. As the number of bookcases the factory produces increases or decreases, average variable costs may change. For example, if the company buys just enough lumber for one bookcase, the lumberyard will charge top dollar. If it buys enough for 100 bookcases, it'll get a better deal. And if it buys enough for thousands of bookcases, it may cut variable costs even more. Even the cost of labor goes down with increased production as manufacturers are likely to invest in labor-saving equipment that allows workers to produce bookcases faster. Figure 11.6 shows this to be the case. By purchasing wood, nails, and paint at a lower price (because of a volume discount) and by providing a means for workers to build bookcases more quickly, the cost per unit of producing 500 bookcases is reduced to $40 each.

Of course, variable costs don't always go down with higher levels of production. Using the bookcase example, at some point the demand for the labor, lumber, or nails required to produce the bookcases may exceed the supply. The bookcase manufacturer may have to pay employees overtime to keep up with production. The manufacturer may have to buy additional lumber from a distant supplier that will charge more to cover the costs of shipping. The cost per bookcase rises. You get the picture.

fixed costs
Costs of production that do not change with the number of units produced.

FIXED COSTS   Fixed costs are costs that do *not* vary with the number of units produced—the costs that remain the same whether the firm produces 1,000 bookcases this month or only 10. Fixed costs include rent or the cost of owning and maintaining the factory, utilities to heat or cool the factory, and the costs of equipment such as hammers, saws, and paint sprayers used in the production of the product. The salaries of a firm's executives and marketing managers also are fixed costs. All these costs are constant no matter how many items are manufactured.

average fixed cost
The fixed cost per unit produced.

Average fixed cost is the fixed cost per unit produced, that is, the total fixed costs divided by the number of units (bookcases) produced. Although total fixed costs remain the same no matter how many units are produced, the average fixed cost will decrease as the number of units produced increases. Say, for example, that a firm's total fixed costs of production are $30,000. If the firm produces one unit, the total of $30,000 is applied to the one unit. If it produces two units, $15,000, or one-half of the fixed costs, is applied to each unit and so on. As we produce more and more units, average fixed costs go down, and so does the price we must charge to cover fixed costs.

Of course, like variable costs, in the long term, total fixed costs may change. The firm may find that it can sell more of a product than it has manufacturing capacity to produce, so it builds a new factory, its executives' salaries go up, and more money goes into manufacturing equipment.

Combining variable costs and fixed costs yields **total costs** for a given level of production. As a company produces more and more of a product, both average fixed costs and average variable costs may decrease. Average total costs may decrease, too, up to a point. As we said, as output continues to increase, average variable costs may start to increase. These variable costs ultimately rise faster than average fixed costs decline, resulting in an increase to average total costs. As total costs fluctuate with differing levels of production, the price that producers have to charge to cover those costs changes accordingly. Therefore, marketers need to calculate the minimum price necessary to cover all costs—the *break-even price*.

Break-Even Analysis

Break-even analysis is a technique marketers use to examine the relationship between cost and price and to determine what sales volume must be reached at a given price before the company will completely cover its total costs and past which it will begin making a profit. Simply put, the **break-even point** is the point at which the company doesn't lose any money and doesn't make any profit. All costs are covered, but there isn't a penny extra. A break-even analysis allows marketers to identify how many units of a product they will have to sell at a given price to be profitable.

Figure 11.7 uses our bookcase manufacturing example to demonstrate break-even analysis. The vertical axis represents the amount of costs and revenue in dollars, and the horizontal axis shows the quantity of goods produced and sold. In this break-even model, we assume that there is a given total fixed cost and that variable costs do not change with the quantity produced.

In this example, let's say that the total fixed costs (the costs for the factory, the equipment, and electricity) are $200,000 and that the average variable costs (for materials and labor) are constant. The figure shows the total costs (variable costs plus fixed costs) and total revenues if varying quantities are produced and sold. The point at which the total revenue and total costs lines intersect is the break-even point. If sales are above the break-even point, the company makes a profit. Below that point, the firm will suffer a loss.

To determine the break-even point, the firm first needs to calculate the **contribution per unit**, or the difference between the price the firm charges for a product (the revenue per unit)

total costs
The total of the fixed costs and the variable costs for a set number of units produced.

break-even analysis
A method for determining the number of units that a firm must produce and sell at a given price to cover all its costs.

break-even point
The point at which the total revenue and total costs are equal and beyond which the company makes a profit; below that point, the firm will suffer a loss.

contribution per unit
The difference between the price the firm charges for a product and the variable costs.

Figure 11.7 Break-Even Analysis

Using break-even analysis, marketers can determine what sales volume to reach before the company makes a profit. This company needs to sell 4,000 bookcases at $100 each to break even.

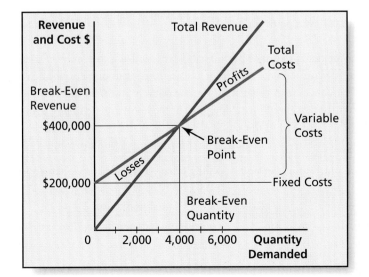

and the variable costs. This figure is the amount the firm has after paying for the wood, nails, paint, and labor to contribute to meeting the fixed costs of production. For our example, we will assume that the firm sells its bookcases for $100 each. Using the variable costs of $50 per unit that we had before, contribution per unit is $100 − $50 = $50. Using the fixed cost for the bookcase manufacturing of $200,000, we can now calculate the firm's break-even point in units of the product:

$$\text{Break-even point (in units)} = \frac{\text{total fixed costs}}{\text{contribution per unit to fixed costs}}$$

$$\text{Break-even point (in units)} = \frac{\$200,000}{\$50} = 4,000 \text{ units}$$

We see that the firm must sell 4,000 bookcases at $100 each to meet its fixed costs and to break even. We can also calculate the break-even point in dollars. This shows us that to break even, the company must sell $400,000 worth of bookcases:

$$\text{Break-even point (in dollars)} = \frac{\text{total fixed costs}}{1 - \dfrac{\text{variable cost per unit}}{\text{price}}}$$

$$\text{Break-even point (in dollars)} = \frac{\$200,000}{1 - \dfrac{\$50}{\$100}} = \frac{\$200,000}{1 - 0.5} = \frac{\$200,000}{0.5} = \$400,000$$

After the firm's sales have met and passed the break-even point, it begins to make a profit. How much profit? If the firm sells 4,001 bookcases, it will make a profit of $50. If it sells 5,000 bookcases, the profit would be calculated as follows:

$$\begin{aligned} \text{Profit} &= \text{quantity above break-even point} \times \text{contribution margin} \\ &= \$1,000 \times 50 \\ &= \$50,000 \end{aligned}$$

Often a firm will set a *profit goal*, which is the dollar profit figure it desires to earn. The break-even point may be calculated with that dollar goal included in the figures. In this case, it is not really a "break-even" point we are calculating because we're seeking profits. It's more of a "target amount." If our bookcase manufacturer feels it is necessary to realize a profit of $50,000, the calculations would be as follows:

$$\text{Break-even point (in units with target profit included)} = \frac{\text{total fixed costs} + \text{target profit}}{\text{contribution per unit to fixed costs}}$$

$$\text{Break-even point (in units)} = \frac{\$200,000 + 50,000}{\$50} = 5,000 \text{ units}$$

Sometimes the target return or profit goal is expressed as a *percentage of sales*. For example, a firm may say that it wants to make a profit of at least 10 percent on sales. In such cases, this profit is added to the variable cost in calculating the break-even point. In our example, the company would want to earn 10 percent of the selling price of the bookcase, or 10% × $100 = $10 per unit. We would simply add this $10 to the variable costs of $50 and calculate the new target amount as we calculated the break-even point before. The contribution per unit becomes

$$\begin{aligned} \text{Contribution per unit} &= \text{selling price} - (\text{variable costs} + \text{target profit}) \\ &= \$100 - (\$50 + \$10) = \$40 \end{aligned}$$

$$\text{Break-even point (in units)} = \frac{\text{total fixed costs}}{\text{contribution per unit to fixed costs}}$$

$$\text{Break-even point (in units)} = \frac{\$200,000}{\$40} = 5,000 \text{ units}$$

Break-even analysis does not provide an easy answer for pricing decisions. It provides answers about how many units the firm must sell to break even and to make a profit, but without knowing whether demand will equal that quantity at that price, companies can make big mistakes. It is, therefore, useful for marketers to estimate the demand for their product and then perform a marginal analysis.

Marginal Analysis

Marginal analysis provides a way for marketers to look at cost and demand at the same time and to identify the output and the price that will generate the maximum profit. Figure 11.8 provides a look at the various cost and revenue elements considered in marginal analysis. Like Figure 11.7, the vertical axis in Figure 11.8 represents the cost and revenues in dollars, and the horizontal axis shows the quantity produced and sold. Figure 11.8 shows the average revenue, average cost, marginal revenue, and marginal cost curves. When doing a marginal analysis, marketers examine the relationship of **marginal cost** (the increase in total costs from producing one additional unit of a product) to **marginal revenue** (the increase in total income or revenue that results from selling one additional unit of a product). Average revenue is also the demand curve and thus represents that amount customers will buy at different prices—people buy more only if price and thus revenue decrease. Thus, both average revenue and marginal revenue decrease with each additional unit sold.

If only one unit is produced, the average total cost per unit is the same as the marginal cost per unit. After the first unit, the cost of *producing each additional unit* (marginal cost) and the average cost at first decrease. Eventually, however, both marginal costs and average costs begin to increase since, as we discussed earlier, both average fixed costs and average variable costs may increase in the long term.

Profit is maximized at the point at which marginal cost is *exactly* equal to marginal revenue. At that point, the cost of producing one unit is exactly equal to the revenue to be realized from selling that one unit. If, however, one additional unit is produced, the cost of producing that unit is *greater than* the revenue from the sale of the unit, and total profit actually begins to decrease. So it just makes sense for firms to keep production and sales at the point of maximum profit.

marginal analysis
A method that uses cost and demand to identify the price that will maximize profits.

marginal cost
The increase in total cost that results from producing one additional unit of a product.

marginal revenue
The increase in total income or revenue that results from selling one additional unit of a product.

Figure 11.8 Marginal Analysis

Marginal analysis allows marketers to consider both costs and demand in calculating a price that maximizes profits.

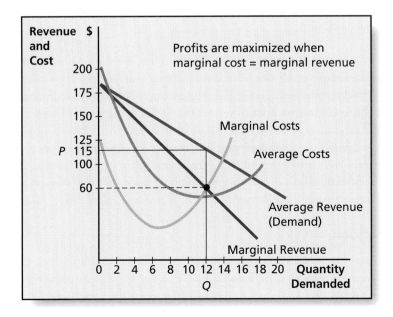

When the economy is hurting, consumers are more interested in paying lower prices—and they're more skeptical about high-priced status symbols.

One word of caution when using marginal analysis: Although in theory the procedure is straightforward, in the real world things seldom are. Production costs may vary unexpectedly because of shortages, inclement weather, unexpected equipment repairs, and so on. Revenues may also unexpectedly move up and down because of the economy, what the competition is doing, or a host of other reasons. Predicting demand, an important factor in marginal analysis, is never an exact science. This makes marginal analysis a less-than-perfect way to determine the best price for a product. Indeed, it is theoretically more sound than break-even analysis, but most firms find the break-even approach more useful.

Evaluating the Pricing Environment

In addition to demand and costs, marketers look at factors in the firm's external environment when they make pricing decisions. Thus, the fourth step in developing pricing strategies is to examine and evaluate the pricing environment. Only then can marketers set a price that not only covers costs but also provides a competitive advantage—a price that meets the needs of customers better than the competition. This section will discuss some important external influences on pricing strategies—the economic environment, competition, and consumer trends.

The Economy

Economic trends tend to direct pricing strategies. The business cycle, inflation, economic growth, and consumer confidence all help to determine whether one pricing strategy or another will succeed. But the upswings and downturns in a national economy do not affect all product categories or all regions equally. Marketers need to understand how economic trends will affect their particular business.

TRIMMING THE FAT: PRICING IN A RECESSION   During recessions, consumers grow more price-sensitive. They switch to generic brands to get a better price and patronize discount stores and warehouse outlets. Even wealthy households, relatively unaffected by the recession, tend to cut back on conspicuous consumption. As a result, during periods of recession, many firms find it necessary to cut prices to levels at which costs are covered but the company doesn't make a profit to keep factories in operation.

INCREASING PRICES: RESPONDING TO INFLATION   There are also some economic trends that allow firms to increase prices, altering what consumers see as an acceptable or unacceptable price range for a product. Inflation may give marketers causes to either increase or decrease prices. First, inflation gets customers used to price increases. They may remain insensitive to price increases, even when inflation goes away, allowing marketers to make real price increases, not just those that adjust for the inflation. Of course, during periods of inflation, consumers may grow fearful of the future and worry about whether they will have enough money to meet basic needs. In such a case, they may cut back on purchases. Then, as in periods of recession, inflation may cause marketers to lower prices and temporarily sacrifice profits in order to maintain sales levels.

The Competition

Marketers try to anticipate how the competition will respond to their pricing actions. They know that consumers' expectations of what constitutes a fair price depend on what the competition is charging. However, it's not always a good idea to fight the competition with lower and lower prices. Pricing wars such as those in the fast-food industry can change consumers' perceptions of what is a "fair" price, leaving them unwilling to buy at previous price levels.

The type of competitive environment in which an industry operates—that is, whether it's an oligopoly, monopolistic competition, or pure competition—also influences price decisions. Generally, firms that do business in an oligopoly (in which the market has few sellers and many buyers) are more likely to adopt *status quo* pricing objectives in which the pricing of all competitors is similar. Such objectives are attractive to oligopolistic firms because avoiding price competition allows all players in the industry to remain profitable. In a state of monopolistic competition, in which there are a lot of sellers each offering a slightly different product, it is possible for firms to differentiate products and to focus on nonprice competition. Then each firm prices its product on the basis of its cost without much concern for matching the exact price of competitors' sweaters.

Firms in a purely competitive market have little opportunity to raise or lower prices. Rather, the price of soybeans, corn, or fresh peaches is directly influenced by supply and demand. When bad weather hurts crops, prices go up. And prices for almost any kind of fish have increased dramatically since health-conscious consumers began turning away from beef and other red meat.

Consumer Trends

Another environmental influence on price is consumer trends. Culture and demographics determine how consumers think and behave and so have a large impact on all marketing decisions. Take, for example, the buying habits of the women who opted for a career in their 20s but who are hearing the ticking of their biological clocks as they enter their late 30s and 40s. Couples having babies later in their lives are often better off financially than younger parents, and on average they will have fewer children to spoil, so they are more willing to spend whatever it costs to give their babies the best.

Another important trend is that even well-off people no longer consider it shameful to hunt for bargains—in fact, it's becoming cool to boast that you found one. As a marketing executive for a chain of shopping malls observed, "Everybody loves to save money. It's a badge of honor today." Luxury consumers are looking for prestigious brands at low prices, though they're still willing to splurge for some high-ticket items. Industry analysts have called this new interest in hunting for sales "strategic shopping."[6]

$15K IS EITHER A VERY LAME YACHT OR A VERY SWEET TV

LG
LIFE'S GOOD

THE 60" WIDE-SCREEN LG PLASMA HDTV MONITOR: A NEXT GENERATION PANEL FOR INCREDIBLE PICTURE. FAROUDJA PROCESSOR, ADVANCED ZOOM AND FLEXIBLE PIP. A BIT MUCH. YES. OVER THE TOP? DEFINITELY. WANT TO KNOW MORE? SEE THE FULL RANGE OF FLATPANELS AT WWW.LGUSA.COM OR CALL 1-800-243-0000.

Consumers today are on the prowl for luxury goods, even if choosing one means delaying getting another.

Choosing a Price Strategy

An old Russian proverb says, "There are two kinds of fools in any market. One doesn't charge enough. The other charges too much."[7] In modern business, there seldom is any one-and-only, now-and-forever, best pricing strategy. Like playing a chess game, making pricing moves and countermoves require thinking two and three moves ahead.

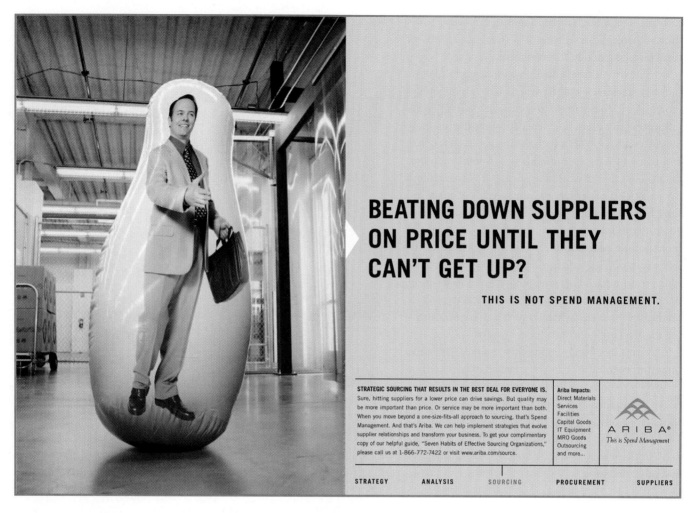

Business purchasers often try to get the supplies they need at the lowest possible price so that they can keep their costs down—sometimes at the expense of quality.

The next step in price planning is therefore choosing a price strategy. Some strategies work for certain products, with certain customer groups, in certain competitive markets. When is it best for the firm to undercut the competition and when to just meet the competition's prices? When is the best pricing strategy one that covers costs only, and when is it best to use one based on demand? Marketers who need to develop pricing strategies will consider many alternatives and try to anticipate their outcomes.

Pricing Strategies Based on Cost

Marketing planners often choose cost-based strategies because they are simple to calculate and relatively risk free. They promise that the price will at least cover the costs the company incurs in producing and marketing the product.

Cost-based pricing methods have drawbacks, however. They do not consider such factors as the nature of the target market, demand, competition, the product life cycle, and the product's image. Moreover, although the calculations for setting the price may be simple and straightforward, accurate cost estimating may prove difficult. Think about firms such as 3M, General Electric, and Nabisco, all of which produce many products. How does cost analysis allocate the costs for the plant, research and development, equipment, design engineers, maintenance, and marketing personnel so that the pricing plan accurately reflects the cost of producing any one product? For example, how do you allocate the salary of a marketing executive who oversees many different products?

Dell Computers uses demand pricing to maintain its annual sales of $40 billion. The computer giant monitors demand on a regular basis and then lowers its prices when necessary to kick-start declining sales.

Should the cost be divided equally among all products? Should costs be based on the actual number of hours spent working on each product? Or should costs be assigned based on the revenues generated by each product? There is no one right answer. Even within these limitations, cost-based pricing strategies often are a marketer's best choice.

The most common cost-based approach to pricing a product is **cost-plus pricing**, in which the marketer totals all the costs for the product and then adds an amount (or marks up the the the cost of the item) to arrive at the selling price. Many marketers, especially retailers and wholesalers, use cost-plus pricing because of its simplicity—users need only estimate the unit cost and add the markup. To calculate cost-plus pricing, marketers usually calculate either a markup on cost or a markup on selling price. With both methods, the price is calculated by adding a predetermined percentage to the cost, but as the names of the methods imply, for one the calculation uses a percentage of the costs and for the other a percentage of the selling price. Which of the two methods is used seems often to be little more than a matter of the "the way our company has always done it." More about cost-plus pricing and how to calculate markup on cost and markup on selling price are in the Marketing Math appendix at the end of this book.

cost-plus pricing
A method of setting prices in which the seller totals all the costs for the product and then adds an amount to arrive at selling price.

Pricing Strategies Based on Demand

Demand-based pricing means that the selling price is based on an estimate of volume or quantity that a firm can sell in different markets at different prices. To use any of the pricing strategies based on demand, firms must determine how much product they can sell in each market and at what price. As noted earlier, marketers often use customer surveys where consumers indicate whether

demand-based pricing
A price-setting method based on estimates of demand at different prices.

they would buy a certain product and how much of it they would buy at various prices. More accurate estimates may be obtained by some type of field experiment. For example, a firm might actually offer the product at different price levels in different test markets and gauge the reaction.

Two specific demand-based pricing strategies are target costing and yield management pricing.

TARGET COSTING   Today, firms are finding that they can be more successful if they match price with demand using a process called **target costing**.[8] A firm first determines the price at which customers would be willing to buy the product and then works backward to design the product in such a way that it can produce and sell the product at a profit.

With target costing, firms first use marketing research to identify the quality and functionality needed to satisfy attractive market segments and what price they are willing to pay *before the product is designed*. As Figure 11.9 shows, the next step is to determine what margins retailers and dealers require as well as the profit margin the company requires. On the basis of this information, managers can calculate the target cost—the maximum it will cost the firm to manufacture the product. If the firm can meet customer quality and functionality requirements and control costs to meet the required price, it will manufacture the product. If not, it abandons the product.

YIELD MANAGEMENT PRICING   **Yield management pricing**, another type of demand-based pricing, is a pricing strategy used by airlines, hotels, and cruise lines. Firms charge different prices to different customers in order to manage capacity while maximizing revenues. Many service firms practice yield management pricing because they recognize that different customers have different sensitivities to price—some customers will pay top dollar for an airline ticket, while others will travel only if there is a discount fare. The goal of yield management pricing is to accurately predict the proportion of customers who fall into each category and allocate the percentages of the airline's or hotel's capacity accordingly so that no product goes unsold.

For example, an airline may charge two prices for the same seat: the full fare ($899) and the discount fare ($299). The airline must predict how many seats it can fill at full fare and how many can be sold only at the discounted fare. The airline begins months ahead of the date of the flight

target costing
A process in which firms identify the quality and functionality needed to satisfy customers and what price they are willing to pay before the product is designed; the product is manufactured only if the firm can control costs to meet the required price.

yield management pricing
A practice of charging different prices to different customers in order to manage capacity while maximizing revenues.

Figure 11.9   Target Costing Using a Jeans Example

With target costing, a firm first determines the price at which customers would be willing to buy the product and then works backward to design the product in such a way that it can produce and sell the product at a profit.

Step 1: Determine the price customers are willing to pay for the jeans
 $39.99

Step 2: Determine the markup required by the retailer
 40% (.40)

Step 3: Calculate the maximum price the retailer will pay, the markup amount

 Formula: Price to the retailer = Selling price × (1.00 − markup percentage)
 Price to the retailer = $39.99   × (1.00 − .40)
 = $39.99   × 0.60 =   **$23.99**

Step 4: Determine the profit required by the firm
 15% (.15)

Step 5: Calculate the target cost, the maximum cost of producing the jeans
 Formula: Target cost = Price to the Retailer × (1.00 − profit percentage)
 Target cost = $23.99 × 0.85 =   **$20.39**

with a basic allocation of seats—perhaps it will place 25 percent in the full-fare "bucket" and 75 percent in the discount-fare "bucket." While the seats in the full-fare bucket cannot be sold at the discounted price, the seats allocated for the discounted price can be sold at the full fare.

As flight time gets closer, the airline might make a series of adjustments to the allocation of seats in the hope of selling every seat on the plane at the highest price possible. If the New York Mets need to book the flight, chances are some of the discount seats will be sold at full fare, decreasing the number available at the discounted price. If, as the flight date nears, the number of full-fare ticket sales falls below the forecast, some of those seats will be moved to the discount bucket. This process continues until the day of the flight as the airline attempts to have every seat filled when the plane takes off. This is why you may be able to get a fantastic price on an airline ticket through an Internet auction site such as Priceline.com if you wait until the last minute to buy your ticket.

Pricing Strategies Based on the Competition

Sometimes a firm's pricing strategy involves pricing its wares near, at, above, or below the competition. In the "good old days," when U.S. automakers had the home market to themselves, pricing decisions were straightforward: Industry giant General Motors would announce its new car prices, and Ford, Chrysler, Packard, Studebaker, and the others got in line or dropped out. A **price leadership** strategy, which usually is the rule in an industry dominated by a few firms and called an oligopoly, may be in the best interest of all firms because it minimizes price competition. Price leadership strategies are popular because they provide an acceptable and legal way for firms to agree on prices without ever talking with each other.

Pricing Strategies Based on Customers' Needs

When firms develop pricing strategies that cater to customers, they are less concerned with short-term results than with keeping customers for the long term. New Era firms constantly assess customers' responses in developing pricing strategies. U.S. Cellular refines its pricing strategies by talking to customers to determine the best blend of minutes, plan features, and price.[9] The firm even designed its FarmFlex Plan to offer farmers one rate during the planting season and a lower rate in the off-season.

Firms that practice **value pricing**, or **everyday low pricing (EDLP)**, develop a pricing strategy that promises ultimate value to consumers. What this really means is that, in the customers' eyes, the price is justified by what they receive.[10] At Wal-Mart Stores, Inc., the world's largest company, everyday low pricing is a fundamental part of the company's success. Wal-Mart has demanded tens of billions of dollars in cost efficiencies from its retail supply chain and passes these savings on to its customers. To compete, other retailers must reduce their prices. For example, in marketers where

EPSON

After all our intensive inspections, there was one thing we didn't need to double check. The price.

Introducing the Epson PowerLite® S1. Finally, an extremely reliable projector with an equally remarkable price.

▷ Bright: 1200 lumens dazzle, even in a well-lit room
▷ Light: 7.0 pounds travel easily wherever you go
▷ Tested: 60 functional tests, 12 image quality tests, 1-hr. lamp-on test
▷ Trusted: Epson is chosen 5 to 1 by leading experts as most reliable

$999

For more information, call 1-800-GO-EPSON or visit epson.com/4presenters

Complete results of the reliability study on Epson projectors are available by calling 1-800-GO-EPSON.
Epson is a registered trademark of Seiko Epson Corp. PowerLite is a registered trademark of Epson America, Inc. © 2003 Epson America, Inc. © Hunter Freeman

Epson expresses confidence that its prices are competitive.

price leadership
A pricing strategy in which one firm first sets its price and other firms in the industry follow with the same or very similar prices.

value pricing
A pricing strategy in which a firm sets prices that provide ultimate value to customers.

everyday low pricing (EDLP)
See value pricing.

MEASURING VALUE
marketing metrics

The consulting firm Booz Allen began to work with a phone company to improve the profitability of its business customer segment, which consists of small to medium businesses with 50 to 200 phone lines. The phone company is small, so it must maximize profit on every customer through personalized, targeted marketing. The project team conducted an experiment where some customers were offered specially designed plans with unique pricing arrangements. The goal was to encourage them to renew contracts so that the phone company wouldn't have to spend a lot to acquire new customers when existing ones switch to other carriers.

They created two metrics: customers' *change-in-spend* (how much more customers spent after accepting the new plan) and customers' *churn rate* (the number of customers who switch their phone plans to a different company). Under the existing plans, the annual churn rate is about 25 percent, meaning that one-fourth of the company's customers switch their plan in a year. Because it costs the company at least $500 in sales and promotional expenses to acquire a new customer, reducing the churn rate would be a major accomplishment. If a customer produces a profit of $1,000 over a 12-month contract, the company nets $500 ($1,000 less the cost of acquiring the customer). If it can get the customer to sign for a second year, net profit will rise sharply because there is no acquisition cost for the second year. Even if the lower-priced calling plan results in less revenue from that customer, the company still comes out ahead.[12]

skimming price
A very high, premium price that a firm charges for its new, highly desirable product.

Wal-Mart sells food products, grocery prices are on the average 14 percent lower. It is estimated that Wal-Mart saved its U.S. customers $20 billion in 2002 alone.[11]

When firms base price strategies solely or mainly on cost, they are operating under the old production orientation and not a marketing orientation. Value-based pricing begins with customers, then considers the competition, and then determines the best pricing strategy. Changing pricing strategies at Procter & Gamble (P&G) in recent years illustrate value pricing in action. Until about a decade ago, P&G watched as sales dollar volume dropped for its Charmin toilet tissue, Dawn dishwashing liquid, Pringles potato chips, and many other well-established brands. More and more shoppers were buying whatever brand was on sale or had a special promotion offer. To rebuild loyalty, P&G switched to an EDLP pricing strategy. It reduced everyday prices 12 to 24 percent on nearly all U.S. brands by cutting the amount it spent on trade promotions. P&G said, in effect, "This really is our best price, and it's a good value for the money. Buy now. There will be no sale next week. We won't do business that way."

New-Product Pricing

As we discussed in Chapter 8, new products are vital to the growth and profits of a firm, but they also present unique pricing challenges. When a product is new to the market or when there is no established industry price norm, marketers may use a skimming price strategy, a penetration pricing strategy, or trial pricing when they first introduce the item to the market.

SKIMMING PRICE Setting a **skimming price** means that the firm charges a high, premium price for its new product with the intention of reducing it in future response to market pressures. For example, when Top-Flite introduced its new Strata golf balls with a new dimple design and more solid core for better flight with metal clubs, the price was three times that of regular balls. Pro shops still couldn't keep them in stock.[13]

If a product is highly desirable and it offers unique benefits, demand is price inelastic during the introductory stage of the product life cycle, allowing a company to recover research-and-development and promotion costs. When rival products enter the market, the price is lowered in order for the firm to remain competitive. Firms focusing on profit objectives in developing their pricing strategies often set skimming prices for new products.

A skimming price is more likely to succeed if the product provides some important benefits to the target market that make customers feel they must have it no matter what the cost. When introduced in the late 1960s, handheld calculators were such a product. To the total astonishment of consumers at that time, these magic little devices could add, subtract, multiply, and divide with just the push of a button. It's equally hard for consumers today to believe that back then these gizmos sold for as high as $200. Today, Hewlett-Packard's new financial calculator allows owners to do symbolic algebra, calculus, and graphing and comes with an 856-page user's guide, all for $176.[14]

Second, for skimming pricing to be successful, there should be little chance that competitors can get into the market quickly. With highly complex, technical products, it may be quite a while before competitors can put a rival product into production. Finally, a skimming pricing strategy is most successful when the market consists of several customer segments with different levels of price sensitivity. There must be a substantial number of initial product customers who have very low price sensitivity. After a period of time, the price can go down, and a second segment of the market with a slightly higher level of price sensitivity will purchase and so on.

PENETRATION PRICING **Penetration pricing** is just the opposite of skimming pricing. This strategy means that a new product is introduced at a very low price in order to sell more in a short period of time, thus gaining market share early on. One reason marketers use penetration pricing is to discourage competitors from entering the market. The firm first out with a new product has an important advantage. Experience has shown that a pioneering brand often is able to maintain dominant market share for long periods of time. Penetration pricing may act as a *barrier to entry* for competitors if the prices the market will bear are so low that the company will not be able to recover development and manufacturing costs. Bayer aspirin and Hoover vacuum cleaners are examples of brands that were first to market decades ago and still dominate their industries today. Such pioneering brands don't need to do much talking to tell consumers who they are.

TRIAL PRICING With **trial pricing**, a new product carries a low price for a limited period of time to attract the customer. The idea is to win customer acceptance first and make profits later, as when a new health club offers an introductory membership to start pulling people in. Microsoft introduced the Access database program at the short-term promotional price of $99; the suggested retail price was $495. Marketers from Microsoft hoped people would be lured to try the product at the lower price and then would be so impressed with the program that they would persuade others to buy it at the full price.

penetration pricing
A pricing strategy in which a firm introduces a new product at a very low price to encourage more customers to purchase it.

trial pricing
Pricing a new product low for a limited period of time in order to lower the risk for a customer.

Developing Pricing Tactics

Once marketers have developed pricing strategies, the last step in price planning is to implement them. The methods companies use to set their strategies in motion are their *pricing tactics*.

Pricing for Individual Products

Once marketers have settled on a product's price, the way they present it to the market can make a big difference. Here are two tactics with examples of each:

- *Two-part pricing* requires two separate types of payments to purchase the product. For example, golf and tennis clubs charge yearly or monthly fees plus fees for each round of golf or tennis. Likewise, cellular phone service providers offer customers a set number of minutes usage for a monthly fee plus a per-minute rate for extra usage.
- *Payment pricing* makes the consumer think the price is "do-able"[15] by breaking up the total price into smaller amounts payable over time. For example, many customers now opt to lease rather than buy a car. The monthly lease amount is an example of payment pricing, which tends to make people less sensitive to the total price of the car (sticker shock).[16]

Pricing for Multiple Products

A firm may sell several products that consumers typically buy at one time. As fast-food restaurants like Taco Bell know, selling a taco for lunch usually invites purchase of a soft drink and maybe a burrito as well. The sale of a paper-cup dispenser usually means a package of cups is not far behind. The two most common tactics for pricing multiple products are price bundling and captive pricing.

Price bundling means selling two or more goods or services as a single package for one price. A music buff can buy tickets to an entire concert series for a single price. A PC typically comes bundled with a monitor, a keyboard, and software. Even an all-you-can-eat special at the local diner is an example of price bundling. Recently, phone service companies including MCI and Verizon have begun offering customers unlimited local and long-distance calls plus such add-on features as call waiting and voicemail for a flat monthly fee.[17]

From a marketing standpoint, price bundling makes sense. If products are priced separately, then it is likely that customers will buy some but not all the items. They might choose to put off

price bundling
Selling two or more goods or services as a single package for one price.

captive pricing
A pricing tactic for two items that must be used together; one item is priced very low, and the firm makes its profit on another, high-margin item essential to the operation of the first item.

some purchases until later, or they might buy from a competitor. Whatever revenue a seller loses from the reduced prices it makes up in increased total purchases.

Captive pricing is a pricing tactic a firm uses when it has two products that work only when used together. The firm sells one item at a very low price and then makes its profit on the second high-margin item. This tactic is commonly used to sell shaving products where the razor is relatively cheap but the blades are not. Similarly, some film manufacturers practically give away the camera in order to keep selling you the film.

Auto manufacturers know that a per-month price for a new car seems a lot easier for consumers to swallow than the "sticker shock" they get when thinking about the total price.

F.O.B. origin pricing
A pricing tactic in which the cost of transporting the product from the factory to the customer's location is the responsibility of the customer.

F.O.B. delivered pricing
A pricing tactic in which the cost of loading and transporting the product to the customer is included in the selling price and is paid by the manufacturer.

Distribution-Based Pricing

Distribution-based pricing is a pricing tactic that establishes how firms handle the cost of shipping products to customers near, far, and wide. Characteristics of the product, the customers, and the competition figure in the decision to charge all customers the same price or to vary according to shipping cost.

F.O.B. PRICING Often a price is given as F.O.B. factory or F.O.B. delivered. F.O.B. stands for "free on board," which means the supplier will pay to have the product loaded onto a truck or some other carrier. Also—and this is important—*title passes to the buyer* at the F.O.B. location. F.O.B. factory or **F.O.B. origin pricing** means that the cost of transporting the product from the factory to the customer's location is the responsibility of the customer. **F.O.B. delivered pricing** means that the seller pays both the cost of loading and the cost of transporting to the customer, which is included in the selling price.

INTERNATIONAL DISTRIBUTION PRICING TERMS OF SALE
Delivery terms for pricing of products sold in international markets are especially important. Some of the more common terms are the following:[18]

- CIF (cost, insurance, freight) is the term used for ocean shipments and means the seller quotes a price for the goods (including insurance), all transportation, and miscellaneous charges to the point of debarkation from the vessel.

- CFR (cost and freight) means the quoted price covers the goods and the cost of transportation to the named point of debarkation but the buyer must pay the cost of insurance. The CFR term is typically used only for ocean shipments.

- CIP (carriage and insurance paid to) and CPT (carriage paid to) include the same provisions as CIF and CFR but are used for shipment by modes other than water.

BASING-POINT PRICING Another distribution-based pricing tactic, **basing-point pricing**, means marketers choose one or more locations to serve as basing points. Customers pay shipping charges from these basing points to their delivery destinations whether the goods are actually shipped from these points or not. For example, a customer in Los Angeles may order a product from a company in San Diego. The product is shipped to Los Angeles from the San Diego warehouse. However, if the designated basing point is Dallas, the customer pays shipping charges from Dallas to Los Angeles, charges that were never incurred by the seller.

UNIFORM DELIVERED PRICING In **uniform delivered pricing**, an average shipping cost is added to the price, no matter what the distance from the manufacturer's plant—within reason. For example, when you order a CD from a music supplier, you may pay the cost of the CD plus $2.99 shipping and handling, no matter what the actual cost of the shipping to your particular location. Internet sales, catalog sales, home television shopping, and other types of nonstore retail sales usually use uniform delivered pricing.

FREIGHT ABSORPTION PRICING **Freight absorption pricing** means the seller takes on part or all of the cost of shipping. This policy is good for high-ticket items when the cost of shipping is a negligible part of the sales price and the profit margin. Marketers are most likely to use freight absorption pricing in highly competitive markets or when such pricing allows them to enter new markets.

Discounting for Members of the Channel

So far we've talked about pricing tactics used to sell to end customers. Now we'll talk about tactics used for pricing to members of the channel of distribution.

Whether a firm sells to businesses or directly to consumers, most pricing structures are built around list prices. A **list price**, also referred to as a *suggested retail price*, is the price that the manufacturer sets as the appropriate price for the end consumer to pay. In pricing for members of the channel, marketers recognize that retailers and wholesalers have costs to cover and profit targets to reach as well. Thus, they often begin with the list price and then use a number of discounting tactics to implement pricing to members of the channel of distribution—wholesalers, distributors, and retailers. Such tactics include the following:

Gillette practices captive pricing with its razors. Once customers have bought the razor, they are a "captive" of the company's blade prices.

- **Trade or functional discounts:** Because the channel members perform selling, credit, storage, and transportation services that the manufacturer would otherwise have to provide, manufacturers often offer **trade or functional discounts**, usually set percentage discounts off list price for each channel level.

- **Quantity discounts:** To encourage larger purchases from distribution channel partners, marketers may use **quantity discounts**, or reduced prices for purchases of larger quantities. **Cumulative quantity discounts** are based on a total quantity bought within a specified time period, often a year, and encourage a buyer to stick with a single seller instead of moving from one supplier to another. Cumulative quantity discounts may be in the form of *rebates*, in which case the firm sends the buyer a rebate check at the end of the discount period or as a credit against future orders.

- **Noncumulative quantity discounts: Noncumulative quantity discounts** are based only on the quantity purchased with each individual order and encourage larger single orders but do little to tie the buyer and the seller together.

- **Cash discounts:** Many firms try to entice their customers to pay their bills quickly by offering cash discounts. For example, a firm selling to a retailer may state that the terms of the sale

basing-point pricing
A pricing tactic where customers pay shipping charges from set basing point locations whether the goods are actually shipped from these points or not.

uniform delivered pricing
A pricing tactic in which a firm adds a standard shipping charge to the price for all customers regardless of location.

freight absorption pricing
A pricing tactic in which the seller absorbs the total cost of transportation.

list price
The price the end customer is expected to pay as determined by the manufacturer; also referred to as the suggested retail price.

trade or functional discounts
Discounts off list price of products to members of the channel of distribution that perform various marketing functions.

quantity discounts
A pricing tactic of charging reduced prices for purchases of larger quantities of a product.

cumulative quantity discounts
Discounts based on the total quantity purchased within a specified time period.

noncumulative quantity discounts
Discounts based only on the quantity purchased with individual orders.

are "2 percent 10 days, net 30 days," meaning that if the retailer pays the producer for the goods within 10 days, the amount due is cut by 2 percent. The total amount is due within 30 days, and after 30 days the payment is late.

- **Seasonal discounts:** Seasonal discounts are price reductions offered only during certain times of the year. For seasonal products such as snowblowers, lawn mowers, and water-skiing equipment, marketers use seasonal discounts to entice retailers and wholesalers to buy off-season and store the product at their locations until the right time of the year. Alternatively, discounts may be offered when products are in-season to create a competitive advantage during periods of high demand.

Pricing with Electronic Commerce

As we have seen, pricing for "bricks-and-mortar" firms is a complex decision process. But the advent of the Internet brought even more options. Because sellers are connected to buyers around the globe as never before through the Internet, corporate networks, and wireless setups, marketers can offer deals tailored to a single person at a single moment.[19]

Many experts suggest that technology is creating a pricing revolution that might change pricing forever—and perhaps create the most efficient market ever. For example, the Internet is creating major changes in the music industry, as paying customers downloaded over 30 million songs in 2003 alone. And many of the sellers find that it is easy to compete on price. While most firms sell single songs for $.99 and albums for $9.99, Wal-Mart Stores Inc. has tested $.88 downloads, while other firms have experimented with prices as low as $.50 per song and $5 per album.[20]

For firms that want to sell to other businesses (B2B firms), the Internet means that they can change prices rapidly to adapt to changing costs. For consumers who have lots of stuff in the attic they need to put in someone else's attic (C2C e-commerce), the Internet means an opportunity for consumers to find ready buyers. And for B2C firms, firms that sell to consumers, the Internet offers other opportunities. In this section, we will discuss some of the more popular Internet pricing strategies.

Dynamic Pricing Strategies

dynamic pricing
A pricing strategy in which the price can easily be adjusted to meet changes in the marketplace.

One of the most important opportunities offered by the Internet is **dynamic pricing**, where the price can easily be adjusted to meet changes in the marketplace. If a retail store wants to change prices, new price tags must be placed on items, new store display signage and media advertising must be created and displayed, and new prices must be input into the store's computer system. For business-to-business marketers, catalogs and price lists must be printed and distributed to salespeople and to customers. These activities can be very costly to a firm, so they simply don't change their prices very often.

Because the cost of changing prices on the Internet is practically zero, firms are able to respond quickly and, if necessary, frequently to changes in costs, changes in supply, and/or changes in demand. For example, Tickets.com periodically adjusts concert ticket prices on the basis of supply and demand so that a sweet seat to see Outkast might cost more or less depending on which day you log on to buy it. As a result, the company reports it has been able to increase revenue as much as 45 percent.[21]

Auctions

online auctions
E-commerce that allows shoppers to purchase products through online bidding.

Hundreds of Internet **online auctions** allow shoppers to bid on everything from bobbleheads to health-and-fitness equipment to a Sammy Sosa home-run ball. Auctions provide a second Internet pricing strategy. Perhaps the most popular auctions are the C2C auctions such as those on eBay. The eBay auction is an open auction, meaning that all the buyers know the highest price bid at any point in time. In many Internet auction sites, the seller can set a reserve price, a price below which the item will not be sold.

Pricing Advantages for Online Shoppers

The Internet also creates unique pricing challenges for marketers because consumers and business customers are gaining more control over the buying process. With the availability of search engines and "shopbots," they no longer are at the mercy of firms that dictate a price they must accept. The result is that customers have become more price sensitive. For example, online drugstores have been stealing customers from traditional pharmacies by offering drastically lower prices: As one illustration, a comparison study found Rogaine priced at $53.99 at Rite Aid while at the same time the antibaldness product could be purchased online for $47.39 at More.com.[22] (That's a hair-raising difference.)

Detailed information about what products actually cost manufacturers, available from sites such as **consumerreports.org**, can give consumers more negotiating power when shopping for new cars and other big-ticket items. Finally, e-commerce potentially can lower consumers' costs because of the gasoline, time, and aggravation saved by avoiding a trip to the mall.

Psychological Issues in Pricing

Much of what we've said about pricing depends on economists' notions of a customer who evaluates price in a logical, rational manner. For example, the concept of demand is expressed by a smooth demand curve, which assumes that if a firm lowers a product's price from $10 to $9.50 and then from $9.50 to $9 and so on, then customers will simply buy more and more. In the real world, though, it doesn't always work that way. Let's look at some psychological factors that keep those economists up at night.

Buyers' Pricing Expectation

Often consumers base their perceptions of price on what they perceive to be the customary or *fair price*. For example, for many years a candy bar or a pack of gum was priced at 5 cents (yes, 5). Consumers would have perceived any other price as too high or low. It was a nickel candy bar—period. So when costs went up or inflation kicked in, some candy makers tried to shrink the size of the bar instead of changing the price. Eventually, inflation prevailed, consumers' salaries rose, and that candy bar goes for 10 to 12 times one nickel today—a price that consumers would have found unacceptable a few decades ago.

When the price of a product is above or even sometimes when it's below what consumers expect, they are less willing to purchase the product. If the price is above their expectations, they may think it as a rip-off. If it is below expectations, consumers may think quality is below par. By understanding the pricing expectations of their customers, marketers are better able to develop viable pricing strategies. These expectations can differ across cultures and countries. For example, one study conducted in southern California found that Chinese supermarkets charge significantly lower prices (only half as much for meat and seafood) than mainstream American supermarkets in the same areas.[23]

INTERNAL REFERENCE PRICES Sometimes consumers' perceptions of the customary price of a product depend on their **internal reference price**. That is, based on past experience, consumers have a set price or a price range in their mind that they refer to in evaluating a product's cost. The reference price may be the last price paid, or it may be the average of all the prices they know of similar products. No matter what the brand, the normal price for a loaf of sandwich bread is about $1.49. In some stores it may be $1.39, and in others it is $1.59, but the average is $1.49. If consumers find a loaf of bread priced much higher than this—say, $2.99—they will feel it is overpriced and grab a competing brand. If they find bread priced significantly lower—say, at $0.59 or $0.69 a loaf—they may shy away from the purchase, wondering "what is wrong" with the bread.

In some cases, marketers try to influence consumers' expectations of what a product should cost by employing reference pricing strategies. For example, manufacturers may show their price

internal reference price
A set price or a price range in consumers' minds that they refer to in evaluating a product's price.

CAFÉ DE QUALITÉ
À UN PRIX BIEN SERRÉ.

CHAT NOIR

Consumers often associate higher prices with higher quality. This Belgian ad for Chat Noir (Black Cat) coffee tries to convince them otherwise. It reads, "Quality coffee. But we've really squeezed the price."

compared to competitors' prices in advertising. Similarly, a retailer will display a product next to a higher-priced version of the same or a different brand. The consumer must choose between the two products with different prices.

Two results are likely: On the one hand, if the prices (and other characteristics) of the two products are fairly close, the consumer will probably feel the product quality is similar. This is called an *assimilation effect*. The customer might think, "The price is about the same, they must be alike. I'll be smart and save a few dollars." And so the customer chooses the item that is priced lower because the low price made it look attractive next to the high-priced alternative. This is why store brands of deodorant, vitamins, pain relievers, and shampoo sit beside national brands, often accompanied by a shelf talker pointing out how much shoppers can save by purchasing the store brands.

On the other hand, if the prices of the two products are too far apart, a *contrast effect* may result in which the customer equates it with a big difference in quality. "Gee, this lower-priced one is probably not as good as the higher-priced one. I'll splurge on the more expensive one." Using this strategy, an appliance store may place an advertised $300 refrigerator next to a $699 model to convince a customer the bottom-of-the-line model just won't do.

PRICE/QUALITY INFERENCES Imagine that you are in a shoe store looking for a pair of running shoes. You notice one pair that is priced at $89.99. On another table you see a second pair looking almost identical to the first pair but priced at only $24.95. Which pair do you want? Which pair do you think is the better quality? Many of us will pay the higher price because we believe the bargain-basement shoes aren't worth the risk at any price.

As we saw in Chapter 5, consumers make *price–quality inferences* about a product when they use price as a cue or an indicator of quality. By inference, we mean that something is believed to be true without any direct evidence. If consumers are unable to judge the quality of a product through examination or prior experience, they usually will assume that the higher-priced product is the higher-quality product.

Psychological Pricing Strategies

Setting a price is part science, part art. Psychological aspects of price are important for marketers to understand in making pricing decisions.

ODD–EVEN PRICING In the U.S. market, we usually see prices in dollars and cents—$1.99, $5.98, $23.67, or even $599.95. We see prices in even dollar amounts—$2, $10, or $600—far less often. The reason? Marketers have assumed that there is a psychological response to odd prices that differs from the responses to even prices. Habit might also play a role here. Research on the difference in perceptions of odd versus even prices supports the argument that prices ending in 99 rather than 00 lead to increased sales.[24]

At the same time, there are some instances in which even prices are the norm or perhaps even necessary. Theater and concert tickets, admission to sporting events, and lottery tickets tend to be priced in even amounts. Professional fees are normally expressed in even dollars. If a doctor or dentist charged $39.99 for a visit, the patient might think the quality of medical care was less than satisfactory. Many luxury items such as jewelry, golf course fees, and resort accommodations use even dollar prices to set them apart.

Advice for Taco Bell

PROFESSOR
DEBORAH BOYCE
State University of New York Institute of Technology, Utica, New York

Price competition is the number-one problem facing the fast food industry. Taco Bell developed a market offering that has positioned itself in the minds of the target consumers as a higher-quality higher-priced quick serve restaurant. Consumers tend to equate higher prices with higher quality and are therefore willing to pay a little more for what they perceive as a better value. Option #3 (Mixed Price Menu #1) provides menu choices and a pricing structure that allows the consumer to discriminate. Nachos and tacos priced at 99 cents are positioned as offering the best values. Taco Bell can benefit from this three-tiered pricing structure if they take advantage of "the unique-value effect." Buyers are less sensitive to price when the more expensive product is also more distinctive. It should be apparent to consumers that the higher-priced burritos and specialty items are indeed of higher quality. This can be achieved through visual display of the food items on the in-store menu as well as advertising media and presentation of the item at the time of service that should include a distinctive more expensive wrapping.

STUDENT
JENNIFER MOSLEY
Rider University, Lawrenceville, New Jersey

I would choose option 3, the Mixed Price Menu #1. Without looking at the three options I had to choose from, I first looked at the menu options that Taco Bell had planned. Both the Mixed Price #1 and Mixed Price #3 options looked like smart choices. If I had to pick from all the options, I would have picked the Mixed Price #3 option first because you would achieve more of a profit than with Mixed Price #1, and you could always decrease some of your prices if they were not working well in the market. Although the pricing structure is complex and many consumers will wonder why certain items cost more than others, as long as the products are each different (i.e., Burrito #1 has beef, Burrito #2 is Veggie, and Burrito #3 has chicken) and the consumer is hungry, the average consumer will not put much thought into the slight variation in price among the products. Options 1 and 2 involve the extremes, and consumers generally like to make purchases that are within the extremes. Therefore, option 3 is the best, and probably the most profitable, menu.

PROFESSOR
MERV YEAGLE
University of Maryland at College Park

I would choose option 3. Consumers need the ability to purchase nutritional items at various prices. This option is also desirable since the purchase intent, overall liking, and uniqueness were all strong for this menu. Taco Bell needs to explain to the consumers why there are three price points on the value menu. Taco Bell must be able to differentiate its fast foods from its competitors justifying the higher prices. Otherwise, some consumers may not be willing to pay premium prices for fast food. They will go to McDonald's and Burger King.

PRICE LINING   Marketers often apply their understanding of the psychological aspects of pricing in a practice called **price lining**, where items in a product line sell at different prices, called *price points*. If you want to buy a new refrigerator, you will find that most manufacturers have one "stripped-down" model for about $400. A better-quality but still moderately priced model will be around $600. A good refrigerator will be about $800, and a large refrigerator with lots of special features will be around $1,000. Recently, some appliance manufacturers have come out with new models, branded and marketed as special premium lines, with price tags of $3,000 or more. Price lining provides the different ranges necessary to satisfy each segment of the market.

price lining
The practice of setting a limited number of different specific prices, called price points, for items in a product line.

Why is price lining a good practice? From the marketer's standpoint, price lining is a way to maximize profits. In theory, a firm would charge each individual customer the highest price that customer was willing to pay. If the maximum one particular person would be willing to pay for a refrigerator is $550, then that would be the price. If another person would be willing to pay $900, that would be his price. But charging each consumer a different price is really not possible. Having a limited number of prices that generally fall at the top of the range customers find acceptable is a more workable alternative.

Legal and Ethical Considerations in Pricing

The free enterprise system is founded on the idea that the marketplace will regulate itself. Prices will rise or fall according to demand. Supplies of goods and services will be made available if there is an adequate profit incentive.

Unfortunately, the business world includes the greedy and the unscrupulous. Federal, state, and local governments have found it necessary to enact legislation to protect consumers and to protect businesses from predatory rivals. For example, under current laws in Europe, car companies are allowed to charge wildly different prices for the same vehicle in different countries—prices can vary by as much as 30 percent. New regulations are now being proposed to create a more level playing field among countries belonging to the European Union—despite fierce opposition by some car manufacturers that want to retain control over their pricing decisions.[25] In this section, we'll talk about deceptive prices, unfair prices, discriminatory prices, price fixing, and some regulations to combat them.

Deceptive Pricing Practices

Unscrupulous businesses may advertise or promote prices in a deceptive way. The Federal Trade Commission (FTC), state lawmakers, and private bodies such as the Better Business Bureau have developed pricing rules and guidelines to meet the challenge. They say retailers (or other suppliers) must not claim that their prices are lower than a competitor's unless that claim is true. A going-out-of-business sale should be the last sale before going out of business. A fire sale should be held only when there really was a fire.

Another deceptive pricing practice is the **bait-and-switch** tactic, where a retailer will advertise an item at a very low price—the *bait*—to lure customers into the store. But it is almost impossible to buy the advertised item—salespeople like to say (privately) that the item is "nailed to the floor." The salespeople do everything possible to get the unsuspecting customers to buy a different, more expensive, item—the *switch*. They might tell the customer "confidentially" that "the advertised item is really poor quality, lacking important features and full of problems." Enforcing laws against bait-and-switch tactics is complicated because bait-and-switch practices are similar to the legal practice of "trading up." Simply encouraging consumers to purchase a higher-priced item is an acceptable sales technique, but it is illegal to advertise a lower-priced item when it's not a legitimate, bona fide offer that is available on demand. The FTC may determine if an ad is a bait-and-switch scheme or a legitimate offer by checking to see if a firm refuses to show, demonstrate, or sell the advertised product; disparages it; or penalizes salespeople who do sell it.

Unfair Sales Acts

Not every advertised bargain is a bait-and-switch. Some retailers advertise items at very low prices or even below cost and are glad to sell them at that price because they know that once in the store, customers may buy other items at regular prices. This is called **loss leader pricing** and is aimed at building store traffic and sales volume.

Some states consider loss leader practices to be wrong and have passed legislation called **unfair sales acts** (also called *unfair trade practices acts*). These laws or regulations prohibit wholesalers and retailers from selling products below cost. These laws are designed to protect small

bait-and-switch
An illegal marketing practice in which an advertised price special is used as bait to get customers into the store with the intention of switching them to a higher-priced item.

loss leader pricing
The pricing policy of setting prices very low or even below cost to attract customers into a store.

unfair sales acts
State laws that prohibit suppliers from selling products below cost to protect small businesses from larger competitors.

wholesalers and retailers from larger competitors because the larger competitors have the financial resources that allow them to offer loss leaders or products sold at very low prices—usually something the smaller firms cannot do.

Illegal Business-to-Business Price Discrimination

The *Robinson-Patman Act* includes regulations against price discrimination in interstate commerce. These price discrimination regulations relate to selling the same product to different retailers and wholesalers at different prices if such practices lessen competition. In addition to regulating the price charged, the Robinson-Patman Act specifically prohibits offering such "extras" as discounts, rebates, premiums, coupons, guarantees, and free delivery to some but not all customers.

There are exceptions, however:

- Robinson-Patman does not apply to final customers—only resellers.
- A discount to a large channel customer is legal if it is based on the quantity of the order and the resulting efficiencies such as transportation savings.
- Differences in prices are allowed if there are physical differences in the product, such as different features. A name-brand appliance may be available through a large national retail chain at a lower price than an almost identical item sold by a higher-priced retailer because that "model" is sold only through that chain.

Price Fixing

Price fixing occurs when two or more companies conspire to keep prices at a certain level. For example, General Electric Co. and De Beers Centenary AG were charged with fixing the prices in the $600-million-per-year world market for industrial diamonds used in cutting tools. This type of illicit agreement can take two forms: horizontal and vertical.

price fixing
The collaboration of two or more firms in setting prices, usually to keep prices high.

HORIZONTAL PRICE FIXING   In 2003, a number of top fashion-modeling agencies were charged with conspiring to fix commissions they charge models. Because such practices mean higher prices for customers, in this case the models who were buying the services of the agencies, such practices are against the regulations of the Sherman Antitrust Act discussed in Chapter 2.[26] *Horizontal price fixing* occurs when competitors making the same product jointly determine what price they each will charge. In industries in which there are few sellers, there may be no specific price-fixing agreement, but sellers will still charge the same price to "meet the competition." Such parallel pricing is not of itself considered price fixing. There must be an exchange of pricing information between sellers to indicate illegal price-fixing actions.

VERTICAL PRICE FIXING   Sometimes manufacturers or wholesalers attempt to force retailers to charge a certain price for their product. This is called *vertical price fixing*. If the retailer wants to carry the product, for example, it has to charge the "suggested" retail price. The *Consumer Goods Pricing Act* of 1976 limited this practice, leaving retail stores free to set whatever price they choose without interference by the manufacturer or wholesaler. Today, retailers don't need to adhere to "suggested" prices.

Predatory Pricing

Predatory pricing means that a company sets a very low price for the purpose of driving competitors out of business. Later, when they have a monopoly, they will increase prices. The Sherman Act and the Robinson-Patman Act prohibit predatory pricing. For example, in 1999 the Justice Department accused American Airlines of predatory pricing at its Dallas–Ft. Worth hub.[27] In the mid-1990s, three small rivals started flying into the airport. American responded by offering cheap seats to scare the rivals away and then raised its prices. That's a no-no, says Uncle Sam.

real people, real choices

How It Worked Out at Taco Bell

Danielle chose option 3, the Mixed Price Menu #1. This configuration featured a strategy that utilizes both the 99¢ and $1.29 price points but that also has some items priced at $1.19 to close the relatively large 30¢ gap between the highest and lowest price points.

The new Big Bell Value Menu went into test market starting in the fall of 2003 with plans to launch it nationally in summer of 2004. So far, consumers have responded very well to this pricing strategy. They seem to understand that items such as burritos, especially those carrying the "half-pound" moniker, are naturally going to be more expensive than some other items such as tacos. Consumers are telling Taco Bell that they like the $1.19 price point because it helps make the menu feel less disjointed, more like a collection of products rather than two separate sets of higher-priced and lower-priced items. The middle price point also allows for some premium pricing where necessary (e.g., on chicken) without resorting to the highest price point of $1.29. By carefully crafting its pricing strategy, Taco Bell is successfully reclaiming its position of offering fast-food value for the money.

How should you handle questions about salary? What can you negotiate to get paid what you're worth? To learn the latest salary trends, go to Chapter 11 in the *Brand You* supplement.

CHAPTER SUMMARY

1. **Explain the importance of pricing and how prices can take both monetary and non-monetary forms.** Pricing is important to firms because it creates profits and influences customers to purchase or not. Prices may be monetary or nonmonetary, as when consumers or businesses exchange one product for another.

2. **Understand the pricing objectives that marketers typically have in planning pricing strategies.** Effective pricing objectives are designed to support corporate and marketing objectives and are flexible. Pricing objectives often focus on sales (to maximize sales or to increase market share), on a desired level of profit growth or profit margin, on competing effectively to increase customer satisfaction or on communicating a certain image.

3. **Describe how marketers use costs, demands, and revenue to make pricing decisions.** In developing prices, marketers must estimate demand and determine costs. Marketers often use break-even analysis and marginal analysis to help in deciding on the price for a product. Break-even analysis uses fixed and variable costs to identify how many units must be sold at a certain price in order to begin making a profit. Marginal analysis uses both costs and estimates of product demand to identify the price that will maximize profits. In marginal analysis, profits are maximized at the point at which the revenue from selling one additional unit of a product equals the costs of producing the additional unit.

4. **Understand some of the environmental factors that affect pricing strategies.** Like other elements of the marketing mix, pricing is influenced by a variety of external environmental factors. This includes economic trends such as inflation and recession and the firm's competitive environment, that is, whether the firm does business in an oligopoly, a monopoly, or a more competitive environment. Pricing may also be influenced by changing consumer trends.

5. **Understand key pricing strategies.** Though easy to calculate and "safe," frequently used cost-based strategies do not consider demand, the competition, the stage in the product life cycle, plant capacity, or product image. The most common cost-based strategy is cost-plus pricing.

   Pricing strategies based on demand such as target costing and yield management pricing can require that marketers estimate demand at different prices in order to be certain they can sell what they produce. Strategies based on the competition may represent industry wisdom but can be tricky to apply. A price leadership strategy is often used in an oligopoly.

   Firms that focus on customer needs may consider everyday low price or value pricing strategies. New products may be priced using a high skimming price to recover research, development and promotional costs, or a penetration price to encourage more customers and discourage competitors from entering the market. Trial pricing means setting a low price for a limited time.

6. **Explain pricing tactics for single and multiple products and for pricing on the Internet.** To implement pricing strategies with individual products, marketers may use two-part pricing or payment pricing tactics. For multiple products, marketers may use price bundling, wherein two or more products are sold and priced as a single package. Captive pricing is often chosen when two items must be used together; one item is sold at a very low price and the other at a high, profitable price.

   Distribution-based pricing tactics, including F.O.B., basing-point, and uniform delivered pricing, address differences in how far products must be shipped. Similar pricing tactics are use for products sold internationally.

Pricing for members of the channel may include trade or functional discounts, cumulative or noncumulative quantity discounts to encourage larger purchases, cash discounts to encourage fast payment, and seasonal discounts to spread purchases throughout the year or to increase off-season or in-season sales.

7. **Understand the opportunities for Internet pricing strategies.** E-commerce may offer firms an opportunity to initiate dynamic pricing—meaning prices can be changed frequently with little or no cost. Auctions offer opportunities for customers to bid on items in C2C, B2C, and B2B e-commerce. The Internet allows buyers to compare products and prices, gives consumers more control over the price they pay for items, and has made customers more price sensitive.

8. **Describe the psychological aspects of pricing, legal, and ethical aspects of pricing.** Consumers may express emotional or psychological responses to prices. Customers may use an idea of a customary or fair price as an internal reference price in evaluating products. Sometimes marketers use reference pricing strategies by displaying products with different prices next to each other. A price–quality inference means that consumers use price as a cue for quality. Customers respond to odd prices differently than to even-dollar prices. Marketers can manipulate pricing with price lining strategies, a practice of setting a limited number of different price ranges for a product line.

Most marketers seek to avoid unethical or illegal pricing practices. One deceptive pricing practice is the illegal bait-and-switch tactic. Many states have unfair sales acts, which are laws against loss leader pricing that make it illegal to sell products below cost or, in some states, to sell at a price less than a certain percentage above cost. Federal regulations prohibit predatory pricing, price discrimination, and horizontal or vertical price fixing.

KEY TERMS

average fixed cost, 334
bait-and-switch, 352
basing-point pricing, 346, 347
break-even analysis, 335
break-even point, 335
captive pricing, 346
contribution per unit, 335
cost-plus pricing, 341
cross-elasticity of demand, 333
cumulative quantity discounts, 347, 348
demand-based pricing, 341
dynamic pricing, 348
elastic demand, 331
everyday low pricing (EDLP), 343
fixed costs, 334
F.O.B. delivered pricing, 346

F.O.B. origin pricing, 346
freight absorption pricing, 347
inelastic demand, 331
internal reference price, 349
list price, 347
loss leader pricing, 352
marginal analysis, 337
marginal cost, 337
marginal revenue, 337
noncumulative quantity discounts, 347, 348
online auctions, 348
penetration pricing, 345
prestige products, 328
price, 325
price bundling, 345

price elasticity of demand, 331
price fixing, 353
price leadership, 343
price lining, 351
quantity discounts, 347, 348
skimming price, 344
target costing, 342
total costs, 335
trade or functional discounts, 347, 348
trial pricing, 345
unfair sales acts, 352
uniform delivered pricing, 347
value pricing, 343
variable costs, 333
yield management pricing, 342

CHAPTER REVIEW

MARKETING CONCEPTS:
TESTING YOUR KNOWLEDGE

1. What is price, and why is it important to a firm? What are some examples of monetary and nonmonetary prices?

2. What are some of the more commonly used pricing objectives?

3. How is demand influenced by price? What is elastic demand? What is inelastic demand?

4. Explain variable costs, fixed costs, average variable costs, average fixed costs, and average total costs.

5. What is break-even analysis? What is marginal analysis? How do marketers use break-even and marginal analyses?

6. How does recession affect consumers' perceptions of prices? How does inflation influence perceptions of prices?

7. Explain cost-plus pricing, target costing, and yield management pricing. Explain how a price leadership strategy works.

8. For new products, when is skimming pricing more appropriate, and when is penetration pricing the best strategy? When would trial pricing be an effective pricing strategy?

9. Explain how marketers use price bunding, captive pricing, and distribution-based pricing tactics.

10. Why do marketers use trade or functional discounts, quantity discounts, cash discounts, and seasonal discounts in pricing to members of the channel?

11. What is dynamic pricing? Why does the Internet encourage the use of dynamic pricing?

12. Explain these psychological aspects of pricing: price–quality inferences, odd–even pricing, internal reference price, and price lining.

MARKETING CONCEPTS: DISCUSSING CHOICES AND ISSUES

1. Governments sometimes provide price subsidies to specific industries; that is, they reduce a domestic firm's costs so that they can sell products on the international market at a lower price. What reasons do governments (and politicians) use for these government subsidies? What are the benefits and disadvantages to domestic industries in the long run? To international customers? Who would benefit and who would lose if all price subsidies were eliminated?

2. Critics of business often accuse marketers of taking advantage of consumers by setting prices that are far above the cost of producing the good or service—sometimes 10 or 20 or more times the cost. How do you feel about this? What reasons might a manufacturer of luxury products have for setting very high prices? Why might a pharmaceutical firm set the prices of its lifesaving medicines higher than the cost of production?

3. Many very successful retailers use a loss leader pricing strategy in which they advertise an item at a price below their cost and sell the item at that price to get customers into their store. They feel that these customers will continue to shop with their company and that they will make a profit in the long run. Do you consider this an unethical practice? Who benefits and who is hurt by such practices? Do you think the practice should be made illegal as some states have done?

4. Consumers often make price–quality inferences about products. What does this mean? What are some products for which you are likely to make price–quality inferences? Do such inferences make sense?

5. Retailers sometimes display, side by side, two similar products carrying different prices, hoping for an assimilation effect or for a contrast effect. Give some examples of products that you have noticed displayed in this manner. What factors do you think make it more likely that one effect versus the other will occur? Do such practices help or hurt the consumer?

MARKETING PRACTICE: APPLYING WHAT YOU'VE LEARNED

1. Assume that you are the director of marketing for a firm that manufactures candy bars. You feel the time is right for your company to increase the price of its candy, but you are concerned that increasing the price might not be profitable. You feel you should examine the elasticity of demand. How would you go about doing this? What findings would lead you to increase the price? What findings would cause you to rethink the decision to increase prices?

2. Assume that you and your friend have decided to go into business together manufacturing wrought-iron birdcages. You know that your fixed costs (rent on a building, equipment, and so on) will be $60,000 a year. You expect your variable costs to be $12 per birdcage.
   a. If you plan on selling the birdcages to retail stores for $18, how many must you sell to break even; that is, what is your break-even quantity?
   b. Assume that you and your partner feel that you must set a goal of achieving a $20,000 profit with your business this year. How many units would you have to sell to make that amount of profit?
   c. What if you feel that you will be able to sell no more than 5,000 birdcages? What price will you have to charge to break even? To make $30,000 in profit?

3. Assume that you have been hired as the assistant manager of a local store that sells fresh fruits and vegetables. As you look over the store, you notice that there are two different displays of tomatoes. In one display the tomatoes are priced at $1.39 per pound, and in the other the tomatoes are priced at $1.29 per pound. The tomatoes look very much alike. You notice that no one is buying the $1.39 tomatoes. Write a report explaining what is happening and give your recommendations for the store's pricing strategy.

4. As the vice president for marketing for a firm that markets computer software, you must regularly develop pricing strategies for new software products. Your latest product is a software package that automatically translates any foreign language e-mail messages to the user's preferred language. You are trying to decide on the pricing for this new product. Should you use a skimming price, a penetration price, or something in between? With a classmate taking the role of another marketing professional with your firm, argue in front of your class the pros and cons for each alternative.

MARKETING MINIPROJECT: LEARNING BY DOING

The purpose of this miniproject is to help you become familiar with how consumers respond to different prices by conducting a series of pricing experiments.

For this project, you should first select a product category that students such as yourself normally purchase. It should be a moderately expensive purchase such as athletic shoes, a bookcase, or a piece of luggage. You should next obtain two photographs of items in this product category or, if possible, two actual items. The two items should not appear to be substantially different in quality or in price.

Note: You will need to recruit separate research participants for each of the activities listed in the next section.

- **Experiment 1: Reference Pricing**
  a. Place the two products together. Place a sign on one with a low price. Place a sign on the other with a high price (about 50 percent higher will do). Ask your research participants to evaluate the quality of each of the items and to tell which one they would probably purchase.
  b. Reverse the signs and ask other research participants to evaluate the quality of each of the items and to tell which one they would probably purchase.
  c. Place the two products together again. This time place a sign on one with a moderate price. Place a sign on the other that is only a little higher (less than 10 percent higher). Again, ask research participants to evaluate the quality of each of the items and to tell which one they would probably purchase.

  d. Reverse the signs and ask other research participants to evaluate the quality of each of the items and to tell which one they would probably purchase.

- **Experiment 2: Odd–Even Pricing** For this experiment, you will only need one of the items from experiment 1.
  a. Place a sign on the item that ends in $.99 (e.g., $59.99). Ask research participants to tell you if they think the price for the item is very low, slightly low, moderate, slightly high, or very high. Also ask them to evaluate the quality of the item and to tell you how likely they would be to purchase the item.
  b. This time place a sign on the item that ends in $.00 (e.g., $60.00). Ask different research participants to tell you if they think the price for the item is very low, slightly low, moderate, slightly high, or very high. Also ask them to evaluate the quality of the item and to tell you how likely they would be to purchase the item.

Develop a presentation for your class in which you discuss the results of your experiments and what they tell you about how consumers view prices.

REAL PEOPLE, REAL SURFERS: EXPLORING THE WEB

Barter exchanges are organizations that facilitate barter transactions between buyers and sellers. Many of these exchanges are members of the National Association of Trade Exchanges (NATE).

First, visit the NATE Web page at **www.nate.org**. Using links on that page to NATE member exchanges or an Internet search engine, locate and explore several barter exchange Web pages. Based on your Internet experience, answer the following questions:

1. What is NATE?
2. What are the benefits to a business of joining a barter exchange?

3. What types of products are bartered?
4. How does a trade actually work with a barter exchange?
5. How does the exchange make its money? Who pays the exchange and how much is charged?
6. Assuming that the goal of barter exchange Web sites is to attract new members, evaluate the different Web sites you visited. Which Web site do you think was best? What features of the site would make you want to join if you were the owner of a small business? What features of the other sites made them less appealing than this one?

MARKETING PLAN EXERCISE

For many service organizations such as restaurants, hotels, airlines, and resorts, pricing strategies are particularly important because of the perishability of services (i.e., services can't be stored). Pricing is a vital part of effective marketing strategies that ensure that a maximum number of seats of the plane or rooms in the hotel are purchased—every day.

Think about a new seaside resort complex that offers vacationers luxury villas, available for rent for a few days, a week, or

longer. Consider possible pricing strategies such as cost-plus, yield management, everyday low pricing, skimming, and penetration and trial pricing.

1. What pricing strategy do you recommend for the resort complex that would maximize their occupancy?
2. What recommendations for pricing tactics or how to implement the strategy do you have?

Marketing in Action Case
Real Choices at the New York Mets

Today's sports world is full of potential hall of famers and other sports celebrities on the rosters of baseball, football, basketball, and hockey teams. In addition, many sports teams, both professional and college, have long-standing rivalries with other teams that make the tickets for games between those two teams highly sought after regardless of either team's current win-loss record. Both of these factors enhance the desirability for tickets to particular games and present an opportunity for sports executives to engage in variable pricing activities.

The New York Mets is one of a reported nine Major League Baseball teams that have adopted variable pricing for its games. In doing so, the team has adopted a pricing strategy that is practiced in many other industries. Movie matinees, airline tickets, and hotel rooms all have been priced on a variable basis for several years, but such a strategy is just now catching on with sports teams.

Until recently, sports teams engaged in a "one-price-for-all" strategy for pricing tickets to their games. In other words, a $43 field-level seat at New York Mets' games remained $43 regardless of the opponent. In addition, seats in the upper level of seating also remained the same price regardless of the opponent. However, under new pricing arrangements followed by the Mets, the "one-price-for-all" strategy has changed. What has changed is that games against the Mets' biggest rivals or against teams featuring the most high-profile athletes have become more expensive for fans, while tickets for the least desirable games have remained the same or in some cases the prices even decreased.

The Mets' pricing scheme now includes four levels of prices called gold, silver, bronze, and value. Gold games are the most highly valued and tickets for these games will get the highest price. For example, the top ticket price for individual games at Shea Stadium on "gold" game nights will be $53. Games against high-profile opponents, such as the New York Yankees, the San Francisco Giants, and strong division rival Atlanta Braves, will be labeled "gold" games and charged the highest price. In addition, games played on opening day of the seasons and on "fireworks" night also will be labeled "gold" games and priced accordingly regardless of opponent.

A "value" game might be a weekday game against the Milwaukee Brewers or Montreal Expos. For value games, tickets will be reduced from their "gold" prices. For example, the "gold" price ticket of $53 will drop to $38, and upper reserved seats will be reduced from their "gold" price of $8 per ticket to just $5. For the 2004 season, the Mets planned 14 "gold" games, 22 silver, 32 bronze, and 13 value.

For the Mets and other professional sports teams that have implemented a variable pricing plan, there are risks involved. Sports fans have for years been used to paying the same ticket price regardless of the opponent. Will they now pay more money to see games against popular foes? One risk teams undertake when adopting a variable pricing plan is the sudden decrease in desirability of a certain opponent. What happens if Barry Bonds, a marquee player and future hall of famer, is injured and will not play when the San Francisco Giants go to play the New York Mets? Will the Mets refund the ticket price increase charged to see the single-season, home-run record holder when that player does not even take the field?

In addition, what about games against perceived lesser opponents like the 2003 version of the Florida Marlins? Games against the Marlins likely were not part of the "gold" package for the Mets, yet the Marlins went on to become world champions in 2003. Furthermore, rival teams may take exception to being classified as "fodder for 'bargain night' at the ballpark." Clearly, team executives must consider many factors when considering a variable pricing plan.

While variable pricing seems to be a way to increase team revenues, questions remain. Will fans continue to pay the higher "gold" prices over the long term? Will bargain value games continue to attract fans even at the lower price? Certainly the Mets must consider the long-term desirability of variable pricing.

Things to Think About

1. What is the decision facing the New York Mets?
2. What factors are important in understanding this decision situation?
3. What are the alternatives?
4. What decision(s) do you recommend?
5. What are some ways to implement your recommendation(s)?

Sources: Bloomberg News, "Baseball's Average Price Boost Is Small," *Milwaukee Journal Sentinel*, March 29, 2003, 8C; Eric Fisher, "Cheapest Seat in Town to Vary on Daily Basis," *Washington Times*, November 26, 2002, C1; Stefan Fatsis, "The Barry Bonds Tax: Teams Raise Prices for Good Games," *Wall Street Journal*, December 3, 2002, D1, D8; and Associated Press, "Mets Ticket Prices Largely Unchanged," December 23, 2003.

the bojangles' recipe

1. No biscuit should ever be older than 20 minutes.

2. Frozen chicken will never be as good as fresh chicken, no matter how much you bread it.

3. Life can be bland. Our food isn't.

4. A piece of chicken should look like a piece of chicken.

5. Fresh ground coffee is always better. Come to think of it, fresh anything is always better.

6. The best chicken 'n biscuits money can buy.

7. Recipes that haven't changed in over 25 years. If it ain't broke, don't fix it.

8. Making sweet tea is an art form.

9. Fixin's as famous as our chicken 'n biscuits.

10. Breakfast should never end.

★ ★ ★

©2005 Bojangles' Restaurants, Inc.

www.pricemcnabb.com

real people, real choices

meet Matt Ferguson, a Decision Maker at PriceMcNabb, Inc.

first job out of school	career high
Writer/account executive at Husebo Advertising, a 12-person shop in the small town of Leesburg, Florida. The lesson is: take your first job anywhere you can to get your foot in the door.	Being part of the 25th anniversary campaign at Walt Disney World, which won an Effie Award.

CONNECTING WITH THE CUSTOMER: INTEGRATED MARKETING COMMUNICATIONS AND INTERACTIVE MARKETING

After graduating from Florida State University in 1991 with a major in advertising, Matt landed at a small agency in Florida called Husebo Advertising as a copywriter and account executive. He soon learned that he preferred the account side of agency work and landed a job as an assistant account executive at PriceMcNabb, Inc. There, he worked on accounts including GE Lighting Systems, Asheville Tourism, and Biltmore Estate. By the time he left PriceMcNabb four years later, he was a senior account executive. Matt's travel and tourism experience led him in 1996 to Walt Disney Attractions, Inc., where he managed national advertising programs for the Walt Disney World destination and Walt Disney World Resorts. While at Disney, Matt was part of the team that worked on the Walt Disney World 25th Anniversary Celebration, the Millennium Celebration, the opening of Disney's Animal Kingdom Park, and the opening of a number of hotel properties, including Disney's Coronado Springs Resort and Disney's Animal Kingdom Lodge. When Matt left Disney, he was account manager of national advertising.

In 2000, Matt returned to his agency roots at PriceMcNabb as account supervisor. He has had the opportunity to manage a range of accounts and project work for such brands as Pine-

hurst Resort, Paramount Parks, Sagebrush Steakhouse, Western Steer, Drexel Heritage Furniture, Nucor Steel, and Bojangles' Restaurants. He has served as vice president with the agency since 2002. Recently, the agency merged with Eric Mower and Associates, New York.

Decision Time at PriceMcNabb

Bojangles' is a chain of 320-plus chicken and biscuit restaurants with stores in the eastern United States and the Caribbean, with the highest concentration in the Southeast. Though they are a regional player, they are forced to compete with national quick-service-restaurant (QSR) chains that have bigger footprints and bigger budgets.

Through the first half of 2003, Bojangles' Restaurants was stuck in a pattern of flat sales, consistent with the rest of the QSR industry. This prompted them to conduct a review to find a new agency for their advertising and other marketing communications. PriceMcNabb was one of the agencies invited to the pitch. Matt and his colleagues immediately went to work to learn about the essence of the Bojangles' brand by visiting stores, conducting consumer focus groups, assessing industry trends,

a job-related mistake i wish i hadn't made	**my hero**	**what drives me**	**don't do this when interviewing with me**
Acting like I knew more than I did early in my career. It's better to be up front about what you *don't* know. That's the only way anyone can teach you something.	Abraham Lincoln. He stood for principle instead of sticking with the status quo.	A coach in college told me that you never stay the same. You're either getting better or worse. No matter how good you are, you must keep getting better, or the other guy will beat you.	Don't make me do all the asking. Ask intelligent questions that show you've done your homework.

1 Understand the role of marketing communications.

2 Understand the communications model.

3 List and describe the elements of the promotion mix.

4 Explain guerrilla marketing, viral marketing, buzz, and hype.

5 Explain integrated marketing communications and its characteristics.

6 Explain the stages in developing the IMC plan.

7 Understand the current trend toward interactive promotion strategies.

8 Explain why database marketing is increasingly popular and how databases are developed and managed.

analyzing the competition, and interviewing employees and franchisees.

In Bojangles', PriceMcNabb found what they believe is a "Krispy Kreme in the making": a gem of a concept just waiting to be discovered by America. Those who know Bojangles' love it and crave its unique flavor. Unlike other fast-food options, Bojangles' makes its chicken and biscuits from scratch. And its secret recipes for chicken and biscuits are deeply rooted in the richness and character of the South. Based on these insights, Matt considered how PriceMcNabb might develop a message strategy to revitalize the Bojangles' brand.

OPTION 1: Position Bojangles' around customers' desire for its uniquely flavorful food.

This strategy would focus on the visceral reason consumers enjoy Bojangles', reminding existing customers to return often and giving prospective customers the desire to try it. Ads would focus on true "moments" when the craving for Bojangles' hits. However, this approach doesn't tell consumers *why* they should crave this particular fast-food option as opposed to other alternatives like Kentucky Fried Chicken (KFC) or Popeye's.

OPTION 2: Position Bojangles' as a quick-serve restaurant where you can actually enjoy the goodness of made-from-scratch, homemade food.

This would be a real point of difference in the world of McNuggets and other "manufactured" fast-food products. But the homemade claim may not be believable or relevant in a fast-food environment where people have become accustomed to eating mass-produced menu items.

OPTION 3: Position Bojangles' around its wholesome, down-home southern roots.

The South has a unique charm that's refreshingly different from our fast-paced society. It's a place where people are invited to slow down and "set a spell." This sets Bojangles' apart from some competitors because KFC and Popeye's have long departed from their southern roots (KFC hasn't been called "Kentucky Fried Chicken" for years). But not everybody thinks of the South in a positive light. Plus, Bojangles' hopes to expand its base to include northern parts of the United States where people are not as familiar with the southern mystique—and many people who now live in the South didn't grow up there either.

Now, put yourself in Matt Ferguson's shoes: Which option would you choose, and why?

Tailoring Marketing Communications to Customers

See how many of the following you can answer:

1. Name the tiger that says, "They're grrrrrreat!"
2. Name one or more products for which Tiger Woods is a spokesperson.
3. What character is featured in Eveready battery ads?
4. At Burger King, you can have it "_____," whereas at Hardee's the burgers are "_____" broiled.
5. Which fast-food chain boasts, "Gottawannaneedagettahava"?

promotion
The coordination of a marketer's communications efforts to influence attitudes or behavior.

Did you get them all right? You owe your knowledge about these and a thousand other trivia questions to the efforts of people who specialize in marketing communications (Hint: We'll give you the answer to question 5 later.). As we said in Chapter 1, the coordination of marketing communications efforts to influence attitudes or behavior is **promotion**. As one of the famous Four Ps of the

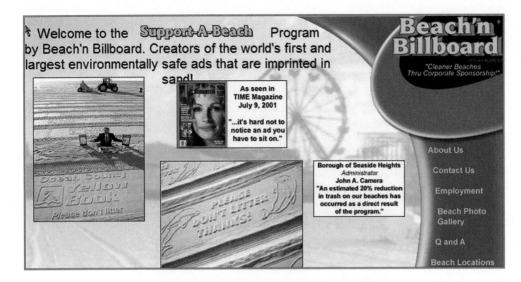

Marketing communications can take many forms. A company called Beach 'N Billboard will even imprint your ad or logo directly into the sand (and then come back to redo it tomorrow).

marketing mix, promotion plays a vital role, whether the goal is to sell hamburgers or to convince consumers to lower their intake of high-cholesterol foods.

Marketing communications can take many forms: quirky television commercials, sophisticated magazine ads, Web banner ads boasting the latest Java-language applications, funky T-shirts, blimps blinking messages over football stadiums, and so on. Some marketing communications push specific products, whereas others try to create or reinforce a corporate image:

- Marketing communications *inform* consumers about new goods and services and where they can purchase them.[1]
- Marketing communications *remind* consumers to continue using certain products.
- Marketing communications *persuade* consumers to choose one product over others.
- Marketing communications *build* relationships with customers.

The traditional forms of marketing communications are advertising (including mass media, direct mail, outdoor advertising, and online advertising); sales promotions such as coupons, samples, rebates, or contests; press releases and special events organized by public relations professionals; and presentations by salespeople. Of course, marketers use all the elements of the marketing mix to communicate with customers. The package in which the product comes, the price of the product, and the type of retail outlet where the product is available all are part of effective marketing communications because they make statements about the nature of the product and the image it intends to convey.

Many marketing experts now believe that integrating all forms of marketing communications is essential for successful marketing. **Integrated marketing communications (IMC)** is the process that marketers use to plan, develop, execute, and evaluate coordinated, measurable, persuasive brand communication programs over time to targeted audiences. As we'll discuss later in this chapter, the IMC approach argues that consumers see the variety of messages they receive from a firm—a TV commercial, a coupon, an opportunity to win a sweepstakes, and a display in a store— as a whole, as a single company speaking to them but in different places and different ways. That's a lot different from how traditional marketing communication programs are created, where little effort is made to coordinate the varying messages consumers receive. An advertising campaign typically is run independently of a sweepstakes, which in turn has no relation to a series of billboard ads. These disjointed efforts can send conflicting messages that leave the consumer confused and unsure of the brand's identity. Just as customer needs are the focus of the marketing concept and of total quality management programs, the customer is also the focus for companies that are adopting

integrated marketing communications (IMC)
A strategic business process that marketers use to plan, develop, execute, and evaluate coordinated, measurable, persuasive brand communication programs over time to targeted audiences.

Figure 12.1 Making and Delivering Value

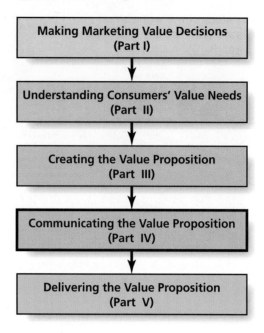

an IMC perspective. With IMC, marketers seek to understand what information consumers want as well as how, when, and where they want it. That's the philosophy that drives PriceMcNabb's desire to craft a clear image for its client, Bojangles'.

As you'll see in Figure 12.1, we are now in Part IV of this book, Communicating the Value Proposition. In today's competitive marketplace, the role of the successful marketer in communicating the value proposition means adopting an IMC perspective. In this chapter, we'll first review the communication process. Next, we'll discuss the characteristics of IMC and the communications planning process. Finally, we'll see how marketers use interactive marketing to truly reach out and touch their customers.

The Communications Model

A good way to understand what marketing communications is all about is to examine the **communications model**, which is shown in Figure 12.2. In this model, a message is transmitted through some medium from a sender to a receiver who (we hope) is listening and understands the message. Regardless of how messages are sent—whether by a hat with a Caterpillar tractor logo on it, a door-to-door sales pitch from a Mary Kay representative, or a televised fashion show with supermodels strutting their stuff for Victoria's Secret—they are designed to capture receivers' attention and relate to their needs.

Any way that marketers reach out to consumers, from a simple highway billboard to a customized message sent via e-mail, is part of the basic communications process. The communications model specifies the elements necessary for communication to occur: a source, a message, a medium, and a receiver.

Encoding by the Source (the Marketer)

Encoding is the process of translating an idea into a form of communication that will convey the desired meaning. The **source** is the organization or individual sending the message. It's one thing for marketers to form an idea about a product in their own minds, but it's not quite as simple to express it so that other people get the same picture. To make their messages more believable or more attractive to consumers, marketers sometimes choose a real person (golf pro Tiger Woods), hire an actor or a model (Catherine Zeta-Jones for Elizabeth Arden), or create a character (Tony the Tiger for Kellogg's Frosted Flakes) to represent the source. Mercedes recently developed an advertising campaign that

communications model
The process whereby meaning is transferred from a source to a receiver.

encoding
The process of translating an idea into a form of communication that will convey meaning.

source
An organization or individual that sends a message.

Figure 12.2 Communications Model

The communications model explains how ideas are translated into messages and transmitted from the marketer (the source) to the consumer (the receiver) who (we hope) understands what the marketer intended to say.

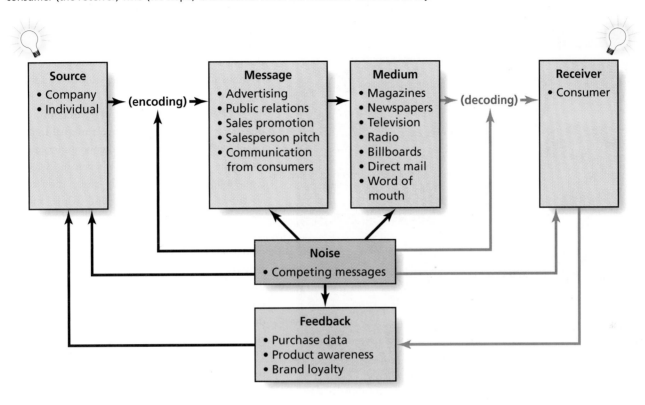

featured photos sent in by Mercedes-Benz owners along with short vignettes of the drivers. These existing owners can be a very convincing source of communication for prospective Mercedes buyers.[2]

The Message

The **message** is the actual communication going from sender to receiver. It must include all the information necessary to persuade, inform, remind, or build a relationship. Messages may include both verbal and nonverbal elements, such as beautiful background scenery or funky music. Messages used in advertising must be carefully constructed so that they can connect with a wide variety of consumers or business customers. In contrast, the message delivered by a salesperson can be carefully tailored for each individual customer, and the salesperson can respond to questions or objections.

message
The communication in physical form that goes from a sender to a receiver.

The Medium

No matter how the message is encoded, it must then be transmitted via a **medium**, a communications vehicle used to reach members of a target audience. This vehicle can be television, radio, a magazine, a Web site, personal contact, a billboard, or even a product logo printed on a coffee mug. Ideally, the attributes of the product should match those of the medium. For example, magazines with high prestige are more effective at communicating messages about overall product image and quality, whereas specialized magazines do a better job of conveying factual information.[3]

medium
A communications vehicle through which a message is transmitted to a target audience.

Decoding by the Receiver

Communication cannot occur unless a **receiver** is there to get the message. The receiver can be any individual or organization that intercepts and interprets the message. Assuming that the customer is even paying attention (a big assumption in our overloaded, media-saturated society),

receiver
The organization or individual that intercepts and interprets the message.

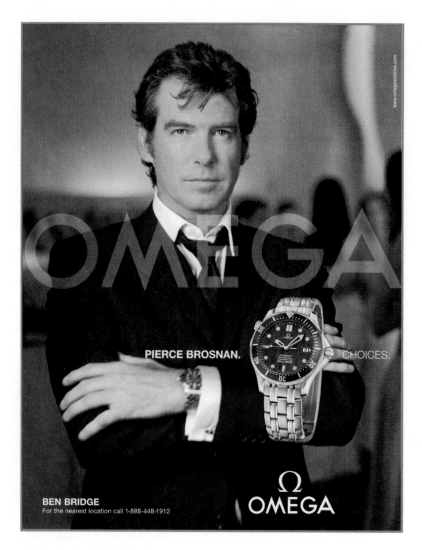

PIERCE BROSNAN.   CHOICES.

BEN BRIDGE
For the nearest location call 1-888-448-1912

Ω
OMEGA

Marketers often hire celebrities as spokespersons for their products, thus adding excitement to the "source" of the message.

the meaning of the message is interpreted in light of that individual's unique experiences. **Decoding** is the process whereby a receiver assigns meaning to a message, that is, translates the message back into an idea. Marketers hope that the target consumer will decode the message the way they intended, that the idea in the mind of the receiver is identical to the idea the source sought to communicate.

Effective communication occurs only when the source and the receiver have a mutual frame of reference. They must share the same understanding about the world. For example, when in 2003 pop icon Bob Dylan showed up in a television ad for Victoria's Secret's "Angels" line while models cavorted to a remixed version of his song "Love Sick," not everyone who saw the commercial interpreted it quite the same way. To die-hard fans who remember the "old Dylan," who wrote song lyrics like "Advertising signs that con you/Into thinking you're the one/That can do what's never been done/That can win what's never been won/Meantime life outside goes on/All around you" in his 1965 song "It's Alright Ma (I'm Only Bleeding)," this wasn't business as usual. One disappointed consumer who is also curator of a collection of Dylan material observed, "I'm going to have to go blow my brains out."[4] Clearly, Victoria's Secret hopes most of the women watching the commercial will have a different reaction.

Noise

The communications model also acknowledges that

decoding
The process by which a receiver assigns meaning to the message.

noise
Anything that interferes with effective communication.

messages can be blocked by **noise**, which is anything that interferes with effective communication. As shown by the many arrows between noise and the other elements of the communication model in Figure 12.2, noise can occur at any stage of communication. It can occur at the encoding stage if the source uses words or symbols that the receiver will not understand. Or, the receiver may be distracted from receiving the message by a nearby conversation. There may be a problem with transmission of the message through the medium—especially if it's drowned out by the chorus of other marketers clamoring for us to look at *their* messages. Marketers try to minimize noise by placing their messages where there is less likely to be distractions or competition for consumers' attention. Calvin Klein, for example, will often buy a block of advertising pages in a magazine so that the reader sees only pictures of its clothing.

Feedback

feedback
Receivers' reactions to the message.

To complete the communications loop, the source receives **feedback** from receivers. These reactions to the message help gauge the effectiveness of the message so that the marketer can fine-tune it. Obtaining feedback reminds us of the importance of conducting marketing research (as we discussed in Chapter 7) to verify that a firm's strategies are working.

Marketing Communication Strategy and the Promotion Mix

As we said earlier, promotion, or marketing communications, is one of the four Ps. But virtually *everything* an organization says and does is a form of marketing communications. The ads it creates, the packages it designs, and even the uniforms its employees wear contribute to the impression people have of the company and its products. In fact, in a broad sense we can argue that *every element of the marketing mix is actually a form of communication.* After all, the price of a product, where it is sold, and even the nature of the product itself contribute to the impression we form of it.

Within the marketing mix, we call the communication elements that the marketer controls the **promotion mix**. These elements include the following:

- Personal selling
- Advertising
- Sales promotions
- Public relations

Just as a DJ combines different songs or phrases to create an entertainment experience, the term mix implies that a company's promotion strategy is focused on more than one element, so part of the challenge is to integrate these different communication tools in an effective way.

Another challenge is to be sure that the promotion mix works in harmony with the overall marketing mix, which combines elements of promotion with place, price, and product information to position the firm's offering in people's minds. For example, ads for luxury products such as Rolex watches or Jaguar automobiles must be designed to communicate that same luxury character of the product.

The messages consumers receive about companies and products vary in the amount of control that the marketer has over the message. As Figure 12.3 shows, mass-media advertising and sales promotion are at one end of the continuum, where the marketer has total control over what message is

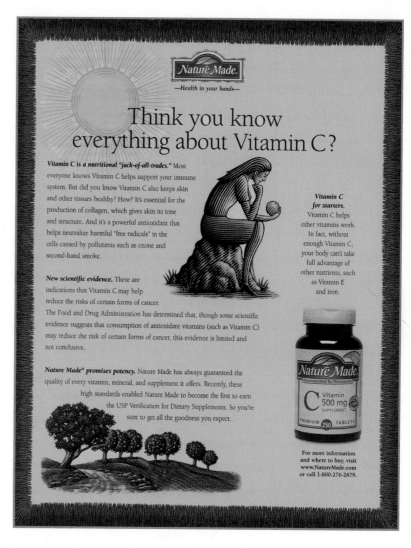

For many products, factual information is essential. Magazine advertising provides an opportunity to deliver the desired information.

promotion mix
The major elements of marketer-controlled communications, including advertising, sales promotions, public relations, and personal selling.

Figure 12.3 Control Continuum

The messages that consumers receive about companies and products differ in the amount of control the marketer has over the message delivered to the consumer.

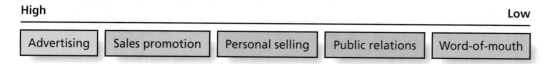

High .... Low

| Advertising | Sales promotion | Personal selling | Public relations | Word-of-mouth |

delivered. At the other end is word-of-mouth communication. Marketers know what consumers hear from one another is a vitally important component of the brand attitudes consumers form—and of their decisions about what and what not to buy. Marketers, however, often have little if any control over word-of-mouth communication. Between the ends we find personal selling, where marketers have much but not total control over the message delivered, and public relations, where marketers have even less control.

In this section, we'll first look at how marketers use various forms of appeals to reach customers. Then we'll briefly describe the elements of the promotion mix, all of which will be covered in detail in later chapters. Table 12.1 presents some of the pros and cons of each element.

Personal Appeals

The most immediate way for a marketer to make contact with customers is simply to tell them how wonderful the product is. This is part of the *personal selling* element of the promotion mix mentioned previously. It is the direct interaction between a company representative and a customer that can occur in person, by phone, or even over an interactive computer link. We'll learn more about this important process in Chapter 14. Salespeople are a valuable source of communications, because customers can ask questions and the salesperson can immediately address objections and describe product benefits.

Table 12.1 A Comparison of Elements of the Promotion Mix

Promotional Element	Pros	Cons
Advertising	• The marketer has control over what the message will say, when it will appear, and who is likely to see it.	• Often expensive to produce and distribute. • May have low credibility and/or be ignored by audience.
Sales promotion	• Provides incentives to retailers to support one's products. • Builds excitement for retailers and consumers. • Encourages immediate purchase and trial of new products. • Price-oriented promotions cater to price-sensitive consumers.	• Short-term emphasis on immediate sales rather than a focus on building brand loyalty. The number of competing promotions may make it hard to break through the promotional clutter.
Public relations	• Relatively low cost. • High credibility.	• Lack of control over the message that is eventually transmitted and no guarantee that the message will ever reach the target. • Hard to track the results of publicity efforts.
Personal selling	• Direct contact with the customer gives the salesperson the opportunity to be flexible and modify the sales message to coincide with the customer's needs. • The salesperson can get immediate feedback from the customer.	• High cost per contact with customer. • Difficult to ensure consistency of message when it is delivered by many different company representatives. • The credibility of salespeople often depends on the quality of their company's image, which has been created by other promotion strategies.

Advice for PriceMcNabb, Inc.

STUDENT
SHERIF FAHMY
Johnson & Wales University

I would choose option 1, to position Bojangles' around customers' desire for its uniquely flavorful food. This option is the most promising because it gives consumers something they're looking for: difference. Popeye's, McDonald's, Burger King, KFC, %they all serve chicken—but Bojangles sells chicken with flavor. All the food sold is made from scratch, many secret recipes, and it's from the South. Furthermore, this chain has the ability to cater itself to a niche market, and option 1 expresses this. "Bojangles' has exactly what you're craving at the exact time you're craving it." When you want a sub, you go to Subway, fries, you go to McDonald's, and so on . . . but when you're in the mood for chicken, Bojangles' will satisfy this need.

PROFESSOR
DEBBIE LAVERIE
Texas Tech University

I would select option 2, position Bojangles' as a quick-serve restaurant where you can actually enjoy the goodness of made-from-scratch, homemade food. All three of the options have merit, and, like many advertising decisions, there is no clear-cut best way to proceed. When evaluating the strategies, I took into consideration the goal of the company, to compete with national quick-service restaurants. Option 2 sets Bojangles' apart from the competition and offers a unique selling proposition. Bojangles' can build on the one clear difference of made-from-scratch, homemade food, which is the essence of the brand. Testimonials could be used in the advertisement to make the claim more believable to consumers. I believe this option is best, as it builds on the strengths of the brand and differentiates Bojangles' from the competition in a cluttered market.

PROFESSOR
THOMAS TANNER
Edinboro University, Pennsylvania

I would choose option 1 because it is vitally important to understand consumerism and what motivates one individual to buy over others. If you remind consumers about the benefits or values of purchasing your product, then, essentially, you are giving them a reason to buy. The key concept here for this type of product is simply more then differentiation. It is more about the understanding of consumer behavior and perceptions. A "soft-sell" strategy that focuses on customer's desires would prove to be more effective in the long term as you focus primarily on what made them purchase your product in the first place.

Personal selling can be tremendously effective, especially for big-ticket consumer items and for industrial products where the "human touch" is essential. It can be so effective that some marketers, if given a choice, might neglect other forms of promotion. Unfortunately, it's often too expensive to personally connect with each and every customer, so we need other forms of promotion as well.

Mass Appeals

The other pieces of the promotion mix are those messages intended to reach many prospective customers at the same time. Whether a company mails an announcement to a few hundred local residents or airs a television commercial to millions, it is promoting itself to a mass audience. The following are the elements of the promotion mix that provide mass appeal strategies:

- **Advertising:** Advertising is for many the most familiar and visible element of the promotion mix. It is nonpersonal communication from an identified sponsor using the mass media. Because it can convey rich and dynamic images, advertising can establish and reinforce a distinctive brand identity. This helps marketers bond with customers and boost sales. Advertising also is useful in communicating factual information about the product or

The product and advertising for it must be combined effectively to create a consistent brand image. Skechers athletic shoes creates an image of excitement for its athletic shoes for women.

reminding consumers to buy their favorite brand. However, advertising sometimes suffers from a credibility problem because cynical consumers tune out messages they think are biased or are intended to sell them something they don't need. Advertising can also be expensive, so firms must take great care to ensure their messages are effective.

- **Sales promotion:** Sales promotions are programs such as contests, coupons, or other incentives that marketers design to build interest in or encourage purchase of a product during a specified time period. Unlike other forms of promotion, sales promotions are intended to stimulate immediate action (often in the form of a purchase) rather than building long-term loyalty. More on this in Chapter 14.

- **Public relations:** Public relations relates to a variety of communications activities that seek to create and maintain a positive image of an organization and its products among various publics, including customers, government officials, and shareholders. As we'll see in Chapter 13, public relations activities include writing press releases about product and company-related issues, dealing with the news media, and organizing special events. Public relations also includes efforts to present negative company news in the most positive way, thus minimizing harmful consequences. In contrast to sales promotions, public relations components of the promotion mix usually do not seek a short-term increase in sales. Instead, they try to influence feelings, opinions, or beliefs for the long term.

New Appeals

In addition to these tried-and-true methods, many marketers are starting to figure out that they must find alternatives to traditional advertising—especially when talking to young consumers who are very cynical about the efforts of big corporations to buy their allegiance. A number of new ways of appealing to customers exist.

guerrilla marketing
Marketing activity in which a firm "ambushes" consumers with promotional content in places they are not expecting to encounter this kind of activity.

GUERRILLA MARKETING A few years back, some companies with smaller advertising budgets developed innovative ways of getting consumers' attention. These activities—from putting stickers on apples and heads of lettuce to placing product-related messages on the backs of theater tickets and flags on a golf course—became known as **guerrilla marketing**. No, this term doesn't refer to marketers making monkeys out of themselves. This strategy involves "ambushing" consumers with promotional content in places where they are not expecting to encounter this kind of activity.[5]

Today, big companies are buying into guerrilla marketing strategies big time. Coca-Cola did it for a Sprite promotion; Nike did it to build interest in a new shoe model.[6] When RCA records wanted to create a buzz around teen pop singer Christina Aguilera, the label hired a team of young people to swarm the Web and chat about her on popular teen sites like Alloy.com, Bolt.com, and Gurl.com. They posted information casually, sometimes sounding like fans. Just before one of Aguilera's albums debuted, RCA also hired a direct marketing company to e-mail electronic postcards filled with song snippets and biographical information to 50,000 Web addresses. The album quickly went to number 1 on the charts.

Guerrilla marketing can be used to promote new drinks, cars, clothing styles—or even computer systems. Much to the annoyance of city officials in San Francisco and Chicago, in 2001 IBM painted hundreds of "Peace Love Linux" logos on sidewalks to publicize the company's adoption of the Linux operating system. Even though the company got hit with a hefty bill to pay for cleaning up the "corporate graffiti," one marketing journalist noted that they "got the publicity they were looking for."[7] Given the success of many of these campaigns that operate on a shoestring budget, expect to see even more of this kind of tactic as other companies climb on the guerrilla bandwagon.

VIRAL MARKETING Another powerful and cheap way of appealing to customers is **viral marketing**. When a company uses this strategy, in essence it recruits customers to be its sales agents by offering them some incentive, such as free e-mail service, to send other consumers a message about the company. In 18 months, Hotmail, which offers free e-mail service, grew to 12 million users using viral marketing.[8] The approach was simple. Hotmail put the message "Get Your Free E-mail at Hotmail.com" at the bottom of every e-mail sent by a Hotmail user. And that's the idea behind viral marketing— messages spread like the flu from one friend to another until "there's a full-blown epidemic and products are flying off the shelves."[9] For companies such as Hotmail, it's a win-win situation. The more free "customers" they have, the more they can charge advertisers who pay to post messages on the Hotmail site.

KitchenAid uses a product giveaway promotion to stimulate purchases.

Although the original users of viral marketing received the word-of-mouth pitches from customers for free, many companies have upped the ante by offering premiums and free products if customers tell friends who become customers. AT&T Wireless San Francisco offered college students a discounted cell phone, a calling plan with free features, and a $25 credit on their bill for every friend who signs up for the service (up to a limit of five).[10] Procter & Gamble generated 2 million referrals when it offered consumers a free styling hair spray and entry into a sweepstakes for every 10 friends who visited the Web site for the company's new Physique shampoo.[11]

BUZZ AND HYPE There's also a lot of buzz these days about buzz-building—generating interest in a product by getting real consumers to talk about it rather than by just producing glitzy ads. **Buzz** is word of mouth that is viewed as authentic and generated by customers. **Hype** is dismissed as inauthentic—corporate propaganda planted by a company with an ax to grind. For example, some video games now feature real live brands, such as Ford, Radio Shack, General Motors, Toyota, Procter & Gamble, and Sony. Quiksilver, a clothing manufacturer for extreme-sport participants, puts its shirts and shorts into video games like Tony Hawk's Pro Skater 3.[12] Table 12.2 compares buzz and hype.

viral marketing
Marketing activity in which a company recruits customers to be sales agents and spread the word about the product.

buzz
Word-of-mouth communication that is viewed as authentic and generated by customers.

hype
Considered corporate propaganda planted by a company with an ax to grind and therefore dismissed by customers.

Table 12.2 Buzz Versus Hype

Buzz	Hype
Word of mouth	Advertising
Grassroots	Corporate
Authentic	Fake
Credibility	Skepticism

Source: Adapted from Michael R. Solomon, *Conquering Consumerspace: Marketing Strategies for a Branded World* (New York: AMACOM Books, 2003).

Integrated Marketing Communications

Marketers have been developing promotion strategies and using the elements of the promotion mix for many years, but the concept of integrated marketing communications (IMC) is relatively new. While IMC has not been adopted by all firms, many marketing experts believe that IMC provides a competitive advantage to firms in the 21st century.

With IMC, marketers plan and then execute marketing communication programs that create and maintain long-term relationships with customers by satisfying customer needs. This means that promotion tools are used in such a way as to build ongoing loyal relationships with customers or other stakeholders, rather than simply causing a one-time product purchase or short-term change in behavior.[13] With IMC, marketers like Matt Ferguson at PriceMcNabb look at communication the way customers see it—as a flow of information from a single source. Thus, marketers who understand the power of IMC seek to "unify all marketing communication tools—from advertising to packaging—to send target audiences a consistent, persuasive message that promotes company goals."[14]

So why is IMC so important today? A few years ago, marketers could effectively communicate with consumers by placing a few ads on major television networks and perhaps in a few popular magazines. Today, with increased global competition, customers are bombarded with more and more marketing messages—in the United States, over 1,400 advertising messages *every day*. And the sheer number of media outlets also is mushrooming. Marketers can choose from literally hundreds of cable and satellite stations, each of which can deliver its messages to a selected portion of the television viewing audience. At the same time, technology now enables even small firms to develop and effectively use customer databases, giving firms greater opportunities for understanding customers and for developing one-to-one communication programs.

Characteristics of IMC

In order to fully understand what IMC is all about and before a firm can begin to implement an IMC program, it is essential that managers understand some important characteristics of IMC.

IMC CREATES A SINGLE UNIFIED VOICE Perhaps the most important characteristic of IMC is that it creates a single unified voice for a firm. If we examine the traditional communication program of a typical consumer goods firm, say, a manufacturer of frozen foods, we see that they often develop communication tactics in isolation. If marketers decide they need advertising, what do they do? They hire an ad agency to produce great advertising. Or they may even hire several different ad agencies to develop advertising aimed at different target markets. They may also realize they need public relations activities, so they hire a public relations firm. Then, some other genius decides they need to sponsor a sweepstakes, so they hire a sales promotion firm to do this. The sales department hires a different firm to develop trade show materials, and some-

Some companies publicize their brands by buying space on blimps. This promotional program might be done independently of an ad campaign.

one in the corporate communication department hires a sports-marketing firm to work with sponsoring an auto race.

Each of these firms may well do a good job, but each may also be sending out a different message. The customer can't help but be confused. What is this product? What is the brand image? Whose needs will this product satisfy? IMC strategies present a unified brand and selling proposition in the marketplace by eliminating duplication and conflicting communication. Because IMC programs are developed as a whole, there is a focus on *all* communications elements—advertising, public relations, sales promotion, and so forth—speaking with one voice, creating a single and powerful brand personality.

Having a single brand message, however, doesn't mean that marketers don't communicate to different segments of the market or different stakeholder groups with different tactics. The same brand message can be communicated to employees with a story in the company newsletter about how local workers have helped flood victims, to loyal customers via direct mail that explains how to make their home safe for toddlers, and to prospective customers through mass media and Internet advertising.

The one-voice/one-message focus of IMC also considers other less obvious forms of communication. For example, a firm's communication with customers includes the letters sent to customers, the way company personnel talk on the phone with clients or customers, the uniforms delivery people or other employees wear, signage, and other policies and procedures that may have an unintended effect on consumers' perceptions of the firm. It's very difficult for a company to convince you that it wants you as a customer when you get nasty letters telling you that you're two days late paying your bill.

IMC BEGINS WITH THE CUSTOMER The customer is the primary focus of the communication, not the goals of the company or the creative genius of the communication specialists. First and foremost, the goal of IMC is to provide the information the customer wants when they want it, where they want it, and in the amount needed. Sometimes that's as simple as letting consumers "vote" on the shows or products they want to see, as when fans of the hit TV comedy *Friends* were allowed to choose their six favorite episodes at a Web site when the producers decided to end the series.[15]

IMC SEEKS TO DEVELOP RELATIONSHIPS WITH CUSTOMERS As mass-marketing activities have become less and less successful, many marketers are finding that the road to success is through one-to-one or relationship marketing, where the focus is on building and maintaining a long-term relationship with each individual customer. To achieve this, marketers must continuously communicate with each customer or else risk losing him or her to the competition.

What we said earlier bears repeating—it simply is easier and less expensive to keep an existing customer than to attract a new one. Thus, IMC firms also measure their success by share of customer, not share of market, and on the lifetime value of a customer. And like we said in Chapter 7, it means prioritizing customers so that greater resources go to communicating with high-value customers.

Because IMC also is much about building and maintaining relationships with customers, IMC strategies often incorporate databases and the CRM programs and practices we talked about in Chapter 7. With these tools, marketers have the information they need to better understand customers and to deliver unique messages to each consumer—messages that meet the needs of each consumer and that build relationships.

IMC INVOLVES TWO-WAY COMMUNICATION Traditional communication programs were built on one-way communication activities. Television, magazine, newspaper, and outdoor advertising spouted clever messages at the consumer, but there was little if any way for the consumer to talk back. Today, we know that one-way, impersonal communication is highly ineffective at building long-term relationships with customers. Instead, marketers seek first to learn what information customers have and what additional information they want and then develop communication tactics that let them share information with their customers.

IMC FOCUSES ON STAKEHOLDERS, NOT JUST CUSTOMERS *Stakeholders* are any individuals or organizations that are important to the long-term health of an organization. Some of these stakeholders include employees, suppliers, stockholders, the media, trade associations, regulators, and even neighbors. One reason these other stakeholders are so important is that customers and prospective customers don't just learn about a company and its products from the firm. Their attitudes, positive or negative, are also heavily influenced by the mass media, government regulatory bodies, or even their local neighbor who happens to work for the firm. Thus, while the primary stakeholder is usually the customer, a myriad of other groups or individuals can significantly influence customer attitudes and behaviors.

IMC GENERATES A CONTINUOUS STREAM OF COMMUNICATION A major characteristic of an IMC strategy is that tactics using many different elements of the communication program—advertising, publicity, personal selling, sales promotion, customer letters, and so on—are included in a single IMC plan. As a result, IMC strategies provide for a continuous stream of communication. Instead of consumers being bombarded with messages from various sources for a week or two and then hearing nothing from the brand for months, IMC planning ensures that consumers receive information on a regular basis and in the right amount.

IMC MEASURES RESULTS BASED ON ACTUAL FEEDBACK Many IMC boosters suggest that the only adequate measure of a promotional campaign's effectiveness is to evaluate the return on investment on communication dollars. This means that if a firm spends $1 million on advertising, it should be able to determine what dollar amount of revenue the firm receives as a result of that expenditure. While this type of relationship between promotion dollars and revenues may be difficult to measure exactly because of such things as the long-term effects of advertising and other communication, most firms are seeking measures of accountability for their communication budgets and demand results.

Figure 12.4 Steps in Developing the IMC Plan

Developing the IMC Plan

Now that we've talked about the characteristics of an IMC strategy, we need to see how to make it happen. How do we go about the complex task of developing an IMC plan—one that delivers just the right message to a number of different target audiences when and where they want it in the most effective and cost-efficient way? Just as with any other strategic decision-making process, the development of this plan includes several steps, as shown in Figure 12.4. Let's review each step.

Step 1: Identify the Target Audiences

An important part of overall marketing planning is to determine who the target market is. This is where a good customer database is most important. With a well-designed database, marketers can know who their target market is as well as the buying behavior of different segments within the total market. This means they can develop targeted messages for each customer. For example, Matt Ferguson had to come up with a way to communicate with "heavy users" of fast-food restaurants, including people who currently patronize Bojangles' competitors.

Step 2: Establish the Communications Objectives

The next step in communications planning is to establish communications objectives. The whole point of communicating with customers and prospective customers is to let them know that the organization has a product to meet their needs in a timely and affordable way. It's bad enough when a product comes along that people don't want or need. But the bigger marketing sin is to have a product that they *do* want—but fail to let them know about it. Of course, seldom can we deliver a single message to a consumer that magically transforms her into a loyal customer. In most cases, it takes a series of messages that move the consumer through several stages.

We might view this process as an uphill climb, such as the one in Figure 12.5, where the consumer is "pushed" through a series of steps, often referred to as a **hierarchy of effects**, from initial awareness of a product to brand loyalty. The task of moving the consumer up the hierarchy becomes more difficult at each step. Many potential buyers may drop out along the way, leaving less of the target group inclined to go the distance and become loyal customers. Each part of this path entails different communication objectives to "push" people to the next level.

hierarchy of effects
A series of steps prospective customers move through, from initial awareness of a product to brand loyalty.

Figure 12.5 The Hierarchy of Effects

Communication objectives seek to move consumers through the hierarchy of effects.

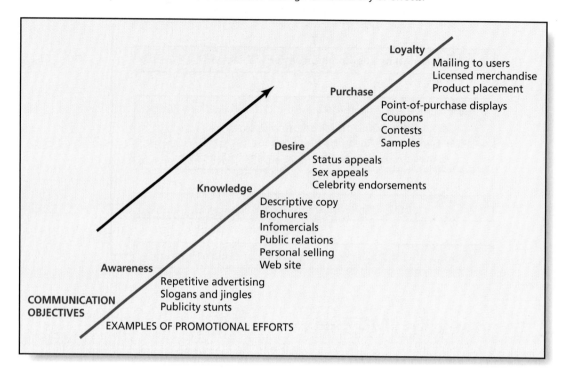

To understand how this process works, consider how a firm would have to adjust its communication objectives as it tries to establish a presence in the market for a new men's cologne called Hunk. Let's say that the primary target market for the cologne is single men aged 18 to 24 who care about their appearance and who are into health, fitness, and working out. The company would want to focus more on some promotion methods (such as advertising) and less on others (such as personal selling). Here are some steps the company might take to promote Hunk:

- **Create awareness:** The first step is to make members of the target market aware that there's a new brand of cologne on the market. Marketers would accomplish this through simple, repetitive advertising in magazines, on television, and on the radio that push the brand name. The company might even consider creating a "teaser" campaign in which interest is heightened by ads that don't reveal the exact nature of the product (e.g., newspaper ads that simply proclaim, "Hunk is coming!"). The promotion objective might be to create an 80 percent awareness of Hunk cologne among 18- to 24-year-old men in the first two months.

- **Inform the market:** The next step would be to provide prospective users with knowledge about the benefits the new product has to offer, that is, how it is positioned relative to other fragrances (see Chapter 7). Perhaps the cologne has a light, slightly mentholated scent with a hint of a liniment smell to remind the wearer of how he feels after a good workout. Promotion would focus on communications that emphasize this position. The objective at this point might be to communicate the connection between Hunk and muscle building so that 70 percent of the target market develops some interest in the product.

- **Create desire:** The next task is to create favorable feelings toward the product and to convince at least some portion of this group that Hunk is preferable to other men's colognes. Communications at this stage might employ splashy advertising spreads in magazines, perhaps including an endorsement by a well-known celebrity "hunk" such as The Rock. The specific objective might be to create positive attitudes toward Hunk cologne among 50 percent of the target market and brand preference among 30 percent of the target market.

- **Encourage trial:** As the expression goes, "How do ya know 'til ya try it?" The company now needs to get some of the men who have formed a preference for the product to try it. A promotion plan might encourage trial by mailing samples of Hunk to members of the target market, inserting "scratch-and-sniff" samples in bodybuilding magazines, placing elaborate displays in stores that dispense money-saving coupons, or even sponsoring a contest in which the winner gets to have The Rock as his personal trainer for a day. The specific objective now might be to encourage trial of Hunk among 25 percent of 18- to 24-year-old men in the first two months.

- **Build loyalty:** Of course, the real test is loyalty: convincing customers to stay with Hunk after they've gone through the first bottle. Promotion efforts must maintain ongoing communications with current users to reinforce the bond they feel with the product. As before, this will be accomplished with some mix of strategies, perhaps including direct-mail advertising to current users, product placements in popular television programs or movies, and maybe even the development of a workout clothing line bearing a Hunk logo. The objective might be to develop and maintain regular usage of Hunk cologne among 10 percent of men from 18 to 24 years old.

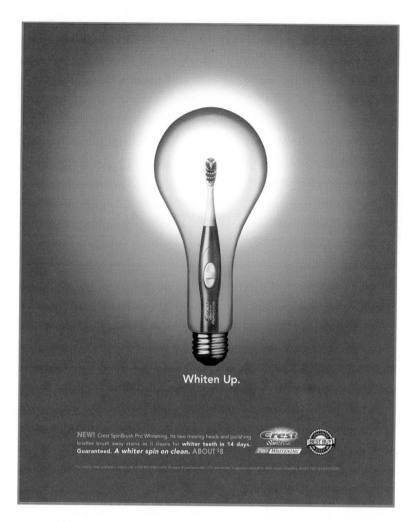

The second step in the hierarchy of effects is knowledge. Crest informs consumers about its new SpinBrush Pro Whitening product.

Step 3: Determine and Allocate the Marketing Communications Budget

While setting a budget for marketing communications might seem easy—you just calculate how much you need to accomplish your objectives—in reality it's not that simple. Determining and allocating communications budgets includes three distinct decisions: determining the total communications budget, deciding whether to use a push strategy or a pull strategy, and allocating how much to spend on specific promotion activities.

DETERMINE THE TOTAL PROMOTION BUDGET In the real world, firms often view communications costs as an expense rather than as an investment leading to greater profits. When sales are declining or the company is operating in a difficult economic environment, it is often tempting to cut costs by reducing spending on advertising, promotions, and other "soft" activities whose contributions to the bottom line are hard to quantify. When this is the case, marketers must work harder to justify these expenses.

Economic approaches to budgeting rely on marginal analysis (discussed in Chapter 11), in which the organization spends money on promotion as long as the revenues realized by these efforts continue to exceed the costs of the promotions themselves. This perspective assumes that promotions are always intended solely to increase sales when in fact these activities may have other objectives, such as enhancing a firm's image.

top-down budgeting techniques
Allocation of the promotion budget based on the total amount to be devoted to marketing communications.

percentage-of-sales method
A method for promotion budgeting that is based on a certain percentage of either last year's sales or on estimates for the present year's sales.

competitive-parity method
A promotion budgeting method in which an organization matches whatever competitors are spending.

bottom-up budgeting techniques
Allocation of the promotion budget based on identifying promotion goals and allocating enough money to accomplish them.

objective-task method
A promotion budgeting method in which an organization first defines the specific communications goals it hopes to achieve and then tries to calculate what kind of promotional efforts it will take to meet these goals.

push strategy
The company tries to move its products through the channel by convincing channel members to offer them.

pull strategy
The company tries to move its products through the channel by building desire for the products among consumers, thus convincing retailers to respond to this demand by stocking these items.

Also, the effects of promotions often lag over time. For example, a firm may have to spend a lot on promotion when it first launches a product without seeing any immediate return. Because of these limitations, most firms rely on two budgeting techniques: top down and bottom up.

Top-down budgeting techniques require top management to establish the overall amount that the organization allocates for promotion activities, and this amount is then divided among advertising, public relations, and other promotion departments.

The most common top-down technique is the **percentage-of-sales method**, in which the promotion budget is based on last year's sales or on estimates for the present year's sales. The percentage may be an industry average provided by trade associations that collect objective information on behalf of member companies. The advantage of this method is that it ties spending on promotion to sales and profits.

Unfortunately, this method can imply that sales cause promotional outlays rather than viewing sales as the *outcome* of promotional efforts. As sales drop, firms might be reluctant to spend more on promotion even though the drop might be due to environmental changes, such as a change in economic conditions or a rival's recent introduction of a new product. If so, cutting promotion spending might not help the firm in the long run.

The **competitive-parity method** is a fancy way of saying "keep up with the Joneses." In other words, match whatever competitors are spending. Some marketers think this approach simply mirrors the best thinking of others in the business. However, this method often sees each player maintaining the same market share year after year. This method also assumes that the same dollars spent on promotion by two different firms will yield the same results, but spending a lot of money doesn't guarantee a successful promotion. Firms certainly need to monitor their competitors' promotion activities, but they must combine this information with their own objectives and capacities.

The problem with top-down techniques is that budget decisions are based more on established practices than on promotion objectives. Another approach is to begin at the beginning: identify promotion goals and allocate enough money to accomplish them. That is what **bottom-up budgeting techniques** attempt. For example, some marketers devise a payout plan that attempts to project the revenues and costs associated with a product over several years and then match promotion expenditures to a pattern—such as spending more on promotion in the first year to build market share and then spending less once the product catches on.

This bottom-up logic is at the heart of the **objective-task method**, which is gaining in popularity. Using this approach, the firm first defines the specific communications goals it hopes to achieve, such as increasing by 20 percent the number of consumers who are aware of the brand. It then tries to figure out what kind of promotional efforts it will take to meet that goal. Although this is the most rational approach, it is hard to implement because it obliges managers to specify their objectives and attach dollar amounts to them. This method requires careful analysis—and a bit of lucky "guesstimating."

DECIDE ON A PUSH OR A PULL STRATEGY   One crucial issue in determining the promotion mix is whether the company is relying on a push strategy or a pull strategy. A **push strategy** means that the company wants to move its products by convincing channel members to offer them and entice their customers to select these items. In this case, promotion efforts will "push" the products from producers to consumer by focusing on personal selling, trade advertising, and sales promotions, such as exhibits at trade shows.

In contrast, a company relying on a **pull strategy** is counting on consumers to desire its products and thus convince retailers to respond to this demand by stocking them. In this case, efforts will focus on media advertising and consumer sales promotion to stimulate interest among end consumers who will "pull" the product onto store shelves and then into their shopping carts.

Whether we use a push or a pull strategy and how the promotion mix for a product is designed must vary over time because some elements work better at different points in the product life cycle than others. As an example, we might think about the state of elecronic audio and video equipment in today's market and the relative positions in the product life cycle.

In the *introduction phase*, the objective is to build awareness of and encourage trial of the product among consumers, often by relying on a push strategy. That's the situation today with WiFi. Advertising is the primary promotion tool for creating awareness, and a publicity campaign to generate news reports about the new product may help as well. Sales promotion (free samples and such, as when retailers like Starbucks set up free WiFi zones for customers) may be used to encourage trial. Business-to-business marketing that emphasizes personal selling, that is, the marketing that a manufacturer does to retailers and other business customers, is important in this phase in order to get channel members to carry the product. For consumer goods sold through retailers, trade sales promotion may be necessary to encourage retailers to stock the product.

In the *growth phase*, promotions must now start stressing product benefits. For products such as MP3 players, advertising increases now, while sales promotions that encourage trial usually decline because people are more willing to try the product without being offered an incentive.

The opposite pattern often occurs with products such as DVD players, now in their *maturity phase*, when many people have already tried the product. As sales stabilize, strategy now shifts to encouraging people to switch from competitors' brands. This can be tough if consumers don't see enough differences to bother. Usually, sales promotions, particularly coupons and special price deals, have greater chances of success than advertising.

All bets are off for products such as VCR players, now in their *decline phase*. As sales plummet, the company dramatically reduces spending on all elements of the promotion mix. Sales will be driven by the continued loyalty of a small group of users who keep the product alive until it is sold to another company or discontinued.

ALLOCATE THE BUDGET TO A SPECIFIC PROMOTION MIX Once the organization decides how much to spend on promotion and whether to use a push or a pull strategy, it must divide its budget among the elements in the promotion mix. Although advertising used to get most of the promotion budget, today sales promotions are playing a bigger role in marketing strategies. For example, companies like Nickelodeon cable network use games to publicize their products.[16]

Reaching the college market is a unique challenge for marketers since students are less likely to be influenced by advertising in traditional media. Instead, the college newspaper and guerrilla or viral marketing have proven effective for many companies.[17]

- **Organizational factors:** Characteristics of the specific firm influence how it allocates its money. These characteristics include the complexity and formality of the company's decision-making process, preferences for advertising versus sales promotions or other elements in the promotion mix, past experiences with specific promotion vehicles, and the "comfort level" of the firm's advertising and promotion agencies with different approaches in marketing communications. For example, Nestlé, the giant Swiss company, shifted 20 percent of its advertising budget into sales promotion and direct-response efforts over a two-year period after determining that its promotion dollars would be more effective there.[18]

- **Market potential:** Some consumer groups are more likely to buy the product than others. For example, the marketers of Hunk might find that men in blue-collar occupations would

Sometimes a company may decide to try to revive a dying brand with a modest promotional budget. Altoids breath mints have been around for 200 years, but the brand was largely unknown. However, it had a devoted following among smokers and coffee drinkers who hung out in the blossoming Seattle club scene during the 1980s. When Altoids' manufacturer (Callard & Bowers) was bought by Kraft, the brand's marketing manager persuaded Kraft (a much larger company) to breathe new life into the mints by funding a quirky campaign that relies on retro imagery to avoid making the product seem too mainstream.

The dance of the
SPLENDA PLUM FAIRY

Now SPLENDA No Calorie Sweetener comes in a large Baker's Bag. Almost anywhere you can use sugar, you can use SPLENDA. Made from sugar, so it tastes like sugar. *Think SUGAR, say SPLENDA.*

A pull strategy tries to create consumer demand for a product in order to convince retailers to carry it in their stores.

AIDA model
The communications goals of attention, interest, desire, and action.

be more interested in the product than men in white-collar occupations. It makes sense for marketers to allocate more resources to areas with more sales potential.

- **Market size:** As a rule, larger markets are more expensive places in which to promote. The costs of buying media (such as local TV spots) are higher in major metropolitan areas, but high population density means it will be easier to reach more consumers at the same time. Advertising is good for mass-market products, while personal selling is good for big-ticket, specialized, or highly technical products.

Step 4: Design the Promotion Mix

Designing the promotion mix is the most complicated step in marketing communication planning. It includes determining the specific communication tools that will be used, what message is to be communicated, and the communication channel(s) to be employed. Planners must ask how advertising, sales promotion, personal selling, and public relations can be used most effectively to communicate with different target audiences. Each element of the promotion mix has benefits and shortcomings, all of which must be considered in making promotion decisions.

The message should ideally accomplish four objectives (though a single message can rarely do all of these): It should get *attention*, hold *interest*, create *desire*, and produce *action*. These communications goals are known as the **AIDA model**. Here we'll review some different forms the message can take as well as how the information in the message might be structured.

TYPE OF APPEAL   There are many ways to say the same thing, and marketers must take care in choosing what type of appeal, or message strategy, they will use when encoding the message. To illustrate, consider two strategies employed by rival car companies to promote similar automobiles: A few years ago, both Toyota and Nissan introduced a large luxury car that sold for more than $40,000. Toyota's advertising for its Lexus model used a rational appeal that focused on the technical advancements in the car's design. This approach is often effective for promoting products that are technically complex and require a substantial investment. Nissan, in contrast, focused on the spiritual fulfillment a driver might feel tooling down the road in a fine machine. Much like Nissan, Volkswagen recently launched an international advertising campaign based on love poems linked to vehicles in an attempt to reach the strong emotions that underlie consumers' preferences for cars. In Germany, double-page newspaper and magazine ads feature a love poem with a paragraph explaining the feelings one of Volkswagen's cars represents.[19]

STRUCTURE OF THE APPEAL   Many marketing messages are similar to debates or trials in which someone presents arguments and tries to convince the receivers to shift their opinions. The way the argument is presented can be important. Most messages merely tout one or more positive attributes of the product or reasons to buy it. These are known as *supportive arguments* or *one-sided messages*.

An alternative is to use a *two-sided message*, with both positive and negative information. Two-sided ads can be quite effective, but marketers seldom use them.[20]

A related issue is whether the argument should draw conclusions. Should the ad say only "our brand is superior," or should it explicitly tell the consumer to buy it? The answer depends on the degree of a consumer's motivation to think about the ad and the complexity of the arguments. If the message is personally relevant, people will pay attention to it and draw their own conclusions. But if the arguments are hard to follow or the person's motivation to follow them is lacking, it is best to make these conclusions explicit.

Even the best message is wasted if it is not placed in communication channels that will reach the target audience effectively. Communication channels include the mass media: newspapers, television, radio, magazines, and direct mail. Other media include outdoor display signs and boards and electronic media, the most important of which is the Internet. Sponsorships provide another channel for communications. In Vermont, skiers can take an Altoids gondola car to the top of Stratton Mountain, while employees at the Whistler ski resort in Canada wear Evian jackets.[21]

The Internet provides a unique environment for promotional messages because it can include text, audio, video, hyperlinking, and personalization, not to mention opportunities for interaction with customers and other stakeholders. Web sites can come alive with the right mix of technical wizardry and good design. One advantage of the Web is that companies can give customers a "feel" for their products or services before they buy. Even nightclubs are going to the Web to draw virtual crowds.[22] Sites like Thewomb.com and Digitalclubnet work.com feature real-time footage of what's happening in the clubs. No more big, beefy bouncers to worry about!

Step 5: Evaluate the Effectiveness of the Communications Program

The final step in managing marketing communications is to decide whether the plan is working. The marketer needs to determine whether the communication objectives are adequately translated into marketing communications that are reaching the right target market.

It would be nice if a marketing manager could simply report, "The $3 million campaign for our revolutionary glow-in-the-dark surfboards brought in $15 million in new sales!" It's not so easy. There are many random factors in the marketing environment: a rival's manufacturing problem, a coincidental photograph of a movie star toting one of the boards, or perhaps a surge of renewed interest in surfing sparked by a cult movie hit like *Blue Crush*.

Still, there are ways to monitor and evaluate the company's communication efforts. The catch is that the effectiveness of some forms of communication is easier to determine than others. As a rule, sales promotions are the easiest to evaluate because they occur over a fixed, usually short period, making it easier to link to sales volume. Advertising researchers measure brand awareness, recall of product benefits communicated through advertising, and even the image of the brand before and after an advertising campaign. The firm can analyze and compare the performance of salespeople in different territories, although again it is difficult to rule out other factors that make one salesperson more effective than another. Public relations activities are more difficult to assess because their objectives relate more often to image building than sales volume.

Interactive Marketing

Some marketers understand that we live in an *attention economy* where the amount of information available seems infinite, but our ability to get the exact information we want is limited by the amount of time we can spend looking for it. Interactive media are in the business of getting people's attention by making the information consumers want easy to access.

The Walt Disney Corporation wanted to boost its profitability by learning more about all the things customers did when they visited one of its theme parks. The company was doing a good job of luring people to its attractions through its advertising and other communications, but management had a feeling that Disney wasn't capturing all the value it could from these visitors. The company developed a metric to tell it more precisely where families actually spend their money during their trips to the parks. It found that while the parks were the primary destinations for vacationers who spent an average of around $3,000 during a visit, Disney was capturing only 25 percent of that amount—the rest was going to independent airlines, taxis, hotels, and restaurants. So Disney focused on building more "tollbooths," or places where visitors would direct their money toward Disney products and services. It built Disney hotels and Disney stores to capture more revenue, and the firm teamed up with airlines to offer travel packages. Now, visitors may be picked up at the airport by a Disney bus and taken to a Disney hotel where they can listen to Disney radio and watch Disney TV. Vacationers now are spending closer to 75 percent of their total vacation budget at Disney properties.[23]

interactive marketing
A promotion practice in which customized marketing communications elicit a measurable response from individual receivers.

That's the key to **interactive marketing**, in which customized marketing communications yield a measurable response from receivers in the form of a purchase or perhaps a request for more information. Let's learn more about interactive marketing.

Customizing the Message

As an executive in charge of exploring interactive marketing applications for the Leo Burnett advertising agency once observed, "Advertising started as . . . one guy with a bullhorn standing 300 yards from the crowd, who had to yell to sell, had to keep his sales pitch real general for the whole audience. . . . Technology brings him closer and closer to the crowd. He can lower his voice now, and talk to the really key customers; and they can talk back, because he's close enough to talk to them without having to yell. So you lower your voice, you target your audience better, you become less manipulative in your advertising."[24]

Indeed, advances in technology continue to improve marketers' ability to customize their messages, especially on the Internet. Online weather sites are experimenting with ads that are triggered by a user's local weather. Toyota Motor Corp. ran ads for its 4Runner during winter weather watch advisories, while American Standard Inc.'s Trane division ran ads for air conditioners when the thermometer was expected to top 80 degrees.[25]

And more Web sites are tracking their users' behavior to let advertisers serve targeted ads. Companies including Reuters, ESPN, and the *Wall Street Journal* track users and tailor the messages they receive. In one campaign, Home & Garden Television tracked about 36 million people who submitted entries for a dream-home giveaway. This gives them the ability to sell advertising on their Web site to specialized companies (say, firms that make accessories for the kitchen) that will be seen by users who visit the Web site and click on the kitchen section.[26] Even small businesses can take advantage of this new technology; for example, a car dealership in Chicago can show ads to people who have accessed articles about cars in the past even when they are currently surfing Web sites that have nothing to do with cars. The technology works through "cookies," small text files stored on Web users' computer containing information about the sites you visit. From this information and user-supplied personal information on location, gender, age, and occupation, sites can divide their audience into segments like mutual-fund investors or travelers and deliver ads accordingly.

Of course, a lot of Internet advertising is more straightforward (and annoying) as we are bombarded with unsolicited pop-up ads and e-mail sales pitches, or "spam." Currently, spam and other Internet marketing activities are protected by the U.S. Constitution's First Amendment rights.[27] Congress is considering legislation that would ban many of the fraudulent practices used by spammers, but few predict that this will do much more than lead to a handful of prosecutions meant to send messages to spammers. Today, big Internet providers are using anti-spam options on their systems while software companies are providing a variety of anti-spam products for smaller systems. Such anti-spam programs allow individual e-mail users to specify which e-mail they wish to receive and which they wish kept out of their mail boxes. Similar software is available that will keep those pesky pop-ups from slowing down your Web browser to a snail's pace.

The wave of offers many of us receive each day for illegal cable descramblers, "male enhancement" potions, and Nigerian money transfer scams may "poison the well" for legitimate advertisers. Still, marketers need the Internet. Postal mail is becoming more expensive. Telemar-

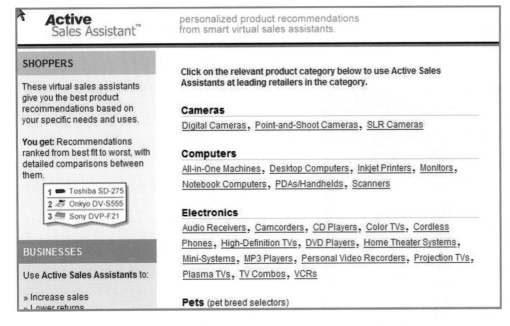

Some Web sites use sophisticated technology called "recommendation agents" that keep track of what you've bought in the past and make suggestions for new purchases based on your purchasing history.

keting is increasingly difficult because of the new national Do-Not-Call List. And young people are shifting their attention from television to the Internet. This forces companies to be more creative. For example, Johnson & Johnson has found that people will read e-mail pitches sent by people they know. So a Web site created for its Clean and Clear brand of acne remedies encourages people to send talking e-mail postcards to their friends. Each contains a coupon for the product. Time will tell if the "bad apples" turn off many consumers and diminish the potential of the Internet to deliver compelling messages about things we actually want when we want to see them.[28]

To improve the abilities of organizations to offer goods and services that better match the characteristics of targeted individuals, companies are slicing the mass market into smaller and smaller pieces. In a truly interactive marketing environment, promotion efforts will look more like door-to-door selling than like television advertising.

With cable television technology, narrowcasting can allow advertisers to make one offer to a consumer and a different one for the customer who lives across the street. Visible World, an ad-targeting technology firm that subdivides the cable world by consumer buying patterns, can produce thousands of versions of commercials that can be changed and updated almost instantly for delivery to unique households.[29]

Levels of Interactive Response

Recall that the goals of promotion include—but are not limited to—purchases. Others include building awareness, informing, reminding, and building a long-term relationship with the product and the firm. To round out our understanding of what interactive marketing is all about, we need to distinguish between two levels of response:

- **First-order response:** In Chapter 13, we will see that direct-marketing vehicles such as catalogs and home shopping television shows are playing a major role in nonstore retailing. These techniques are interactive. If successful, they result in an order (which is most definitely a response),

By creating e-mail using HTML (the same programming language used to create Web pages), firms can send customers messages that look like their corporate Web pages. This helps communicate a consistent image.

transactional data
An ongoing record of individuals or organizations that buy a product.

and the record of these responses is called **transactional data**. So let's think of a product offer that directly yields a transaction as a first-order response.

- **Second-order response:** Customer feedback other than a transaction in response to a promotional message is a *second-order response*. This may take the form of a request for more information about a good, service, or organization.

A second-order response may also take the form of criticism that may even result in changes to the offering. In some cases, consumers literally play a role in shaping the goods or services they will receive before making a transaction. When the director of the movie *The Hulk* hinted that the superhero might not wear his trademark purple pants in the movie (or any pants at all), irate fans filled Web sites with protests and vowed to boycott the film. The Hulk wound up wearing the pants in the final version. Moviegoers are influencing the films that get produced as never before. Special-interest sites like SuperHeroHype.com and DarkHorizons.com are giving a powerful voice to fans of fantasy, horror, and comic-based films. *The Blair Witch Project* was propelled to greatness based on Internet buzz.[30]

It may sound weird, but another kind of second-order response is a request not to receive any more information from the company. We assume that a priority of any promotion campaign is to get more customers. Interactive marketers sometimes operate with the opposite goal in mind: to *reduce* their customer base. No, they have not lost their minds. They know that future efforts will be more efficient when they connect with customers who are interested in what they have to promote. The amount of effort required to sell the same item gets progressively greater as the target's interest in it gets lower. An expression of no interest is valuable information, because it enables the firm to concentrate its resources on customers who are the most likely to buy.

Now, let's see what interactive marketers do with all this feedback.

Database Marketing

The secret to effective interactive marketing is the development of a customer database that allows the organization to learn about the preferences of its customers, fine-tune its offerings, and build an ongoing relationship with its market. And as we said, this same effective use of databases is important to building relationships with consumers, a key characteristic of IMC.

While some companies have maintained a customer database for years, until recently most have not linked the database with their marketing communication activities. **Database marketing** is the creation of an ongoing relationship with a set of customers with an identifiable interest in a product or service and whose responses to promotion efforts become part of the ongoing communications process.

We can look at an example of how an IMC firm might make effective use of database marketing. What if you ordered a dozen roses to be delivered to a friend for his or her birthday last year? You (and your friend) have become a part of the florist's database. What are the possibilities for the florist? First, the database is a gold mine of information. By examining (or *mining* as it is often called) the records of thousands of customers including you, the florist can find out which customers order flowers frequently (heavy users) and which order only occasionally (light users). They can identify customers who order flowers for themselves, usually when they entertain. They know which customers order flowers only for funerals, and which send flowers to their sweethearts. And they can determine what type of customer accounts for their greatest sales and their greatest profits. This helps them to develop a better understanding of their target markets.

"Facing the Facts About Adult Acne"

Successful IMC strategies rely on a customer database. If you fill out and return this reply card that goes along with an ad for BenzaClin adult acne medicine, your name will be entered in the company's database.

Of course, using the information in the database for understanding a firm's market is only the beginning. Even more important is how firms such as our florist use the database to create that one-to-one communication with their target markets. So you, our florist's customer, may get a call or a postcard next year reminding you of your friend's birthday and asking if you want the same dozen roses (well, actually, fresh ones of the same type) sent again this year. The customer who entertains may receive a brochure before the New Year's holiday season that shows various table arrangements. Heavy users might receive a special thank-you for their business and an offer to receive a free arrangement after purchasing 12 arrangements. And by the way, what about your friend who received flowers but who has never purchased from our florist? Since we may assume that a consumer who likes to receive flowers will sooner or later want to purchase them as well, she becomes part of the florist's prospective customer database. As such, she may receive a catalog of the most popular arrangements or perhaps a coupon for a discount on her first order.

The following list explains what database marketing can do:[31]

database marketing
The creation of an ongoing relationship with a set of customers who have an identifiable interest in a product or service and whose responses to promotional efforts become part of future communications attempts.

- **Database marketing is interactive:** Recall that interactive marketing requires a response from consumers, be it filling out an order form or calling an 800 number for product information. For example, H.J. Heinz sent a mail piece to female cat owners that asked the provocative question, "Does he sleep with you?" If the woman completes a brief survey that tells the company more about her pet food preferences, she receives a personalized thank-you note that mentions her pet by name.[32] She is also entered into the company's database so that she will receive future communications about her feline friend. This type of interactivity gives marketers more than one opportunity to develop a dialogue with the customer and possibly to create add-on sales by engaging the customer in a discussion about the product and related items or services in which she might be interested.

- **Database marketing builds relationships:** It's easier for the marketer to build promotion programs that continue over time with database marketing because the marketer can best adapt them in light of consumers' responses. *The best predictor of who will buy a product is knowing who bought it in the past.* That's why *Reader's Digest*'s 12 full-time statisticians sort its customers by likelihood of purchase and predict the probability that each will respond to a given offer.[33] Once sophisticated database marketers know who has already purchased, they can keep in touch with these consumers on an ongoing basis. They can reward loyal customers with money-saving coupons and keep them informed of upcoming prizes and promotions. As one executive whose company tracks big-ticket customers explained, "They are members of a club, but they don't know they are members."[34]

- **Database marketing locates new customers:** In some cases, a marketer can create new customers by focusing communications on likely prospects with characteristics similar to current users. For example, Dial sent coupon mailings about rust stains to neighbors of people in Des Moines, Iowa, and Omaha, Nebraska, who use its Sno Bol toilet bowl cleaner. The brand's sales volume jumped 81 percent in a 12-week period.[35]

- **Database marketing stimulates cross-selling:** Database marketers can find it easy to offer related products to their customers. Interest in one product category boosts the odds that the customer is a good candidate for similar items. This explains why consumers are bombarded with mail offers for computer software, magazines, or clothing after they purchase a similar product over the phone or through a catalog. Hershey Direct, a division of Hershey Foods Corp. that sells limited-edition collectible elf figurines (not the edible kind), tested its database by sending some mailings to only its most serious collectors, while its other mailings measure the potential of other database segments.[36] Some mailings have included questionnaires regarding specific collectible interests such as plates and music boxes to help the company decide on future product offerings.

- **Database marketing is measurable:** A common complaint of many marketers is the difficulty in pinpointing the impact a promotion had on the target market. Who can say for sure that a single TV commercial motivated people to switch colas? But the database marketers know exactly who received a specific message, so they are able to measure the effectiveness of each communication.

- **Responses are trackable:** The marketer can assess the proportion of message recipients that responded, compare the effectiveness of different messages, and compile a history of which consumers are most likely to respond over time. Farm equipment manufacturer John Deere targeted 20,000 farmers who were loyal to other brands. Using a list of farmers who owned competing equipment, Deere sent prospects a series of four mailings spaced over eight weeks, each with an inexpensive gift such as a stopwatch that was related to the theme of saving time and money by replacing existing equipment. The campaign brought 5,800 farmers into the showroom, yielding a 29 percent response rate. Nearly 700 of these consumers bought new equipment, resulting in more than $40 million in new business.[37]

real people, real choices
How It Worked Out at PriceMcNabb

Matt and his team tested all three options in focus groups. Option 2, "made-from-scratch/homemade," proved to be a ho-hum idea. Most consumers didn't care if their fast food was homemade. They just wanted it to taste good. Option 3, which capitalized on the concept of "southern," was quite polarizing. Those who had moved from the North didn't perceive southern cooking to be that appealing. And the South—particularly the Old South—had negative connotations that tended to drown out the positive ones. However, option 1, the "desire" concept, really hit some hot buttons: Virtually everyone who had ever tried Bojangles' could describe a "Bojangles' moment" when they craved Bojangles' so much that they would do anything to have it.

After they collected this customer feedback, PriceMcNabb realized that the made-from-scratch and southern characteristics of Bojangles' weren't reasons enough to compel people to eat there. However, they were important "ingredients" behind the desirability of Bojangles' food. PriceMcNabb developed

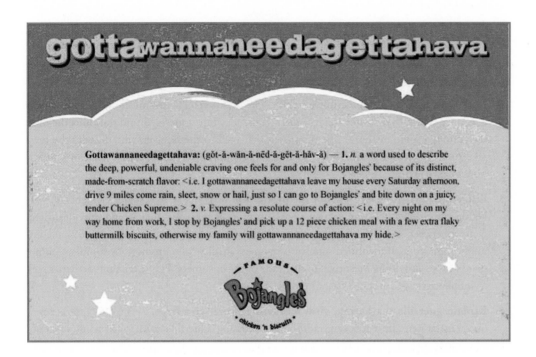

Gottawannaneedagettahava: (gŏt-ă-wăn-ă-nĕd-ă-gĕt-ă-hăv-ă) — **1.** *n.* a word used to describe the deep, powerful, undeniable craving one feels for and only for Bojangles' because of its distinct, made-from-scratch flavor: <i.e. I gottawannaneedagettahava leave my house every Saturday afternoon, drive 9 miles come rain, sleet, snow or hail, just so I can go to Bojangles' and bite down on a juicy, tender Chicken Supreme.> **2.** *v.* Expressing a resolute course of action: <i.e. Every night on my way home from work, I stop by Bojangles' and pick up a 12 piece chicken meal with a few extra flaky buttermilk biscuits, otherwise my family will gottawannaneedagettahava my hide.>

"The Bojangles' Recipe" in a uniquely down-home, southern style to celebrate those aspects. This recipe is now displayed in Bojangles' stores.

PriceMcNabb discovered that it's those unique ingredients that lead to the intense cravings people feel for Bojangles'—a desire so strong that there are no words to describe it. So they introduced a new word to the English language: Gottawannaneedagettahava. (See the tray liner shown here for the "definition" that appears in Bojangles' stores.) This "new word" turns the not-so-proprietary idea of crave-ability into something Bojangles' can own. PriceMcNabb used it as the basis for its IMC campaign. It reinforces the utter desire for Bojangles' in all marketing communication materials, including television and radio commercials, print ads, coupon inserts, store signage—even company letterhead. Television and radio spots focus on moments where people are overtaken by their desire for Bojangles.'

The new creative campaign launched in October 2003. The result? Same-store sales immediately spiked the week the campaign broke and resulted in fourth-quarter gains of 6 percent. Same-store sales in early 2004 consistently jumped into the double digits. Bojangles' QSR chicken rivals continued to deal with flat to declining sales. In this case, Gottawannaneedagettahava translated into a successful IMC campaign for Bojangles.'

How can relationships help you achieve your goals? Posting your resume on the web isn't the only way to search for work. To learn effective ways to connect directly with employers (the people who have the power to hire you) go to Chapter 12 in the *Brand You* supplement.

CHAPTER SUMMARY

1. **Understand the role of communications for successful marketing.** Firms use promotion and other forms of marketing communication to influence attitudes and behavior. Through marketing communications, marketers inform consumers about new products, remind them

of familiar products, persuade them to choose one alternative over another, and build strong customer relationships. Today, firms believe that the integration of marketing communications, where firms look at the communication needs of customers, is essential for successful marketing communication programs.

2. **Understand the communication model.**   The traditional communications model includes a message source that creates an idea, encodes the idea into a message, and transmits the message through some medium. The message is delivered to the receiver, who decodes the message and may provide feedback to the source. Anything that interferes with the communication is called "noise."

3. **List and describe the elements of the promotion mix.**   The four major elements of marketing communications are known as the promotion mix. Personal selling provides direct contact between a company representative and a customer. Advertising is nonpersonal communication from an identified sponsor using mass media. Sales promotions stimulate immediate sales by providing incentives to the trade or to consumers. Public relations activities seek to influence the attitudes of various publics.

4. **Explain guerrilla marketing, viral marketing, buzz, and hype.**   Marketers have developed several new alternatives to traditional advertising. Guerrilla marketing includes promotional strategies that "ambush" consumers in places they are not expecting it. In viral marketing, a company uses incentives to recruit customers to be sales agents. Buzz is word-of-mouth communication generated by consumers and is viewed as authentic, whereas hype is corporate propaganda planted by a company.

5. **Explain integrated marketing communications and its characteristics.**   Integrated marketing communications (IMC) includes the planning, development, execution, and evaluation of coordinated, measurable persuasive brand communications. IMC programs mean a firm's marketing communication programs include a single unified voice, begin with the customer, seek to develop relationships with customers, use targeted communications, use two-way communications, focus on all stakeholders rather than customers only, rely on the effective use of databases, generate a continuous stream of communications, and measure results based on actual feedback.

6. **Explain the stages in developing the IMC plan.**   The IMC plan begins with communication objectives, usually stated in terms of communications tasks such as creating awareness, knowledge, desire, product trial, and brand loyalty. Which promotion mix elements will be used depends on the overall strategy (i.e., a push versus a pull strategy, the type of product, and the stage of the product life cycle).

   Promotion budgets are often developed from such rules of thumb as the percentage-of-sales method, the competitive-parity method, and the objective-task method. Monies from the total budget are then allocated to various elements of the promotion mix. Designing the promotion mix includes determining what communication tools will be used and the message that will be delivered.

   Marketing messages use a variety of different appeals, including those that are rational and others that are emotional in nature. The message may provide one- or two-sided arguments and may or may not draw conclusions. Communication channels must be selected. The Internet provides both challenges and opportunities for communication. Finally, marketers monitor and evaluate the promotion efforts to determine if the objectives are being reached.

7. **Explain the current trend toward interactive promotion strategies.**   Today, marketers are focusing on interactive marketing in which customized marketing communications elicit a measurable response from receivers. Specialized market segments can now be identified and reached. Increasingly, marketers are tailoring messages to individual consumers, decreasing the use of mass-marketing programs. An important part of interactive marketing is the response of the consumer. Product purchases provide first-order responses, but marketers also

seek second-order responses such as requests for information or suggestions for product improvements.

8. **Explain why database marketing is increasingly popular and how databases are developed and managed.** Database marketing is interactive marketing that utilizes a customer database. Database marketing allows marketers to develop dialogues and build relationships with customers. Marketers use database marketing to create programs that are more flexible, reward loyal users, locate new customers, offer related products to existing customers (cross selling), and track customer responses.

KEY TERMS

AIDA model, 380
bottom-up budgeting techniques, 378
buzz, 371
communications model, 364
competitive-parity method, 378
database marketing, 385
decoding, 366
encoding, 364
feedback, 366
guerrilla marketing, 370

hierarchy of effects, 375
hype, 371
integrated marketing communications (IMC), 363
interactive marketing, 382
medium, 365
message, 365
noise, 366
objective-task method, 378
percentage-of-sales method, 378

promotion, 362
promotion mix, 367
pull strategy, 378
push strategy, 378
receiver, 365
source, 364
top-down budgeting techniques, 378
transactional data, 384
viral marketing, 371

CHAPTER REVIEW

MARKETING CONCEPTS: TESTING YOUR KNOWLEDGE

1. How is IMC different from traditional promotion strategies?
2. Describe the traditional communications model.
3. List the elements of the promotion mix and describe how they are used to deliver personal and mass appeals. Describe guerrilla marketing, viral marketing, buzz, and hype.
4. What is IMC? Explain the characteristics of IMC.
5. List and explain the steps in the development of an IMC strategy.
6. Explain how marketers develop communication objectives using the hierarchy of effects.
7. Describe some of the methods firms use to develop marketing communications budgets.
8. How does the promotion mix vary with push versus pull strategies? How does it vary in different stages of the product life cycle?
9. What is interactive marketing?
10. What is database marketing? What are some reasons that database marketing is growing in popularity?

MARKETING CONCEPTS: DISCUSSING CHOICES AND ISSUES

1. Some people would argue that there is really nothing new about IMC. What do you think?

2. Guerrilla marketing, viral marketing, and hype are new methods companies use to get their messages to consumers. Are these effective forms of communications? Will they survive long-term, or are they just fads?
3. Implementation of IMC strategies requires major changes in the way marketers and agencies think and do business. Why do you think people resist these changes?
4. Consumers are becoming concerned that the proliferation of databases is an invasion of an individual's privacy. Do you feel this is a valid concern? How can marketers use databases effectively and, at the same time, protect the rights of individuals?

MARKETING PRACTICE: APPLYING WHAT YOU'VE LEARNED

1. As a marketing consultant, you are frequently asked by clients to develop recommendations for marketing communication strategies. Outline your recommendations for the use of different marketing communication elements for one of the following clients:
   a. A new online banking service
   b. A health spa and resort
   c. A political candidate
   d. A brand of photocopy equipment
2. Again, assume that you are a marketing consultant for one of the clients in question 1. You believe that the client would benefit from guerrilla marketing. Develop several

ideas for guerrilla marketing tactics that you feel would be successful for the client.

3. As the director of marketing for a small firm that markets environmentally friendly household cleaning supplies, you are developing a marketing communication plan. With one or more of your classmates, provide suggestions for each of the following items. Then, in a role-playing situation, present your recommendations to the client:
   a. Marketing communication objectives
   b. A method for determining the communication budget
   c. The use of a push strategy or a pull strategy
   d. Elements of the promotion mix you will use

4. Assume that you are an account executive with an advertising agency. Your assignment is to develop recommendations for a new client, a health-and-fitness center. Give your recommendations for the following:
   a. How to use interactive marketing
   b. How to develop a database for interactive marketing

5. As a member of the marketing department for a manufacturer of handheld power tools for home improvement, you have been directed to select a new agency to do the promotion for your firm. Of two agencies solicited, one recommends an IMC plan, and the other has developed recommendations for a traditional advertising plan. Write a memo to your boss explaining each of the following:
   a. What is different about an IMC plan?
   b. Why is the IMC plan superior to conventional advertising?

MARKETING MINIPROJECT: LEARNING BY DOING

This miniproject is designed to help you understand how organizations use database marketing.

1. Visit your campus admissions office and ask to discuss how it uses database marketing to recruit students. Some of the questions you might ask include the following:
   a. How the office obtains names for an initial or expanded database
   b. What information is included in the initial database
   c. What information is added to the database
   d. How the office uses the database for communicating with prospective students

2. Based on what you learn, consider other ways the school might use database marketing for recruiting students.

3. Make a presentation of your findings and recommendations to your class.

REAL PEOPLE, REAL SURFERS: EXPLORING THE WEB

A vast majority of traditional media (television stations, newspapers, magazines, and radio stations) are now using the Internet to build relationships with readers and viewers. For the media, the Internet provides an excellent way to build a database and to communicate one on one with customers.

Although individual sites change frequently, some media sites that have provided opportunities for interactive communications with customers and for building a database are the following:

Business Week (**www.businessweek.com**)
New York Times (**www.nytimes.com**)
Advertising Age (**www.advertisingage.com**)
Newsweek (**www.newsweek.com**)

Explore these or other sites that provide opportunities for consumers to register, answer questionnaires, or in some other way use the Internet to build a database. After completing your exploration of each site, answer the following questions:

1. In what ways does each Web site facilitate interactive communications between the firm and customers?

2. How does each firm use the Internet to gather information on customers? What information is gathered? Which site does a superior job of gathering information, and why?

3. How do you think the firm might use the information it gathers through the Internet in database marketing activities? How can the information be used to build relationships with customers and prospective customers?

4. What recommendations do you have for each company to improve the interactive opportunities on its Web site?

MARKETING PLAN EXERCISE

In this chapter, you learned that with IMC, marketers plan and execute marketing communications programs using promotion tools to build ongoing loyal relationships with customers or other stakeholders and unifying all marketing communication tools—from advertising to packaging—to send target audiences a consistent, persuasive message. Think about a firm that markets product that you as a university student commonly buy (e.g., toothpaste, shampoo, a computer, a cell phone, and so on).

1. What different promotion tools would you recommend the firm use in its communication program?

2. What steps should the firm take to ensure that the various promotion tools provide a consistent persuasive message?

3. What can the firm do to build long-term relationships with customers?

Marketing in Action Case

Real Choices at Apple Computer Inc.

It seems that Steve Jobs, chief executive officer at Apple Computer Inc., is at it again. Twenty years after reinventing the personal computer industry with the Macintosh computer and operating system, Jobs is now changing the music industry with the iPod, a small personal music device that is smaller than a deck of cards but can store up to 10,000 songs. Industry analysts indicate that the iPod is the most radical change in how people listen to music since Sony Corporation introduced the Walkman in 1979.

Since introducing the iPod in 2001, Apple has sold over 3 million iPods at prices ranging from $249 to $499, making it the most popular music player on the market. In fact, as of June 2004, the recently introduced iPod Mini had a six-week waiting list on the Apple Web site. Furthermore, Apple's iTunes online music store accounts for 70 percent of all legal downloads of music from the Internet. With iTunes providing the content and iPod providing the means to take advantage of the content, Jobs has staked out a formidable position in the digital music marketplace.

Much of the success of iPod came from the use of a savvy marketing communications program. First, iPod's image was communicated by an ad campaign depicting a fun yet unobtrusive means to enjoy music in almost any setting. Creative ads showing dark silhouettes of individuals against different colored backgrounds dancing to music that only they could hear generated interest in the product. Judging by the results for both the iPod and the iTunes download service, the ads have led to the feedback (increased sales and market share) that Apple was seeking.

However, advertising is not Apple's only means of promoting the iPod and iTunes service. Through the use of personal selling, Apple has developed a relationship with Hewlett-Packard (HP) whereby HP will sell the music player under the HP brand name while also installing the iTunes software on 9 million personal computers per year. Equally important to the promotion of iTunes is Apple's sales promotion agreement with Pepsi-Cola to give away 100 million songs from the iTunes Web site. When one includes Apple's use of press releases announcing product and service upgrades to the advertising, personal selling, and sales promotion elements of the promotion mix already mentioned, it adds up to a very impressive use of integrated marketing communications.

However, maintaining the level of success Apple has enjoyed so far with the iPod and iTunes will be a challenge. Apple's competition includes almost 60 other digital music players and some of the biggest companies in the world. For example, Sony has $66 billion in annual sales, nearly 10 times more than Apple's anticipated 2004 sales of $7.6 billion. In addition, Samsung, Cisco, Dell, Microsoft, and Wal-Mart are all looking to increase their stake in the market for digital music and/or digital music players.

Consequently, Apple and Steve Jobs will be under intense pressure to continue upgrading not only its products and services but also the promotion of those items. While innovators and early adopters of a product may react positively to hip and innovative advertising, early and late majority adopters of a product make more reasoned buying decisions. As a result, Apple may have to change future advertising to appeal to these groups of people. In addition, some industry experts have suggested that Apple partner with other companies such as cell phone manufacturers and online retailers (like Amazon.com) to extend its reach. Others have suggested that Apple provide more price promotions so that more people can afford the iPod. Regardless of how Apple reacts to the challenges it will face in the future, one thing is for sure: its continued use of the various promotion mix elements will play a key role in the company's success or failure in the digital music marketplace.

Things to Think About

1. What is the decision facing Apple?
2. What factors are important in understanding the decision situation?
3. What are the alternatives?
4. What decision(s) do you recommend?
5. What are some ways to implement your recommendation(s)?

Sources: Mae Anderson, "The Fine Print," *Adweek*, June 7, 2004, 24–25; Peter Burrows and Tom Lowry, "Rock On, iPod," *Business Week*, June 7, 2004, 130–31; Peter Burrows, Ronald Grover, and Tom Lowry, "Show Time!" *Business Week*, February 2, 2004, 56–64; and Stephen Gandel, "Why iPod Can't Save Apple," *Money*, April 2004, 90–93.

www.zenogroup.com

real people, real choices
meet Jerry Epstein,
a Decision Maker at the Zeno Group
(previously PR21)

first job out of school

Delivering pizzas in Union,
New Jersey.

what i do when i'm not working

Run marathons, skydive,
listen to classic rock.

ADVERTISING AND PUBLIC RELATIONS

Jerry Epstein is president and chief executive officer of the Zeno Group (previously PR21), one of the world's fastest-growing marketing communications agencies. With 25 years of experience in strategic positioning and brand development, Jerry is one of the leading authorities in the public relations industry. Prior to joining the Zeno Group, Jerry spent 17 years in senior positions with the PR firm Fleishman-Hillard International, Inc., until he left there to start an incentive management company, The PeopleTrends Network, in 1999.

Jerry has directed numerous strategic corporate positioning, branding, and marketing campaigns for clients such as Anheuser-Busch, Oracle Corporation, Sirius Satellite Radio, Johnson & Johnson, Whirlpool, KIA Automobiles, America Online, Sony Playstation, Honda, Pioneer Electronics, Eagle Snacks, Nestlé, and several major Las Vegas hotel properties. His international sports marketing clients included World Cup '94, ISL Marketing (the rights holder of the Olympic Games), and the 2002 Japanese World Cup Bidding Committee.

Jerry also served as strategic counsel for President Ronald Reagan and orchestrated public and media relations for the opening of the Reagan Presidential Library—the first-ever gathering of five living U.S. presidents. He also assisted President Reagan with, among other projects, a visit to the United States by former Soviet Union leader Mikhail Gorbachev and the presentation of the Reagan Presidential Freedom award to Colin Powell. In 1996 he was named the Industry Marketing Communications Executive of the Year by *Inside PR*. He also has served on a number of charitable boards, including the Muscular Dystrophy Association.

Decision Time at the Zeno Group

Satellite radio is the radio industry's first technological change since FM radio gained national acceptance in the 1970s. This broadcast medium—transmitted by satellite—has the potential to replace traditional AM and FM radio. Sirius Satellite Radio is one of only two companies licensed to offer this new national audio service and provide subscription-based programming to listeners across the country.

When Sirius launched a new public relations campaign in January 2003, its public relations challenges were twofold. First, satellite radio is an emerging category with little awareness among the general public. And, similar to the introduction of cable TV, it requires consumers to purchase hardware and pay a monthly subscription fee for radio—a service that historically has been free. Thus, a compelling case needed to be made to introduce and legitimize the category itself, position satellite radio as the future of music and audio entertainment, and educate

career high	business book i'm reading now	my heroes	my motto to live by
The opening of the Ronald Reagan Library.	*The Secret* by Ken Blanchard and Mark Miller.	Benjamin Franklin and Robert Kennedy.	The quote by Ralph Waldo Emerson, "Do not go where the path may lead, go instead where there is no path and leave a trail."

objectives

1 Tell what advertising is and describe the major types of advertising.

2 Describe the process of developing an advertising campaign.

3 Explain how marketers evaluate advertising.

4 Explain the role of public relations.

5 Describe the steps in developing a public relations campaign.

6 Understand direct marketing.

7 Discuss the future of m-commerce.

consumers about the value of satellite radio over traditional commercial stations.

Second, Sirius's competitor had a first-to-market advantage and a substantial lead in consumer awareness and market share. At the time of its PR campaign in 2003, the company had low consumer awareness and minimal market penetration, and it faced significant financial challenges, with public speculation about possible bankruptcy and negative coverage from every major financial and business publication covering the satellite radio space. Sirius's success or failure also had significant ramifications for the future of the category itself—an industry cannot be sustained with only one provider.

Jerry knew that Sirius needed an aggressive PR strategy to increase awareness and credibility of both satellite radio as a category and, at the same time, effectively communicate the advantages of Sirius's service over its competitor. For Sirius, and potentially the category itself, to survive, the PR campaign had to make an immediate impact that not only raised awareness of the value proposition but also directly translated to the company's bottom-line performance. Jerry considered his options:

OPTION 1: Maintain a low profile until Sirius's subscription numbers increase to enable a more credible story to be told.

While delaying public relations outreach until the company was on more solid footing would provide greater opportunities for positive stories, better messaging, and a stronger media platform, it also had inherent risks. The situation demanded immediate positive market exposure; public relations played a critical role in generating that exposure. Delaying outreach could result in a continuing downward spiral for the company, with little chance of future recovery.

OPTION 2: Position Sirius as *the* premium satellite radio entertainment and information company, highlighting its innovative programming advantages over both traditional radio and its satellite competitor.

This positioning would enable Sirius to target the mass market as well as a wide variety of niche audiences by music genre. But choosing this option would carry the risk of target audiences questioning the credibility of the company and its claim to be the "premium" market leader, given its current position. Downplaying the technology advantages also had the potential to weaken the sales proposition, as advanced technology can be a key factor in deciding to "purchase" radio for the first time.

OPTION 3: Position Sirius as a technology company rather than an entertainment company by emphasizing its hardware product quality.

The rationale for this strategy would be to target audiophiles as "early adopters" to drive the marketing effort, particularly on a grassroots level, and position the company as cutting edge. One potential problem with this strategy was that Sirius's competitor, which at that point had a more sophisticated hardware product, had also taken this position to target this very narrow market. For Sirius to be successful by using this approach, the company would have to go head to head with its only competitor.

Now put yourself in Jerry Epstein's shoes: Which option would you choose, and why?

Advertising: The Image of Marketing

Advertising is so much a part of marketing that many people think of the two as the same thing. As we saw in Chapter 12, that's not the case—there are many ways to get a message out to a target audience. Advertising is still very important—analysts estimated that in 2004 alone, marketers spent over $265 billion to do it. Still, in today's competitive environment, even the big guys are rethinking how much they want to invest in pricey ad campaigns as they search for alternative ways to get their messages out there. This is especially true as the number of media outlets mushrooms along with the number of TV viewers who use their trusty remote control or perhaps even TiVo to skip over ads. "Personal video recorders" that let viewers skip through commercials are now in roughly just 2 percent of U.S. households but growing fast, and increasingly these gadgets are available as part of cable-TV boxes.[1] That's why in-show product plugs (known as *product placement*) are turning up much more often (no, it's no accident that the logos are so visible!):[2]

- Cars made by Ford are prominently featured in the hit drama *24* on the FOX Network.
- Ragu Express, a packaged pasta-and-sauce meal, got an eye-catching role on *Everybody Loves Raymond* when Ray stalked his wife in a supermarket and knocked over an entire display of the product.
- Rolling Rock beer showed up on an episode of *Ed*.
- Microsoft Corp.'s Xbox game machine made it onto CBS's *Two and a Half Men*.
- Products from Sears, Roebuck, including Craftsman tools and Kenmore appliances, play a prominent role on *Extreme Makeover: Home Edition* on ABC.

Meanwhile, other marketers are taking their messages to the streets as they rely on public relations events in addition to traditional advertising. For example, Coca-Cola Co. opened lounges for teens at malls, while the Campbell Soup Co. unveiled "Soup Sanctuaries" that offer weary shoppers a chance to relax while enjoying free soup. BMW scored big points with its series of short films from famous directors that appear on its Web site.[3] There are many ways to communicate with a mass audience. In this chapter, we'll learn about some of the major approaches, beginning with advertising.

It's An Ad Ad Ad World

Wherever we turn, we are bombarded by advertising. Television commercials, radio spots, banner ads for Web sites such as PR21, and huge billboards scream, "Buy me!!" **Advertising** is nonpersonal communication paid for by an identified sponsor using mass media to persuade or inform an audience.[4] Advertising can be fun, glamorous, annoying, informative—and hopefully an effective way to let consumers know what they're selling and why people should run out and buy it *today*.

A long-running Virginia Slims cigarettes advertising campaign proclaims, "You've come a long way, baby!" The same could be said about advertising itself. Advertising has been with us a long time. In ancient Greece and Rome, advertisements appeared on walls and were etched on stone tablets. Would the ancients have believed that today we get messages about products almost wherever we are, whether cruising down the road or around the Web? Some of us even get advertising messages on our mobile phones. It's hard to find a place where ads don't try to reach us.

Advertising is also a potent force that creates desire for products by transporting us to imaginary worlds where the people are happy, beautiful, or rich. In this way, advertising allows the organization to communicate its message in a favorable way and to repeat the message as often as it deems necessary to have an impact on receivers.

Types of Advertising

Although almost every business advertises, some industries are bigger spenders than others. In 2003, the automotive industry was the top ad spender in the United States, with expenditures of over $18.4 billion. Retail ad spending topped $16.2 billion, and spending by the food and beverage industry and the financial sector was over $6 billion each.[5] Because so much is spent on advertising, marketers must decide which type of ad will work best given their organizational and marketing goals. The advertisements an organization runs can take many forms, so let's review the most common kinds.

PRODUCT ADVERTISING When people give examples of advertising, they are likely to recall the provocative poses in Victoria's Secret ads or the ever-present messages for cell phone services: "Can you hear me now?" These are examples of **product advertising**, where the message focuses on a specific good or service.

advertising
Nonpersonal communication paid for by an identified sponsor using mass media to persuade or inform.

product advertising
An advertising message that focuses on a specific good or service.

institutional advertising
An advertising message that promotes the activities, personality, or point of view of an organization or company.

While not all advertising focuses on a product or a brand, most of the advertising we see and hear is indeed product advertising.

INSTITUTIONAL ADVERTISING   Rather than focusing on a specific brand, **institutional advertising** promotes the activities, personality, or point of view of an organization or company. Unlike many older ad campaigns that consisted largely of "fluff" ("We're Company X. Look how wonderful we are!"), today institutional ads are likely to offer one cohesive message, such as when financial service company ING tells consumers they are "Someone looking out for you" with a variety of products including life insurance, banking, retirement plans, and mutual funds.

Some institutional messages state a firm's position on an issue to sway public opinion, a strategy called **advocacy advertising**.[6] For example, prior to the 2004 U.S. presidential elections, MTV's "Choose or Lose" campaign encouraged the more than 20 million young people aged 18 to 30 to learn about the issues, to vote, and to be a deciding factor in the election.[7] Other messages called **public service advertisements (PSAs)** are advertisements the media run free of charge. These messages promote not-for-profit organizations that serve society in some way, or they champion an issue such as increasing literacy or discouraging drunk driving. Advertising agencies often take on one or more public service campaigns on a *pro bono* (for free) basis.

RETAIL AND LOCAL ADVERTISING   Both major retailers and small, local businesses advertise to encourage customers to shop at a specific store or use a local service. Much local advertising informs us about store hours, location, and products that are available or on sale. Retail advertisers spend more than any other type of advertiser per year (almost $8 billion).

Product advertising like this ad for Keds focuses on a specific good or service.

advocacy advertising
A type of public service advertising provided by an organization that is seeking to influence public opinion on an issue because it has some stake in the outcome.

public service advertisements (PSAs)
Advertising run by the media without charge for not-for-profit organizations or to champion a particular cause.

Who Creates Advertising?

An **advertising campaign** is a coordinated, comprehensive plan that carries out promotion objectives and results in a series of advertisements placed in media over a period of time. Although a campaign may be based around a single ad, most employ multiple messages with all ads in the campaign having the same look and feel. For example, UPS's recent campaign "What can Brown do for you?" utilized both television and print advertising to position UPS for small and midsize businesses as a "solution company."

Creating and executing an advertising campaign often means many companies work together, and it requires a broad range of skilled people to do the job right. Some firms may do their own advertising. In many cases, though, the firm will retain outside *advertising agencies* to develop advertising messages on its behalf. A **limited-service agency** provides one or more specialized services, such as media buying or creative development (we'll see what these tasks are a bit later). A **full-service agency** provides most or all of the services needed to mount a campaign, including research, creation of ad copy and art, media selection, and production of the final messages. The five largest American agencies are the J. Walter Thompson Co., Leo Burnett Worldwide, McCann-Erickson Worldwide, BBDO Worldwide, and Grey Worldwide.[8]

Many different tasks are required to produce a campaign. Big or small, an advertising agency hires a range of specialists to craft a message and make the communications concept a reality:

- **Account management:** The *account executive,* or account manager, is the "soul" of the operation. This person develops the campaign's strategy for the client, supervises the day-to-day activities on the account, and is the primary liaison between the agency and the client. The account executive has to ensure that the client is happy while verifying that people within the agency are executing the desired strategy.

- **Creative services:** *Creatives* are the "heart" of the communications effort. These are the people who actually dream up and produce the ads. They include the agency's creative director, copywriter, and art director. Creatives are the artists who breathe life into marketing objectives and craft messages that (hopefully) will interest consumers.

- **Research and marketing services:** *Researchers* are the "brains" of the campaign. They collect and analyze information that will help account executives develop a sensible strategy. They assist creatives in getting consumer reactions to different versions of ads or by providing copywriters with details on the target group.

- **Media planning:** The *media planner* is the "legs" of the campaign. He or she helps to determine which communication vehicles are the most effective, and recommends the most efficient means for delivering the ad by deciding where, when, and how often it will appear.

ASTHMA. APPEARING WITHOUT NOTICE. Are you using your rescue inhaler more than twice a week? If so, your asthma may not be under control. See your doctor to find out about preventative medications that can help keep your asthma from acting up. Call 1.800.2.BREATHE or log on to controlasthma.com. And help put asthma in its place

In this ad, a drug company is sponsoring a PSA on behalf of the American Lung Association.

As we saw in Chapter 12, more and more agencies practice integrated marketing communication (IMC) in which advertising is only one element of a total communications plan. Because IMC includes more than just advertising, client teams composed of people from account services, creative services, media planning, research, public relations, sales promotion, and direct marketing may work together to develop a plan that best meets the communications needs of each client.

Developing the Advertising Campaign

The advertising campaign is about much more than creating a cool ad and hoping people notice it. It should be intimately related to the organization's overall communications goals. That means the firm (and its outside agency if it uses one) must have a good idea of whom it wants to reach, what it will take to appeal to this market, and where and when the messages should be placed. Let's examine the steps required to do this, as shown in Figure 13.1.

advertising campaign
A coordinated, comprehensive plan that carries out promotion objectives and results in a series of advertisements placed in media over a period of time.

limited-service agency
An agency that provides one or more specialized services, such as media buying or creative development.

full-service agency
An agency that provides most or all of the services needed to mount a campaign, including research, creation of ad copy and art, media selection, and production of the final messages.

This PSA discusses how kids can use courage to fight drug use.

Step 1: Identify the Target Audiences

The best way to communicate with an audience is to understand as much as possible about them and what turns them on and off. An ad that uses the latest "hip-hop" slang may relate to teenagers but not to their parents—and this strategy may backfire if the ad copy reads like an "ancient" 40-year-old trying to sound like a 20-year-old.

Most advertising is directed toward customers, whether the target market is college students or industry executives. As we discussed in Chapter 7, the target market for an advertising campaign often is identified from research related to the client's segmentation strategy. Researchers try to get inside the customer's head to understand just how to create a message that he or she will understand and respond to. For example, an account executive working on a campaign for Pioneer Stereo was assigned to hang out with guys who were likely prospects to buy car stereos. His observations resulted in an advertising campaign that incorporated the phrases they actually used to describe their cars: "My car is my holy temple, my love shack, my drag racer of doom."[9]

Step 2: Establish Message and Budget Objectives

Advertising objectives should be consistent with the overall communications plan. That means that both the underlying message and its costs need to be related to what the marketer is trying to say about the product and what the marketer is willing or able to spend. Thus, advertising objectives generally will include objectives for both the message and the budget.

SETTING MESSAGE OBJECTIVES As we noted earlier, because advertising is the most visible part of marketing, many people assume that marketing *is* advertising. In truth, advertising alone is quite limited in what it can achieve. What advertising *can* do is to inform, persuade, and remind. Accordingly, some advertising objectives are informational; they seek to make the customer knowledgeable about features of the product or how to use it. At other times, advertising seeks to persuade consumers to like a brand or to prefer one brand over the competition. But many, many ads are simply aimed at keeping the name of the brand in front of the consumer—reminding consumers that this brand is the one to choose when they go looking for a soft drink or a hamburger or a candy bar.

SETTING BUDGET OBJECTIVES Advertising is expensive. In 2003, businesses spent over $245 billion on advertising in the United States alone. General Motors Corp., which led all U.S. companies in advertising expenditures, spent over $3 billion. Other companies that spent over $3 billion in 2003 were Procter & Gamble Corp. and Time Warner.[10]

A firm often has as an objective of allocating a percentage of its overall communication budget to advertising, depending on how much and what type of advertising the company can afford. Major corporations like General Motors advertise heavily, using expensive media such as television to promote multiple products throughout the year. Other companies may seek to be more selective, and smaller firms may want to put their advertising dollars into cheaper media outlets, such as direct mail or trade publications.

Figure 13.1 Steps in Developing an Advertising Campaign

Developing an advertising campaign includes a series of steps that will ensure the advertising meets communication objectives.

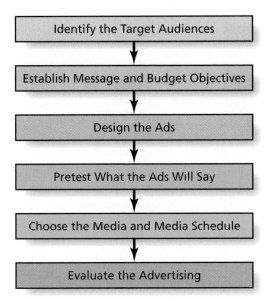

Identify the Target Audiences

↓

Establish Message and Budget Objectives

↓

Design the Ads

↓

Pretest What the Ads Will Say

↓

Choose the Media and Media Schedule

↓

Evaluate the Advertising

The major approaches and techniques to setting overall promotional budgets, such as the percentage-of-sales and objective-task methods discussed in Chapter 12, also set advertising budgets.

Step 3: Design the Ads

Creative strategy is the process that turns a concept into an advertisement. It's one thing to know *what* a company wants to say about itself and its products, and another to figure out *how* to say it. Some marketers like to think of the creative process for an advertising campaign as the "spark between objective and execution."

The goal of an advertising campaign is to present a series of messages and repeat it to a sufficient degree to meet the desired objectives. To do this, advertising creatives (art directors, copywriters, photographers, and others) must develop a "big idea," a concept that expresses aspects of the product, service, or organization in a tangible, attention-getting, memorable manner.

An **advertising appeal** is the central idea of the ad. Some advertisers use an emotional appeal complete with dramatic color or powerful images, while others bombard the audience with facts. Some feature sexy people or stern-looking experts (even professors from time to time). Different appeals can work for the same product, from a bland "talking head" to a montage of animated special effects. An attention-getting way to say something profound about cat food or laundry detergent is more art than science, but we can describe some common appeals:

- **Reasons why: The USP:** A **unique selling proposition (USP)** gives consumers a single, clear reason why one product is better at solving a problem. The format focuses on a need and points out how the product can satisfy it. For example, "M&Ms melt in your mouth, not in your hands" is a USP. In general, a USP strategy is best if there is some clear product advantage that consumers can readily identify and that is important to them.

- **Comparative advertising:** A comparative advertisement explicitly names one or more competitors. Comparative ads can be very effective, but there is a risk of turning off consumers who don't like the negative tone. While in many countries comparative advertising is illegal, it's a widely used tactic in the United States. Comparative advertising is best for brands that have a smaller share of the market, and for those firms that can focus on a specific feature

creative strategy
The process that turns a concept into an advertisement.

advertising appeal
The central idea or theme of an advertising message.

unique selling proposition (USP)
An advertising appeal that focuses on one clear reason why a particular product is superior.

USP strategies clearly communicate the reason why the product can satisfy a need.

Scoop Away

Tidy Cats®

Scoop Away® cat litter controls stinky odors better.
(according to the most sophisticated noses)

Scoop Away cat litter controls litter box odors better than Tidy Cats cat litter. If you don't believe us, ask your own nose.

that makes them superior to a major brand. When market leaders use comparative advertising, there is the risk of consumers feeling they are "picking on" the littler guy.

- **Demonstration:** The ad shows a product "in action" to prove that it performs as claimed. "It slices, it dices!" Demonstration advertising is most useful when consumers are unable to identify important benefits except by seeing the product in use.

- **Testimonial:** A celebrity, an expert, or a "man in the street" states the product's effectiveness. The use of *celebrity endorsers* is a common but expensive strategy. It is particularly effective for mature products that need to differentiate themselves from competitors, such as Coke and Pepsi that enlist celebrities to tout one cola over another.[11]

- **Slice of life:** A slice-of-life format presents a (dramatized) scene from everyday life. Slice-of-life advertising can be effective for everyday products such as peanut butter and headache remedies that consumers may feel good about if they see "real" people buying and using them.

- **Lifestyle:** A lifestyle format shows a person or persons attractive to the target market in an appealing setting. The advertised product is "part of the scene," implying that the person who buys it will attain the lifestyle. For example, a commercial shown on MTV might depict a group of "cool" California skateboarders who take a break for a gulp of milk and say, "It does a body good."

- **Fear appeals:** This tactic highlights the negative consequences of *not* using a product. Some fear appeal ads focus on physical harm, while others try to create concern for social harm or disapproval. Mouthwash, deodorant, dandruff shampoo makers, and life insurance companies have successfully used fear appeals, as have ads aimed at changing behaviors, such as messages discouraging drug use or encouraging safe sex.

- **Sex appeals:** Some ads appear to be selling sex rather than products. In a Guess jeans ad, a shirtless man lies near an almost shirtless woman. Ads such as these rely on sexuality to get consumers' attention. Sex appeal ads are more likely to be effective when there is a connection between the product and sex (or at least romance). For example, sex appeals will work well with a perfume but are less likely to be effective when selling a lawn mower.

- **Humorous appeals:** Humorous ads can be an effective way to break through advertising clutter. But humor can be tricky, because what is funny to one person may be offensive or stupid to another. Different cultures also have different senses of humor. A recent Reebok commercial showed women at a basketball game checking out the all-male cheerleading squad—people from countries who don't have cheerleaders (you don't find too many pom-poms at soccer matches) might not "get it." Perhaps the major benefit of humorous advertising is that it attracts consumers' attention and leaves them with a pleasant feeling.

- **Slogans and jingles:** Slogans link the brand to a simple linguistic device that is memorable. Jingles do the same but set the slogan to music. Some popular slogans that have been used for successful advertising campaigns are "Please don't squeeze the Charmin," "Double your pleasure, double your fun," and "Can you hear me now?"

Step 4: Pretest What the Ads Will Say

Now that the creatives have worked their magic, how does the agency know if the campaign ideas will work? Advertisers try to minimize mistakes by getting reactions to ad messages before they actually place them. Much of this **pretesting**, the research that goes on in the early stages of a campaign, centers on gathering basic information that will help planners be sure they've accurately defined the product's market, consumers, and competitors. As we saw in Chapter 4, this information comes from quantitative sources, such as syndicated surveys, and qualitative sources, such as focus groups.

As the campaign takes shape, the players need to determine how well the advertising concepts will perform. **Copy testing** measures the effectiveness of ads. This process determines whether consumers are receiving, comprehending, and responding to the ad according to plan.

NICHT ÜBERALL, WO'S DUNKEL IST, LAUFEN TOLLE FILME.

CINEMAXX Der Filmpalast

AB 3. AUGUST IN BRAUNSCHWEIG, LANGE STRASSE 60.

Sense of humor is different across cultures. This German ad for a movie theater chain reminds us that "Not everywhere that's dark shows great movies."

Step 5: Choose the Media and Media Schedule

Media planning is a problem-solving process for getting a message to a target audience in the most effective way. Planning decisions include audience selection and where, when, and how frequent the exposure should be. Thus, the first task for a media planner is to find out when and where people in the target market are most likely to be exposed to the communication. This is called an **aperture**, the best "window" to reach the target market. Many college students read the campus newspaper in the morning, so their aperture would include this medium at this time.

There is no such thing as one perfect medium for advertising. The choice depends on the specific target audience, the objective of the message, and, of course, the budget. For the advertising campaign to be effective, the media planner must match up the profile of the target market with specific media vehicles. For example, many African American consumers are avid radio listeners, so marketers wishing to reach this segment might allocate a relatively large share of their advertising budget to buying time on radio stations.

Choosing the right mix of media is no laughing matter, especially as new options including videos and DVDs, video games, personal computers, the Internet, MP3 players, hundreds of new TV channels, and even satellite radio now vie for our attention. Consider that in 1965, 80 percent of 18- to 49-year-olds in the United States could be reached with three 60-second TV spots. In 2002, it required 117 prime-time commercials to produce the same result. While viewing of traditional broadcast TV is down dramatically in recent years, people are spending a lot more time watching cable and satellite channels, which explains why the companies that own broadcast networks are buying up major cable channels—General Electric's NBC owns Bravo; Walt Disney Co., which owns ABC, also owns ESPN and ABC Family channel; and Viacom Inc. owns MTV and Nickelodeon along with CBS.[12] Figure 13.2 shows how dramatic some of these changes are.

WHERE TO SAY IT: TRADITIONAL MEDIA What does a 52-inch television with Dolby SurroundSound have in common with a matchbook? Each is a media vehicle that permits an advertiser to communicate with a potential customer. Depending on the intended message, each

pretesting
A research method that seeks to minimize mistakes by getting consumer reactions to ad messages before they appear in the media.

copy testing
A marketing research method that seeks to measure the effectiveness of ads by determining whether consumers are receiving, comprehending, and responding to the ad according to plan.

media planning
The process of developing media objectives, strategies, and tactics for use in an advertising campaign.

aperture
The best place and time to reach a person in the target market group.

Figure 13.2 Changes in Media Usage

An ever-growing array of entertainment options are competing for consumers' time. This figure shows the hours the average American spent per week tuning into various media.

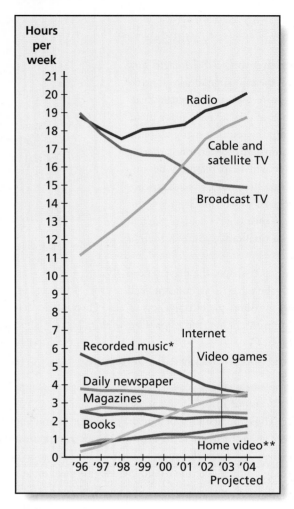

Note: Ages varied by survey subject
*Excludes MP3s and Internet downloading, which is included in Internet
**Playback of prerecorded VHS cassettes and DVDs.

Source: Veronis Suhler Stevenson Communications Industry Forecast

medium has its advantages and disadvantages. Let's take a look at the major categories of media. Table 13.1 summarizes some of the pros and cons of each type.

- **Television:** Because of television's ability to reach so many people at once, it's the medium of choice for regional or national companies. Today there are literally hundreds of television choices available to advertisers. However, advertising on a television network can be very expensive. The cost to place a 30-second ad on a popular prime-time TV show one time normally ranges between $200,000 and $500,000, depending on the size of the show's audience. Advertisers may prefer to buy cable, satellite, or local television time rather than network time because it's cheaper or because they want to reach a more targeted market, such as "foodies" who are into cooking.

- **Radio:** Radio as an advertising medium goes back to 1922, when a New York City apartment manager went on the air to advertise properties for rent. One advantage of radio adver-

Table 13.1 Pros and Cons of Media Vehicles

Vehicle	Pros	Cons
Television	• Extremely creative and flexible. • Network TV is the most cost-effective way to reach a mass audience. • Cable and satellite TV allow the advertiser to reach a selected group at relatively low cost. • A prestigious way to advertise. • Can demonstrate product in use. • Can provide entertainment and generate excitement. • Messages have high impact because of the use of sight and sound.	• The message is quickly forgotten unless it is repeated often. • The audience is increasingly fragmented. • Although the relative cost of reaching the audience is low, prices are still high on an absolute basis—often too high for smaller companies. A 30-second spot on a prime-time TV sitcom costs well over $250,000. • Fewer people viewing network television. • People switch from station to station zapping commercials. • Rising costs have led to more and shorter ads, causing more clutter.
Radio	• Good for selectively targeting an audience. • Is heard out of the home. • Can reach customers on a personal and intimate level. • Can use local personalities. • Relatively low cost, both for producing a spot and for running it repeatedly. • Because of short lead time, radio ads can be modified quickly to reflect changes in the marketplace. • Use of sound effects and music allows listeners to use their imagination to create a vivid scene.	• Listeners often don't pay full attention to what they hear. • Difficulty in buying radio time, especially for national advertisers. • Not appropriate for products that must be seen or demonstrated to be appreciated. • The small audience of individual stations means ads must be placed with many different stations and must be repeated frequently.
Newspapers	• Wide exposure provides extensive market coverage. • Flexible format permits the use of color, different sizes, and targeted editions. • Ability to use detailed copy. • Allows local retailers to tie in with national advertisers. • People in the right mental frame to process advertisements about new products, sales, etc. • Timeliness, i.e., short lead time between placing ad and having it run.	• Most people don't spend much time reading the newspaper. • Readership is especially low among teens and young adults. • Short life span—people rarely look at a newspaper more than once. • Very cluttered ad environment. • The reproduction quality of images is relatively poor. • Not effective in reaching specific audiences.
Magazines	• Audiences can be narrowly targeted by specialized magazines. • High credibility and interest level provide a good environment for ads. • Advertising has a long life and is often passed along to other readers. • Visual quality is excellent. • Can provide detailed product information with a sense of authority.	• With the exception of direct mail, the most expensive form of advertising. The cost of a full-page, four-color ad in a general-audience magazine typically exceeds $100,000. • Long deadlines reduce flexibility. • The advertiser must generally use several magazines to reach the majority of a target market. • Clutter.
Outdoor	• Most of the population can be reached at low cost. • Good for supplementing other media. • High frequency when signs located in heavy traffic areas. • Effective for reaching virtually all segments of the population. • Geographic flexibility.	• Hard to communicate complex messages because of short exposure time. • Difficult to measure advertisement's audience. • Controversial and disliked in many communities. • Cannot pinpoint specific market segments.
Direct response	• Ads can target extremely narrow audiences. • Messages can be timed by the advertiser at his or her convenience. • Easy to measure the effectiveness of ads.	• High cost per exposure. • Target lists must be constantly updated. • Ads lack credibility among many consumers.

Sources: Adapted form Thomas J. Russell and Ron Lane, *Kleppner's Advertising Procedure*, 15th ed. (Upper Saddle River, N.J.: Prentice Hall, 2002); Terence A. Shimp, *Advertising, Promtion and Supplemental Aspects of Integrated Marketing Communications*, 6th ed. (Australia: Thomson Southwestern, 2003); and William Wells, John Burnett, and Sandra Moriarty, *Advertising: Principles and Practice*, 6th ed. (Upper Saddle River, N.J.: Prentice Hall, 2003). .

Out-of-home media provide an excellent way to reach consumers on the go. Billboards such as this one certainly grab our attention.

tising is flexibility. Marketers can change commercials quickly, often on the spot by an announcer and a recording engineer.[13] Radio is attractive to advertisers seeking low cost and the ability to reach specific consumer segments.

- **Newspapers:** The newspaper is among the oldest types of media. Retailers in particular have relied on newspaper ads since before the turn of the 20th century to inform readers about sales and deliveries of new merchandise. Newspapers are an excellent medium for local advertising and for events (such as sales) that require a quick response. Today, most newspapers also offer online versions of their papers to expand their exposure.

- **Magazines:** Approximately 92 percent of adults look through at least one magazine per month. New technologies such as *selective binding* allow publishers to personalize their editions, so that advertisements for local businesses can be included in issues mailed to specific locations only.

- **Directories:** Directory advertising is the most "down-to-earth," information-focused advertising medium. In 1883, a printer in Wyoming ran out of white paper while printing part of a telephone book, so he substituted yellow paper instead. Today, the Yellow Pages has revenues of more than $9.5 billion, and more than 6,000 directories are published in North America alone. Often consumers look through directories when or just before they are ready to buy.

out-of-home media
A communication medium that reaches people in public places.

- **Out-of-home media: Out-of-home media**, such as blimps, transit ads, and billboards, reach people in public places. This medium works best when it tells a simple, straightforward story.[14] For example, four Houston men rented a billboard with the message "4 Middle Class White Males, 32–39, Seek Wives." These "advertisers" got responses from almost 800 women.[15]

place-based media
Advertising media that transmit messages in public places, such as doctors' offices and airports, where certain types of people congregate.

- **Place-based media:** Marketers are constantly searching for new ways to get their messages out to busy people. **Place-based media** like "The Airport Channel" transmit messages to "captive audiences" in public places, such as doctors' offices and airports. Another example of place-based media is *in-store TV*. Retailers from around the globe, including Wal-Mart, Best Buy, Circuit City, and Tesco (Britain's biggest supermarket chain), have installed TV monitors in their aisles to show ads for products sold in the stores.[16]

And now, some retailers can even follow you around the store to deliver more up-close and personal messages: A new technology called RFID (radio frequency identifica-

Deciding on the best place for an advertising message is often a key element of any strategy. This Spanish ad for a media company asks, "Is your product in the right place?"

tion) tracks customers as they make their way through the aisles. So a shopper might receive a beep to remind her she just passed her family's favorite peanut butter.[17] You're not paranoid; they really *are* watching you!

INTERNET ADVERTISING   The Web gives marketers the ability to reach customers in new and exciting ways. Online advertising offers several advantages. First, the Internet provides new ways to finely target customers. Web user registrations and *cookies* allow sites to track user preferences and deliver ads based on previous Internet behavior. In addition, because the Web site can track how many times an ad is "clicked," advertisers can measure how people are responding to online messages. Finally, online advertising can be interactive—it lets consumers participate in the advertising campaign, and in some cases they can even become part of the action. Viewers who logged on to a special Web site were able to "direct" TV commercials for the Ford Probe by picking the cast and plotlines that would be used to create actual spots. Similarly, during its "whatever.com" campaign, Nike sent consumers to the Web to pick the endings of three cliffhanger TV spots.[18]

Specific forms of Internet advertising include banners, buttons, pop-up ads, search engines and directories, and e-mail:

- **Banners: Banners**, rectangular graphics at the top or bottom of Web pages, were the first form of Web advertising. Although the effectiveness of banners remains in question (banners now receive less than a one percent click-through rate), they still remain the most popular form of Web advertising.

- **Buttons: Buttons** are small banner-type advertisements that can be placed anywhere on a page. Early in the life of the Internet, buttons encouraging surfers to "Download Netscape

banners
Internet advertising in the form of rectangular graphics at the top or bottom of Web pages.

buttons
Small banner-type advertisements that can be placed anywhere on a Web page.

Now" became a standard on many Web sites and were responsible for much of Netscape's early success.

- **Search engine and directory listings:** Just as the Yellow Pages and other directories are advertising media, so too are search engines and online directory listings. Increasingly, firms are paying search engines for more visible or higher placement on results lists. Who have you Googled today?

- **Pop-up ads:** A pop-up ad is an advertisement that appears on the screen while a Web page is being loaded or after it is loaded. Because pop-up ads take the center of the screen while surfers are waiting for the desired page to load, they are difficult to ignore. A pop-up ad opens a separate Internet window. Web advertisers are typically charged only if people actually click through to the ad.

- **E-mail:** For advertising, e-mail is becoming as pervasive as radio and television. It is one of the easiest ways of communicating with consumers because marketers can send unsolicited e-mail advertising messages to thousands of users by *spamming*—sending unsolicited e-mail to five or more people not personally known to the sender. Many Web sites that offer e-mail give surfers the opportunity to refuse unsolicited e-mail. This **permission marketing** gives the consumer the power to opt in or out. Marketers in the United States send about 200 billion e-mails to consumers every year, so they hope that a good portion of these will be opened and read rather than being sent straight to the recycle bin.[19]

MEDIA SCHEDULING: WHEN TO SAY IT   After choosing the advertising media, the planner then creates a **media schedule** that specifies the exact media to use for the campaign as well as when and how often the message should appear. Figure 13.3 shows a hypothetical media schedule for the promotion of a new video game. Note that much of the advertising reaches its target audience in the months just before Christmas and that much of the expensive television budget is focused on advertising during specials just prior to the holiday season.

The media schedule outlines the planner's best estimate of which media will be most effective in attaining the advertising objective(s) and which specific media vehicles will do the most effective job. The media planner considers such factors as the match between the demographic and psychographic profile of a target audience and the people reached by a media vehicle, the advertising patterns of competitors, and the capability of a medium to convey the desired information adequately. The planner must also consider such factors as the compatibility of the product with editorial content. For example, viewers might not respond well to a lighthearted ad for a new snack food during a somber documentary on world hunger.

When analyzing media, the planner is interested in assessing **advertising exposure**, the degree to which the target market will see an advertising message in a specific medium. Media planners speak in terms of **impressions**; the number of people who will be exposed to a message placed in one or more media vehicles. For example, if 5 million people watch *MTV Total Request Live* on television, then each time an advertiser runs an ad during that program it receives 5 million impressions. If the advertiser's spot runs four times during the program, the impression count would be 20 million (even though some of these impressions would represent repeated exposure to the same viewers).

To calculate the exposure a message will have if placed in a certain medium, planners consider two factors: reach and frequency. **Reach** is the percentage of the target market that will be exposed to the media vehicle at least one time. This measure is particularly important for widely used products when the message needs to get to as many consumers as possible. **Frequency** is the number of times a person in the target group will be exposed to the message. This measure is important for products that are complex or those that are targeted to relatively small markets for which multiple exposures to the message are necessary to make an impact.

Say that a media planner wants to be sure her advertising for Club Med effectively reaches college students. She learns that 25 percent of the target market reads at least a few issues of *Rolling*

permission marketing
E-mail advertising where online consumers have the opportunity to accept or refuse the unsolicited e-mail.

media schedule
The plan that specifies the exact media to use and when.

advertising exposure
The degree to which the target market will see an advertising message placed in a specific vehicle.

impressions
The number of people who will be exposed to a message placed in one or more media vehicles.

reach
The percentage of the target market that will be exposed to the media vehicle.

frequency
The number of times a person in the target group will be exposed to the message.

Figure 13.3 Media Schedule for a Video Game

Media planning includes decisions on where, when, and how much advertising will be done. A media schedule such as this one for a video game shows the plan visually.

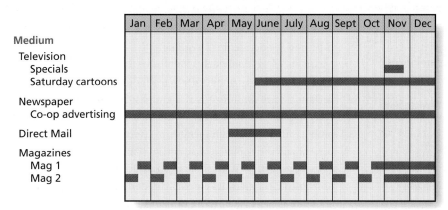

Stone each year (that's reach). She may also determine that these students are likely to see three of the 12 monthly ads that Club Med will run in *Rolling Stone* during the year (that's frequency). Now, the planner calculates the magazine's **gross rating points (GRPs)** by multiplying reach times frequency, which in this case compares the effectiveness of *Rolling Stone* to alternative media. By using this same formula, the planner could then compare this GRP number to another magazine or to the GRP of placing an ad on television or on a bus or any other advertising medium.

Although some media vehicles deliver superior exposure, they may not be cost-efficient. More people will see a commercial aired during the Super Bowl than during a 3:00 A.M. rerun of a Tarzan movie. But the advertiser could run late-night commercials every night for a year for the cost of one 30-second Super Bowl spot. To compare the relative cost effectiveness of different media and of spots run on different vehicles in the same medium, media planners use a measure called **cost per thousand (CPM)**. This figure reflects the cost to deliver a message to 1,000 people and allows advertisers to compare the relative cost-effectiveness of different media vehicles that have different exposure rates.

A medium's popularity with consumers determines how much advertisers must pay to put their message there. Television networks are concerned about the size of their audiences because their advertising rates are determined by how many viewers their programming attracts. Similarly, magazines and newspapers try to boost circulation to justify the ad rates they charge to their advertising clients.

MEDIA SCHEDULING: HOW OFTEN TO SAY IT   After deciding where and when to advertise, the planner must decide how often. What time of day? And what overall pattern will the advertising follow?

A *continuous schedule* maintains a steady stream of advertising throughout the year. This is most appropriate for products that we buy on a regular basis, such as shampoo or bread. The American Association of Advertising Agencies, an industry trade group, maintains that continuous advertising sustains market leadership even if total industry sales fall.[20] On the downside, some messages can suffer from *advertising wear-out* because people tune out the same old ad messages.

A *pulsing schedule* varies the amount of advertising throughout the year based on when the product is likely to be in demand. A suntan lotion might advertise year-round but more heavily during the summer months. *Flighting* is an extreme form of pulsing in which advertising appears in short, intense bursts alternating with periods of little to no activity. It can produce as much brand awareness as a steady dose of advertising at a much lower cost if the messages from the previous flight were noticed and made an impact.

gross rating points (GRPs)
A measure used for comparing the effectiveness of different media vehicles: average reach × frequency.

cost per thousand (CPM)
A measure used to compare the relative cost-effectiveness of different media vehicles that have different exposure rates; the cost to deliver a message to 1,000 people or homes.

As more and more companies start to allocate some of their advertising budgets to the online space, they need to know whether this is an effective strategy and to learn more about which kinds of Internet ads are more likely to have an impact on Web surfers. A metric called "stickiness" is the Holy Grail for many Web advertisers. A "sticky" Web site is one that holds people's attention so that they are motivated to stay at the site for a long time—which in turns means they are more likely to absorb the advertising information they see there and/or make a purchase. Stickiness can be computed by combining some of the same metrics (like reach and frequency) that marketers use to calculate the effectiveness of other forms of advertising:[26]

Frequency = the number of visitors to a Web site divided by the number of unique visitors (since the same person can click on a Web site as much as she wants).

Duration = the total number of minutes visitors spend viewing Web pages divided by the number of visits during the month.

Reach = the number of unique visitors during the month divided by the total number of visitors to the site.

Stickiness = frequency × duration × reach.

Consider the following example of visits to a company's Web site in two successive months. Although more people visited the Web site in February, this basic measure of Web site attractiveness can be misleading. In reality, the content on the Web site in January was "stickier."

	January	February
Number of visits	10,000	11,000
Number of unique visitors during month	4,000	5,000
Total unique visitors acquired by site	8,000	9,000
Frequency	2.5	2.2
Total number of viewing minutes	1,920,000	2,112,000
Duration	192.00	192.00
Reach	50%	55.6%
Monthly stickiness	240.00	234.67

posttesting
Research conducted on consumers' responses to actual advertising messages they have seen or heard.

unaided recall
A research technique conducted by telephone survey or personal interview that asks whether a person remembers seeing an ad during a specified period of time.

Step 6: Evaluate the Advertising

John Wanamaker, a famous Philadelphia retailer, once complained, "I am certain that half the money I spend on advertising is completely wasted. The trouble is, I don't know which half."[21] Now that we've seen how advertising is created and executed, let's step back and consider how we decide if it's working.

There's no doubt that a lot of advertising is ineffective. Ironically, as marketers try harder and harder to reach their customers, these efforts can backfire. Many consumers have a love–hate relationship with advertising. Over half the respondents in a recent major survey said they "avoid buying products that overwhelm them with advertising and marketing," and 60 percent said their opinion of advertising "is much more negative than just a few years ago."[22] With so many messages competing for the attention of frazzled customers, it's especially important for firms to evaluate their efforts to increase the impact of their messages. How can they do that? Often advertisers do this by posttesting their advertising campaigns.

Posttesting means conducting research on consumers' responses to advertising messages they have seen or heard (as opposed to *pretesting*, which as we've seen collects reactions to messages *before* they're actually placed in "the real world"). Ironically, many creative ads that are quirky or even bizarre make an advertising agency look good within the industry, but are ultimately unsuccessful because they don't communicate what needs to be said about the product itself. As one consultant observed, "There is so much emphasis on the creative aspect of the ads, sort of 'Aren't we clever?' that the message is lost."[23]

In some cases, the ads are popular, but they send the wrong message to consumers. For example, a lot of people remember Joe Isuzu, the lying car salesman whose television commercials were popular for two years but were no help to Isuzu's car sales during that time.[24] As one advertising executive explained, "The humor got in the way. All you remembered was that car salesmen are dishonest, and the car salesman you remembered most was from Isuzu."[25]

Three ways to measure the impact of an advertisement are *unaided recall*, *aided recall*, and *attitudinal measures*. **Unaided recall** tests by telephone survey or personal interview whether a person remembers seeing an ad during a specified period of time without giving the person the name of the brand. An **aided recall** test uses the name of the brand and sometimes other clues to prompt answers. For example, a researcher might show a group of consumers a list of brands and ask them to choose which items they have seen advertised within the past week. **Attitudinal measures** probe a bit more deeply by testing consumer beliefs or feelings about a product before and after being exposed to messages about it. If, for example, Pepsi's messages about "freshness-dating" make enough consumers believe that freshness of soft drinks is important, marketers can consider the advertising campaign successful.

Public Relations

Public relations (PR) is the communication function that seeks to build good relationships with an organization's publics. These include consumers, stockholders, legislators, and others who have a stake in the organization. Today marketers use PR activities, like those PR21 develops, to influence the attitudes and perceptions of various groups not only toward companies and brands but also toward politicians, celebrities, and not-for-profit organizations.

The basic rule of good PR is: *Do something good, then talk about it.* A company's efforts to get in the limelight—and stay there—can range from humanitarian acts to more lighthearted "exposure." Consider, for example, the Homemade Bikini Contest sponsored by the makers of Cruzan Rum: Each year, hundreds of competitors nationwide show up in bathing suits made of anything but cloth—including jelly beans, Express Mail tape, dog biscuits, and picnic baskets.[27]

The big advantage of this kind of communication is that when PR messages are placed successfully, they are more credible than if the same information appeared in a paid advertisement. As one marketing executive observed, "There's a big difference between hearing about a product from a pitchman and from your trusted local anchorman."[28] The value of publicity was clearly demonstrated by the huge success of Mel Gibson's controversial film *The Passion of the Christ.* Frequent news stories, TV appearances by Mr. Gibson, radio debates, and even a *Newsweek* cover that asked "Who Really Killed Jesus?" built momentum. Even before the movie opened, 81 percent of moviegoers were aware of it. This high level of interest didn't just "happen"—a year before the movie's release, Gibson toured churches with a rough cut of his movie, giving speeches and charming pastors. His production company, Icon, signed up consultants to advise pastors on how best to use the movie to promote the church and recruit new members.[29]

Public relations is crucial to an organization's ability to establish and maintain a favorable image. Some types of PR activities, referred to as *proactive PR*, stem from the company's marketing objectives. For example, marketers create and manage **publicity**, which is unpaid communication about an organization that gets media exposure. This strategy helps to create awareness about a product or an event, as when a local newspaper reporting on an upcoming concert features an interview with the band's lead guitarist around the time that tickets go on sale. Although some publicity happens naturally, more typically a "buzz" needs to be created by a firm's publicists.

Public relations may be even more important when the company's image is at risk due to negative publicity, for example, product tampering.[30] The goal here is to manage the flow of information to address concerns so that consumers don't panic and distributors don't abandon the product. For example, a few years ago PepsiCo was rocked by claims that hypodermic needles had been found in Diet Pepsi cans. The company assembled a crisis team to map out a response and supplied video footage of its bottling process showing that foreign objects could not find their way into cans before they were sealed at the factory. The claims proved false, and PepsiCo ran follow-up ads reinforcing the findings. Pepsi's calm, coordinated response averted a PR disaster.

Whether it's product tampering or an accident at a company's facilities or some other company-related problem, a crisis can do permanent damage to a company, the success of its products, and its stockholder equity. Public relations professionals know that when a firm handles crises well, damage can be minimized. Thus, a vitally important role of PR is to prepare a *crisis management plan*, a document that details what an organization will do *if* a crisis occurs—who will be the spokesperson for the organization, how the organization will deal with the press, and what sort of messages will be delivered.

In August 2003, both Coca-Cola Co. and PepsiCo Inc. were the targets of a report by a local environmental group in New Delhi, India, that their products contain potentially harmful levels of pesticides. In the weeks that followed, sales of Coke and Pepsi products dropped between 30 and 40 percent, and in at least one city, Coke property was vandalized.[31] In response, the two companies stood together to fight the claims of the group, vehemently denying the allegations and even holding a joint press conference to refute the charges. Both companies stated that worldwide the water they use in their products meets local, U.S., and European safety guidelines. In addition, the companies sought legal remedies through the court in New Delhi, which agreed to conduct new tests on the colas in a government laboratory to determine the level of pesticides in the colas. Coke also filed a defamation suit against the environmental group.

aided recall
A research technique that uses clues to prompt answers from people about advertisements they might have seen.

attitudinal measures
A research technique that probes a consumer's beliefs or feelings about a product before and after being exposed to messages about it.

public relations (PR)
Communication function that seeks to build good relationships with an organization's publics, including consumers, stockholders, and legislators.

publicity
Unpaid communication about an organization appearing in the mass media.

Control yourself.

Bleach what you want to bleach.

CLOROX Bleach Pen

©2003 The Clorox Company. Based on results with leading detergent.

When companies introduce new products—such as a bleach pen—they often use news releases and other PR activities in addition to advertising to publicize the new product.

The Internet has expanded the capabilities of the traditional PR function.[32] Corporate Web sites post testimonials from customers, make new product announcements, and respond quickly to important events. The Internet also can be very effective in handling crises. Companies can respond to a crisis online in far less time than other forms of communication, such as press releases or conferences.[33] When Alaska Airlines flight 261 crashed off the California coast in January 2000, the company turned its Web site into a crash-information site, posting updates hourly, a reaction most PR professionals feel is the best way to minimize damage from a disaster.[34]

Objectives of Public Relations

Public relations specialists need to operate at many levels to ensure that various *publics* of a company receive coordinated, positive messages about the firm. These groups include customers, suppliers, employees, the media, stockholders, and government regulators.

Why are all these publics important in marketing communication? Companies, brands, and customers do not exist in isolation. As we noted in Chapter 12, customers receive information about the company and its products from many different sources. Thus, a company must establish and maintain a positive image with all these publics because they influence market attitudes and consumer behavior, perhaps even more than communications that come directly from corporate headquarters.

Companies that practice IMC know that PR strategies are best used in concert with advertising, sales promotions, and personal selling to send a consistent message to customers and other stakeholders. As part of the total IMC plan, PR is often used to accomplish the following objectives:

- **Introducing new products to manufacturers:** When Weyerhaeuser Co. introduced Cellulon, a new biotechnology product, it distributed information kits that clearly explained the technical product and its applications in each of 12 markets to ensure that the trade press properly covered the introduction.[35]

- **Introducing new products to consumers:** When Chrysler Corp. rolled out its trio of LH sedans, the market was already anticipating their arrival. Working months ahead of time, Chrysler's PR teams exposed journalists to the LH project through factory and laboratory tours as well as discussions with designers. These efforts were successful in garnering favorable reviews in automotive magazines.[36]

- **Influencing government legislation:** Concerned about attempts to limit the amount that could be reimbursed for prescriptions in health care plans, the Pharmaceutical Manufacturers Association initiated an $8 million print campaign arguing that such drugs represent just 5 percent of national health care expenditures and save lives.[37]

- **Enhancing the image of a city, region, or country:** Faced with international criticism about possible human rights abuses and restriction of trade, the Chinese government established an office in charge of "overseas propaganda" to present a more favorable image of China to the rest of the world.[38]

- **Calling attention to a firm's involvement with the community:** Each year, an estimated 4,500 firms spend some $3.7 billion to sponsor sporting events, rock concerts, museum exhibits, and the ballet. "We're touching customers in their life-style, when they are more relaxed," said the national director of sponsorships and promotions for AT&T's consumer long-distance division.[39] PR specialists work behind the scenes to ensure that sponsored events receive ample press coverage and exposure.

Planning a Public Relations Campaign

A public relations campaign is a coordinated effort to communicate with one or more of the firm's publics. This is a three-step process of developing objectives, executing, and evaluating. Let's review each step.

Like an advertising campaign, the organization must first develop clear objectives for the PR program that define the message it wants people to hear. Next, the PR specialists must develop a campaign strategy that includes the following:

- A statement of objectives

- A situation analysis

- Specification of target audiences (publics), messages to be communicated, and specific program elements to be used

- A timetable and budget

- Discussion of how the program will be evaluated

For example, the International Apple Institute, a trade group devoted to increasing the consumption of apples, had to decide if a campaign should focus on getting consumers to cook more with apples, drink more apple juice, or simply to buy more fresh fruit. Because fresh apples brought a substantially higher price per pound to growers than apples used for applesauce or apple juice, the group decided to push the fresh-fruit angle. It used the theme "An apple a day . . . " (sound familiar?) and mounted a focused campaign to encourage people to eat more apples by placing articles in consumer media extolling the fruit's health benefits.

Execution of the campaign means deciding precisely how the message should be communicated to the targeted public(s). An organization can get out its positive messages in many ways: news conferences, sponsorship of charity events, and other attention-getting promotions.

One of the barriers to greater reliance on PR campaigns is the difficulty of gauging their effectiveness. Who can say precisely what impact appearances by company executives on talk shows or sponsoring charity events has on sales? It is possible to tell if a PR campaign is getting media exposure, though compared to advertising it's more difficult to gauge bottom-line impact. Table 13.2 describes some of the most common measurement techniques.

Public Relations Activities

Public relations professionals engage in a wide variety of activities. While some of these may seem more related to marketing and to marketing communications than others, they all lead to the same goal—creating and maintaining that positive image the organization needs. Some of these activities are as follows:

- **Press releases:** The most common way for PR specialists to communicate is a **press release**, which is a report of some event that an organization writes itself and sends to the media in the hope that it will be published for free. A newer version of this idea is a video news release

press release
Information that an organization distributes to the media intended to win publicity.

Table 13.2 Measuring the Effectiveness of Public Relations (PR) Efforts

Method	Description	Pros	Cons
In-house assessments conducted by a PR manager	Analyze media coverage in publications, looking for number of mentions and prominence of mentions	Relatively inexpensive because the major cost is the manager's time	Cannot guarantee objectivity in the analysis; crucial to specify up front what the relevant indicators are
Awareness and preference studies	Assess company's standing in the minds of customers relative to competition	Good for broad-based strategy setting or to demonstrate the progress of a large program	Difficult to connect results to specific PR events and to identify which actions had what level of impact on awareness; very expensive
Measurement of print and broadcast coverage generated by PR activities	The basic measurement tool in PR	Provides a quantifiable measure of press coverage; relatively inexpensive	Quantitative only; does not consider the *content* of the press coverage
Impression counts	Measure the size of the potential audience for a given article	Because a similar measure is used to assess advertising effectiveness, this method provides a common measure for comparison	Usually limited to the circulation of selected publications, so this method does not include pass-along readership; can be expensive

Source: Adapted from Deborah Holloway, "How to Select a Measurement System That's Right for You," *Public Relations Quarterly*, Fall 1992, 15–17.

(VNR) that tells the story in a film format instead. Some of the most common types of press releases include the following:

- *Timely topics* deal with topics in the news, such as Levi Strauss's efforts to promote "casual" Fridays to boost sales of its Dockers and Slates casual dress pants by highlighting how different corporations around the country are adopting a relaxed dress code.

- *Research project stories* are published by universities highlighting breakthroughs by faculty researchers.

- *Consumer information releases* provide information to help consumers make product decisions, such as helpful tips from a turkey company about preparing dishes for Thanksgiving dinner.

- **Internal PR:** These activities aimed at employees often include company newsletters and closed-circuit television. Internal releases help keep employees informed about company objectives, successes, or even plans to "downsize" the workforce. Often company newsletters also are distributed outside the firm to suppliers or other important publics.

- **Lobbying:** Lobbying means talking with and providing information to government officials to persuade them to vote a certain way on pending legislation or even to initiate legislation that would benefit the organization.

- **Speech writing:** An important job of the PR department of a firm is to write speeches on a topic for a company executive to deliver. While some executives do actually write their own

Many company Web sites allow surfers to access recent press releases.

speeches, it is more common for a speechwriter on the PR staff to develop an initial draft of a speech after which the executive might add his own input.

- **Corporate identity:** PR specialists may provide input on corporate identity materials, such as logos, brochures, building design, and even stationery, that communicate a positive image for the firm.

- **Media relations:** One of the tasks of the PR professional is to work to develop and maintain positive relationships with the media. Of course, this is important if the company is going to receive the best media exposure possible for positive news, such as publicizing the achievements of an employee who has done some notable charity work or for a

Oscar Meyer created an eye-catching promotion with its Wienermobile—guaranteed to draw attention from hot dog lovers.

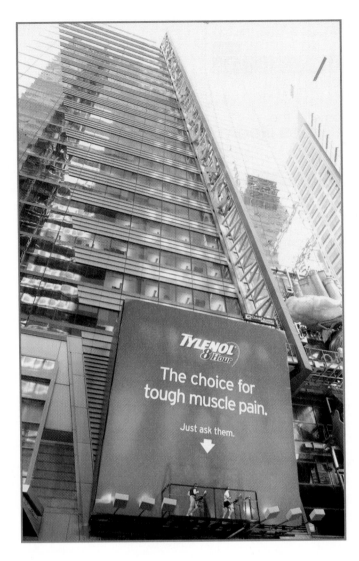

To promote its sponsorship of the New York City Marathon, Tylenol hired flesh-and-blood people to run on treadmills on a billboard above Times Square.

sponsorships
PR activities through which companies provide financial support to help fund an event in return for publicized recognition of the company's contribution.

product it developed that saved someone's life. For example, a Canadian pharmaceutical firm called Boerhinger Ingelhim Ltd. sent large dolls wearing respirator masks to Canadian pediatricians. The idea was to help doctors ease the fears of their young patients about putting a mask over their mouths and noses. Boerhinger won considerable favorable publicity when the campaign was featured in many Canadian newspapers. And, as we've seen, good media relations can be even more important when things go wrong. News editors are simply less inclined to present a story of a crisis in its most negative way if they have a good relationship with PR people in the organization.

- **Sponsorships: Sponsorships** are PR activities through which companies provide financial support to help fund an event in return for publicized recognition of the company's contribution. Many companies today find that their promotion dollars are well spent to sponsor a golf tournament, a NASCAR driver, a symphony concert, or global events such as the Olympics or World Cup soccer competition. These sponsorships are particularly effective because consumers often connect their enjoyment of the event with the sponsor, thus creating brand loyalty. Because different events cater to different consumers, sponsorships are a good way to target specific market segments. Rolling Rock beer, a product that brags about its roots in Latrobe, a small Pennsylvania town, attracted 35,000 consumers to a Rolling Rock town fair complete with headlining rock bands the Red Hot Chili Peppers, Moby, and Fuel.[40] Sponsorships also help build interest in an entire product or activity. In Huntington Beach, California, corporate sponsors are rediscovering the allure of surfing in a big way. Companies such as Toyota, Washington Mutual, Seagram's, and Microsoft are catching the wave because they want to associate their brand with this legendary and cool extreme sport.[41]

- **Special events:** Another job of a PR department is the planning and implementation of special events. Whether it is the visit of a group of foreign investors to a firm's manufacturing facilities, a Fourth of July picnic for company employees, or a hospitality booth set up during a motorcycle race where the company is a sponsor, the PR staff's job is to make sure the event happens without a glitch and people go home happy.

- **Advice and counsel:** When the importance of the PR function is fully understood and appreciated, firms and the people who run them recognize that PR professionals have much more to offer than just planning parties and writing news releases. Because of their expertise and understanding of the effects of communication in the crafting of public opinion, PR professionals also play the role of consultants to top management. So when a firm needs to shut down a plant or to build a new one, to discontinue a product or add to the product line, to fire a vice president, or to give an award to an employee who spends hundreds of hours a year doing volunteer work in his community, it needs the advice of its PR staff. What is the best way to handle the situation? How should the announcement be made? Who should be told first? What is to be said and how?

Advice for the Zeno Group

STUDENT
CONROD KELLY
Florida A&M University

I would choose option 2 because the company needs to pursue an aggressive advertising strategy. The company should utilize the advertising campaign to highlight the points of difference between Sirius satellite radio, conventional radio, and its major competitor, XM satellite. Consumers are interested more in the benefits they can receive from the product than in the technology behind it. With Sirius positioning itself as an entertainment and information company, it is able to reach a broad audience base because of the diversity of options that consumers have. Consumer empowerment translates to sales. Additionally, with the premium positioning, Sirius could work with premium car manufacturers to include the satellite radio as a standard option, therefore providing an opportunity for brand leveraging and guaranteed sales.

PROFESSOR
SHELLY MCCALLUM
Saint Mary's University of Minnesota

I would choose option 2. Because of Sirius's competitive position being second to market and the inherent difficulty competing head to head with a first to market competitor, Sirius needs to reposition itself. The approach to redefine its "premium" position based on programming versus its main competitor and traditional radio offers Sirius an opportunity to attract the broader market of music/sports/information lovers (mass market) versus only tech-savvy listeners (micromarket). As the industry is in its early stages, Sirius needs to actively build its share of mind as a unique delivery service (satellite radio) as well as a unique brand. Through active promotion, Sirius has a greater opportunity to build its subscriber base (increasing revenues) and to establish a leadership position in the area of programming excellence (grow and maintain a competitive position in the market).

Direct Marketing

Are you one of those people who loves to get lots of catalogs in the mail, pore over them for hours, and then order just exactly what you want without leaving home? Do you order CDs, computer software, and books on the Web? Have you ever responded to an infomercial on TV? All these are examples of direct marketing, the fastest-growing type of marketing communications. **Direct marketing** refers to "any direct communication to a consumer or business recipient that is designed to generate a response in the form of an order, a request for further information, and/or a visit to a store or other place of business for purchase of a product."[42] The Direct Marketing Association reports that in a recent six-month period, 39 percent of Americans bought or sought information from a catalog, while 21 percent responded to a direct-mail offer.[43]

Let's look at the most popular types of direct marketing, starting with the oldest—buying through the mail.

Mail Order

In 1872, Aaron Montgomery Ward and two partners put up $1,600 to mail a one-page flyer that listed their merchandise with prices, hoping to spur a few more sales for their retail store.[44] The mail-order industry was born. Today, consumers can buy just about anything through the mail, and mail orders account for 3 percent of overall retail sales in the United States.[45] Mail order comes in two forms: catalogs and direct mail.

CATALOGS A **catalog** is a collection of products offered for sale in book form, usually consisting of product descriptions accompanied by photos of the items. Catalogs came on the scene

direct marketing
Any direct communication to a consumer or business recipient that is designed to generate a response in the form of an order, a request for further information, and/or a visit to a store or other place of business for purchase of a product.

catalog
A collection of products offered for sale in book form, usually consisting of product descriptions accompanied by photos of the items.

within a few decades of the invention of movable type over 500 years ago, but they've come a long way since then.[46]

The early catalogs pioneered by Montgomery Ward and other innovators such as Sears were designed for people in remote areas who lacked access to stores. Today, the catalog customer is likely to be an affluent career woman with access to more than enough stores but without the time or desire to go to them. According to the Direct Marketing Association, over two-thirds of the U.S. adult population orders from a catalog at least once a year.[47] Catalog mania extends well beyond clothing and cosmetics purchases. Dell and Gateway 2000, direct-selling computer companies, each have annual sales of over $1 billion. Although established retailers such as Bloomingdale's or JCPenney publish catalogs, others are start-ups by ambitious entrepreneurs who cannot afford to open a store. That's how housewife Lillian Hochberg began—by selling handbags through the mail. Today the Lillian Vernon catalog mails out more than 137 million copies each year.[48]

Many stores use catalogs to complement their in-store efforts—Neiman-Marcus is famous for featuring one-of-a-kind items like diamond-encrusted bras or miniature working versions of Hummers in its mailings as a way to maintain the store's image as a purveyor of unique and upscale merchandise.

A catalog strategy allows the store to reach people who live in areas too small to support a store. However, catalogs can be an efficient and expensive way to do business. Catalog retailers mail out 10 to 20 books for every order they receive, and paper and printing costs are rising steadily. Still, catalog sales are a successful form of nonstore retailing, and U.S. firms are using them to reach overseas markets as well. Companies like Lands' End and Eddie Bauer are doing brisk sales in Europe and Asia, where consumers tend to buy more products through the mail than do Americans in the first place. Lands' End opened up a central warehouse in Berlin and attacked the German market with catalogs. The company trained phone operators in customer service and friendliness and launched an aggressive marketing campaign to let consumers know of the Lands' End lifetime warranty (German catalog companies require customers to return merchandise within two weeks). Although local competitors protested and even took the company to court, the case was settled in the American company's favor, and the Yankee invasion continues.[49]

direct mail
A brochure or pamphlet offering a specific product or service at one point in time.

DIRECT MAIL Unlike a catalog retailer that offers a variety of merchandise through the mail, **direct mail** is a brochure or pamphlet offering a specific product or service at one point in time. For example, Saab Cars U.S.A. started a program to sell cars using letters and a coupon for $2,000. A pilot program that cost only $200,000 helped generate sales of $62 million in new Saabs.[50] A direct-mail offer has an advantage over a catalog because it can be personalized. Direct mail also is widely used by charities, political groups, and other not-for-profit organizations.

Just as with e-mail spamming, many Americans get overwhelmed with direct-mail offers and don't open all their "junk mail." This problem was amplified following the anthrax scare of 2001, when a lot of people became more reluctant to open mail from a source they couldn't identify. One solution was to create an industry-wide, nonproprietary Web site (**www.whatsmailing.org**) so mail recipients can check the legitimacy of packages that cross their desks or land in their home mailboxes.

Even so, after the attacks of September 11, 2001, adjustments had to be made. Procter & Gamble halted shipments of samples of Always Maxi Pads because consumers received lumpy packages without a clearly identified sender. Nissan canceled a direct-mail push for its new Altima model because the unusual packages spurred calls from fearful consumers.[51] The direct-mail industry is always working on ways to monitor what is sent through the mail and provides some help by allowing consumers to "opt out" of at least some mailing lists (you can learn more about this at the Direct Marketing Association's Web site at **www.the-dma.org**).

Telemarketing

Telemarketing is direct selling conducted over the telephone. Especially compared to door-to-door selling, this method is cheap and easy. Surveys indicate that one out of six Americans finds it difficult to resist a telemarketing pitch. However, about one in three complained of feeling cheated at one time by a telemarketer.[52] And do they always have to call during dinner? Telemarketing actually is more profitable for organizational markets than for consumer markets. When business-to-business marketers use the telephone to keep in contact with smaller customers, it costs far less than personal sales calls and lets small customers know they are important to the company.

As noted in Chapter 2, in 2003, the Federal Trade Commission established the National Do Not Call registry in an attempt to allow consumers to limit the number of telemarketing calls they receive. Consumers sign up on the registry indicating they do not wish to be called. The idea is that telemarketing firms will check the registry at least every 31 days and clean their phone lists accordingly. Consumers responded very positively to the regulation, with over 58 million phone numbers on the registry in the first eight months.[53] Direct marketers have challenged the registry, stating that it will put the legitimate companies out of business while unethical companies will not abide by the regulation and will continue to harass consumers.

Infomercials, or program-length advertisements, are widely used to promote goods ranging from fitness products and kitchen knives to luxury items and real estate.

Direct-Response Advertising

Another way companies do direct marketing is through advertising. Direct advertising can be very successful. For example, Richard Thalheimer, founder of high-tech retailer Sharper Image, began his business with a full-page ad in *Runners World* for a chronograph watch.[54] Other products, sold through creative direct-response advertising, continued the success. While the Internet has for many companies become the media of choice for direct marketing, direct advertising in magazines, newspapers, and television is still alive and well.

As early as 1950, a channel called Television Department Stores brought the retailing environment into the television viewer's living room by offering a limited number of products the viewer could buy by calling the advertised company. Television sales picked up in the 1970s when two companies, Ronco Incorporated and K-Tel International, began to hawk such products as the Kitchen Magician, the Mince-O-Matic, and the Miracle Broom on television sets around the world.[55] A simple phone call, and one of these wonders could be yours. The form of advertising called **direct-response TV (DRTV)** includes short commercials of less than two minutes, 30-minute or longer infomercials, and home shopping networks such as QVC and HSN. Top-selling DRTV product categories include exercise equipment, self-improvement products, diet and health products, kitchen appliances, and music. And this is hardly just an American phenomenon—DRTV sales in Japan of $1.5 billion per year equal those in the United States.[56]

INFOMERCIALS Today these primitive sales pitches have mostly been replaced by slick **infomercials**, which are half-hour or hour commercials that resemble a talk show but in actuality are intended to sell something. Although some infomercials still carry a low-class, sleazy stereotype, in fact more than 40 major companies have used this format, including heavyweights from American Airlines and Apple Computer to Visa and Volkswagen. A survey by *TV Guide* found that 72 percent of respondents have watched at least one infomercial, and about one-third made a purchase as a result.[57] Top-selling categories include cosmetics, self-improvement products, fitness products, kitchen appliances, music, and videos.

HOME SHOPPING NETWORKS Television channels that exist solely to sell products let shopping junkies indulge themselves without leaving their living rooms.[58] In the United States, the QVC

direct-response TV (DRTV)
Advertising on TV that seeks a direct response, including short commercials of less than two minutes, 30-minute or longer infomercials, and home shopping networks.

infomercials
Half-hour or hour commercials that resemble a talk show but in actuality are intended to sell something.

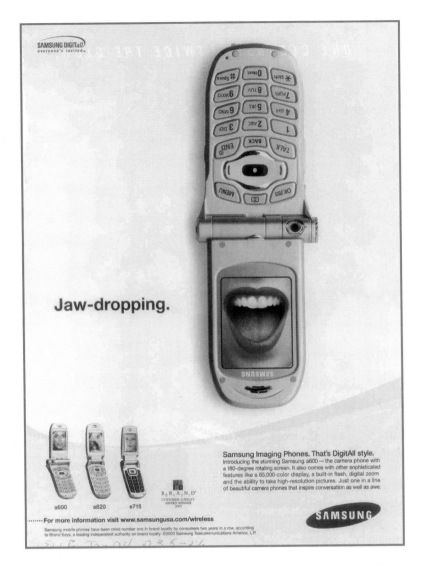

Jaw-dropping.

Samsung Imaging Phones. That's DigitAll style.
Introducing the stunning Samsung a600 — the camera phone with
a 180-degree rotating screen. It also comes with other sophisticated
features like a 65,000-color display, a built-in flash, digital zoom
and the ability to take high-resolution pictures. Just one in a line
of beautiful camera phones that inspire conversation as well as awe.

a600   a820   e715

········ For more information visit www.samsungusa.com/wireless

Samsung mobile phones have been rated number one in brand loyalty by consumers two years in a row, according
to Brand Keys, a leading independent authority on brand loyalty. ©2003 Samsung Telecommunications America, L.P.

Improvements in mobile phone technology are making M-commerce more attractive to consumers and thus to marketers.

m-commerce
Promotional and other e-commerce activities transmitted over mobile phones and other mobile devices, such as personal digital assistants (PDAs).

channel alone sells products at the rate of $39 per second around the clock. To date, the typical American home shopping customer is in a low-income bracket, and the most frequently purchased product is inexpensive jewelry. Some upscale retailers, such as Saks Fifth Avenue and Donna Karan, have experimented with this format, but these efforts have largely been unsuccessful.[59]

M-Commerce

In this age of the Internet, it seems like we just get used to a dozen or so new terms when they are replaced by an equal number of new ones. M-commerce is such a term. The "M" stands for mobile. **M-commerce** refers to the promotional and other e-commerce activities transmitted over mobile phones and other mobile devices, such as personal digital assistants (PDAs).[60] With about a billion mobile phones in use worldwide, many of them Internet-enabled, it makes sense that marketers would want to reach out and touch this large target audience.

While M-commerce hasn't yet caught on big time in the United States, it is quite prevalent in Europe and Asia. For example, approximately half of Japan's 30 million Internet users gain access to the Web by using their wireless phones because that's a cheaper way to do it there.[61] Although only a small proportion of the millions of users of mobile phones worldwide use their phones to check e-mail, stock quotes, and so on, that number is expected to grow dramatically in the next few years. Young people in particular are big users of cell phones (how many are ringing in your class today?), which explains why cell phone companies such as Nokia are aggressively advertising on high school and college campuses.[62]

Of course, some American companies do have m-commerce strategies. For example, *Vibe*, a magazine that targets young, hip readers, is experimenting with creating magazine content for cell phone users. For $2.99 a month, subscribers can download photos of their favorite rock stars at parties, get instant music reviews, and even read short magazine articles.[63]

Another type of m-commerce simply involves sending text messages such as an ad for a concert or a new restaurant to customers. This technique, known as *short-messaging system marketing* (SMS), is becoming a popular way to reach customers in the United Kingdom and throughout Europe. MTV promoted its Music Video Awards with a wireless advertising campaigns that sent messages to millions of consumers urging them to tune in.[64]

Indeed, text messaging is very popular in many parts of the world. In 2003, there were an estimated 162 million consumer text messaging accounts worldwide.[65] In the Philippines, text messaging is even replacing traditional phone calls because of convenience and cost savings—an estimated 1 million text messages are sent everyday in that country alone![66] Mobile phone users find "SMSing" a fun way to communicate with friends and business contacts even when they are not available to talk. And with most mobile phone systems, customers are charged much less for text messages than for voice communications.

In the United Kingdom, Nestlé conducted an m-commerce campaign for its Kit Kat candy bar. The firm's ad agency sent text messages to the cell phones of 6,000 consumers ages 18 to 25 that alerted them when ads for the candy would air, and invited them to take a quiz about the ad that would in turn enter them into a drawing to win a month's supply of Kit Kats (about 94 percent of British youth have cell phones with wireless messaging capability). A campaign for readers of *Men's Health* magazine sent a customized daily menu via cell phone to help interested readers curb calories (doubtful those Kit Kats were on the list).[67]

As with e-mail, unfortunately there is a dark side. Some unscrupulous marketers have figured out a new scam called *spim* (the instant messaging version of spam). In some cases when your America Online Buddy List sends you a link to a news article (e.g., Osama bin Laden has been captured), instead you're taken to an advertising site or to a place to download a game. Clicking on the link not only installs the game but also sends the program without your knowing it to contacts on your buddy list. You may also wind up installing *adware*—software that runs undetected, tracking your Web habits and interests, presenting pop-up advertisements, and resetting the home page.[68]

So what are the advantages of m-commerce to consumers? First, it provides incredible consumer convenience. You can use your mobile phone to buy tickets for a concert without standing in line. You can even buy soft drinks from a vending machine through the phone—a service already available in Europe.[69]

But the potential for m-commerce is even greater. Perhaps you're in the market for a new computer. You visit a local retailer and decide what you want. While you're there, you use your mobile phone or PDA to check prices of the same computer on the Internet. If you decide you have the best price, you'll be able to handle the transaction on your phone as well, paying for the computer through a secure Internet connection.

For marketers, the opportunities for m-commerce are even more exciting. Using sophisticated *location-based technologies* including satellites, a retailer will be able to know when you are only a few blocks away from her store, and she can send you messages about a special sale.[70] And as you pass McDonald's, your phone will beep to remind you how great a Big Mac combo would taste right about now. Of course, such opportunities bring a whole host of privacy issues that must be settled before these scenarios can become a reality.

Many of the technological barriers that have slowed the growth of m-commerce in the past are being overcome. Today's wireless phones have cameras, a keyboard for typing e-mail, access to e-mail accounts, and a Web browser. And the price is right—top-of-the-line products sell for $600 to $700.[71] Overall, the future is bright for m-commerce: One study predicts that despite the slow start, about 90 million Americans will be participating by 2007, generating more than $50 billion in revenues.[72] That's opportunity calling!

real people, real choices
How It Worked Out at the Zeno Group

Jerry selected option 2, to position Sirius as an entertainment company with superior programming rather than focusing on its line of consumer electronics. By emphasizing Sirius's programming as superior to the competition, the marketing team was able to differentiate the two companies in the

eyes of the press and, ultimately, purchasing consumers. Specific objectives of the campaign included the following:

- Differentiate Sirius from its competitor
- Raise awareness of Sirius among entertainment industry and consumer audiences
- Drive awareness of benefits of Sirius versus other forms of in-car entertainment
- Position Sirius as an economically viable company

To make a significant and measurable impact with limited resources, campaign tactics focused exclusively on intensive media outreach to generate immediate reach and frequency to change consumer mindset, emphasizing the programming offering of the two services in head-to-head reviews. The team also focused on providing exposure of the various products that supported the Sirius service and positioning the company as a player in the entertainment business. This strategy proved extremely successful with numerous publications. Several, including *Fortune*, *Business Week*, *SmartMoney*, and *Sound & Vision*, decided Sirius had superior programming. the Zeno Group also targeted other specialized audiences, including holiday gift guide buyers, new car buyers, music lovers, and sports junkies. Selected campaign tactics included the following:

- An aggressive presence at the national Consumer Electronics Show to introduce consumer and trade media to the new Sirius marketing campaign and product offerings
- Special events specifically designed to generate media coverage, such as an event at the House of Blues in Los Angeles
- Satellite Media Tours timed around the New York Auto Show, Father's Day, and back-to-school and holiday gift guides
- Press teleconference events announcing the launch of a new channel targeted to gay listeners called OutQ and Sirius's partnerships with the NHL and the NFL

Before the PR campaign began in January 2003, Sirius was on the verge of bankruptcy and had fewer than 27,000 customers. By June 2004, the company had more than 500,000 customers and is on target to reach one million by the end of the year. According to one media report, "Sirius . . . has gone from dead to brilliant in a matter of weeks." During 2003, Sirius garnered 1,563,589,034 media impressions, and the company appeared in nearly 5,000 press articles and more than 400 broadcast segments. Influential publications such as *Fortune*, *Business Week*, *SmartMoney*, *Radio & Records*, and *Sound & Vision* recommended Sirius programming over the competition, and it was featured as a cover story in *Billboard Magazine* and *Electronic Design*. And consumer awareness of Sirius increased significantly. According to the *Hollywood Reporter*, "Consumer awareness for XM has remained a constant 37 percent over the year, whereas Sirius jumped from 8 percent in January [2003] to 24 percent in July [2003]." This was done with less than $25 million spent in advertising during the year. Public relations clearly boosted Sirius's signal in the competition for the ears of the American public.

How do you write a resume that gets noticed? Learn how to communicate your brand to create a dynamic resume and cover letter in Chapter 13 of the *Brand You* supplement.

CHAPTER SUMMARY

1. **Tell what advertising is and describe the major types of advertising.** Advertising is non-personal communication from an identified sponsor using mass media to persuade or influence an audience. Advertising informs, reminds, and creates consumer desire. Product advertising is used to persuade consumers to choose a specific product or brand. Institutional advertising is used to develop an image for an organization or company, to express opinions (advocacy advertising), or to support a cause (public service advertising). Advertising begins with the client or advertiser that may be a manufacturer, a distributor, a retailer, or an institution. Most companies rely on the services of advertising agencies.

2. **Describe the process of developing an advertising campaign.** Development of an advertising campaign begins with identifying the target audiences and developing advertising objectives. Next, advertisers design the advertising, choosing an effective type of advertising appeal. Pretesting advertising before placing it in the media prevents costly mistakes. A media plan determines where and when advertising will appear. Media options include broadcast media (network and spot television and radio), print media (newspapers, magazines, and directories), out-of-home media (outdoor advertising and place-based media), and Internet advertising. A media schedule specifies when and how often the advertising will be seen or heard.

3. **Explain how marketers evaluate advertising.** Marketers evaluate advertising through posttesting. Posttesting research may include aided or unaided recall tests that examine whether the message had an influence on the target market.

4. **Explain the role of public relations.** The purpose of PR is to maintain or improve the image of an organization among various publics. An important part of this is managing publicity. Public relations is useful in introducing new products; influencing legislation; enhancing the image of a city, region, or country; and calling attention to a firm's community involvement.

5. **Describe the steps in developing a public relations campaign.** The steps in a PR campaign begin with setting objectives, creating and executing a campaign strategy, and planning how the PR program will be evaluated. PR specialists often use print or video news releases to communicate timely topics, research stories, and consumer information. Internal communications with employees include company newsletters and internal TV programs. Other PR activities include lobbying, developing corporate identity materials, media relations, arranging sponsorships and special events, and providing advice and counsel for management.

6. **Understand direct marketing.** Direct marketing refers to any direct communication designed to generate a response from a consumer or business customer. Some of the types of direct-marketing activities are mail order (catalogs and direct mail), telemarketing, and direct-response advertising, including infomercials and home shopping networks.

7. **Discuss the future of m-commerce.** M-commerce is e-commerce done over mobile devices such as phones and personal digital assistants (PDAs). M-commerce can provide great convenience for consumers and gives marketers the opportunity for location-based commerce. In the next few years, m-commerce is expected to grow as marketers overcome technological barriers.

KEY TERMS

advertising, 395
advertising appeal, 399
advertising campaign, 397
advertising exposure, 406
advocacy advertising, 396
aided recall, 408, 409
aperture, 401
attitudinal measures, 408, 409
banners, 405
buttons, 405
catalog, 415
copy testing, 401
cost per thousand (CPM), 407
creative strategy, 399

direct mail, 416
direct marketing, 415
direct-response TV (DRTV), 417
frequency, 406
full-service agency, 397
gross rating points (GRPs), 407
impressions, 406
infomercials, 417
institutional advertising, 396
limited-service agency, 397
m-commerce, 418
media planning, 401
media schedule, 406
out-of-home media, 404

permission marketing, 406
place-based media, 404
posttesting, 408
press release, 411
pretesting, 401
product advertising, 395
public relations (PR), 408, 409
public service advertisements (PSAs), 396
publicity, 409
reach, 406
sponsorships, 414
unaided recall, 408
unique selling proposition (USP), 399

CHAPTER REVIEW

MARKETING CONCEPTS: TESTING YOUR KNOWLEDGE

1. What is advertising, and what is its role in marketing?

2. What are the types of advertising that are most often used?

3. How is an advertising campaign developed? Describe some of the different advertising appeals used in campaigns.

4. What are the strengths and weaknesses of television, radio, newspapers, magazines, directories, out-of-home media, and the Internet for advertising? What are the ways marketers advertise on the Internet?

5. Describe the media planning process. How do marketers pretest their ads? How do they posttest ads?

6. What is the purpose of PR? What is proactive PR? What is a crisis management plan?

7. What are the steps in planning a PR campaign?

8. Describe some of the activities that are a part of PR.

9. What is direct marketing? Describe the more popular types of direct marketing.

10. What is m-commerce?

MARKETING CONCEPTS: DISCUSSING CHOICES AND ISSUES

1. Some people are turned off by advertising because they say it is obnoxious, that it insults their intelligence, and that

advertising claims are untrue. Others argue that advertising is beneficial and actually provides value for consumers. What are some arguments on each side? How do you feel?

2. Technology through television remotes, VCRs, computers, and cable television is giving today's consumers more and more control over the advertising images they see. How has this affected the advertising industry so far, and do you think this will affect it in the future? What are some ways that advertising can respond to this?

3. M-commerce will allow marketers to engage in location commerce where they can identify where consumers are and send them messages about a local store. Do you think consumers will respond positively to this? What do you think the benefits for consumers of m-commerce are?

4. Some critics denounce PR specialists, calling them "flacks" or "spin doctors" whose job is to hide the truth about a company's problems. What is the proper role of PR within an organization? Should PR specialists try to put a good face on bad news?

MARKETING PRACTICE: APPLYING WHAT YOU'VE LEARNED

1. As an account executive for an advertising agency, you have been assigned to a new client, a new mobile phone service. As you begin development of the creative strategy, you are considering different types of appeals:
   a. USP
   b. Comparative advertising
   c. A fear appeal
   d. A celebrity endorsement
   e. A slice-of-life ad
   f. Sex appeal
   g. Humor
   Outline the strengths and weaknesses of using each of these appeals for advertising the sports phone service.

2. Spend some time looking through magazines. Find an ad that fits each of the following categories:
   a. USP strategy
   b. Testimonial
   c. Lifestyle format
   d. Humor appeal
   Critique each ad. Tell who the target market appears to be. Describe how the appeal is executed. Discuss what is good and bad about the ad. Do you think the ad will be effective? Why or why not?

3. Assume that you are the head of PR for a furniture company. There has been a fire in one of your plants, and several people have been seriously injured. As the director of PR, what recommendations do you have for how the firm might handle this crisis?

4. As a PR professional employed by your university, you have been asked to develop strategies for improving your school's PR program. Write a memo to your university president with your recommendations.

MARKETING MINIPROJECT: LEARNING BY DOING

The purpose of this miniproject is to give you an opportunity to experience the advertising creative process.

1. With one or more classmates, create (imagine) a new brand of an existing product (such as a laundry detergent, toothpaste, perfume, soft drink, or the like).

2. Decide on an advertising appeal for your new product.

3. Create a series of at least three different magazine ads for your product, using the appeal you selected. Your ads should have a headline, a visual, and copy to explain your product and to persuade customers to purchase your brand.

4. Present your ads to your class. Discuss the advertising appeal you selected and explain your ad executions.

REAL PEOPLE, REAL SURFERS: EXPLORING THE WEB

Much of the advertising you see every day on television and in magazines is created by a small number of large advertising agencies. To make their agency stand out from the others, the different agencies develop unique personalities or corporate philosophies. Visit the Web sites of several advertising agencies:

Leo Burnett Worldwide (**www.leoburnett.com**)
BBDO Worldwide (**www.bbdo.com**)
The Martin Agency (**www.martinagency.com**)
Fallon Worldwide (**www.fallon.com**)
J. Walter Thompson (**www.jwt.com**)

Explore the Web sites to see how they differ. Then answer the following questions:

1. What is the mission of each agency? How does each agency attempt to position itself compared to other agencies?

2. Who are some of the major clients of the agency?

3. How does the site demonstrate the creative ability of the agency? Does the site do a good job of communicating the mission of the agency? Explain.

4. If available, tell a little about the history of the agency.

5. Of the agencies you visited, which would you most like to work for, and why?

6. As a client, based on your exploration of the Web sites, which agency would you choose for your business, and why?

MARKETING PLAN EXERCISE

An advertising campaign consists of a series of advertisements placed in media over time. While ads may be placed in different media, all will have the same look, feel, and message. Think about one of the following products:

1. A new brand of toothpaste
2. Your local city or state
3. Your university

Assume that you are developing an advertising campaign for the product. Outline how you would develop the campaign. Be sure to discuss the following:

1. The type of appeal you would use
2. The main message you will seek to communicate
3. The media you would use (be sure to include at least one print and one broadcast medium)
4. How you will develop the ads so that they have the same look and feel

Marketing in Action Case

Real Choices at Premier Retail Networks

Premier Retail Networks (PRN) is a privately held company that operates in-store TV networks in 5,700 locations around the United States, including in Wal-Mart, Circuit City, and Best Buy. The company got its start when executives at Wal-Mart became annoyed at their competitors' ads airing in Wal-Mart stores while the TVs were tuned to network programming. PRN solves this problem. The company provides a dedicated television network located in the stores of large retailer chains.

Advertisers on the PRN network are some of the world's largest consumer products companies, including Gillette, Disney, Sony, Procter & Gamble, Unilever, Nintendo, and Levi Strauss. These companies and many others rely on PRN's network of in-store TVs to distribute some of their newest ad content—often relying on the network to introduce new products in-store before national ad campaigns for those same products are begun.

Indeed, the Disney-released video *Monsters Inc.* became the record holder for one-day and one-week sales as a result of the advertising the Disney did through PRN on Wal-Mart's in-store television network. Levi Strauss relied on the network to introduce its new Signature line of low-priced jeans in Wal-Mart stores. Other packaged-goods companies have used the network to launch approximately 350 new products.

The ads on PRN's network run in a loop three times per hour. Ads can be tailored for each specific retail chain and cost between $50,000 and $300,000 for a four-week time period depending on the frequency with which the ads run. The PRN network provides many advantages to advertisers, including high levels of reach. For example, more than half of all American shoppers visit a Wal-Mart every month, and one-third visit every week. That's roughly 100 million people on a weekly basis and 150 million over the course of a month. Thus, the reach of PRN is higher than almost any other single TV network available to advertisers.

One problem with traditional advertising on television, in magazines and newspapers, and on the radio is that consumers are rarely in "buying mode" when they see the ads. Advertisers recognize a need to reach customers with advertisements at the point in time when they are more likely to pay attention and when they are deciding to make a purchase. The PRN system reaches customers as they are making buying decisions. Since roughly three out of four buying decisions are made in the store itself, having an ad run on the in-store TV is a last chance to sway buying decisions as customers are "getting their wallets out."

However, not everything associated with PRN is positive. One of the problems the network faces is how to increase the number of consumers who actually notice the ads. Many retail customers comment that they often go into stores to get what they went for and then get out—that they are not in the store to watch TV. Because of this, some advertising media buyers question whether enough customers, especially those shopping with children, pay attention to the spots to justify the expense. In Wal-Mart stores, the TVs are suspended from the ceiling, and hearing the ads over the din of noise created by all the activity often is a major challenge.

To counter such questions, PRN needs to determine the effectiveness of ads running on the network. Is it possible to do a posttest on these ads, and, if not, how would PRN convince advertising executives of the networks advertising effectiveness? Even though the *Monsters Inc*. release saw fabulous results, not every new product introduction is as successful. When sales results like those experienced for the Disney movie are not available, gauging the impact of individual ads becomes much more difficult.

And what about the future? Like most companies, PRN wants and needs to grow. For PRN, this means increasing its share of total U.S. advertising spending. To do this, the company needs more than just a handful of retailers using its services, and it needs more advertisers choosing to have their ads seen on PRN. Both of these growth opportunities provide challenges for PRN as the company tries to capitalize on its early success.

Things to Think About

1. What is the decision(s) facing Premier Retail Networks?
2. What factors are important in understanding this decision situation?
3. What are the alternatives?
4. What decision(s) do you recommend?
5. What are some ways to implement your recommendation(s)?

Sources: Alice Z. Cuneo, "Challenge for Wal-Mart TV: Getting Shoppers' Attention," *Advertising Age*, October 6, 2003, 30; Alice Z. Cuneo, Wayne Friedman, and Bradley Johnson, "Levi's Stays In-Store for Signature Launce, *Advertising Age*, June 30, 2003, 4, 25; Louis Chunovic, "He's Got Some Surprises in Store," *Television Week*, March 3, 2003, 16; and Matthew Boyle, "Hey, Shoppers: Ads on Aisle 7!," *Fortune*, November 24, 2003, 50.

IBM
ibm.com/bcsondemand
IBM BUSINESS CONSULTING SERVICES

BREADTH
IS ON

AUTOMOTIVE
RETAIL
PHARMACEUTICALS
DEFENSE
GOVERNMENT
UTILITIES
ELECTRONICS
TELECOM
INSURANCE
BANKING
CHEMICALS
ENERGY
CONSUMER PRODUCTS
MEDIA
AEROSPACE
TRAVEL
TRANSPORTATION

ON DEMAND BUSINESS

EDUCATION
HEALTHCARE
FINANCIAL MARKETS
LIFE SCIENCES
PETROLEUM
ENTERTAINMENT

IBM
ibm.com/bcsondemand
IBM BUSINESS CONSULTING SERVICES

DEPTH
IS ON

BUSINESS STRATEGY
CHANGE MANAGEMENT
HUMAN RESOURCE SERVICES
GROWTH STRATEGY
STRATEGIC SOURCING
ORGANIZATIONAL CHANGE
FINANCE STRATEGY
PERFORMANCE LEADERSHIP
CUSTOMER RELATIONSHIP MANAGEMENT
PEOPLE STRATEGY
BRANDING AND DESIGN

ON DEMAND BUSINESS

OPERATIONS STRATEGY
CUSTOMER ANALYTICS
SUPPLY CHAIN STRATEGY
SALES FORCE EFFECTIVENESS
LEARNING AND DEVELOPMENT

www.ibm.com

real people, real choices
meet Esther Ferre,
a Decision Maker at IBM

what I do when I'm not working

career high

Being a mother, exercising, cooking, collecting art, and traveling.

Appointment to senior management team.

SALES PROMOTION, PERSONAL SELLING, AND SALES MANAGEMENT

Esther Ferre is a managing director at IBM, where she is responsible for global revenue in excess of $500 million. Based in Dallas, she has been with the company for 25 years in sales and sales-related roles, including 20 years in sales and executive management. She completed her professional education at Harvard and Boston University. In addition to her work with IBM, Esther serves on the board of directors for Girl Scouts Tejas Council and as vice chairman of the board of directors for the Center for BrainHealth at the University of Texas at Dallas.

Decision Time at IBM

Sales managers and executives are often faced with the challenge of balancing the importance of long-term client relationships with short-term business results. Just how do you invest in long-term customer relationships when the short-term business results do not support the investment? How long can you afford to invest sales resources in developing and maintaining client relationships to maximize longer-term revenue opportunities?

As a managing director at IBM, Esther Ferre is responsible for developing and managing the overall business relationship between IBM and a single, large client in the information technology (IT) consulting and services industry. This client has over 125,000 employees in over 60 countries. It uses IBM's technology to help it service its own clients, which include large companies in many industries as well as governments around the world. Esther and her team must establish and develop a relationship with this client and identify opportunities in which the client can use IT to reduce costs, improve productivity, or provide a unique market advantage.

To meet these goals, the sales team must have an in-depth understanding of the client's business and be able to successfully integrate IBM products, services, and solutions to solve the client's business issues. Esther is responsible for all aspects of the IBM relationship with the client and she is evaluated on how well her team is able to maximize revenue, generate profits, and satisfy the customer while minimizing sales expense. She must also ensure that her team is meeting its sales objectives through the delivery of high-value IT solutions.

A recent slowdown in corporate spending resulted in companies reducing their expenditures for IT and related consulting and services, which lowered her client's revenue, profits, and new contract signings. To make matters worse, the client also lost money when a few of its own clients in the telecommunications and airlines sectors filed bankruptcy, which further eroded its

my motto to live by	**what drives me**	**don't do this when interviewing with me**	**my pet peeve**
Achieve balance in all aspects of your life to accomplish the most from each part of it.	Sense of accomplishment and bringing value to the client.	Tell me you're a "people person."	People who can't write letters or memos.

objectives

1 Explain what sales promotion is and describe the different types of trade and consumer sales promotion activities.

2 Explain the important role of personal selling in the marketing effort.

3 List the steps in the personal selling process.

4 Explain the role of the sales manager.

revenues and profits. The client took significant actions to cut back on its expenses by reducing head-counts, eliminating redundant functions, and streamlining certain business processes. However, the client also significantly reduced its expenditures for IT technology, including IBM's products, which directly affected the IBM team's ability to achieve its revenue and profit objectives.

Although it was declining, the revenue IBM generated from Esther's client was still significant, and Esther understood that maintaining a long-term relationship with the client was critical. Doing so would provide future revenue opportunities when the client's business recovered. Thus, Esther had to review her sales expenses such as salary, benefits, office space, phone, and travel against expected revenues in order to lower IBM's sales expenses through reduced head-count, reduced travel, and other cost-cutting measures. Meanwhile, Esther had to make such cost-cutting decisions while minimizing the impact to her client. This is a delicate balancing act, because the investment of sales resources must be balanced among existing and prospective customers to ensure an adequate overall pipeline of sales opportunities. Relationships with established customers must be maintained to ensure customer satisfaction and the opportunity to compete for new sales opportunities. Concurrently, relationships with prospective customers must be developed to identify new sales opportunities. Esther considered her options:

OPTION 1: Reduce IBM's sales and support resources to an affordable level.

This would mean curtailing investment in marketing resources and retaining only a minimum sales team to provide technical support and maintain the relationship with the client. With this option, IBM sales and support resources could immediately be assigned to other, higher-growth revenue opportunities. On the other hand, the client would not be satisfied with the reduced level of sales resources and support, which could jeopardize future revenue opportunities for IBM with this major client.

OPTION 2: Maintain the current level of sales and support resources.

Maintaining the status quo would allow IBM to keep the client satisfied and would better position the IBM team to compete for future revenue opportunities when the client's business improved. However, with this option, Esther and her team would not be able to achieve their short-term revenue and expense objectives. Meanwhile, other revenue opportunities might not have adequate sales resources, and IBM could lose revenue.

OPTION 3: Evaluate lower-cost ways to provide sales and support resources, such as call centers, Web support, and resource sharing.

By choosing this option, Esther and her team could maintain the client relationship, and the sales model would be more cost effective. On the other hand, the loss of face-to-face client relationships could reduce client satisfaction, leading the client to turn elsewhere in the future.

Now, put yourself in Esther Ferre's shoes: Which option would you choose, and why?

Advertising Is Not the Only Game in Town!

Esther Ferre's dilemma is to find the best way for IBM to service its clients' needs. Similarly, when it comes to promoting a product, there's more than one way to skin a cat—or, in one case, a goose: A liquor company once sent attractive models into trendy cigar bars to push Grey Goose, a pricey French vodka being introduced in the U.S. market. To get customers to try it, the women dropped a cherry soaked with the liquor into people's martinis and then gave surprised barflies a sales pitch about the vodka. When word of this "guerrilla marketing" hit the newspapers, the company got some free publicity for its efforts. To paraphrase Agent 007, the company apparently hopes potential customers will be stirred, not shaken.[1]

We saw in Chapter 13 that traditional advertising efforts are steadily being supplemented with other communication methods, such as public relations campaigns and various forms of direct marketing such as direct mail as companies work harder and harder to get through the clutter. In this chapter, we'll look at other forms of promotion—sales promotion and personal selling—that are commonly used in addition to advertising, public relations, and direct marketing in a firm's promotion mix.

Sales Promotion

Sometimes taking a simple walk through your student union on campus puts you in contact with a variety of people eager for you to enter a contest, taste a new candy bar, or take home a free T-shirt with a local bank's name on it. These are examples of **sales promotion**, programs that marketers design to build interest in or encourage purchase of a product or service during a specified time period.[2] Marketers have been placing an increasing amount of their total marketing communication budget into sales promotion for one simple reason—these strategies deliver short-term sales results.

Sales promotion sometimes can be elaborate and high-profile. For example, a successful effort by Burger King called "Spidey Sense" capitalized on the enormous popularity of the movie *Spider Man 2*. During the Spidey Sense promotion, customers obtained game pieces at Burger King restaurants and were told to "use their Spidey sense to scratch off the right spider web" that would let them win one of several possible prizes ranging from sodas at Burger King to $50,000 in cash.

How does sales promotion differ from advertising? Both are paid messages from identifiable sponsors intended to change consumer behavior or attitudes. In some cases, the sales promotion itself is publicized using a traditional advertising medium, such as the Burger King Spidey Sense game commercials that came out in conjunction with the introduction of *Spider Man 2*. Although many advertising campaigns are carefully crafted to create long-term positive feelings about a brand, company, or store, sales promotion tends to focus on more short-term objectives, such as an immediate boost in sales or the introduction of a new product.

Sales promotion is very useful if the firm has an *immediate* objective, such as bolstering sales for a brand quickly or encouraging consumers to try a new product. The objective of sales promotion may be to generate enthusiasm among retailers to take a chance on a new product or provide more shelf space for an item they already carry. Thus, like advertising, sales promotion can target channel partners (the "trade") or the selling firm's own employees, as well as end consumers.

As you learned in Chapter 12, sales promotion is but one part of a firm's integrated marketing communication program and, thus, must be coordinated with other promotion activities. For example, if a brand's marketing communication tries to position the product as an expensive, luxury item (think BMW), a sales promotion activity that reduces the price or involves giving away free fried chicken and lemonade at the BMW dealer served by a guy dressed in a clown suit will undoubtedly send conflicting messages to the customer about the BMW brand. And, importantly, sales promotion rarely if ever is used by itself as the sole form of marketing communication. By its nature, sales promotion is most often used to support a more extensive advertising, direct marketing, public relations, and/or personal selling initiative.

Table 14.1 summarizes key sales promotion techniques. Sales promotion is directed to two key groups: trade and consumers. Let's start with trade promotions and then learn about consumer promotions.

Sales Promotion Directed Toward the Trade

Trade promotions focus on members of the trade, which includes distribution channel members, such as retail salespeople or wholesale distributors, that a firm must work with in order to sell its products. (We'll discuss these and other distribution channel members in more detail in Chapters 15 and 16.)

sales promotion
Programs designed to build interest in or encourage purchase of a product during a specified time period.

trade promotions
Promotions that focus on members of the "trade," which includes distribution channel members, such as retail salespeople or wholesale distributors, that a firm must work with in order to sell its products.

Table 14.1 Sales Promotion Techniques: A Sampler

Technique	Primary Target	Description	Example
Trade shows	Trade	Many manufacturers showcase their products to convention attendees.	The National Kitchen and Bath Association organizes several shows a year. Manufacturers display their latest wares to owners of kitchen and bath remodeling stores.
Incentive programs	Trade	A prize is offered to employees who meet a prespecified sales goal or who are top performers in a given time period.	Mary Kay cosmetics awards distinctive pink cars to its top-selling representatives.
Point-of-purchase displays	Trade and consumers	In-store exhibits make retail environments more interesting and attract consumers' attention.	As somber music plays in the background, a huge plastic rat draped in a black shroud lies next to a tombstone to promote the Farnam Company's Just One Bite rat poison.
Push money	Trade	Salespeople are given a bonus for selling a specific manufacturer's product.	A retail salesperson at a cosmetics counter at a Nordstrom store in Seattle gets $5 every time she sells a bottle of Glow by JLo.
Promotional products	Trade	A company builds awareness and reinforces its image by giving out items with its name on them.	Coors distributors provide bar owners with highly sought-after "Coors Light" neon signs.
Cross promotion/ cooperative promotions	Trade and consumers	Companies team up to promote their products jointly.	Burger King promotes its Spidey Man game in conjunction with Columbia Pictures' *Spider Man 2*.
Coupons	Consumers	Certificates for money off on selected products, often with an expiration date, are used to encourage product trial.	Crest offers $5 off its WhiteStrips.
Samples	Consumers	Retailers might get a demonstration product to help in sales presentations; consumers get a free trial size of the product.	A small bottle of Clairol Herbal Essences shampoo arrives for free in the mail.
Contests/ sweepstakes	Consumers	A sales contest rewards wholesalers or retailers for performance; consumers participate in games or drawings to win prizes; builds awareness and reinforces image.	Publisher's Clearing House announces its zillionth sweepstakes.
Special/bonus packs	Consumers	Additional product is given away with purchase; rewards users. Note that bonus packs usually mean the package must be altered in some way to accommodate the extra merchandise.	Maxell provides 10 free blank CDs with purchase of a pack of 50.
Gifts with purchase	Consumers	A consumer gets a free gift when a product is bought; reinforces product image and rewards users.	A free makeup kit comes with the purchase of $20 worth of Clinique products.

Trade promotions take one of two forms: (1) discounts and deals and (2) increasing industry visibility. Discount promotions (deals) reduce the cost of the product to the retailer or help defray its advertising expenses. They are designed to encourage stores to stock the item and be sure it's given a lot of attention. Trade promotions that focus on increasing awareness and sales (increasing industry visibility) do so by creating enthusiasm among salespeople and customers. Let's take a look at both types of trade promotions in more detail.

DISCOUNTS AND DEALS One form of trade promotion is a *price break*. A manufacturer can reduce a channel partner's costs through sales promotions that discount its products. For example, a manufacturer can offer a **merchandising allowance**, which reimburses the retailer for in-store support of a product, such as an off-shelf display. Another way in which a manufacturer can reduce a channel partner's cost is through a **case allowance**, which provides a discount to the retailer or wholesaler based on the sales volume of a product it orders from the manufacturer.

However, allowances and deals have a downside. As with all sales promotion activities, the manufacturer's expectation is that they will be of limited duration after which the distribution channel partner will again pay full price for the items. Unfortunately, some channel members engage in a practice called *forward buying*, in which large quantities of the product are purchased during a discount period, warehoused, and not bought again until another discount is offered. Some large retailers and wholesalers take this to an extreme by engaging in *diverting*, an ethically questionable practice. Here the retailer buys the product at the discounted promotional price, warehouses it, and, after the promotion has expired, sells the inventory to other retailers at a price that is lower than the manufacturer's nondiscounted price but high enough to turn a profit for the retailer. Both forward buying and diverting go against the manufacturer's intent in offering the sales promotion.

INCREASING INDUSTRY VISIBILITY Other types of trade sales promotions increase the visibility of a manufacturer's products to channel partners within the industry. Whether an elaborate exhibit at a convention or a coffee mug with the firm's logo sent out to clients, these efforts seek to keep the company's name topmost when distributors and retailers make decisions about which products to stock and push. These forms of sales promotions include the following:

- **Trade shows:** The thousands of industry **trade shows** held in the United States and around the world each year are major vehicles for manufacturers to show off their product lines to wholesalers and retailers. Usually, large trade shows are held in big convention centers where many companies set up elaborate exhibits to show their products, give away samples, distribute product literature, and troll for new business contacts. One example of how technology is changing traditional marketing is the advent of online trade shows where potential customers can preview a manufacturer's wares remotely. This idea is growing in popularity, though many industry people are finding it a challenge to "schmooze" in cyberspace. An important benefit of traditional trade shows is the opportunity to develop customer leads that are then given to the company's sales force for follow-up. We'll talk more about the role of a sales force later in this chapter.

- **Promotional products:** We have all seen them: coffee mugs, visors, T-shirts, ball caps, key chains, refrigerator magnets, and countless other doodads emblazoned with a company logo. They are examples of **promotional products**. Unlike licensed merchandise sold in stores, these goodies are given away to build awareness for the sponsor. Although some of these freebies are distributed directly to consumers and business customers, many are intended for channel partners such as retailers and vendors to build name recognition and loyalty.

- **Incentive programs:** Mary Kay cosmetics is famous for giving its more productive distributors pink cars to reward their efforts. In addition to motivating distributors and customers, some promotions are designed to light a fire under the firm's own sales force. These incentives, known as **push money**, may come in the form of cash bonuses, trips, or other prizes. Recently, Starbucks got into the incentive program business by providing gift cards that can be given by salespeople to clients as a small "thank you" for closing a sale.

Sales Promotion Directed Toward Consumers

Some sales promotion directed toward consumers creates a buzz in the form of a contest or a special event. For example, Red Bull, the high-octane energy drink (and popular mixer), has became famous for this approach by making its auspicious Red Bull vans available at rave and hip-hop clubs to raise

merchandising allowance
Reimburses the retailer for in-store support of the product.

case allowance
A discount to the retailer or wholesaler based on the volume of product ordered.

trade shows
Events at which many companies set up elaborate exhibits to show their products, give away samples, distribute product literature, and troll for new business contacts.

promotional products
Goodies such as coffee mugs, T-shirts, and magnets given away to build awareness for a sponsor. Some freebies are distributed directly to consumers and business customers; others are intended for channel partners such as retailers and vendors.

push money
A bonus paid by a manufacturer to a salesperson, customer, or distributor for selling its product.

MEASURING VALUE
marketing metrics

The consulting firm Booz Allen revamped the way the Kellogg Company uses trade promotions in its overall strategy to promote its cereal products. In the 1990s, the company was losing market share to competitors despite spending $600 million annually on trade promotions. Meanwhile, Kellogg's managers knew almost nothing about the effectiveness of their promotions, and it seemed they were just blindly throwing money at the problem to boost sales.

Thus, Kellogg launched its Trade Excellence Program (TEP) to increase the return on its huge promotion investment. The TEP program used sophisticated software tools to create an effectiveness metric that precisely tracked where Kellogg's promotional dollars were going and how much revenue was produced by each individual trade promotion. The analysis showed that 59 percent of Kellogg's trade promotion events actually *lost* money, and, as a result, the profit generated by the other 41 percent that were successful promotion events was almost entirely eaten away. Booz Allen projected that Kellogg could save at least $64 million per year if it spent its money differently. While Kellogg still does a lot of trade promotions, now the company monitors these activities closely to determine which kinds actually contribute to sales growth and profitability and which are a waste of time and money.[3]

the party atmosphere profile for the venue. Red Bull's consistent efforts at consumer sales promotion became the signature aspect of its marketing communication to consumers, and for the early stages of Red Bull's product life cycle the company did very little traditional consumer advertising. The word-of-mouth advertising (also known as "buzz") created by these special events added to the mystique of the brand, fueling popularity among its young target market much more effectively than would traditional advertising. Let's take a closer look at several popular forms of consumer-targeted sales promotion.

PRICE-BASED CONSUMER SALES PROMOTION   Many sales promotions target consumers where they live: their wallets. They emphasize short-term price reductions or rebates that encourage people to choose a brand—at least during the deal period. Price-based consumer promotion, however, has a downside similar to the price break trade promotion. If used too frequently, consumers become conditioned to purchase the product only at the lower promotional price. Price-based consumer sales promotions include the following:

- **Coupons:** Try to pick up any Sunday newspaper without spilling some coupons. These certificates, redeemable for money off on a purchase, are the most common price promotion. Indeed, they are the most popular form of sales promotion overall, with billions distributed annually. One company, Valpak, has created an entire business around coupons. You've probably received a Valpak envelope in the mail—it's the one with dozens of coupons and other offers inside. Even industries such as pharmaceuticals that never tried this approach before are turning to it in a big way. Coupons that can be redeemed for free initial supplies of drugs are being mailed and are also available through sites such as Viagra.com

Cooking contests (such as the "Bourboncuing" contest sponsored by Jim Beam) are a popular way to let consumers "strut their stuff" and create a buzz about the company's products.

and Purplepill.com. Companies use the coupons to prompt patients to ask their physician for the specific brand instead of a competing brand or a more economical generic version.[4]

Today, many firms simply send consumers to their Web site for coupons. Wolf Camera (also branded as Ritz Camera) has been a leader in online couponing in the film processing arena, providing coupon promotions for a variety of products and film processing options on its Web site. The online couponing trend has sparked a cottage industry of online coupon consolidators. SmartSource.com, for example, has users register with the site, including details about family members' ages, gender, and pets along with the names of stores where they shop. After that, users have free access to 30 to 35 coupons on a given day, worth about $14. Manufacturers pay SmartSource a fee each time a consumer redeems a coupon accessed through the Web site. The average savings on an online coupon is about 97 cents, compared with 81 cents for newspaper coupons.[5]

- **Price deals, refunds, and rebates:** In addition to coupons, manufacturers often offer a temporary price reduction to stimulate sales. This *price deal* may be printed on the package itself, or it may be a price-off flag or banner on the store shelf. Alternatively, companies may offer **rebates**, which allow the consumer to recover part of the purchase price via mail-ins to the manufacturer. Today, many retailers, such as Best Buy and Circuit City, print the rebate form for you along with your sales receipt. After you mail the rebate form in, you can track whether the check has been sent to you by visiting the retailer's Web site.

- **Frequency (loyalty/continuity) programs: Frequency programs**, also referred to as loyalty or continuity programs, offer a consumer a discount or a free product for multiple purchases over time. Mike Gunn, former vice president of marketing at American Airlines, is widely credited with developing this concept in the early 1980s, coining the phrase "frequent flyer" miles. Of course, all the other airlines were quick to follow suit, as were a host of other firms, including retailers, auto rental companies, hotels, restaurants—you name it, they have a customer loyalty program. For example, T.G.I. Friday's boasts more than a million members in its Friday's Gold Points program, which allows customers to redeem gifts from a variety of cosponsors, including Radisson hotels.[6]

- **Special/bonus packs:** Another form of price promotion involves giving the shopper more product instead of lowering the price.[7] How nice to go to Walgreen's and find an eight-ounce bottle of Nivea lotion with four ounces free! A *special pack* also can be a separate product given away along with another product, such as a GoodNews! Razor wrapped with a can of Gillette Foamy shaving cream.

ATTENTION-GETTING CONSUMER PROMOTIONS   Attention-getting consumer promotions stimulate interest in and publicity for a company's products. Some typical types of attention-getting promotions include the following:

- **Contests and sweepstakes:** According to their legal definitions, a contest is a test of skill, and a sweepstakes is based on chance. Guinness Import Company's "Win Your Own Pub in Ireland" contest gave away an actual pub to the winner of an essay contest titled "Why Guinness Is My Perfect Pint."[8]

Promotional products are giveaways with the company logo. Companies find that promotional products, such as 3M Post-Its, imprinted with their company logo, are a good way to keep their name in front of both their customers and channel partners.

rebates
Sales promotions that allow the customer to recover part of the product's cost from the manufacturer.

frequency programs
Consumer sales promotion programs that offer a discount or free product for multiple purchases over time; also referred to as loyalty or continuity programs.

To encourage consumers to buy more Chiquita products, the producer held a sweepstakes to win a Ford Windstar.

The dairy industry's popular and ongoing milk mustache advertising campaign was also the basis for an innovative consumer contest.[9] Consumers collected under-the-cap game pieces on gallons of milk, and winners of the "Milk Mustache Fame Game" were featured in a milk mustache ad. Chiquita Brands, marketer of Chiquita bananas, included a Ford Windstar, $5,000 in cash, and other items as grand prizes in its "Miss Chiquita's Summer Fun on the Run" contest.[10]

premiums
Items offered free to people who have purchased a product.

- **Premiums:** **Premiums** are items offered free to people who have bought a product. They usually are novelty items, such as the removable tattoos called Barqtoos that Barq's root beer gave away. The prize in the bottom of the box of cereal—the reason many college students open the box from the bottom—is a premium. Prepaid phone cards have become highly popular premiums. Companies jumping on the phone card bandwagon offer cards emblazoned with pictures of sports heroes, products, and even rock bands. Phone cards make ideal premiums because they are compact, they can display brand logos or attractive graphics, and they provide opportunities for repeat exposure. And an important benefit for the marketer is the ability to build databases by tracking card usage.[11] Your good neighbor State Farm agent used to send you a calendar on your birthday—now you're likely to get a phone card with 30 long-distance minutes on it, adorned with a reminder of your agent's phone number and product lines.

sampling
Distributing free trial-size versions of a product to consumers.

- **Sampling:** How many people at one time or another have managed to scrape together an entire meal by scooping up free food samples at their local grocery store? Some stores, like Publix and Sam's Club, actually promote Saturdays as sampling day in their advertising. **Sampling** encourages people to try a product by distributing trial-size versions in stores, in public places such as student unions, or through the mail. Hawaiian Tropic, the suntan lotion people, follows spring breakers to current hot spots such as Panama City, Florida; South Padre Island, Texas; and Cancun, Mexico, to offer students free samples coupled with coupons for purchasing a regular-size bottle.

Many marketers now distribute free samples through sites on the Internet.[12] Companies such as Procter & Gamble, Unilever, S.C. Johnson & Son, and SmithKline Beecham are readily taking advantage of Web sites such as **www.freesamples.com** and **www.startsampling.com** that not only distribute the firms' samples but also follow up with consumer satisfaction surveys.

- **Point-of-purchase promotion:** A **point-of-purchase (POP) promotion** attempts to influence consumers while they are in the store by catching their attention with creative displays or signs.[13] Marketers are challenged to come up with new and innovative POP displays that will grab attention, such as the promotion Bausch & Lomb ran in Spain. The company wanted to encourage consumers with good vision to buy contact lenses that changed their eye color. By letting shoppers upload their pictures to a computer in the store and digitally altering the photos, the promotion allowed people to see how they would look with five different eye colors without actually inserting the contacts.[14]

  POP activities also include the use of *in-store media*, such as placards on shopping carts or closed-circuit television, to promote specific products. As the chief executive officer of one company that produces these in-store messages put it, "Does it make any sense to spend millions of dollars talking to people in their living rooms and cars and then let them wander around a supermarket with 30,000 product choices without something to remind them to buy your product?"[15] The most noticeable of this genre of POP promotion uses a motion detector box that flashes lights in the coupon dispenser as a shopper approaches a section of the shelf.

- **Product/brand placements:** As we mentioned in Chapter 13, *product placement* refers to getting your brand featured in movies or television shows. When consumers see a brand being used by a popular celebrity or shown in a favorite movie or TV program, they might develop a more positive attitude toward the brand. Successful brand placements have included the BMW Z3 driven by James Bond, the Nike shoes worn by Forrest Gump, and the Ray-Ban sunglasses worn by Tom Cruise in *Risky Business*.

  Beyond movies and television shows, what better way to promote to the video generation than through brand placements in video games, an approach called **advergaming**. If you are a video game hound, watch for placements of real-life brands such as Ford, Radio Shack, General Motors, Toyota, and Sony embedded in the action of your game. Quiksilver, a clothing manufacturer for extreme-sport participants, now puts its shirts and shorts into video games such as Tony Hawk's Pro Skater 3.

- **Cross-promotion:** In **cross-promotion** (or **cooperative promotion**), marketers of two or more products or services join forces to create interest using a single promotional tool. In a way, this is similar to product/brand placement in that each promoted products appears on each other's turf. Cross-promoted products should share some logical connection, be compatible in image, and put forth a message that helps both brands. The Burger King/*Spider Man 2* sales promotion mentioned earlier is an example of a cross-promotion that worked. In the theaters, moviegoers got a dose of the Burger King "Spidey Sense" contest in the trailers that play before the feature. Then, when consumers went to their nearby Burger King to chow down and get a game piece, they saw *Spider Man 2* cups and all sorts of Spidey decor throughout the restaurant.

Personal Selling

As you have learned, sales promotion usually isn't the only form of marketing communications used by a company. In fact, sales promotion nearly always supports other forms of marketing communications, including personal selling. **Personal selling** occurs when a company representative interacts directly with a customer or prospective customer to communicate about a good or service. Personal selling is a far more intimate way to talk to the market. Many organizations rely heavily on

point-of-purchase (POP) promotion
In-store displays or signs.

advergaming
Brand placements in video games.

cross-promotion (cooperative promotion)
Two or more products or services combine forces to create interest using a single promotional tool.

personal selling
Marketing communication by which a company representative interacts directly with a customer or prospective customer to communicate about a good or service.

A cross-promotion lets companies join forces to push their products using a single promotional tool. That's the plan behind this cross-promotion between Hard Candy and Visa.

this approach because at times the "personal touch" can carry more weight than mass-media material. For a business-to-business market situation, such as that of Esther Ferre at IBM, the personal touch translates into developing relationships with clients. Also, many industrial products and services are too complex or expensive to market effectively in impersonal ways (such as through mass advertising).

Another advantage of personal selling is that salespeople are the firm's eyes and ears in the marketplace. They learn which competitors are talking to customers, what is being offered, what new rival products are on the way—all sorts of competitive intelligence. As such, salespeople perform a vital role in the success of a firm's customer relationship management system that we discussed in Chapter 7—providing a source of timely and accurate informational input about customers and the market.

Personal selling has special importance for students because many graduates with a marketing background will enter professional sales jobs. The Bureau of Labor Statistics estimates that 17.4 million people will be employed in sales and related occupations by 2010, up from 15.5 million in 2000.[16] Jobs in selling and sales management often provide high upward mobility if you are successful because firms value employees who understand customers and who can communicate well with them. The old business adage "nothing happens until something is sold" translates into quite a bit of emphasis being placed on personal selling by many firms.

Sold on selling? Alright then, let's take a close look at how personal selling works and how professional salespeople develop long-term relationships with customers.

The Role of Personal Selling

When a man calls an 800 number to order a new desktop PC configured with a DVD drive so his kids can play the latest version of Doom, he is dealing with a salesperson. When he sits in on a presentation by a computer technician presenting a new spreadsheet software package, he is dealing with a salesperson. And when that same man agrees over a business dinner at a swanky restaurant to buy a new computer network for his company, he also is dealing with a salesperson. For many firms, some element of personal selling is essential to land a commitment to purchase or a contract, making this type of marketing communication an important part of any marketing plan. Table 14.2 summarizes some of the factors that make personal selling relatively more or less important in an organization's promotion mix.

Generally, a personal selling effort is more important when a firm engages in a *push strategy*, in which the goal is to "push" the product through the channel of distribution so that it is available to consumers. As a vice president at Hallmark Cards observed, "We're not selling to the retailer, we're selling *through* the retailer. We look at the retailer as a pipeline to the hands of consumers."[17]

Personal selling also is likely to be crucial in business-to-business contexts when direct interaction with a client's management is required to clinch a big deal—and often when intense negotiations about price and other factors will occur before the deal is signed. In consumer contexts, inexperienced customers may need the hands-on assistance that a professional salesperson can provide. Firms selling products that consumers buy infrequently—houses, cars, computers, lawn mowers, even college educations—often rely heavily on personal selling. (Hint: Your school didn't just pick

Table 14.2 Factors Influencing a Firm's Emphasis on Personal Selling

Factors Increasing Emphasis on Personal Selling	Factors Limiting Emphasis on Personal Selling
• If a push strategy is used	• If the dollar amount of individual orders will be small
• If the decision maker has higher status within the organization	• If there are many small customers
• If the purchase is a "new task" for the customer	• If the image of the salesperson is poor
• If the product is highly technical or complex	
• If the customer is very large	
• If the product is expensive	
• If the product is a custom good or personalized service	
• If there are trade-in products	
• If negotiation is required	

any student at random to conduct campus tours for prospective attendees.) Likewise, firms whose products or services are complex or very expensive often need a salesperson to explain, justify, and sell them—in both business and consumer markets.[18]

If personal selling is so useful, why don't firms just scrap their advertising and sales promotion budgets and hire more salespeople? Because there are some drawbacks that limit the role played by personal selling in the marketing communications mix. First, when the dollar amount of individual purchases is low, it doesn't make sense to use personal selling. In personal selling, the cost per contact with each customer is very high compared to other forms of communication. Analysts estimate that in 2005, the average total cost for a sales call with a consultative (or problem-solving) approach to selling to be about $270, and this cost is increasing at a rate of 5 percent per year. In contrast, the per-contact cost of a national television commercial is miniscule by comparison. A 30-second, prime-time commercial may be $300,000 to $500,000 (or even over $2 million during the Super Bowl), but with millions of viewers, the cost per contact may be only $10 or $15 per 1,000 viewers. For low-priced consumer goods, personal selling to end users simply doesn't make good financial sense.

Salespeople—even the *really* energetic—can make only so many calls a day. Thus, reliance on personal selling is effective only when the success ratio is at its highest. Because the cost of fielding salespeople is high, **telemarketing** (sometimes called *teleselling* in this context), in which person-to-person communication takes place via the telephone, is growing in popularity (much to the dismay of many prospects who are interrupted by dinnertime calls). Of course, as you learned in earlier chapters, no-call legislation and do-not-call lists at the state and federal levels have given consumers a powerful weapon to ward off unwanted telephone selling.

Ironically, consumer resistance to telemarketing has provided a powerful boost for a form of selling that has been around for a long time: *direct selling*. Direct sellers bypass channel intermediaries and sell directly from manufacturer to consumer. Typically, independent sales representatives do the selling in person in a customer's home or place of business. Well-known examples include Avon, Mary Kay, and the Pampered Chef. Many of these firms utilize a *party plan* approach to selling in which products are demonstrated in front of groups of neighbors or friends. Direct selling is on a big upswing, with domestic sales volume doubling in the past 10 years to over $30 billion annually. We'll discuss direct selling in more detail in Chapter 16.[19]

telemarketing
The use of the telephone to sell directly to consumers and business customers.

Technology and Personal Selling

Personal selling is supposed to be, well, "personal." By definition, a company uses personal selling for marketing communication in which one person (the salesperson) interacts directly with another person (the customer or prospective customer) to communicate about a good or service. All sorts of technologies are available to enhance the personal selling process. However, as anyone making sales calls knows, technology cannot *replace* personal selling. As we'll discuss later in this chapter, the main role of personal selling in New Era marketing firms is to manage customer *relationships*—and remember, relationships occur between people, not between technologies.

However, without a doubt, a bevy of technological advancements have made it easier for salespeople to do their jobs more effectively. One such technological advance is customer relationship management (CRM) software. For years now, salespeople have used and benefited from account management software such as ACT and GoldMine. Account management software is inexpensive, easy to navigate, and allows salespeople to track all aspects of customer interaction. Currently, many firms are turning to online CRM applications that are more integrative than ACT or GoldMine yet less expensive than major company-wide CRM installations such as those provided by Siebel Systems. Examples of widely used online CRM products include SalesForce.com and SalesNet, both of which are user-friendly for salespeople. A key benefit of online CRM systems is that the firm "rents" them for a flat fee per month, avoiding major capital outlays.[20]

Beyond CRM, numerous other technology applications are enhancing personal selling, including teleconferencing, videoconferencing, and improved corporate Web sites that include FAQ pages that answer many customer queries. In the following sections, we'll mention many of these and other technologies salespeople use to do their jobs more efficiently.

Types of Sales Jobs

As you might imagine, types of sales jobs vary considerably. The person who processes a computer purchase over the phone is an **order taker**—a salesperson whose primary function is to process transactions that the customer initiates. Many retail salespeople are order takers, but often wholesalers, dealers, and distributors also employ salespeople to wait on customers. Because little creative selling is involved in order taking, this type of sales job typically is the lowest-paying sales position.

In contrast, a computer technician is a **technical specialist** who contributes expertise in the form of product demonstrations, recommendations for complex equipment, and setup of machinery. The technical specialist's job is to provide *sales support* rather than to actually close the sale. The technical specialist promotes the firm and works to stimulate demand for a product to make it easier for colleagues to actually gain the sale.

Sometimes a person whose job is to stimulate clients to buy is called a **missionary salesperson**.[21] Like technical specialists, missionary salespeople promote the firm and work to stimulate demand for its products but don't actually take orders for products. Pfizer salespeople do missionary sales work when they call on physicians to influence them to prescribe the latest and greatest Pfizer medication over competing products. However, no "sale" is made until doctors call prescriptions into pharmacies, which then place orders through their drug wholesalers.

The **new-business salesperson** is responsible for finding new customers and calling on them to present the company's products or services. As you might imagine, gaining the business of a new customer usually means that customer stops doing business with one of the firm's competitors. New-business selling requires a high degree of creativity and professionalism, so this type of salesperson is usually very well paid. Once a new-business salesperson establishes a relationship with a client, she often continues to service that client as the primary contact as long as the client continues to buy from the company. In that long-term relationship building role, this type of salesperson is an **order getter**. Order getters are usually the people most directly responsible for a particular client's business and may also have titles such as "account manager."[22]

More and more, firms are finding that the selling function is best handled by **team selling**. A selling team may consist of a salesperson, a technical specialist, someone from engineering and

---

order taker
A salesperson whose primary function is to facilitate transactions that the customer initiates.

technical specialist
A sales support person with a high level of technical expertise who assists in product demonstrations.

missionary salesperson
A salesperson who promotes the firm and tries to stimulate demand for a product but does not actually complete a sale.

new-business salesperson
The person responsible for finding new customers and calling on them to present the company's products or services.

order getter
A salesperson who works to develop long-term relationships with particular customers or to generate new sales.

team selling
The sales function when handled by a team that may consist of a salesperson, a technical specialist, and others.

design, and other players who work together to develop products and programs that satisfy the customer's needs. At IBM, for example, Esther Ferre manages the relationship with her large client by deploying a customized sales team that includes a variety of functional experts from inside IBM.

Approaches to Personal Selling

Personal selling is one of the oldest forms of marketing communication. Unfortunately, its image was tarnished by smooth-talking pitchmen who would say anything to make a sale. The profession was not helped by Pulitzer Prize–winning playwright Arthur Miller's famous character Willie Loman in *Death of a Salesman*. For generations of students, middle school and high school English and drama courses have required *Death of a Salesman* as a must-read. In the play, Willie Loman (as in "low man" on the totem pole—get it?) is a pathetic, burned-out peddler who leaves home for the road on Monday morning and returns late Friday evening, selling "on a smile and a shoeshine." His personal life is in shambles with two dysfunctional sons and a disaffected wife who hardly knows him. Great public relations for selling as a career, right?

Fortunately, personal selling today is nothing like Arthur Miller's harsh portrayal. Selling has moved from a transactional, hard-sell approach to an approach based on relationships with customers. Let's see how.

TRANSACTIONAL SELLING: PUTTING ON THE HARD SELL The *hard sell* practiced by Willy Loman is a high-pressure process. We've all been exposed to the pushy electronics salesperson who puts down the competition by telling shoppers that if they buy elsewhere they will be stuck with an inferior sound system apt to fall apart in six months. Or how about the crafty used car salesman who plays good cop/bad cop games using the sales manager or finance manager at the dealership as a foil? These hard-sell tactics reflect **transactional selling**, an approach that focuses on making an immediate sale with no concern for developing a long-term relationship with the customer.

As customers, the hard sell makes us feel manipulated and resentful and thwarts customer satisfaction and loyalty. It is a very short-sighted approach to selling—constantly finding new customers is much more expensive than getting repeat business from the customers you already have. And the behaviors promoted by transactional selling (i.e., doing anything to get the order) contribute to the negative image many of us have of "obnoxious salespeople." Such salespeople engage in these behaviors because they don't care if they ever have the chance to sell to you again. This is really bad business!

RELATIONSHIP SELLING: BUILDING LONG-TERM CUSTOMERS Today's professional salesperson is more likely to practice relationship selling than transactional selling. This means that the salesperson seeks to develop a mutually satisfying relationship with the customer. **Relationship selling** involves securing, developing, and maintaining long-term relationships with profitable customers.[23] *Securing* a customer relationship means converting an interested prospect into someone who is convinced that the product or service holds value for him. *Developing* a customer relationship means ensuring that you and the customer find more ways to add value. *Maintaining* a customer relationship means building customer satisfaction and loyalty so that the customer can be counted on to provide future business and won't switch to another source to purchase the products or services you sell.

The Selling Process

Many people find selling to be a great profession, partly because something different is always going on. Every customer, every sales call, and every salesperson is unique. Some salespeople are successful primarily because they know so much about what they sell. Others are successful because they've built strong relationships with customers so that they're able to add value to both the customer and their own firm—a win-win approach to selling. Successful salespeople understand and engage in a series of activities to make the sales encounter mutually beneficial.

transactional selling
A form of personal selling that focuses on making an immediate sale with little or no attempt to develop a relationship with the customer.

relationship selling
A form of personal selling that involves securing, developing, and maintaining long-term relationships with profitable customers.

Figure 14.1 Steps in the Creative Selling Process

In the creative selling process, salespeople follow a series of steps to ensure successful long-term relationships with customers.

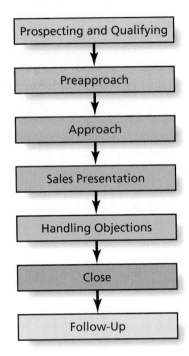

Successful personal selling is more likely if the salesperson undergoes a systematic series of steps called the **creative selling process**. These steps require the salesperson to seek out potential customers, analyze their needs, determine how product attributes provide benefits, and then decide how best to communicate this to the prospects. As Figure 14.1 shows, there are seven steps in the process. Let's take a look at each step.

STEP 1: PROSPECTING AND QUALIFYING **Prospecting** is the process of identifying and developing a list of potential customers, called *prospects* or *sales leads*. Leads can come from existing customer lists, telephone directories, and commercially available databases. The local library usually contains directories of businesses (including those published by state and federal agencies) and directories of association memberships. Sometimes companies generate sales leads through their advertising or sales promotion by letting customers request more information (in Chapter 12, we called this a *second-order response*). As we said earlier, trade shows are often an important source of sales leads, as are Web site visits by potential customers that are tracked by companies such as Accela Communications. Sales organizations turn to Accela to monitor, analyze, and summarize visitors to a company's Web site—in essence, to develop prospect lists. The lists are then turned over to salespeople for follow-up by phone or in person.

An emerging technology available to salespeople for prospecting is the development of online *social networks*. These are not "friendship" social networks, such as Friendster and Tribe, but rather business networks, such as LinkedIn, Ryze, and Spoke. These sites enable salespeople to create profiles, upload their personal address books to the site, and invite business colleagues to join the network. The site protocol then provides for contact, request for formal introductions, and information exchange. Business social networks are growing fast—LinkedIn boasts membership of over 200,000 and a join rate of over 25,000 per week.[24]

Another way to generate leads is through *cold calling*, when the salesperson simply contacts prospects "cold" without prior introduction or arrangement. It always helps to know the prospect, so salespeople might rely instead on *referrals*. Current clients who are satisfied with their purchase often give referrals—yet another reason to maintain good customer relationships.

creative selling process
The process of seeking out potential customers, analyzing needs, determining how product attributes might provide benefits for the customer, and then communicating that information.

prospecting
A part of the selling process that includes identifying and developing a list of potential or prospective customers.

However, the mere fact that someone is willing to talk to a salesperson doesn't guarantee a sale. Along with identifying potential customers, salespeople need to **qualify prospects** to determine how likely they are to become customers by asking questions such as the following: Are the prospects likely to be interested in what I'm selling? Are they likely to switch their allegiance from another supplier or product? Is the potential sales volume large enough to make a relationship profitable? Can they afford the purchase? If they must borrow money to buy the product, what is their credit history?

STEP 2: PREAPPROACH The **preapproach** consists of compiling background information about prospective customers and planning the sales interview. Important purchases are not made lightly, so it is foolish for a salesperson to blindly call on a qualified prospect and risk losing the sale because of a lack of preparation. Salespeople try to learn as much as possible about qualified prospects early on. They may probe prior purchase history, current needs, or, in some cases, information about their interests.

Salespeople can draw information about a prospect from a variety of sources. In the case of larger companies, financial data, names of top executives, and other information about a business may be found in such publications as *Standard & Poor's 500 Directory* or Dun & Bradstreet's *Million Dollar Directory*. A great deal of information needed for the preapproach can be found on customers' Web sites as well.

And if the salesperson's firm has a CRM system, he or she can use it to see whether information on the prospect exists in the system's database. Say, for example, a salesperson at Mike's Bikes is planning a call on a buyer at Greg's Rentals. If Mike's Bikes has had a CRM system in place for some time, any contacts with customers and potential customers (prospects) will have been recorded in the CRM database. The salesperson can simply run an inquiry about Greg's Rentals, and, with luck, the CRM database will have information on the company, prior purchases from Mike's Bikes, when and why they stopped buying from Mike's Bikes, and even the preferences of the particular buyer (if he was with Greg's Rentals at the time the data were recorded).

As useful as external databases and internal CRM systems are, the inside scoop on a prospect often comes from informal sources, such as noncompeting salespeople who have dealt with the prospect before. This background information helps salespeople set their goals and plan their strategy for the sales call.

STEP 3: APPROACH After the groundwork has been laid with the preapproach, it is time to **approach**, or contact, the prospect. During these important first minutes when the salesperson initiates contact with the prospective customer, several key events occur. The salesperson tries to learn even more about the prospect's needs, create a good impression, and build rapport. If the salesperson made contact with the prospect through a referral, the salesperson will probably say so up

Turn your web site visitors into customers.

LEADS Create web response programs quickly, easily and inexpensively.

Web-based marketing programs can be complicated and often involve people and departments you don't control. With LEADS (Lead Evaluation and Delivery System), no special programming, database skills, hardware or software is needed. LEADS can be used on a one-off basis with no annual contract or license fees.

LEADS is a web-based tool that gives you the power to:
- Quickly create data capture forms
- Publish them to the web
- Filter and classify information in real-time
- Analyze response data
- Automatically route leads for follow-up

Learn more now. Watch our brief interactive demonstration at **http://www.accelacommunications.com/leads** Or call Jeff Bodenmann at 646.486.9870.

A product of: **Accela** COMMUNICATIONS

Today, many leads come from visits to a company's Web site. Companies like Accela Communications work with sales organizations to develop Web response programs to effectively develop these leads and hopefully turn them into customers.

qualify prospects
A part of the selling process that determines how likely prospects are to become customers.

preapproach
A part of the selling process that includes developing information about prospective customers and planning the sales interview.

approach
The first step of the actual sales presentation in which the salesperson tries to learn more about the customer's needs, create a good impression, and build rapport.

INCREASED POWER AND FLEXIBILITY FOR YOUR SALES FORCE

Comprehensive customer management with GoldMine® 6.5

For more than 15 years, GoldMine software has helped over 50% of the FORTUNE 500¹ and over a million satisfied users manage their business relationships and increase productivity.

¥ Get instant access to customer and contact information with complete histories.

¥ Manage time with reminders, alerts and a full view of your schedule.

¥ Generate targeted, personalized correspondence from a centralized location.

¥ Receive immediate updates for your pipeline, and track the entire sales life cycle in real time.

¥ Share information across the whole team, inside and outside the office.

¥ Compatible with Palm OS¹ and Pocket PC mobile devices for anytime-anywhere access.

Maximize your sales opportunities now! Save up to $100¹ on GoldMine 6.5 at CompUSA or Office Depot.

GoldMine®

GoldMine 6.5
Free e-learning session with purchase!

Contact us:
800.776.7889
www.frontrange.com

COMP USA
WHERE AMERICA BUYS TECHNOLOGY.

Office DEPOT
What you need.
What you need to know.

FrontRange
SOLUTIONS®

*Subject to complete rebate and purchase terms and conditions.
Copyright ¹ 2 004 FrontRange Solutions USA Inc. All Rights Reserved. GoldMine, HEAT and other FrontRange Solutions products, brands and trademarks are property of FrontRange Solutions USA Inc. and/or its affiliates in the United States and/or other countries. Other products, brands and trademarks are property of their respective owners/companies.

CRM systems such as GoldMine are very popular because they help the sales force organize and utilize information about their customers, thus making salespeople better prepared to make the sales presentation.

sales presentation
The part of the selling process in which the salesperson directly communicates the value proposition to the customer, inviting two-way communication.

front: "Kevin Keenan with Hamdy Industries suggested I call on you."

During the approach, the customer is deciding whether the salesperson has something to offer that is of potential value to him. Also, the old saying, "You never get a second chance to make a good first impression," rings true here. A professional appearance tells the prospect that the salesperson means business and is competent to handle the sale. A good salesperson is well-groomed and wears appropriate business dress. He doesn't chew gum, use poor grammar or inappropriate language, mispronounce the customer's name, or seem uninterested in the call.

STEP 4: SALES PRESENTATION Many sales calls involve a formal **sales presentation** that lays out the benefits of the product and its advantages over the competition. The focus of the sales presentation should always be on ways the salesperson, her products, and her company can add value to the customer (and, in a business-to-business setting, to the customer's company). It is important for the salesperson to present this value proposition clearly, inviting involvement by the customer in the conversation. Let the customer ask questions, give feedback, and discuss her needs. Canned or formulated approaches to sales presentations are a poor choice for salespeople attempting to build long-term relationships. In fact, sales managers rate *listening* skills, not talking skills, as the single most important attribute they look for when hiring relationship salespeople.[25]

Where possible and appropriate, salespeople should incorporate technology such as laptops and DVDs to facilitate demonstrations into their sales presentations.

STEP 5: HANDLING OBJECTIONS It is rare when a prospect accepts everything the salesperson has to say without question. The effective salesperson anticipates *objections*, or reasons why the prospect is reluctant to make a commitment, and is prepared to respond with additional information or persuasive arguments. Actually, the salesperson should *welcome* objections because they show the prospect is at least interested enough to have considered the offer and seriously weigh its pros and cons. Handling the objection successfully can move a prospect to the decision stage. For example, the salesperson might say, "Ms. Robbins, you've said before that you don't have room to carry our new line of trail bikes, although you mentioned that you may be losing some sales by carrying only one brand with very few different models. If we could come up with an estimate of how much business you're losing, I'd be willing to bet you'd consider making room for our line, wouldn't you?"

STEP 6: CLOSE The win-win nature of relationship selling should take some of the pressure off salespeople to make "the dreaded close." But there still comes a point in the sales call where one or the other party has to move toward gaining commitment to the objectives of the call—presumably a purchase. This is the decision stage, or **close**. Directly asking the customer for his business doesn't need to be painful or awkward: If the salesperson has done a great job in the previous five steps in the creative selling process, closing the sale should be a natural progression of the dialogue between the buyer and seller.

There are a variety of approaches salespeople can use to close the sale. For example, a *last objection close* asks customers if they are ready to purchase, providing any concerns they have about the product can be addressed: "Are you ready to order if we can prove our delivery time frames meet your expectations?" Using an *assumptive* or *minor points close*, the salesperson acts as if the purchase is inevitable with only a small detail or two to be settled: "What quantity would you like to order?" In some cases, the salesperson interjects urgency by using a *standing-room-only* or *buy-now close* that suggests the opportunity might be missed if the customer hesitates. "This price is good through Saturday only, so to save 20 percent we should book the order now." When making such closes, salespeople must be sure the basis they state for buying now is truthful. Relationship selling–minded salespeople don't stretch the truth for short-term gain—they know the customer's long-term loyalty to them, their company, and its products is worth much more than booking one order today.

STEP 7: FOLLOW-UP **Follow-up** after the sale includes arranging for delivery, payment, and purchase terms. It also means the salesperson makes sure the customer received delivery and is satisfied. Follow-up also allows the salesperson to *bridge* to the next purchase. Once a relationship develops, the selling process is only beginning. Even as one cycle of purchasing draws to a close, a good salesperson is already laying the foundation for the next one.

A new technology called *voice-over Internet protocol (VoIP)*—using a data network to carry voice calls—is beginning to get a lot of use in day-to-day correspondence between salespeople and customers. With VoIP, the salesperson on the road can just plug into a fast Internet connection and then start making and receiving calls just as if he or she is in the office. Unlike using cell phones, there are no bad reception areas, and unlike using hotel phones, there are no hidden charges. Predictions are that by 2007, about 20 percent of U.S. firms will employ VoIP.[26] Of course, wireless technology in general is being used more and more by salespeople to provide seamless communication process with clients. BlackBerry has been around a while, but predictions are that as wireless becomes more and more predominant, the various devices used by salespeople to communicate (cell phone, fax, laptop, and so on) will become more and more integrated. Anyone for a software-packed personal digital assistant (PDA) with cell-phone capabilities, Internet access, and a global positioning system to help you find your way around? And can it also make a cup of coffee? [27]

Preparing demonstrations and video presentations for use in sales calls has been made much more user friendly by new software such as Visual Communicator, produced by Serious Magic.

close
The stage of the selling process in which the salesperson actually asks the customer to buy the product.

follow-up
Activities after the sale that provide important services to customers.

Sales Management

Few, if any, firms can succeed with just one star salesperson. Personal selling is a team effort that requires careful planning and salespeople available when and where customers need them. **Sales management** is the process of planning, implementing, and controlling the personal selling function. Let's review some of the major decisions sales managers who oversee this function must make, as outlined in Figure 14.2.

sales management
The process of planning, implementing, and controlling the personal selling function of an organization.

Setting Sales Force Objectives

Sales force objectives state what the sales force is expected to accomplish and when. Sales managers develop such sales force performance objectives as "acquire 100 new customers," "generate $100 million in sales," or even "reduce travel expenses by 5 percent." Firms engaged in relationship selling also state objectives related to customer satisfaction, loyalty, and retention (or turnover). Other common objectives are new customer development, new product suggestions, training, reporting on competitive activity, and community involvement.

Esther Ferre and her team at IBM have an objective of establishing and developing a relationship with their key client and identifying opportunities where the client can use IBM's IT products to reduce costs, improve productivity, or provide a unique market advantage. To meet these objectives, the sales team must have an in-depth understanding of the client's business and be able to successfully integrate IBM products, services, and solutions to solve the client's business issues.

Sales managers also work with their salespeople to develop *individual* objectives. We can identify two types of individual objectives. *Performance objectives* are readily measurable outcomes, such as total sales and total profits per salesperson. *Behavioral objectives* specify the actions salespeople must accomplish, such as the number of prospects to identify, the number of sales calls, and the number of follow-up contacts she should make.

Creating a Sales Force Strategy

sales territory
A set of customers often defined by geographic boundaries for whom a particular salesperson is responsible.

A sales force strategy establishes important specifics such as the structure and size of a firm's sales force. Each salesperson has the responsibility for a set group of customers—her **sales territory**. The territory structure allows salespeople to have an in-depth understanding of customers and their needs through frequent contact, both business and personal. The most common way to allot territories is geographically, minimizing travel and other field expenses. A *geographic sales force structure* usually is sized according to how many customers are found in a given area.

Figure 14.2 The Sales Force Management Process

Personal selling is a team effort that requires careful planning to place salespeople in the best locations at the best times.

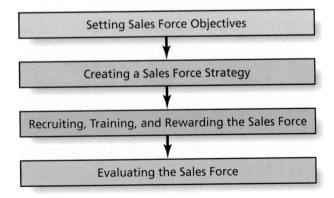

Setting Sales Force Objectives

↓

Creating a Sales Force Strategy

↓

Recruiting, Training, and Rewarding the Sales Force

↓

Evaluating the Sales Force

If the product line is diverse or technically complex, however, a better approach may be to structure sales territories based on different classes of products to enable the sales force to provide more product expertise to customers. Procter & Gamble has separate sales forces for its major product areas, such as beauty care, pharmaceuticals, food products, and so on.

Still another structure is *industry specialization*, in which salespeople focus on a single industry or a small number of industries. Esther Ferre's group at IBM takes the industry-specialized sales structure to an extreme level, focusing on only one very large customer for IBM. Such large clients are often referred to as *key accounts* or *major accounts*.

Putting salespeople out into the field is an expensive proposition that greatly impacts a company's profitability. Remember, the cost per customer contact is by far higher for personal selling than for any other approach to marketing communication. Thus, determining the optimal number of salespeople is an important decision. A larger sales force may increase sales, but at what cost? A smaller sales force will keep costs down, but this could backfire if competitors move in with larger sales forces and are able to develop strong customer relationships because each of their salespeople doesn't have to call on as many customers.

Today, many company sales meetings take place in virtual settings. This trend has reduced non-customer-related travel time of salespeople and their managers substantially and thus increased time available for making sales calls.

A very important contributor to the success of a sales force is keeping salespeople in front of customers as much of the time as possible—as opposed to spending their time traveling, in meetings, doing paperwork, or otherwise engaging in nonselling activities. Fortunately, the advent of *virtual meetings* (or *videoconferencing*) has cut down substantially on nonselling time for salespeople. Also, the ability to videoconference—to have members of a geographically diverse sales team hold meetings from their home offices—can cut non-customer-related travel costs substantially. Along the same lines, more and more companies are allowing salespeople to work from virtual offices through telecommuting. This trend keeps salespeople from having to make trips back and forth from home to some office location, allowing them instead to use precious travel time visiting customers.[28]

Recruiting, Training, and Rewarding the Sales Force

Because the quality of a sales force can make or break a firm, a top priority for sales managers is to recruit and hire the right set of people to do the job. These are people who have good listening skills, effective follow-up skills, the ability to adapt their sales style from situation to situation, tenacity (sticking with a task), and a high level of personal organization, among a variety of other well-documented key factors for salesperson success.[29] Companies screen potential salespeople to reveal these skills, along with useful information about interests and capabilities. Pencil-and-paper tests can determine quantitative skills and competencies in areas not easily assessed through interviews.

Are successful salespeople born or made? Probably elements of both inherent ability and trainable skills combine for success. *Sales training* teaches salespeople about the organization and its products and how to develop the skills, knowledge, and attitudes to facilitate success. For example, IBM's extensive sales training program helps Esther Ferre's salespeople focus on ways to identify customer needs and satisfy those needs through IBM's integrated IT solutions.

Advice for IBM

PROFESSOR
MIKE GATES
South Hills School of Business and Technology

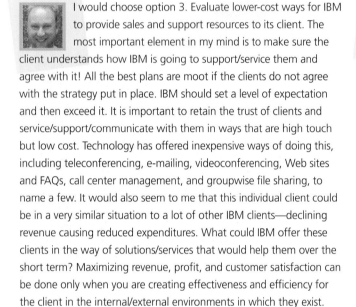

I would choose option 3. Evaluate lower-cost ways for IBM to provide sales and support resources to its client. The most important element in my mind is to make sure the client understands how IBM is going to support/service them and agree with it! All the best plans are moot if the clients do not agree with the strategy put in place. IBM should set a level of expectation and then exceed it. It is important to retain the trust of clients and service/support/communicate with them in ways that are high touch but low cost. Technology has offered inexpensive ways of doing this, including teleconferencing, e-mailing, videoconferencing, Web sites and FAQs, call center management, and groupwise file sharing, to name a few. It would also seem to me that this individual client could be in a very similar situation to a lot of other IBM clients—declining revenue causing reduced expenditures. What could IBM offer these clients in the way of solutions/services that would help them over the short term? Maximizing revenue, profit, and customer satisfaction can be done only when you are creating effectiveness and efficiency for the client in the internal/external environments in which they exist.

STUDENT
KATHERINE GRAHSLER
Drexel University

I would choose option 3. The decision to evaluate lower-cost channels would be the solution that most benefits IBM and its client. Developing a more cost-effective sales model would be the best option to sustain an adequate level of client satisfaction. The nature of IBM's business allows for the use of Web support, call centers, and resource sharing as efficient means of sales support. The client would accept this solution as a way to continue doing business at a fair price. Esther Ferre must consider the opportunity costs of the choices before she decides. Although minimizing face-to-face client interaction may not be ideal, it is far better than the ramifications of Esther's other two options. Option 3 would have the least damaging effect on the relationship, and it would allow IBM to continue the pursuit of future high-growth revenue opportunities.

Sales organizations desiring to improve performance often turn to firms such as Synygy, which provides software and services designed to create performance-driven organizations. Here they advertise that their clients achieve a return on investment of up to 173 percent by investing in their solutions.

Closely related to training, *development* strives to prepare salespeople personally and professionally for new challenges, such as promotions and management responsibilities. And training and development at IBM, like most great sales forces, takes place not just after the initial hire but rather on an ongoing basis throughout the salesperson's career. Many sales organizations turn to outside consultants to help them develop sales force training and development programs. Sometimes a boost in creative thinking from the outside can do wonders for developing more productive salespeople. Today, with budgets tighter than ever, sales organizations are expecting identifiable returns on investments in training, and outside firms can often deliver these quantifiable results.[30]

Of course, a way to motivate salespeople is to pay them well. This can mean tying compensation to performance. A *straight commission plan* is based solely on a percentage of sales the person closes. Under a *commission-with-draw plan*, earnings are based on commission plus a regular payment, or "draw," that may be charged against future commissions if current sales are inadequate to cover the draw. With a *straight salary plan*, the salesperson is paid a set amount regardless of sales performance. Sometimes straight salary plans are augmented with a *quota-bonus plan*, in which salespeople are paid a salary *plus* a bonus for sales above an assigned quota or for selling certain products that may be new or more profitable. Table 14.3 shows some average sales compensation figures.

Sales contests provide prizes (cash or otherwise) for selling specific products during a specific time period and can provide a needed short-term boost to sales. However, sales contests can be easily overused, motivating salespeople to simply wait to sell subject products until the contest period, resulting in no real long-term sales increase. Popular prizes for contest winners include cruises, other types of travel, and product selections from prize catalogs.

Incentives available to motivate salespeople come in all types. One popular approach is to use contests that provide possible travel rewards, such as a cruise on the *Queen Mary 2*.

Although many salespeople like to work independently, supervision is essential to an effective sales force. Sales managers often require salespeople to develop monthly, weekly, or daily *call reports*, a plan of action detailing which customers were called on and how things went. These call reports are likely generated electronically, often on laptop computers or even as a part of the firm's overall CRM initiative. They allow the sales manager to track what the salespeople are doing in the field, and they provide marketing managers with timely information about customers' responses, competitive activity, and any changes in the firm's customer base.

Evaluating the Sales Force

Of course, the job of sales management isn't complete until the total effort of the sales force is evaluated. First, it is important to determine if the sales force is meeting its objectives. If not, the sales manager must figure out the causes. Is it due to flaws in the design and/or implementation of the sales force strategy, or are there uncontrollable factors that have contributed? An overall downturn in the economy, such as the recession of 2000–2002, can make it impossible for the best of sales force plans to meet its original sales objectives.

Advice for IBM

PROFESSOR
GUNDARS KAUPINS
Boise State University

 I would choose option 2. Maintain the current level of sales and support resources, because of strategic and human resource management–related considerations. Part of the mission statement of IBM is to translate "advanced technologies into value for our customers through our professional solutions, services, and consulting businesses worldwide." Option 2, maintaining the current level of resources, allows the company to continue to build long-term, strong client relationships based on trust, considerable training, and detailed knowledge of the clients' business. This option best appears to coincide with the corporate mission.

Option 1, reducing the sales force, may be appealing in the short term. However, the long-term implications may be devastating. With downsizing, the survivors might be left with significant amount of extra work. If there is an upturn in the market, training new individuals with an in-depth knowledge of the client's business may be difficult. Option 3 also would be problematic because an in-depth knowledge of the client's business is required. In my opinion, call centers, Web support, and resource sharing might not provide the customer with sufficient service.

Critical strategic and human resource–related factors that could help IBM management choose between the options include the mission and objectives of IBM, short- and long-term objectives, economic projections, workload of the sales force, time and cost of training and replacing the sales force, and the short- or long-term nature of the sales compensation and incentives program.

Table 14.3	Average Salaries for Sales Personnel		
	Total Compensation	Base Salary	Bonus Plus Commissions
Executive	$144,653	$95,170	$49,483
Top Performer	$153,417	$87,342	$66,075
Mid-Level Performer	$ 92,337	$58,546	$33,791
Low-Level Performer	$ 63,775	$44,289	$19,486
Average of All Reps	$111,135	$70,588	$40,547

Source: "2004 Compensation Survey," *Sales and Marketing Management*, May 2001, 28–34.

Individual salesperson performance is normally measured against sales quotas for individual sales territories, even when compensation plans do not include bonuses or commissions based on the quotas. Other quantitative measures, such as number of sales calls and sales reports, may also be used in the evaluation.

In addition to quantitative measures, many firms also evaluate their salespeople on qualitative indicators of performance, such as salesperson attitude, product knowledge, and communication skills. Increasingly, as firms focus on relationship selling, the level of several important customer metrics such as customer satisfaction, loyalty, and retention/turnover have become key measures of superior salesperson performance.

Finally, the salesperson's expense account for travel and entertainment may be considered since the best sales record can mean little to a company's bottom line if the salesperson is gouging the company with outrageous expenses. You think you're creative when spending money? Here are some expenses a few salespeople actually submitted according to *Sales and Marketing Management* magazine:[31] chartering a private plane to make an appointment after missing a regularly scheduled flight, a Jaguar convertible rental car, a $2,300 round of golf for four people, a set of china for a salesperson's wife to use for a client dinner party, a "meeting" in the Virgin Islands during Christmas and New Year's, a $3,100 elk-hunting trip, a three-day houseboat rental with a crew and chef for $30,000, and season baseball tickets for $6,000. Wow! These sales jobs really do sound pretty good!

MEASURING VALUE
marketing metrics

How does a firm know whether a salesperson is effective? Obviously, the short answer is that she gets high sales volume and meets or exceeds sales goals. But just increasing total dollar or unit sales volume is not always a good indicator of salesperson success. The problem is, everything else being equal, salespeople who are compensated strictly on sales volume will simply sell whatever products are easiest in order to maximize total sales—these may not be the products with the highest profit margins, and they may not be important new products or other products that the firm has identified as key to grow for future success in the market.

Because of the problems with using raw sales volume as the sole indicator of salesperson success, some firms have turned to a variety of other metrics, including input and output measures. Input measures are *effort* measures—things that go into selling like the number and type of sales calls, expense account management, and a variety of nonselling activities, such as follow-up work and client service. Output measures, or the *results* of the salesperson's efforts, include sales volume but also can be number of orders, size of orders, number of new accounts, level of repeat business, customer profitability, and customer satisfaction.

Ultimately, the best approach to measuring salesperson success is to employ a variety of metrics that are consistent with the goals of the firm, to ensure the salesperson understands the goals and related metrics, and to link rewards to the achievement of those goals.

real people, real choices
How It Worked Out at IBM

Esther selected option 3. After completing an assessment on customer support requirements and revenue projections for the next few years, she developed a resource allocation plan. She also assessed what functions could be moved to the call centers and Web support functions, where the function could be supported at a lower cost. Some of the sales personnel were moved to other customer accounts where more revenue opportunities existed. Noncritical support functions were eliminated, transferred to remaining team members, or delivered through call center and Web support. Those resources in customer critical roles were maintained but were realigned to increase productivity.

This coverage model minimized the impact to the customer but improved the cost structure of the sales and support team. This new approach maintained customer satisfaction with a lower cost of sales and support.

How can you communicate your value in an interview? Learn what to expect on job interviews and a simple system for nailing the interview every time. Go to Chapter 14 in the *Brand You* supplement.

CHAPTER SUMMARY

1. **Explain what sales promotion is and describe some of the different types of trade and consumer sales promotion activities.** A sales promotion is a short-term program designed to build interest in or encourage purchase of a product. Trade sales promotions include merchandising and case allowances, trade shows, incentive programs, push money, and promotional products, among others. Consumer sales promotions include coupons, samples, contests/sweepstakes, bonus packs, and gifts with purchase, among others.

2. **Explain the important role of personal selling in the marketing effort.** Personal selling occurs when a company representative interacts directly with a prospect or customer to communicate about a good or service. Many organizations rely heavily on this approach because at times the "personal touch" can carry more weight than mass-media material. Generally, a personal selling effort is more important when a firm engages in a push strategy, in which the goal is to "push" the product through the channel of distribution so that it is available to consumers. Today's salespeople are less likely to employ transactional selling (hard-sell tactics) in favor of relationship selling in which they pursue win-win relationships with customers.

3. **List the steps in the personal selling process.** The steps in the personal selling process include prospecting and qualifying, preapproach, approach, sales presentation, handling objections, close, and follow-up. These steps combine to form the basis for communicating the company's message to the customer. Learning the intricacies of each step can aid the salesperson in developing successful relationships with clients and in bringing in the business for their companies.

4. **Explain the role of the sales manager.** Sales management includes planning, implementing, and controlling the selling function. The responsibilities of a sales manager include the following: creating a sales force strategy, including the structure and size of the sales force; recruiting, training, and compensating the sales force; and evaluating the sales force.

KEY TERMS

advergaming, 435
approach, 441
case allowance, 431
close, 443
creative selling process, 440
cross-promotion (cooperative promotion), 435
follow-up, 443
frequency programs, 433
merchandising allowance, 431
missionary salesperson, 438
new-business salesperson, 438

order getter, 438
order taker, 438
personal selling, 435
point-of-purchase (POP) promotion, 435
preapproach, 441
premiums, 434
promotional products, 431
prospecting, 440
push money, 431
qualify prospects, 441
rebates, 433
relationship selling, 439

sales management, 444
sales presentation, 442
sales promotion, 429
sales territory, 444
sampling, 434
team selling, 438
technical specialist, 438
telemarketing, 437
trade promotions, 429
trade shows, 431
transactional selling, 439

CHAPTER REVIEW

MARKETING CONCEPTS: TESTING YOUR KNOWLEDGE

1. What is sales promotion?

2. Explain some of the different types of trade sales promotions frequently used by marketers.

3. Explain some of the different types of consumer sales promotions frequently used by marketers.

4. What is the role played by personal selling within the marketing function?

5. What is relationship selling? How is it different from transactional selling?

6. What is prospecting? What does it mean to qualify the prospect? What is the preapproach? Why are these steps in the creative selling process that occur before you ever even contact the buyer so important to the sale?

7. What are some different ways you might approach a customer? Would some work better in one situation or another?

8. What is the objective of the sales presentation? How might you overcome buyer objections?

9. Why is follow-up after the sale so important in relationship selling?

10. Describe the role of sales managers. What key functions do they perform?

MARKETING CONCEPTS: DISCUSSING CHOICES AND ISSUES

1. Companies sometimes teach consumers a "bad lesson" with the overuse of sales promotion. As a result, consumers expect the product always to be "on deal" or have a rebate available. What are some examples of products where this has occurred? How do you think companies can prevent this?

2. In general, professional selling has evolved from hard-sell to relationship selling. Is the hard-sell style still used? If so, in what types of organizations? What do you think the future holds for these organizations? Will the hard sell continue to succeed—that is, are there instances where transactional selling is still appropriate? If so, when?

3. One reason cited by experts for the increase in consumer catalog shopping is the poor quality of service available at retail stores. What do you think about the quality of most retail salespeople you come in contact with? What are some ways retailers can improve the quality of their sales associates?

4. Based on the salesperson compensation figures supplied in the chapter, do think professional salespeople are appropriately paid? Why or why not? What is it that salespeople do that warrant the compensation indicated?

5. Would training and development needs of salespeople vary depending on how long they have been in the business? Why or why not? Would it be possible (and feasible) to have different training programs for salespeople at different career stages?

6. What would be the best approach for a sales manager to take in determining the appropriate rewards program to implement for his or her salespeople? What issues are important when determining the rewards to make available?

MARKETING PRACTICE: APPLYING WHAT YOU'VE LEARNED

1. Assume that you are a member of the marketing department for a firm that produces several brands of household cleaning products. Your assignment is to develop recommendations for trade and consumer sales promotion activities for a new laundry detergent. Develop an outline of your recommendations for these sales promotions.

2. Timing is an important part of a sales promotion plan. Marketers must decide when the best time is to mail out samples, to offer trade discounts, or to sponsor a sweepstakes. Assume that the introduction of the new laundry detergent in question 1 is planned for April 1. Place the activities you recommended in question 1 on a 12-month calendar. In a role-playing situation, present your plan to your supervisor. Be sure to explain why you have included certain types of promotions and the reasons for your timing of each sales promotion activity.

3. Assume that you have just been hired as a field salesperson by a firm that markets university textbooks. As part of your training, your sales manager has asked you to develop an outline of what you will say in a typical sales presentation. Write that outline.

4. In this chapter, you were introduced to several key success factors sales managers look for when hiring relationship salespeople. Are there other key success factors you can identify for relationship salespeople? Explain why each is important.

5. For you personally, what are the pros and cons of personal selling as a career choice? Make a list under the two columns and be as specific as you can in explaining each pro and con.

MARKETING MINIPROJECT: LEARNING BY DOING

The purpose of this miniproject is to help you understand the impact of different sales promotion activities.

1. With several of your classmates, first select a product that most college students buy regularly (e.g., toothpaste, shampoo, pens, pencils, soft drinks, and so on).

2. Develop a questionnaire that describes scenarios in which students find a new brand of the product with different sales promotion offers (e.g., a price-off package, a bonus pack, a coupon, and so on). Ask whether the students would buy the new brand with each offer and how many units of the product they would buy.

3. Report the results to your class along with recommendations you would give a company planning to introduce a new brand to the market.

REAL PEOPLE, REAL SURFERS: EXPLORING THE WEB

A problem that has confronted marketers for several years is how to efficiently distribute coupons. Some companies find the Internet to be a useful medium. In fact, a number of Web sites have been developed solely for the purpose of distributing coupons. Some of these follow:

> **www.hotcoupons.com**
> **www.valupage.com**
> **www.suzicoupon.com**
> **www.couponsonline.com**
> **www.couponcraze.com**

Visit several of these Web sites or use an Internet search engine to identify other coupon sites. Then evaluate the different sites you've visited by answering the following questions:

1. Generally describe each coupon Web site you visited. What kinds of coupons were there? How do consumers take advantage of the offers?

2. What in the design of each Web site is most useful to you as a consumer?

3. Do you think the coupons offered by the Web sites are useful to many consumers? Do you think consumers visit the Web site on a regular basis? What do you think would be some of the characteristics of the type of consumer most likely to be a regular visitor to these sites?

4. As a marketer, would you be likely to try to distribute coupons for your products over the Web sites? Why or why not?

5. How would you improve each of the Web sites you visited?

MARKETING PLAN EXERCISE

Assume for a moment that you are Esther Ferre at IBM. Consider the nature of her business—its products and services and the markets in which she competes for business. In developing her marketing plan, she must be very careful to use the elements of the marketing communication mix (1) in an integrated way so that she communicates a consistent message and (2) in a way that represents the best investment of promotional dollars that will give her the greatest returns.

1. Would personal selling be a high priority for Esther in her marketing plan? Why or why not?

2. What approach to personal selling would you recommend she build into her plan? Why do you recommend this approach?

3. Is there any place for sales promotion within Esther's marketing plan? Justify your answer. If you believe sales promotion should be planned for, what type(s) do you recommend, and why?

Marketing in Action Case

Real Choices at Amazon.com

What can the undisputed leader in Internet commerce, Amazon.com, do now that it has finally (at least temporarily) turned a profit? Well, for starters it can generate more sales volume and make more money than it has in the past. How? Sales promotion, of course.

Internet entrepreneur Jeff Bezos founded Amazon.com in a suburban Seattle, Washington, garage in July 1994. The time line of significant events for Amazon is quite impressive and belies the company's inability for so many years to actually generate a consistent profit. In July 1995, the company Web site was launched, and before the end of the month, Amazon had shipped product to all 50 states and 40 different countries. In 1996, the company's first full year of operations, sales totaled $15.7 million, and after just four full years of business, annual sales surpassed $1 billion. In May 1997,

Amazon.com generated $54 million with its first stock offering to the public, and in October of that year the company received its one-millionth order.

As these numbers indicate, the growth of the company has been staggering. Furthermore, Bezos has stated publicly that Amazon's strategy for the future is to continue getting bigger and to create more reasons why consumers would make Amazon their first choice for shopping rather than the local mall or discount store. Bezos believes that "the better you can make your customer experience, the more customers you'll attract, and the larger share of that household's purchases you will attract."

Amazon's approaches to sales promotion come in a variety of forms. For example, in the fall of 2003, it opened an online sporting goods store offering a variety of products from some of the biggest names in that line of merchandise. In conjunction with this opening, Amazon offered a $10 promotional certificate toward a future Amazon.com purchase for every $50 spent on items in the sporting goods store. Since Amazon's prices already are discounted from manufacturer-suggested prices, consumer premiums such as this have been rare in the past. But the company now provides gifts to customers in the form of free shipping on orders greater than $25. Another sales promotion provided by Amazon is free samples of its books and music offerings. To provide the samples, the company greatly upgraded its Web site to include several sample pages from the books it sells and sample tracks of music from the CDs that it sells. Spending money to improve the Web site represents an investment the company made to enhance the customer experience.

Finally, Amazon has started dropping coupon packs in every shipment it sends to customers. The coupons included in the pack often are for services or other products Amazon offers, but they also can include coupons from other companies outside of Amazon. Providing these coupons represent yet another way that Amazon is attempting to bring customers back to its Web site after an initial or follow-up purchase.

Despite the efforts Amazon has undertaken to attract new customers and increase sales through sales promotion, the company continues to struggle with an inability to consistently generate profits. Even though Amazon offers premiums, coupons, and free samples to boost volume, it is not yet generating enough business to eke out a profit with its slim profit margins. Consequently, the development of some sort of long-term customer loyalty program may be in order for the company.

Determining how to structure a loyalty program is tricky. Just look at the airlines, all of whom have costly loyalty (frequent flier) programs, giving none a competitive advantage. Amazon's Web site already provides a few aspects of a loyalty program, such as allowing customers to create wish lists in order to generate incremental business. However, is it really possible to generate long-term customer relationships, the type that keep customers coming back to your company to make additional purchases, when customers have no direct contact with a human being? Whether the actions Amazon.com has taken thus far to generate new customers, greater sales volume, and more consistent profits are enough is yet to be determined.

Things to Think About

1. What is the decision facing Amazon.com?
2. What factors are important in understanding the decision situation?
3. What are the alternatives?
4. What decision(s) do you recommend?
5. What are some ways to implement your recommendation(s)?

Sources: "Amazon.com Launches Sporting Goods Store," *Business Wire, Inc.*, September 22, 2003; Christine Frey and John Cook, "Amazon Posts Its First Annual Profits," *Seattle Post-Intelligencer*, January 28, 2004, News section, A1; David Stires, "Amazon's Secret," *Fortune*, April 19, 2004, 144; and Ken Ma Gill, "Amazon Customers Will Receive Other Merchants' Advertisements with Their Orders," *New York Sun*, October 10, 2003, Business section, 11.

Reflections | You need a special occasion to dress up. Being out of milk and oranges counts as a special occasion.

riveted
By Lee®

The Painter Jean. To find a store call 1-800-453-3348 or visit www.rivetedbylee.com

www.vfcorporation.com

real people, real choices

meet Mackey McDonald,
a Decision Maker at VF Corporation

first job out of school	what i do when i'm not working
Pilot for the U.S. Army.	Exercise and hang out with my children.

CREATING VALUE THROUGH SUPPLY CHAIN MANAGEMENT: CHANNELS OF DISTRIBUTION, LOGISTICS, AND WHOLESALING

Mackey McDonald is president, chairman, and chief executive officer (CEO) of VF Corporation. He was appointed chairman in October 1998, capping a distinguished career with the company where he began in 1983 as assistant vice president, merchandising services. He received a BA from Davidson College and an MBA in marketing management from Georgia State University.

Decision Time at VF Corporation

VF Corporation is the largest apparel manufacturer in the world. It is the parent company of Lee, Wrangler, Vanity Fair, JanSport, The North Face, and other well-known brands. A big corporation like VF relies on its partners to be sure its products make their way from its factories into consumers' shopping bags. These companies devote a great deal of attention to their partners, including suppliers, shipping companies, and retailers, to ensure that they are efficiently moving merchandise down the chain.

JCPenney is a major distributor for VF. VF could always count on the department store to move many of its products, especially garments made by VF's Lee division. In 1997, womenswear accounted for 40 percent of Lee's total retail sales

nationwide. Womenswear accounted for 75 percent of Lee's business with JCPenney, and sales were up 22 percent over the previous year. In 1998 and 1999, however, Lee's womenswear sales at JCPenney stores started to drop off. This was a puzzling problem since Lee's overall business, including womenswear, was strong (and growing) with its other retail distributors—May Company, Federated Department Stores, Kohl's, and Sears.

At the time, JCPenney was not competing well against specialty clothing retailers such as Gap, Old Navy, and The Limited Express, whose product lines were tailored to the lifestyle of the typical shopper at that store. In contrast, shoppers seemed to be visiting Penney's only to find bargains; the chain was struggling to convince its customers that it was a good place to find clothing that defined a specific lifestyle. During this time period, JCPenney allowed individual store managers to select and order products from the manufacturers with which the store did business. As a result, JCPenney was confusing customers by selling different brands at different stores.

When Lee's sales at Penney outlets dropped 20 percent between 1998 and 1999, Mackey knew VF had to take action. The ordering process had to be simplified so that shoppers wouldn't be confused about what they found in each Penney store. That meant paying attention to the way products were

career high

Becoming CEO of VF Corporation.

motto

Find solutions, not problems.

management style

Collaborative effort from a diversified team.

don't do this when interviewing with me

Camouflage the tough questions.

objectives

1 Understand the concept of the value chain and the key elements in a supply chain.

2 Explain what a distribution channel is and what functions distribution channels perform.

3 Describe the types of wholesaling intermediaries found in distribution channels.

4 Describe the types of distribution channels and the steps in planning distribution channel strategies.

5 Explain how logistics is used in the supply chain.

distributed as they made their way through the links in the chain that eventually connected VF with end consumers. Mackey and his team needed to strengthen links in the chain to boost sales of womenswear. But how to help? The team considered these options:

OPTION 1: Use VF's customized delivery program.

Implement VF's already-in-place Retail Floor Space Management program, which it had used successfully at other retail outlets including Wal-Mart and Shopko. VF developed this system to match product selection to the demographics and psychographic profiles of consumers shopping in each store. This customized approach was an innovation in the retail industry. The idea is to centralize product selection and be sure that product assortments available at each store would be clearly focused and easily replenished. However, JCPenney would give up control of its Lee's womenswear inventories. The store chain had balked at this system in the past because it just was not the way it did business. Penney's management felt it could run its business better than could an outside vendor.

OPTION 2: Deliver a bargain message.

Focus on volume and reduce the price of Lee and other VF national brands at Penney's, delivering a "bargain" message to the consumer. This option would help attract the price-driven consumer and probably boost sales in the short term. But it could reduce JCPenney's operating margins and devalue brand equity by sending the message that the jeans are a discount brand.

OPTION 3: Institute a pull strategy.

Maintain the status quo. JCPenney would continue to allow individual stores to buy and manage their own product assortments. It would be up to VF to engineer a "pull strategy" to lure consumers into the stores with national brand advertising promoting the availability of Lee products at Penney stores. JCPenney would not have to change its procedures and would maintain control of its inventory. However, the stores would continue to operate with inconsistent product lines, risking consumer loyalty and further eroding the effectiveness of the VF/Penney relationship.

Now, put yourself in Mackey McDonald's shoes: Which option would you choose, and why?

Place: The Final Frontier

As VF Corporation knows, you can make the best products in the world, but if the right clothes aren't available in the right assortment at the right prices and in the stores where customers are inclined to look for them, you have a problem.

Distribution may be the "final frontier" for marketing success. After years of hype, many consumers no longer believe that "new and improved" products really *are* new and improved. Nearly everyone, even upscale manufacturers and retailers, tries to gain market share through aggressive pricing strategies. Advertising and other forms of promotion are so commonplace they have lost some of their impact. Marketers know that *place* may be the only one of the Four Ps to offer an opportunity for competitive advantage.

That's why savvy marketers are always on the lookout for novel ways to distribute their products. For example, a new company called LidRock is prospering because it figured out a unique way to get music, video games, and movies into the hands of consumers: on mini CDs tucked into the lids of soft drinks. Based on the strategy "Hear It First, See It First, Play It First," LidRock sold 10 million of these lids within a year to fast-food outlets, theme parks, and movie theaters. They contain new music samples from such artists as Britney Spears, Avril Lavigne, 3 Doors Down, and Ashanti; clips and extras from movies such as *BarberShop 2* and *Scooby-Doo 2*; and video games such as *The Sims 2* and *Medal of Honor*.[1]

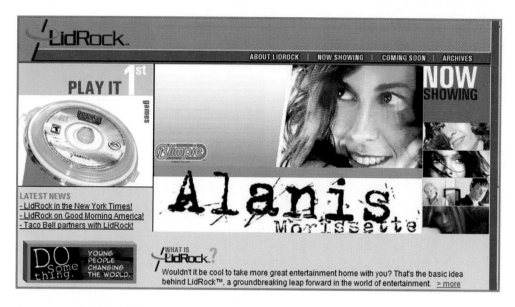

A company called LidRock discovered a competitive advantage by devising a novel way for record companies and movie studios to distribute samples—mini CDs stuck in the lids of beverage cups.

This chapter is about the science and art of getting goods and services to customers. As you'll see in Figure 15.1, we are now in Part V of the book: "Delivering the Value Proposition." A large part of the marketer's role in delivering the value proposition deals with understanding and developing effective distribution strategies. In this chapter, we will begin with a broad view of the company through the lens of the value chain concept. The *value chain* is a broad concept that spans all the activities involved in designing, producing, marketing, delivering, and supporting any product. Then we focus on the supply chain, which spans activities across multiple firms. The *supply chain* includes all the activities necessary to turn raw materials into a good or service and put it into the hands of the consumer or business customer. Often, of course, these activities are accomplished by firms outside your own company—firms with whom your company has likely developed some form of partnership or cooperative business arrangement.

Figure 15.1 Making and Delivering Value

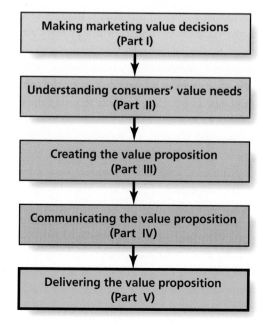

Making marketing value decisions
(Part I)

↓

Understanding consumers' value needs
(Part II)

↓

Creating the value proposition
(Part III)

↓

Communicating the value proposition
(Part IV)

↓

Delivering the value proposition
(Part V)

Figure 15.2 The Generic Value Chain

The value chain (a concept first proposed by Professor Michael Porter) encompasses all the activities a firm does to create products and services that in turn create value for the consumer and make a profit for the company.

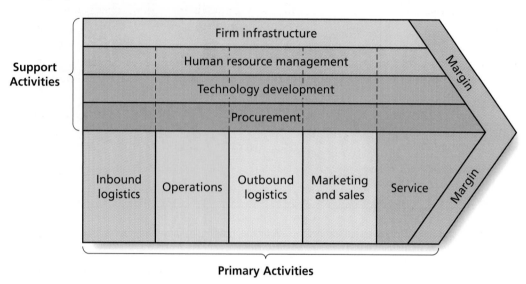

Source: Reprinted withs the permission of The Free Press, an imprint of Simon & Schuster, from Michael E. Porter, Competitive Advantage: *Creating and Sustaining Superior Performance*. Copyright 1985 by Michael Porter.

Next, we talk about distribution channels, which are a subset of the supply chain. Distribution channels are important because a large part of the marketer's role in delivering the value proposition deals with understanding and developing effective distribution strategies. Finally, we look at logistics management, which is the process of actually moving goods through the supply chain. We will define each of these terms in greater detail in subsequent sections of this chapter, but for now let's look at the broader activities of the value chain.

The Value Chain

Delivering value to the customer is of primary importance. As we saw way back in Chapter 1, the **value chain** concept is a way of looking at how firms deliver value. Companies deliver value by coordinating a range of activities that result in providing a product or service to the customer. As we can see in Figure 15.2, the value chain consists of five primary activities (inbound logistics, operations, outbound logistics, marketing and sales, and service) and four support activities (procurement, technology development, human resource management, and firm infrastructure).

Specifically, during the stage of *inbound logistics* activity, the company receives materials it needs to manufacture its products. This activity includes receiving the input materials, warehousing, and inventory control. In *operations*, activities transform the materials into final product form, such as by machining, packaging, and assembly. *Outbound logistics* activities ship the product out to customers, while *marketing and sales* handle advertising, promotion, channel selection, and pricing. *Service* activities enhance or maintain the value of the product, such as by installation or repair. The process is called a value chain because each of these activities adds value to the product or service the customer eventually buys.

Links in the Supply Chain

Whereas the value chain is an overarching concept of how firms create value, the **supply chain** also encompasses components external to the firm itself, including all activities that are necessary to convert raw materials into a good or service and put it in the hands of the consumer or

value chain
Encompasses all the activities a firm does to create products and services that in turn create value for the consumer and make a profit for the company.

supply chain
All the firms that engage in activities necessary to turn raw materials into a good or service and put it in the hands of the consumer or business customer.

business customer. Thus, **supply chain management** is the management of flows among the firms in a supply chain to maximize total profitability. These "flows" include not only the physical movement of goods but also the sharing of information about the goods. That is, supply chain partners must coordinate their activities with one another. For example, they need to communicate information about which goods they want to purchase (the procurement function), about which marketing campaigns they plan to execute (so that the supply chain partners can ensure there will be enough product to supply the increased demand from the promotion), and about logistics (such as sending advance shipping notices alerting their partners that products are on their way). Through these information flows, a company can effectively manage all the links in its supply chain, from sourcing to retailing.

The difference between a supply chain and a *channel of distribution* (a term we introduced back in Chapter 1) is the number of members and their function. A supply chain is broader; it consists of those firms that supply the raw materials, component parts, and supplies necessary for a firm to produce a good or service plus the firms that facilitate the movement of that product to the ultimate users of the product. This last part—the firms that get the product to the ultimate users—is the **channel of distribution**. (More on channels of distribution in a bit.)

In Chapter 1, we looked at a value chain for Hewlett-Packard. Now, let's take a closer look at the company's supply chain, shown in Figure 15.3. Of course, Hewlett-Packard uses hundreds of suppliers in manufacturing its computers and it sells those items through hundreds of online and off-line retailers worldwide. And it is noteworthy that the role of individual firms within the supply chain depends on your perspective. If we are looking at Hewlett-Packard's supply chain, Intel is a supplier, and Best Buy is a member of its channel of distribution. From Intel's perspective, Hewlett-Packard is a customer. From the perspective of Best Buy, Hewlett-Packard is a supplier.

In our example, Intel takes raw materials such as silicon and adds value by turning them into Pentium chips. Intel ships these chips to Hewlett-Packard, which combines them with the other components of a computer, again adding value. Best Buy takes the finished product and adds value by providing display, sales support, repair service, financing, and so forth for the customer.

Now that you understand the basics of the value chain and the supply chain, let's dig into the importance of distribution.

supply chain management
The management of flows among firms in the supply chain to maximize total profitability.

channel of distribution
The series of firms or individuals that facilitates the movement of a product from the producer to the final customer.

Figure 15.3 Supply Chain

The supply chain for computer maker Hewlett-Packard includes firms that supply component parts for the machines as well as retailers such as Best Buy and CompUSA. Each firm in the chain adds value to its inputs to provide the PC the consumer wants at the lowest cost.

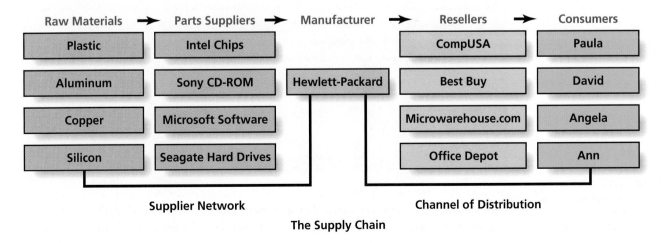

The Importance of Distribution: You Can't Sell What Isn't There!

So you've created your product. Priced it, too. And you've done the research to understand your target market and created a marketing message. Sorry, you're still not done—now you need to get what you make out into the marketplace. As noted earlier, a channel of distribution is a series of firms or individuals that facilitates the movement of a product from the producer to the final customer. In many cases, these channels include an organized network of producers (also called manufacturers), wholesalers, and retailers that develop relationships and work together to make products conveniently available to eager buyers.

Distribution channels come in different shapes and sizes. The bakery around the corner where you buy your cinnamon rolls is a member of a channel, as is the baked goods section at the local supermarket, the espresso bar at the mall that sells biscotti to go with your double mocha cappuccino, and the bakery outlet store that sells day-old rolls at a discount.

A channel of distribution consists of, at a minimum, a producer—the individual or firm that manufactures or produces a good or service—and a customer. This is a *direct channel*. For example, when you buy a gallon of strawberries at a farm where they're grown, that's a direct channel. Firms that sell their own products through catalogs, 800 numbers, or factory outlet stores use direct channels.

But life (or marketing) usually isn't that simple: Channels often are *indirect* because they include one or more **channel intermediaries**, firms or individuals such as wholesalers, agents, brokers, and retailers who in some way help move the product to the consumer or business user. For example, our strawberry farmer may choose to sell his acres of berries to a produce wholesaler that will in turn sell cases of the berries to supermarkets and restaurants that in turn sell to consumers.

Functions of Distribution Channels

Distribution channels perform a number of functions that make possible the flow of goods from the producer to the customer. These functions must be handled by someone, be it the producer or a channel intermediary. Sometimes the activities are delegated to the customer, like the person who picks up a new chair from the warehouse instead of having it delivered to his home.

Channels that include one or more organizations or intermediaries often can accomplish certain distribution functions more effectively and efficiently than can a single organization. This is especially true in international distribution channels where differences in countries' customs, beliefs, and infrastructures can make global marketing a nightmare. Even small companies can be successful in global markets by relying on distributors that know local customs and laws.

channel intermediaries
Firms or individuals such as wholesalers, agents, brokers, or retailers who help move a product from the producer to the consumer or business user.

Supermarkets like this one are channel intermediaries. They buy fresh fruits and vegetables from farmers and make them available to consumers on a daily basis.

Overall, channels provide the time, place, and ownership utility we described in Chapter 1. They make desired products available when, where, and in the sizes and quantities customers desire. Suppose, for example, you want to buy that perfect bouquet of flowers for a special someone. You *could* grow them yourself or even "liberate" them from a cemetery if you were really desperate (let's hope not!). Fortunately, you can probably just accomplish this task with a simple phone call or a few mouse clicks, and "like magic" the flowers are delivered to your honey's door.

Just think about what happened behind the scenes to make this possible. Many flowers, for example, are harvested and electronically sorted by growers, auctioned to buyers at a huge wholesale flower market in Amsterdam, shipped by air to importers in New York where they are inspected for insects and disease, transported to over 170 wholesalers around the country, and finally distributed to local florists who make them available to their customers. The channel members—the growers, the auction house, the importers, the wholesalers, and the local florists—all work together to create just the right bouquet for budding lovers—and save you a lot of time and hassles.

Distribution channels provide a number of logistics or physical distribution functions that increase the efficiency of the flow of goods from producer to customer. How would we buy groceries without our modern system of supermarkets? We'd have to get our milk from a dairy, our bread from a bakery, our tomatoes and corn from a local farmer, and our flour from a flour mill. And forget about specialty items such as Twinkies or Coca-Cola. The companies that make these items would have to handle literally millions of transactions to sell to every individual who craved a junk-food fix.

Distribution channels create *efficiencies* by reducing the number of transactions necessary for goods to flow from many different manufacturers to large numbers of customers. This occurs in two ways. The first is called **breaking bulk**. Wholesalers and retailers purchase large quantities (usually cases) of goods from manufacturers but sell only one or a few at a time to many different customers. Second, channel intermediaries reduce the number of transactions by **creating assortments**—providing a variety of products in one location—so that customers can conveniently buy many different items from one seller at one time.

Figure 15.4 provides a simple example of how distribution channels work. This simplified illustration includes five producers and five customers. If each producer sold its product to each

breaking bulk
Dividing larger quantities of goods into smaller lots in order to meet the needs of buyers.

creating assortments
Providing a variety of products in one location to meet the needs of buyers.

Figure 15.4 Reducing Transactions via Intermediaries

One of the functions of distribution channels is to provide an assortment of products. Because the customers can buy a number of different products at the same location, this reduces the total costs of obtaining a product.

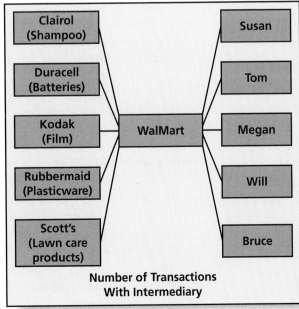

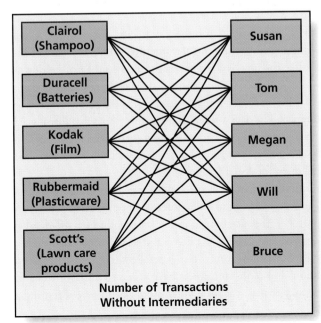 Number of Transactions Without Intermediaries

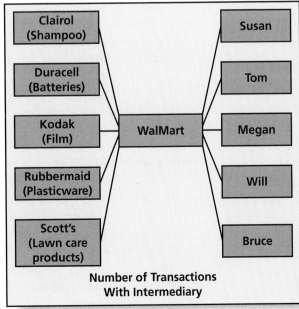 Number of Transactions With Intermediary

individual customer, 25 different transactions would have to occur, which is not an efficient way to distribute products. But with a single intermediary who buys from all five manufacturers and sells to all five customers, the number of transactions is cut to 10. If there were 10 manufacturers and 10 customers, an intermediary would reduce the number of transactions from 100 to just 20. Do the math: Channels are efficient.

The transportation and storage of goods is another type of physical distribution function. Retailers and other channel members move the goods from the production point to other locations where they can be held until they are wanted by consumers.

facilitating functions
Functions of channel intermediaries that make the purchase process easier for customers and manufacturers.

Channel intermediaries also perform a number of **facilitating functions**, functions that make the purchase process easier for customers and manufacturers. For example, intermediaries often provide customer services such as offering credit to buyers. Many of us like to shop at department stores because if we are not happy with the product, we can take it back to the store, where cheerful customer service personnel are happy to give us a refund (at least in theory). These same customer services are even more important in business-to-business markets where customers purchase larger quantities of higher-priced products.

Some wholesalers and retailers assist the manufacturer by providing repair and maintenance service for products they handle. An appliance, television, stereo, or computer dealer may serve as an authorized repair center, provide maintenance contracts, and sell essential supplies to customers. And channel members perform a risk-taking function. If a retailer buys a product from a manufacturer and it just sits on the shelf because no customers want it, she is stuck with the item and must take a loss. Perishable items present an even greater risk of spoilage.

Finally, intermediaries perform a variety of communication and transaction functions. Wholesalers buy products to make them available for retailers and sell products to other channel members. Retailers handle transactions with final consumers. Channel members can provide two-way communication for manufacturers. They may supply the sales force, advertising, and other types of marketing communication necessary to inform consumers and persuade them that a product will meet their needs. And, the channel members can be invaluable sources of information on consumer complaints, changing tastes, and new competitors in the market.

The Internet in the Distribution Channel

The Internet has become an important place for consumers to shop for everything from tulip bulbs to exotic vacations. By using the Internet, even small firms with limited resources enjoy the same market opportunities as their largest competitors in making their products available to customers around the globe.

E-commerce has resulted in radical changes in distribution strategies. For example, when Stephen King experimented with distributing his writing on the Internet, 400,000 copies of his novel *Riding the Bullet* were distributed free the first day, while other readers paid $2.50 to download it.[2] And many consumers find it far more convenient to read their daily newspapers or to receive their magazine subscriptions via the Internet. Even the *haute couture* fashion industry is evolving to meet the needs of cyber-shoppers: Just days after its 2004 runway show that introduced its current designs, the hot designer firm Proenza Schouler actually put its new styles up for auction on eBay. These clothes usually sell only at Neiman-Marcus and other luxury chains, some for more than $10,000. Bidders on eBay snagged them for deep discounts.[3]

Today most goods are mass-produced, and in most cases end users don't obtain products directly from manufacturers. Rather, goods flow from manufacturers to intermediaries and then on to the final customers. With the Internet, this need for intermediaries and much of what we assume about the need and benefits of channels is changing. For example, an increasing number of consumers are buying downloadable MP3 files from Internet retailers like iTunes, making retail music stores less necessary. As more and more consumers have access to faster broadband Internet service, downloadable DVDs may replace the local video store as a means of renting a favorite movie.

In the future, channel intermediaries that physically handle the product may become obsolete. Already, many traditional intermediaries are being eliminated as companies question the value added by layers in the distribution channel—a process called **disintermediation (of the channel of distribution)** (see Chapter 10). For marketers, disintermediation reduces costs in many ways: fewer employees, no need to buy or lease expensive retail property in high-traffic locations, and no need to furnish a store with fancy fixtures and decor. You can also see this process at work when you dine at many restaurants—anytime you choose a serve-yourself buffet or salad bar that reduces or even eliminates the need for an intermediary (otherwise known in this case as a server).

Some companies are using the Internet to make coordination among members of a supply chain more effective—in ways that end consumers never see. These firms are developing better ways to implement **knowledge management**, which refers to a comprehensive approach to collecting, organizing, storing, and retrieving a firm's information assets. These assets include both databases and company documents and the practical knowledge of employees whose past experience may be relevant to solving a new problem. If a firm tries to share this knowledge with other supply chain members, this can result in a win-win situation for all the partners.

For example, the supply chain in the textile and apparel industry begins with a raw material extraction or production stage (i.e., harvesting cotton or developing new synthetic fibers) that supplies the second stage of primary manufacturing. The second stage usually produces a standardized output of commodity material (fibers and fabrics) used to fabricate commodity products. Progressing downstream, commodity products from the previous stage are used by manufacturers, who apply product development technologies, patents, and proprietary features to further add value. The next stage includes marketers of consumer products, followed by distributors and, finally, the retailers who sell to the final consumer.

Many distribution channel members provide customer services. Appliance and electronics retailers like Best Buy offer repair and warranty services for many of the products they sell.

As technology continues to evolve, some companies are capitalizing on the ability of the Internet to link partners in the supply chain quickly and easily. For example, the textile and apparel division of DuPont (now a separate company known as Invista) manufactures such products as Lycra® and Coolmax® that usually go into activewear and outerwear products. Invista works closely with companies like Nike, Donna Karan, and Levi Strauss to develop fibers and fabrics that meet the needs of consumers. Invista's Lycra Assured® program helps to differentiate Invista's "stretch and recover" Lycra® fiber from low-cost competitors that sell the generic version (called Spandex) by providing manufacturers with extensive information they can access online about performance characteristics of their products.[4]

So far, we've learned what a distribution channel is and about some of the functions it performs. Now let's find out about different types of channel intermediaries and channel structures.

disintermediation (of the channel of distribution)
The elimination of some layers of the channel of distribution in order to cut costs and improve the efficiency of the channel.

knowledge management
A comprehensive approach to collecting, organizing, storing, and retrieving a firm's information assets.

The Composition of Channels: Types of Wholesaling Intermediaries

How can you get your hands on a new Dave Matthews T-shirt? You could pick one up at your local music store, at a trendy clothing store like Hot Topic, or directly over the Internet. You might buy an "official Dave Matthews concert T-shirt" from vendors during a show. Alternatively,

Advice for VF Corporation

PROFESSOR ROBERT COSENZA
University of Mississippi

I would choose option 1 since it allows VF and JCPenney to forge a stronger relationship/bond and create better value/profitability for both. Option 2 would seem to hamper the brand image and devalue it so should only be used as a desperate measure. Option 3 (favored status) might create conflict with JCPenney's other channel members. However, the implementation of option 3 would not be easy because of the "control" issues at JCPenney. Therefore, I would suggest that VF provide a testing framework (show how sales/profitability would be increased over a period of time) to convince JCPenney's management of this new approach rather than dictating it to them.

PROFESSOR THEODORE WALLIN
Syracuse University

I would choose option 1. It would be the best way of directly solving VF's problems and bring consistency and cost-saving possibilities to the direction it gives its supply chain. The other solutions are indirect and could lead to a splintering of VF's marketing thrust, particularly insofar as conflicting pricing policies were established. Certainly, other VF retailers, such as Wal-Mart, would also be in a discounting medium, and special attention to JCPenney would be disruptive. There are substantial benefits to JCPenney in the Retail Floor Space Management program, making the work of local managers simpler and, likely, more effective; these benefits should be put across to the management at JCPenney. The other proposed solutions deal with issues of pricing and advertising, whereas the key problem here is in supply chain: inventories, delivery, space utilization, and customer supply with relevant merchandise.

you might get a "deal" on a bootlegged, unauthorized version of the same shirt being sold from a suitcase by a shady guy standing *outside* the stadium. It might even be possible to buy it on the Home Shopping Network. Each of these distribution alternatives traces a different path from producer to consumer. Let's look at the different types of wholesaling intermediaries and at different channel structures. We'll hold off focusing on retailers, which are usually the last link in the chain, until the next chapter.

wholesaling intermediaries
Firms that handle the flow of products from the manufacturer to the retailer or business user.

Wholesaling intermediaries are firms that handle the flow of products from the manufacturer to the retailer or business user. There are many different types of consumer and business-to-business wholesaling intermediaries. Some of these are independent, but manufacturers and retailers can own them, too. Table 15.1 summarizes the important characteristics of each.

independent intermediaries
Channel intermediaries that are not controlled by any manufacturer but instead do business with many different manufacturers and many different customers.

Independent Intermediaries

Independent intermediaries do business with many different manufacturers and many different customers. Because they are not owned or controlled by any manufacturer, they make it possible for many manufacturers to serve customers throughout the world while keeping prices low.

merchant wholesalers
Intermediaries that buy goods from manufacturers (take title to them) and sell to retailers and other business-to-business customers.

MERCHANT WHOLESALERS **Merchant wholesalers** are independent intermediaries that buy goods from manufacturers and sell to retailers and other business-to-business customers. Because merchant wholesalers take title to the goods (i.e., they legally own them), they assume certain risks and can suffer losses if products get damaged, become outdated or obsolete, are stolen, or just don't sell. On the other hand, because they own the products, they are free to develop their own marketing strategies, including setting the prices they charge their customers.

Table 15.1 Types of Intermediaries

Intermediary Type	Description	Advantages
INDEPENDENT INTERMEDIARIES	Do business with many different manufacturers and many different customers	Used by most small- to medium-size firms
Merchant Wholesalers	Buy (take title to) goods from producers and sell to organizational customers; either full or limited function	Allow small manufacturers to serve customers throughout the world while keeping costs low
Cash-and-carry wholesalers	Provide products for small-business customers who purchase at wholesaler's location	Distribute low-cost merchandise for small retailers and other business customers
Truck jobbers	Deliver perishable food and tobacco items to retailers	Ensure perishable items are delivered and sold efficiently
Drop shippers	Take orders from and bill retailers for products drop-shipped from manufacturer	Facilitate transactions for bulky products
Mail-order wholesalers	Sell through catalogs, telephone, or mail order	Provide reasonable price selling options to small organizational customers
Rack jobbers	Provide retailers with display units, check inventories, and replace merchandise for the retailers	Provide merchandising services to retailers
Merchandise Agents and Brokers	Provide services in exchange for commissions	Maintain legal ownership of product by the seller
Manufacturers' agents	Utilize independent salespeople; carry several lines of noncompeting products	Supply sales function for small and new firms
Selling agents, including export/import agents	Handle entire output of one or more products	Handle all marketing functions for small manufacturers
Commission merchants	Receive commission on sales price of product	Provide efficiency primarily in agricultural products market
Merchandise brokers, including export/import brokers	Identify likely buyers and bring buyers and sellers together	Enhance efficiency in markets where there are lots of small buyers and sellers
MANUFACTURER-OWNED INTERMEDIARIES	Limit operations to one manufacturer	Create efficiencies for large firms
Sales branches	Maintain some inventory in different geographic areas (similar to wholesalers)	Provide service to customers in different geographic areas
Sales offices	Carry no inventory; availability in different geographic areas	Reduce selling costs and provide better customer service
Manufacturers' showrooms	Display products attractively for customers to visit	Facilitate examination of merchandise by customers at a central location

- *Full-service merchant wholesalers* provide a wide range of services for their customers, including delivery, credit, product-use assistance, repairs, advertising, and other promotional support—even market research. Full-service wholesalers often have their own sales force to call on businesses and organizational customers. Some general merchandise wholesalers carry a large variety of different items, whereas specialty wholesalers carry an extensive assortment of a single product line. For example, a candy wholesaler would carry only candy and gum but stock enough different varieties to give your dentist nightmares for a year.

- In contrast, *limited-service merchant wholesalers* provide fewer services for their customers. Like full-service wholesalers, limited-service wholesalers **take title** to merchandise but are

take title
To accept legal ownership of a product and the accompanying rights and responsibilities of ownership.

Rack jobbers are full-service merchant wholesalers. These intermediaries own and maintain product display racks in retail stores.

less likely to provide such services as delivery, credit, or marketing assistance to retailers. Specific types of limited-service wholesalers include the following:

- *Cash-and-carry wholesalers* provide low-cost merchandise for retailers and industrial customers that are too small for other wholesalers' sales representatives to call on. Customers pay cash for products and provide their own delivery. Some popular cash-and-carry product categories include groceries, office supplies, and building materials.

- *Truck jobbers* carry their products to small business customer locations for their inspection and selection. Truck jobbers often supply perishable items such as fruit and vegetables to small grocery stores. For example, a bakery truck jobber calls on supermarkets, checks the stock of bread on the shelves, removes outdated items, and suggests how much bread the store needs to reorder.

- *Drop shippers* are limited-function wholesalers that take title to the merchandise but never actually take possession of it. Drop shippers take orders from and bill retailers and industrial buyers, but the merchandise is shipped directly from the manufacturer. Because they take title to the merchandise, they assume the same risks as other merchant wholesalers. Drop shippers are important to both the producers and the customers of bulky products, such as coal, oil, or lumber.

- *Mail-order wholesalers* sell products to small retailers and other industrial customers, often located in remote areas, through catalogs rather than a sales force. They usually carry products in inventory and require payment in cash or by credit card before shipment. Mail-order wholesalers supply such products as cosmetics, hardware, and sporting goods.

- *Rack jobbers* supply retailers with such specialty items as health and beauty products, and magazines. Rack jobbers get their name because they own and maintain the product display racks in grocery stores, drugstores, and variety stores. These wholesalers visit retail customers on a regular basis to maintain levels of stock and refill their racks with merchandise.

merchandise agents or brokers
Channel intermediaries that provide services in exchange for commissions but never take title to the product.

MERCHANDISE AGENTS OR BROKERS **Merchandise agents or brokers** are a second major type of independent intermediary. Agents and brokers provide services in exchange for commissions. They may or may not take possession of the product, but they never take title; that is, they do not

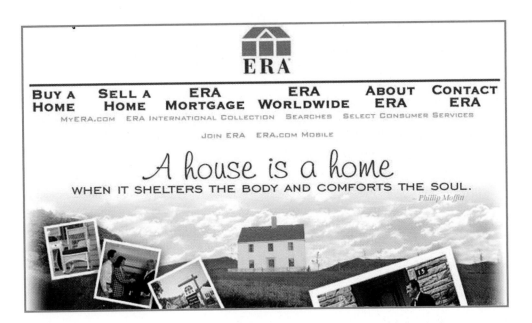

Real estate brokers are independent intermediaries whose job it is to identify likely buyers and sellers and to bring the two together.

accept legal ownership of the product. Agents normally represent buyers or sellers on an ongoing basis, whereas brokers are employed by clients for a short period of time.

- *Manufacturers' agents*, also referred to as *manufacturers' reps*, are independent salespeople who carry several lines of noncompeting products. They have contractual arrangements with manufacturers that outline territories, selling prices, and other specific aspects of the relationship. These agents have little if any supervision and are compensated with commissions based on a percentage of what they sell. Manufacturers' agents often develop strong customer relationships and provide an important sales function for small and new companies.

- *Selling agents*, including export/import agents, market a whole product line or one manufacturer's total output. They are often seen as independent marketing departments because they perform the same functions as full-service wholesalers but do not take title to products. Unlike manufacturers' agents, selling agents have unlimited territories and control the pricing, promotion, and distribution of their products. Selling agents are found in such industries as furniture, clothing, and textiles.

- *Commission merchants* are sales agents who receive goods, primarily agricultural products such as grain or livestock, on *consignment*. That is, they take possession of products without taking title. Although sellers may state a minimum price they are willing to take for their products, commission merchants are free to sell the product for the highest price they can get. Commission merchants receive a commission on the sales price of the product.

- *Merchandise brokers*, including export/import brokers, are intermediaries that facilitate transactions in markets such as real estate, food, and used equipment in which there are lots of small buyers and sellers. Brokers identify likely buyers and sellers and bring the two together in return for a fee received when the transaction is completed.

Manufacturer-Owned Intermediaries

Sometimes manufacturers set up their own channel intermediaries. In this way, they are able to have separate business units that perform all the functions of independent intermediaries while at the same time maintaining complete control over the channel.

- *Sales branches* are manufacturer-owned facilities that, like independent wholesalers, carry inventory and provide sales and service to customers in a specific geographic area. Sales branches are found in such industries as petroleum products, industrial machinery and equipment, and motor vehicles.
- *Sales offices* are manufacturer-owned facilities that, like agents, do not carry inventory but provide selling functions for the manufacturer in a specific geographic area. Because they allow members of the sales force to be located close to customers, they reduce selling costs and provide better customer service.
- *Manufacturers' showrooms* are manufacturer-owned or leased facilities in which products are permanently displayed for customers to visit. Manufacturers' showrooms are often located in or near large merchandise marts, such as the furniture market in High Point, North Carolina. Merchandise marts are often multiple buildings in which one or more industries hold trade shows and many manufacturers have permanent showrooms. Retailers can come either during a show or all year long to see the manufacturer's merchandise and make business-to-business purchases.

Types of Distribution Channels

Firms face many choices when structuring distribution channels. Should they sell directly to consumers and business users? Would they benefit by including wholesalers, retailers, or both in the channel? Would it make sense to sell directly to some customers but use retailers to sell to other customers? Of course, there is no single best channel for all products. The marketing manager must select a channel structure that creates a competitive advantage for the firm and its products based on the size and needs of the target market. Let's consider some of the factors these managers need to think about.

channel levels

The number of distinct categories of intermediaries that populate a channel of distribution.

When developing place or distribution strategies, marketers first consider different **channel levels**, or the number of distinct categories of intermediaries that make up a channel of distribution. Many different factors have an impact on this decision. What channel members are available? How large is the market, how frequently do consumers purchase the product, and what services do they require? Figure 15.5 summarizes the different structures a distribution channel can take. The producer and the customer are always members, so the shortest channel possible has two levels. Using a retailer adds a third level, a wholesaler adds a fourth level, and so on. Different channel structures exist for both consumer and business-to-business markets.

Consumer Channels

As we noted earlier, the simplest channel is a direct channel. Why do some producers sell directly to customers? One reason is that a direct channel may allow the producer to serve its customers better and at a lower price than is possible using a retailer. By using a direct channel, the strawberry farmer makes sure his customers have fresher strawberries than if he sells the berries through a local supermarket. Furthermore, if the farmer sells the berries through a supermarket, the price will be higher because of the supermarket's costs of doing business and required profit on the berries. In fact, sometimes this is the *only* way to sell the product, because using channel intermediaries may boost the price above what consumers are willing to pay.

For both large and small firms, one of the newest means of selling in a direct channel is the Internet. For example, small entrepreneurs Richard Lodico and Vinny Barbieri, owners of Eastern Meat Farms Italian Market, have found Internet sales are a great way to expand their business to new markets.[5] For years, Lodico and Barbieri shipped sausages and cheeses across the country but they didn't feel there was enough volume to justify the expense of direct marketing. However, when the Internet offered them the opportunity to sell to customers all around the globe with only $1,800 per month in Web charges, **www.salami.com** was born. The company ships each order using styrofoam

Figure 15.5 Different Types of Channels of Distribution

Channels differ in the number of channel members that participate.

Major Types of Channels of Distribution

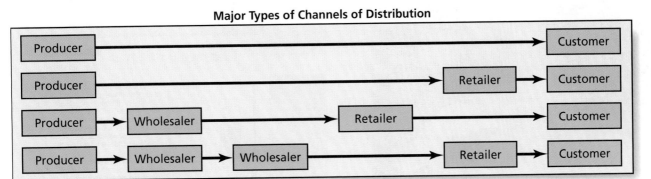

Typical Consumer Channels

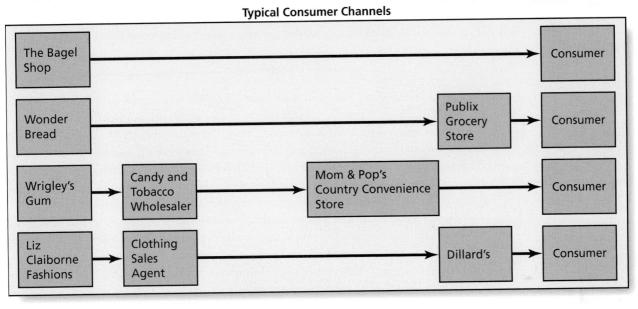

Business-to-Business Channels

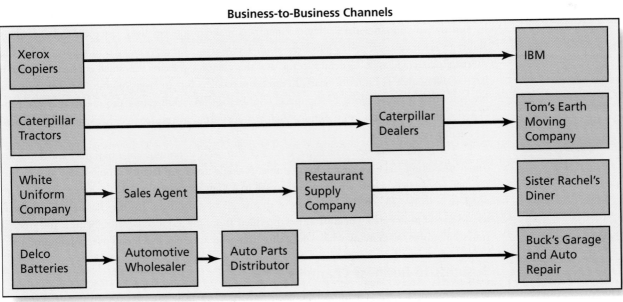

Richard Lodico and Vinny Barbieri, owners of Eastern Meat Farms Italian Market, used the Internet to expand their business as Salami.com. It's turned out to be a meaty distribution strategy.

and ice packs to ensure that customers from around the globe receive high-quality, fresh products, often for less than half the price they would have to pay for similar delicacies locally. Hot dog!

Another reason to use a direct channel is control. When the producer handles distribution, it maintains control of pricing, service, and delivery—all elements of the transaction. Because distributors and dealers carry many products, it can be difficult to get their sales forces to focus on selling one product. In a direct channel, a producer works directly with customers, gaining insights into trends, customer needs and complaints, and the effectiveness of its marketing strategies.

Why do producers choose to use indirect channels to reach consumers? A reason in many cases is that customers are familiar with certain retailers or other intermediaries—it's where they always go to look for what they need. That's why a big company like VF relies so much on well-known retailers. Getting customers to change their normal buying behavior, for example, convincing consumers to buy their laundry detergent or frozen pizza from a catalog or over the Internet instead of from the corner supermarket, would be difficult.

In addition, intermediaries help producers in all the ways described earlier. By creating utility and transaction efficiencies, channel members make producers' lives easier and enhance their ability to reach customers. The *producer–retailer–consumer channel* portrayed in Figure 15.5 is the shortest indirect channel. General Electric uses this channel when its sells small appliances through large retailers such as Target or Sears. Because the retailers buy in large volume, they can buy at a low price that is passed along to shoppers. The size of these retail giants also means they can provide the physical distribution functions such as transportation and storage that wholesalers handle for smaller retail outlets.

The *producer–wholesaler–retailer–consumer channel* is a common distribution channel in consumer marketing. Take ice cream, for example. A single ice-cream factory supplies, say, four or five regional wholesalers. These wholesalers then sell to 400 or more retailers such as grocery stores. The retailers in turn each sell the ice cream to thousands of customers. In this channel, the regional wholesalers combine many manufacturers' products to supply to grocery stores. Because the grocery stores do business with many wholesalers, this arrangement results in a broad selection of products.

Business-to-Business Channels

Business-to-business distribution channels, as the name suggests, facilitate the flow of goods from a producer to an organizational or business customer. Generally, business-to-business channels parallel consumer channels in that they may be direct or indirect. For example, the simplest indirect channel in industrial markets occurs when the single intermediary—a merchant wholesaler referred to as an industrial distributor rather than a retailer—buys products from a manufacturer and sells them to business customers.

Direct channels are more common to business-to-business markets than to consumer markets. This is because business-to-business marketing often means selling high-dollar, high-profit items (a single piece of industrial equipment may cost hundreds of thousands of dollars) to a market made up of only a few customers. In such markets, it makes sense financially for a company to develop its own sales force and sell directly to customers—that is, the investment in an in-house sales force pays off.

Distribution Channels for Services

Because services are intangible, there is no need to worry about storage, transportation, and the other functions of physical distribution. In most cases, the service travels directly from the producer to the customer. However, some services do need an intermediary, often called an *agent*, who helps the parties complete the transaction. Examples include insurance agents, stockbrokers, and travel agents.

Dual Distribution Systems

Figure 15.5 shows simple distribution channels. Well, once again we are reminded that life (or marketing) is rarely that simple: Producers, dealers, wholesalers, retailers, and customers alike may actually interact with more than one type of channel. We call these *dual* or *multiple distribution systems.*

The pharmaceutical industry provides a good example of multiple-channel usage. Pharmaceutical companies distribute their products in at least three types of channels. First, they sell to hospitals, clinics, and other organizational customers directly. These customers buy in quantity, purchasing a wide variety of products. Because in hospitals and clinics pills are dispensed one at a time rather than in bottles of 50, hospitals and clinics require different product packaging than when the products are sold to other types of customers. Pharmaceuticals' second channel is an indirect consumer channel in which the manufacturer sells to large drug store chains like Walgreens that distribute the medicines to their stores across the country. Alternatively, some of us would rather purchase our prescriptions in a more personal manner from the local independent drugstore where we can still get an ice-cream soda while we wait. In this version of the indirect consumer channel, the manufacturer sells to drug wholesalers that in turn supply these independents. Finally, third-party payers such as HMOs, PPOs, and insurance companies are a third type of channel to which pharmaceutical companies sell directly.

A new development in the drug arena is the emergence of online sales of drugs from Canadian companies that are offering pharmaceuticals at much lower prices than available in the United States. U.S. drug manufacturers are pushing to halt this practice, while state legislatures are considering setting up state-run Web sites to let consumers find and buy drugs from Canada in order to save money. States like Wisconsin and Minnesota already run Web sites that help consumers shop for Canadian drugs.[6]

Hybrid Marketing Systems

Instead of serving a target market with a single channel, some companies have added new channels—direct sales, distributors, retail sales, and direct mail. As they add channels and communications methods, they create a **hybrid marketing system**.[7] For example, at one time, IBM ThinkPads were available only from IBM salespeople. Today, IBM ThinkPads are sold through dealers, catalog operations, direct mail, and retail stores. Hybrid marketing systems can offer companies certain competitive advantages, including increased coverage of the market, lower marketing costs, and a greater potential for customization.

hybrid marketing system
A marketing system that uses a number of different channels and communication methods to serve a target market.

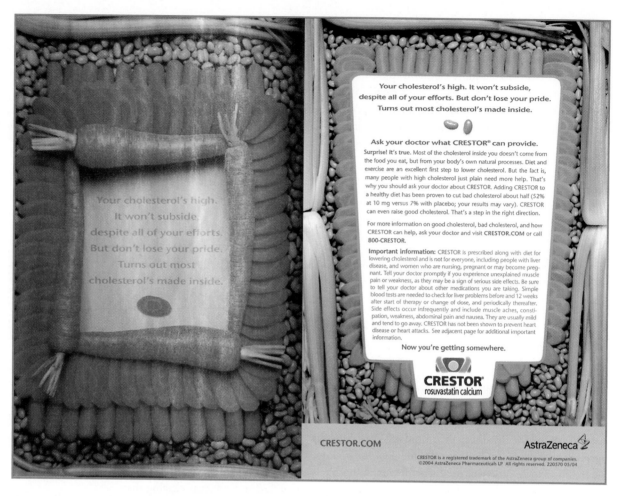

Pharmaceutical companies usually interact with more than one channel. They may sell directly to hospitals, while consumers often buy their prescription medicines from retail drugstores.

Now we know what distribution channels and channel intermediaries are and the role of channel members in the distribution of goods and services. We also know that not all channels are alike. Some channels are direct while others are indirect, and indirect channels can be quite complex. The next section is about how marketers plan channel strategies to meet customer needs better than the competition—that is, seeking the all-important competitive advantage.

Planning a Channel Strategy

Do customers want products in large or small quantities? Do they insist on buying them locally, or will they purchase from a distant supplier? How long are they willing to wait to get the product? Inquiring marketers want to know!

Distribution planning is best accomplished when marketers follow the steps in Figure 15.6. In this section, we will first look at how manufacturers decide on distribution objectives and then examine what influences distribution decisions. Finally, we'll talk about how firms select different distribution strategies and tactics.

Firms that operate within a channel of distribution—manufacturers, wholesalers, and retailers—do *distribution planning*. In this section, our perspective focuses on distribution planning by producers and manufacturers rather than intermediaries because they, more often than intermediaries, take a leadership role in creating a successful distribution channel.

Figure 15.6 Steps in Distribution Planning

Distribution planning begins with setting channel objectives and includes developing channel strategies and tactics.

1. **Develop Distribution Objectives**

2. **Evaluate Internal and External Environmental Influences**

3. **Choose a Distribution Strategy**
   - Number of Channel Levels
   - Conventional, Vertical, or Horizontal System
   - Intensive, Exclusive, or Selective Distribution

4. **Develop Distribution Tactics**
   - Select Channel Partners
   - Manage the Channel
   - Develop Logistics Strategies
     - Order Processing
     - Warehousing
     - Materials Handling
     - Transportation
     - Inventory Control

Step 1: Develop Distribution Objectives

The first step in deciding on a distribution plan is to develop objectives that support the organization's overall marketing goals. How can distribution work with the other elements of the marketing mix to increase profits? To increase market share? To increase volume of sales? In general, the overall objective of any distribution plan is to make a firm's product available when, where, and in the quantities customers want at the minimum cost. More specific distribution objectives, however, depend on the characteristics of the product and the market.

For example, if the product is bulky, a primary distribution objective may be to minimize shipping costs. If the product is fragile, a goal may be to develop a channel that minimizes handling. In introducing a new product to a mass market, a channel objective may be to provide maximum product exposure or to make the product available close to where customers live and work. Sometimes marketers make their product available where similar products are sold so that consumers can compare prices.

Step 2: Evaluate Internal and External Environmental Influences

After setting the distribution objectives, marketers must consider their internal and external environments to develop the best channel structure. Should the channel be long or short? Is intensive, selective, or exclusive distribution best? Short, often direct, channels may be better suited for business-to-business marketers where customers are geographically concentrated and require high levels of technical know-how and service. Expensive or complex products are frequently sold directly to final customers. Short channels with selective distribution also make more sense with perishable products, since getting the product to the final user quickly is a priority. However,

Blue Diamond is a cooperative of over 4,000 almond growers who market together.

longer channels with more intensive distribution are generally best for inexpensive, standardized consumer goods that need to be distributed broadly and where little technical expertise is required.

The organization must also examine such issues as its own ability to handle distribution functions, what channel intermediaries are available, the ability of customers to access these intermediaries, and how the competition distributes its products. Should a firm use the same retailers as its competitors? It depends. Sometimes, to ensure customers' undivided attention, a firm sells its products in outlets that don't carry the competitors' products. In other cases, a firm uses the same intermediaries as its competitors because customers expect to find the product there. For example, you will only find Harley-Davidson bikes in selected Harley "boutiques," but you can expect to find Coca-Cola, Colgate toothpaste, and a Snickers bar in every store that sells these types of items.

Finally, by studying competitors' distribution strategies, marketers can learn from their successes and failures and avoid repeating them. If the biggest complaint of competitors' customers is delivery speed, developing a system that allows same-day delivery can make the competition pale in comparison.

Step 3: Choose a Distribution Strategy

Planning distribution strategies means making at least three decisions. First, of course, distribution planning includes decisions about the number of levels in the distribution channel. But distribution strategies also involve decisions about channel relationships—that is, whether a conventional system or a highly integrated system will work best. A third decision relates to the distribution intensity or the number of intermediaries at each level of the channel.

CONVENTIONAL, VERTICAL, AND HORIZONTAL MARKETING SYSTEMS Participants in any distribution channel form an interrelated system. In general, these systems take one of three forms: conventional, vertical, and horizontal marketing systems.

A **conventional marketing system** is a multilevel distribution channel in which members work independently of one another. Their relationships are limited to simply buying and selling from one another. Each firm seeks to benefit with little concern for other channel members. Even

conventional marketing system
A multiple-level distribution channel in which channel members work independently of one another.

though channel members work independently, most conventional channels are highly successful. For one thing, all members of the channel are working toward the same goals—to build demand, reduce costs, and improve customer satisfaction. And each channel member knows that it's in everyone's best interest to treat other channel members fairly.[8]

A **vertical marketing system (VMS)** is a channel in which there is formal cooperation among channel members at two or more different levels: manufacturing, wholesaling, and retailing. Vertical marketing systems were developed as a way to meet customer needs better by reducing costs incurred in channel activities. Often a vertical marketing system can provide a level of cooperation and efficiency not possible with a conventional channel, maximizing the effectiveness of the channel while also maximizing efficiency and keeping costs low. Members share information and provide services to other members, recognizing that such coordination makes everyone more successful in reaching a desired target market.

There are three types of vertical marketing systems: administered, corporate, and contractual:

- In an *administered VMS*, channel members remain independent but voluntarily work together because of the power of a single channel member. Strong brands are able to manage an administered VMS because resellers are eager to work with the manufacturer to carry the product.

- In a *corporate VMS*, a single firm owns manufacturing, wholesaling, and retailing operations. Thus, the firm has complete control over all channel operations. Retail giant Sears, for example, owns a nationwide network of distribution centers and retail stores.

- In a *contractual VMS*, cooperation is enforced by contracts (legal agreements) that spell out each member's rights and responsibilities and how they will cooperate. This arrangement means that the channel members can have more impact as a group than they could alone. In a wholesaler-sponsored VMS, wholesalers get retailers to work together under their leadership in a voluntary chain. Retail members of the chain use a common name, cooperate in advertising and other promotion, and even develop their own private-label products. Examples of wholesaler-sponsored chains are IGA (Independent Grocers' Alliance) food stores and Ace Hardware stores.

In other cases, retailers themselves organize a cooperative marketing channel system. A *retailer cooperative* is a group of retailers that has established a wholesaling operation to help them compete more effectively with the large chains. Each retailer owns shares in the wholesaler operation and is obligated to purchase a certain percentage of inventory from the cooperative operation. Associated Grocers and True Value Hardware stores are examples of retailer cooperatives.

Franchise organizations are a third type of contractual VMS. In these organizations, channel cooperation is explicitly defined and strictly enforced through contractual arrangements in which a franchiser (a manufacturer or a service provider) allows an entrepreneur (the franchisee) to use the franchise name and marketing plan for a fee. In most franchise agreements, the franchiser provides a variety of services for the franchisee, such as helping to train employees, giving access to lower prices for needed materials, and selecting a good location. In return, the franchiser receives a percentage of revenue from the franchisee. Usually the franchisees are obligated to follow the franchiser's business format very closely in order to maintain the franchise.[9] Table 15.2 lists a sampling of both long-standing and newer franchise operations.

From the manufacturer's perspective, franchising a business is a way to develop widespread product distribution with minimal financial risk while at the same time maintaining control over product quality. From the entrepreneur's perspective, franchises are a popular way to get a start in business.

In a **horizontal marketing system**, two or more firms at the same channel level agree to work together to get their product to the customer. Sometimes these agreements are between unrelated businesses. For example, many supermarkets now have formed a horizontal marketing system with banks that maintain a manned branch in the store. Publix leases Bank of America space in

vertical marketing system (VMS)
A channel of distribution in which there is formal cooperation among members at the manufacturing, wholesaling, and retailing levels.

horizontal marketing system
An arrangement within a channel of distribution in which two or more firms at the same channel level work together for a common purpose.

Table 15.2   A Sampler of Franchises in the Personal Care Services Industry

Company Name	Description	Start-Up Costs
Barbizon School of Modeling	Modeling and related creative arts education	$47.9K–106K
Executive Tans Inc.	Tanning salon	$125K–499K
Foot Solutions Inc.	Custom insoles and specialty shoes	$171.7K–230.8K
Right at Home Inc.	Senior home care and medical staffing	$28.5K–64.9K
Safety Watch Inc.	First aid/emergency products and training	$50K
Sarah Adult Day Services Inc.	Adult day services	$170K
Visiting Angels	Non-medical home-care services for seniors	$22.4K–41.6K
Women's Health Boutique Franchise System Inc.	Women's health care products and services	$197.4K–225.4K
Woodhouse Day Spa	Day spa services/bath and body retail products	$153.7K–226.9K

Source: "Franchise 500®," Entrepreneur, January 2004, http://www.entrepreneur.com/franchise500.

some of its stores and customers like it because they can do their food shopping and their banking in one stop.

Most airlines today are members of a horizontal alliance that allows them to cooperate in providing passenger air service. For example, American Airlines is a member of the "oneworld Alliance," which also includes Aer Lingus, British Airways, Cathay Pacific Airways, Finnair, Iberia, LanChile/LanPeru, and Qantas Airways. These alliances increase passenger volume for all airlines because travel agents who book passengers on one of the airline's flights will be more likely to book a connecting flight on the other airline. To increase customer benefits, they also share frequent-flyer programs and airport clubs.[10]

INTENSIVE, EXCLUSIVE, AND SELECTIVE DISTRIBUTION   How many wholesalers and retailers will carry the product within a given market? This may seem like an easy decision: Distribute the product through as many intermediaries as possible. But guess again. If the product goes to too many outlets, there may be inefficiency and duplication of efforts. For example, if there are too many Honda dealerships in town, there will be a lot of unsold Hondas sitting on dealer lots, and no single dealer will be successful. But if there are not enough wholesalers or retailers carrying a product, total sales of the manufacturer's products (and profits) will not be maximized. If customers have to drive hundreds of miles to find a Honda dealer, they may settle for a Ford or a Chevy. Thus, a distribution objective may be to either increase or decrease the level of distribution in the market..

The three basic choices are intensive, exclusive, and selective distribution. Table 15.3 summarizes five decision factors—company, customers, channels, constraints, and competition—and how they help marketers determine the best fit between distribution system and marketing goals.

intensive distribution

Selling a product through all suitable wholesalers or retailers that are willing to stock and sell the product.

Intensive distribution aims at maximizing market coverage by selling a product through all wholesalers or retailers that will stock and sell the product. Marketers use intensive distribution for products such as chewing gum, soft drinks, milk, and bread that are quickly consumed and must be frequently replaced. Intensive distribution is necessary for these products because availability is more important than any other consideration in customers' purchase decisions.

Table 15.3 Characteristics that Favor Intensive Over Exclusive Distribution

Decision Factor	Intensive Distribution	Exclusive Distribution
Company	Oriented toward mass markets	Oriented toward specialized markets
Customers	High customer density	Low customer density
	Price and convenience are priorities	Service and cooperation are priorities
Channels	Overlapping market coverage	Non-overlapping market coverage
Constraints	Cost of serving individual customers is low	Cost of serving individual customers is high
Competition	Based on a strong market presence, often through advertising and promotion	Based on individualized attention to customers, often through relationship marketing

In contrast to intensive distribution, **exclusive distribution** means limiting distribution to a single outlet in a particular region. Marketers often sell pianos, cars, executive training programs, television programs, and many other products with high price tags through exclusive distribution arrangements. These strategies are typically used with products that are high priced, that have considerable service requirements, and when there are a limited number of buyers in any single geographic area. Exclusive distribution enables wholesalers and retailers to better recoup the costs associated with long selling processes for each customer and, in some cases, extensive after-sale service.

Of course, not every situation neatly fits a category in Table 15.3. (You didn't *really* think it would be that simple, did you?) For example, consider professional sports. Customers might not shop for games in the same way they shop for pianos. They might go to a game on impulse, and they don't require much individualized service. Nevertheless, professional sports teams employ exclusive distribution. The team's cost of serving customers is high because of those million-dollar player salaries and multimillion-dollar stadiums.

The alert reader (and/or sports fan) may note that there are some exceptions to the exclusive distribution of sports teams. New York has two football teams and two baseball teams, Chicago fields two baseball teams, and so on. Market coverage that is less than intensive distribution but more than exclusive distribution is called **selective distribution**. Selective distribution fits when demand is so large that exclusive distribution is inadequate, but selling costs, service requirements, or other factors make intensive distribution a poor fit. Although a White Sox baseball fan may not believe that the Cubs franchise is necessary (and vice versa), major league baseball and even some baseball fans think the Chicago market is large enough to support both teams.

Selective distribution strategies are suitable for so-called *shopping products* such as household appliances and electronic equipment for which consumers are willing to spend time visiting different retail outlets to compare alternatives. For producers, selective distribution means freedom to choose only those wholesalers and retailers that have a good credit rating, provide good market coverage, serve customers well, and cooperate effectively. Wholesalers and retailers like selective distribution because it results in higher profits than are possible with intensive distribution where sellers often have to compete on price.

Step 4: Develop Distribution Tactics

As with planning for the other marketing Ps, the final step in distribution planning is developing the distribution tactics necessary to implement the distribution strategy. These decisions are usually about the type of distribution system to use, such as a direct or indirect channel or a conventional

exclusive distribution
Selling a product only through a single outlet in a particular region.

selective distribution
Distribution using fewer outlets than in intensive distribution but more than in exclusive distribution.

New Yorkers get to debate the merits of the Mets versus the Yankees because of selective distribution in that market.

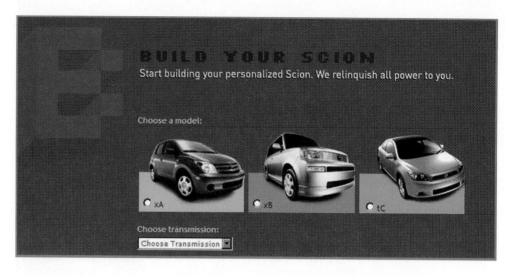

The new, youth-oriented Scion brand, a new line of vehicles from Toyota, gets delivered faster because the car company's new streamlined distribution strategy lets buyers customize the car online.

or an integrated channel. Distribution tactics relate to the implementation of these strategies, such as selecting individual channel members and managing the channel. These decisions are important because they often have a direct impact on customer satisfaction—nobody wants to have to wait for something they've bought! Toyota's plans for its new youth-oriented Scion model included a new way to distribute the cars. The car company's goal was to cut delivery time to its impatient young customers to no more than a week by offering fewer model variations and doing more customization at the dealer rather than at the factory.[11]

SELECTING CHANNEL PARTNERS   When firms agree to work together in a channel relationship, they become partners in what is normally a long-term commitment. Like a marriage, it is important to both manufacturers and intermediaries to select channel partners wisely, or they'll regret the matchup later. In evaluating intermediaries, manufacturers try to answer questions such as these: Will the channel member contribute substantially to our profitability? Does the channel member have the ability to provide the services customers want? What impact will a potential intermediary have on channel control?

For example, what small to midsize firm wouldn't jump at the chance to have its products distributed by retail giant Wal-Mart? With Wal-Mart as a channel partner, a small firm could double, triple, or quadruple its business. Actually, some firms, recognizing that size means power in the channel, have decided against selling to Wal-Mart because they are not willing to relinquish control of their marketing decision making. There is also a downside to choosing one retailer and selling only through that one retailer. If that retailer stops carrying the product, for example, the company will lose all its customers and it will be back to square one.

Another consideration in selecting channel members is competitors' channel partners. Because people spend time comparing different brands when purchasing a shopping product, firms need to make sure their products are displayed near similar competitors' products. If most competitors distribute their electric drills through mass merchandisers, a manufacturer has to make sure its brand is there also.

A firm's dedication to social responsibility may also be an important determining factor in the selection of channel partners. Many firms have developed extensive programs to recruit minority-owned channel members. For example, Gillette Company was named Corporation of the Year by the New England Minority Supplier Development Council in 2003 for its exemplary leadership and support of minority businesses as suppliers.[12]

Haggar works closely with its retailers to maintain tight inventory control.

MANAGING THE CHANNEL OF DISTRIBUTION Once a manufacturer develops a channel strategy and aligns channel members, the day-to-day job of managing the channel begins. The **channel leader**, sometimes called a *channel captain*, is the dominant firm that controls the channel. A firm becomes the channel leader because it has power relative to other channel members. This power comes from different sources:

- A firm has *economic power* when it has the ability to control resources.
- A firm such as a franchiser has *legitimate power* if it has legal authority to call the shots.
- A producer firm has *reward or coercive power* if it engages in exclusive distribution and has the ability to give profitable products and to take them away from the channel intermediaries.

In the past, producers traditionally held the role of channel captain. Procter & Gamble, for example, developed customer-oriented marketing programs, tracked market trends, and advised retailers on the mix of products most likely to build sales. As large retail chains evolved, giant retailers such as Wal-Mart began to assume a leadership role because of the sheer size of their operations. Today it is much more common for the big retailers to dictate their needs to producers instead of producers controlling what product is available to retailers.

Because producers, wholesalers, and retailers depend on one another for success, channel cooperation helps everyone. Channel cooperation is also stimulated when the channel leader takes actions that help make its partners more successful. High intermediary profit margins, training programs, cooperative advertising, and expert marketing advice are invisible to end customers but are motivating factors in the eyes of wholesalers and retailers.[13] Haggar Apparel, for example, finds ways to help its retail channel partners become more successful. By improving the speed and accuracy of reorders, retailers are able to maintain inventory levels necessary to satisfy customers while avoiding ordering errors.

Of course, relations among members in a channel are not always full of sweetness and light. Because each firm has its own objectives, channel conflict may threaten a manufacturer's distribution strategy. Such conflict most often occurs between firms at different levels of the same distribution channel. Incompatible goals, poor communication, and disagreement over roles, responsibilities, and functions cause conflict. For example, a producer is likely to feel the firm would enjoy greater success and profitability if intermediaries carry only its brands, but many intermediaries believe they will do better if they carry a variety of brands.

channel leader
A firm at one level of distribution that takes a leadership role, establishing operating norms and processes based on its power relative to other channel members.

Distribution Channels and the Marketing Mix

How are decisions regarding place related to the other three Ps? For one thing, place decisions affect pricing. Marketers that distribute products through low-priced retailers such as Wal-Mart, T.J. Maxx, and Marshalls, will have different pricing objectives and strategies than will those that sell to specialty stores.

Distribution decisions can sometimes give a product a distinct position in its market. For example, Enterprise Rent-a-Car avoids being overly dependent on the cutthroat airport rental car market by also seeking locations in residential areas and local business centers. This strategy takes advantage of the preferences of those customers who are not flying and who want short-term use of a rental vehicle.[14] And, of course, the choice of retailers and other intermediaries is strongly tied to the product itself. Manufacturers select mass merchandisers to sell mid-price-range products while they distribute top-of-the-line products such as expensive jewelry through high-end department and specialty stores.

In this section, we've been concerned with the distribution channels firms use to get their products to customers. In the next section, we'll look at the area of logistics—physically moving products through the supply chain.

Logistics: Implementing the Supply Chain

Some marketing textbooks tend to depict the practice of marketing as 90 percent planning and 10 percent implementation. Not so! In the "real world," many managers would argue that this ratio should be reversed. Marketing success is very much the art of getting the timing right and delivering on promises—*implementation*. That's why marketers place so much emphasis on efficient **logistics**, the process of designing, managing, and improving the movement of products through the supply chain. Logistics includes purchasing, manufacturing, storage, and transport.[15] As mentioned at the start of the chapter, the supply chain is implemented via logistics.

The Lowdown on Logistics

Logistics was originally a military term used to describe everything needed to deliver troops and equipment to the right place, at the right time, and in the right condition.[16] In business, logistics is similar in that its objective is to deliver exactly what the customer wants—at the right time, in the right place, and at the right price. The application of logistics is essential to the efficient management of the supply chain. Just as it's said "an army travels on its stomach" (meaning it can't function without adequate supplies, such as food), so a business relies on efficient logistics to be sure it has the resources it needs to successfully compete in the marketplace.

The delivery of goods to customers involves **physical distribution**, which refers to the activities used to move finished goods from manufacturers to final customers. Physical distribution activities include order processing, warehousing, materials handling, transportation, and inventory control. This process impacts how marketers physically get products where they need to be, when they need to be there, and at the lowest possible cost. Effective physical distribution is at the core of successful logistics.

When doing logistics planning, however, the focus also is on the customer. When managers thought of logistics as physical distribution only, the objective was to deliver the product at the lowest cost. Today, firms consider the needs of the customer first. The customer's goals become the logistics provider's goals. And this means that with most logistics decisions, firms must decide on the best trade-off between low costs and high customer service.

The focus on the customer is especially important when customer goals and "lowest price" goals conflict. Take, for example, a business-to-business customer who demands just-in-time (JIT) delivery—receiving the product exactly when they need it. The appropriate goal is not just to deliver what is needed at the lowest cost but rather to provide the product at the lowest cost possi-

logistics
The process of designing, managing, and improving the movement of products through the supply chain. Logistics includes purchasing, manufacturing, storage, and transport.

physical distribution
The activities used to move finished goods from manufacturers to final customers, including order processing, warehousing, materials handling, transportation, and inventory control.

ble *so long as* the JIT delivery requirements are met. Although it would be nice to transport all goods quickly by air, that is certainly not practical. But sometimes air transport is necessary to meet the needs of the customer, no matter the cost.

Logistics Functions

When developing logistics strategies, marketers must make decisions related to the five functions of logistics: order processing, warehousing, materials handling, transportation, and inventory control. For each decision, managers must consider how to minimize costs while maintaining the service customers want.

ORDER PROCESSING   *Order processing* includes the series of activities that occurs between the time an order comes into the organization and the time a product goes out the door. After an order is received, it is typically sent electronically to an office for record keeping and then on to the warehouse to be filled. When the order reaches the warehouse, personnel there check to see if the item is in stock. If it is not, the order is placed on *back-order status.* That information is sent to the office and then to the customer. If the item is available, it is located in the warehouse, packaged for shipment, and scheduled for pickup by either in-house or external shippers.

Fortunately, many firms have automated this process through **enterprise resource planning (ERP) systems**. An ERP system is a software solution that integrates information from across the entire company, including finance, order fulfillment, manufacturing, and transportation. Data only need to be entered into the system once, and then the data are automatically shared throughout the organization and linked to other information. For example, information on inventories of products is tied to sales information so that a sales representative can immediately tell a customer whether the product is in stock.

SEE THROUGH TRUCK TRAILERS!
PEER INTO CARGO CONTAINERS!
KNOW WHAT'S GOING ON
BEHIND WAREHOUSE WALLS!

No, we haven't brought back x-ray glasses. But we do have technology that lets you see deep into your supply chain, so you'll know your products and orders are right where they're supposed to be, and be alerted immediately if for any reason they're not. That's the sort of thing we do at Menlo Worldwide. We're constantly finding more efficient ways to transport supplies, manage inventories, and distribute products around the world. We offer unparalleled expertise in air and ocean forwarding, 3rd and 4th party logistics, supply chain technologies and integrated customs and trade solutions. To get the full picture, look us up at menloworldwide.com. (No funny glasses required.)

FORWARDING   LOGISTICS   VECTOR SCM   MENLO WORLDWIDE   EXPEDITE!   TECHNOLOGIES   TRADE SERVICES

Transporting and storing products requires companies to carefully track the movement of goods through the supply chain.

WAREHOUSING   Whether we speak of fresh-cut flowers, canned goods, or computer chips, at some point goods (unlike services) must be stored. Storing goods allows marketers to match supply with demand. For example, toys and other gift items are big sellers at Christmas, but toy factories operate 12 months of the year. **Warehousing**—storing goods in anticipation of sale or transfer to another member of the channel of distribution—enables marketers to provide time utility to consumers by holding on to products until consumers need them.

Part of developing effective logistics means deciding how many warehouses a firm needs and where and what type of warehouse each should be. A firm determines the location of its warehouse(s) by the location of customers and access to major highways, airports, or rail transportation. The number of warehouses often depends on the level of service customers require. If customers generally require fast delivery (today or tomorrow at the latest), then it may be necessary to store products in a number of different locations where they can be delivered to the customer quickly.

Firms use private and public warehouses to store goods. Those that use *private warehouses* have a high initial investment, but they also lose less inventory due to damage. *Public warehouses* are an alternative, allowing firms to pay for a portion of warehouse space rather than having to own an entire storage facility. Most countries offer public warehouses in all large cities and many smaller cities to support domestic and international trade. A *distribution center* is a warehouse that stores goods for short periods of time and that provides other functions, such as breaking bulk.

enterprise resource planning (ERP) systems
A software system that integrates information from across the entire company. Data need to be entered into the system only once, at one point, and then the data are automatically shared throughout the organization.

warehousing
Storing goods in anticipation of sale or transfer to another member of the channel of distribution.

Companies can track a wide range of metrics within the supply chain area. Some of the most common ones are the following:

- On-time delivery
- Forecast accuracy
- Value-added productivity per employee
- Returns processing cost as a percentage of product revenue
- Customer order actual cycle time
- Perfect order measurement

Let's take a look at the last measure in more detail. The perfect order measure calculates the error-free rate of each stage of a purchase order.[17] This measure helps managers track the multiple steps involved in getting a product from a manufacturer to a customer so that they can pinpoint processes in need of improvement. For example, a company can calculate its error rate at each stage and then combine these rates to create an overall metric of order quality. Suppose the company identifies the following error rates:

Order entry accuracy: 99.95% correct (5 errors per 1,000 order lines)
Warehouse pick accuracy: 99.2%
Delivered on time: 96%
Shipped without damage: 99%
Invoiced correctly: 99.8%

The company can then combine these individual rates into an overall perfect order measure by multiplying them together: $99.95\% \times 99.2\% \times 96\% \times 99\% \times 99.8\% = 94.04\%$.

MATERIALS HANDLING   Materials handling is the moving of products into, within, and out of warehouses. When goods come into the warehouse, they must be physically identified, checked for damage, sorted, and labeled. Next they are taken to a location for storage. Finally, they are recovered from the storage area for packaging and shipment. All in all, the goods may be handled over a dozen separate times. Procedures that limit the number of times a product must be handled decrease the likelihood of damage and reduce the cost of materials handling.

TRANSPORTATION   Logistics decisions take into consideration the modes of transportation and the individual freight carriers a firm needs to use to move products among channel members. Again, making transportation decisions entails a compromise between minimizing cost and providing the service customers want. As Table 15.4 shows, modes of transportation, including railroads, water transportation, trucks, airways, pipelines, and the Internet, differ in the following ways:

- **Dependability:** The ability of the carrier to deliver goods safely and on time
- **Cost:** The total transportation costs for moving a product from one location to another, including any charges for loading, unloading, and in-transit storage
- **Speed of delivery:** The total time for moving a product from one location to another, including loading and unloading
- **Accessibility:** The number of different locations the carrier serves
- **Capability:** The ability of the carrier to handle a variety of different products such as large or small, fragile or bulky
- **Traceability:** The ability of the carrier to locate goods in shipment

materials handling
The moving of products into, within, and out of warehouses.

Each mode of transportation has strengths and weaknesses that make it a good choice for different transportation needs. Table 15.4 summarizes the pros and cons of each mode.

RAILROADS   Railroads are best for carrying heavy or bulky items, such as coal and other mining products, over long distances. Railroads are about average in their cost and provide moderate speed of delivery. Although rail transportation provides dependable, low-cost service to many locations, trains cannot carry goods to every community.

WATER   Ships and barges carry large, bulky goods and are very important in international trade. Water transportation is quite low in cost but can be slow.

TRUCKS   Trucks or motor carriers are the most important transportation mode for consumer goods, especially for shorter hauls. Motor carrier transport allows flexibility because trucks can travel to locations missed by boats, trains, and planes. Trucks are also able to carry a wide variety of products, including perishable items. Although costs are fairly high for longer-distance shipping, trucks are economical for shorter deliveries. Because trucks provide door-to-door service, product handling is minimal, reducing the chance of product damage.

AIR   Air transportation is the fastest and most expensive transportation mode. It is ideal to move high-value items such as some mail, fresh-cut flowers, and live lobsters. Passenger airlines, air-freight carriers, and express delivery firms such as FedEx provide air transportation. Ships remain the major mover of international cargo, but air transportation networks are becoming more important in the development of international markets.

Table 15.4 A Comparison of Transportation Modes

Transportation Mode	Dependability	Cost	Speed of Delivery	Accessibility	Capability	Traceability	Most Suitable Products
Railroads	Average	Average	Moderate	High	High	Low	Heavy or bulky goods, such as automobiles, grain, and steel
Water	Low	Low	Slow	Low	Moderate	Low	Bulky, nonperishable goods, such as automobiles
Trucks	High	High for long distances; low for short distances	Fast	High	High	High	A wide variety of products, including those that need refrigeration
Air	High	High	Very fast	Low	Moderate	High	High-value items, such as electronic goods and fresh flowers
Pipeline	High	Low	Slow	Low	Low	Moderate	Petroleum products and other chemicals
Internet	High	Low	Very fast	Potentially very high	Low	High	Services such as banking, information, and entertainment

PIPELINE   Pipelines are used to carry petroleum products such as oil and natural gas and a few other chemicals. Pipelines flow primarily from oil or gas fields to refineries. They are very low in cost, require little energy, and are not subject to disruption by weather.

THE INTERNET   As we discussed earlier in this chapter, marketers of services such as banking, news, and entertainment are taking advantage of distribution opportunities provided by the Internet.

INVENTORY CONTROL   Another component of logistics is **inventory control**, which means developing and implementing a process to ensure that the firm always has sufficient quantities of goods available to meet customers' demands—no more and no less. That explains why firms work so hard to track merchandise so they know where their products are and where they are needed in case a low inventory situation appears imminent.

Some companies are even phasing in a sophisticated technology (similar to that used in the E-Z Pass system many drivers use to speed through tollbooths) known *as radio-frequency identification (RFID),* which lets them tag clothes, pharmaceuticals, or virtually any kind of product with tiny chips containing information about the item's content, origin, and destination. This new technology has the potential to revolutionize inventory control and help marketers ensure that their products are on the shelves when people want to buy them. In one test of the system, Gap put these tags on denim apparel at one of its stores. Sales jumped because the tags prevented the store from experiencing *stockouts*—running out of popular items. Typically, 15 percent of shoppers leave clothing stores without getting what they want; during the test, fewer than 1 percent of Gap shoppers left empty-handed.[18]

Firms store goods (i.e., create an inventory) for many reasons. For manufacturers, the pace of production may not match seasonal demand, and it may be more economical to produce snow skis year around than to produce them only during the winter season. For channel members that purchase goods from manufacturers or other channel intermediaries, it may be economical to

inventory control
Activities to ensure that goods are always available to meet customers' demands.

MAERSK SEALAND

A new dimension in shipping

Unmatched in experience
Resourceful
Dedicated to giving customers value for money

MAERSK EGYPT S.A.E.
For Maritime Transport

Cairo office:	68, El Merghany St., 3rd floor, Heliopolis
	Tel: 20-24144950 Fax: 20-24144974
Alexandria office:	9, El Fawatem St., 5th floor, Azarita
	Tel: 20-34843315 Fax: 20-34143319

Transportation by water, such as that provided by Maersk Sealand, is best for large, bulky, nonperishable goods and is vital to international trade.

order a product in quantities that don't exactly parallel demand. For example, delivery costs make it prohibitive for a retail gas station to place daily orders for just the amount of gas people will use that day. Instead, stations usually order truckloads of gasoline, holding their inventory in underground tanks. The consequences of stockouts may be very negative. Hospitals must keep adequate supplies of blood, IV fluids, drugs, and other supplies on hand to meet emergencies, even if some items go to waste.

Inventory control has a major impact on the overall costs of a firm's logistics initiatives. If supplies of products are too low to meet fluctuations in customer demand, a firm may have to make expensive emergency deliveries or lose customers to competitors. If inventories are above demand, unnecessary storage expenses and the possibility of damage or deterioration occur. To balance these two opposing needs, manufacturers are turning to JIT inventory techniques with their suppliers. As noted earlier, JIT sets up delivery of goods just as they are needed on the production floor, minimizing the cost of holding inventory while ensuring the inventory will be there when it is needed.

VF Corporation is at the forefront of this new technology.[19] VF makes sure customers find what they're looking for by use of a computerized market-response system that keeps records on what consumers buy so that VF can rapidly restock stores with popular items. The system is hooked up to the computers of large retail customers such as JCPenney. Every night, retailers transmit sales data collected at register scanners straight to VF, where the market-response system automatically enters an order based on what items have been sold. VF jeans arrive within three days.[20] Manufacturers that provide their channel partners with this type of fast service are way ahead of the competition.

real people, real choices
How It Worked Out at VF Corporation

Mackey convinced JCPenney to choose option 1. In May 2000, the store chain implemented Lee's Retail Floor Space Management (RFSM) program in its womenswear division. In the six months following the implementation of this program, Lee's womenswear business at JCPenney increased 15 percent. In June 2001, Lee expanded the RFSM to include JCPenney's menswear and boyswear departments. Owing to the success of the rollout, JCPenney expanded implementation of the plan from 300 to 650 stores. JCPenney also began to test the program in men's casuals. Lee's RFSM has proven to be a success for JCPenney as well. For 2000, total brand sales were up over 5 percent. And in 2001, things got even better; Lee ended the year up 15 percent.

Mackey's experience illustrates how retailers and manufacturers within a *channel of distribution* can work together to improve profitability for all channel members: In the flow of value from producer to consumer, fixing one link makes the chain stronger for everyone.

Think like a supply chain manager to uncover hidden work opportunities. Chapter 15 in the *Brand You* supplement is full of ideas for expanding your work options.

CHAPTER SUMMARY

1. **Understand the concept of the value chain and the key elements in a supply chain.** The value chain consists of five primary activities (inbound logistics, operations, outbound logistics, marketing and sales, and service) and four support activities (procurement, technology development, human resource management, and firm infrastructure). The process is called a value chain because each of these activities adds value to the product or service the customer eventually buys. Whereas the value chain is an overarching concept of how firms create value, the supply chain also encompasses components external to the firm itself, including all activities that are necessary to convert raw materials into a good or service and put it in the hands of the consumer or business customer.

2. **Explain what a distribution channel is and what functions distribution channels perform.** A distribution channel is a series of firms or individuals that facilitates the movement of a product from the producer to the final customer. Channels provide time, place, and ownership utility for customers and reduce the number of transactions necessary for goods to flow from many manufacturers to large numbers of customers by breaking bulk and creating assortments. Channel members make the purchasing process easier by providing important customer services. Today the Internet is becoming an important player in distribution channels.

3. **Describe the types of wholesaling intermediaries found in distribution channels.** Wholesaling intermediaries are firms that handle the flow of products from the manufacturer to the retailer or business user. Merchant wholesalers are independent intermediaries that take title to a product and include both full-function wholesalers and limited-function wholesalers. Merchandise agents and brokers are independent intermediaries that do not take title to products. Manufacturer-owned channel members include sales branches, sales offices, and manufacturers' showrooms.

4. **Describe the types of distribution channels and the steps in planning distribution channel strategies.** Distribution channels vary in length from the simplest two-level channel to longer channels with three or more channel levels. Distribution channels include direct distribution, in which the producer sells directly to consumers, and indirect channels, which may include a retailer, wholesaler, or other intermediary. Marketers begin channel planning by developing channel objectives and considering important environmental factors. The next step is to decide a distribution strategy, which involves determining the type of distribution channel that is best. Distribution tactics include the selection of individual channel members and management of the channel.

5. **Explain how logistics is used in the supply chain.** The supply chain includes all the firms that engage in activities that are necessary to turn raw materials into a good or service for a consumer or business customer, including those in the marketing channel of distribution. Every firm occupies a position on a value chain. Companies add value to inputs received from firms upstream. Logistics is the process of designing, managing, and improving supply chains, including all those activities that are required to move products through the supply chain. Logistics activities include order processing, warehousing, materials handling, transportation, and inventory control.

KEY TERMS

CHAPTER REVIEW

MARKETING CONCEPTS: TESTING YOUR KNOWLEDGE

1. What is a value chain?

2. What is a supply chain, and how is it different from a channel of distribution?

3. What is a channel of distribution? What are channel intermediaries?

4. Explain the functions of distribution channels.

5. List and explain the types of independent and manufacturer-owned wholesaling intermediaries.

6. What factors are important in determining whether a manufacturer should choose a direct or indirect channel? Why do some firms use hybrid marketing systems?

7. What are conventional, vertical, and horizontal marketing systems?

8. Explain intensive, exclusive, and selective forms of distribution.

9. Explain the steps in distribution planning.

10. What is logistics? Explain the functions of logistics.

MARKETING CONCEPTS: DISCUSSING CHOICES AND ISSUES

1. The supply chain concept looks at both the inputs of a firm and the means of firms that move the product from the manufacturer to the consumer. Do you think *marketers* should be concerned with the total supply chain concept? Why or why not?

2. You have probably heard someone say, "The reason products cost so much is because of all the intermediaries." Do intermediaries increase the cost of products? Would consumers be better off or worse off without intermediaries?

3. Many entrepreneurs choose to start a franchise business rather than "go it alone." Do you think franchises offer the typical businessperson good opportunities? What are some positive and negative aspects of purchasing a franchise?

4. As colleges and universities are looking for better ways to satisfy their customers, an area of increasing interest is the distribution of their product—education. Describe the characteristics of your school's channel(s) of distribution. What types of innovative distribution might make sense for your school to try?

MARKETING PRACTICE: APPLYING WHAT YOU'VE LEARNED

1. Assume that you have recently been hired by a firm that manufactures furniture. You feel that marketing should have an input into supplier selection for the firm's products, but the purchasing department says that should not be a concern for marketing. You need to explain to him the importance of the value chain perspective. In a role-playing exercise, explain to the purchasing agent the value chain concept, why it is of concern to marketing, and why the two of you should work together.

2. Assume that you are the director of marketing for a firm that manufactures cleaning chemicals used in industries. You have traditionally sold these products through manufacturer's reps. You are considering adding a direct Internet channel to your distribution strategy, but you aren't sure whether this will create channel conflict. Make a list of the pros and cons of this move. What do you think is the best decision?

3. As the one-person marketing department for a candy manufacturer (your firm makes high-quality, hand-dipped chocolates using only natural ingredients), you are considering making changes in your distribution strategy. Your products have previously been sold through a network of food brokers that call on specialty food and gift stores. But

you think that perhaps it would be good for your firm to develop a corporate vertical marketing system (i.e., vertical integration). In such a plan, a number of company-owned retail outlets would be opened across the country. The president of your company has asked that you present your ideas to the company executives. In a role-playing situation with one of your classmates, present your ideas to your boss, including the advantages and disadvantages of the new plan compared to the current distribution method.

4. Assume that you have recently been given a new marketing assignment by your firm. You are to head up development of a distribution plan for a new product line—a series of do-it-yourself instruction videos for home gardeners. These videos would show consumers how to plant trees, shrubbery, and bulbs; how to care for their plants; how to prune; and so on. You know that in developing a distribution plan, it is essential that you understand and consider a number of internal and external environmental factors. Make a list of the information you will need before you can begin developing the distribution plan. How will you adapt your plan based on each of these factors?

MARKETING MINIPROJECT: LEARNING BY DOING

In the United States, the distribution of most products is fairly easy. There are lots of independent intermediaries (wholesalers,

dealers, distributors, and retailers) that are willing to cooperate to get the product to the final customer. Our elaborate interstate highway system combines with rail, air, and water transportation to provide excellent means for moving goods from one part of the country to another. In many other countries, the means for distribution of products are far less efficient and effective.

For this miniproject, you and one or more of your classmates should first select a consumer product, probably one you normally purchase. Then use either library sources or other people or both (retailers, manufacturers, dealers, classmates, and so on) to gather information to do the following:

1. Describe the path the product takes to get from the producer to you. Draw a model to show each of the steps the product takes. Include as much as you can about transportation, warehousing, materials handling, order processing, inventory control, and so on.

2. Select another country in which the same or a similar product is sold. Describe the path the product takes to get from the producer to the customer in that country.

3. Determine if the differences between the two countries cause differences in price, availability, or quality of the product.

4. Make a presentation to your class on your findings.

REAL PEOPLE, REAL SURFERS: EXPLORING THE WEB

Visit a Web site for a logistics company such as NYK Line (**http://www2.nykline.com/home/index.html**). Then answer the following questions:

1. What logistics services does the logistics firm offer its customers?

2. What does the company say to convince prospective customers that its services are better than those of the competition?

MARKETING PLAN EXERCISE

Avon is a company that has traditionally used a fairly simple supply chain system. Avon manufactured the products and shipped them to independent Avon representatives who in turn delivered them directly to their customers.

In planning for the future, Avon is very interested in making use of other distribution channels and outlets. Their Web site can aid in promoting alternative means of getting product into the hands of users. Yet they certainly don't want to negatively impact the backbone of their supply chain process—the independent Avon representative.

1. If you were a marketing executive at Avon, what supply chain options would you suggest in designing a marketing plan beyond their traditional distribution model?

2. Can Avon successfully coexist in retail store distribution and in distribution through their traditional means (catalogs and direct sellers)? Justify your answer.

3. Assume that your plan recommends Avon become more aggressive in pursuing distribution through retail stores and other means beyond their traditional direct-selling approach. What intermediaries do you recommend become part of their supply chain?

Marketing in Action Case

Real Choices at Ben & Jerry's

Chubby Hubby, Chunky Monkey, Karamel Sutra, Phish Food, and the ever-popular Cherry Garcia are just a few of the many innovative ice cream flavors being produced and sold by Ben & Jerry's Homemade, Inc., a Vermont-based manufacturer of ultrapremium ice cream, frozen yogurt, and sorbet. Two childhood friends, Ben Cohen and Jerry Greenfield, started the company in 1978 with a $12,000 investment in a renovated gas station located in Burlington, Vermont. Since then, the company has become known for its high-quality ice cream products, its memorable and innovative ice cream flavors, and the involvement of its employees in local community projects. Ben & Jerry's success led to the company being purchased by Unilever, an international consumer products company, for $326 million in 2000.

Ben & Jerry's has enjoyed great success as a company since its founding in 1978, but one of the most important aspects of its marketing plan success has been the company's use of effective supply chain management practices to make its product available in the right quantities, at the right time, to the right customers. Ben & Jerry's follows a fairly intensive distribution strategy with its products, selling its many ice cream flavors via a multichannel strategy in supermarkets, grocery stores, convenience stores, franchised Ben & Jerry's Scoop Shops, restaurants, and other locations, including college dorms.

An important aspect Ben & Jerry's had to consider when designing their distribution strategy and the type of consumer channel they would rely on was whom to select as channel partners. Channel partners/intermediaries provide a number of valuable services to a manufacturer, including functions that help facilitate the completion of transactions. As with many manufactured products, retailers selling Ben and Jerry's products take a financial risk that the product will sell, not only by acquiring inventory but also by putting some of their own money behind promoting the product. Consequently, Ben & Jerry's must be very careful when selecting its retail partners and ensure that the companies they choose have sufficient resources to properly display, promote, and sell the products.

In addition to using a great deal of care to select its retail partners, the company also is concerned with its supply chain and where it gets the raw materials it needs to produce the premium ice cream products. Early in its history, Ben & Jerry's realized that high-quality finished products require a steady supply of equally high-quality raw materials. As a result, the company has spent a great deal of time working with the Vermont dairy farmers from which it purchases the milk and cream that are used in the production process. Ben & Jerry's is a very environmentally friendly firm and is committed to using milk and cream that come from cows not treated with the synthetic hormone rBGH. Such a commitment requires that company purchasing agents communicate this policy to potential suppliers and take steps to ensure that the milk products they purchase do not contain the unwanted hormone.

As Ben & Jerry's continues to expand the distribution base of its products, the company also will have to continue to search for new retail and franchise partners. The company recently has embarked on an effort to expand the number of franchisees willing to open a Ben & Jerry's Scoop Shop. Scoop Shops are stand-alone retail outlets that sell a variety of Ben & Jerry's products. In 2000 there were only 200 franchised shops, but by 2007 the company hopes to have 1,000 Scoop Shops. However, the competition for stand-alone retail outlets selling ice cream is extremely intense. Practically every community has at least one local ice cream parlor that sells a variety of ice cream treats. In addition, well-known and well-financed competitors, such as Baskin-Robbins, Braum's, Häagen Dazs, and Dairy Queen, make the expansion of Ben & Jerry's Scoop Shops a risky undertaking.

Another concern for Ben & Jerry's is that they require their franchisees to open three to 10 stores within their assigned territory. With the average investment for just one Scoop Shop equaling about $200,000, the number of entrepreneurs who can afford to become a franchisee is severely limited. Finally, it's likely that Ben & Jerry's will have to significantly upgrade its supply chain management system to handle the additional business the huge planned increase in franchised outlets will produce. The average Scoop Shop will generate roughly 7,000 to 10,000 transactions per month. Growing from 200 to 1,000 Scoop Shops could generate as much as another 8 million customer transactions per month.

Being able to properly support the Scoop Shops, along with all the other retail outlets, with inventory will become a daunting task for the company's existing supply chain management system.

Things to Think About

1. What is the decision facing Ben & Jerry's?
2. What factors are important in understanding the decision situation?
3. What are the alternatives?
4. What decision(s) do you recommend?
5. What are some ways to implement your recommendation(s)?

Sources: "Ben and Jerry's Marks Five Years of Customer Service Success with RightNow's on Demand CRM Solutions," *PR Newswire*, May 3, 2004; "Ben and Jerry's Scoop Shops to Dish Out Near Real-Time Sales Data via MICROS RES3000, Eclipse POS Terminals and mymicros.net," *PR Newswire*, February 24, 2004; and Sherri C. Goodman, "Scooping Out a Dream Couple's Persistence Leads to State's First Ben & Jerry's," *Birmingham News*, June 13, 2004, Business section.

www.limitedbrands.com

real people, real choices

meet Subha Ramesh,
a Decision Maker at LimitedBrands

first job out of
school   my hero

Research analyst for a retail   Colin Powell.
real estate consulting firm.

RETAILING: BRICKS AND CLICKS

Subha S. Ramesh is vice president of strategy–real estate for LimitedBrands. In that role, she is responsible for coordinating the company's strategic decisions regarding the purchase and development of real estate as it opens new stores. She has been with LimitedBrands for the past five years. Subha started her career as a senior analyst for a retail real estate consulting company. During her 13 years at The Green Group, she developed numerous market strategies and sales forecasts for retailers such as Ann Taylor, Williams-Sonoma, Pottery Barn, and American Eagle Outfitters. She left The Green Group in 1999 as partner and executive vice president.

Decision Time at LimitedBrands

Starting with one store in 1963, LimitedBrands operates about 4,500 stores today that include Bath & Body Works, Express, The Limited, and Victoria's Secret. In addition to its Internet and catalog sales, the company operates retail stores primarily in malls throughout the continental United States. In the 1970s and 1980s, LimitedBrands increased its store count (and sales) through the roughly 50 new malls built during these two decades. By the beginning of the 1990s, however, the number of new malls decreased dramatically. The reduc-

tion in new malls was due principally to lack of suitable sites and a reduction in viable anchors as department store consolidation continued.

Despite the significant reduction in new malls, Limited-Brands continued to add new properties by opening more of its Victoria's Secret and Bath & Body Works stores in both existing and new malls. By 2000, however, attractive new store opportunities for both of these brands had also significantly diminished. The issue for LimitedBrands was how to grow square footage (and yield higher sales and profits) for its existing brands. Subha and the LimitedBrands real estate group considered the following options:

OPTION 1: Focus on expanding floor space in existing stores in upscale malls, with the objectives of increasing sales and increasing productivity (sales per gross square foot).

If she chose this option, Subha and her team would be able to increase floor space in only those locations that had proven they were able to attract a steady flow of customers who wanted the latest fashions. However, it is difficult to expand store size and increase sales per gross square foot. To do so would require more time and money devoted to merchandising, marketing, and store

what drives me	my management style	don't do this when interviewing with me	my pet peeve
At this point in my career, watching and helping a junior person be successful.	Influence and teaming.	Not know about the company or department.	Ignorance.

objectives

1 **Define retailing and understand how retailing evolves.**

2 **Describe how retailers are classified.**

3 **Describe the more common forms of nonstore retailing.**

4 **Describe B2C e-commerce and its benefits, limitations, and future promise.**

5 **Understand the importance of store image to a retail positioning strategy and explain how a retailer can create a desirable image in the marketplace.**

design. In addition, the greater investment would bring with it greater risk.

OPTION 2: Open new stores in nonmall venues, such as strip centers, specialty centers, and street locations.

This option would provide the increase in square footage needed to accommodate the company's growing stable of stores. However, it might not yield adequate sales and profit growth as Limited-Brands reached diminishing incremental returns in a given market. Subha also thought about The Gap's experience when that company opened more than 50 stores in Manhattan—she was concerned that having too many stores in proximity to one another would make the retail brands too commonplace.

OPTION 3: Open new stores for some brands in lower-tier malls.

Again, this would provide the square footage growth Limited-Brands required. And these deals could be more attractive financially because the less desirable locations would not charge the high rents demanded by premium malls. However, while these stores could be profitable, the sales opportunities were likely low. In addition, adding stores in downscale locations might diminish the fashion image of the company's brands. Also, as department stores consolidate, they tend to close anchor stores in lower-tier malls first—a death knell for the specialty stores in those malls.

Now, put yourself in Subha Ramesh's shoes: Which option would you choose, and why?

Retailing: Special Delivery

Shop 'til you drop! For many people, obtaining the product is only half the fun. Others, of course, would rather walk over hot coals than spend time in a store. Marketers like Subha Ramesh need to find ways to deliver products and services that please both types of consumers. **Retailing** is the final stop on the distribution path—the process by which goods and services are sold to consumers for their personal use.

retailing
The final stop in the distribution channel by which goods and services are sold to consumers for their personal use.

A retail outlet is more than a place to buy something. The retailer adds or subtracts value from the offering with its image, inventory, service quality, location, and pricing policy. In many cases, the shopping experience is what is being bought as well as the products we take home. For example, Bass Pro Shops, a chain of outdoor sports equipment stores, features giant aquariums, waterfalls, trout ponds, archery and rifle ranges, putting greens, and free classes on topics from ice fishing to conservation.[1]

This chapter will explore the many different types of retailers, keeping one question in mind: How does a retailer—whether store or nonstore (selling via television, phone, or computer)—lure the consumer? Answering this question isn't getting any easier, as the competition for customers continues to heat up, fueled by the explosion of Web sites selling branded merchandise (or auctioning it like eBay), the "overstoring" of many areas as developers continue to build elaborate malls and strip centers, and improvements in communications and distribution that make it possible for retailers from around the world to enter local markets. So, this chapter has plenty "in store" for us. Let's start with an overview of where retailing has been and where it's going.

Retailing: A Mixed (Shopping) Bag

Retailing is big business. About one of every five U.S. workers is employed in retailing. There are over 1.2 million retail firms, but only about 8 percent of them have annual sales greater than $2.5 million. Although we tend to associate huge stores such as Wal-Mart and Sears with retailing activity, in reality most retailers are small businesses.[2] Certain retailers such as Home Depot also are wholesalers, because they provide goods and services to businesses as well as to end consumers.

As we said in Chapter 15, retailers are one of the members of a channel of distribution and as such they provide time, place, and ownership utility to customers. Some retailers save people time or money by providing an assortment of merchandise under one roof. Others search the world for the most exotic delicacies, allowing shoppers access to goods they would otherwise never see. Still others, such as Barnes & Noble café/bookstores, provide us with interesting environments in which to spend our leisure time and, they hope, our money.

The Evolution of Retailing

Retailing has taken many forms over time, including the peddler who hawked his wares from a horse-drawn cart, a majestic urban department store, an intimate boutique, and a huge "hyper-store" that sells everything from potato chips to snow tires. But now the horse-drawn cart has been replaced by the cart you see at your local mall, selling new-age jewelry or monogrammed golf balls to passersby. As the economic, social, and cultural times change, different types of retailers emerge—often replacing older, outmoded types. How can marketers know what the dominant types of retailing will be tomorrow or 10 years from now?

THE WHEEL OF RETAILING   One of the oldest and simplest explanations for these changes is the **wheel-of-retailing hypothesis**. This states that new types of retailers find it easiest to enter the market by offering goods at lower prices than competitors.[3] After they gain a foothold, they gradually trade up, improving their facilities, increasing the quality and assortment of merchandise, and offering amenities such as parking and gift wrapping. This upscaling results in greater investment and operating costs, so the store must raise its prices to remain profitable, which then makes it vulnerable to still newer entrants that can afford to charge lower prices. And so the wheel turns. That's the story behind Pier 1 Imports. Pier 1 started as a single store in San Mateo, California, offering low-priced beanbags, love beads, and incense to post–World War II baby boomers. Today it sells quality home furnishings and decorative accessories to the same customers who are now the most affluent segment of the American population.[4]

The wheel of retailing helps explain the development of some but not all forms of retailing. For example, some retailers never trade up; they simply continue to occupy a niche as discounters. Others, such as upscale specialty stores, start out at the high end. Of course, some retailers move down after experiencing success at the high end. Sometimes they open sister divisions that sell lower-priced products (as when Gap Stores opened Old Navy), and other times they develop outlets that sell lower-priced versions of their own products (as when Nordstrom creates the Nordstrom Rack or Anne Taylor opens Anne Taylor Loft).

THE RETAIL LIFE CYCLE   Of course, retailers sell products. But in a way retailers also are products because they provide benefits such as convenience or status to consumers, and they must offer a competitive advantage over other retailers to survive. And sometimes where a product is bought either adds to or takes away from its allure (which explains why some people replace shopping bags from bargain stores with those from upscale stores to create the "right" impression).

From the value chain perspective, the selection of a retail location by a manufacturer means value is added in two ways: by the utility provided and by enhancing the image of the product. When a manufacturer makes its product available at Wal-Mart, the value added is primarily the time, place, and ownership utility it provides. But when a product is available at Neiman-Marcus or Saks, the value of the product is also increased because the high-end image of the retailer is transferred to the product.

So, another way to understand how retailers evolve is the **retail life cycle**. Like the product life cycle, this perspective recognizes that (like people, soft-drink brands, and vacation destinations) retailers are born, they grow and mature, and eventually they die or become obsolete. The life cycle

wheel-of-retailing hypothesis
A theory that explains how retail firms change, becoming more upscale as they go through their life cycle.

retail life cycle
A theory that focuses on the various stages that retailers pass through from introduction to decline.

Pier 1 Imports exemplifies the wheel of retailing. The stores initially sold low-priced beanbags and love beads, but today shoppers can find quality home furnishings.

approach allows us to categorize retail stores by the conditions they face at different points in the cycle.[5]

In the *introduction* stage, the new retailer often is an aggressive entrepreneur who takes a unique approach to doing business. This may mean competing on the basis of low price, as the wheel of retailing suggests. However, the new guy on the block may also enter the market by offering a distinctive assortment or a different way to distribute items, such as through the Internet. That's what Samuel Wurtzel did in 1949 when he opened Richmond, Virginia's first retail television store. Today, Circuit City has over 600 stores and sells a wide variety of electronics and home appliances.[6]

In the introduction stage, profits are low because of high development costs. As the business enters the *growth* stage, the retailer (hopefully) catches on with shoppers, and sales and profits rise. But a new idea doesn't stay new for long. Others start to copy it and competition increases, so the store needs to expand what it offers. Often the retailer responds by opening more outlets and develops systems to distribute goods to these new stores—which may in turn cut profits as the firm invests in new buildings and fixtures.

By the time the business reaches the *maturity* stage, many other individual retailers have copied the unique idea of the original entrepreneur to form an entire industry. The industry has overexpanded, and intense competition makes it difficult to maintain customer loyalty. Profits decline as competitors resort to price cutting to keep their customers. We can observe this pattern in department stores like Macy's and fast-food chains like McDonald's.

In the *decline* stage, retail businesses, like the general store or the peddler, become obsolete as newer ways of doing business emerge. Of course, the outmoded retailer does not have to fold its tent at this stage. Marketers who anticipate these shifts can avert decline by changing to meet the times. For example, full-service gas stations had difficulty competing with self-service discount outlets. Many responded by adding variety stores to their retail mix to let drivers buy groceries while they're filling their tanks. Or, how about a store that plans to close even as it opens? That's just what happened recently in Berlin with the launch of a new concept called the Comme des Garçons Guerrilla Store. The store plans to close in a year—even if it is making money! Instead of spending millions to build or renovate a building, Comme des Garçons spent just $2,500 to fix up a former bookshop. This "here today, gone tomorrow" strategy acknowledges consumers' desires to have different shopping experiences all the time in a unique way.[7]

The Evolution Continues: What's "In Store" for the Future?

As our world continues to change rapidly, retailers are scrambling to keep up. Three factors motivate innovative merchants to reinvent the way they do business: demographics, technology, and globalization.

DEMOGRAPHICS   As we noted in Chapter 7, keeping up with changes in population characteristics is at the heart of many marketing developments. Retailers can no longer afford to stand by and assume that their customer base is the same as it has always been. They must come up with new ways to sell their products to diverse groups.

For example, although many retailers chase after the same set of affluent customers, others are carving out markets by targeting lower-income households. Stores like Dollar General, Dollar Tree, and Family Dollar profit by serving the needs of the 4 out of 10 U.S. households that earn less than $25,000 per year. These "value retailers," operating stores with bare-bones fixtures and offering cash-and-carry checkout only (no credit cards), rack up total sales of over $8 billion in merchandise per year.

Here are some of the ways changing demographics are altering the face of retailing:

- **Convenience for working consumers:** Some retailers are expanding their operating hours because consumers no longer have time to shop during the day. Other retailers, including dry cleaners and pharmacies, are adding drive-up windows. In areas from financial services to interior decorating, enterprising individuals have turned time shortage into a business opportunity by becoming shopping consultants for busy consumers. Many major department stores offer in-house consultants at no charge.

- **Catering to specific age segments:** Retailers are seeing the benefits of serving specific age-groups. For example, several companies such as Pacific Sunwear and Hot Topic have prospered by targeting suburban teenagers who are prowling the mall for the latest in cool fashions. More recently, Pacific Sunwear opened a new chain called D.e.m.o. that's intended to deliver a hip-hop flavor to the mainstream youth market. The stores stock brands such as Ecko Unlimited, Enyce, Sean John, and Phat Farm. As one analyst observed, "You have to realize that teenagers are bored, and mainstream American mall culture is mostly boring. Hip hop, and to a different degree, snowboard and surf life, have an exciting, rebellious quality that kids in the suburbs may not be able to access where they live."[8] It's the job of retailers to provide that excitement—and sell a lot of products while doing so.

- **Recognizing ethnic diversity:** Although members of every ethnic group can usually find local retailers that cater to their specific needs, larger companies must tailor their strategies to the cultural makeup of specific areas. For example, in Texas, California, and Florida, where there are large numbers of customers who speak only Spanish, many retailers make sure that there are sales associates who *habla Español.*

TECHNOLOGY   In addition to demographics, technology is revolutionizing retailing. As we all know, the Internet has brought us the age of e-tailing. Whether it's a store that sells only on the Web or a traditional retailer such as Banana Republic or J. Crew that *also* sells on the Web, retailing is steadily evolving from bricks to clicks. Our personal computers have turned our homes into virtual malls. There are other technological advances that have little to do with the Internet that are also helping to change our shopping experiences.

Cutting-edge retailers and mall developers understand that stores of the future will double as entertainment centers and social hubs that will let shoppers hungry for stimulation shop, eat, network and have a good time all at once. This is the CocoWalk mall in Coconut Grove, Florida.

point-of-sale (POS) systems
Retail computer systems that collect sales data and are hooked directly into the store's inventory control system.

Some of the most profound changes are not even visible to shoppers, such as advanced electronic **point-of-sale (POS) systems**, which contain computer brains that collect sales data and are connected directly into the store's inventory control system. For example, every day 500 gigabytes of data are sent from JCPenney stores across the United States to its corporate headquarters in Dallas. From there, computer programs analyze patterns of demand for different products and automatically send orders to vendors.[9] This makes stores such as Penney's or Macy's more efficient. If shoppers in your area are buying a lot of wide-legged jeans, for example, the company can be sure that its store there will offer an ample selection for every hip-hop shopper.

And how about skipping the checkout altogether? At the Extra Future Store in Rheinberg, Germany, shoppers are given a small touch-screen computer with a built-in bar code scanner when they enter. The cart-top computer also allows shoppers to scan their purchases for payment as they move through the store. For items like produce that require weighing, the store has installed scales equipped with digital cameras that use image-recognition software to figure out and then price the kind of object they are weighing.[10] Central to the concept are the quarter-size radio-frequency identification (RIFD) tags we discussed in Chapter 15. These tags are attached to individual products, tracking their movement from storeroom to shelves to shopping cart. While only relatively few products now carry these tags, retailers say eventually they will appear on all items, replacing bar codes. Welcome to the future!

Other technological innovations will radically change the way we shop in the future. JCPenney International makes these predictions about retailing in the year 2010: "Each consumer will have a personal preference card, so a store will know your tastes, clothing sizes, and even your current household decor. When shopping for furniture, a design consultant will call up a 3-D image of your living room, and show you how your new purchases will actually look in the room. Or, forget about endlessly trying on clothes—holographic imaging will let you 'see' yourself in a new suit or dress."[11] Sophisticated body scanners will be able to read a person's exact dimensions and send this information to machines that produce clothing precisely tailored to individual proportions.

American retailers need to go global if they want to continue to grow. Starbucks is fast becoming a household name in Japan.

GLOBALIZATION   As we saw in Chapter 3, the world is becoming a much smaller place. Retailers are busy expanding to other countries and bringing with them innovations and new management philosophies. McDonald's, T.G.I. Friday's, and Blockbuster Entertainment are among the global success stories for U.S. retailers. Starbucks has become a household name in Japan (where it's pronounced STAH-buks-zu). The coffee shops feature comfortable sofas, American hip-hop music, and large servings of gourmet brew. These are relatively new concepts in Japan, where café patrons had been accustomed to sitting in dimly lit shops and sipping tea from thimble-size cups.[12]

Still, retailers need to adjust to different conditions around the world. While the Japanese are embracing Starbucks, for example, Wal-Mart is finding that it needs to change some of its tried-and-true practices to conform to that country's local customs. Its employees there have balked at Wal-Mart's "10 foot" rule, which encourages them to offer assistance to any customer within 10 feet. In Japan, grocery clerks usually wait for the customer to ask a question. In addition, Japanese consumers assume that an item that's low-priced must be of low quality—they must be convinced that the chain can offer cheaper sashimi (fish meant to be eaten raw) because it got a better price by buying in volume, not that the fish is several days old.[13]

Globalization is a two-way street. Innovative retailing concepts developed overseas are influencing U.S. retailing. For example, Sephora operates stores that sell nothing but cosmetics and beauty products made by many companies conveniently organized by category (need 1,000 different shades of lipstick from which to choose?).

Of course, understanding global retailing means recognizing that the way things are sold differs from country to country. In many developing countries, the retailing industry is made up of small individual retailers who sell cigarettes, soft drinks, snacks, cassette tapes, batteries, and just about anything else you can think of from some kiosks or street carts. In Shanghai, Internet orders for water are delivered by a 19th-century-style pedicart—a kind of bicycle with a cart over the rear wheel.[14]

From Mom-and-Pop to Super Wal-Mart: Classifying Retail Stores

We've seen that exciting things are happening in the world of retailing. But the field of retailing covers a lot of ground—from mammoth department stores to sidewalk vendors to Web sites. Retail marketers need to understand all the possible ways they might offer their products in the market, and they also need a way to benchmark their performance to other similar retailers.

Classifying Retailers by What They Sell

One of the most important strategic decisions a retailer makes is *what* to sell—its **merchandise mix**. This choice is similar to settling on a market segment (as discussed in Chapter 7): If a store's merchandise mix is too limited, it may not have enough potential customers, whereas if it is too broad, the retailer runs the risk of being a "jack of all trades, master of none." Because what the retailer sells is central to its identity, we will describe some retail types by merchandise mix.

While we learned in Chapter 9 that a manufacturer's product line consists of product offerings that satisfy a single need, in retailing a *product line* is a set of related products offered by a retailer, such as kitchen appliances or leather goods. The Census of Retail Trade, conducted by the U.S. Bureau of the Census, classifies all retailers by North American Industry Classification System (NAICS) codes (the same system we described in Chapter 6 that is used to classify industrial firms). A retailer that wants to identify direct competition can find other firms that are classified by the same NAICS codes.

However, a word of caution: As retailers experiment with different merchandise mixes, these direct comparisons are getting harder to make. For example, even though marketers like to distinguish between food and nonfood retailers, in reality these lines are blurring. Supermarkets are adding hardware product lines, and some department stores offer gourmet food.

For a while, British shoppers could pick up a pair of cut-rate-priced Levi's jeans while food shopping.[15] In 2001, Levi Strauss sued Tesco, a big U.K. grocery store chain, to prevent it from buying jeans at a low price in the United States, importing them into the United Kingdom, and then selling the jeans at very low prices along with scones and tea. Levi's argument was that it allows the sale of its jeans only in selected outlets that agree to provide the service and selection that customers want. Similar situations are common in retailing, such as warehouse stores that are not authorized dealers of designer clothing but are able to obtain the items at a low price and then stack the designer clothing on wooden palettes next to economy-size boxes of pretzels or jars of pickles.

The strategy of carrying a combination of food and nonfood items is called **scrambled merchandising**. This strategy is exemplified by Blockbuster Entertainment Group, which defines its merchandise mix in terms of products a customer might want when spending an evening at home. In addition to stocking your favorite James Bond video, the stores sell candy, soda, and even private-label popcorn to complete the couch potato experience.

Classifying Retailers by Level of Service

Retailers differ in the amount of service they provide for consumers. Firms recognize that there is a tradeoff between service and low prices, so they tailor their strategies to the level of service they offer. Customers who demand higher levels of service must be willing to pay for that service, and those who want lower prices must be willing to give up services.

Retailers like Sam's Club that promise bottom-dollar prices are often self-service operations. When customers shop at *self-service retailers*, they make their product selection without any assistance, they often must bring their own bags or containers to carry their purchases, and they may even handle the checkout process with self-service scanners.

Contrast that experience to visiting a *full-service retailer*. Many of us prefer to shop at major department stores like Bloomingdale's and specialty stores like Victoria's Secret because they pro-

merchandise mix
The total set of all products offered for sale by a retailer, including all product lines sold to all consumer groups.

scrambled merchandising
A merchandising strategy that offers consumers a mixture of merchandise items that are not directly related to each other.

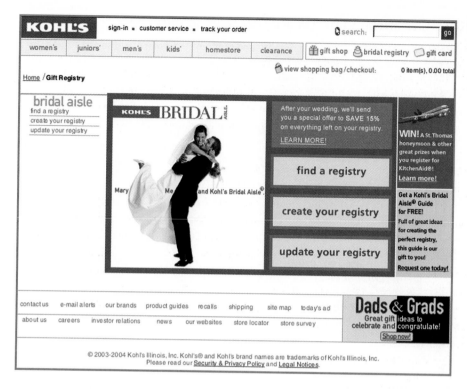

At limited-service retailers like Kohl's, customers select the merchandise themselves and in exchange save a buck or two.

vide supporting services such as gift wrapping, and they offer trained sales associates who can help us select that perfect present. Other specialized services are available based on the merchandise offered. For example, many full-service clothing retailers will provide alterations services. Retailers likes Macy's that carry china, silver, housewares, and other items brides might want offer special bridal consultants and bridal gift registries.

Falling in between self-service and full-service retailers are *limited-service retailers*. Stores like Wal-Mart, Target, Old Navy, and Kohl's offer credit and merchandise return but little else. Customers select merchandise without much assistance, preferring to pay a bit less rather than be waited on a bit more.

Classifying Retailers by Merchandise Selection

Another way to classify retailers is in terms of the selection they offer. A retailer's **merchandise assortment**, or selection of products sold, has two dimensions: breadth and depth. **Merchandise breadth**, or variety, is the number of different product lines available. A *narrow assortment*, such as that found in convenience stores, means that shoppers will find only a limited selection of product lines such as candy, cigarettes, and soft drinks. A *broad assortment*, such as that in a warehouse store, means there is a wide range of items from eyeglasses to barbecue grills.

Merchandise depth is the variety of choices available for each specific product. A *shallow assortment* means that the selection within a product category is limited, so a factory outlet store may sell only white and blue men's dress shirts (all made by the same manufacturer, of course) and only in standard sizes. In contrast, a men's specialty store may feature a *deep assortment* of dress shirts (but not much else) in varying shades and in hard-to-find sizes. Figure 16.1 illustrates these assortment differences for one product, science fiction books.

Now that we've seen how retailers differ in the breadth and depth of their assortments, let's review some of the major forms these retailers take.

merchandise assortment
The range of products sold.

merchandise breadth
The number of different product lines available.

merchandise depth
The variety of choices available for each specific product line.

Figure 16.1 Classification of Retailers by Merchandise Selection

Retail stores are often classified based on the breadth and depth of their merchandise assortment. In this figure, the two dimensions are used to classify types of bookstores that carry science fiction books.

Depth \ Breadth	Narrow	Broad
Shallow	Airport Bookstore: A few *Lord of the Rings* books	Sam's Club: A few *Lord of the Rings* books and a limited assortment of *Lord of the Rings* T-shirts and toys
Deep	www.legendaryheroes.com: Internet retailer selling only merchandise for *Lord of the Rings, The Highlander, Zena: Warrior Princess, Legendary Swords, Conan,* and *Hercules*	Barnes & Noble: Many titles in each of many categories from sci-fi to romance to cook books

convenience stores
Neighborhood retailers that carry a limited number of frequently purchased items and cater to consumers willing to pay a premium for the ease of buying close to home.

CONVENIENCE STORES **Convenience stores** carry a limited number of frequently purchased items, including basic food products, newspapers, and sundries. They cater to consumers willing to pay a premium for the ease of buying staple items close to home. In other words, they meet the needs of those who are pressed for time, who buy items in smaller quantities, or who shop at irregular hours. But these stores are starting to change, especially in urban areas where many time-pressed shoppers prefer to visit these outlets even for specialty items.

A new design for 7-Eleven stores illustrates that convenience stores aren't just for Slurpee drinks anymore. The chain, whose stores rack up $41 billion in sales worldwide and a daily average of 6 million customers alone in the United States, decided to pull out all the stops when it opened its 25,000th store. The new "urban" version boasts a huge coffee bar, flanked by cases of fresh-made deli sandwiches and pastries delivered fresh every day of the year. The wall is painted in "grasslands," not off-white. Pendant lamps hang from faux tin ceilings, and the porcelain-tile floors are meant to look like wood. At the opening, waiters in tuxedos served doughnut centers and taquitos while a high school choir belted "Oh Thank Heaven" (for 7-Eleven . . .).[16]

supermarkets
Food stores that carry a wide selection of edibles and related products.

SUPERMARKETS **Supermarkets** are food stores that carry a wide selection of edibles and nonedible products. Although the large supermarket is a fixture in the United States, it has not caught on to the same extent in other parts of the world. Europeans, for example, are used to walking or biking to small stores near their homes. They tend to have smaller food orders per trip and to shop more frequently, partly because many lack the freezer space to hoard a huge inventory of products at home. Wide variety is less important than quality and local ambiance, though, as we'll see shortly, those habits are changing as huge hypermarkets are becoming popular around the globe.

specialty stores
Retailers that carry only a few product lines but offer good selection within the lines that they sell.

SPECIALTY STORES **Specialty stores** have narrow and deep inventories. They do not sell a lot of product lines, but they offer good selection of brands within the lines they do sell. For many women with less-than-perfect figures, shopping at a store that sells only swimsuits means there will be an adequate selection to find a suit that really fits. The same is true for larger, taller men who can't find suits that fit in regular department stores but have lots of choices in stores that cater to big and tall guys. Specialty stores can tailor their assortment to the specific needs of a targeted consumer, and they often offer a high level of knowledgeable service.

7-Eleven's new "urban store" concept upgrades the convenience store experience for a new generation of sophisticated customers who want more than just Slurpees and speed.

DISCOUNT STORES   **General merchandise discount stores**, such as Sears, Kmart, and Wal-Mart, offer a broad assortment of items at low prices and with minimal service and are the dominant outlet for many products. Discounters are tearing up the retail landscape because they appeal to price-conscious shoppers who want easy access to a lot of merchandise. Kohl's, for example, is one of the nation's fastest-growing retailers. These stores increasingly carry designer name clothing at bargain prices as companies like Liz Claiborne are creating new lines just for discount stores.[17]

Some discount stores, such as Loehmann's, are **off-price retailers**. These stores obtain surplus merchandise from manufacturers and offer these brand-name, fashion-oriented goods at low prices.

Warehouse clubs such as Costco and BJ's are a newer version of the discount store. These establishments do not even pretend to offer any of the amenities of a full-service store; a bargain mentality is reinforced by merchandise that is displayed (often in its original box) in a cavernous, bare-bones facility. These clubs often charge a membership fee to consumers and small businesses. The typical warehouse shopper is likely to have a large family and a relatively high income and can afford to pay several hundred dollars to "stock up" on staples during one shopping trip.[18] Nothing like laying in a three-year supply of paper towels or five-pound boxes of pretzels—even if you have to build an extra room in your house to store all this stuff! And, consistent with the wheel of retailing, even these stores are "trading up" in terms of what they sell—today shoppers can purchase fine jewelry and other luxury items at many of these stores. Costco now sells fine art, including limited-edition lithographs by Pablo Picasso, Marc Chagall, and Joan Miró.[19] Take a few home today!

The **factory outlet store** is still another type of discount retailer. These stores are owned by a manufacturer. Some factory outlets enable the manufacturer to sell off defective merchandise or excess inventory, while others carry items not available at full-price retail outlets and are designed to provide an additional distribution channel for the manufacturer. Although the assortment is not wide because a store carries only products made by one manufacturer, most factory outlet stores are located in *outlet* malls where a large number of factory outlet stores cluster together in the same location. And, in keeping with the wheel-of-retailing idea, we are starting to see outlet malls adding amenities such as elaborate food courts and local entertainment.

general merchandise discount stores
Retailers that offer a broad assortment of items at low prices with minimal service.

off-price retailers
Retailers that buy excess merchandise from well-known manufacturers and pass the savings on to customers.

warehouse clubs
Discount retailers that charge a modest membership fee to consumers that buy a broad assortment of food and nonfood items in bulk and in a warehouse environment.

factory outlet store
A discount retailer, owned by a manufacturer, that sells off defective merchandise and excess inventory.

Warehouse clubs continue to expand their range of offerings. Today shoppers can stock up on doughnuts, deodorants, dust ruffles, and even expensive watches and diamonds on the same trip.

department stores
Retailers that sell a broad range of items and offer a good selection within each product line.

DEPARTMENT STORES   Department stores sell a broad range of items and offer a deep selection organized into different sections of the store. Grand department stores dominated urban centers in the early part of the 20th century. In their heyday, these stores sold airplanes and auctioned fine art. Lord & Taylor even offered its customers a mechanical horse to ensure the perfect fit of riding habits.

In many countries, department stores are thriving and remain consumers' primary place to shop. In Japan, department stores are always crowded with shoppers buying everything from a takeaway sushi dinner to a string of fine pearls. In Spain, a single department store chain, El Corte Engles, dominates retailing. Its branch stores include store-size departments for electronics, books, music, and gourmet foods, and each has a vast supermarket covering one or two floors of the store. In the United States, however, department stores have struggled in recent years. Specialty stores have lured department store shoppers away with deeper, more cutting-edge fashion selections and better service. Department stores have also been squeezed by mass merchandisers and catalogs that can offer the same items at lower prices because they don't have the expense of rent, elaborate store displays and fixtures, or high salaries for salespeople.

Because of these recent problems, department stores are searching for different strategies to compete. Some retail stores have pruned their assortments to concentrate more on *soft goods*, such as clothing and home furnishings, and less on *hard goods*, such as appliances. Macy's dropped its electronics department altogether and used the space instead to create its highly successful Macy's Cellar, which features tastefully displayed cooking items and food.

Some department stores are trying to go upscale by introducing amenities such as valet parking; others are competing more directly with discount stores by offering shopping carts. Nordstrom and Saks Fifth Avenue are cutting prices, while May Company is targeting specific types of customers like brides. Federated is trying still a different strategy: To increase sales for young women's clothing, the chain is enhancing young women's departments with new sound systems and Internet access. The chain is also placing these departments near the young men's department to create more of a social atmosphere.[20]

HYPERMARKETS   **Hypermarkets** combine the characteristics of warehouse stores and supermarkets. Originally introduced in Europe, these are huge establishments several times larger than other stores. A supermarket might be 40,000 to 50,000 square feet, whereas a hypermarket takes up 200,000 to 300,000 square feet, or four football fields. They offer one-stop shopping, often for over 50,000 items, and feature restaurants, beauty salons, and children's play areas. Hypermarkets, such as those run by the French firm Carrefours, are popular in Europe and Latin America, where big stores are somewhat of a novelty. More recently, Carrefours has expanded to developing countries such as Egypt, where a burgeoning population and a lack of large retailers provides hyper-opportunities. Hypermarkets have been less successful in the United States, where so many discount stores, malls, and supermarkets are available. Consumers in the United States find the hypermarkets to be too large and shopping in them too time consuming.

Nonstore Retailing

Stores like The Limited succeed because they put cool merchandise in the hands of young shoppers who can't get it elsewhere. But competition for shoppers' dollars comes from sources other than traditional stores, ranging from bulky catalogs to dynamic Web sites. Debbie in Dubuque can easily log on to Alloy.com at 3:00 A.M. and order the latest belly-baring fashions without leaving home.

As the founder of the Neiman-Marcus department store once noted, "If customers don't want to get off their butts and go to your stores, you've got to go to them."[21] Indeed, many products are readily available in places other than stores. Think of the familiar Avon Lady selling beauty products to millions of women around the world. Avon allows customers to place orders by phone, fax, or catalog or through a sales representative.

Avon's success at giving customers alternatives to traditional store outlets illustrates the increasing importance of **nonstore retailing**, which is any method a firm uses to complete an exchange that does not require a customer visit to a store. Indeed, many conventional retailers—from upscale specialty stores such as Tiffany's to discounter Wal-Mart—offer nonstore alternatives such as catalogs and Web sites for customers interested in buying their merchandise. For other companies such as catalog merchandisers L.L. Bean and Lands' End, nonstore retailing is their entire business.

We talked about direct marketing done through the mail, the telephone, and television in Chapter 13. In this section, we'll look at two other types of nonstore retailing: direct selling and automatic vending.

Direct Selling

Direct selling occurs when a salesperson presents a product to one individual or a small group, takes orders, and delivers the merchandise. This form of nonstore retailing works well for vacuum cleaners, nutritional products, and educational materials—products that require a great deal of information to sell. Most people involved in direct selling are independent agents who buy the merchandise from the company and then resell it to consumers.

DOOR-TO-DOOR SALES   Although door-to-door selling is popular in some countries such as China, it is declining in the United States because fewer women are home during the day and those

hypermarkets
Retailers with the characteristics of both warehouse stores and supermarkets; hypermarkets are several times larger than other stores and offer virtually everything from grocery items to electronics.

nonstore retailing
Any method used to complete an exchange with a product end user that does not require a customer visit to a store.

direct selling
An interactive sales process in which a salesperson presents a product to one individual or a small group, takes orders, and delivers the merchandise.

Experience the taste.
Taste the experience.

Receive a **FREE** recipe book when hosting "A Taste of Tupperware" Party.

recipes

Tupperware

Contact your Consultant or call **1-888-TUPWARE** or visit **www.tupperware.com** to locate a local Distributor.

Tupperware®

Surprising products. Tantalizing tastes and aromas.
Simple solutions for everyday living. Discover the new
Tupperware party experience, **"A Taste of Tupperware."**
You'll be delighted by how fresh we've become.

In USA contact 1-888-TUPWARE or visit www.tupperware.com
In Canada contact 1-800-567-0400 or visit www.tupperware.ca

A Taste of Tupperware

The new party experience

Tupperware was built on the party plan system.

party plan system
A sales technique that relies heavily on people getting caught up in the "group spirit," buying things they would not normally buy if alone.

multilevel network
A system in which a master distributor recruits other people to become distributors, sells the company's product to the recruits, and receives a commission on all the merchandise sold by the people recruited.

pyramid schemes
An illegal sales technique in which the initial distributors profit by selling merchandise to other distributors, with the result that consumers buy very little product.

who are home are reluctant to open their doors to strangers. Companies that used to rely on door-to-door sales have had to adapt their retailing strategies. Avon now sells to women at the office during lunch and coffee breaks.

PARTIES AND NETWORKS   About three-quarters of direct sales are made in the consumer's home, sometimes at a *home shopping party*, at which a company representative makes a sales presentation to a group of people who have gathered in the home of a friend. People who attend may get caught up in the "group spirit," buying things they would not normally buy if alone—even Botox injections to get rid of those nasty wrinkles. This technique is called a **party plan system**.

Perhaps the most famous party products are Tupperware. Tupperware parties "became synonymous with American suburban life in the 1950s."[22] Today, Tupperware has over a million salespeople in more than 100 countries and sells its plasticware through the Internet, infomercials, and mall kiosks. Tupperware parties are now more likely to be a rush-hour office event at the end of the workday.

Another form of nonstore retailing, epitomized by the Amway Company, is called a **multilevel network**, or *network marketing*. In this system, a master distributor recruits other people to become distributors. The master distributor sells the company's products to the people she entices to join, then she receives commissions on all the merchandise sold by the people she recruits. Today, Amway has more than 3.6 million independent business owners who distribute personal care, home care, and nutrition and commercial products in more than 80 countries and territories.[23] Amway and other companies like it use revival-like techniques to motivate distributions to sell products and find new recruits.[24]

One of the advantages of multilevel marketing is that it allows firms to reach consumers who belong to tightly knit groups that are not so easy to reach. Salt Lake City–based Nu Skin Enterprises relies on Mormons to sell its products in Mormon communities. Shaklee (which sells food supplements, cleaning products, and personal care items) recruits salespeople in isolated religious communities, including Amish and Mennonite people (who receive "bonus buggies" instead of cars as prizes for superior salesmanship).[25] Despite the growing popularity of this technique, some network systems are illegal. They are really **pyramid schemes** in which the initial distributors profit by selling merchandise to other distributors—very little product ever gets to consumers.[26]

Automatic Vending

Coin-operated vending machines are a tried-and-true way to sell convenience goods, especially cigarettes and drinks. These machines are appealing because they require minimal space and personnel to maintain and operate. Some of the most interesting innovations are state-of-the-art vending machines, which dispense everything from Ore-Ida french fries to software. French consumers can even purchase Levi's jeans from a machine called Libre Service that offers the pants in 10 different sizes.

Modern vending machines are capable of selling a broad range of products. The bait machine on the right dispenses prepackaged minnows, night crawlers, red wigglers, and crickets in styrofoam containers that keep bait fresh for up to one week. The one on the left dispenses cigars, and it features a direct line customers can use to order boxes of the cigars they purchase from the vending machine. Important: Do not mix up these two machines!

In general, vending machines are best suited to the sales of inexpensive merchandise and food and beverages. Most consumers are reluctant to buy pricey items from a machine. New vending machines may spur more interest, however, as technological developments loom on the horizon, including video kiosk machines that let people see the product in use, the ability to accept credit cards as payment, and inventory systems that signal the operator when malfunctions or stockouts occur.

B2C E-Commerce

Business-to-consumer (B2C) e-commerce is the online exchange between companies and individual consumers. Forrester Research reports that in 2003 over 67 million U.S. households were connected to the Internet, spending an average of 8.5 hours per week online for personal reasons.[27] Over half of these (51 percent) or 33 million households buy online (they spent $76 billion online in 2002), and almost 24 million bank online. This compares with only 17 million online shoppers reported in 1999.[28]

What is powering this online retail growth? As more people shop, more retailers will enter the Web marketplace, making more types of products available. At the same time, enhanced technology and improvements in delivery and security entice even more consumers to shop online. Table 16.1 shows 2003 and predicted 2008 B2C sales in various product categories.

business-to-consumer (B2C) e-commerce
Online exchanges between companies and individual consumers.

Table 16.1 B2C Sales by Product Category

Product Category	2003 Online Sales (in $billions)	Projected 2008 Online Sales (in $billions)
Computer hardware	7.4	8.5
Computer software	2.1	2.9
Books	2.8	5.5
Music	1.2	2.5
Videos	1.8	5.6
General apparel	6.3	18.7
Footwear	1.5	4.8
Health and beauty	1.5	4.5
Toys and video games	2.8	5.5
Food and beverage	3.7	17.4
Furniture	1.4	5.1
Travel	27.3	53.0

Source: Adapted from Carfrie A. Johnson, Kate Delhagen, and Esther H. Yuen, *U.S. eCommerce Overview: 2003–2008*, Forrester Research, Inc., July 25, 2003.

Electronic commerce in retailing has enormous potential. The continued success of this non-store format will depend on the ability of retailers to offer sites that are entertaining and informative and that are worth surfing to even after the novelty wears off. Lands' End, for example, offers a virtual model on its Web site that you can customize to your own body type as you let it "try on" that blouse or shorts before you buy.

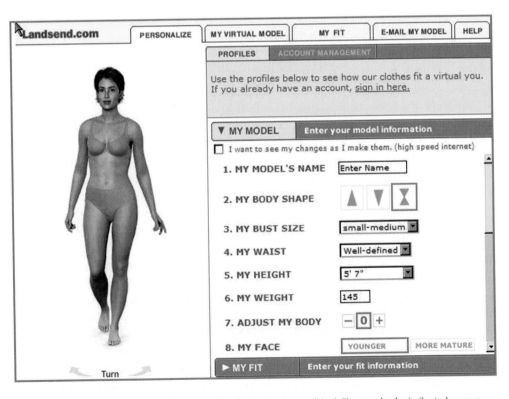

Lands' End's virtual model enables a shopper to "see" what an item will look like on a body similar to her own.

Table 16.2 Benefits and Limitations of E-Commerce

Benefits	Limitations
For the consumer:	**For the consumer:**
Shop 24 hours a day	Lack of security
Less traveling	Fraud
Can receive relevant information in seconds from any location	Can't touch items
More product choices	Exact colors may not reproduce on computer monitors
More products available to less developed countries	Expensive to order and then return
Greater price information	Potential breakdown of human relationships
Lower prices so that less affluent can purchase	**For the marketer:**
Participate in virtual auctions	Lack of security
Fast delivery	Must maintain site to reap benefits
Electronic communities	Fierce price competition
For the marketer:	Conflicts with conventional retailers
The world is your marketplace	Legal issues not resolved
Decreases costs of doing business	
Very specialized businesses can be successful	
Real-time pricing	

Benefits of B2C E-Commerce

For both consumers and marketers, B2C e-commerce provides a host of benefits and some limitations. Some of these are listed in Table 16.2. E-commerce allows consumers and marketers to easily find and make exchanges in a global marketplace. Consumers can choose from hundreds of thousands of sellers worldwide, while marketers can tap into consumer and business markets with virtually no geographic limitations.

From the consumer's perspective, electronic marketing has increased convenience by breaking down many of the barriers caused by time and location. You can shop 24/7 without leaving home. Electronic marketing makes more products available to consumers. Consumers in even the smallest of communities can purchase funky shoes or a hot swimsuit from Bloomingdales.com just like big-city dwellers. In less developed countries, the Internet lets consumers purchase products that may not be available at all in local markets. Thus, the Internet can improve the quality of life without the necessity of developing costly infrastructure, such as opening retail stores in remote locations.

Understanding just what online shoppers really desire and why they are shopping online can help marketers be more successful. For some consumers, online shopping provides an additional benefit by fulfilling their experiential needs, that is, their need to shop for fun.[29] Consumers who are collectors or who enjoy hobbies are most likely to be **experiential shoppers**. While most online consumers engage in goal-directed behavior—they wish to satisfy their shopping goal as quickly as possible—between 20 and 30 percent of online consumers shop online because they enjoy the "thrill of the hunt" as much or more than the actual acquisition of the item. Experiential shoppers stick to sites longer and are motivated by a desire to be entertained. Consequently, marketers who wish to attract these customers must design Web sites that offer surprise, uniqueness, and excitement. Land-sEnd.com gives frequent markdowns on overstock items encouraging bargain-hunter experiential

experiential shoppers
Consumers who engage in online shopping because of the experiential benefits they receive.

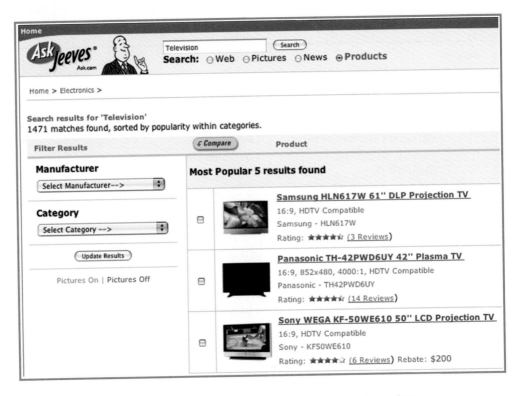

Comparison sites like Ask Jeeves scour the Web for competitive prices and product reviews.

shoppers to visit the site more frequently. How well a site satisfies experiential needs might determine how much money consumers will choose to spend at that site.

Marketers realize equally important benefits from e-commerce. Because marketers can reach such a large number of consumers with electronic commerce, it is possible to develop very specialized businesses that could not be profitable if limited by geographic constraints. For example, although your town may not have enough fanatic dog owners to support a doggie toy store, there are a number of sites on the Web, including Dogtoys.com and Petexpo.net, that cater to the needs of pampered pooches.

As we discussed in Chapter 11, one of the biggest advantages of e-commerce is that it's easy to get price information. Want to buy a new Hellboy action figure, a mountain bike, an MP3 player, or just about anything else you can think of? Instead of plodding from store to store to compare prices, many Web surfers use search engines or "shop bots" like Ask Jeeves that compile and compare prices from multiple vendors. With readily available pricing information, shoppers can browse brands, features, reviews, and information on where to buy that particular product—the benefit being that consumers can find all of this information in one central location, making it easy to spend their dollars more efficiently.

E-commerce also allows businesses to reduce costs. Compared to traditional bricks-and-mortar retailers, cost for e-tailers is minimal—no expensive mall sites and no need for in-store sales associates. And, for some products, such as computer software and digitized music, e-commerce provides fast, almost instantaneous delivery. Beginning in 2000, consumers could download music at no charge, thanks to a program created by 19-year-old college dropout Shawn Fanning. Although Napster didn't store music on its own servers, the Napster program allowed its members to download music that other Napster members had on their computers. After being sued by the Recording Industry Association of America as well as the heavy-metal band Metallica, Napster closed its service in July 2001. In 2003, after years of dealing with such digital piracy, the music industry began licensing music to a host of legal download services. Music fans responded by buying over 30 million downloads from sites including iTunes (an Apple Computer site), Dell, and Wal-Mart Stores, Inc. Even Napster has been reopened—although today the downloads no longer are free.[30]

Limitations of B2C E-Commerce

Alas, all is not perfect in the virtual world. E-commerce does have its limitations. One drawback relative to shopping in a store is that customers still must wait a few days to receive most products, which are often sent via private delivery services, so shoppers can't achieve instant gratification by walking out of a store clutching their latest "finds." And many e-commerce sites still suffer from poor design that people find confusing or irritating. One study found that 65 percent of online shoppers empty their carts before they complete their purchase because they find the process hard to follow and there are no "flesh and blood" customer service people available to answer questions. To make matters worse, 30 percent of online shoppers who have problems with a Web site say they won't shop there again, and 10 percent say they won't shop online at all anymore.[32]

Security is a concern to both consumers and marketers. We hear horror stories of consumers whose credit cards and other identity information have been stolen. Although an individual's financial liability in most theft cases is limited to $50, the damage to one's credit rating can last for years.

Consumers also are concerned about Internet fraud. Although most of us feel competent to judge a local bricks-and-mortar business by its physical presence, by how long it's been around, and from the reports of friends and neighbors who shop there, we have little or no information on the millions of Internet sites offering their products for sale—even though sites like eBay try to address these concerns by posting extensive information about the reliability of individual vendors.

Another problem is that people need "touch-and-feel" information before buying many products. Although it may be satisfactory to buy a computer or a book on the Internet, buying clothing and other items where touching the item or trying it on is essential may be less attractive. As with catalogs, even though most online companies have liberal return policies, consumers can still get stuck with large delivery and return shipping charges for items that don't fit or simply aren't the right color. Although online sales account for more than a quarter of the personal computers sold, less than 2 percent of apparel sales are transacted this way—and 30 percent of this clothing bought online will be returned.[33] In some cases, ingenious businesspeople find ways to combine electronic retailing with traditional shopping to overcome this barrier. For example, Peapod.com offers home delivery of groceries that have been selected by a "personal shopper" who fills Internet orders based on customers' exact preferences, even squeezing fruit to be sure they correspond to the person's ripeness specifications.[34]

Traditional bricks-and-mortar companies such as The Limited are actually *more* likely to be successful in cyberspace than are Internet-only start-ups because they already have established brand names and a base of loyal customers. From Wal-Mart to Circuit City, traditional retailers are going online, many combining their Web retailing with existing stores. For example, at Circuit City and Office Depot, customers can check the inventories of stores near them for availability of an item and then pick the item up at the store.[35]

MEASURING VALUE
marketing metrics

E-commerce marketers often want to measure a metric they call the *conversion rate*, which is the percentage of visitors to an online store who purchase from it. This is a useful metric, but if this rate is low, it doesn't help the retailer understand the possible factors affecting the Web site's performance. So, in addition to knowing the conversion rate, researchers at IBM compute other metrics called *microconversion rates* that enable them to pinpoint more precisely what may need to be improved in the online shopping process[31]. This technique breaks down the shopping experience into the stages that are involved between visiting a site and actually making a transaction:

Product impression: Viewing a hyperlink to a Web page presenting a product
Click-through: Clicking on the hyperlink and viewing the product's Web page
Basket placement: Placing the item in the "shopping basket"
Purchase: Actually buying the item

These researchers calculate microconversion rates for each adjacent pair of measures to come up with additional metrics that can pinpoint specific problems in the shopping process:

- **Look-to-click rate:** How many product impressions are converted to click-throughs? This can help the e-tailer determine if the products featured on the Web site are the ones that customers want to see.
- **Click-to-basket rate:** How many click-throughs result in a product being placed in the shopping basket? This metric helps to determine if the detailed information provided about the product is appropriate.
- **Basket-to-buy rate:** How many basket placements are converted to purchases? This metric can tell the e-tailer which kinds of products are more likely to be abandoned in the shopping cart instead of being bought. It can also pinpoint possible problems with the checkout process, such as forcing the shopper to answer too many questions or making her wait too long for her credit card to be approved.

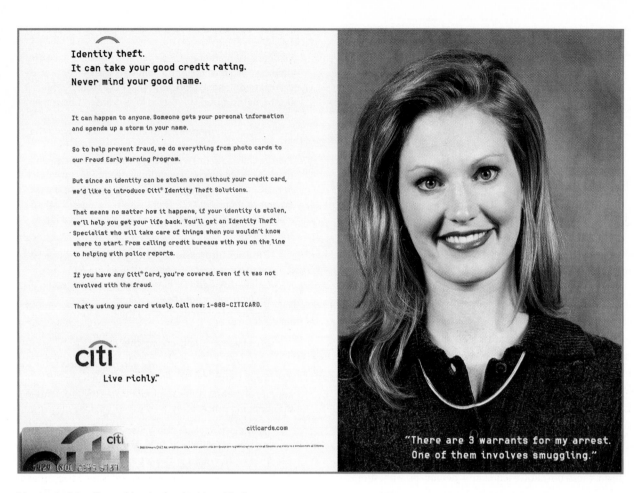

Identity theft is still a problem in the virtual world of e-commerce.

Catalog companies have had the easiest time making the transition to the Web since they have the most experience delivering goods directly to consumers. That explains why almost three-quarters of these firms have profitable e-commerce sites, whereas less than 40 percent of other Web retailers are in the black so far.[36]

We're also seeing movement in the opposite direction. Online travel companies like Expedia.com are adding off-line operations and buying traditional travel agencies (recently Expedia paid $48 million to acquire a retail chain called Classic Custom Vacations). These businesses recognize that many shoppers use the Web to research their travel options but then actually purchase their tickets off-line because of concerns about security and privacy. As one online analyst observed, "A lot of folks who used to think we live in a milk-or-meat world are now realizing that travelers aren't kosher. They'll buy the type of travel they want through the channel they want."[37]

Developing countries with primarily cash economies pose yet another obstacle to the success of B2C e-commerce. In these countries, few people use credit cards, so they can't easily pay for items they purchase over the Internet. An alternative for payments that may gain popularity in the future is *digital cash*. Currently, digital cash is available on prepaid cards and smart cards such as a prepaid phone card. Another alternative is e-cash, developed by Digicash of Amsterdam. E-cash provides secure payments between computers using e-mail or the Internet. You can use e-cash to buy a pizza or to get money from home. To do so, you need e-cash client software and a *digital bank account*, a Web-based account that allows you to make payments to Internet

Advice for LimitedBrands

VISITING LECTURER
LISA GANGADEEN
University of Miami

I would choose option 2, open new stores in nonmall venues, such as strip centers, specialty centers, and street locations. The issue deals primarily with one of the four Ps of marketing: place or location, in addition to changing demographics. Before LimitedBrands chooses a new store location, more market analysis is recommended for demographic shifts, market segmentation, and target marketing. Getting back to the basics, there needs to be clarity at the store level of the market segment, target market, and image. One such real-life success story is Starbucks. They have a proven formula for expanding profitably with new store locations in urban, more affluent areas, such as South Miami Beach and San Francisco. In these cities, it is not uncommon to see upwards of five Starbucks locations within a three-mile radius. In conclusion, it is recommended that LimitedBrands implement option 2 with a delicate balance of modeling the success of Starbucks while not reliving Gap's experience.

STUDENT
TOM LACNY
University of Notre Dame

I would choose option 2. With the ongoing consolidation and decreased draw of malls and mall department stores in recent years, LimitedBrands must look to new markets to ensure future success. Even in the unlikely event that adjoining space was available at a reasonable price, option 1 would not address the changing face of the retail industry. In addition, option 1 involves altering LimitedBrands' current model, which is clearly successful given the company's desire for growth. By instead targeting heavily trafficked, upscale areas with high disposable incomes, LimitedBrands can achieve its goals of increasing square footage as well as revenue and profits without diminishing its brand prestige with less desirable locations. Establishing locations in new and expanding downtowns or business districts would allow the retailer to effectively reach new and existing customers more frequently. With its growth in Internet and catalog sales, LimitedBrands might also look to international markets, where its upscale brands, "American identity," and specialty retailing expertise could prove to be very successful.

PROFESSOR
ERIC NELSON
Saint Michael's College

I would choose option 1. Increasing volume within existing stores is consistent with LimitedBrands' current positioning strategy as a high-end specialty retailer. Expansion for brand names such as Tiffany's and Banana Republic is a tricky balancing act that can mean consolidating into fewer profit centers. Adding a significant number of stores could result in "cheapening" the brand name in consumers' eyes and could result in reaching a completely different, and possibly unwanted, target market. While star performers such as Victoria's Secret and Bath & Body Works could look to adding sites in nontraditional mall settings such as airports, high-end hotel minimalls, and upscale entertainment meccas (golf resorts, casinos, and vacation resorts), LimitedBrands needs to keep in mind that people associate the quality of the products offered with the quality of the mall or area surrounding the retail location.

retailers directly from the account while online. You withdraw money from your bank account, store it on your computer, and spend it when you need to. When the going gets tough, the tough go shopping!

As major marketers beef up their presence on the Web, they worry that inventory they sell online will cannibalize their store sales. This is a big problem for companies like bookseller Barnes & Noble, which has to be careful about steering customers toward a Web site and away from its chain of stores bursting with inventory. Barnes & Noble has to deal with competitors such as

Advice for LimitedBrands

PROFESSOR
W. ROCKY NEWMAN
Department of Management, Miami University of Ohio

From an operational standpoint, I would go with option 1 and look to expand in the best (and assumed most profitable) stores. While greater investments are required, sticking to a proven strategy helps mitigate the risk associated with scaling the operations larger. Operationally, issues of staffing, compensation, scheduling, inventory management, and logistics would be the least affected by this strategy.

Diversifying the approach taken by the chain to include either "nonmall venues" or "lower-tier malls" could be introducing unexpected complexity into their business model. What demographic differences will they find in the clientele frequenting those new venues? Will new demographics mean a change in the typical product mix sold at those stores? How will that mix change the services provided as part of what they "sell"? While applying multiple approaches to operating different venues is not always a bad idea (i.e., Holiday Inns vs. Holiday Inn Express, Wal-Mart vs. Sam's Club), it must be based on a clear identification of the differences and what market segments they are targeted toward. That does not seem to be established in this case. The goal here seems to be growth rather than diversification from an established marketplace.

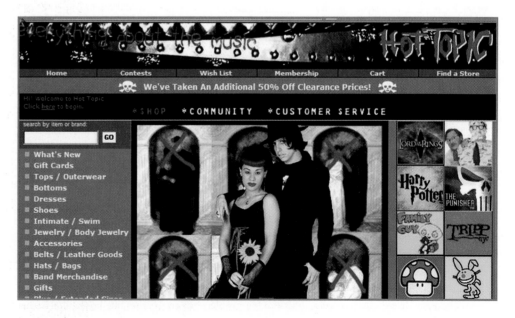

Retailers like youth-oriented Hot Topic reinforce their identities with Web sites that mirror their bricks-and-mortar store personalities.

Amazon.com (with 40 million worldwide customers and annual sales of not only books but a myriad of products from apparel to cell phones of over $6 billion in 2004), which sells its books and music exclusively over its six global Web sites.[38]

B2C's Effect on the Future of Retailing

Does the growth of B2C e-commerce mean the death of bricks-and-mortar stores as we know them? Don't plan any funerals for your local stores prematurely. Although some argue that virtual distribution channels will completely replace traditional ones because of their cost advantages, this is unlikely. For example, although a bank saves 80 percent of its costs when customers do business online from their home computers, Wells Fargo found that it could not force its customers to use PC-based banking services. At least in the short term, too many people are accustomed to obtaining goods and services from stores—and, of course, shopping provides a social outlet that (at least now) can't be replaced by solitary surfing. At least in the near future, clicks will have to coexist with bricks.[39]

Stores as we know them will have to continue to evolve to lure shoppers away from their computer screens. In the future, the trend will be "destination retail." Many retailers are already developing ways to make the shopping in bricks-and-mortar stores an experience rather than just a place to pick up stuff. For example, Levi Strauss opened a retail store in San Francisco that features a "shrink-to-fit" hot tub, fabric painting and ornamentation services, and a showcase of new music, art, and Levi's product samples from around the world. At the General Mills Cereal Adventure in the Mall of America, children of all ages can cavort in the Cheerios Play Park and the Lucky Charms Magical Forest.[40] Sony's Metreon in San Francisco is a high-tech mall featuring futuristic computer games and cutting-edge electronics.[41]

Developing a Store Positioning Strategy: Retailing as Theater

A "destination retail" strategy reminds us that shopping often is part buying, part entertainment, and part social outlet. So far we've seen that stores can be distinguished in several ways, including the types of products they carry and the breadth and depth of their assortments. But recall that a store is itself a product that adds to or subtracts from the goods the shopper came to buy there.

When we are deciding which store to patronize, many of us are less likely to say "I'll go there because their assortment is broad," and more likely to say "That place is so cool. I really enjoy hanging out there." Stores can entertain us, bore us, make us angry, or even make us sad (unless it's a funeral parlor, that kind probably won't be in business for long). In today's competitive marketplace, retailers have to do more than offer good inventory at reasonable prices. They need to position their stores so that they offer a competitive advantage over other stores also vying for the shopper's attention—not to mention the catalogs, Web sites, and shopping channels that may offer the same or similar merchandise without having to leave home. Let's see next how bricks-and-mortar retailers are competing.

Walk into REI, a Seattle-based retailer with over 70 stores in 24 states, and you'll find gear for camping, climbing, cycling, skiing, outdoor cross-training, paddling, snow sports, and travel. REI is more than that, though. The Seattle store, for example, features a 65-foot-high, artificial climbing rock, while other REI stores include a vented area for testing camp stoves and an outdoor trail to check out mountain bikes. Buying a water pump? Test it in an indoor river. Want to try out those boots before you walk in them? Take a walk on hiking boot test trails.[42]

In Chapter 10, we saw that staging a service is much like putting on a play. Similarly, many retailers recognize that much of what they do is theater. At a time when it is possible to pick up a phone or log on to a computer to buy many items, a customer must have a reason to make a trip to

REI creates a stimulating, interactive shopping environment. Some stores, like this one in Seattle, even include a rock-climbing pinnacle.

a store instead. True, you can probably buy that jacket over the Web, but try getting your computer to rain on it.

Shoppers are an audience to entertain. The "play" can cleverly employ stage sets (store design) and actors (salespeople) that together create a "scene." For example, think about buying a pair of sneakers. Athletic shoe stores are a far cry from the old days, when a tired shoe salesman (much like Al Bundy in the TV show *Married with Children*) waded through box after box of shoes as kids ran amuck across dingy floors. Now salespeople (actors) are dressed in costumes such as black-striped referee outfits. Stores like Woolworth's World Foot Locker are ablaze with neon, with the shoes displayed in clear acrylic walls so that they appear to be floating.[43] All these special effects make the buying occasion less about buying and more about having an experience. As one marketing strategist commented, "The line between retail and entertainment is blurring."[44] In this section, we'll review some of the tools available to the retailing playwright.

Store Image

When people think of a store, they often have no trouble portraying it in the same terms they might use in describing a person. They might use words such as *exciting, depressed, old-fashioned, tacky,* or *elegant.* **Store image** is how the target market perceives the store—its market position relative to the competition. Even stores operated by the same parent company such as Federated can be quite different from one another: Bloomingdale's department store is seen by many as chic and fashionable, especially compared to a more traditional competitor such as Macy's. These images don't just happen. Just as brand managers do for products, store managers work hard to create a "personality."

To appreciate this idea, consider the dramatic makeover now in place at Selfridges, long a well-known but dowdy British department store chain. At the newly renovated flagship store in London, shoppers can wander over to a body-piercing salon staffed by teenagers in dreadlocks. In the children's department, giant white plastic blobs hold racks of shocking-pink playsuits. Need a break from browsing? Go to one of the store's 14 restaurants, which often share a theme with the adjacent selling floor. Base Bar, a stripped-down cafeteria full of gleaming aluminum, is next to computers; Lab Cafe is minimalist, next to young designers' clothes. The store's makeover is accented by periodic events that scream cutting edge, including one called "Body Craze," where thousands of shoppers flocked to see 650 naked people ride the escalators. Do not attempt this at home.[45]

Not every store can (or wants!) to have naked people running around the store, but even more modest strategies to enliven the atmosphere make a big difference. In developing a desirable store image, the resourceful retailer has a number of choices. Ideally, all these elements should work together to create a clear, coherent picture that meets consumers' expectations of what that particular shopping experience should be. Figure 16.2 illustrates one attempt to identify and compare the store images of eight different department stores in the New York City area.

Atmospherics is the use of color, lighting, scents, furnishings, sounds, and other design elements to create a desired setting. Marketers manipulate these to create a certain "feeling" about the retail environment.[46] Kinney's Colorado Stores, which sell high-end outdoor clothing, for example, are designed to make the shoppers feel they're out in nature. The stores pipe in New Age background music, interrupted occasionally by the sound of a thunderstorm or a babbling brook.

store image
The way a retailer is perceived in the marketplace relative to the competition.

atmospherics
The use of color, lighting, scents, furnishings, and other design elements to create a desired store image.

Figure 16.2 Mapping a Store's Personality

Marketers can use perceptual mapping to chart the personality of retail stores.

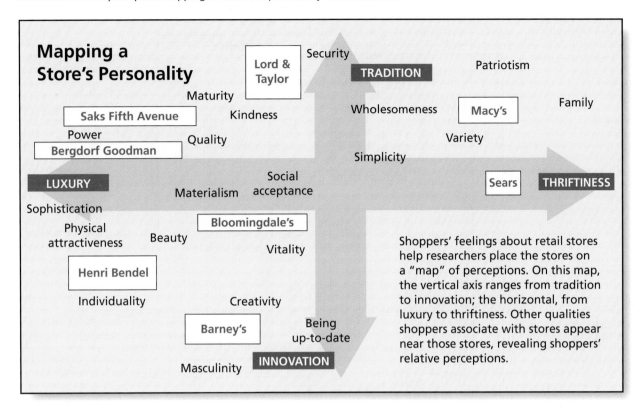

Source: Adapted from BBDO; Stephanie From, "Image and Attitude Are Department Stores' Draw," *New York Times*, August 12, 1993, B1.

Motion sensors in the ceiling activate displays as a shopper approaches, so, for example, a person who walks near an arrangement of beach shoes may hear the sound of waves crashing.[47] The owners of these stores believe that getting people "in the mood" makes them more likely to buy what they see. Recently, Taco Bell sought to use decor to change its image from cheap fast food to a kind of "Starbucks with a Spanish accent."[48] To attract a wider range of customers, Taco Bell used more wood, natural fibers, and new colors.

STORE DESIGN: SETTING THE STAGE The elements of store design should correspond to management's desired image. A bank lobby needs to convey respectability and security because people need to be reassured about the safety of their money. In contrast, a used bookstore might create a disorderly look so that shoppers think treasures lie buried beneath piles of tattered novels. Chili's Grill & Bar restaurant recently opened a new restaurant in Denver. Because of heightened competition from other restaurants with similar menus, Chili's is using radical store design (a restaurant in the shape of a huge chili pepper) to woo customers who are looking for a "hot" dining experience.[49]

Here are some other design factors that retailers consider:

- **Store layout:** This is the arrangement of merchandise in the store. The placement of fixtures such as shelves, racks, and cash registers is important because store layout determines **traffic flow**, that is, how shoppers will move through the store and what areas they will pass or avoid. A *grid layout*, usually found in supermarkets and discount stores, consists of rows of neatly spaced shelves that are at right angles or parallel to one another. This configuration is useful when management wants to systematically move shoppers down each aisle, being sure that they pass through such high-margin sections as deli and meat. Figure 16.3 illustrates how a grid layout in a supermarket helps regulate traffic flow.

traffic flow

The direction in which shoppers will move through the store and what areas they will pass or avoid.

Figure 16.3 Grid Layout

A grid layout encourages customers to move up and down the aisles, passing many different products, and is often used by supermarkets and discount stores.

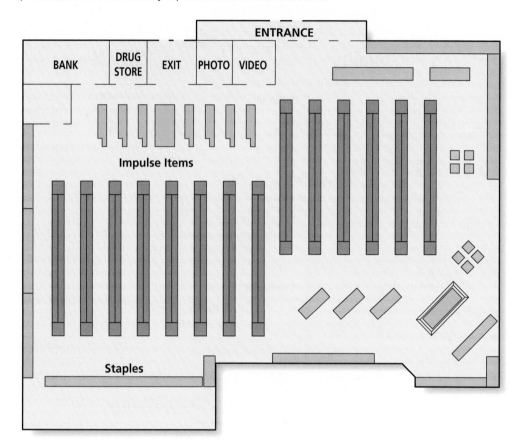

A typical strategy is to place staple goods in more remote areas. The designers know that traffic will move to these areas because these are frequently purchased items. They try to place impulse goods in spots shoppers will pass on their way elsewhere. Then they place eye-catching displays to rope people in, such as the signs for Mountain Dew that PepsiCo puts above the cash registers in convenience stores that look like a mountain biker dropped through the ceiling.[50]

In contrast, a *free-flow layout* is more often used in department and specialty stores because it is conducive to browsing. A retailer might arrange merchandise in circles or arches or perhaps in separate areas, each with its own distinct image and merchandise mix.

- **Fixture type and merchandise density:** Just as we may form impressions of people from their home decor, our feelings about stores are affected by furnishings, fixtures (shelves and racks that display merchandise), and even how much "stuff" is packed into the sales area. Generally, clutter conveys a store with lower-priced merchandise. Upscale stores allocate space for sitting areas, dressing rooms, and elaborate displays of merchandise. A shopping center called The Lab in southern California attracts its target audience of mall rats aged 18 to 30 by using unusual furnishings such as concrete walls, a fountain made of oil drums, and an open-air living room filled with thrift-shop furniture to craft a laid-back image its patrons call "the antimall."

- **The sound of music:** An elegant restaurant softly playing Mozart in the background is worlds apart from a raucous place such as the Hard Rock Café, where loud rock-and-roll is essential to the atmosphere. The music playing in a store has become so central to its personality that many retailers, including Ralph Lauren, Victoria's Secret, Au Bon Pain, Starbucks, and Pottery Barn, are even selling the soundtracks specially designed for them.[51]

- **Color and lighting:** Marketers use color and lighting to set a mood. Red, yellow, and orange are warm colors (fast-food chains use a lot of orange to stimulate hunger), whereas blue, green, and violet signify elegance and cleanliness. Light colors make one feel more serene, whereas bright colors convey excitement. Fashion designer Norma Kamali replaced fluorescent lights with pink ones after management found that pink lighting is more flattering and made female customers more willing to try on bathing suits.[52]

STORE PERSONNEL   Store personnel (the actors) should complement a store's image. Each employee has a part to play, complete with props and costumes. Movie theaters often dress ushers in tuxedos, and many store employees are provided with scripts to use when they present products to customers.

Although the presence of knowledgeable sales personnel is important to shoppers, they generally rate the quality of service they receive from retail personnel as low, often because stores don't hire enough people to wait on their customers. Retailers are working hard to upgrade service quality, though they often find that the rapid turnover of salespeople makes this a difficult goal to achieve. Perhaps they can learn from Japanese retailers. A visitor to a Japanese store is greeted by an enthusiastic, cheerful, polite, and immaculately dressed employee who, no matter how busy she is, tells each new customer they are welcome and bows to them.

Some U.S. firms have taken customer service and made it into a competitive advantage. Nordstrom's chain of department stores is legendary for its service levels. In fact, some "Nordies" have even been known to warm up customers' cars while they are paying for merchandise! The store motivates its employees by paying them substantially more than the average rate and deducting sales commissions if the merchandise is returned. This encourages the salesperson to be sure the customer is satisfied the first time.

PRICING POLICY: HOW MUCH FOR A TICKET TO THE SHOW?   When consumers form an image of a store in their minds, the *price points*, or price ranges, of its merchandise often play a role. A chain of off-price stores in the Northeast called Daffy's advertises with such slogans as, "Friends Don't Let Friends Pay Retail," implying that anyone who buys at the full, nondiscounted price needs help. Discount stores and general merchandisers are likely to compete on a price basis by offering brand names for less.

In recent years, department stores have been hurt by consumers' desires for bargains. The response of many department stores was to run frequent sales, a strategy that often backfired because many consumers would buy *only* when the store held a sale. Some stores have instead reduced the number of sales they run in favor of lowering prices across the board. Many, such as Home Depot and Wal-Mart, offer an everyday-low-pricing (EDLP) strategy in which they set prices that are between the list price suggested by the manufacturer and the deeply discounted price offered by stores that compete on price only (see Chapter 10).

Building the Theater: Store Location

Any real estate agent will tell you the three most important factors in buying a home are "location, location, and location." As Subha Ramesh at The Limited knows very well, the same is true in retailing. Wal-Mart's success is due to not only what it is but also to *where* it is. Wal-Mart was the first mass merchandiser to locate in small and rural markets. When choosing a site, Wal-Mart's planners consider such factors as proximity to highways and major traffic routes. By carefully selecting "undiscovered" areas, the company has been able to negotiate cheap leases in towns with expanding populations, an important strategy for Wal-Mart because it means access to markets hungry for a store that offers such a wide assortment of household goods.[53] This section will review some important aspects of retail locations.

Figure 16.4 Types of Store Locations

Different types of store locations are best for different types of retailers. Retailers choose from central business districts, shopping centers, freestanding stores, or nontraditional locations.

A central business district is often found in downtown areas. Although U.S. retailers have been deserting impoverished center cities in droves for the past 20 years, these downtown areas are now staging a comeback. Sophisticated developments such as festival marketplaces including New York City's South Street Seaport, Union Station in St. Louis, Harborplace in Baltimore, and Boston's Fanueil Hall (shown here) are contributing to the renaissance of American cities.

A shopping center is a group of commercial establishments owned and managed as a single property. They range in size from strip centers to superregional centers such as the Mall of America, which covers 4.2 million square feet of shopping space. Shopping malls offer the ability to combine shopping with entertainment.

A freestanding store is not located near other stores. This locational strategy, used by some big chains like Kids "R" Us, has the advantage of offering a lack of direct competition, lower rents, and adaptability. The store has the freedom to alter its selling space to accommodate its own needs. On the other hand, the store had better be popular because it cannot rely on the drawing power of neighbor stores to provide it with customer traffic.

A nontraditional location offers products to shoppers in convenient places. For example, Taco Bell now has locations inside Target stores, tempting shoppers to take a taquito break.

TYPES OF STORE LOCATIONS As Figure 16.4 shows, there are four basic types of retail locations. A store can be found in a business district, in a shopping center, as a freestanding entity, or in a nontraditional location:

- **Business districts:** A central business district (CBD) is the traditional downtown business area found in a town or city. Many people are drawn to the area to shop or work, and public transportation is usually available. CBDs have suffered in recent years because of concerns about security, lack of parking, and the lack of customer traffic on evenings and weekends. To combat these problems, many cities provide incentives such as tax breaks to encourage the opening of stores and entertainment areas such as Boston's Quincy Marketplace. These vibrant developments are called *festival marketplaces*, and they have done a lot to reverse the fortunes of aging downtown areas from Boston to Baltimore.

- **Shopping centers:** A shopping center is a group of commercial establishments owned and managed as a single property. They range in size and scope from *strip centers* to massive *superregional centers* such as Minneapolis's Mall of America, which offers 4.2 million square feet of shopping plus such attractions as a seven-acre Knott's Camp Snoopy Theme Park.

Strip centers offer quick and easy access to basic conveniences such as dry cleaners and video rentals, though shoppers seeking more exotic goods need to look elsewhere. Shopping malls offer variety and the ability to combine shopping with entertainment. Rents tend to be high in shopping malls, making it difficult for many stores to be profitable. In addition, small specialty stores may find it hard to compete with a mall's *anchor stores*, the major department stores that typically draw many shoppers.

A new form of store location called a *lifestyle center* combines the feel of a neighborhood park with the convenience of a strip mall. Typically located in affluent neighborhoods and featuring expensive landscaping, these more intimate centers are an appealing way for retailers to blend in to residential areas. Retailers including Williams-Sonoma and Talbot's are investing heavily in this concept.[54]

- **Freestanding retailers:** Some stores, usually larger ones such as IKEA, are freestanding, located by themselves in a separate building. These retailers benefit from lower rents and fewer parking problems. However, the store must be attractive enough on its own to be a destination point for shoppers because it can't rely on spillover from consumers visiting other stores at the same place.

- **Nontraditional store locations:** Innovative retailers find new ways to reach consumers. Many entrepreneurs use *carts*, which are small, movable stores that can be set up in many locations including inside malls, in airports, or in other public facilities, or *kiosks*, which are slightly larger and offer storelike facilities including telephone hookups and electricity. Carts and kiosks are relatively inexpensive and a good way for new businesses to get started.

SITE SELECTION: CHOOSING WHERE TO BUILD Sam Walton, the founder of Wal-Mart, used to fly over an area in a small plane until he found a spot that appealed to him. That's a story from the past. Now such factors as long-term population patterns, the location of competitors, and the demographic makeup of an area enter into retailers' decisions. The choice of where to open a new store should reflect the company's overall growth strategy. It should be consistent with long-term goals and be in a place that allows the company to best support the outlet. For example, a chain with stores and an extensive warehouse system in the Northeast may not be wise to open a new store in California because the store would be an "orphan" cut off from the company's supply lines.

Location planners like Subha Ramesh look at many factors when selecting a site. They want to find a place that is convenient to customers in the store's **trade area**, the geographic zone that accounts for the majority of its sales and customers.[55] A *site evaluation* considers such specific factors as traffic flow; number of parking spaces available; ease of delivery access; visibility from the street; local zoning laws that determine the types of buildings, parking, and signage allowed; and such cost factors as the length of the lease and the amount of local taxes.

Planners also consider such population characteristics as age profile (is the area witnessing an influx of new families?), community life cycle (is the community relatively new, stable, or in decline?), and mobility (how often are people moving in and out of the area?). This information is available from a variety of sources, including the U.S. Bureau of the Census, the buying power index (BPI) published each year by the trade magazine *Sales and Marketing Management*, and research firms such as Urban Decision Systems and Claritas that analyze many forms of demographic data to create profiles of selected areas.

Planners also have to consider the degree of competition they will encounter by locating in one place versus another. One strategy followed, for example, by fast-food outlets is to locate in a *saturated trade area*. This is a site where a sufficient number of stores already exist so that high customer traffic is present but where the retailer believes it can compete successfully by going head to head with the competition. As one fast-food industry executive put it, "Customers are lazybones. They absolutely will not walk one more step. You literally have to put a store where people are going to smack their face against it." However, that task is getting harder and harder because at this point many of the good sites are already taken: The United States has 277,208 fast-food outlets

trade area
A geographic zone that accounts for the majority of a store's sales and customers.

from coast to coast—one for every 1,000 people in the country. Subway Restaurants opens a new store in the United States every three hours on average. Starbucks unveils a new store every 11 hours and Quiznos Sub every 16 hours.[56]

Another strategy is to find an *understored trade area*, where too few stores exist to satisfy the needs of the population (this was Wal-Mart's strategy) and the retailer can establish itself as a dominant presence in the community. Over time, these areas may become *overstored* so that too many stores exist to sell the same goods. Those that can't compete are forced to move or close, as has happened to many small mom-and-pop stores that can't beat the Wal-Marts of the world at their sophisticated retailing games.

A store's targeted consumer segment also determines where it locates. For example, a new, growing community would be appealing for hardware stores that can supply hammers and drywall to home owners, while upscale dress stores and travel agencies might find better locations in more established areas because people living there have the income to spend on fashion items and vacations. The Buckle, a clothing store chain, successfully sells designer clothing in 200 small towns across the United States. This retailer specifically targets high school and college students who want cutting-edge fashion but who live in relatively isolated areas.

real people, real choices

How It Worked Out at LimitedBrands

LimitedBrands chose option 1. The company focused on expanding some of its brands in the upscale malls, an effort known as the Top 160. To date, the company has repositioned several of its stores in the Top 160 malls in the United States (the best fashion and traffic malls in the country). As the gross size of these stores increased, so did sales and productivity.

Women waiting at a Victoria's Secret reopening.

To achieve these results, LimitedBrands focused on initiatives for brand expansion such as a store grand reopening program; new subbrands like Pink, Henri Bendel Home, and Express Design Studio; new store designs; and new promotional strategies for some of its brands. For example, at Victoria's Secret, the new subbrand Pink (aimed at 19- to 22-year-olds) has created tremendous buzz and added new customers to the brand (without cannibalizing existing subbrands).

The grand reopening program at Victoria's Secret has also been a huge success—each time the company "reopened" one of its Victoria's Secret stores, it staged an event to call attention to this. Because the company heavily advertised the event and offered a strong gift-with-purchase program, women stood in line for over an hour to catch a glimpse of the new store and the tantalizing products waiting within. Through a combination of merchandising, marketing, and store design efforts, the stores have boosted sales and productivity along with square-footage increases.

You may not believe it today, but graduation will be here before you know it. Follow the easy steps in Chapter 17 to create your *Brand You* marketing plan. The plan will help you land internships, part-time jobs in college, and best of all, that first professional job when you graduate.

CHAPTER SUMMARY

1. **Define retailing and understand how retailing evolves.** Retailing is the process by which goods and services are sold to consumers for their personal use. The wheel-of-retailing hypothesis suggests that new retailers compete on price and over time become more upscale, leaving room for other new, low-price entrants. The retail life cycle theory suggests retailing institutions are introduced, grow, reach maturity, and then decline. Three factors that motivate retailers to evolve are changing demographics, technology, and globalization.

2. **Describe how retailers are classified.** Retailers are classified by NAICS codes based on product lines sold. Retailers may also be classified by the level of service offered (self-service, full-service, and limited-service retailers) and by the merchandise assortment offered. Merchandise assortment is described in terms of breadth and depth, which refer to the number of product lines sold and the amount of variety available for each. Thus stores are classified as convenience stores, supermarkets, specialty stores, discount stores, warehouse clubs, factory outlets, department stores, and hypermarkets.

3. **Describe the more common forms of nonstore retailing.** The two more common types of nonstore retailing are direct selling and automatic vending machines. In direct selling, a salesperson presents a product to one individual or a small group, takes orders, and delivers the merchandise. Direct selling includes door-to-door sales and party or network sales. With state-of-the-art self-service vending machines, products from french fries to blue jeans can be dispensed.

4. **Describe B2C e-commerce and its benefits, limitations, and future promise.** B2C e-commerce, online exchanges between companies and consumers, is growing rapidly. B2C benefits include greater convenience and greater product variety for consumers and opportu-

nities for specialized businesses, lower business costs, and instantaneous delivery of some products for marketers. For consumers, the downside of B2C e-commerce includes having to wait to receive products, security issues, and the inability to touch and feel products. For Internet-only marketers, success on the Internet may be difficult to achieve, whereas cannibalization may be a problem with traditional retailers' online operations.

5. **Understand the importance of store image to a retail positioning strategy and explain how a retailer can create an image in the marketplace.** Store image is how the target market perceives the store relative to the competition and results from many different elements working together to create the most desirable shopping experience and to ensure that shoppers view a store favorably relative to the competition. Color, lighting, scents, furnishings, and other design elements, called atmospherics, are used to create a "feel" for a store environment. Use of atmospherics includes decisions on (1) store layout, which determines traffic flow and influences the desired customer behavior in the store; (2) the use of store fixtures and open space; (3) the use of sound to attract (or repel) certain types of customers; and (4) the use of color and lighting that can influence customers' moods. The number and type of store personnel are selected to complement the store image. Pricing of products sold in the store contributes to shoppers' perceptions. A store's location also contributes to its image. Major types of retail locations include central business districts, shopping centers, freestanding retailers, and nontraditional locations such as kiosks.

KEY TERMS

atmospherics, 514

business-to-consumer (B2C)
  e-commerce, 505

convenience stores, 500

department stores, 502

direct selling, 503

experiential shoppers, 507

factory outlet store, 501

general merchandise discount stores, 501

hypermarkets, 503

merchandise assortment, 499

merchandise breadth, 499

merchandise depth, 499

merchandise mix, 498

multilevel network, 504

nonstore retailing, 503

off-price retailers, 501

party plan system, 504

point-of-sale (POS) systems, 496

pyramid schemes, 504

retail life cycle, 493

retailing, 492

scrambled merchandising, 498

specialty stores, 500

store image, 514

supermarkets, 500

trade area, 519

traffic flow, 515

warehouse clubs, 501

wheel-of-retailing hypothesis, 493

CHAPTER REVIEW

MARKETING CONCEPTS: TESTING YOUR KNOWLEDGE

1. Define retailing. What is the role of retailing in today's world?

2. How do the wheel-of-retailing and retail life cycle theories explain the evolution of retailing? How do demographics, technology, and globalization affect the future of retailing?

3. Explain how retail stores differ in terms of their merchandise mix.

4. How do retailers vary in terms of services offered?

5. Describe the differences in merchandise assortments for convenience stores, supermarkets, specialty stores, discount stores, department stores, and hypermarkets.

6. Explain the different types of direct selling. What is the role of automatic vending in retailing?

7. What is B2C e-commerce? What are some benefits of B2C e-commerce for consumers and for marketers? What are the limitations of B2C e-commerce?

8. What are some possible effects of B2C e-commerce on traditional retailing?

9. What is store image? Why is it important? What is meant by store atmospherics? How can the elements of atmospherics be used to increase the store's success? How are store personnel a part of store image?

10. What are some of the different types of store locations? What are their advantages and disadvantages?

MARKETING CONCEPTS: DISCUSSING CHOICES AND ISSUES

1. The wheel-of-retailing theory suggests that the normal path for a retailer is to enter the marketplace with lower-priced goods and then to increase quality, services, and prices. Why do you think this happens? Is it the right path for all retailers? Why or why not?

2. Wal-Mart has become a dominant retailer in the American marketplace, accounting for the sales of over 30 percent of the total sales of some products. Is this a good thing for consumers? For the retail industry as a whole? Some communities try to prevent Wal-Mart from building a store in their area. Why do you think people feel this way?

3. Owners of stores that make effective use of atmospherics believe that getting people "in the mood" makes them more likely to buy. Do you feel that store atmospherics influence your purchase behavior? Is this sort of planned store setting ethical?

4. Experts predict the future of B2C e-commerce to be very rosy indeed with exponential increases of Internet sales of some product categories within the next few years. What effect do you think the growth of e-retailing will have on traditional retailing? In what ways will this be good for consumers, and in what ways will it not be so good?

MARKETING PRACTICE: APPLYING WHAT YOU'VE LEARNED

1. As a college graduate, you think the career you really would enjoy means being your own boss—you want to start your own business. You feel the future of e-commerce is the place for you to make your fortune. You are considering two options: (1) a business that sells wines from around the world online and (2) a blue-jean online store that offers consumers many different brands of blue jeans at prices slightly less than in traditional retail outlets. Outline the pros and cons of each of these two online retail businesses.

2. All your life you've wanted to be an entrepreneur and to own your own business. Now you're ready to graduate from college, and you've decided to open a combination coffee shop and bookstore in a location near your college. You know that to attract both the college student market and other customers from the local community, it will be necessary to carefully design the store image. Develop a detailed plan that specifies how you will use atmospherics to create the image you desire.

3. In your job with a marketing consulting firm, you often are asked to make recommendations for store location. Your current client is a local caterer that is planning to open a new retail outlet for selling take-out gourmet dinners. You are examining the possible types of locations: the central business district, a shopping center, a freestanding entity, or some nontraditional location. Outline the advantages and disadvantages of each type of location. Present your recommendations to your client.

4. Assume that you are the director of marketing for a national chain of convenience stores. Your firm has about 200 stores located in 43 states. The stores are fairly traditional both in design and in the merchandise they carry. Because you want to be proactive in your marketing planning, you are concerned that your firm may need to consider making significant changes because of the current demographic, technological, and global trends in the marketplace. You think it is important to discuss these things with the other executives at your firm. Develop a presentation that includes the following:
   a. A discussion of the demographic changes that will impact your stores
   b. A discussion of the technological changes that will impact your stores
   c. A discussion of how global changes may provide problems and opportunities for your organization
   d. Your recommendations for how your firm might meet the challenges faced in each of these areas

MARKETING MINIPROJECT: LEARNING BY DOING

This project is designed to help you understand how store atmospherics play an important role in consumers' perceptions of a retail store.

1. First, select two retail outlets where students in your college are likely to shop. It will be good if you can select two outlets that you feel are quite different in terms of store image but that sell the same types of products.

2. Visit each of the stores and write down a detailed description of the store atmosphere—colors, materials used, types of displays, lighting fixtures, product displays, store personnel, and so on.

3. Survey some of the students in your college. Develop a brief questionnaire asking about the perceptions of the two stores you are studying. You may want to ask about such things as the quality of merchandise, prices, competence and friendliness of the store personnel, the attitude of management toward customer service, and so on. What is the "personality" of each store?

4. Develop a report of your findings. Compare the description of the stores with the results of the survey. Attempt to explain how the different elements of the store atmosphere create each store's unique image.

REAL PEOPLE, REAL SURFERS: EXPLORING THE WEB

Many traditional retailers now have Internet sites. Other online retailers such as Lands' End and L.L. Bean do not have actual stores but practice only direct selling. Visit the sites of one or two popular retailers such as Gap, Pottery Barn, Williams-Sonoma, J. Crew, Banana Republic, or others. Then visit the site of a direct-only retailer.

1. Describe each retailer's Web site. What information is available on each site? How easy was each to navigate? What information did you find interesting and useful on each site? What did you find that you didn't expect to find at a retailer site? What did you find lacking at each site?

2. What differences are there for sites that have traditional bricks-and-mortar stores from those that do not? Does the site encourage consumers to visit the physical store or just to remain an online shopper?

3. How do the retailers' Web sites communicate the image or personality of their stores? How are they alike? How are they different? If you had no information except that available on the Web, would you know what types of products are sold; whether the products sold are expensive, prestige products, or low-priced products; and what types of consumers each retailer is attempting to attract to its stores? How does each site use graphics or other design elements to represent the "setting" as retailers do in their stores? How do they communicate the type of consumer they consider their primary market?

4. What recommendations would you make to each retailer to improve its Web site?

MARKETING PLAN EXERCISE

The wheel of retailing suggests that new retailers enter the marketplace by offering goods at lower prices than competitors and that after they gain a foothold they "trade up," improving their facilities and their merchandise assortment. Think about a new retail venture, a specialty store that sells timepieces, such as men's and ladies' watches and clocks.

1. What retailing strategies do you recommend for the new retailer for their first two years in business—what merchandise, what store image, and what location(s)?

2. What long-term retailing strategies do you recommend?

Marketing in Action Case

Real Choices at IKEA

Ingvar Kamprad founded IKEA, now the world's largest furniture store, in Sweden in 1943 when he was just 17 years old and while the world was embroiled in World War II. He began by selling pens, picture frames, wallets, and other bargain items out of a catalog. Eight years after starting the company, Kamprad began selling furniture made by local carpenters, and in 1957 he opened his first IKEA furniture store in Sweden. Today, IKEA is a discount specialty furniture store selling home furniture and accessories and generating $12.2 billion in annual sales from stores located all over the world. As such, the company carries a wide variety of items—furniture, decorative items, lighting fixtures, and so on for all rooms of the house—that individuals and couples can use to decorate their homes.

How IKEA became the furniture store juggernaut that it is today is a testament to implementing a solid retail strategy. In designing its stores, IKEA considers what customers are looking for in their furniture selections and any changes in shopping trends. For example, many shoppers today are interested in one-stop shopping for the convenience it offers and because it allows customers to find what they want without having to visit numerous stores.

Also, IKEA makes it easier for customers to shop once they enter the store. Furniture displays are set up in "lifestyle" themes showing the type of furniture that singles, couples, or young families might need in a single grouping. The company uses vignette displays to suggest how various items sold in the store can be put together to create a certain look. These types of displays are perfect for consumers no longer interested in buying furniture to last for a lifetime but rather to find something that fits their lifestyle now.

In addition, IKEA recognizes that its customers have very busy lifestyles. Thus, IKEA provides added convenience by making its products available in catalogs and on the Internet in addition to its traditional retail locations.

IKEA also effectively uses pricing and promotion as part of its retail strategy. Because the company is a relatively low-priced provider of quality home furnishings, IKEA is perfect for those renewing their homes on a small budget. From a promotion standpoint, IKEA has been extremely innovative. For example, in China company representatives decorated the inside of apartment building elevators to illustrate how products available at IKEA can help transform old, stodgy homes into modern, pleasant living spaces. In Singapore the company went after younger age-groups by partnering with Nickelodeon for a "Nick Takes Over Your Room" promotion. For this promotion, IKEA redecorated a child's room, and then Nickelodeon allowed the kids to host TV specials from their redecorated rooms. Such promotions generate much excitement among the target audience that translates into greater awareness of and more sales for IKEA.

Today, IKEA, like many companies, must consider its future. The company hopes to add 50 additional store locations in North America over the next decade. Given the many considerations and expense that go into building retail stores, such decisions are fraught with peril. It often is said that the three most important aspects of retail strategy are location, location, and location. Consequently, where IKEA decides to expand is extremely important. So far, IKEA has limited itself in terms of store locations to some of the most heavily populated markets in the countries in which it competes. To continue its growth trends, IKEA may have to begin investigating alternative (smaller) communities as locations in which to place its stores.

As IKEA expands, it must continue to compete successfully in many different countries with very different cultures. But are the IKEA product assortment and quirky promotions appropriate for all of them? In the future, company managers may need to adapt their merchandise and promotion strategies to appeal to differing consumer tastes and preferences.

Clearly, despite the history of success the company has enjoyed thus far, there are no guarantees for the future. One thing about IKEA's future is certain: future success will come from providing value to the public. To ensure that the future is as rosy as the past, IKEA must keep innovating and executing a successful retailing strategy.

Things to Think About

1. What is the decision facing IKEA?
2. What factors are important in understanding the decision situation?
3. What are the alternatives?
4. What decision(s) do you recommend?
5. What are some ways to implement your recommendation(s)?

Sources: Cora Daniels and Adam Edström, "Create IKEA, Make Billions, Take Bus," *Fortune*, May 3, 2004, 44; Emma Hall and Normandy Madden, "Ikea Courts Buyers with Offbeat Ideas," *Advertising Age*, April 12, 2004, 10; Mercedes M. Cardona, "Retailers Work to Brand Home Goods," *Advertising Age*, April 5, 2004, S7–S8; and Mike Duff, "IKEA Eyes Aggressive Growth," *DSN Retailing Today*, January 27, 2003, 3, 22.

UNDER ARMOUR IN ACTION
Implementing a Marketing Plan

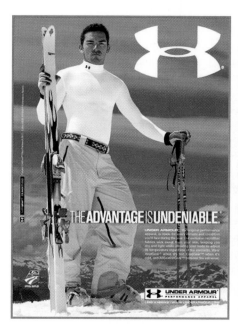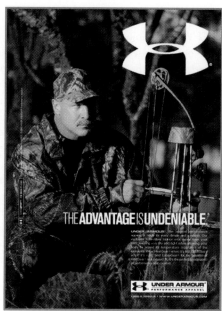

In Chapter 2, "Strategic Planning and the Marketing Environment: The Advantage Is Undeniable," you read a "Real People, Real Choices" feature about Steve Battista, director of marketing at Under Armour. Take a look back at the feature on Steve. As the senior brand marketing executive reporting directly to Under Armour founder and president Kevin Plank, remember that Steve oversees all aspects of marketing, including buying and placement strategy, public relations, merchandising, promotions, virtual marketing, and corporate communications.

Great marketing planning has been a key ingredient in Under Armour's success in the performance apparel category. Now we're going to take a closer look at just how Steve and his colleagues planned for this success. Chapter 2 gave us insights on the following issues:

- The overall process of strategic planning
- The steps in marketing planning
- The elements of operational planning
- The aspects of an organization's internal environment
- The issues involved in scanning an organization's external business environment

After we discussed all these topics, we gave you a framework for marketing planning, which is summarized at the end of Chapter 2 in a foldout template for a marketing plan. The template references which chapters in *Marketing: Real People, Real Choices* are most relevant to each aspect of the plan. It also provides some questions to guide your research and thinking as you approach the task of developing a marketing plan. In addition, as you take another look through Chapter 2, you will notice that we asked a number of questions about marketing planning at Under Armour throughout the various topical sections in the chapter.

Now, with a little help from Steve Battista, we're going to get the answers to those and other pertinent questions relating to marketing planning. In fact, believe it or not, you are ready to try your hand at a marketing planning project yourself. And we will use our friends at Under Armour as a case study.

Questions for Steve Battista

To help you get started, we asked Steve Battista some questions about key elements of his marketing plan. The responses Steve provided give insight into why Under Armour has done so well, and they provide information you can use to develop a marketing plan of your own for Under Armour.

1. *List a few of your key overall marketing objectives. Why did you set each?*
   STEVE: The objective for Under Armour's marketing is simple: *Tell a great story*. Use all the tools in your arsenal, including advertising, point-of-purchase displays, and public relations. Tell the story about the gear, about the company, about the brand. It's all connected.

   The first objective with marketing for a company as young as ours is about building a brand experience for the end user. We are about performance, and we use only authentic, intense athletes in our advertising and marketing. Our print campaign features an oversize logo in the upper right-hand corner. You definitely will see the logos on athletes during games, so our advertising is meant to educate consumers about what the brand is and why athletes insist on wearing Under Armour gear during competition.

   One of the most difficult aspects of planning is coordinating all our activities to be sure we meet our objectives. For example, it's a real challenge to be sure that product hits the shelves at the same time fixtures reach the stores, with the proper POS (point-of-sale) materials, while the advertising is breaking on television and landing on the newsstands.

   But, when you get it right, *the advantage is undeniable:*
   - 60,000 people asked for copies of one of our commercials to run during pep rallies, games, player introductions, sales meetings, and employee retreats.
   - We were rated the second fastest growing private company in America (*Inc.* magazine, 2003).

2. *How does your marketing plan support the overall strategic plan for Under Armour?*
   STEVE: By consistently telling the great Under Armour story. Our gear lines are tied closely to the story of CEO Kevin Plank and his creation of the company—our overall objective is to have everything tied together in a clear package. The basic story is simple yet powerful: Wear our HeatGear when it's hot, ColdGear when it's cold, AllSeason gear during other times. HeatGear POS materials, hangtags, and ads are red, ColdGear materials are blue, and those for AllSeason gear are orange. We may have high-tech, complex fabrications and highly technological gear on the racks, but we market it with a simple color scheme and naming convention that makes it easy for any and all of our customers to understand. It's all tied together throughout.

3. *Can you point to one of Under Armour's key internal strengths or weaknesses?*
   STEVE: A key to our success on the surface may seem like a weakness: we're small in the overall context of a market ruled by an 800-pound gorilla like Nike. This is actually an advantage because it means we're *quick* to market and very nimble, and we have a personal touch with our sales force. People love doing business with us.

4. *What issues drive your marketing planning here?*
   STEVE: We stick with a performance base ("the universal guarantee of performance"). We don't play in the "fashion" game where there are big changes every season, and we never plan to. We focus on finding the best fabrics to make the best performance apparel that will let you play your best on the field or on the job.

5. *Tell us a little about your approach to market segmentation, target markets, and positioning.*
   STEVE: We're efficient because we don't waste a lot of effort developing lots of different products for different sports. For example, the ColdGear shirt that all-pro athlete LaVar

Arrington wears on the football field is the same shirt (just a different color!) as the one hall-of-famer Randy White wears when he's hunting ducks, and it's the same shirt Mark Prior and Roger Clemens are wearing when they take the mound to pitch. What's more, U.S. Olympic freestyle ski team member Jeremy Bloom can wear this shirt when he competes, and we use the same fabric to make a ColdGear shirt for Olympic soccer player Heather Mitts.

For us, product line extensions are about finishing off the overall apparel and "look" for athletes who want to be sure they have the gear they need to compete at a major league level. Alan Iverson wants to wear a sleeve on his arm during games—we're the compression guys, so let's make him a tight sleeve. We look for people who can take advantage of performance apparel and who need it, we make sure it's within our brand mission, and we go design our products for the most elite levels in every sport. This means that we started working with the NFL for football apparel and with MLB for baseball jerseys. We designed our military gear specifically for the Navy SEALS.

Female athletes have always worn our gear, but to appeal to women at the retail level, we needed to add more colors and more style to the line. We needed more LooseGear and more outerwear. Women don't want just undergarments; they want the stuff you wear to the gym, while you work out, and after you shower and head home.

I can summarize our positioning strategy as follows:

Product: New technology or, at the very least, better technology than what's currently available

Price: Best *value* in our category

Promotion: Build the brand by stressing authenticity and intensity

Distribution: Confined to high-end sporting goods retailers

6. *The finest marketing plans are only as successful as their implementation. Please share some of your experiences in implementing your marketing plan—making it actually happen. Hopefully you can include some successful and less successful examples from which we can learn.*
STEVE: I'll start with one of our "less successful" examples. Since we do all our advertising in-house rather than using an advertising agency, we farmed out a catalog to a local ad firm. They came back with something that looked like every other brand. It didn't have the connection to our brand and it didn't feel right. It also came in way over budget and after our sales meeting deadline. The lesson was simple: Your have to *earn* the right to work on the Under Armour brand. Now, we don't delegate our business to anyone who doesn't live the Under Armour brand and really understand it.

Now for a more positive example of how we put our plan into action: With our first "Protect This House" commercial, we wanted to create something very sticky, an experience, or a feeling or a slogan that people around the country could share—and hopefully repeat to one another to get a buzz going about Under Armour. So, we came up with the war cry: "Protect This House!" Before we knew it, sports fans far and wide were adopting this phrase. And we used it as a message to the big guys out there (our competitors) that this is our house and we're not backing down.

7. *What marketing metrics do you have in place to gauge the success of your marketing activities?*
STEVE: We have a small marketing research budget, so I look for things like a spike in sales after we get our product exposed in a sports program. We do tons of focus groups, we have our Web site set up for surveys and feedback, and we listen to our vendors. And by tracking direct sales on our Web site, we can tell when things are working and when they're not.

8. *Can you give us an example of a situation when you have had to alter your objectives or strategies within your marketing plan because the results you hoped for were just not happening?*
STEVE: The first time we tried women's gear, we got the first shipment in, and Kevin didn't like it one bit. We pulled the plug, took a huge bite to the bottom line, went back to the drawing board, did even more research and development, and came up with something spectacular. It was devastating at first, but we wouldn't and still won't come out with anything less than the very best for our customers.

Now It's Your Turn to Do Some Marketing Planning

OK, you've learned about planning in Chapter 2, you know something about Steve Battista's marketing planning so far at Under Armour, and you have the resources in the *Marketing: Real People, Real Choices* book available. You also will find a great deal more about Under Armour on their Web site (**www.UnderArmour.com**). And, of course, a personal "field trip" to an Under Armour dealer could be in order.

Your job is to fill in the elements of the marketing plan template presented in Chapter 2 for Under Armour. Use the questions in the template to help guide your work. Be thorough in your research and creative in your ideas. Your goal is to be a marketing consultant to Steve Battista at Under Armour and provide him with a great plan so he can continue the Under Armour success story well into the future. Your instructor will give you all the process details on the assignment (how long the paper should be, whether you will give an oral presentation, when the plan is due, and so on). Now, go have fun developing an Under Armour marketing plan!

SAMPLE MARKETING PLAN
The S&S Smoothie Company

Situation Analysis

The S&S Smoothie Company* was founded in September 1998 in New York with the goal of creating and marketing healthy "smoothie" beverages for sale to health-conscious consumers. S&S Smoothie expects to take advantage of an increasing desire for healthy foods both in the United States and internationally—and to ride the wave of the latest low-carb craze. While there are other companies both large and small competing in this market, S&S Smoothie feels it has the expertise to create and market superior products that will appeal to its target market.

INTERNAL ENVIRONMENT

Mission statement. The strategic direction and actions of the S&S Smoothie Company are driven by its mission:

> *S&S Smoothie seeks to meet the needs of discriminating, health-conscious consumers for high-quality, superior-tasting smoothie beverages and other similar products.*

Organizational structure. As an entrepreneurial company, S&S Smoothie does not have a very sophisticated organizational structure. Key personnel include the following:

- Patrick Small, founder and co-president. Small is responsible for the creation, design, packaging, and production management of all S&S Smoothie products.
- William "Bill" Sartens, founder and co-president. Sartens is responsible for international and domestic distribution and marketing.
- Gayle Humphries, chief financial officer. Humphries develops financial strategy and keeps the company's books.
- Alex Johnson, national sales manager. Johnson is responsible for maintaining the sales force of independent sales reps. He also advises on product development.
- Bob LeMay, Pam Sartens, and Paul Sartens, shareholders. Next to Patrick Small and William Sartens, Bob, Pam, and Paul own the largest number of shares. They consult and sit on the company's board of directors. Bob is a lawyer and also provides legal services.

Corporate culture. S&S Smoothie is an entrepreneurial organization. Thus, a key element of the internal environment is a culture that encourages innovation, risk taking, and individual creativity. The company's beginning was based on a desire to provide a unique, superior product, and company decisions have consistently emphasized this mission.

Products. The original S&S Smoothie, introduced in mid-1999, was a fruit- and yogurt-based beverage that contained only natural ingredients (no additives) and was high in essential nutrients. Because of the company's patented manufacturing process, S&S Smoothie beverages do not have to be refrigerated and have a shelf life of over a year. Therefore, the product can be shipped and delivered via nonrefrigerated carriers. The S&S Smoothie beverages are sold exclusively through gyms, health clubs, and smaller upscale food markets.

As a producer of dairy-based beverages, S&S Smoothie's NAICS classification is 311511, Fluid Milk Manufacturers. At present the single product line is the S&S Smoothie fruit and yogurt beverage. This health beverage product has a flavor and nutritional content that makes it superior to other

---

*S&S Smoothie Company is a fictitious company created to illustrate a sample marketing plan.

Table B.1   Nutritional Information: S&S Smoothie Beverage

Serving Size: 12 ounces
For 20-ounce sizes, multiply the amounts by 1.67.

	Amount per Serving	% Daily Value
Calories	140	
Calories from fat	6	
Total Fat	<0.5 g	1%
Saturated fat	<0.5 g	2%
Cholesterol	6 mg	2%
Sodium	70 mg	3%
Potassium	100 mg	3%
Total carbs	10 g	3%
Dietary fiber	5 g	20%
Sugar	1 g	
Protein	25 g	50%
Vitamin A		50%
Vitamin C		50%
Calcium		20%
Iron		30%
Vitamin D		40%
Vitamin E		50%
Thiamin		50%
Riboflavin		50%
Niacin		50%
Vitamin B6		50%
Vitamin B12		50%
Biotin		50%
Pantothenic acid		50%
Phosphorus		10%
Iodine		50%
Chromium		50%
Zinc		50%
Folic acid		50%

competing products on the market. The present product comes in five flavors: strawberry, blueberry, banana, peach, and cherry. Each is offered in a 12-ounce and a 20-ounce size. The product is packaged in a unique hourglass-shaped, frosted glass bottle with a screw-off cap. The bottle design makes the product easy to hold, even with sweaty hands after workouts. The frosted glass allows the color of the beverage to be seen but at the same time communicates an upscale image. The labeling and lid visually denote the flavor with an appropriate color. Labeling includes complete nutritional information. In the future, S&S Smoothie plans to expand its line of products in order to grow its market share of the health drink market.

Pricing of S&S Smoothie beverages is as follows:

	12 oz.	20 oz.
Suggested retail price	$4.00	$6.00
Price to retail outlets (health clubs, etc.)	$2.00	$3.00
Price to distributor/discount to sales agent	$1.00	$1.50

Thus, S&S Smoothie receives $1.00 in revenue for each 12-ounce bottle and $1.50 in revenue for each 20-ounce bottle it sells.

Table B.2 Company Sales Performance

Year	Gross Sales
1999	$ 87,000
2000	$238,000
2001	$311,000
2002	$436,000
2003	$618,000
2004	$650,000

At present, S&S Smoothie outsources actual production of the product. Still, the company takes care to oversee the entire production process to ensure consistent quality of its unique product. With this method of production, variable costs for the 12-ounce S&S Smoothie beverages are $0.63, and variable costs for the 20-ounce size are $0.71. Current annual fixed costs for S&S Smoothie office space, management salaries, and professional services are as follows:

Salaries and employee benefits	$275,000
Office rental, equipment, and supplies	$24,600
Expenses related to sales (travel, etc.)	$32,000
Advertising and other marketing communications	$50,000
Total fixed costs	**$381,600**

Sales of the two sizes of the product are approximately equal; that is, half of sales are for the 12-ounce size and half for the 20-ounce size. Thus, there is an average contribution margin of $0.58 per bottle. Based on this, in order to achieve breakeven, S&S Smoothie must sell

$$\frac{\$381,600}{.58} = 657,931 \text{ units}$$

Again, assuming equal sales of the two size products, breakeven in dollars is $822,413.

Previous sales. Sales of S&S Smoothie products have continued to grow since introduction to the market in 1999.

Markets. The consumer market for S&S Smoothie products is anyone who is interested in healthy food and a healthy lifestyle. While research has shown that nearly 70 percent of American consumers say they are interested in living a healthy lifestyle, the number of those who actually work to achieve that goal is much smaller. It is estimated that approximately 80 million Americans actually engage in exercise and/or follow nutritional plans that would be described as healthy.

As the trend toward healthier living is expected to grow globally, the domestic market and the international market for S&S Smoothie products is expected to expand for some time. While the world economy has suffered in recent years, current predictions are that the worst is over, and the economies of the United States and other developed countries should begin a slow upward trend.

Within the U.S. consumer market, S&S Smoothie is targeting upscale consumers who frequent gyms and health clubs. While these consumers are primarily younger, there is also a growing older segment that also seeks to be physically fit and that also patronizes health clubs. To reach this market, S&S Smoothie targets two broad reseller markets: (1) gyms and health clubs and (2) smaller upscale food markets.

Channels. S&S Smoothie's primary emphasis is on health clubs and other physical fitness facilities and small, upscale specialty food markets. The company began developing channel relationships with these outlets through individual contacts by company personnel. As sales developed, the company solicited the services of manufacturers' agents and specialty food distributors. Manufacturers' agents are individuals who sell products for a number of different noncompeting manufacturers. By contracting with these agents in various geographic regions, the company can expand its product distribution to a significant portion of the United States and Canada. Similar arrangements with agents in the United Kingdom have allowed it to begin distribution in that country.

Large accounts such as Gold's Gym and World Gyms are handled directly by the company. While total sales to these chains are fairly substantial, when considering the large number of facilities within each chain, the sales are very small with much room for growth.

The Internet is a secondary channel for S&S Smoothie. Online retail outlets currently account for only 5 percent of S&S Smoothie sales. While this channel is useful for individuals who wish to purchase S&S Smoothie products in larger quantities, it is not expected that online sales will become a significant part of the business in the near future.

EXTERNAL ENVIRONMENT

Competitive environment. S&S Smoothie faces several different levels of competition. Direct competitors are companies that also market smoothie-type beverages and include the following:

1. Franchise smoothie retail operations
2. Online-only smoothie outlets
3. Other smaller manufacturers
4. Larger companies such as Nestlé that produce similar products

Indirect competition comes from the following:

1. Home-made smoothie drinks made from powders sold in retail outlets and over the Internet
2. Home-made smoothie drinks made using a multitude of available recipes
3. Other healthy beverages, such as juices

Economic environment. S&S Smoothie products were introduced during a period of relative prosperity. Even with the economic downturn following the dot.com bust and 9/11, the product was able to maintain and in some geographic areas actually increase its level of sales. As the economy of the United States is improving, sales have correspondingly begun to increase. Analysts estimate that the total U.S. gross domestic product (GDP) will only increase a little over 2 percent annually for the next three years. A similar percentage increase is anticipated for the European Union, while Canada's GDP is expected to grow slightly over 3 percent annually.

Technological environment. Because S&S Smoothie produces a simple food product, its operations are not closely tied to technological advances. Nevertheless, many of the company's operations are enabled and enhanced by the use of current technology. For example, S&S Smoothie uses the Internet to enhance its operations in two ways. First, the Internet provides an additional venue for sales. In addition, sales agents and channel members can keep in contact with the company, allowing for fewer problems with deliveries, orders, and so on.

Demographic environment. There are approximately 125 million American adults aged 15 to 44. This age-group is projected to remain stable for the foreseeable future, with an increase of less than 8 percent projected to 2025. Similarly, incomes are not expected to either decrease or increase significantly within the near future in this segment of the population.

Political and legal environment. Because they are advertised as nutritional products, all S&S Smoothie products must be approved by the U.S. Food and Drug Administration (FDA). Labeling must include ingredients and nutritional information also regulated by the FDA. In addition, the S&S Smoothie products are regulated by the U.S. Department of Agriculture.

While there are no specific regulations about labeling or advertising products as low carb, there is potential for such regulations to come into play in the future. In addition, there are numerous regulations that are country specific in current and prospective global markets of which the company must constantly remain aware. Any future advertising campaigns developed by S&S Smoothie will have to conform to regulatory guidelines both in the United States and internationally.

Social and cultural environment. The social and cultural environment continues to provide an important opportunity for S&S Smoothie. The trend toward healthy foods and a healthier lifestyle has grown dramatically for the past decade or longer. In response to this, the number of health clubs across the country and the number of independent resorts and spas that offer patrons a healthy holiday have also grown. In addition, many travelers demand that hotels offer health club facilities.

During the past three years, consumers around the globe have become aware of the advantages of a low-carbohydrate diet. Low-carb menu items abound in restaurants, including fast-food chains such as McDonald's. Supermarket store shelves are filled with a vast number of low-carb foods, including low-carb candy.

SWOT ANALYSIS

Strengths. The following are the strengths identified by S&S Smoothie:

- A creative and skilled employee team
- A high-quality product recipe that provides exceptional flavor with high levels of nutrition
- Because of its entrepreneurial spirit, the ability to remain flexible and to adapt quickly to environmental changes
- A strong network of sales agents and distributors
- The growth of a high-quality reputation among health clubs, other retail outlets, and targeted consumer groups

Weaknesses. The following are the weaknesses identified by S&S Smoothie:

- Limited financial resources for growth and for advertising and other marketing communications
- Little flexibility in terms of personnel due to size of the firm
- Reliance on external production to maintain quality standards and to meet any unanticipated surges in demand for the product

Opportunities. The following are the opportunities identified by S&S Smoothie:

- A strong and growing interest in healthy living, both among young, upscale consumers and among older consumers
- A low-carb craze that offers opportunities for additional product lines

Threats. The following are the threats identified by S&S Smoothie:

- The potential for competitors, especially those with large financial resources who can invest more in promotion, to develop products that consumers will find superior
- A major economic downturn that might affect potential sales
- Fizzling of the low-carb craze if other forms of dieting gain in popularity

Marketing Objectives

The following are the marketing objectives set by S&S Smoothie:

- To increase the awareness of S&S Smoothie products among the target market
- To increase gross sales by 50 percent over the next two years
- To introduce two new product lines over the next three years: a line of low-carb smoothies and a line of gourmet flavored smoothies
- To increase distribution of S&S Smoothie products to include new retail outlets both in the United States and globally

Marketing Strategies

TARGET MARKETS

Consumer markets. S&S Smoothies will continue to target its existing consumer markets. The primary consumer target market for S&S Smoothie beverages can be described as follows:

Demographics

- Male and female teens and young adults
- Ages: 15–44

- Household income: $50,000 and above
- Education of head of household: College degree or above
- Primarily located in midsize to large urban areas or college towns

Psychographics

- Health-conscious, interested in living a healthy lifestyle
- Spend much time and money taking care of their bodies
- Enjoy holidays that include physical activities
- Live very busy lives and need to use time wisely to enjoy all they want to do
- Enjoy spending time with friends
- According to the VALS™ typology, many are in the Achievers and Experiencers categories

Media Habits

- The target market is more likely to get their news from television or the Internet than from newspapers. They are likely to view not only the news channels but also the financial news networks.
- They prefer watching cable television stations to the programming provided by the more traditional major networks and enjoy shows, such as *Sex and the City* and *Nip/Tuck*.
- They are likely to have satellite radio installed in their automobiles.
- Magazines frequently read include *Men's Health, Business Week, Sports Illustrated,* and *The New Yorker.*

Organizational markets. In the past, S&S Smoothie has targeted two categories of reseller markets: (1) health clubs and gyms and (2) small upscale specialty food markets. In order to increase distribution and sales of its products, S&S Smoothie will target the following in the future:

1. Hotels and resorts in the United States and in selected international markets
2. Golf and tennis clubs
3. College and university campuses

Upscale young professionals frequently visit hotels and resorts and they demand that even business travel includes quality accommodations and first-rate health club facilities. The membership of golf and tennis clubs, while including many older consumers, also is an excellent means of providing products conveniently for the targeted groups. College and university students, probably more than any other consumer group, are interested in health and in their bodies. In fact, many universities have built large fairly elaborate health and recreational facilities as a means of attracting students. Thus, providing S&S Smoothie beverages on college campuses is an excellent means of meeting the health beverage needs of this group.

POSITIONING THE PRODUCT

S&S Smoothie seeks to position its products as the first-choice smoothie beverage for the serious health-conscious consumer, including those who are seeking to lower their carbohydrate intake. Justification: A lot of smoothie beverages are available. The S&S Smoothie formula provides superior flavor and nutrition in a shelf-stable form. S&S Smoothie has developed its product, packaging, and promotion to communicate a superior, prestige image. This positioning is thus supported by all its marketing strategies.

PRODUCT STRATEGIES

In order to increase its leverage in the market and to meet its sales objectives, S&S Smoothie needs additional products. Two new product lines are planned:

1. **S&S Smoothie Gold:** This product will be similar to the original S&S Smoothie beverages but will come in six unique flavors:
   a. Piña Colada
   b. Chocolate Banana
   c. Apricot Nectarine Madness

d. Pineapple berry crash

e. Tropical tofu cherry

f. Peaches and dreams

In order to set the product apart from the original-flavor Smoothie beverages in store refrigerator cases, labels will include the name of the beverage and the logo in gold lettering. The bottle cap will be black.

2. **Low-Carb S&S Smoothie:** The Low-Carb S&S Smoothie beverage will have approximately 50 percent fewer grams of carbohydrate than the original Smoothie beverage or the S&S Smoothie Gold. Low-Carb S&S Smoothie will come in the following four flavors:

a. Strawberry

b. Blueberry

c. Banana

d. Peach

Packaging for the Low-Carb S&S Smoothie will be similar to other S&S Smoothie beverages but will include the term "Low-Carb" in large type. The label will state that the beverage has 50 percent fewer carbs than regular smoothies.

PRICING STRATEGIES

The current pricing strategy will be maintained for existing and new products. This pricing is appropriate for communicating a high-quality product image for all S&S Smoothie products. The company feels that creating different pricing for the new beverages would be confusing and create negative attitudes among consumers. Thus, there is no justification for increasing the price for the new products.

PROMOTION STRATEGIES

In the past, S&S Smoothie has used mainly personal selling to promote its products to the trade channel. To support this effort, signage has been provided for the resellers to promote the product at the point of purchase. Posters and stand-alone table cards show appealing photographs of the product in the different flavors and communicate the brand name and the healthy benefits of the product. Similar signage will be developed for use by those resellers who choose to stock the S&S Smoothie Gold and the Low-Carb Smoothies.

Selling has been handled by a team of over 75 manufacturers' agents who sell to resellers. In addition, in some geographic areas, an independent distributor does the selling.

To support this personal selling approach, S&S Smoothie plans for additional promotional activities to introduce its new products and meet its other marketing objectives. These include the following:

1. **Television advertising:** S&S Smoothie will purchase a limited amount of relatively inexpensive and targeted cable channel advertising. A small number of commercials will be shown during prime-time programs with high viewer ratings by the target market. Television advertising can be an important means of not only creating awareness of the product but also enhancing the image of the product. Indeed, consumers are prone to feeling that if a product is advertised on prime-time TV, it must be a good product.

2. **Magazine advertising:** Because consumers in the target market are not avid magazine readers, magazine advertising will be limited and will supplement other promotion activities. During the next year, S&S Smoothie will experiment with limited magazine advertising in such titles as *Sports Illustrated.* The company will also investigate the potential of advertising in university newspapers.

3. **Sponsorships:** S&S Smoothie will attempt to sponsor several marathons in major cities. The advantage of sponsorships is that they provide visibility for the product while at the same time showing that the company supports activities of interest to the target market.

4. **Sampling:** Sampling of S&S Smoothie beverages at select venues will provide an opportunity for prospective customers to become aware of the product and to taste the great flavor. Sampling will include only the two new products being introduced. Venues for sampling will include the following:

a. Marathons

b. Weightlifting competitions

    c. Gymnastics meets

    d. Student unions located on select college campuses

DISTRIBUTION STRATEGIES

As noted earlier, S&S Smoothie beverages are distributed primarily through health clubs and gyms and small upscale specialty food stores. S&S Smoothie plans to expand its target reseller market to include the following:

1. Hotels and resorts in the United States and in targeted international markets
2. Golf and tennis clubs
3. College campuses

To increase leverage in larger health clubs, S&S Smoothie will offer free refrigerated display units. This will encourage the facility to maintain a high level of inventory of S&S Smoothie beverages.

Implementation Strategies

Table B.3 shows an example of one objective, i.e., to increase distribution venues, and the action items S&S Smoothie will use to accomplish it. Note that the final marketing plan should include objectives, action items, timing information, and budget imformation necessary to accomplish all marketing strategies. We have only one objective in this sample marketing plan.

Monitoring and Control Strategies

RESEARCH

Continuous market research is needed to understand brand awareness and brand attitudes among the target market. S&S Smoothie will therefore commission exploratory research and descriptive benchmark studies of its target consumer and reseller markets.

TREND ANALYSIS

S&S Smoothie will do a monthly trend analysis to examine sales by reseller type, geographic area, chain, agent, and distributor. These analyses will allow S&S Smoothie to take corrective action when necessary.

MARKETING AUDIT

A marketing audit will be conducted two years following introduction of the company's planned new products.

Table B.3

Objectives/Action Items	Beginning Date	Ending Date	Responsible Party	Cost	Remarks
Objective: Increase distribution venues					
1. Identify key hotels and resorts, golf, and tennis clubs where S&S Smoothies might be sold	July 1	September 1	Bill Sartens (consulting firm will be engaged to assist in this effort)	$25,000	Key to this strategy is to selectively choose resellers so that maximum results are obtained from sales activities. Because health club use is greater during the months of January to May, efforts will be timed to have product in stock no later than January 15.
2. Identify 25 key universities where S&S Smoothies might be sold	July 1	August 1	Bill Sartens	0	Information about colleges and universities and their health club facilities should be available on the university Web pages.
3. Make initial contact with larger hotel and resort chains	September 1	November 1	Bill Sartens	Travel: $10,000	
4. Make initial contact with larger individual (nonchain) facilities	September 1	November 1	Bill Sartens	Travel: $5,000	
5. Make initial contact with universities	August 15	September 15	Sales agents	0	Sales agents will be assigned to the 25 universities and required to make an initial contact and report back to Bill Sartens on promising prospects.
6. Follow up to initial contacts with all potential resellers and obtain contracts for coming 6 months	September 15	Ongoing	Bill Sartens, sales agents	$10,000	$10,000 is budgeted for this item, although actual expenditures will be on an as-needed basis, as follow-up planning travel cannot be preplanned.

MARKETING MATH

To develop marketing strategies to meet the goals of an organization effectively and efficiently, it is essential that marketers understand and use a variety of financial analyses. This appendix provides some of these basic financial analyses, including a review of the income statement and balance sheet as well as some basic performance ratios. In addition, this appendix includes an explanation of some of the specific calculations that marketers use routinely in setting prices for their products and services.

Income Statement and Balance Sheet

The two most important documents used to analyze the financial situation of a company are the income statement and the balance sheet. The **income statement** (which is sometimes referred to as the *profit and loss statement*) provides a summary of the revenues and expenses of a firm—that is, the amount of income a company received from sales or other sources, the amount of money it spent, and the resulting income or loss that the company experienced.

The major elements of the income statement are

- **Gross sales:** the total of all income the firm receives from the sales of goods and services.
- **Net sales revenue:** the gross sales minus the amount for returns and promotional or other allowances given to customers.
- **Cost of goods sold (sometimes called the *cost of sales*):** the cost of inventory or goods that the firm has sold.
- **Gross margin (also called *gross profit*):** the amount of sales revenue that is in excess of the cost of goods sold.
- **Operating expenses:** expenses other than the cost of goods sold that are necessary for conducting business. These may include salaries, rent, depreciation on buildings and equipment, insurance, utilities, supplies, and property taxes.
- **Operating income (sometimes called *income from operations*):** the gross margin minus the operating expenses. Sometimes accountants prepare an *operating statement,* which is similar to the income statement except that the final calculation is the operating income—that is, other revenues or expenses and taxes are not included.
- **Other revenue and expenses:** income and/or expenses other than those required for conducting the business. These may include such items as interest income/expenses and any gain or loss experienced on the sale of property or plant assets.
- **Taxes:** the amount of income tax the firm owes calculated as a percentage of income.
- **Net income (sometimes called *net earnings* or *net profit*):** the excess of total revenue over total expenses.

Table C.1 shows the income statement for an imaginary company, DLL Incorporated. DLL is a typical merchandising firm. Note that the income statement is for a specific year and includes income and expenses from January 1 through December 31 inclusive. The following comments explain the meaning of some of the important entries included in this statement.

- DLL, Inc. has total or gross sales during the year of $253,950. This figure was adjusted, however, by deducting the $3,000 worth of goods returned and special allowances given to customers and by $2,100 in special discounts. Thus, the actual or net sales generated by sales is $248,850.
- The cost of goods sold is calculated by adding the inventory of goods on January 1 to the amount purchased during the year and then subtracting the inventory of goods on

Table C.1 DLL Income Statement for the Year Ended December 31, 20XX

Gross Sales		$253,950	
Less: Sales Returns and Allowances	$ 3,000		
Sales Discounts	2,100	5,100	
Net Sales Revenue			$248,850
Cost of Goods Sold			
Inventory, January 1, 20XX		$ 60,750	
Purchases	$135,550		
Less: Purchase Returns and Allowances	1,500		
Purchase Discounts	750		
Net Purchases	$133,300		
Plus: Freight-In	2,450	135,750	
Goods Available for Sale		196,500	
Less: Inventory, December 31, 20XX		60,300	
Cost of Goods Sold			$136,200
Gross Margin			112,650
Operating Expenses			
Salaries and Commissions		15,300	
Rent		12,600	
Insurance		1,500	
Depreciation		900	
Supplies		825	
Total Operating Expenses			31,125
Operating Income			81,525
Other Revenue and (Expenses)			
Interest Revenue		1,500	
Interest Expense		(2,250)	(750)
Income Before Tax			80,775
Taxes (40%)			32,310
Net Income			$ 48,465

December 31. In this case, DLL had $60,750 worth of inventory on hand on January 1. During the year the firm made purchases in the amount of $135,550. This amount, however, was reduced by purchase returns and allowances of $1,500 and by purchase discounts of $750, so the net purchase is only $133,300.

There is also an amount on the statement labeled "Freight-In." This is the amount spent by the firm in shipping charges to get goods to its facility from suppliers. Any expenses for freight from DLL to its customers (Freight-Out) would be an operating expense. In this case, the Freight-In expense of $2,450 is added to net purchase costs. Then these costs of current purchases are added to the beginning inventory to show that during the year the firm had a total of $196,500 in goods available for sale. Finally, the inventory of goods held on December 31 is subtracted from the goods available, for the total cost of goods sold of $136,200.

For a manufacturer, calculation of the cost of goods sold would be a bit more complicated and would probably include separate figures for such items as inventory of finished goods, the "work-in-process" inventory, the raw materials inventory, and the cost of goods delivered to customers during the year.

- The cost of goods sold is subtracted from the net sales revenue to get a gross margin of $112,650.

- Operating expenses for DLL include the salaries and commissions paid to its employees, rent on facilities and/or equipment, insurance, depreciation of capital items, and the cost of operating supplies. DLL has a total of $31,125 in operating expenses, which is deducted from the gross margin. Thus, DLL has an operating income of $81,525.
- DLL had both other income and expenses in the form of interest revenues of $1,500 and interest expenses of $2,250, making a total other expense of $750, which was subtracted from the operating income, leaving an income before tax of $80,775.
- Finally, the income before tax is reduced by 40 percent ($32,310) for taxes, leaving a net income of $48,465. The 40 percent is an average amount for federal and state corporate income taxes incurred by most firms.

The **balance sheet** lists the assets, liabilities, and stockholders' equity of the firm. Whereas the income statement represents what happened during an entire year, the balance sheet is like a snapshot; it shows the firm's financial situation at one point in time. For this reason, the balance sheet is sometimes called the *statement of financial position.*

Table C.2 shows DLL, Inc.'s balance sheet for December 31. Assets are any economic resource that is expected to benefit the firm in the short or long term. *Current assets* are items that are normally

Table C.2 DLL, Inc. Balance Sheet: December 31, 20XX

Assets

Current Assets			
Cash		$ 4,275	
Marketable Securities		12,000	
Accounts Receivable		6,900	
Inventory		60,300	
Prepaid Insurance		300	
Supplies		150	
Total Current Assets			84,525
Long-Term Assets—Property, Plant and Equipment			
Furniture and Fixtures	$42,300		
Less: Accumulated Depreciation	4,500	37,800	
Land		7,500	
Total Long-Term Assets			45,300
Total Assets			$129,825

Liabilities

Current Liabilities			
Accounts Payable	$70,500		
Unearned Sales Revenue	1,050		
Wages Payable	600		
Interest Payable	300		
Total Current Liabilities		72,450	
Long-Term Liabilities			
Note Payable		18,900	
Total Liabilities			91,350
Stockholders' Equity			
Common Stock		15,000	
Retained Earnings		23,475	
Total Stockholders' Equity			38,475
Total Liabilities and Stockholders' Equity			$129,825

expected to be turned into cash or used up during the next 12 months or during the firm's normal operating cycle. Current assets for DLL include cash, securities, accounts receivable (money owed to the firm and not yet paid), inventory on hand, prepaid insurance, and supplies: a total of $84,525. *Long-term assets* include all assets that are not current assets. For DLL, these are furniture and fixtures (less an amount for depreciation) and land, or $45,300. The *total assets* for DLL are $129,825.

A firm's *liabilities* are its economic obligations, or debts that are payable to individuals or organizations outside the firm. *Current liabilities* are debts due in the coming year or in the firm's normal operating cycle. For DLL, the current liabilities—the accounts payable, unearned sales revenue, wages payable, and interest payable—total $72,450. *Long-term liabilities* (in the case of DLL, a note in the amount of $18,900) are all liabilities that are not due during the coming cycle. *Stockholders' equity* is the value of the stock and the corporation's capital or retained earnings. DLL has $15,000 in common stock and $23,475 in retained earnings for a total stockholders' equity of $38,475. Total liabilities always equal total assets—in this case, $129,825.

Important Financial Performance Ratios

How do managers and financial analysts compare the performance of a firm from one year to the next? How do investors compare the performance of one firm with that of another? As the book notes, managers often rely upon various metrics to measure performance. Often a number of different financial ratios provide important information for such comparisons. Such *ratios* are percentage figures comparing various income statement items to net sales. Ratios provide a better way to compare performance than simple dollar sales or cost figures for two reasons. They enable analysts to compare the performance of large and small firms, and they provide a fair way to compare performance over time, without having to take inflation and other changes into account. In this section we will explain the basic operating ratios. Other measures of performance that marketers frequently use and that are also explained here are the inventory turnover rate and return on investment (ROI).

OPERATING RATIOS

Measures of performance calculated directly from the information in a firm's income statement (sometimes called an operating statement) are called the *operating ratios*. Each ratio compares some income statement item to net sales. The most useful of these are the *gross margin ratio, the net income ratio, the operating expense ratio*, and *the returns and allowances ratio*. These ratios vary widely by industry but tend to be important indicators of how a firm is doing within its industry. The ratios for DLL Inc. are shown in Table C.3.

- The **gross margin ratio** shows what percentage of sales revenues is available for operating and other expenses and for profit. With DLL, this means that 45 percent, or nearly half, of every sales dollar is available for operating costs and for profits.
- The **net income ratio** (sometimes called the *net profit ratio*) shows what percentage of sales revenues is income or profit. For DLL, the net income ratio is 19.5 percent. This means that the firm's profit before taxes is about 20 cents of every dollar.

Table C.3 Hypothetical Operating Ratios for DLL, Inc.

Gross margin ratio	=	gross margin / net sales	=	$112,650 / 248,850	=	45.3%
Net income ratio	=	net income / net sales	=	$48,465 / 248,850	=	19.5%
Operating expense ratio	=	total operating expenses / net sales	=	$31,125 / 248,850	=	12.5%
Returns and allowances ratio	=	returns and allowances / net sales	=	$3,000 / 248,850	=	1.2%

- The **operating expense ratio** is the percentage of sales needed for operating expenses. DLL has an operating expense ratio of 12.5 percent. Tracking operating expense ratios from one year to the next or comparing them with an industry average gives a firm important information about how efficient its operations are.
- The **returns and allowances ratio** shows what percentage of all sales is being returned, probably by unhappy customers. DLL's returns and allowances ratio shows that only a little over 1 percent of sales are being returned.

INVENTORY TURNOVER RATE

The *inventory turnover rate,* also referred to as the stockturn rate, is the number of times inventory or stock is turned over (sold and replaced) during a specified time period, usually a year. Inventory turnover rates are usually calculated on the basis of inventory costs, sometimes on the basis of inventory selling prices, and sometimes by number of units.

In our example, for DLL, Inc., we know that for the year the cost of goods sold was $136,200. Information on the balance sheet enables us to find the average inventory. By adding the value of the beginning inventory to the ending inventory and dividing by 2, we can compute an average inventory. In the case of DLL, this would be

$$\frac{\$60,750 + \$60,300}{2} = \$60,525$$

Thus,

$$\frac{\text{Inventory turnover rate}}{\text{(in cost of goods sold)}} = \frac{\text{costs of goods sold}}{\text{average inventory at cost}} = \frac{\$136,200}{\$60,525} = 2.25 \text{ times}$$

RETURN ON INVESTMENT (ROI)

Firms often develop business objectives in terms of return on investment, and ROI is often used to determine how effective (and efficient) the firm's management has been. First, however, we need to define exactly what a firm means by investment. In most cases, firms define investment as the total assets of the firm. In order to calculate the ROI, we need the net income found in the income statement and the total assets (or investment) found in the firm's balance sheet.

Return on investment is calculated as follows:

$$\text{ROI} = \frac{\text{net income}}{\text{total investment}}$$

For DLL, Inc., if the total assets are $129,825, then the ROI is

$$\frac{\$48,465}{\$129,825} = 37.3\%$$

Sometimes return on investment is calculated by using an expanded formula.

$$\text{ROI} = \frac{\text{net profit}}{\text{sales}} \times \frac{\text{sales}}{\text{investment}}$$
$$= \frac{\$48,465}{\$248,850} \times \frac{\$248,850}{\$129,825} = 37.3\%$$

This formula makes it easy to show how ROI can be increased and what might reduce ROI. For example, there are different ways to increase ROI. First, if the management focuses on cutting costs and increasing efficiency, profits may be increased while sales remain the same.

$$\text{ROI} = \frac{\text{net profit}}{\text{sales}} \times \frac{\text{sales}}{\text{investment}}$$
$$= \frac{\$53,277}{\$248,850} \times \frac{\$248,850}{\$129,825} = 41.0\%$$

But ROI can be increased just as much without improving performance simply by reducing the investment—by maintaining less inventory, for instance.

$$ROI = \frac{\text{net profit}}{\text{sales}} \times \frac{\text{sales}}{\text{investment}}$$

$$= \frac{\$48,465}{\$248,850} \times \frac{\$248,850}{\$114,825} = 42.2\%$$

Sometimes, however, differences among the total assets of firms may be related to the age of the firm or the type of industry, which makes ROI a poor indicator of performance. For this reason, some firms have replaced the traditional ROI measures with *return on assets managed* (ROAM), *return on net assets* (RONA), or *return on stockholders' equity* (ROE).

Price Elasticity

Price elasticity, discussed in Chapter 11, is a measure of the sensitivity of customers to changes in price. Price elasticity is calculated by comparing the percentage change in quantity to the percentage change in price.

$$\text{Price elasticity of demand} = \frac{\text{percentage change in quantity}}{\text{percentage change in price}}$$

$$E = \frac{(Q_2 - Q_1)/Q_1}{(P_2 - P_1)/P_1}$$

where Q = quantity and P = price.

For example, suppose a manufacturer of jeans increased its price from $30.00 a pair to $35.00. But instead of 40,000 pairs being sold, sales declined to only 38,000 pairs. The price elasticity would be calculated as follows:

$$E = \frac{(38,000 - 40,000)/40,000}{(\$35.00 - 30.00)/\$30.00} = \frac{-0.05}{0.167} = 0.30$$

Note that elasticity is usually expressed as a positive number even though the calculations create a negative value.

In this case, a relative small change in demand (5 percent) resulted from a fairly large change in price (16.7 percent), indicating that demand is inelastic. At 0.30, the elasticity is less than 1.

On the other hand, what if the same change in price resulted in a reduction in demand to 30,000 pairs of jeans? Then the elasticity would be

$$E = \frac{(30,000 - 40,000)/40,000}{(\$35.00 - 30.00)/\$30.00} = \frac{-0.25}{0.167} = 1.50$$

In this case, because the 16.7 percent change in price resulted in an even larger change in demand (25 percent), demand is elastic. The elasticity of 1.50 is greater than 1.

Note: Elasticity may also be calculated by dividing the change in quantity by the average of Q_1 and Q_2 and dividing the change in price by the average of the two prices. We, however, have chosen to include the formula that uses the initial quantity and price rather than the average.

Cost-Plus Pricing

As noted in Chapter 11, the most common cost-based approach to pricing a product is **cost-plus pricing**, in which a marketer figures all costs for the product and then adds an amount to cover profit and, in some cases, any costs of doing business that are not assigned to specific products. The most frequently used type of cost-plus pricing is *straight markup pricing*. The price is calculated by

Table C.4 Markup Pricing Using a Jeans Example

Step 1: Determine Total Fixed Costs

Management and other non-production-related salaries	$750,000	
Rental of factory	600,000	
Insurance	50,000	
Depreciation on equipment	100,000	
Advertising	500,000	
Total Fixed Costs	**$2,000,000**	

Step 2: Determine Fixed Costs Per Unit

   Number of Units Produced = 200,000

   Fixed Cost Per Unit ($2,000,000/200,000) $10.00

Step 3: Determine Variable Costs Per Unit

Cost of materials (fabric, zipper, thread, etc.)	$7.00	
Cost of production labor	10.00	
Cost of utilities and supplies used in production process	3.00	
Variable Cost Per Unit		**$20.00**

Step 4: Determine Total Cost Per Unit

   $10.00 + $20.00 = $30.00

   Total Cost Per Unit   **$30.00**

Step 5: Determine Price

   Mark-up on Cost (assuming 40% markup percentage)

   Formula: Price = total cost + (total cost × markup percentage)

   Price = $30.00 + ($30.00 × .40) = $30.00 + $12.00 =   **$42.00**

   Mark-up on Selling Price (assuming 40% markup percentage)

   Formula: $\text{Price} = \dfrac{\text{total cost}}{(1.00 - \text{markup percentage})}$

   $\text{Price} = \dfrac{\$30.00}{(1.00 - .40)} = \dfrac{\$30.00}{.60} =$ **$50.00**

adding a predetermined percentage to the cost. Most retailers and wholesalers use markup pricing exclusively because of its simplicity—users need only estimate the unit cost and add the markup.

The first step requires that the unit cost be easy to estimate accurately and that production rates are fairly consistent. As Table C.4 shows, we will assume a jeans manufacturer has fixed costs (the cost of the factory, advertising, managers' salaries, etc.) of $2,000,000. The variable cost, per pair of jeans (the cost of fabric, zipper, thread, and labor) is $20.00. With the current plant, the firm can produce a total of 200,000 pairs of jeans, so the fixed cost per pair is $10.00. Combining the fixed and variable costs per pair means that the jeans are produced at a total cost of $30.00 per pair.

The second step is to calculate the markup. There are two methods for calculating the markup percentage: markup on cost and markup on selling price. Using *markup on cost pricing,* just as the name implies, a percentage of the cost is added to the cost to determine the firm's selling price.

Markup on cost.   For markup on cost, the calculation is:

Price = total cost + (total cost × markup percentage)

But how does the manufacturer or reseller know the markup percentage to use? One way is to base the markup on the total income needed for profits, for shareholder dividends, and for investment in the business. In our jeans example, the total cost of producing the 200,000 pairs of jeans is $10,000,000. If the manufacturer wants a profit of $4,000,000, what markup percentage would it use? The $4,000,000 is 40 percent of the $10 million total cost, so 20 percent. To find the price, the calculations would be:

$$Price = \$30.00 + (\$30.00 \times 0.40) = \$30.00 + \$12.00 = \$42.00$$

(Note that in the calculations, the markup percentage is expressed as a decimal; that is, 20% = 0.20, 25% = 0.25, 30% = 0.30, and so on.

Markup on selling price. Wholesalers and retailers more generally use markup on selling price. The markup percentage here is the seller's gross margin, the difference between the cost to the wholesaler or retailer and the price needed to cover such overhead items as salaries, rent, utility bills, advertising, and profit. For example, if the wholesaler or retailer knows it needs a margin of 40 percent to cover its overhead and reach its target profits, that margin becomes the markup on the manufacturer's selling price.

So now let's say a retailer buys the jeans from the supplier (wholesaler or manufacturer) for $30 per pair. If the retailer requires a 40 percent markup on its cost, the calculation would be as follows:

$$Price = \frac{total\ cost}{(1.00 - markup\ percentage)}$$

As we see in Table C.4, the price of the jeans with the markup on selling price is $50.00.

Just to compare the difference in the final prices of the two markup methods, Table C.5 also shows what would happen if the retailer uses a markup on cost method. Using the same product cost and price with a 40 percent markup on cost would yield $42.00, a much lower price. The markup on selling price gives you the percentage of the selling price that the markup is. The markup on cost gives you the percentage of the cost that the mark up is. In the markup on selling price the markup amount is $20, which is 40 percent of the selling price of $50. In the markup on cost, the markup is $12, which is 40 percent of the cost of $42.

But what happens when costs go up? Do marketers increase their prices? If they do, consumers may rebel and buy competing products or services instead. One solution is to keep the price constant but provide a bit less of the product. Frito-Lay, maker of salty snack foods, offset increasing production costs by cutting the contents by 6.7 to 7.5 percent per bag of Fritos, Cheetos, and potato chips. To keep consumers from complaining that packages aren't full, a company may make the package ever so slightly smaller. In a similar move, Procter & Gamble once reduced the number of disposable diapers in its Luvs and Pampers packages by an average of 13 percent. Let the buyer beware!

Economic Order Quantity

The amount a firm should order at one time is called the *economic order quantity* (EOQ). Every time a firm places an order, there are additional costs. By ordering larger quantities less frequently, the firm saves on these costs. But it also costs money to maintain large inventories of needed materials. The EOQ is the order volume that provides both the lowest processing costs and the lowest inventory costs. The EOQ can be calculated as follows:

1. Determine the **order processing cost**. This is the total amount it costs a firm to place an order from beginning to end. Typically, this might include the operating expenses for the purchasing department, costs for follow-up, costs of record keeping of orders (data processing), costs for the receiving department, and costs for the processing and paying of invoices from suppliers. The simplest way to calculate this is to add up all these yearly costs and then divide by the number of orders placed during the year.
2. Next, calculate the **inventory carrying cost**. This is the total of all costs involved in carrying inventory. These costs include the costs of capital tied up in inventory, the cost of waste (merchandise that becomes obsolete or unuseable), depreciation costs, storage costs, insurance premiums, property taxes, and opportunity costs.

The formula for calculating EOQ is

$$EOQ = \sqrt{\frac{2 \times \text{units sold (or annual usage)} \times \text{ordering cost}}{\text{unit cost} \times \text{inventory carrying cost (\%)}}}$$

For example, suppose an office supply store sells 6,000 cases of pens a year at a cost of $12.00 a case. The cost to the store for each order placed is $60.00. The cost of carrying the pens in the warehouse is 24 percent per year (this is a typical inventory carrying cost in many businesses.) Thus, the calculation is

$$EOQ = \sqrt{\frac{2 \times 6000 \times \$60}{\$12 \times 0.24}} = \sqrt{\frac{\$720,000}{\$2.88}} = 500$$

The firm should order pens about once a month (it sells 6,000 cases a year or 500 cases a month).

NOTES

CHAPTER 1

1. John W. Schouten, "Selves in Transition: Symbolic Consumption in Personal Rites of Passage and Identity Reconstruction," *Journal of Consumer Research*, March 17, 1991, 412–25; Michael R. Solomon, "The Wardrobe Consultant: Exploring the Role of a New Retailing Partner," *Journal of Retailing* 63 (1987): 110–28; Michael R. Solomon and Susan P. Douglas, "Diversity in Product Symbolism: The Case of Female Executive Clothing," *Psychology & Marketing* 4 (1987): 189–212; Joseph Z. Wisenblit, "Person Positioning: Empirical Evidence and a New Paradigm," *Journal of Professional Services Marketing* 4, no. 2 (1989): 51–82.

2. www.marketingpower.com, 2004

3. Michael R. Solomon, "Deep-Seated Materialism: The Case of Levi's 501 Jeans," in *Advances in Consumer Research*, ed. Richard Lutz (Las Vegas, Nev.: Association for Consumer Research, 1986), 13:619–22.

4. Peter F. Drucker, *Management: Tasks, Responsibilities, Practices* (New York: Harper & Row, 1972), 64–65.

5. Sal Randazzo, "Advertising as Myth-Maker; Brands as Gods and Heroes," *Advertising Age*, November 8, 1993, 32.

6. Lee D. Dahringer, "Marketing Services Internationally: Barriers and Management Strategies," *Journal of Service Marketing* 5 (1991): 5–17.

7. Stuart Elliott, "Introducing Kentucky, the Brand," June 9, 2004, www.nyt.com.

8. Jean Halliday, "Mustang Fans Help Ford Give New Model Free Ride," *Advertising Age*, May 24, 2004, 4.

9. Michael E. Porter, *Competitive Advantage: Creating and Sustaining Superior Performance* (New York: Free Press, 1985).

10. "Dear Chrysler: Outsiders' Advice on Handling the Odometer Charge," *Wall Street Journal*, June 26, 1987, 19.

11. Larry Edwards, "The Decision Was Easy," *Advertising Age*, August 26, 1987, 106. For research and discussion related to public policy issues, see Paul N. Bloom and Stephen A. Greyser, "The Maturing of Consumerism," *Harvard Business Review*, November/December 1981, 130–39; George S. Day, "Assessing the Effect of Information Disclosure Requirements," *Journal of Marketing*, April 1976, 42–52; Dennis E. Garrett, "The Effectiveness of Marketing Policy Boycotts: Environmental Opposition to Marketing," *Journal of Marketing* 51 (January 1987): 44–53; Michael Houston and Michael Rothschild, "Policy-Related Experiments on Information Provision: A Normative Model and Explication," *Journal of Marketing Research* 17 (November 1980): 432–49; Jacob Jacoby, Wayne D. Hoyer, and David A. Sheluga, *Misperception of Televised Communications* (New York: American Association of Advertising Agencies, 1980); Gene R. Laczniak and Patrick E. Murphy, *Marketing Ethics: Guidelines for Managers* (Lexington, Mass.: Lexington Books, 1985): 117–23; Lynn Phillips and Bobby Calder, "Evaluating Consumer Protection Laws: Promising Methods," *Journal of Consumer Affairs* 14 (summer 1980): 9–36; Donald P. Robin and Eric Reidenbach, "Social Responsibility, Ethics, and Marketing Strategy: Closing the Gap between Concept and Application," *Journal of Marketing* 51 (January 1987): 44–58; Howard Schutz and Marianne Casey, "Consumer Perceptions of Advertising as Misleading," *Journal of Consumer Affairs* 15 (winter 1981): 340–57; and Darlene Brannigan Smith and Paul N. Bloom, "Is Consumerism Dead or Alive? Some New Evidence," in *Advances in Consumer Research*, ed. Thomas C. Kinnear (Provo, Utah: Association for Consumer Research, 1984): 11:569–73.

12. Gerry Khermouch, "Virgin's 'Va Va' Bottle Has 'Voom'; First Ads via Long Haymes Carr," *Brandweek*, July 10, 2000, 13.

13. http://abclocal.go.com/kgo/business/050704ap_business_adidas.html, May 7, 2004.

14. "Henry Ford and The Model T," in *Forbes Greatest Business Stories* (New York: John Wiley & Sons, 1996), www.wiley.com/legacy/products/subject/business/forbes/ford.html.

15. Theodore Levitt, "Marketing Myopia," *Harvard Business Review*, July–August 1960, 45–56.

16. Rahul Jacob, "How to Retread Customers," *Fortune*, autumn/winter 1993, 23–24.

17. Bob Tedeschi, "Brand Building on the Internet," August 25, 2003, www.nyt.com.

18. Kate Fitzgerald, "Avon Adds 3 Venues to Anti-Cancer Walk," *Advertising Age*, May 1, 2000, 54.

19. Jeff Lowe, *The Marketing Dashboard: Measuring Marketing Effectiveness* (Venture Communications, February 2003) accessed at www.brandchannel.com/images/papers/dashboard.pdf; G. A. Wyner, "Scorecards and More: The Value Is in How You Use Them," *Marketing Research*, Summer, 6–7; C. F. Lunbdy, and C. Rasinowich, "The Missing Link: Cause and Effect Linkages Make Marketing Scorecards More Valuable," *Marketing Research*, winter 2003, 14–19.

CHAPTER 2

1. www.madd.org.

2. Devin Freiberg and Jackie Freiberg, *NUTS! Southwest Airlines' Crazy Recipe for Business and Personal Success* (Austin, Tex.,: Bard Press, 1996).

3. Quoted in James Hookway, "Philippine Balut Goes Gourmet with an Appeal to Elite Class," *Wall Street Journal Interactive Edition*, May 2, 2002.

4. David Barboza, "Versatility Helps Oreo Fill Gaps in Market," *New York Times Online*, October 4, 2003.

5. Ian P. Murphy, "Southwest Emphasizes Brand as Others Follow the Low-Fare Leader," *Marketing News*, November 4, 1996, 1–2.

6. www.fortune.com/fortune/bestcompanies.

7. www.russell.com/services/individual/employee/articles/scarticle3b.htm and http://woodrow.mpls.frb.fed.us/economy/calc/cpihome.html.

8. Stan Crock, Geoffrey Smith, Joseph Weber, Richard A. Melcher, and Linda Himelstein, "They Snoop to Conquer," *BusinessWeek*, October 28, 1996, 172–76.

9. Anthony Bianco and Wendy Zellner, "Is Wal-Mart Too Powerful," *Business Week* (October 6, 2003): 100-110.

10. www.eggland.com/egg.html.

11. www.bbb.org.

12. Warren St. John, "On the Final Journey, One Size Doesn't Fit All," *New York Times Online*, September 28, 2003.

13. Sarah Ellison, "Sexy-Ad Reel Shows What Tickles in Tokyo Can Fade Fast in France," *Wall Street Journal Interactive Edition*, March 31, 2000.

CHAPTER 3

1. *1992 Annual Report*, Rockwell International.

2. "Ben & Jerry's Social & Environmental Assessment, 2002," www.benjerry.com/our_company/about_us/environment/social_audit/final_socialaudit.pdf.

3. "Government Lifts Ban on Contracts with MCI," *USA Today*, www.usatoday.com/money/industries/telecom/2004-01-07-mci-contracts_x.htm (accessed January 20, 2004).

4. "Italians Struggle to Grasp Fall of Beloved Parmalat, *USA Today*, www.usatoday.com/money/world/2004-01-06-parmalat_x.htm, January 20, 2004.

5. Philip R. Cateora, *Strategic International Marketing* (Homewood, Ill.: Dow Jones-Irwin, 1985).

6. "Capital Wrap-Up: Competitiveness," *BusinessWeek*, November 1, 1993, 47.

7. U.S. Department of Justice, "Foreign Corrupt Practices Act Antibribery Provisions," October 24, 2001, www.usdoj.gov/criminal/fraud/fcpa/dojdocb.htm (accessed January 15, 2002).

8. www.dow.com/webapps/lit/litorder.asp?filepath=about/pdfs/noreg/473-00001.pdf&pdf=true.

9. Rajendra S. Sisodia, "We Need Zero Tolerance toward Ethics Violations," *Marketing News*, March 1990, 4, 14.

10. "Retail Theft and Inventory Shrinkage," http://retailindustry.about.com/library/weekly/02/aa021126a.htm (accessed January 20, 2004).

11. Kenneth N. Gilpin, "Firestone Will Recall an Additional 3.5 Million Tires," *New York Times,* Section C, p. 3, Column 3.

12. *Facts on File*, March 17, 1978, 185; April 14, 1978, 264; May 19, 1978, 366; July 28, 1978, 569; September 22, 1978, 718–19.

13. Consumer Product Safety Council, "CPSC, Window Covering Industry Announce Recall to Repair Window Blinds, New Investigation of Children's Deaths Leads to Redesigned Window Blinds," press release, November 1, 2000, www.cpsc.gov/cpscpub/prerel/prhtml01/01023.html.

14. "Gateway Fined for False Ads," *Advertising Age*, July 23, 1998, www.adage.com/news.cms?newsId=23418.

15. Federal Trade Commission, *FTC Policy Statement on Deception*, October 14, 1983, www.ftc.gov/bcp/policystmt/ad-decept.htm; Dorothy Cohen, *Legal Issues in Marketing Decision Making* (Cincinnati: South-Western College Publishing, 1995).

16. Federal Trade Commission, *FTC Policy Statement on Deception*, October 14, 1983, www.ftc.gov/bcp/policystmt/ad-decept.htm; Dorothy Cohen, *Legal Issues in Marketing Decision Making* (Cincinnati: South-Western College Publishing, 1995).

17. Ira Teinowitz, "FTC Faces Test of Ad Power," *Advertising Age*, March 30, 1998, 26.

18. "Business Ethics' 100 Best Corporate Citizens for 2004," www.businessethics.com/chart_100_best_corporate_citizens_for_2004.htm (accessed May 14, 2004).

19. "Business Ethics' 100 Best Corporate Citizens for 2004."

20. Excerpted from www.stonyfield.com/AboutUs/PartnershipSummary.shtml (accessed May 19, 2004).

21. Sharon Begley, "The Battle for Planet Earth," *Newsweek*, April 24, 2000, 50–53.

22. "Office Depot Releases New 'Green Products' Catalog," December 23, 2003, www.greenbiz.com/news/printer.cfm?NewsID=26260 (accessed May 14, 2004).

23. "Office Depot Releases New 'Green Products' Catalog."

24. Nancy Arnott, "Marketing with a Passion," *Sales & Marketing Management* (January 1994); 64–71.

25. "Avon Breast Cancer Crusade," www.avoncompany.com/women/avoncrusade/background/overview.html (accessed January 24, 2004).

26. Laura Bird, "Denny's TV Ad Seeks to Mend Bias Image," *Wall Street Journal*, June 21, 1993, B3.

27. Chuck Hawkins, "Denny's: The Stain That Isn't Coming Out," *BusinessWeek*, June 28, 1993, 98–99.

28. Sonya Thorpe Brathwaite, "Denny's: A Diversity Success Story," *Franchising*, www.franchise.org/news/fw/aug2002b.asp (accessed May 14, 2004).

29. "Diversity Facts," www.dennys.com/aboutus/Diversity.asp (accessed May 14, 2004).

30. "Community Support," www.tjx.com/corprespons/commsupp.html (accessed May 24, 2004).

31. Patricia Digh, "America's Largest Untapped Market: Who They Are, the Potential They Represent," *Fortune*, March 2, 1998, S1–S12; "Hertz Offers a Full Range of Services for the Physically Challenged, www.hertz.com/serv/us/services_phys.html.

32. Press Release, Nike, "Nike Reports Second Quarter Earnings Up Nine Percent; Worldwide Futures Orders Increase Eight Percent," press release, December 20, 2001, www.nikebiz.com/media/n_q202.shtml (accessed February 18, 2002).

33. World Trade Organization, "Stronger Than Expected Growth Spurs Modest Trade Recovery," press release, April 5, 2004, www.wto.org/english/news_e/pres04_e/pr373_e.htm (accessed May 12, 2004).

34. Sak Onkvisit and John J. Shaw, *International Marketing: Analysis and Strategy*, 2nd ed. (New York: Macmillan, 1993).

35. Charles Goldsmith, "MTV Seeks Global Appeal," July 21, 2003, www.wsj.com.

36. P. D. Harveston and P. S. Davis, "Entrepreneurship and the Born Global Phenomenon: Theoretical Foundations and a Research Agenda," in *E-Commerce and Entrepreneurship: Research in Entrepreneurship and Management,* vol. 1., ed. John Butler (City, State: Information Age Publishing, 2001), 1–30; text adapted from www.campbell.berry.edu/faculty/pharveston/bornglobal.html (accessed February 11, 2004).

37. Michael R. Czinkota and Masaaki Kotabe, "America's New World Trade Order," *Marketing Management* 1, no. 3 (1992): 47–54.

38. "Russia: Introduction of Mean Import Quotas," www.iet.ru/afe/english/apk/january03.pdf (accessed January 22, 2004).

39. "U.S. Moves to Limit Textile Imports from China," November 19, 2003, www.wsj.com.

40. "The WTO in Brief," www.wto.org/english/thewto_e/whatis_e/inbrief_e/inbr02_e.htm (accessed January 22, 2004).

41. "The WTO in Brief."

42. Nic Hopkins, "Software Piracy Microsoft's Big Threat," February 7, 2001, www.cnn.com/2001/WORLD/asiapcf/east/02/07/hongkong.microsoft (accessed February 18, 2002).

43. "Delivering Lisbon: Reforms for the Enlarged Union," www.wto.org/english/thewto_e/ whatis_e/inbrief_e/inbr02_e.htm (accessed January 22, 2004).

44. William C. Symonds, "Border Crossings," *BusinessWeek*, November 22, 1993, p. 40; "Fact Sheet: North American Free Trade Agreement," July 2001, www.fas.usda.gov/info/factsheets/nafta.html (accessed February 18, 2002).

45. Geri Smith, Elisabeth Malkin, Jonathan Wheatley, Paul Magnusson, and Michael Arnds, "Betting on Free Trade," *BusinessWeek*, April 23, 2001, 60–62; "Free Trade Area of the Americas: FTAA," www.ftaa-alca.org/View_e.asp#PREPARATORY (accessed January 22, 2004).

46. Geri Smith, Elisabeth Malkin, Jonathan Wheatley, Paul Magnusson, and Michael Arnds, "Betting on Free Trade," *BusinessWeek*, April 23, 2001, 60–62; "Free Trade Area of the Americas: FTAA," www.ftaa-alca.org/View_e.asp#PREPARATORY (accessed January 22, 2004).

47. Peter Fuhrman and Michael Schuman, "Where Are the Indians? The Russians?" *Forbes*, July 17, 1995, 126–127.

48. "Peru: Privatization Is Principal Policy for Attracting Foreign Investment," *Wall Street Journal*, October 27, 1993, B7.

49. Keith Bradsher, "Consumerism Grows in China, with Beijing's Blessing," *New York Times*, www.bdachina.com/content/about/pressquotes/P1070443598/en?portal_skin=printable (accessed February 11, 2004).

50. Sara Hope Franks, "Overseas, It's What's Inside That Sells," *Washington Post National Weekly Edition*, December 5–11, 1994, 21.

51. William C. Symonds, "Border Crossings," *BusinessWeek*, November 22, 1993, 40.

52. Thomas L. Friedman, "U.S. Prods Indonesia on Rights," *New York Times*, January 18, 1994, D1(2).

53. Amy Merrick, "Gap Offers Unusual Look at Factory Conditions," May 12, 2004, www.wsj.com.

54. Cecilie Rohwedder, "The Chic of Arabia," January 23, 2004, www.wsj.com.

55. Richard W. Pollay, "Measuring the Cultural Values Manifest in Advertising," *Current Issues and Research in Advertising* 6 (1983): 71–92.

56. Daniel Goleman, "The Group and the Self: New Focus on a Cultural Rift," December 25, 1990, www.nyt.com, 37; Harry C. Triandis, "The Self and Social Behavior in Differing Cultural Contexts," *Psychological Review* 96 (July 1989): 506; Harry C. Triandis, Robert Bontempo, Marcelo J. Villareal, Masaaki Asai, and Nydia Lucca, "Individualism and Collectivism: Cross-Cultural Perspectives on Self-Ingroup Relationships," *Journal of Personality and Social Psychology* 54 (February 1988): 323.

57. David Carr, "Romance, In Cosmo's World, Is Translated in Many Ways," May 26, 2002, *New York Times*, Section 1, p. 1, Column 1., adapted from Michael R. Solomon, *Consumer Behavior: Buying, Having, and Being*, 6th ed. (Upper Saddle River, N.J.: Prentice Hall, 2003).

58. George J. McCall and J. L. Simmons, *Social Psychology: A Sociological Approach* (New York: Free Press, 1982).

59. Alison Leigh Cowan, "Caterpillar: Worldwide Watch for Opportunities," *New York Times*, January 4, 1994, C4.

60. Steve Rivkin, "The Name Game Heats Up," *Marketing News*, April 22, 1996, 8.

61. Items excerpted from Terence A. Shimp and Subhash Sharma, "Consumer Ethnocentrism: Construction and Validation of the CETSCALE," *Journal of Marketing Research* 24 (August 1987): 282.

62. Evan Perez, "Argentina's Middle Class Goes Suburban Thanks to Vision of a U.S. Home Builder," January 16, 2002, www.wsj.com.

63. Lizette Alvarex, "London Journal: U.S. Eating Habits and Europeans Are Spreading Visibly," *New York Times*, October 31, 2003, Section A, p. 4, Column 3.; Ellen Hale, "Krispy Kreme's Sweet on Britain," *USA Today*, August 12, 2003, 1B(2).

64. Eric Pfanner, "Foreign Policy and Marketing," January 20, 2004, www.nyt.com.

65. Charles Goldsmith, "How 'Idols' around the World Harmonize with Local Viewers," September 23, 2003, www.wsj.com.

66. Michael Skapinker, "Brand Strength Proves Its Worth," *Financial Times*, January 20, 2004, www.ge.com/en/company/news/ft_brand_strength.htm?category=News (accessed January 22, 2004).

67. Alexander Hiam and Charles D. Schewe, *The Portable MBA in Marketing* (New York: John Wiley & Sons, 1992).

68. Harvey S. James Jr. and Murray Weidenbaum, *When Businesses Cross International Borders* (Westport, Conn.: Praeger, 1993).

69. Rebecca Buckman, "China's Cheeseman Is No Longer Alone," December 11, 2003, www.wsj.com.

70. www.mcdonalds.com/corporate/index.html.

71. Saritha Rai, "Tastes of India in U.S. Wrappers," April 29, 2003, www.nyt.com.

72. www.gm.com/company/corp_info/profiles.

73. Onkvisit and Shaw, *International Marketing*.

74. Jeremy Kahn, "The World's Most Admired Companies," *Fortune*, October 26, 1998, 206–216.

75. One of the most influential arguments for this perspective can be found in Theodore Levitt, "The Globalization of Markets," *Harvard Business Review*, May–June 1983, 92–102.

76. Juliana Koranteng, "Reebok Finds Its Second Wind as It Pursues Global Presence," *Advertising Age International*, January 1998, 18.

77. Terry Clark, "International Marketing and National Character: A Review and Proposal for an Integrative Theory," *Journal of Marketing* 54 (October 1990): 66–79.

78. Norihiko Shirouzu, "Snapple in Japan: How a Splash Dried Up," *Wall Street Journal*, April 15, 1996, B1(2).

79. Richard C. Morais, "The Color of Beauty," *Forbes*, November 27, 2000, 170–76.

80. Franks, "Overseas, It's What's Inside That Sells."

81. Bradley Johnson, "Unisys Touts Service in Global Ads," *Advertising Age*, February 15, 1993, 59.

82. Sheryl WuDunn, "An Uphill Journey to Japan," *New York Times*, May 16, 1995, D1(2).

83. Better Business Bureau, "Gray Market Goods," www.newyork.bbb.org/library/publications/subrep45.html (accessed January 22, 2004).

84. "Kodak Alleges Fuji Photo Is Dumping Color Photographic Paper in the U.S.," *Wall Street Journal*, February 22, 1993, B6.

85. Wendy Zellner, "How Well Does Wal-Mart Travel?" *BusinessWeek*, September 3, 2001, 82(2).

CHAPTER 4

1. Alan J. Greco and Jack T. Hogue, "Developing Marketing Decision Support Systems in Consumer Goods Firms," *Journal of Consumer Marketing* 7 (1990): 55–64.

2. Michelle Krebs, "50-Plus and King of the Road," *Advertising Age*, May 1, 2000, S18; Daniel McGinn and Julie Edelson Halpert, "Driving Miss Daisy—and Selling Her the Car," *Newsweek*, February 3, 1997, 14.

3. Norm Alster, "Business: It's Just a Game, but Hollywood Is Paying Attention," November 23, 2003, www.nyt.com.

4. www.qscores.com (accessed May 17, 2004).

5. Yumiko Ono, "An Ad for Smudge-Proof Makeup Rubs a Big Marketer Wrong Way," *Wall Street Journal*, April 12, 1996, B1.

6. Laurie Hays, "Using Computers to Divine Who Might Buy a Gas Grill," *Wall Street Journal*, August 16, 1994, B1(2).

7. Peter R. Peacock, "Data Mining in Marketing: Part I," *Marketing Management*, winter 1998, 9–18.

8. Peacock, "Data Mining in Marketing."

9. Frederick F. Reichheld, *Loyalty Rules! How Leaders Build Lasting Relationships in the Digital Age* (Cambridge, Mass.: Harvard Business School Press, 2001).

10. Paul C. Judge, "Do You Know Who Your Most Profitable Customers Are?," September 14, 1998, www.Businessweek.Com/1998/37/B3595144.Htm?$Se.

11. Robert Baxter, Mercedes-Benz North America, personal communication, June 1996.

12. Michael R. Solomon, *Conquering Consumerspace: Marketing Strategies for a Branded World* (New York: AMACOM Books, 2003).

13. Ronald B. Lieber, "Storytelling: A New Way to Get Close to Your Customer," *Fortune*, February 3, 1997, 102–8.

14. Lieber, "Storytelling."

15. Lieber, "Storytelling."

16. Michael R. Solomon, *Consumer Behavior: Buying, Having, and Being*, 5th ed. (Upper Saddle River, N.J.: Prentice Hall, 2001).

17. www.brawny.com (accessed June 18, 2004); Jack Weber, "Absorbing Some Changes," November 1994, www.quirks.com (accessed January 26, 1998).

18. Jean Halliday, "Nissan Delves into Truck Owner Psyche," *Advertising Age*, December 1, 2003, 11.

19. Kelly Shermach, "Art of Communication," *Marketing News*, May 8, 1995, 2.

20. Srikumar Rao, "Diaper–Beer Syndrome," *Forbes*, April 6, 1998, 128(3).

21. Clive Thompson, "There's a Sucker Born in Every Medial Prefrontal Cortex," October 26, 2003, www.nyt.com.

22. www.the-dma.org/government/donotcalllists.shtml.

23. Kim Bartel Sheehan, "Online Research Methodology: Reflections and Speculations," *Journal of Interactive Advertising* 3, no. 1, (fall 2002): accessed at jiad.org/vol3/no1/Sheehan.

24. Basil G. Englis and Michael R. Solomon, *Life/Style OnLine ©: A Web-Based Methodology for Visually-Oriented Consumer Research*," *Journal of Interactive Marketing* 14, no. 1 (2000): 2–14; Basil G. Englis, Michael R. Solomon, and Paula D. Harveston, "Web-Based, Visually Oriented Consumer Research Tools," in *Online Consumer Psychology: Understanding How to Interact with Consumers in the Virtual World*, ed. Curt Haugtvedt, Karen Machleit, and Richard Yalch (Hillsdale, N.J.: Lawrence Erlbaum Associates, in press).

25. David Goetzl, "O&M Turns Reality TV into Research Tool," *Advertising Age*, July 10, 2000, 6.

26. Matt Richtel, "A New on-the-Job Hazard: Turning into a Mall Rat," May 3, 2004, www.nyt.com.

27. Mike Galetto, "Turning Trash to Research Treasure," *Advertising Age*, April 17, 1995, 1–16.

28. Bruce L. Stern and Ray Ashmun, "Methodological Disclosure: The Foundation for Effective Use of Survey Research," *Journal of Applied Business Research* 7 (1991): 77–82.

29. Alan E. Wolf, "Most Colas Branded Alike by Testy Magazine," *Beverage World*, August 31, 1991, 8.

30. Gary Levin, "New Adventures in Children's Research," *Advertising Age*, August 9, 1993, 17.

31. Stephanie Strom, "How Gap Inc. Spells Revenge," *New York Times*, April 24, 1994, 1(2).

32. 2004 Honomichl Top 50 Report, *Marketing News*, June 15, 2004, H4.

33. Jack Honomichl, "Research Cultures Are Different in Mexico, Canada," *Marketing News*, May 10, 1993, 12.

34. Honomichl, "Research Cultures Are Different in Mexico, Canada," 12.

35. Tara Parker-Pope, "Nonalcoholic Beer Hits the Spot in Mideast," *Wall Street Journal*, December 6, 1995, B1(2).

36. Steve Rivkin, "The Name Game Heats Up," *Marketing News*, April 22, 1996, 8.

37. Catherine Arnold, "Cast Your Net—Survey Customers, Partners Online," *Marketing News*, November 24, 2003, 15, 19.

38. Jean Halliday, "Automakers Involve Consumers," *Advertising Age*, January 31, 2000, 82.

39. Tobi Elkin, "Virtual Test Market, *Advertising Age*, October 27, 2003, 6.

40. Jack Neff, "P&G Weds Data, Sales," *Advertising Age*, October 23, 2000, 76.

41. James Heckman, "Turning the Focus Online," *Marketing News*, February 28, 2000, 15; Judith Langer, "'On' and 'Offline' Focus Groups: Claims, Questions," *Marketing News*, June 5, 2000, H38.

42. Dana James, "Precision Decision," *Marketing News*, September 27, 1999, 24–25.

CHAPTER 5

1. James R. Bettman, "The Decision Maker Who Came in from the Cold," Presidential Address, in *Advances in Consumer Research*, vol. 20, ed. Leigh McAllister and Michael Rothschild (Provo, Utah: Association for Consumer Research, 1990); John W. Payne, James R. Bettman, and Eric J. Johnson, "Behavioral Decision Research: A Constructive Processing Perspective," *Annual Review of Psychology* 4 (1992): 87–131; for an overview of recent developments in individual choice models, see Robert J. Meyer and Barbara E. Kahn, "Probabilistic Models of Consumer Choice Behavior," in *Handbook of Consumer Behavior*, ed. Thomas S. Robertson and Harold H. Kassarjian (Englewood Cliffs, N.J.: Prentice Hall, 1991), 85–123.

2. Constance L. Hays, "Targeting the Toddler Market," July 11, 2003, www.nyt.com.

3. Christopher Lawton, "Pushing Faux Foreign Beer in U.S.: Can Anheuser-Busch Tap Imports' Growth with Beers Produced in Land of Budweiser?," June 27, 2003, www.wsj.com.

4. "Touch Looms Large as a Sense That Drives Sales," *Brand Packaging*, May/June 1999, 39–40.

5. Michael Lev, "No Hidden Meaning Here: Survey Sees Subliminal Ads," *New York Times*, May 3, 1991, D7.

6. Bruce Orwall, "Disney Recalls 'The Rescuers' Video Containing Images of Topless Woman," January 11, 1999, www.wsj.com.

7. Robert M. McMath, "Image Counts," *American Demographics*, May 1998, 64.

8. Abraham H. Maslow, *Motivation and Personality*, 2nd ed. (New York: Harper & Row, 1970).

9. Robert A. Baron and Donn Byrne, *Social Psychology: Understanding Human Interaction*, 5th ed. (Boston: Allyn & Bacon, 1987).

10. Stuart Elliott, "Pepsi's New Campaign Leaves Left Brain for Right," November 20, 2003, www.nyt.com.

11. Rebecca Piirto Heath, "You Can Buy a Thrill: Chasing the Ultimate Rush," *American Demographics*, June 1997, 47–51.

12. Richard E. Petty and John T. Cacioppo, "Need for Cognition and Advertising: Understanding the Role of Personality Variables in Consumer Behavior," *Journal of Consumer Psychology* 1, no. 3 (1992): 239–60.

13. Mercedes M. Cardona, "Kenra Restyles Idea of 'Good/Bad' Hair," *Advertising Age*, August 16, 1999, 27.

14. Jeffrey F. Durgee, "Self-Esteem Advertising," *Journal of Advertising* 14 (1986): 4–21.

15. Nancy Keates, "Baby-Boomers Relive Spring Break, but MTV Is Conspicuously Absent," March 26, 1998, www.wsj.com.

16. Cate T. Corcoran, "Shares of Teen Hub iTurf Surge on Traffic Numbers," January 24, 2000, www.wsj.com.

17. Benjamin D. Zablocki and Rosabeth Moss Kanter, "The Differentiation of Life-Styles," *Annual Review of Sociology* (1976): 269–97.

18. Kate Zernike and Marian Burros, "Low-Carb Boom Isn't Just for Dieters Anymore," February 19, 2004, www.nyt.com; Richard Gibson, "McDonald's to Phase Out 'Super Size' from Menus," March 3, 2004, www.wsj.com.

19. Brian Sternberg, "Pioneer's Hot-Rod Ads Too Cool for Mainstream," March 14, 2003, www.wsj.com.

20. Alfred S. Boote, "Psychographics: Mind Over Matter," *American Demographics*, April 1980, 26–29; William D. Wells, "Psychographics: A Critical Review," *Journal of Marketing Research* 12 (May 1975): 196–213.

21. Alan R. Hirsch, "Effects of Ambient Odors on Slot-Machine Usage in a Las Vegas Casino," *Psychology & Marketing* 12, no. 7 (October 1995): 585–94.

22. Marianne Meyer, "Attention Shoppers!" *Marketing and Media Decisions* 23 (May 1988): 67.

23. See Eben Shapiro, "Need a Little Fantasy? A Bevy of New Companies Can Help," *New York Times*, March 10, 1991, F4.

24. Janet Ginsburg, "Xtreme Retailing," *Business Week*, December 20, 1999, 120(7).

25. Stephanie Grunier, "An Entrepreneur Chooses to Court Cafe Society (Cyber Version, Actually)," September 24, 1999, www.wsj.com.

26. John P. Cortez, "Media Pioneers Try to Corral On-the-Go Consumers," *Advertising Age*, August 17, 1992, 25.

27. Quoted in John P. Cortez, "Ads Head for Bathroom," *Advertising Age*, May 18, 1992, 24.

28. John P. Robinson, "Time Squeeze," *Advertising Age*, February 1990, 30–33.

29. Leonard L. Berry, "Market to the Perception," *American Demographics*, February 1990, 32.

30. Neil MacFarquhar, "A Kiss Is Not Just a Kiss to an Angry Arab TV Audience," March 5, 2004, www.nyt.com.

31. Richard W. Pollay, "Measuring the Cultural Values Manifest in Advertising," *Current Issues and Research in Advertising* (1983): 71–92.

32. Becky Ebenkamp, "Chicks and Balances," *Brandweek*, February 12, 2001, 16.

33. Norihiko Shirouzu, "Japanese 'Hygiene Fanatics' Snap Up Low-Smoke Cigarette," September 8, 1997, www.wsj.com.

34. Nicole Crawford, "Getting Street-Smart," *PROMO Magazine*, March 1998, 61(3), quoted on p. 62.

35. Bob Jones, "Black Gold," *Entrepreneur*, July 1994, 62–65; Fred Thompson, "Blacks Spending Potential Up 54 Percent Since 1990," *Montgomery Advertiser*, May 9, 1997, 1.

36. J. Michael Munson and W. Austin Spivey, "Product and Brand-User Stereotypes among Social Classes: Implications for Advertising Strategy," *Journal of Advertising Research* 21 (August 1981): 37–45.

37. Stuart U. Rich and Subhash C. Jain, "Social Class and Life Cycle as Predictors of Shopping Behavior," *Journal of Marketing Research* 5 (February 1968): 41–49.

38. Alessandra Galloni, "Armani, Mercedes to Form Marketing, Design Venture," September 30, 2003, www.wsj.com.

39. Nathan Kogan and Michael A. Wallach, "Risky Shift Phenomenon in Small Decision-Making Groups: A Test of the Information Exchange Hypothesis," *Journal of Experimental Social Psychology* 3 (January 1967): 75–84; Arch G. Woodside and M. Wayne DeLozier, "Effects of Word-of-Mouth Advertising on Consumer Risk Taking," *Journal of Advertising*, Fall 1976, 12–19.

40. Nancy Keates and Charles Passy, "Tailgating, Inc.," August 29, 2003, www.wsj.com.

41. Jack Neff, "Door-to-Door Sellers Join the Party Online," *Advertising Age*, September 27, 1999, www.adage.com/news.cms?newsId =1100.

42. Everett M. Rogers, *Diffusion of Innovations*, 3rd ed. (New York: Free Press, 1983).

43. Cecile Rohwedder, "In Step with Famous Feet: How Wealthy Entrepreneur Used Celebrities to Create Buzz before His Shoes Hit Stores," June 27, 2003, www.wsj.com.

44. Kathleen Debevec and Easwar Iyer, "Sex Roles and Consumer Perceptions of Promotions, Products, and Self: What Do We Know and Where Should We Be Headed," in *Advances in Consumer Research*, vol. 13, ed. Richard J. Lutz (Provo, Utah: Association for Consumer Research, 1986), 210–14; Lynn J. Jaffe and Paul D. Berger, "Impact on Purchase Intent of Sex-Role Identity and Product Positioning," *Psychology & Marketing* (fall 1988): 259–71.

45. Becky Ebenkamp, "Battle of the Sexes," *Brandweek*, April 17, 2000, accessed online at http://www.findarticles.com/p/articles/mi_m0BDW/is_16_41/ai_61860406.

46. Debevec and Iyer, "Sex Roles and Consumer Perceptions of Promotions, Products and Self"; Deborah E. S. Frable, "Sex Typing and Gender Ideology: Two Facets of the Individual's Gender Psychology That Go Together," *Journal of Personality and Social Psychology* 56 (1989): 95–108; Jaffe and Berger, "Impact on Purchase Intent of Sex-Role Identity and Product Positioning"; Keren A. Johnson, Mary R. Zimmer, and Linda L. Golden, "Object Relations Theory: Male and Female Differences in Visual Information Processing," in *Advances in Consumer Research*, vol. 14, ed. Melanie Wallendorf and Paul Anderson (Provo, Utah: Association for Consumer Research, 1986), 83–87; Leila T. Worth, Jeanne Smith, and Diane M. Mackie, "Gender Schematicity and Preference for Gender-Typed Products," *Psychology & Marketing* 9, (January 1992): 17–30.

47. Kara K. Choquette, "Not All Approve of Barbie's MasterCard," *USA Today*, March 30, 1998, 6B.

48. Adam Lashinsky, "Meg and the Machine" *Fortune*, August 11, 2–3, www.fortune.com/fortune/subs/print/0,15935,473553,00.html (accessed May 20, 2004).

49. This section adapted from Michael R. Solomon, *Consumer Behavior: Buying, Having and Being*, 5th ed. (Upper Saddle River, N.J.: Prentice Hall, 2001).

50. S. Lee Jamison, "An Online Search for Fun without a Look for Love," *New York Times*, December 12, 2003, www.craigslist.org/about/press/searchforfun.html (accessed May 20, 2004).

51. Robert V. Kozinets, "E-Tribalized Marketing?: The Strategic Implications of Virtual Communities of Consumption," *European Management Journal* 17, no. 3 (June 1999): 252–64.

52. Hassan Fattah and Pamela Pual, "Gaming Gets Serious," *American Demographics*, May 2002, 39–43.

53. "Dunkin' Donuts Buys Out Critical Web Site," August 27, 1999, www.nyt.com.

54. Bradley Johnson, "febrezekillsdogs.com (and birds, too)," *Advertising Age* (May 10, 1999): 8.

55. Nicholas Kulish, "Still Bedeviled by Satan Rumors, P&G Battles Back on the Web," The *Wall Street Journal Interactive Edition*, September 21, 1999.

CHAPTER 6

1. B. Charles Ames and James D. Hlaracek, *Managerial Marketing for Industrial Firms* (New York: Random House Business Division, 1984); Edward F. Fern and James R. Brown, "The Industrial/Consumer Marketing Dichotomy: A Case of Insufficient Justification," *Journal of Marketing*, Spring 1984, 68–77.

2. Andy Reinhardt, Joan O'C. Hamilton, and Linda Himelstein, "Silicon Valley: How It Really Works," *Business Week*, August 18, 1997, 64–147.

3. www.bmwusa.com/welcome.cfm?page=&bottom=0.

4. *Statistical Abstract of the United States*, 2001, 303.

5. Mark Amtower, "There's Room for Players of All Types and Sizes," *Business Marketing*, July 1994, G-1.

6. www.census.gov/pub/epcd/www/naics/html.

7. Timothy Aeppel, "Low-Profile Widget Maker Mainly Targets Engineers Watching Their Favorite Shows," August 7, 2003, www.wsj.com.

8. Catherine Arnold, "Reference Programs Keep B-to-B Customers Satisfied," *Marketing News*, August 18, 2003, 4.

9. Faye W. Gilbert, Joyce A. Young, and Charles R. O'Neal, "Buyer-Seller Relationships in Just-in-Time Purchasing Environments," *Journal of Organizational Research*, February 1994, 29, 111–20.

10. Gilbert et al., "Buyer-Seller Relationships in Just-in-Time Purchasing Environments."

11. Steven J. Kafka, Bruce D. Temkin, Matthew R. Sanders, Jeremy Sharrard, and Tobias O. Brown, "eMarketplaces Boost B2B Trade," *The Forrester Report*, February 2000.

12. "The Whole Enchilada," *Intranet Design*, http://idm.internet.com/rweb/tacobell/shtml.

13. Andy Reinhardt, "Log On, Link Up, Save Big," *Business Week*, June 22, 1998, 132–38.

14. Reinhardt, "Log On, Link Up, Save Big."

15. Nicole Harris, " 'Private Exchanges' May Now Allow B-to-B Commerce to Thrive After All," March 16, 2001, www.wsj.com.

CHAPTER 7

1. Stanley C. Hollander and Richard Germain, *Was There a Pepsi Generation before Pepsi Discovered It?: Youth-Based Segmentation in Marketing* (New York: NTC Business Books, 1992).

2. Conway Lackman and John M. Lanasa, "Family Decision-Making Theory: An Overview and Assessment," *Psychology & Marketing* 10 (March/April 1993): 81–93.

3. Mary Beth Grover, "Teenage Wasteland," *Forbes*, July 28, 1997, 44–45.

4. Amy Barrett, "To Reach the Unreachable Teen," *Business Week*, September 18, 2000, 78–80.

5. Bruce Horovitz, "Gen Y: A Tough Crowd to Sell," *USA Today*, May 21, 2002, www.usatoday.com/money/covers/2002-04-22-geny.htm (accessed June 1, 2002).

6. T. L. Stanley, "Age of Innocence . . . Not," *PROMO*, February 1997, 28–33; Douglas Coupland, *Generation X: Tales for an Accelerated Culture* (New York: St. Martin's Press, 1991).

7. Quoted in Karen Lowry Miller, "You Just Can't Talk to These Kids," *Business Week*, April 19, 1993, 104.

8. Robert Scally, "The Customer Connection: Gen X Grows Up, They're in Their 30s Now," *Discount Store News*, October 25, 1999, 38(20), (accessed February 13, 2000).

9. Scally, "The Customer Connection," 38(20).

10. www.census.gov/dmd/www/2khome.htm.

11. Jennifer Lawrence, "Gender-Specific Works for Diapers—Almost Too Well," *Advertising Age*, February 8, 1993, S-10.

12. Charles M. Schaninger and William D. Danko, "A Conceptual and Empirical Comparison of Alternate Household Life Cycle Markets," *Journal of Consumer Research* 19 (March 1993): 580–94.

13. Christy Fisher, "Census Data May Make Ads More Single-Minded," *Advertising Age*, July 20, 1992, 2.

14. Susan Carey, "Not All That's Gold Glitters in a $14,000 Pinstriped Suit," December 13, 1999, www.wsj.com.

15. "Religion Reshapes Realities for U.S. Restaurants in Middle East," *Nation's Restaurant News*, February 16, 1998, 32(7), (accessed February 13, 2000).

16. "Burger King Will Alter Ad That Has Offended Muslims," March 15, 2000, www.wsj.com.

17. Tom Morganthau, "The Face of the Future," *Newsweek*, January 27, 1997, 58.

18. Michael E. Ross, "At Newsstands, Black Is Plentiful," *New York Times*, December 26, 1993, F6.

19. Eleena DeLisser, "Romance Books Get Novel Twist and Go Ethnic," *Wall Street Journal*, September 6, 1994, B1.

20. Brad Edmondson, "Asian Americans in 2001," *American Demographics*, February 1997, 16–17.

21. Dorinda Elliott, "Objects of Desire," *Newsweek*, February 12, 1996, 41.

22. Joe Schwartz, "Hispanic Opportunities," *American Demographics*, May 1987, 56–59.

23. Carolyn Shea, "The New Face of America," *PROMO*, January 1996, 53.

24. Schwartz, "Hispanic Opportunities."

25. Lucette B. Comer and J. A. F. Nicholls, "Communication between Hispanic Salespeople and Their Customers: A First Look," *Journal of Personal Selling & Sales Management* 20 (Summer 2000): 121–27.

26. Rick Wartzman, "When You Translate 'Got Milk' for Latinos, What Do You Get?," June 3, 1999, www.wsj.com.

27. Wartzman, "When You Translate 'Got Milk' for Latinos, What Do You Get?"

28. Quoted in George Rathwaite, "Heileman's National Impact with Local Brews," *Marketing Insights*, premier issue (1989): 108.

29. Rick E. Bruner, "Sites Help Marketers Think Global, Advertise Local," *Advertising Age*, March 24, 1997, 30.

30. Tara Weingarten, "Life in the Fastest Lane," *Newsweek*, February 21, 2000, 60–61.

31. See Lewis Alpert and Ronald Gatty, "Product Positioning by Behavioral Life Styles," *Journal of Marketing* 33 (April 1969): 65–69; Emanuel H. Demby, "Psychographics Revisited: The Birth of a Technique," *Marketing News*, January 2, 1989, 21; and William D. Wells, "Backward Segmentation," in *Insights into Consumer Behavior*, ed. Johan Arndt (Boston: Allyn & Bacon, 1968), 85–100.

32. Rebecca Piirto Heath, "You Can Buy a Thrill: Chasing the Ultimate Rush," *American Demographics*, June 1997, 47–51.

33. Richard Trubo, "Metrosexuals: It's a Guy Thing," http://content.health.msn.com/content/article/71/81366.htm.

34. Judann Pollack, "Kraft's Miracle Whip Targets Core Consumers with '97 Ads," *Advertising Age*, February 3, 1997, 12.

35. Reported in Michael R. Solomon and Elnora W. Stuart, *Marketing: Real People, Real Choices*, 1st ed. (Upper Saddle River, N.J.: Prentice Hall, 1997).

36. Anthony Ramirez, "New Cigarettes Raising Issue of Target Market," *New York Times*, February 18, 1990, 28.

37. William Echikson, "Aiming at High and Low Markets," *Fortune*, March 22, 1993, 89.

38. Chip Bayers, "The Promise of One to One (a Love Story)," *Wired*, May 1998, 130.

39. www.dell.com.

40. Becky Ebenkamp, "No Dollars for Bowling," *Brandweek*, March 27, 2000, 56–58.

41. For an example of how consumers associate food brands with a range of female body shapes, see Martin R. Lautman, "End-Benefit Segmentation and Prototypical Bonding," *Journal of Advertising Research*, June/July 1991, 9–18.

42. Ian P. Murphy, "Beverages Don't Mean a Thing if They Ain't Got That Zing."

43. "A Crash Course in Customer Relationship Management," *Harvard Management Update*, March 2000 (Harvard Business School reprint U003B).

44. Don Peppers and Martha Rogers, *The One-to-One Future* (New York: Doubleday, 1996).

45. Don Peppers, Martha Rogers, and Bob Dorf, "Is Your Company Ready for One-to-One Marketing?," *Harvard Business Review*, January–February 1999, 151–160.

46. Quoted in Cara B. DiPasquale, "Navigate the Maze," Special Report on 1:1 Marketing, *Advertising Age*, October 29, 2001, S1(2).

47. Jim Middlemiss, "Users Say CRM Is Worth the Effort," www.wallstreetandtech.com, third quarter 2001, 17–18.

48. Mel Duvall, "Charting Customers: Why CRM Spending Remains Strong Even in Tight Times," *Interactive Week* 8 (August 20, 2001): 23.

49. Todd R. Weiss, "PeopleSoft Delivers CRM Apps to a Friendlier IRS," *Computerworld* 35 (August 27, 2001): 12(3).

50. Marc L. Songini, "Dimmed Utilities Plug into CRM," *Computerworld* 35 (August 6, 2001): 1(2).

51. Kate Fitzgerald, "Events a Big 1st Step," *Advertising Age*, October 29, 2001, S4.

52. Rodney Moore, "1-to-1 an Ethnic Star," *Advertising Age*, October 29, 2001, S8.

53. Susan Fournier, Susan Dobscha, and David Glen Mick, "Preventing the Premature Death of Relationship Marketing," *Harvard Business Review*, January–February 1998, 42–44.

54. Duvall, "Charting Customers," 23.

55. Momentum Research Group, *Customer Selection: Finding the "Best" Customers*, www.momentumresearchgroup.com (accessed June 5, 2004).

56. Robert C. Blattberg, Gary Getz, and Mark Pelofsky, "What to Build Your Business? Grow Your Customer Equity," *Harvard Management Update*, August 2001 (Harvard Business School reprint U0108B), 3.

57. Tonia Bruyns, "Banking on Targeted Marketing," November 7, 2001, www.business2.co.za.

CHAPTER 8

1. Information obtained from the Woodstream Corporation.

2. Paul Sweeting, "Netflix Shrugs Off Growing Pains," *Video Business*, March 1, 2004, 1(2); Erik Gruenwedel, "Netflix CEO Cheers Market," *Video Store*, February 29, 2004, 1.

3. Walter S. Mossberg, "Lots of Laptop Choices Mean Shoppers Have to Identify Their Needs," *Wall Street Journal*, April 29, 2004, B1.

4. George Anders, "Vital Statistic: Disputed Cost of Creating a Drug," *Wall Street Journal*, November 9, 1993, B1.

5. "The Replacements," *Newsweek*, June 25, 2001, 50.

6. www.top100musclecarsites.com/Volvo-V40.html.

7. Steve Traiman, "Goin' Digital," *Billboard*, May 1, 2004, 45(2); John Markoff, "Oh, Yeah, He Also Sells Computers," *New York Times*, April 25, 2004, Section 3, 1; Devin Leonard, "Songs in the Key of Steve," *Fortune*, May 12, 2003, 52 ff.

8. John Morris, "The PDA/Phone Advances from Hype to Handy," *Computer Shopper*, January 2004, 55.

9. Bill Hoffmann, "$5,000 Toilet Does All the 'Hand'iwork for You," *New York Post*, January 14, 2004, 19.

10. F. Keenan, "G.I. Joe Heroics at Hasbro," *BusinessWeek*, November 26, 2001, 16.

11. Roman G. Hiebing and Scott W. Copper, "Instructor's Manual," in *The Successful Marketing Plan* (Lincolnwood, Ill.: NTC Business Books, 1992).

12. Richard Rapaport, "Reinventing the Heel: Nike and the Culture of Endless Invention," *Forbes ASAP*, June 24, 2002, 114–19.

13. James Dao, "From a Collector of Turkeys, a Tour of a Supermarket Zoo," *New York Times*, September 24, 1995, F12.

14. Jennifer Ordonez, "Burger King's Decision to Develop French Fry Has Been a Whopper," http://interactive.wsj.com/articles/SB97960472517999878 (accessed January 16, 2001).

15. Robert Berner, "Why P&G's Smile Is So Bright," *BusinessWeek*, August 12, 2002, 58–60.

16. Dan Cray and Maggie Sieger, "Inside the Food Labs," *Time*, October 6, 2003, 56–60.

17. "Test Marketing a New Product: When It's a Good Idea and How to Do It," *Profit Building Strategies for Business Owners*, March 1993, 14.

18. Andrew Pollack, "Nasal Spray Mishaps," November 19, 2003, www.nyt.com.

19. Malcolm Gladwell, *The Tipping Point* (New York: Little, Brown, 2000).

20. Alice Z. Cuneo, "Microsoft Taps 'Puffy' for Xbox," *Advertising Age*, October 20, 2004, 4.

21. Ellen Byron, "Will Kids Buy Organic Food in School Vending Machines?," October 15, 2003, www.wsj.com.

22. "It's Back," *Campaign*, April 8, 2004, 10.

23. Jennifer Alsever, "Soy Milk and Saturation," April 12, 2004, www.denverpost.com and www.silkissoy.com.

24. "Deere Puts Consumers in the Demo Tractor Seat," *Brandweek*, April 12, 2004, 16(1).

25. Amy Gilroy, "More Players Enter Portable Nav Market," *TWICE*, April 5, 2004, 28(2).

26. Everett Rogers, *Diffusion of Innovations* (New York: Free Press, 1983), 247–51.

27. Sources used in this section: "Wi-Fi's Big Brother," *Economist*, March 13, 2004, 65; "Burgers, Fries and Wi-Fi," *Informationweek*, http://www.informationweek.com/showarticle.jhtml?articleID=8700269 (accessed October 25, 2004); William J. Gurley, "Why Wi-Fi Is the Next Big Thing," *Fortune*, March 5, 2001, 184; Joshua Quittner, "Cordless Capers," *Time*, May 1, 2000, 85; Scott Van Camp, "Intel Switches Centrino's Gears," *Brandweek*, April 26, 2004, 16; Benny Evangelista, "SBC Park a Hot Spot for Fans Lugging Laptops," *San Francisco Chronicle*, April 26, 2004, A1; Todd Wallack, "Santa Clara Ready for Wireless," *San Francisco Chronicle*, April 19, 2004, D1; http://wifinetnews.com.

28. Christine Chen and Tim Carvell, "Hall of Shame," *Fortune*, November 22, 1999, 140.

29. Rogers, *Diffusion of Innovations*, chap. 6.

30. Thomas S. Robertson and Yoram Wind, "Organizational Psychographics and Innovativeness," *Journal of Consumer Research* 7 (June 1980): 24–31.

31. David Pringle, Jesse Drucker, and Evan Ramstad, "Cellphone Makers Pay a Heavy Toll for Missing Fads," October 30, 2003, www.wsj.com.

32. Scott R. Gourley, "Army Terrain Vehicles," *Army Magazine*, February 2004, http://www.ausa.org/www/armymag.nsf(soldier)/20042?opendocument (accessed May 26, 2004); Sandra I. Erwin, "Success of 'Lessons Learned' Process Based on Truthfulness," *National Defense Magazine*, July 2002, 24–26; Harold Kennedy, "Military Units Experiment with Ultralight Vehicles," *National Defense Magazine*, June 2003, 42.

CHAPTER 9

1. Geoff Gasior, "Adidas Puts Microprocessor in Running Shoe," *The Tech Report*, May 21, 2004, http://tech-report.com/onearticle.x/6756; Sean Gregory, "Get Your Electric Kicks," *Time*, May 17, 2004, 82; Jessie Scanlon, "The Shoe with the 20-MHz Brain," *Wired*, June 2004, 28.

2. Anthony Vagnoni, "Overused and Misunderstood." *Print*, November–December 2003, 42(2).

3. www.rollsroycemotorcars.co.uk/rolls-royce/index.html (accessed March 24, 2002).

4. Larry Armstrong, "And Now, a Luxury Hyundai," *Business Week*, February 26, 2001, 33.

5. "Nabisco Snak Saks Mini Cookies," *International Product Alert*, March 15, 2004, v21, i6, 0.

6. Daniel Thomas, "Relaunches: New Life or Last Gasps?" *Marketing Week*, January 29, 2004, 20(2).

7. Mark Hyman, "Nike: Great Balls Afire. Will Golf Clubs Be Next?," *Business Week*, February 26, 2001, 109.

8. Material adapted from a presentation by Glenn H. Mazur, QFD Institute, 2002.

9. Geoffrey Colvin, "The Ultimate Manager," *Fortune*, November 22, 1999, 185–87.

10. The Malcolm Baldrige National Quality Improvement Act of 1987—Public Law 100–107, www.quality.nist.gov/Improvement_Act.htm.

11. "ISO 9000 and ISO 14000 in Plain Language," www.iso.ch/iso/en/iso9000-14000/tour/magical.html.

12. John Holusha, "Global Yardsticks Are Set to Measure 'Quality,'" *New York Times*, December 23, 1992, D6.

13. "The Sabre System of the Appliance Service Industry," *Appliance*, March 2004, 69(2).

14. Erik Sherman, "Heavy Lifting," *Chief Executive*, March 2004, 52(4).

15. Mohanbir Sawhney et al., "Creating Growth with Services," *MIT Sloan Management Review*, winter 2004, 34(10).

16. Al Ries and Laura Ries, *The Origin of Brands* (New York: HarperBusiness, 2004).

17. Robert J. Thomas, *New Product Development* (New York: John Wiley & Sons, 1993), 17.

18. "Today's Buzzword: Low-Carb," *Chain Drug Review*, February 2, 2004, 40.

19. Chana R. Schoenberger, "The Money Factory," *Forbes*, October 13, 2003, 72.

20. Ed Brown, "Thwacking Away for 66 Years," *Fortune*, August 4, 1997, 40.

21. Emily Nelson, "Procter & Gamble Tries to Hide Wrinkles in Aging Beauty Fluid," May 16, 2000, www.wsj.com.

22. "P&G Joins Forces with MTV Asia to Attract Young Chinese," *European Cosmetic Markets*, March 2004, 84; "Will P&G's Moisturinse Boost Personal Cleanser Sales?," *Household & Personal Products Industry*, April 2004, 125.

23. "Skippy Peanut Butter Launches New Advertising Campaign," *PR Newswire*, May 13, 2004; www.peanutbutter.com/video/video.html; www.peanutbutter.com.

24. Julian Hunt, "Making Great Ideas Pay Off," *Grocer*, March 27, 2004, 2; Glen L. Urban, *Digital Marketing Strategies* (Englewood Cliffs, N.J.: Prentice Hall, 2004).

25. Gail Tom, Teresa Barnett, William Lew, and Jodean Selmonts, "Cueing the Consumer: The Role of Salient Cues in Consumer Perception," *Journal of Consumer Marketing* (1987): 23–27.

26. "Jell-O Sugar Free Gelatin," *Product Alert*, May 10, 2004, v34, i9, 0.

27. Susan Fournier, "Consumers and Their Brands: Developing Relationship Theory in Consumer Research," *Journal of Consumer Research* 24 (March 1998): 343–73.

28. "The Most Famous Name in Music," *Music Trades*, September 2003, 118(12).

29. Kevin Lane Keller, "The Brand Report Card," *Harvard Business Review*, January–February 2000 (Harvard Business School reprint R00104).

30. David Goetz, "A Hangover Helper," *Advertising Age*, November 5, 2001, 8.

31. www.harrisinteractive.com/solutions/equitrend.asp (accessed June 5, 2004).

32. www.harrisinteractive.com/news/newscats.asp?NewsID=665 (accessed June 5, 2004).

33. Kusum L. Ailawadi, Donald R. Lehmann, and Scott A. Neslin, "Revenue Premium as an Outcome Measure of Brand Equity," *Journal of Marketing* 67 (October 2003): 1–17.

34. Bill Virgin, "Safeway Makes Investment in Store-Brand Branch Banks," *Seattle Post-Intelligencer*, March 16, 2002, www.marketingpower.com/index.php?&Session_ID=f21e39f3e0653e0b590a3414a6850986 (accessed March 26, 2002).

35. "Psst! Wanna See Loblaws' New Products?," *Private Label Buyer*, January 2003, 10(1); Len Lewis, "Turf War!," *Grocery Headquarters*, November 2002, 13(6).

36. Emily Scardino, "Target Assortment Taps into Wider Demographics," *DSN Retailing Today*, April 5, 2004, 19(20).

37. Ron Ruggless, "T.G.I. Friday's Beefs Up Menu with New Atkins Partnership," *Nation's Restaurant News*, December 15, 2003, 1(2).

38. "Putting Zoom into Your Life," *Time International*, March 8, 2004, 54.

39. D. C. Denison, "The Boston Globe Business Intelligence Column," *Boston Globe*, May 26, 2002, http://marketingpower.yellowbrix.com/pages/marketingpower/Story.nsp?story_id=30186718&ID=marketingpower (accessed June 5, 2002).

40. Stephanie Thompson, "Brand Buddies," *Brandweek*, February 23, 1998, 26–30; Jean Halliday, "L.L. Bean, Subaru Pair for Co-Branding," *Advertising Age*, February 21, 2000, 21.

41. Ed Brown, "I Scream You Scream—Saaay, Nice Carton!," *Fortune*, October 26, 1998, 60.

42. "Labels to Include Trans Fat," *San Fernando Valley Business Journal*, January 19, 2004, 15; www.cfsan.fda.gov/label.html.

43. Jack Neff, "P&G Redefines the Brand Manager," *Advertising Age*, October 13, 1997, 1, 18, 20.

44. Pam Weisz, "Lever Plans P&G-Like Moves," *Brandweek*, January 10, 1994, 1, 6.

45. Gary Hoover, Alta Campbell, and Patrick J. Spain, *Hoover's Handbook of American Business* (Austin, Tex,: Reference Press, 1994).

46. Professor Jakki Mohr, University of Montana, personal communication (April 2004).

CHAPTER 10

1. Deborah L. Vence, "Boston Orchestra Tunes Up Net Campaign," *Marketing News*, June 23, 2003, 5–6.

2. Ross Kerber and Benjamin A. Holden, "Power Struggle: Deregulation Sparks Marketing Battle," *Wall Street Journal*, May 13, 1996, B1(2); Rebecca Piirto Heath, "The Marketing of Power," *American Demographics*, September 1997, 59–63.

3. Associated Press, "Astros Airbrush Reference to Enron Field," March 16, 2002, www.marketingpower.com/index.php?&Session_ID=13af9ba667c21450aee9ed04b6b91ba1 (accessed March 29, 2002).

4. Laura Koss Feder, "Branding Culture," *Marketing News*, January 5, 1998, 1(2).

5. Based on a discussion in Gene R. Laczniak, "Product Management and the Performing Arts," in *Marketing the Arts*, ed. Michael P. Mokwa, William M. Dawson, and E. Arthur Prieve (New York: Praeger Publishers, 1980), 124–38.

6. "Service Sector Jumps," June 4, 2003, http://money.cnn.com/2003/06/04/news/economy/ism/ (accessed March 9, 2004); Bureau of Labor Statistics, "Employment Situation Summary: The Employment Situation: May 2004," www.bls.gov/news.release/empsit.t14.htm (accessed June 12, 2004).

7. Robert E. Yuskavage and Erich H. Strassner, "Gross Domestic Product by Industry for 2002," www.ita.doc.gov/td/sif/U.S.%20GDP%20by%20Industry%20(2-002).pdf (accessed June 12, 2004).

8. Marj Charlier, "Bikers Give Ski Resorts Summertime Life," *Wall Street Journal*, July 7, 1994, B1(2).

9. Eleena de Lisser, "Rock 'n' Roll Hits the Multiplex," March 25, 2004, www.wsj.com.

10. John A. Czepiel, Michael R. Solomon, and Carol F. Surprenant, eds., *The Service Encounter: Managing Employee/Customer Interaction in Service Businesses* (Lexington, Mass.: D.C. Heath and Company, 1985).

11. Lou W. Turkey and Douglas L. Fugate, "The Multidimensional Nature of Service Facilities: Viewpoints and Recommendations," *Journal of Services Marketing* 6 (Summer 1992): 37–45.

12. David H. Maister, "The Psychology of Waiting Lines," in Czepiel et al., *The Service Encounter*, 113–24.

13. Michael T. Kaufman, "About New York: The Nail Salon of the 90's: Massages for the Clothed," *New York Times*, December 1, 1993, B3.

14. Jennifer Chao, "Airports Open Their Gates to Profits," *Montgomery Advertiser*, January 26, 1997, 16A.

15. Greg Winter, "Jacuzzi U.? A Battle of Perks to Lure Students," *New York Times*, October 5, 2003, www.nyt.com (accessed January 21, 2004).

16. Jared Sandbert, "NoChores.com," *Newsweek*, August 30, 1999, 64–66.

17. Jim Kerstetter and Jay Greene, "Pay-As-You-Go Is Up and Running," *Business Week*, January 12, 2004, 69–70; Peter Burrows, Ronald Grover, and Jay Greene, "Tuning Up For the Online Music Business," *Business Week*, October 13, 2003, 48.

18. Heather Green, "Downloads: The Next Generation," *Business Week*, February 16, 2004, 54.

19. "True Love? Let a Computer Matchmaker Decide," May 28, 2004, www.cnn.com (accessed June 12, 2004).

20. John McCormick, "The New School," *Newsweek*, April 24, 2000, 60–62.

21. Katherine Yung, "For University of Phoenix, College Is Big Business—and Growing," March 22, 2004, www.kansascity.com/mld/kansascity/news/nation/8250727.htm?1c.

22. Wayne J. Guglielmo, "Take Two Aspirin and Hit the Send Key: Doctor E-Mail," *Newsweek*, June 25, 2001, 61.

23. Cengiz Haksever, Barry Render, Roberta S. Russell, and Robert G. Murdick, *Service Management and Operations* (Englewood Cliffs, N.J.: Prentice Hall, 2000), 25–26.

24. Stephen J. Grove, Raymond P. Fisk, and Joby John, "Surviving in the Age of Rage," *Marketing Management*, March/April 2004, 41–45.

25. Wendy Zellner, "Is JetBlue's Flight Plan Flawed?," *BusinessWeek*, February 16, 2004, 56–58.

26. Cynthia Webster, "Influences upon Consumer Expectations of Services," *Journal of Services Marketing* 5 (winter 1991): 5–17.

27. Mary Jo Bitner, "Evaluating Service Encounters: The Effects of Physical Surroundings and Employee Responses," *Journal of Marketing* 54 (April 1990): 69–82.

28. Michael Selz, "Chain Aims to Hammer Dents Out of Auto-Collision Repair," July 31, 1998, www.wsj.com.

29. Lewis P. Carbone and Stephan H. Haeckel, "Engineering Customer Experiences," *Marketing Management* 3 (winter 1994), reprint, exhibit 4.

30. Valarie A. Zeithaml, "How Consumer Evaluation Processes Differ between Goods and Services," in *Services Marketing* (2nd ed.), ed. Christopher H. Lovelock (Englewood Cliffs, N.J.: Prentice Hall, 1991), 39–47.

31. Kenneth Wylie, "Customer Satisfaction Blooms; Rivalry at Top Grows," *Advertising Age*, October 18, 1993, S1 (2).

32. Valarie A. Zeithaml, Leonard L. Berry, and A. Parasuraman, "Communication and Control Processes in the Delivery of Service Quality," *Journal of Marketing* 52 (April 1988): 35–48.

33. Jody D. Nyquist, Mary F. Bitner, and Bernard H. Booms, "Identifying Communication Difficulties in the Service Encounter: A Critical Incident Approach," in Czepiel et al., *The Service Encounter*, 195–212.

34. Nyquist et al., "Identifying Communication Difficulties in the Service Encounter," 195–212.

35. "Market Metrix Third Quarter 2003 Hospitality Index Results," November 4, 2003, www.hotel-online.com/News (accessed May 4, 2004).

36. Ron Zemke, "The Art of Service Recovery: Fixing Broken Customers—and Keeping Them on Your Side," in *The Service Quality Handbook*, ed. Eberhard E. Scheuing and William F. Christopher (New York: American Management Association, 1993).

37. Haksever et al., *Service Management and Operations*, 342–43.

38. Stephen J. Grove, Raymond P. Fisk, and Joby John, "Surviving in the Age of Rage," *Marketing Management*, March/April 2004, 41–45.

39. Frederik Balfour, Manjeet Kripalani, Kerry Capell, and Laura Cohn, "Over the Sea, Then Under the Knife," *BusinessWeek*, February 16, 2004, 20–22.

40. Joe Sharkey, "Hotels to Flaunt Brands and Add Amenities," December 1, 2003, www.nyt.com.

41. Kathleen V. Schmidt, "E-Giving: Charity Begins at the Home Page," *Marketing News*, October 11, 1999, 13.

42. Michael R. Solomon, "The Wardrobe Consultant: Exploring the Role of a New Retailing Partner," *Journal of Retailing* 63 (summer 1987): 110–28.

43. Irving J. Rein, Philip Kotler, and Martin R. Stoller, *High Visibility* (New York: Dodd, Mead, 1987).

44. Michael R. Solomon, "Celebritization and Commodification in the Interpersonal Marketplace," unpublished manuscript, Rutgers University, 1991.

45. Adapted from a discussion in Rein et al., *High Visibility*.

46. "New York Rolls Out Tourism Ad Campaign," November 8, 2001, http://cnn.com/travel.

47. Gustav Niebuhr, "Where Religion Gets a Big Dose of Shopping-Mall Culture," *New York Times*, April 16, 1995, 1(2).

48. Philip Kotler and Nancy Lee, "Best of Breed,"www.ssireview.com/pdf_files/kotler_lee_spring_2004.pdf (accessed June 12, 2004).

CHAPTER 11

1. Leslie Vreeland, "How to Be a Smart Shopper," *Black Enterprise*, August 1993, 88.

2. Kenneth Labich, "What Will Save the U.S. Airlines," *Fortune*, June 14, 1993, 98–101.

3. "Airlines Face Continued Tough Times, According to Air Transport World Magazine," press release, Penton Media, Inc., www.Penton.com/cgi-bin/news/display_news pl?id=475 (accessed June 13, 2004).

4. Wendy Zellner, "Is JetBlue's Flight Plan Flawed?" *BusinessWeek*, February 16, 2004, 56–58.

5. Melanie Trottman, "First Class at Coach Prices," February 17, 2004, http://online.wsj.com/article_email?article?pring/O,,SB107698413620331110-H0je4Nhl (accessed February 18, 2004).

6. Quoted in Mercedes M. Cardonna, "Affluent Shoppers Like Their Luxe Goods Cheap," *Advertising Age*, December 1, 2003, 6.

7. Steward Washburn, "Pricing Basics: Establishing Strategy and Determining Costs in the Pricing Decision," *Business Marketing*, July 1985, reprinted in Valerie Kijewski, Bob Donath, and David T. Wilson, eds., *The Best Readings from Business Marketing Magazine* (Boston: PWS-Kent Publishing, 1993), 257–69.

8. Robin Cooper and W. Bruce Chew, "Control Tomorrow's Costs Through Today's Design," *Harvard Business Review*, January–February 1996, 88–97.

9. Nikki Swartz, "Rate-Plan Wisdom," *Wireless Review*, June 15, 2001, http://industryclick.com/magazinearticle.asp?releaseid=2921&magazinearticleid=17552&siteid=3&magazineid=9 (accessed February 22, 2002).

10. Swartz, "Rate-Plan Wisdom."

11. Anthony Bianco, Wendy Zellner, Diane Brady, Mike France, Tom Lowry, Nanette Byrnes, Susan Zegel, Michael Arndt, Robert Berner, and Ann Therese Palmer, "Is Wal-Mart Too Powerful?," *Business Week*, October 6, 2003, 100–10.

12. "When Art Meets Science: The Challenge of ROI Marketing," *Strategy + Business*, New York: Booz Allen Hamilton, Inc., December 17, 2003.

13. Jennifer Merritt, "The Belle of the Golf Balls," *Business Week*, July 29, 1996, 6.

14. "Numerical Nirvana," *Business Week*, November 10, 2003, 13.

15. "Numerical Nirvana."

16. Douglas Lavin, "Goodbye to Haggling: Savvy Consumers Are Buying Their Cars Like Refrigerators," *Wall Street Journal*, August 20, 1993, B1, B3.

17. Ryan Chittum, "MCI's Uniform Pricing Is a Hit Even as Parent World Com Falls," July 2, 2002, www.wsj.com.

18. "Pricing, Quotations, and Terms," *Advertising & Marketing Review*, http://www.ad-mkt-review.com/public_html/govdocs/bge/bgec10.html (accessed March 20, 2004).

19. Amy E. Cortese and Marcia Stepanek, "Good-Bye to Fixed Pricing?," *Business Week*, May 4, 1998, 71–84.

20. Heather Green, "Downloads: The Next Generation," *Business Week*, February 16, 2004, 54; Peter Burrows, Ronald Grover, and Jay Greene, "Tuning Up Like Nobody's Business," *Business Week*, October 13, 2003, 48.

21. Walter Baker, Mike Marn, and Craig Zawada, "Price Smarter on the Net," *Harvard Business Review*, February 2001, www.hbsp.harvard.edu/rcpt/filestream.asp?otype=s&key=69541836&prodno=R0102J&order_id=1136431&type=.pdf (accessed February 22, 2002).

22. Jennifer Gilbert, "Drugstores Wage a Pricey Online Battle," *Advertising Age*, August 30, 1999, 26.

23. David Ackerman and Gerald Tellis, "Can Culture Affect Prices? A Cross-Cultural Study of Shopping and Retail Prices," *Journal of Retailing* 77 (2001): 57–82.

24. Robert M. Schindler and Thomas M. Kibarian, "Increased Consumer Sales Response through Use of 99-Ending Prices," *Journal of Retailing* 72 (1996): 187–99.

25. Edmund L. Andrews, "Europe to Seek Uniformity in Car Pricing," February 5, 2002, www.nyt.com.

26. John R. Wilke, "Top Modeling Agencies Face Federal Price-Fixing Inquiry," August 4, 2003, www.wsj.com.

27. Adam Bryant, "Aisle Seat Bully?" *Newsweek*, May 24, 1999, 56.

CHAPTER 12

1. Leiss et al., *Social Communication*; George Stigler, "The Economics of Information," *Journal of Political Economy* (1961): 69.

2. Fara Weiner," A New Campaign for Mercedes-Benz," *New York Times*, March 24, 2004, www.nytimes.com/2004/03/24/business/media/24adco.html (accessed March 24, 2004).

3. Gert Assmus, "An Empirical Investigation into the Perception of Vehicle Source Effects," *Journal of Advertising* 7 (Winter 1978): 4–10; for a more thorough discussion of the pros and cons of different media, see Stephen Baker, *Systematic Approach to Advertising Creativity* (New York: McGraw-Hill, 1979).

4. Quoted in Brian Steinberg, "Bob Dylan Gets Tangled Up in Pink," April 2, 2004, www.wsj.com.

5. T. L. Stanley, "Guerrilla Marketers of the Year," *Brandweek*, March 27, 2000, 28; Jeff Green, "Down with the Dirt Devils," *Brandweek*, March 27, 2000, 41–44; Stephanie Thompson, "Pepsi Favors Sampling Over Ads for Fruit Drink," *Advertising Age*, January 24, 2000, 8.

6. Constance L. Hays, "Guerrilla Marketing Is Going Mainstream," October 7, 1999, www.nytimes.com.

7. Quoted in Michelle Kessler, "IBM Graffiti Ads Gain Notoriety," *USA Today*, April 26, 2001, 3B.

8. Amanda Beeler, "Virus without a Cure," *Advertising Age*, April 17, 2000, 54, 60.

9. Erin Kelly, "This Is One Virus You Want to Spread," *Fortune*, November 27, 2000, 297–300.

10. Kelly, "This Is One Virus You Want to Spread."

11. Kelly, "This Is One Virus You Want to Spread."

12. Karen J. Bannan, "Companies Look to Video Games for Product Placements," March 5, 2002, www.nytimes.com.

13. Tom Eppes, "From Theory to Practice," Price/McNabb corporate presentation, 2002.

14. John Burnett and Sandra Moriarty, *Marketing Communications: An Integrated Approach* (Upper Saddle River, N.J.: Prentice Hall, 1998).

15. "NBC to Hold Online Vote for Top 'Friends' Episodes," January 7, 2004, www.wsj.com.

16. Ellen Edwards, "Plug (the Product) and Play," *Washington Post*, January 26, 2003, www.washingtonpost.com/ac2/wp-dyn/A43992-2003Jan25 (accessed January 29, 2003).

17. Sandra Yin, "Degree of Challenge," *American Demographics*, May 2003, 20–22.

18. Patricia Sellers, "Winning Over the New Consumer," *Fortune*, July 27, 1991, 113.

19. Bill Britt, "Volkswagen Waxes Poetic to Stir Up Emotions and Sales," *Advertising Age*, September 29, 2003, 8.

20. Linda L. Golden and Mark I. Alpert, "Comparative Analysis of the Relative Effectiveness of One- and Two-Sided Communication for Contrasting Products," *Journal of Advertising* 16 (1987): 18–25; Robert B. Settle and Linda L. Golden, "Attribution Theory and Advertiser Credibility," *Journal of Marketing Research* 11 (May 1974): 181–85.

21. Paul Tolme, "Sponsoring the Slopes," *Newsweek*, December 8, 2003, 10.

22. Khanh T. L. Tran, "Lifting the Velvet Rope: Nightclubs Draw Virtual Throngs with Webcasts," August 30, 1999, www.wsj.com.

23. "When Art Meets Science: The Challenge of ROI Marketing," *Strategy + Business* (New York: Booz Allen Hamilton, Inc., December 17, 2003).

24. Quoted in Beth Spethman, "Closer and Closer to the Crowd," *Mediaweek*, October 17, 1994, 24–27.

25. Carl Bialik, "Weather Sites Run Ads Based on Local Conditions," August 22, 2003, www.wsj.com.

26. Carl Bialik, "More Web Sites Plan Ads Based on What Users Read," March 11, 2004, www.wsj.com.

27. Lorraine Woellert, "Will the Right to Pester Hold Up?," *Business Week*, November 10, 2003, 58–59.

28. Saul Hansell, "Marketers Adjust as Spam Clogs the Arteries of E-Commerce," December 1, 2003, www.nytimes.com.

29. Allison Fass, "Spot On," *Forbes*, June 23, 2003, 140.

30. Scott Bowles, "Fans Use Their Muscle to Shape the Movie," *USA Today*, June 20–22, 2003, 1A(2).

31. Curt Barry, "Building a Database," *Catalog Age*, August 1992, 65–68.

32. Martin Everett, "This One's Just for You," *Sales and Marketing Management*, June 1992, 119–26.

33. Ian P. Murphy, "Reader's Digest Links Profits Directly to Research," *Marketing News*, March 31, 1997, 7.

34. Elaine Santoro, "NBO Markets with Style," *Direct Marketing*, February 1992, 28–31, quoted on p. 30.

35. Gary Levin, "Package-Goods Giants Embrace Databases," *Advertising Age*, November 2, 1992, 1.

36. Carol Krol, "New Window of Opportunity in Hershey Direct's Elf Push," *Advertising Age*, May 10, 1999, 30, 34.

37. Everett, "This One's Just for You."

CHAPTER 13

1. Martin Peers, "Buddy Can You Spare Some Time?," January 26, 2004, www.wsj.com.

2. Stuart Elliott, "On ABC, Sears Pays to Be Star of New Series," December 3, 2003, www.nytimes.com; Brian Steinberg and Suzanne Vranica, "Prime-Time TV's New Guest Stars: Products," January 12, 2004, www.wsj.com.

3. Brian Steinberg and Suzanne Vranica, "Five Key Issues Could Alter the Ad Industry," January 4, 2004, www.wsj.com.

4. William Wells, John Burnett, and Sandra Moriarty, *Advertising: Principles and Practice,* 5th ed. (Englewood Cliffs, N.J.: Prentice Hall, 2000).

5. "Domestic Advertising Spending by Category," *Advertising Age,* June 28, 2004.

6. Bob D. Cutler and Darrel D. Muehling, "Another Look at Advocacy Advertising and the Boundaries of Commercial Speech," *Journal of Advertising* 20 (December 1991): 49–52.

7. "Choose or Lose," www.mtv.com/chooseorlose (accessed July 21, 2004).

8. "Top 25 U.S. Agency Brands by Core Advertising Revenue," *Advertising Age,* April 19, 2004.

9. Leslie Kaufman, "Enough Talk," *Newsweek,* August 18, 1997, 48–49.

10. Craig R. Endicott, "100 Leading National Advertisers," *Advertising Age,* June 28, 2004.

11. Douglas C. McGill, "Star Wars in Cola Advertising," *New York Times,* March 22, 1989, D1.

12. Martin Peers, "Buddy Can You Spare Some Time?" January 26, 2004, www.wsj.com.

13. Phil Hall, "Make Listeners Your Customers," *Nation's Business,* June 1994, 53R.

14. Lisa Marie Petersen, "Outside Chance," *Mediaweek,* June 15, 1992, 20–23.

15. Petersen, "Outside Chance."

16. Erin White, "Look Up for New Products in Aisle 5," March 23, 2004, www.wsj.com (accessed March 23, 2004).

17. Jeremy Wagstaff, "Loose Wire," July 31, 2003, www.wsj.com (accessed January 21, 2004).

18. Michael McCarthy, "Companies Are Sold on Interactive Ad Strategy," *USA Today,* March 3, 2000, 1B.

19. Ann M. Mack, "Got E-Mail," *Brandweek,* March 20, 2000, 84–88.

20. Bristol Voss, "Measuring the Effectiveness of Advertising and PR," *Sales and Marketing Management,* October 1992, 123–24.

21. This remark has also been credited to a British businessman named Lord Leverhulme; see Charles Goodrum and Helen Dalrymple, *Advertising in America: The First 200 Years* (New York: Harry N. Abrams, 1990).

22. Stuart Elliott, "New Survey on Ad Effectiveness," April 14, 2004, www.nytimes.com.

23. Carol Moog, president, Creative Focus, quoted in Kevin Goldman, "The Message, Clever as It May Be, Is Lost in a Number of High-Profile Campaigns," *Wall Street Journal,* July 27, 1993, B1(2).

24. Goodrum and Dalrymple, *Advertising in America.*

25. Quoted in Kevin Goldman, "Knock, Knock. Who's There? The Same Old Funny Ad Again," *Wall Street Journal,* November 2, 1993, B10.

26. Embellix Software, *eMarketing Planning: Accountability and eMetrics,* www.templatezone.com/pdfs/ems_whitepaper.pdf (accessed June 6, 2004).

27. Kate Fitzgerald, "Homemade Bikini Contest Hits Bars, Beach for 10th Year," *Advertising Age,* April 13, 1998, 18.

28. Fitzgerald, "Homemade Bikini Contest Hits Bars, Beach for 10th Year," 18.

29. Melissa Marr, "Publicity, PR and 'Passion,'" February 20, 2004, www.wsj.com.

30. Willie Vogt, "Shaping Public Perception," *Agri Marketing,* June 1992, 72–75.

31. Joanna Slater, "Coke, Pepsi Fight Charges of Product-Contamination," August 15, 2003, www.wsj.com (accessed January 21, 2004).

32. Steve Jarvis, "How the Internet Is Changing Fundamentals of Publicity," *Marketing News,* July 17, 2000, 6–7.

33. Dana James, "When Your Company Goes Code Blue," *Marketing News,* November 6, 2000, 1, 15.

34. James, "When Your Company Goes Code Blue."

35. Judy A. Gordon, "Print Campaign Generates Sales Leads for Biotechnology Product," *Public Relations Journal,* July 1991, 21.

36. Lindsay Chappell, "PR Makes Impressions, Sales," *Advertising Age,* March 22, 1993, S–18, S–32.

37. Patricia Winters, "Drugmaker Portrayed as Villains, Worry about Image," *Advertising Age,* February 22, 1993, 1, 42.

38. Ni Chen and Hugh M. Culbertson, "Two Contrasting Approaches of Government Public Relations in Mainland China," *Public Relations Quarterly,* fall 1992, 36–41.

39. Stephen Kindel, "Gentlemen, Flash Your Logos," *Financial World,* April 13, 1993, 46–48.

40. Gerry Khermouch, "Long Live Roll 'n' Rock!" *Brandweek,* July 17, 2000, 20–23.

41. Matt Krantz, "Sponsors Get Gnarly Idea: Surf Sells, Dude," August 6, 2001, www.usatoday.com (accessed August 25, 2001).

42. Direct Marketing Association, "What Is Direct Marketing," www.the-dma.org/aboutdma/whatisthedma.shtml#whatis (accessed April 6, 2002).

43. Direct Marketing Association, *Statistical Fact Book 2003* (New York: Direct Marketing Association, 2004).

44. Frances Huffman, "Special Delivery," *Entrepreneur,* February 1993, 81(3).

45. Cacilie Rohwedder, "U.S. Catalog Firms Target Avid Consumers Overseas," January 6, 1998, www.wsj.com.
46. Paul Hughes, "Profits Due," *Entrepreneur,* February 1994, 74(4).
47. Direct Marketing Association, *1996 Statistical Fact Book* (New York: Direct Marketing Association, 1996).
48. Huffman, "Special Delivery."
49. Rohwedder, "U.S. Catalog Firms Target Avid Consumers Overseas."
50. Stuart Elliott, "A Mail Campaign Helps Saab Find, and Keep, Its Customers," *New York Times,* June 21, 1993, D7.
51. C. B. DiPasquale, "Direct Hit after Anthrax Threat," *Advertising Age,* October 22, 2001, 1, 60.
52. Linda Lipp, "Telephones Ringing Off the Hook," *Journal and Courier,* May 19, 1994; Denise Gillene, "FBI Launches 12-State Telemarketing Sweep," *Los Angeles Times,* March 5, 1993, D1.
53. Federal Trade Commission, "FTC Amends Telemarketing Sales Rule Regarding Access to National Do Not Call Registry," www.ftc.gov/bcp/conline/pubs/buspubs/calling.htm (accessed July 21, 2004).
54. "How We Got Started, Richard Thalheimer," *Fortune,* accessed at http://www.fortune.com/fortune/fsb/specials/innovators/thalheimer.html, August 31, 2004.
55. Alison J. Clarke, "'As Seen on TV': Socialization of the Tele-Visual Consumer" (paper presented at the Fifth Interdisciplinary Conference on Research in Consumption, University of Lund, Sweden, August 1995).
56. Gary Arlen, "DRTV: Beyond the Fringe!," *Marketing Tools,* October 1997, 37–42.
57. Tim Triplett, "Big Names Crowd the Infomercial Airwaves," *Marketing News,* March 28, 1994, 1(2).
58. "How Videotex Offers Special Potential in France," *Business Marketing Digest* 17 (1992): 81–84.
59. Scott McMurray, "Television Shopping Is Stepping Up in Class," *New York Times,* March 6, 1994, F5.
60. William Safire, "M-Commerce," www.nytimes.com/library/magazine/home/20000319mag-onlanguage.html (accessed February 27, 2002).
61. Randall Frost, "M-Commerce: Is the Line Dead," March 8, 2004, www.marketingprofs.com.
62. Sheree R. Curry, "Wireless Trend Taking Hold," *Advertising Age,* June 25, 2001, 2.
63. Claire Atkinson, "'Vibe,' 'Blender' Can Now Dial in Content," *Advertising Age,* April 5, 2004, 29.
64. "MTV Adds Wireless Ads to Mix," August 23, 2001, http://archives.cnn.com/2001/TECH/industry/08/23/mtv.wireless.ads.idg.
65. Sandeep Junnarkar, "When Instant Messages Come Bearing Malice," March 25, 2004, www.nytimes.com.
66. Michael Bociurkiw, "Text Messaging Thrives in the Philippines," *Forbes,* September 10, 2001, 28.
67. Dana James, "RU PYNG ATTN?: Europeans Find Text Messaging the Right Marketing Call," *Marketing News,* January 7, 2002, 4.
68. Junnarkar, "When Instant Messages Come Bearing Malice."
69. Olga Kharif, "Online Extra: Mobile Commerce Is Coming—Modestly, Eventually," May 14, 2001, www.businessweek.com (accessed February 26, 2002).
70. Kharif, "Online Extra."
71. Stephen H. Wildstrom, "Handhelds That You'll Always Want to Hold," *Business Week,* November 10, 2003, 76–77.
72. Mike Dano, "M-Commerce Will Outperform E-Commerce," *RCR Wireless News* 20 (April 2, 2001): 4.

CHAPTER 14

1. James B. Arndorfer, "Models to Troll Taverns for Pricey French Vodka," *Advertising Age,* May 5, 1997, 8.
2. Howard Stumpf and John M. Kawula, "Point of Purchase Advertising," in *Handbook of Sales Promotion,* ed. S. Ulanoff (New York: McGraw-Hill, 1985); Karen A. Berger, *The Rising Importance of Point-of-Purchase Advertising in the Marketing Mix* (Englewood Cliffs, N.J.: Point-of-Purchase Advertising Institute).
3. "When Art Meets Science: The Challenge of ROI Marketing," *Strategy + Business* (New York: Booz Allen Hamilton, Inc., December 17, 2003).

4. Gardiner Harris, "Drug Makers Offer Consumers Coupons for Free Prescriptions," March 13, 2002, www.wsj.com.
5. Bob Tedeschi, "Consumers Downloading Coupons," www.nytimes.com (accessed December 13, 2003).
6. Amanda Beeler, "Restaurateurs Learn to Savor Loyalty Plans," *Advertising Age,* June 5, 2000, 35–36.
7. This section based on material presented in Don E. Schultz, William A. Robinson, and Lisa A. Petrison, *Sales Promotion Essentials,* 2nd ed. (Lincolnwood, Ill.: NTC Business Books, 1993).
8. Kate Fitzgerald, "Guinness Looks to Its Past to Fresh 5th Pub Giveaway," *Advertising Age,* March 30, 1998, 46.
9. Stephanie Thompson, "New Milk Effort Promises Fame with Cap Game," *Advertising Age,* April 24, 2000, 34.
10. Sonia Reyes, "Chiquita Appeals to Health-Minded Consumers with Ford Giveaway," *Brandweek,* March 19, 2001, 15.
11. Kerry J. Smith, "It's for You," *PROMO: The International Magazine for Promotion Marketing,* August 1994, 41(4); Sharon Moshavi, "Please Deposit No Cents," *Forbes,* August 16, 1993, 102.
12. Amanda Beeler, "Package-Goods Marketers Tune in Free-Sampling Sites," *Advertising Age,* June 12, 2000, 58.
13. *The Point-of-Purchase Advertising Industry Fact Book* (Englewood Cliffs, N.J.: Point-of-Purchase Advertising Institute, 1992).
14. "Bausch & Lomb Makes Eyes with Consumers in Spain," *PROMO: The International Magazine for Promotion Marketing,* October 1994, 93.
15. Patricia Sellers, "Winning Over the New Consumer," *Fortune,* July 29, 1991, 113.
16. Bureau of Labor Statistics, "Employment by Major Occupational Group, 2000 and Projected 2010," http://stats.bls.gov/news.release/ecopro.t02.htm (accessed March 8, 2002).
17. Quoted in Jaclyn Fierman, "The Death and Rebirth of the Salesman," *Fortune,* July 25, 1994, 38(7), 88.
18. Michelle Marchetti, "The Cost of Doing Business," *Sales and Marketing Management,* September 1999, 56.
19. Scott Reeves, "'Do Not Call' Revives Door-to-Door Sales," *Marketing News,* December 8, 2003, 13; Maria Puente, "Direct Selling Brings It All Home," *USA Today,* October 28, 2003, 5D.
20. Daniel Tynan, "CRM Software: Who Needs It?," *Sales and Marketing Management,* July 2003, 30; Daniel Tynan, "CRM: Buy or Rent?," *Sales and Marketing Management,* March 2004, 41–45.
21. Dan C. Weilbaker, "The Identification of Selling Abilities Needed for Missionary Type Sales," *Journal of Personal Selling and Sales Management* 10 (Summer 1990): 45–58.
22. Derek A. Newton, *Sales Force Performance and Turnover* (Cambridge, Mass.: Marketing Science Institute, 1973), 3.
23. Mark W. Johnston and Greg W. Marshall, *Relationship Selling and Sales Management* (Boston: McGraw-Hill, 2005).
24. www.Linked/n.com (Accessed October 21.2004).
25. Greg W. Marshall, Daniel J. Goebel, and William C. Moncrief, "Hiring for Success at the Buyer-Seller Interface," *Journal of Business Research* 56 (April 2003): 247–55.
26. Daniel Tynan, "Tech Advantage," *Sales and Marketing Management,* April 2004, 47–51.
27. Jennifer Gilbert, "No Strings Attached," *Sales and Marketing Management,* July 2004, 22–27.
28. Andy Cohen, "Selling from Home Base," *Sales and Marketing Management,* November 2003, 12.
29. Marshall et al., "Hiring for Success at the Buyer-Seller Interface."
30. Julia Chang, "Making the Grade," *Sales and Marketing Management,* March 2004, 24–29.
31. Adapted from Erin Strout, "The Top 10 Most Outrageous T&E Expenses," *Sales and Marketing Management,* February 2001, 60.

CHAPTER 15

1. Monte Burke, "Pop Music," *Forbes,* January 12, 2004, 192(2).
2. David Gates and Ray Sawhill, "A Thriller on the Net," *Newsweek,* March 27, 2000, 46–47.

3. Tracie Rozhon, "High Fashion Prepares to Put a Digital Foot Forward," February 3, 2004, www.nytimes.com.

4. Paula D. Harveston, Basil G. Englis, Michael R. Solomon, and Marla Goldsmith, "Knowledge Management as Competitive Advantage: Lessons from the Textile and Apparel Value Chain," *Journal of Knowledge Management* 2005 Volume 9, No 3, (in press).

5. Kathy Rebello, "Italian Sausage That Sizzles in Cyberspace," *Business Week*, September 23, 1996, 118.

6. Mark Martin, "Legislature Taking Seriously Desire to Buy Drugs in Canada," *San Francisco Chronicle*, May 27, 2004, B3.

7. Rowland T. Moriarty and Ursula Moran, "Managing Hybrid Marketing Systems," *Harvard Business Review*, November–December 1990, 2–11.

8. Brent H. Felgner, "Retailers Grab Power, Control Marketplace," *Marketing News*, (January 16, 1989): 1–2.

9. Jeffrey A. Tannenbaum, "Chain Reactions," *Wall Street Journal*, October 15, 1993, R6.

10. www.delta.com/prog_serv/global_alliance/index.jsp (accessed April 13, 2002); Robert L. Rose and Bridget O'Brian, "United, Lufthansa Form Marketing Tie, Dealing a Setback to American Airlines," *Wall Street Journal*, October 4, 1993, A4.

11. Norihiko Shirouzu, "Toyota's New Scion Brand to Offer 'New Model' of Auto Distribution," March 27, 2002, www.wsj.com.

12. "GM Minority Supplier Spending Reaches $7.2 Billion in 2003," *PR Newswire*, March 22, 2004.

13. Allan J. Magrath, "The Gatekeepers," *Across the Board*, April 1992, 43–46.

14. Gabriella Stern, "If You Don't Feel Like Fetching the Rental Car, It Fetches You," *Wall Street Journal*, June 9, 1995, B1(2).

15. Richard Norman and Rafael Ramirez, "From Value Chain to Value Constellation: Designing Interactive Strategy," *Harvard Business Review*, July–August 1993, www.hbsp.harvard.edu/rcpt/filestream.asp?otype=s&key=69541836& prodno=93408&order_id=1151389&type=.pdf (accessed March 9, 2002).

16. Institute of Logistics and Transport, "Transport, Logistics, and All That," www.iolt.org.uk/whoweare/who_fr.htm (accessed March 7, 2002).

17. www.supplychainmetric.com/perfect.htm (accessed July 10, 2004).

18. Claudia H. Deutsch and Barnaby J. Feder, "A Radio Chip in Every Consumer Product," February 25, 2003, www.nytimes.com.

19. Joseph Weber, "Just Get It to the Stores on Time," *Business Week*, March 6, 1995, 66–67.

20. Scott Woolley, "Replacing Inventory with Information," *Forbes*, March 24, 1997, 54–58.

CHAPTER 16

1. Janet Ginsburg, "Xtreme Retailing," *Business Week*, December 20, 1999, 120.

2. Michael Levy and Barton A. Weitz, *Retailing Management*, 3rd ed. (Boston: Irwin/McGraw-Hill, 1998).

3. Stanley C. Hollander, "The Wheel of Retailing," *Journal of Retailing*, July 1960, 41.

4. "About Us," www.pier1.com/company/history.asp (accessed April 17, 2004).

5. William R. Davidson, Albert D. Bates, and Stephen J. Bass, "The Retail Life Cycle," *Harvard Business Review*, November–December 1976, 89.

6. "About Circuit City," www.circuitcity.com/cs_contentdisplay.jsp?c=1&b=g& u=c&incat= 84526 (accessed April 17, 2004).

7. Cathy Horyn," A Store Made for Right Now: You Shop until It's Dropped," February 17, 2004, www.nytimes.com.

8. Quoted in Stephanie Kang, "Pacific Sunwear's d.e.m.o. Chain Sells Hip-Hop Lite to Teenagers," February 20, 2004, www.wsj.com.

9. Levy and Weitz, *Retailing Management*.

10. Ian Austen, "In Germany, Customers Scan as They Shop," May 12, 2003, www.nytimes.com; Annick Moes, "Technology Rules 'Future Store' by Tracking Shoppers and Sales," June 19, 2003, www.wsj.com.

11. Alfred F. Lynch, "Training for a New Ball Game: Retailing in the 21st Century," *The Futurist*, July/August 1992, 36–40.

12. K. Belson, "As Starbucks Grows, Japan, Too, Is Awash," October 21, 2001, http://query.nytimes.com/search/abstract?res=F50F14FF3B5A0C728EDDA 90994D9404482 (accessed April 10, 2002).

13. Ann Zimmerman and Martin Fackler, "Wal-Mart's Foray into Japan Spurs a Retail Upheaval," September 19, 2003, www.wsj.com.

14. Grace Fan, "Pedicarts Link Shanghai's Streets to the Internet," March 29, 2000, www.nytimes.com/library/tech/00/03/biztech/technology/29fan.html (accessed January 2, 2001).

15. "Levi Wins Designer Shopping Battle," November 20, 2001, www.cnn.com/ 2001/ WORLD/europe/11/20/designer.goods/index.html.

16. Jodi Wilgoren, "In the Urban 7-Eleven, the Slurpee Looks Sleeker," July 31, 2003, www.nytimes.com.

17. Amy Merrick, "Kohl's Woos Tony Upscale Brands, Jolting Battered Department Stores," March 12, 2002, www.wsj.com.

18. Julie Liesse, "Welcome to the Club," *Advertising Age*, February 1, 1993, 3(2).

19. Martin Forstenzer, "In Search of Fine Art amid the Paper Towels," February 22, 2004, www.nytimes.com.

20. Amy Merrick, Jeffrey A. Trachtenberg, and Ann Zimmerman, "Department Stores Fight to Save a Model That May Be Outdated," March 12, 2002, www.wsj.com.

21. Quoted in Stratford Sherman, "Will the Information Superhighway Be the Death of Retailing?" *Fortune*, April 18, 1994, 99(5), 110.

22. Julie Krippel, "Tupperware Corporation," April 17, 2004, www.hoovers.com/ free/co/factsheet.xhtml?COID=48028.

23. "History," www.amway.com/pourstory/0-history.asp (accessed April 17, 2004).

24. Catherine Colbert, "Amway Corporation," April 17, 2004, http://www.hoovers.com/ amway/--ID_103441--/free-co-factsheet.xhtml.

25. H. J. Shrager, "Close Social Networks of Hasidic Women, Other Tight Groups, Boost Shaklee Sales," November 19, 2001, www.wsj.com.

26. Mario Brossi and Joseph Marino, *Multilevel Marketing: A Legal Primer* (Washington, D.C.: Direct Selling Association, 1990).

27. James E. McQuivey, Kate Delhagen, and Esther H. Yuen, "RIP: The Online Consumers 1998–2003," July 25, 2003, www.forrester.com/ER/Research?Brief/ 0,1317.17225,00.html.

28. Seema Williams, David M. Cooperstein, David E. Weisman, and Thalika Oum, "Post-Web Retail," *The Forrester Report*, Forrester Research, Inc., September 1999.

29. Stuart Elliott, "Betty Crocker: Can She Cook in Cyberspace?," December 13, 2000, www.nytimes.com/library/tech/00/12/biztech/technology/13elli.html (accessed January 14, 2001).

30. Heather Green, "Downloads: The Next Generation," *Business Week*, February 16, 2004, 54.

31. Juhnyoung Lee, Robert Hoch, Mark Podlaseck, Edith Schonberg, and Stephen Gomory, "Analysis and Visualization of Metrics for Online Merchandising," www.research.ibm.com/iac/papers/Incs.pdf (accessed May 2004).

32. B. Tedeschi, "Selling Made-to-Order Clothing Online," November 5, 2001, www.nytimes.com.

33. Lisa Napoli, February 26, 1998, www.nytimes.com.

34. M. Slatalla, "Voyeur-Cams Come to Home Furnishings," www.nytimes.com/ library/tech/00/07/circuits/articles/06shop.html (accessed July 6, 2000).

35. Rebecca Quick, "Hope Springs Anew for Web Retailers: Study Shows Many Are Making Money," April 18, 2000, www.wsj.com; Randy Myers, "E-Tailers & Space Invaders," *e-CFO*, April 2000, 47(7).

36. Quoted in Bob Tedeschi, "Online Travel Agents Expand Offline," March 18, 2002, www.nytimes.com.

37. Michael Krantz, "Click till You Drop," *Time* (20 July 1998):34-39.

38. 2003 Annual Report, Amazon.com, http://phx.corporate-ir.net/phoenix. zhtml?c=97664&p=irol-annualreports (accessed July 16, 2004).

39. Kathryn Waskom, "Destination Retail Is on Its Way," *Marketing News*, March 13, 2000, 15.

40. Vanessa O'Connell, "Fictional Hershey Factory Will Send Kisses to Broadway," August 5, 2002, www.wsj.com.

41. Jennifer Steinhauer, "Interactive Stores Make Shopping an Experience" February 28, 1998, www.nytimes.com

42. "A Wide World of Sports Shoes: Fixtures Enhance Appeal of World Foot Locker," *Chain Store Age Executive*, January 1993, 176–81.

43. Quoted in Wendy Marx, "Shopping 2000," *Brandweek*, January 9, 1995, 20(2).

44. L. W. Turley and Ronald E. Milliman, "Atmospheric Effects on Shopping Behavior: A Review of the Experimental Evidence," *Journal of Business Research* 49 (2000): 193–211.

45. Tracie Rozhon, "High Fashion, from Front Door to the Top Floor," July 31, 2003, www.nytimes.com.

46. "The Sound of Retail," *Chain Store Age*. January 1996, 3C–6C.

47. Louise Dramer, "Taco Bell Tests Improved Taste—in Interior Design," *Advertising Age*, July 19, 1999, 1, 26.

48. Emily Nelson, "Chili's Hopes Customers Warm to Pepper-Shaped Restaurant," April 8, 1998, www.wsj.com.

49. Yumiko Ono, "Food, Beverage Makers Set Up Traps to Increase Number of Impulse Buys," September 8, 1998, www.wsj.com.

50. Julie Flaherty, "Ambient Music Has Moved to Record Store Shelves," July 4, 2001, www.nytimes.com.

51. Deborah Blumenthal, "Scenic Design for In-Store Try-Ons," *New York Times*, April 1988.

52. "Service: Retail's No. 1 Problem," *Chain Store Age*, January 19, 1987.

53. Dean Starkman, "Lifestyle Centers Are New Mall Concept: Part Main Street and Part Fifth Avenue," July 25, 2001, www.wsj.com.

54. Levy and Weitz, *Retailing Management*.

55. Rekha Balu, "The Buckle Finds Rural Kids Will Pay Dearly for Hip Clothes," January 14, 1998, www.wsj.com.

56. Quoted in Shirley Leung, "A Glutted Market Is Leaving Food Chains Hungry for Sites," September 1, 2003, www.wsj.com.

GLOSSARY

80/20 rule A marketing rule of thumb that 20 percent of purchasers account for 80 percent of a product's sales.

A

advergaming Brand placements in video games.

advertising appeal The central idea or theme of an advertising message.

advertising campaign A coordinated, comprehensive plan that carries out promotion objectives and results in a series of advertisements placed in media over a period of time.

advertising exposure The degree to which the target market will see an advertising message placed in a specific vehicle.

advertising Nonpersonal communication paid for by an identified sponsor using mass media to persuade or inform.

advocacy advertising A type of public service advertising provided by an organization that is seeking to influence public opinion on an issue because it has some stake in the outcome.

AIDA model The communications goals of attention, interest, desire, and action.

aided recall A research technique that uses clues to prompt answers from people about advertisements they might have seen.

aperture The best place and time to reach a person in the target market group.

approach The first step of the actual sales presentation in which the salesperson tries to learn more about the customer's needs, create a good impression, and build rapport.

atmospherics The use of color, lighting, scents, furnishings, and other design elements to create a desired store image.

attitude A learned predisposition to respond favorably or unfavorably to stimuli on the basis of relatively enduring evaluations of people, objects, and issues.

attitudinal measures A research technique that probes a consumer's beliefs or feelings about a product before and after being exposed to messages about it.

augmented services The core service plus additional services provided to enhance value.

average fixed cost The fixed cost per unit produced.

B

baby boomers The segment of people born between 1946 and 1964.

back-translation The process of translating material to a foreign language and then back to the original language.

bait-and-switch An illegal marketing practice in which an advertised price special is used as bait to get customers into the store with the intention of switching them to a higher-priced item.

banners Internet advertising in the form of rectangular graphics at the top or bottom of Web pages.

basing-point pricing A pricing tactic where customers pay shipping charges from set basing point locations whether the goods are actually shipped from these points or not.

BCG growth–market share matrix A portfolio analysis model developed by the Boston Consulting Group that assesses the potential of successful products to generate cash that a firm can then use to invest in new products.

behavioral learning theories Theories of learning that focus on how consumer behavior is changed by external events or stimuli.

behavioral segmentation A technique that divides consumers into segments on the basis of how they act toward, feel about, or use a good or service.

benefit The outcome sought by a customer that motivates buying behavior—that satisfies a need or want.

born-global firms Companies that try to sell their products in multiple countries from the moment they're created.

bottom-up budgeting techniques Allocation of the promotion budget based on identifying promotion goals and allocating enough money to accomplish them.

brand A name, a term, a symbol, or any other unique element of a product that identifies one firm's product(s) and sets them apart from the competition.

brand competition When firms offering similar goods or services compete on the basis of their brand's reputation or perceived benefits.

brand equity The value of a brand to an organization.

brand extensions A new product sold with the same brand name as a strong existing brand.

brand loyalty A pattern of repeat product purchases, accompanied by an underlying positive attitude toward the brand, that is based on the belief that the brand makes products superior to its competition.

brand manager An individual who is responsible for developing and implementing the marketing plan for a single brand.

brand personality A distinctive image that captures a good's or service's character and benefits.

break-even analysis A method for determining the number of units that a firm must produce and sell at a given price to cover all its costs.

break-even point The point at which the total revenue and total costs are equal and beyond which the company makes a profit; below that point, the firm will suffer a loss.

breaking bulk   Dividing larger quantities of goods into smaller lots in order to meet the needs of buyers.

business analysis   The step in the product development process in which marketers assess a product's commercial viability.

business cycle   The overall patterns of change in the economy—including periods of prosperity, recession, depression, and recovery—that affect consumer and business purchasing power.

business ethics   Rules of conduct for an organization.

business plan   A plan that includes the decisions that guide the entire organization.

business planning   An ongoing process of making decisions that guide the firm both in the short term and for the long haul.

business portfolio   The group of different products or brands owned by an organization and characterized by different income-generating and growth capabilities.

business-to-business (B2B) e-commerce   Internet exchanges between two or more businesses or organizations.

business-to-business marketing   The marketing of those goods and services that business and organizational customers need to produce other goods and services, for resale or to support their operations.

business-to-business markets   The group of customers that include manufacturers, wholesalers, retailers, and other organizations.

business-to-consumer (B2C) e-commerce   Online exchanges between companies and individual consumers.

buttons   Small banner-type advertisements that can be placed anywhere on a Web page.

buy class   One of three classifications of business buying situations that characterizes the degree of time and effort required to make a decision.

buying center   The group of people in an organization who participate in a purchasing decision.

buzz   Word-of-mouth advertising that is viewed as authentic and generated by customers.

C

cannibalization   The loss of sales of an existing brand when a new item in a product line or product family is introduced.

capacity management   The process by which organizations adjust their offerings in an attempt to match demand.

captive pricing   A pricing tactic for two items that must be used together; one item is priced very low, and the firm makes its profit on another, high-margin item essential to the operation of the first item.

case allowance   A discount to the retailer or wholesaler based on the volume of product ordered.

case study   A comprehensive examination of a particular firm or organization.

catalog   A collection of products offered for sale in book form, usually consisting of product descriptions accompanied by photos of the items.

causal research   A technique that attempts to understand cause-and-effect relationships.

cause marketing   Marketing activities in which firms seek to have their corporate identity linked to a good cause through advertising, public service, and publicity.

channel intermediaries   Firms or individuals such as wholesalers, agents, brokers, or retailers who help move a product from the producer to the consumer or business user.

channel leader   A firm at one level of distribution that takes a leadership role, establishing operating norms and processes based on its power relative to other channel members.

channel levels   The number of distinct categories of intermediaries that populate a channel of distribution.

channel of distribution   The series of firms or individuals that facilitates the movement of a product from the producer to the final customer.

classical conditioning   The learning that occurs when a stimulus eliciting a response is paired with another stimulus that initially does not elicit a response on its own but will cause a similar response over time because of its association with the first stimulus.

close   The stage of the selling process in which the salesperson actually asks the customer to buy the product.

cobranding   An agreement between two brands to work together in marketing a new product.

codes of ethics   Written standards of behavior to which everyone in the organization must subscribe.

cognitive learning theory   Theory of learning that stresses the importance of internal mental processes and that views people as problem solvers who actively use information from the world around them to master their environment.

collectivist cultures   Cultures in which people subordinate their personal goals to those of a stable community.

commercialization   The final step in the product development process in which a new product is launched into the market.

communications model   The process whereby meaning is transferred from a source to a receiver.

competitive advantage   The ability of a firm to outperform the competition, thereby providing customers with a benefit the competition can't.

competitive intelligence   The process of gathering and analyzing publicly available information about rivals.

competitive-parity method   A promotion budgeting method in which an organization matches whatever competitors are spending.

component parts   Manufactured goods or subassemblies of finished items that organizations need to complete their own products.

concentrated targeting strategy   Focusing a firm's efforts on offering one or more products to a single segment.

conformity   A change in beliefs or actions as a reaction to real or imagined group pressure.

consumer behavior   The process involved when individuals or groups select, purchase, use, and dispose of goods, services, ideas, or experiences to satisfy their needs and desires.

Consumer Bill of Rights   The rights of consumers to be protected by the federal government.

consumer goods The goods purchased by individual consumers for personal or family use.

consumer interviews One-on-one discussions between a consumer and a researcher.

consumer orientation A management philosophy that focuses on ways to satisfy customers' needs and wants.

consumer satisfaction/dissatisfaction The overall feelings or attitude a person has about a product after purchasing it.

consumer The ultimate user of a good or service.

consumerism A social movement that attempts to protect consumers from harmful business practices.

consumer-to-consumer (C2C) e-commerce Communications and purchases that occur among individuals without directly involving the manufacturer or retailer.

continuous innovation A modification of an existing product that sets one brand apart from its competitors.

contribution per unit The difference between the price the firm charges for a product and the variable costs.

control A process that entails measuring actual performance, comparing this performance to the established marketing objectives, and then making adjustments to the strategies or objectives on the basis of this analysis.

convenience product A consumer good or service that is usually low priced, widely available, and purchased frequently with a minimum of comparison and effort.

convenience stores Neighborhood retailers that carry a limited number of frequently purchased items and cater to consumers willing to pay a premium for the ease of buying close to home.

conventional marketing system A multiple-level distribution channel in which channel members work independently of one another.

conventions Norms regarding the conduct of everyday life.

convergence The coming together of two or more technologies to create a new system with greater benefits than its parts.

cookies Text files inserted by a Web site sponsor into a Web surfer's hard drive that allow the site to track the surfer's moves.

copy testing A marketing research method that seeks to measure the effectiveness of ads by determining whether consumers are receiving, comprehending, and responding to the ad according to plan.

core service The basic benefit of having a service performed.

corporate culture The set of values, norms, and beliefs that influence the behavior of everyone in the organization.

corrective advertising Advertising that clarifies or qualifies previous deceptive advertising claims.

cost per thousand (CPM) A measure used to compare the relative cost-effectiveness of different media vehicles that have different exposure rates; the cost to deliver a message to 1,000 people or homes.

cost-plus pricing A method of setting prices in which the seller totals all the costs for the product and then adds an amount to arrive at selling price.

countertrade A type of trade in which goods are paid for with other items instead of with cash.

creating assortments Providing a variety of products in one location to meet the needs of buyers.

creative selling process The process of seeking out potential customers, analyzing needs, determining how product attributes might provide benefits for the customer, and then communicating that information.

creative strategy The process that turns a concept into an advertisement.

credence qualities Product characteristics that are difficult to evaluate even after they have been experienced.

critical incident technique A method for measuring service quality in which marketers use customer complaints to identify critical incidents; specific face-to-face contacts between consumer and service providers that cause problems and lead to dissatisfaction.

cross-promotion (cooperative promotion) Two or more products or services combine forces to create interest using a single promotional tool.

cross-elasticity of demand When changes in the price of one product affect the demand for another item.

cross-sectional design A type of descriptive technique that involves the systematic collection of quantitative information.

cultural diversity A management practice that actively seeks to include people of different sexes, races, ethnic groups, and religions in an organization's employees, customers, suppliers, and distribution channel partners.

cultural values A society's deeply held beliefs about right and wrong ways to live.

culture The values, beliefs, customs, and tastes valued by a group of people.

cumulative quantity discounts Discounts based on the total quantity purchased within a specified time period.

custom A norm handed down from the past that controls basic behaviors.

custom marketing strategy An approach that tailors specific products and the messages about them to individual customers.

custom research Research conducted for a single firm to provide specific information its managers need.

customer equity The financial value of a customer relationship throughout the lifetime of the relationship.

customer relationship management (CRM) A philosophy that sees marketing as a process of building long-term relationships with customers to keep them satisfied and to keep them coming back. A concept that involves systematically tracking consumers' preferences and behaviors over time in order to tailor the value proposition as closely as possible to each individual's unique wants and needs.

D

data mining Sophisticated analysis techniques to take advantage of the massive amount of transaction information now available.

database marketing The creation of an ongoing relationship with a set of customers who have an identifiable interest in a product or service and whose responses to promotional efforts become part of future communications attempts.

decline stage The final stage in the product life cycle in which sales decrease as customer needs change.

decoding The process by which a receiver assigns meaning to the message.

demand Customers' desire for products coupled with the resources to obtain them.

demand-based pricing A price-setting method based on estimates of demand at different prices.

demographics Statistics that measure observable aspects of a population, including size, age, gender, ethnic group, income, education, occupation, and family structure.

department stores Retailers that sell a broad range of items and offer a good selection within each product line.

derived demand Demand for business or organizational products derived from demand for consumer goods or services.

descriptive research A tool that probes more systematically into the problem and bases its conclusions on large numbers of observations.

developed country A country that boasts sophisticated marketing systems, strong private enterprise, and bountiful market potential for many goods and services.

developing countries Countries in which the economy is shifting its emphasis from agriculture to industry.

differential benefit Properties of products that set them apart from competitors' products by providing unique customer benefits.

differentiated targeting strategy Developing one or more products for each of several distinct customer groups and making sure these offerings are kept separate in the marketplace.

diffusion The process by which the use of a product spreads throughout a population.

direct mail A brochure or pamphlet offering a specific product or service at one point in time.

direct marketing Any direct communication to a consumer or business recipient that is designed to generate a response in the form of an order, a request for further information, and/or a visit to a store or other place of business for purchase of a product.

direct selling An interactive sales process in which a salesperson presents a product to one individual or a small group, takes orders, and delivers the merchandise.

direct-response TV (DRTV) Advertising on TV that seeks a direct response, including short commercials of less than two minutes, 30-minute or longer infomercials, and home shopping networks.

discontinuous innovation A totally new product that creates major changes in the way we live.

discretionary income The portion of income people have left over after paying for necessities such as housing, utilities, food, and clothing.

disintermediation (of the channel of distribution) The elimination of some layers of the channel of distribution in order to cut costs and improve the efficiency of the channel.

disintermediation Eliminating the interaction between customers and salespeople so as to minimize negative service encounters.

distinctive competency A superior capability of a firm in comparison to its direct competitors.

diversification strategies Growth strategies that emphasize both new products and new markets.

dumping A company tries to get a toehold in a foreign market by pricing its products lower than they are offered at home.

durable goods Consumer products that provide benefits over a long period of time, such as cars, furniture, and appliances.

dynamic pricing A pricing strategy in which the price can easily be adjusted to meet changes in the marketplace.

dynamically continuous innovation A change in an existing product that requires a moderate amount of learning or behavior change.

E

early adopters Those who adopt an innovation early in the diffusion process but after the innovators.

early majority Those whose adoption of a new product signals a general acceptance of the innovation.

e-commerce The buying or selling of goods and services electronically, usually over the Internet.

economic communities Groups of countries that band together to promote trade among themselves and to make it easier for member nations to compete elsewhere.

economic infrastructure The quality of a country's distribution, financial, and communications systems.

economic sanctions Trade prohibitions imposed by one country against another.

elastic demand Demand in which changes in price have large effects on the amount demanded.

e-marketers Marketers who use e-commerce in their strategies.

embargo A quota completely prohibiting specified goods from entering or leaving a country.

encoding The process of translating an idea into a form of communication that will convey meaning.

enterprise resource planning (ERP) systems A software solution that integrates information from across the entire company. Data need to be entered into the system only once, at one point, and then the data are automatically shared throughout the organization.

environmental stewardship A position taken by an organization to protect or enhance the natural environment as it conducts its business activities.

equipment Expensive goods that an organization uses in its daily operations that last for a long time.

ethnocentrism The tendency to prefer products or people of one's own culture.

ethnography A detailed report based on observations of people in their own homes or communities.

European Union (EU) Economic community that now includes most of Europe.

evaluative criteria The dimensions used by consumers to compare competing product alternatives.

everyday low pricing (EDLP) See value pricing.

exchange The process by which some transfer of value occurs between a buyer and a seller.

exclusive distribution Selling a product only through a single outlet in a particular region.

experience qualities   Product characteristics that customers can determine during or after consumption.

experiential shoppers   Consumers who engage in online shopping because of the experiential benefits they receive.

experiments   Techniques that test prespecified relationships among variables in a controlled environment.

exploratory research   A technique that marketers use to generate insights for future, more rigorous studies.

export merchants   Intermediaries used by a firm to represent them in other countries.

expropriation   A domestic government's seizure of a foreign company's assets without any compensation.

external environment   The uncontrollable elements outside an organization that may affect its performance either positively or negatively.

extranet   A private, corporate computer network that links company departments, employees, and databases to suppliers, customers, and others outside the organization.

F

F.O.B. delivered pricing   A pricing tactic in which the cost of loading and transporting the product to the customer is included in the selling price and is paid by the manufacturer.

F.O.B. origin pricing   A pricing tactic in which the cost of transporting the product from the factory to the customer's location is the responsibility of the customer.

facilitating functions   Functions of channel intermediaries that make the purchase process easier for customers and manufacturers.

factory outlet store   A discount retailer, owned by a manufacturer, that sells off defective merchandise and excess inventory.

family brand   A brand that a group of individual products or individual brands share.

family life cycle   A means of characterizing consumers within a family structure on the basis of different stages through which people pass as they grow older.

feedback   Receivers' reactions to the message.

fixed costs   Costs of production that do not change with the number of units produced.

focus group   A product-oriented discussion among a small group of consumers led by a trained moderator.

follow-up   Activities after the sale that provide important services to customers.

franchising   A form of licensing involving the right to adapt an entire system of doing business.

freight absorption pricing   A pricing tactic in which the seller absorbs the total cost of transportation.

frequency   The number of times a person in the target group will be exposed to the message.

frequency programs   Consumer sales promotion programs that offer a discount or free product for multiple purchases over time; also referred to as loyalty or continuity programs.

full-service agency   An agency that provides most or all of the services needed to mount a campaign, including research, creation of ad copy and art, media selection, and production of the final messages.

functional planning   A decision process that concentrates on developing detailed plans for strategies and tactics for the short term that support an organization's long-term strategic plan.

G

gap analysis   A marketing research methodology that measures the difference between a customer's expectation of a service quality and what actually occurred.

General Agreement on Tariffs and Trade (GATT)   International treaty to reduce import tax levels and trade restrictions.

general merchandise discount stores   Retailers that offer a broad assortment of items at low prices with minimal service.

Generation X   The group of consumers born between 1965 and 1976.

Generation Y   The group of consumers born between 1977 and 1994.

geodemography   A segmentation technique that combines geography with demographics.

good   A tangible product that we can see, touch, smell, hear, or taste.

government markets   The federal, state, county, and local governments that buy goods and services to carry out public objectives and to support their operations.

gray market goods   Items manufactured outside a country and then imported without the consent of the trademark holder.

green marketing   A marketing strategy that supports environmental stewardship by creating an environmentally founded differential benefit in the minds of consumers.

gross domestic product (GDP)   The total dollar value of goods and services produced by a nation within its borders in a year.

gross national product (GNP)   The value of all goods and services produced by a country's citizens or organizations, whether located within the country's borders or not.

gross rating points (GRPs)   A measure used for comparing the effectiveness of different media vehicles: average reach x frequency.

growth stage   The second stage in the product life cycle during which the product is accepted and sales rapidly increase.

guerilla marketing   Marketing activity in which a firm "ambushes" consumers with promotional content in places they are not expecting to encounter this kind of activity.

H

heuristics   A mental rule of thumb that leads to a speedy decision by simplifying the process.

hierarchy of effects   A series of steps prospective customers move through, from initial awareness of a product to brand loyalty.

hierarchy of needs   An approach that categorizes motives according to five levels of importance, the more basic needs being on the bottom of the hierarchy and the higher needs at the top.

horizontal marketing system   An arrangement within a channel of distribution in which two or more firms at the same channel level work together for a common purpose.

hybrid marketing system   A marketing system that uses a number of different channels and communication methods to serve a target market.

hype Considered corporate propaganda planted by a company with an ax to grind and therefore dismissed by customers.

hypermarkets Retailers with the characteristics of both warehouse stores and supermarkets; hypermarkets are several times larger than other stores and offer virtually everything from grocery items to electronics.

I

idea generation The first step of product development in which marketers brainstorm for products that provide customer benefits and are compatible with the company mission.

idea marketing Marketing activities that seek to gain market share for a concept, philosophy, belief, or issue by using elements of the marketing mix to create or change a target market's attitude or behavior.

import quotas Limitations set by a government on the amount of a product allowed to enter or leave a country.

impressions The number of people who will be exposed to a message placed in one or more media vehicles.

impulse purchase A purchase made without any planning or search effort.

independent intermediaries Channel intermediaries that are not controlled by any manufacturer but instead do business with many different manufacturers and many different customers.

individualist cultures Cultures in which people tend to attach more importance to personal goals than to those of the larger community.

industrial goods Goods bought by individuals or organizations for further processing or for use in doing business.

inelastic demand Demand in which changes in price have little or no effect on the amount demanded.

infomercials Half-hour or hour commercials that resemble a talk show but in actuality are intended to sell something.

information search The process whereby a consumer searches for appropriate information to make a reasonable decision.

ingredient branding A form of cobranding in which branded materials are used as ingredients or component parts of other branded products.

innovation A product that consumers perceive to be new and different from existing products.

innovators The first segment (roughly 2.5 percent) of a population to adopt a new product.

inseparability The characteristic of a service that means that it is impossible to separate the production of a service from the consumption of that service.

institutional advertising An advertising message that promotes the activities, personality, or point of view of an organization or company.

intangibility The characteristic of a service that means customers can't see, touch, or smell the service.

intangibles Experienced-based products that cannot be touched.

integrated marketing communications (IMC) A strategic business process that marketers use to plan, develop, execute, and evaluate coordinated, measurable, persuasive brand communication programs over time to targeted audiences.

intensive distribution Selling a product through all suitable wholesalers or retailers that are willing to stock and sell the product.

interactive marketing A promotion practice in which customized marketing communications elicit a measurable response from individual receivers.

internal environment The controllable elements inside an organization, including its people, its facilities, and how it does things that influence the operations of the organization.

internal reference price A set price or a price range in consumers' minds that they refer to in evaluating a product's price.

intranet An internal corporate communication network that uses Internet technology to link company departments, employees, and databases.

introduction stage The first stage of the product life cycle in which slow growth follows the introduction of a new product in the marketplace.

inventory control Activities to ensure that goods are always available to meet customers' demands.

involvement The relative importance of perceived consequences of the purchase to a consumer.

ISO 14000 Standards of the International Organization for Standardization concerned with "environmental management" aimed at minimizing harmful effects on the environment.

ISO 9000 Criteria developed by the International Organization for Standardization to regulate product quality in Europe.

J

joint demand Demand for two or more goods that are used together to create a product.

joint venture A strategic alliance in which a new entity owned by two or more firms is created to allow the partners to pool their resources for common goals.

just in time (JIT) Inventory management and purchasing processes that manufacturers and resellers use to reduce inventory to very low levels and ensure that deliveries from suppliers arrive only when needed.

K

Kansei engineering A Japanese philosophy that translates customers' feelings into design elements.

knockoff A new product that copies with slight modification the design of an original product.

knowledge management A comprehensive approach to collecting, organizing, storing, and retrieving a firm's information assets.

L

laggards The last consumers to adopt an innovation.

late majority The adopters who are willing to try new products when there is little or no risk associated with the purchase, when the purchase becomes an economic necessity, or when there is social pressure to purchase.

learning A relatively permanent change in behavior caused by acquired information or experience.

less developed country (LDC)   A country at the lowest stage of economic development.

licensing (in foreign markets)   An agreement in which one firm gives another firm the right to produce and market its product in a specific country or region in return for royalties.

licensing   An agreement in which one firm sells another firm the right to use a brand name for a specific purpose and for a specific period of time.

lifestyle   The pattern of living that determines how people choose to spend their time, money, and energy and that reflects their values, tastes, and preferences.

lifetime value of a customer   How much profit companies expect to make from a particular customer, including each and every purchase she will make from them now and in the future. To calculate lifetime value, companies estimate the amount the person will spend and then subtract what it will cost the company to maintain this relationship.

limited-service agency   An agency that provides one or more specialized services, such as media buying or creative development.

list price   The price the end customer is expected to pay as determined by the manufacturer; also referred to as the suggested retail price.

local content rules   A form of protectionism stipulating that a certain proportion of a product must consist of components supplied by industries in the host country.

logistics   The process of designing, managing, and improving the movement of products through the supply chain. Logistics includes purchasing, manufacturing, storage, and transport.

longitudinal design   A technique that tracks the responses of the same sample of respondents over time.

loss leader pricing   The pricing policy of setting prices very low or even below cost to attract customers into a store.

M

maintenance, repair, and operating (MRO) products   Goods that a business customer consumes in a relatively short time.

marginal analysis   A method that uses cost and demand to identify the price that will maximize profits.

marginal cost   The increase in total cost that results from producing one additional unit of a product.

marginal revenue   The increase in total income or revenue that results from selling one additional unit of a product.

market   All the customers and potential customers who share a common need that can be satisfied by a specific product, who have the resources to exchange for it, who are willing to make the exchange, and who have the authority to make the exchange.

market development strategies   Growth strategies that introduce existing products to new markets.

market fragmentation   The creation of many consumer groups due to a diversity of distinct needs and wants in modern society.

market manager   An individual who is responsible for developing and implementing the marketing plans for products sold to a particular customer group.

market penetration strategies   Growth strategies designed to increase sales of existing products to current customers, nonusers, and users of competitive brands in served markets.

market position   The way in which the target market perceives the product in comparison to competitors' brands.

market segment   A distinct group of customers within a larger market who are similar to one another in some way and whose needs differ from other customers in the larger market.

marketing   An organizational function and a set of processes for creating, communicating and delivering value to customers and for managing customer relationships in ways that benefit the organization and its stakeholders.

marketing concept   A management orientation that focuses on identifying and satisfying consumer needs to ensure the organization's long-term profitability.

marketing decision support system (MDSS)   The data, analysis software, and interactive software that allow managers to conduct analyses and find the information they need.

marketing information system (MIS)   A procedure developed by a firm to continuously gather, sort, analyze, store, and distribute relevant and timely marketing information to its managers.

marketing intelligence system   A method by which marketers get information about everyday happenings in the marketing environment.

marketing mix   A combination of the product itself, the price of the product, the place where it is made available, and the activities that introduce it to consumers that creates a desired response among a set of predefined consumers.

marketing plan   A document that describes the marketing environment, outlines the marketing objectives and strategy, and identifies who will be responsible for carrying out each part of the marketing strategy.

marketing research   The process of collecting, analyzing, and interpreting data about customers, competitors, and the business environment in order to improve marketing effectiveness.

marketplace   Any location or medium used to conduct an exchange.

mass customization   An approach that modifies a basic good or service to meet the needs of an individual.

mass market   All possible customers in a market, regardless of the differences in their specific needs and wants.

materials handling   The moving of products into, within, and out of warehouses.

maturity stage   The third and longest stage in the product life cycle in which sales peak and profit margins narrow.

m-commerce   Promotional and other e-commerce activities transmitted over mobile phones and other mobile devices, such as personal digital assistants (PDAs).

media planning   The process of developing media objectives, strategies, and tactics for use in an advertising campaign.

media schedule   The plan that specifies the exact media to use and when.

medium   A communications vehicle through which a message is transmitted to a target audience.

merchandise agents or brokers Channel intermediaries that provide services in exchange for commissions but never take title to the product.

merchandise assortment The range of products sold.

merchandise breadth The number of different product lines available.

merchandise depth The variety of choices available for each specific product line.

merchandise mix The total set of all products offered for sale by a retailer, including all product lines sold to all consumer groups.

merchandising allowance Reimburses the retailer for in-store support of the product.

merchant wholesalers Intermediaries that buy goods from manufacturers (take title to them) and sell to retailers and other business-to-business customers.

message The communication in physical form that goes from a sender to a receiver.

metrosexual A man who is heterosexual, sensitive, educated, and an urban dweller who is in touch with his feminine side.

mission statement A formal statement in an organization's strategic plan that describes the overall purpose of the organization and what it intends to achieve in terms of its customers, products, and resources.

missionary salesperson A salesperson who promotes the firm and tries to stimulate demand for a product but does not actually complete a sale.

modified rebuy A buying situation classification used by business buyers to categorize a previously made purchase that involves some change and that requires limited decision making.

monopolistic competition A market structure in which many firms, each having slightly different products, offer unique consumer benefits.

monopoly A market situation in which one firm, the only supplier of a particular product, is able to control the price, quality, and supply of that product.

mores A custom with a strong moral overtone.

motivation An internal state that drives us to satisfy needs by activating goal-oriented behavior.

multilevel network A system in which a master distributor recruits other people to become distributors, sells the company's product to the recruits, and receives a commission on all the merchandise sold by the people recruited.

multiple sourcing The business practice of buying a particular product from many suppliers.

myths Stories containing symbolic elements that express the shared emotions and ideals of a culture.

N

national or manufacturer brands Brands that the manufacturer of the product owns.

nationalization A domestic government's takeover of a foreign company for its assets with some reimbursement, though often not for the full value.

need The recognition of any difference between a consumer's actual state and some ideal or desired state.

new era orientation A management philosophy in which marketing means a devotion to excellence in designing and producing products that benefit the customer plus the firm's employees, shareholders, and communities.

new-business salesperson The person responsible for finding new customers and calling on them to present the company's products or services.

new-task buy A new business-to-business purchase that is complex or risky and that requires extensive decision making.

noise Anything that interferes with effective communication.

noncumulative quantity discounts Discounts based only on the quantity purchased with individual orders.

nondurable goods Consumer products that provide benefits for a short time because they are consumed (such as food) or are no longer useful (such as newspapers).

nonprobability sample A sample in which personal judgment is used in selecting respondents.

nonstore retailing Any method used to complete an exchange with a product end user that does not require a customer visit to a store.

norms Specific rules dictating what is right or wrong, acceptable or unacceptable.

North American Free Trade Agreement (NAFTA) The world's largest economic community composed of the United States, Canada, and Mexico.

North American Industry Classification System (NAICS) The numerical coding system that the United States, Canada, and Mexico use to classify firms into detailed categories according to their business activities.

not-for-profit organizations/institutions Organizations with charitable, educational, community, and other public service goals that buy goods and services to support their functions and to attract and serve their members.

O

objective-task method A promotion budgeting method in which an organization first defines the specific communications goals it hopes to achieve and then tries to calculate what kind of promotional efforts it will take to meet these goals.

off-price retailers Retailers that buy excess merchandise from well-known manufacturers and pass the savings on to customers.

oligopoly A market structure in which a relatively small number of sellers, each holding a substantial share of the market, compete in a market with many buyers.

online auctions E-commerce that allows shoppers to purchase products through online bidding.

operant conditioning Learning that occurs as the result of rewards or punishments.

operational planning A decision process that focuses on developing detailed plans for day-to-day activities that carry out an organization's functional plans

operational plans Plans that focus on the day-to-day execution of the marketing plan. Operational plans include detailed directions for the specific activities to be carried out, who will be responsible for them, and timelines for accomplishing the tasks.

opinion leader A person who is frequently able to influence others' attitudes or behaviors by virtue of his or her active interest and expertise in one or more product categories.

order getter A salesperson who works to develop long-term relationships with particular customers or to generate new sales.

order taker A salesperson whose primary function is to facilitate transactions that the customer initiates.

organizational markets Another name for business-to-business markets.

out-of-home media A communication medium that reaches people in public places.

outsourcing The business buying process of obtaining outside vendors to provide goods or services that otherwise might be supplied in-house.

P

package The covering or container for a product that provides product protection, facilitates product use and storage, and supplies important marketing communication.

party plan system A sales technique that relies heavily on people getting caught up in the "group spirit," buying things they would not normally buy if alone.

patent Legal documentation granting an individual or firm exclusive rights to produce and sell a particular invention.

penetration pricing A pricing strategy in which a firm introduces a new product at a very low price to encourage more customers to purchase it.

perceived risk The belief that choice of a product has potentially negative consequences, either financial, physical, or social.

percentage-of-sales method A method for promotion budgeting that is based on a certain percentage of either last year's sales or on estimates for the present year's sales.

perception The process by which people select, organize, and interpret information from the outside world.

perceptual map A vivid way to construct a picture of where products or brands are "located" in consumers' minds.

perfect competition A market structure in which many small sellers, all of whom offer similar products, are unable to have an impact on the quality, price, or supply of a product.

perishability The characteristic of a service that makes it impossible to store for later sale or consumption.

permission marketing E-mail advertising where online consumers have the opportunity to accept or refuse the unsolicited e-mail.

personal selling Marketing communication by which a company representative interacts directly with a customer or prospective customer to communicate about a good or service.

personality The psychological characteristics that consistently influence the way a person responds to situations in his or her environment.

physical distribution The activities used to move finished goods from manufacturers to final customers, including order processing, warehousing, materials handling, transportation, and inventory control.

place marketing Marketing activities that seek to attract new businesses, residents, or visitors to a town, state, country, or some other site.

place The availability of the product to the customer at the desired time and location.

place-based media Advertising media that transmit messages in public places, such as doctors' offices and airports, where certain types of people congregate.

point-of-purchase (POP) promotion In-store displays or signs.

point-of-sale (POS) systems Retail computer systems that collect sales data and are hooked directly into the store's inventory control system.

popular culture The music, movies, sports, books, celebrities, and other forms of entertainment consumed by the mass market.

portfolio analysis A management tool for evaluating a firm's business mix and assessing the potential of an organization's strategic business units.

positioning Developing a marketing strategy aimed at influencing how a particular market segment perceives a good or service in comparison to the competition.

posttesting Research conducted on consumers' responses to actual advertising messages they have seen or heard.

preapproach A part of the selling process that includes developing information about prospective customers and planning the sales interview.

premiums Items offered free to people who have purchased a product.

press release Information that an organization distributes to the media intended to win publicity.

prestige products Products that have a high price and that appeal to status-conscious consumers.

pretesting A research method that seeks to minimize mistakes by getting consumer reactions to ad messages before they appear in the media.

price The assignment of value, or the amount the consumer must exchange to receive the offering.

price bundling Selling two or more goods or services as a single package for one price.

price elasticity of demand The percentage change in unit sales that results from a percentage change in price.

price fixing The collaboration of two or more firms in setting prices, usually to keep prices high.

price leadership A pricing strategy in which one firm first sets its price and other firms in the industry follow with the same or very similar prices.

price lining The practice of setting a limited number of different specific prices, called price points, for items in a product line.

primary data Data from research conducted to help in making a specific decision.

private exchanges Systems that link an invited group of suppliers and partners over the Web.

private-label brands Brands that are owned and sold by a certain retailer or distributor.

probability sample A sample in which each member of the population has some known chance of being included.

problem recognition The process that occurs whenever the consumer sees a significant difference between his or her current state of affairs and some desired or ideal state; this recognition initiates the decision-making process.

processed materials Products created when firms transform raw materials from their original state.

producers The individuals or organizations that purchase products for use in the production of other goods and services.

product A tangible good, service, idea, or some combination of these that satisfies consumer or business customer needs through the exchange process; a bundle of attributes including features, functions, benefits, and uses.

product adoption The process by which a consumer or business customer begins to buy and use a new good, service, or idea.

product advertising An advertising message that focuses on a specific good or service.

product category managers Individuals who are responsible for developing and implementing the marketing plan for all the brands and products within a product category.

product competition When firms offering different products compete to satisfy the same consumer needs and wants.

product concept development and screening The second step of product development in which marketers test product ideas for technical and commercial success.

product development strategies Growth strategies that focus on selling new products in served markets.

product life cycle A concept that explains how products go through four distinct stages from birth to death: introduction, growth, maturity, and decline.

product line A firm's total product offering designed to satisfy a single need or desire of target customers.

product mix The total set of all products a firm offers for sale.

product specifications A written description of the quality, size, weight, and so forth required of a product purchase.

production orientation A management philosophy that emphasizes the most efficient ways to produce and distribute products.

projective techniques Tests that marketers use to explore people's underlying feelings about a product, especially appropriate when consumers are unable or unwilling to express their true reactions.

promotion The coordination of a marketer's marketing communications efforts to influence attitudes or behavior; the coordination of efforts by a marketer to inform or persuade consumers or organizations about goods, services, or ideas.

promotion mix The major elements of marketer-controlled communications, including advertising, sales promotions, public relations, and personal selling.

promotional products Goodies such as coffee mugs, T-shirts, and magnets given away to build awareness for a sponsor. Some freebies are distributed directly to consumers and business customers; others are intended for channel partners such as retailers and vendors.

prospecting A part of the selling process that includes identifying and developing a list of potential or prospective customers.

protectionism A policy adopted by a government to give domestic companies an advantage.

prototypes Test versions of a proposed product.

psychographics The use of psychological, sociological, and anthropological factors to construct market segments.

public relations (PR) Communication function that seeks to build good relationships with an organization's publics, including consumers, stockholders, and legislators.

public service advertisements (PSAs) Advertising run by the media without charge for not-for-profit organizations or to champion a particular cause.

publicity Unpaid communication about an organization appearing in the mass media.

puffery Claims made in advertising of product superiority that cannot be proven true or untrue.

pull strategy The company tries to move its products through the channel by building desire for the products among consumers, thus convincing retailers to respond to this demand by stocking these items.

push money A bonus paid by a manufacturer to a salesperson, customer, or distributor for selling its product.

push strategy The company tries to move its products through the channel by convincing channel members to offer them.

pyramid schemes An illegal sales technique in which the initial distributors profit by selling merchandise to other distributors, with the result that consumers buy very little product.

Q

qualify prospects A part of the selling process that determines how likely prospects are to become customers.

quantity discounts A pricing tactic of charging reduced prices for purchases of larger quantities of a product.

R

raw materials Products of the fishing, lumber, agricultural, and mining industries that organizational customers purchase to use in their finished products.

reach The percentage of the target market that will be exposed to the media vehicle.

rebates Sales promotions that allow the customer to recover part of the product's cost from the manufacturer.

receiver The organization or individual that intercepts and interprets the message.

reciprocity A trading partnership in which two firms agree to buy from one another.

reference group An actual or imaginary individual or group that has a significant effect on an individual's evaluations, aspirations, or behavior.

relationship selling A form of personal selling that involves securing, developing, and maintaining long-term relationships with profitable customers.

reliability The extent to which research measurement techniques are free of errors.

repositioning Redoing a product's position to respond to marketplace changes.

representativeness The extent to which consumers in a study are similar to a larger group in which the organization has an interest.

research design A plan that specifies what information marketers will collect and what type of study they will do.

resellers The individuals or organizations that buy finished goods for the purpose of reselling, renting, or leasing to others to make a profit and to maintain their business operations.

retail life cycle A theory that focuses on the various stages that retailers pass through from introduction to decline.

retailing The final stop in the distribution channel by which goods and services are sold to consumers for their personal use.

return on investment (ROI) The direct financial impact of a firm's expenditure of a resource such as time or money.

reverse marketing A business practice in which a buyer firm attempts to identify suppliers who will produce products according to the buyer firm's specifications.

S

sales management The process of planning, implementing, and controlling the personal selling function of an organization.

sales presentation The part of the selling process in which the salesperson directly communicates the value proposition to the customer, inviting two-way communication.

sales promotion Programs designed to build interest in or encourage purchase of a product during a specified time period.

sales territory A set of customers often defined by geographic boundaries for whom a particular salesperson is responsible.

sampling Distributing free trial-size versions of a product to consumers.

scenarios Possible future situations that futurists use to assess the likely impact of alternative marketing strategies.

scrambled merchandising A merchandising strategy that offers consumers a mixture of merchandise items that are not directly related to each other.

search qualities Product characteristics that the consumer can examine prior to purchase.

secondary data Data that have been collected for some purpose other than the problem at hand.

segment profile A description of the "typical" customer in a segment.

segmentation The process of dividing a larger market into smaller pieces based on one or more meaningful, shared characteristics.

segmentation variables Dimensions that divide the total market into fairly homogeneous groups, each with different needs and preferences.

selective distribution Distribution using fewer outlets than in intensive distribution but more than in exclusive distribution.

self-concept An individual's self-image that is composed of a mixture of beliefs, observations, and feelings about personal attributes.

selling orientation A managerial view of marketing as a sales function, or a way to move products out of warehouses to reduce inventory.

service encounter The actual interaction between the customer and the service provider.

services Intangible products that are exchanged directly from the producer to the customer.

servicescape The actual physical facility where the service is performed, delivered, and consumed.

sex roles Society's expectations regarding the appropriate attitudes, behaviors, and appearance for men and women.

share of customer The percentage of an individual customer's purchase of a product that is a single brand.

shopping product A good or service for which consumers spend considerable time and effort gathering information and comparing alternatives before making a purchase.

single sourcing The business practice of buying a particular product from only one supplier.

single-source data Information that is integrated from large consumer panels comprised of people who agree to participate in ongoing research.

skimming price A very high, premium price that a firm charges for its new, highly desirable product.

slotting allowance A fee paid by a manufacturer to a retailer in exchange for agreeing to place products on the retailer's shelves.

social class The overall rank or social standing of groups of people within a society according to the value assigned to such factors as family background, education, occupation, and income.

social profit The benefit an organization and society receive from the organization's ethical practices, community service, efforts to promote cultural diversity, and concern for the natural environment.

social responsibility A management practice in which organizations seek to engage in activities that have a positive effect on society and promote the public good.

source An organization or individual that sends a message.

specialized services Services purchased from outside suppliers that are essential to the operation of an organization but are not part of the production of a product.

specialty product A good or service that has unique characteristics and is important to the buyer and for which the buyer will devote significant effort to acquire.

specialty stores Retailers that carry only a few product lines but offer good selection within the lines that they sell.

sponsorships PR activities through which companies provide financial support to help fund an event in return for publicized recognition of the company's contribution.

stakeholders Buyers, sellers, investors in a company, community residents, and even citizens of the nations where goods and services are made or sold—in other words, any person or organization that has a "stake" in the outcomes.

standard of living An indicator of the average quality and quantity of goods and services consumed in a country.

stimulus generalization Behavior caused by a reaction to one stimulus occurs in the presence of other, similar stimuli.

store image The way a retailer is perceived in the marketplace relative to the competition.

straight rebuy A buying situation in which business buyers make routine purchases that require minimal decision making.

strategic alliance Relationship developed between a firm seeking a deeper commitment to a foreign market and a domestic firm in the target country.

strategic business units Individual units within the firm that operate like separate businesses, with each having its own mission, business objectives, resources, managers, and competitors.

strategic planning A managerial decision process that matches an organization's resources and capabilities to its market opportunities for long-term growth and survival.

subculture A group within a society whose members share a distinctive set of beliefs, characteristics, or common experiences.

supermarkets Food stores that carry a wide selection of edibles and related products.

supply chain All the firms that engage in activities necessary to turn raw materials into a good or service and put it in the hands of the consumer or business customer.

supply chain management The management of flows among firms in the supply chain to maximize total profitability.

SWOT analysis An analysis of an organization's strengths and weaknesses and the opportunities and threats in its external environment.

syndicated research Research by firms that collect data on a regular basis and sell the reports to multiple firms.

T

take title To accept legal ownership of a product and the accompanying rights and responsibilities of ownership.

target costing A process in which firms identify the quality and functionality needed to satisfy customers and what price they are willing to pay before the product is designed; the product is manufactured only if the firm can control costs to meet the required price.

target market A group or groups that a firm selects to turn into customers as a result of segmentation and targeting.

target marketing strategy Dividing the total market into different segments on the basis of customer characteristics, selecting one or more segments, and developing products to meet the needs of those specific segments.

tariffs Taxes on imported goods.

team selling The sales function when handled by a team that may consist of a salesperson, a technical specialist, and others.

technical development The step in the product development process in which a new product is refined and perfected by company engineers and the like.

technical specialist A sales support person with a high level of technical expertise who assists in product demonstrations.

telemarketing The use of the telephone to sell directly to consumers and business customers.

top-down budgeting techniques Allocation of the promotion budget based on the total amount to be devoted to marketing communications.

total costs The total of the fixed costs and the variable costs for a set number of units produced.

total quality management (TQM) A management philosophy that focuses on satisfying customers through empowering employees to be an active part of continuous quality improvement.

trade area A geographic zone that accounts for the majority of a store's sales and customers.

trade or functional discounts Discounts off list price of products to members of the channel of distribution that perform various marketing functions.

trade promotions Promotions that focus on members of the "trade," which includes distribution channel members, such as retail salespeople or wholesale distributors, that a firm must work with in order to sell its products.

trade shows Events at which many companies set up elaborate exhibits to show their products, give away samples, distribute product literature, and troll for new business contacts.

trademark The legal term for a brand name, brand mark, or trade character; trademarks legally registered by a government obtain protection for exclusive use in that country.

traffic flow The direction in which shoppers will move through the store and what areas they will pass or avoid.

transactional data An ongoing record of individuals or organizations that buy a product.

transactional selling A form of personal selling that focuses on making an immediate sale with little or no attempt to develop a relationship with the customer.

trial pricing Pricing a new product low for a limited period of time in order to lower the risk for a customer.

U

unaided recall A research technique conducted by telephone survey or personal interview that asks whether a person remembers seeing an ad during a specified period of time.

undifferentiated targeting strategy Appealing to a broad spectrum of people.

unfair sales acts State laws that prohibit suppliers from selling products below cost to protect small businesses from larger competitors.

uniform delivered pricing A pricing tactic in which a firm adds a standard shipping charge to the price for all customers regardless of location.

unique selling proposition (USP) An advertising appeal that focuses on one clear reason why a particular product is superior.

Universal Product Code (UPC) The set of black bars or lines printed on the side or bottom of most items sold in grocery stores and other mass-merchandising outlets. The UPC, readable by scanners, creates a national system of product identification.

unsought products Goods or services for which a consumer has little awareness or interest until the product or a need for the product is brought to his or her attention.

usage occasions An indicator used in one type of market segmentation based on when consumers use a product most.

utility The usefulness or benefit consumers receive from a product.

V

validity The extent to which research actually measures what it was intended to measure.

VALS™ (Values and Lifestyles) A psychographic system that divides the entire U.S. population into eight segments.

value The benefits a customer receives from buying a product or service.

value chain A series of activities involved in designing, producing, marketing, delivering, and supporting any product. Each link in the chain has the potential to either add or remove value from the product the customer eventually buys.

value pricing or everyday low pricing (EDLP) A pricing strategy in which a firm sets prices that provide ultimate value to customers.

value proposition A marketplace offering that fairly and accurately sums up the value that will be realized if the product or service is purchased.

variability The characteristic of a service that means that even the same service performed by the same individual for the same customer can vary.

variable costs The costs of production (raw and processed materials, parts, and labor) that are tied to and vary depending on the number of units produced.

venture teams Groups of people within an organization who work together focusing exclusively on the development of a new product.

vertical marketing system (VMS) A channel of distribution in which there is formal cooperation among members at the manufacturing, wholesaling, and retailing levels.

viral marketing Marketing activity in which a company recruits customers to be sales agents and spread the word about the product.

W

want The desire to satisfy needs in specific ways that are culturally and socially influenced.

warehouse clubs Discount retailers that charge a modest membership fee to consumers that buy a broad assortment of food and nonfood items in bulk and in a warehouse environment.

warehousing Storing goods in anticipation of sale or transfer to another member of the channel of distribution.

wheel-of-retailing hypothesis A theory that explains how retail firms change, becoming more upscale as they go through their life cycle.

wholesaling intermediaries Firms that handle the flow of products from the manufacturer to the retailer or business user.

World Trade Organization (WTO) An organization that replaced GATT, the WTO sets trade rules for its member nations and mediates disputes between nations.

world trade The flow of goods and services among different countries—the value of all the exports and imports of the world's nations.

Y

yield management pricing A practice of charging different prices to different customers in order to manage capacity while maximizing revenues.

CREDITS

CHAPTER 1

1 Courtesy of Monster and Jeff Taylor. ©2004 Monster. All Rights Reserved; **6** Courtesy of Johnson & Johnson; **8** © The Procter & Gamble Company. Used by permission; **9** Elnora Stuart; **9** David Young-Wolff/PhotoEdit; **10** Courtesy of the National Peanut Board; **10** AP Wide World Photos; **11** Courtesy of the Oregon Zoo and Cole and Weber. Photographer: Lars Topleman **12** Used with permission of the National Sports Center of the Disabled; **16** Courtesy of Tchoia Brown; **16** Courtesy of Professor Linda Jane Coleman; **16** Courtesy of Robert J. Strassheim; **17** Courtesy of The Center for Consumer Freedom; **18** Courtesy of Under Armour. Photographer: Brendan Mattingly Photography; **19** Used with permission of the Tourism Authority of Thailand; **22** Ford Motor Company; **23** Courtesy of Reflect; **24** Courtesy of Oris USA Inc.; **26** Courtesy of Monster and Jeff Taylor. ©2004 Monster. All Rights Reserved

CHAPTER 2

32 Courtesy of Under Armour; **40** © Procter & Gamble Company, Inc. All rights reserved; **44** Courtesy of Amethyst Howell; **44** Courtesy of Professor Dan Robertson; **46** Courtesy of Under Armour. Photographer: Brendan Mattingly; **47** Getty Images, Inc.; **49** Courtesy of the Xerox Corporation; **52** © 2004 Maxell Corporation of America. All rights reserved; **55** © Kraft Foods, Inc. Mr. Peanut® is a registered trademark of Kraft Foods, Inc. All rights reserved; **56** Courtesy of Under Armour

CHAPTER 3

62 Courtesy of SweatX and Rick Roth; **70** Courtesy of the Muir Heritage Land Trust; **71** Denny's; **74** MTV, Music Television; **75** © Continental Corporation. All rights reserved; **79** AP Wide World Photos; **80** © Sunkist Growers, Inc. All rights reserved; **82** J. Nordell/The Image Works; **83** Courtesy of Hyun-Joo Rachel Lee; **83** Courtesy of Carlos M. Rodriguez; **83** Courtesy of Sandie Lakin; **84** AP Wide World Photos; **87** © P. Samuelsson. Toyota Iceland. Photographer Ragnar Th Sigurdsson. Courtesy of Islenska auglysingastofan ehf; **88** © HSBC. All rights reserved; **89** © Adidas. All rights reserved; **90** © DHL International, Ltd. All rights reserved; **91** Courtesy of SweatX and Rick Roth

CHAPTER 4

98 Courtesy of RBC Centura Bank and Cathy Burrows; **104** Ford Motor Company; **109** © DaimlerChrysler. All rights reserved; **112** Used with permission of Jerry Zaltman; **113** © Delve. All rights reserved; **115** © Diesel. All rights reserved. Courtesy KesselsKramer, Amsterdam; **118** Mark Graham; **119** Matrix International, Inc.; **120** Reprinted from *Marketing Tools* magazine, January/February, 1998; **123** Photo Researchers, Inc.; **125** © Harris Interactive. All rights reserved; **126** © Coremetrics, Inc. All rights reserved; **126** © MCI. All rights reserved; **127** © Coremetrics, Inc. All rights reserved; **127** © MCI. All rights reserved; **128** Courtesy of Adel Sakr; **128** Courtesy of Professor Nancy M. Puccinelli; **129** Courtesy of RBC Centura Bank and Cathy Burrows

CHAPTER 5

134 Courtesy of Wild Planet and Daniel Grossman, CEO; **140** Used with permission of Konica Minolta Corporation. All rights reserved; **142** © 2004 Ask Jeeves, Inc. All rights reserved; **143** © 2004 General Motors. All rights reserved; **146** © 2004 General Motors. All rights reserved; **148** Alvarez; **149** © Allen Edmonds. All rights reserved; **151** © Holland America. All rights reserved; **153** AP Wide World Photos; **155** AP Wide World Photos; **156** Courtesy of Dr. Paul G. Farnham; **157** Courtesy of Dr. David L. Moore; **157** Courtesy of Dr. Jeff Murray; **157** Courtesy of Diane H. Sappenfield; **157** Courtesy of Professor Susan Geringer; **159** Schick; **160** Courtesy of Hollywood Stock Exchange; Solomon Boovin; **161** Courtesy of Wild Planet and Daniel Grossman, CEO

CHAPTER 6

166 Courtesy of E. I. duPont de Nemours and Company and Steve McCracken. Corian® is a registered trademark of E. I. duPont de Nemours and Company. All rights reserved; **169** Courtesy of WestLB AG; **172** Used with permission of Central States Fire Apparatus; **175** Courtesy of Dassault Aviation; **176** Courtesy of FedBizOpps; **177** © DHL International, Ltd. All rights reserved; **178** Courtesy of the Xerox Corporation; **178** © General Electric Company. All rights reserved; **179** Courtesy of Alka Varma Citrin; **179** Courtesy of Eshan Salek; **181** © VERITAS Software Company. All rights reserved; **185** © Rackspace Managed Hosting. All rights reserved; **186** © Groove Networks, Inc. All rights reserved; **188** Courtesy of E. I. duPont de Nemours and Company and Steve McCracken. Corian® is a registered trademark of E. I. duPont de Nemours and Company. All rights reserved

CHAPTER 7

194 © Reebok International, Ltd. All rights reserved; **199** © 2004 VANS, Inc. All rights reserved; **200** © Avon Products, Inc. All rights reserved; **201** © 2004 FX Networks. All rights reserved; **202** ™ & © 2002, 2003, 2004 Burger King Brands, Inc. (USA only); **207** © palm One, Inc. All rights reserved. Courtesy of AKQA; **208** © 2004 Tropicana Products, Inc.; **209** Courtesy of Kelly Birchler; **209** Courtesy of Professor Joan Giese; **209** Courtesy of Dr. Erin Wilkinson; **213** © 2004 BC Ethic USA. All rights reserved; **214** © Exxon Mobil Corporation. All rights reserved. Courtesy of McCann-Erickson Rio; **216** © Maui and Sons. All rights reserved. Courtesy of Zegers DDB; **218** © 2004 Siebel Systems, Inc. All Rights Reserved; **221** © Reebok International, Ltd. All rights reserved

CHAPTER 8

226 Courtesy of The Black & Decker Corporation and Eleni Rossides. Black & Decker®, SteamBuster®, ScumBuster®, and DustBuster® are registered trademarks of The Black & Decker Corporation. All rights reserved;

234 © 2004 Samsung Electronics. All rights reserved; 235 © 2004 Johnson & Johnson. All rights reserved; 236 Sony Electronics Inc.; 240 Jessica Wecker Photography; 242 Corbis/SABA Press Photos, Inc.; 244 Courtesy of Tracy Rickman; 244 Courtesy of Ted Atkinson; 245 Courtesy of Texwood. Used with permission of Ogilvy & Mather, Hong Kong; 246 Courtesy of Greenfield Online, Inc.; 247 © 2004 Pfizer Inc. All rights reserved; 249 Courtesy of Michelle Beauty Centre. Used with permission of Ogilvy & Mather, Hong Kong; 250 Courtesy of White Wave, Inc. Used with permission of Arnold Worldwide; 253 Courtesy of Swatchplanet.com. All rights reserved; 254 Courtesy of Deere & Company, Moline, IL; 255 Courtesy of The Black & Decker Corporation and Eleni Rossides. Black & Decker®, SteamBuster®, ScumBuster®, and DustBuster® are registered trademarks of The Black & Decker Corporation. All rights reserved

CHAPTER 9

260 Courtesy of Nissan USA and Mario A. Polit; 264 MINI USA; 267 © 2004 Toshiba America, Inc. All rights reserved; 268 © Fuji Photo Film (UK) Ltd. All rights reserved; 271 © 2004 Planet Feedback. All rights reserved; 275 Courtesy of Brian Larson; 275 Courtesy of Michael Munro; 276 American Alphabet © 2004 Heidi Cody; 279 © 2004 Bayer Corporation. All rights reserved; 281 National Pictures/Topham/The Image Works; 284 © Playtex Products, Inc. All rights reserved; 286 Courtesy of Nissan USA and Mario A. Polit

CHAPTER 10

292 Courtesy of Universal Orlando® and Robyn Eichenholz. © Universal Studios. All rights reserved; 296 © City Harvest. All rights reserved. Special thanks to Harrison Ford. Photo: Timothy White; 298 Courtesy of Avis; 299 Courtesy of Mastercard; 303 Courtesy of todaysmilitary.com, U.S. Department of Defense; 304 Michael Stravato/The New York Times; 305 © Napster, LLC. All rights reserved; 306 © Shangri-La Hotels and Resorts. All rights reserved; 307 Reprinted with permission; 311 Courtesy of Laura Borden; 311 Courtesy of Janice M. Karlen; 312 © 2004 Veterinary Pet Services, Inc. All rights reserved; 313 © (Beyoncé with Pepsi) 2004 PepsiCo, Inc. All rights reserved; 313 (Beyoncé at Superbowl) Globe Photos, Inc.; 314 © India Department of Tourism. All rights reserved; 315 The Richards Group; 316 Courtesy of Universal Orlando® and Robyn Eichenholz

CHAPTER 11

323 Courtesy of TACO BELL Corp. ©2004 TACO BELL Corp. All rights reserved; 323 Courtesy of TACO BELL Corp. and Danielle Blugrind. ©2004 TACO BELL Corp. All rights reserved; 325 MADD; 327 © The Dial Corporation. All rights reserved; 328 Courtesy of Seiko Epson Corp.; 333 © Toyota Motor Sales, U.S.A., Inc. All rights reserved; 338 © Daffy's. All rights reserved; 339 © LG Electronics. All rights reserved; 340 © Ariba Inc. All rights reserved; 341 © Dell Inc. All rights reserved; 343 Courtesy of Seiko Epson Corp.; 346 Courtesy of the American Suzuki Motor Corporation; 347 © The Gillette Company. All rights reserved; 350 Intellectual copyrights by Hans Kroeskamp Photography; 351 Courtesy of Deborah Boyce; 351 Courtesy of Jennifer Mosley; 351 Courtesy of Merv Yeagle; 354 Courtesy of TACO BELL Corp. ©2004 TACO BELL Corp. All rights reserved; 354 Courtesy of TACO BELL Corp. and Danielle Blugrind. ©2004 TACO BELL Corp. All rights reserved

CHAPTER 12

360 Courtesy of Bojangles' Restaurants, Inc., and Price McNabb, Inc.; 360 Courtesy of Bojangles' Restaurants, Inc., Price McNabb, Inc., and Matt Ferguson.; 363 © Beach 'N Billboard. All rights reserved; 366 © OMEGA Ltd. All rights reserved; 367 © Pharmavite LLC. All rights reserved; 368 Courtesy of Sherif Fahmy; 368 Courtesy of Professor Debbie Laverie; 368 Courtesy of Thomas Tanner; 370 © Skechers USA, Inc. All rights reserved; 371 Used with permission of KitchenAid Home Appliances; 373 John Barrett/Globe Photos, Inc.; 377 © Procter & Gamble Company, Inc. All rights reserved; 379 Altoids/Hunter & Associates; 380 Courtesy of McNeil; 383 © Active Decisions, Inc. All rights reserved; 384 © 2004 Eddie Bauer, Inc. All rights reserved; 385 Courtesy of Demik Labs; 387 © Bojangles' Restaurants, Inc. All rights reserved; 387 Courtesy of Bojangles' Restaurants, Inc., Price McNabb, Inc., and Matt Ferguson

CHAPTER 13

392 Courtesy of Jerry Epstein, Zeno Group, and SIRIUS Satellite Radio; 396 © The Stride Rite Corporation. All rights reserved. 397 Courtesy of the American Lung Association and Glaxo Smith Kline; 398 Courtesy of the Office of National Drug Control Policy; 400 © The Clorox Company. All rights reserved; 401 Courtesy of Jung von Matt and CinemaxX Cinema GmbH & Co.; 404 Seaworld; 404 Leo Burnett/Madrid; 410 © The Clorox Company. All rights reserved; 413 © Intel Corporation. All rights reserved; 413 Oscar Mayer Foods; 414 Thomas Johnson/Camera 1; 415 Courtesy of Conrod Kelly; 415 Courtesy of Shelly McCallum; 417 © Ronco Inventions, LLC All rights reserved. Courtesy of R. P. Productions; 418 © 2004 Samsung Telecommunications American LLP. All rights reserved; 420 Courtesy of Jerry Epstein, Zeno Group, and SIRIUS Satellite Radio

CHAPTER 14

426 Courtesy of IBM Corp. and Ogilvy & Mather. © 2004 International Business Machines Corporation. All rights reserved 426 Courtesy of IBM Corp. and Esther Ferre. © 2004 International Business Machines Corporation. All rights reserved; 432 Jim Beam Bourbon/Joseph D'Amore; 433 © 2004 3M Corporation. All rights reserved; 434 Used with permission of Chiquita ® Brands; 436 © Copyright 1996-2004, Visa International Service Association. Copyright © 2004 Hard Candy, LLC. All rights reserved; 441 © 2004 Accela Communications. All rights reserved; 442 Copyright © 2004, FrontRange Solutions Inc. All Rights Reserved; 443 © Copyright 2004 Serious Magic. All Rights Reserved; 445 Copyright © 2004 WebEx Communications, Inc. All rights reserved; 446 Courtesy of Mike Gates; 446 Courtesy of Katherine Grahsler; 447 Courtesy of Gundars Kaupins; 447 © 2004 Synygy, Inc., All Rights Reserved; 448 © 2004 Cunard. All rights reserved; 449 Courtesy of IBM Corp. and Ogilvy & Mather. © 2004 International Business Machines Corporation. All rights reserved; 449 Courtesy of IBM Corp. and Esther Ferre

CHAPTER 15

454 Courtesy of VF Corporation and Mackey McDonald; 457 Courtesy of Alanis Morrisette and Maverick Records. © The Convex Group. All rights reserved; 460 David Lassman/The Image Works; 463 AP Wide World Photos; 464 Courtesy of Robert Cosenza; 464 Courtesy of Theodore Wallin; 466 AP Wide World Photos; 467 © ERA Franchise Systems, Inc. All rights reserved; 470 Larry Ford Foto; 472 © 2004 AstraZeneca. All rights reserved; 474 © Blue Diamond Growers. All rights reserved; 477 (NY Yankees and NY Mets logos) Major League Baseball Properties, Inc.; 478 Scion is a Marque Of Toyota Motor Sales, U.S.A., Inc. © Toyota Motor Sales, U.S.A., Inc. All rights reserved; 479 Courtesy of Haggar Clothing Co.; 481 © Copyright 2004 Menlo

Worldwide. All Rights Reserved; **484** Maersk Sealand; **484** Courtesy of VF Corporation and Mackey McDonald

CHAPTER 16

490 Courtesy of Limited Brands. © 2004 Limited Brands. All rights reserved; **490** Courtesy of Limited Brands and Subha Ramesh. © 2004 Limited Brands. All rights reserved; **494** Pier 1 Imports; **496** Cummins/CORBIS-NY; **497** AP Wide World Photos; **499** Courtesy of Kohl's Department Stores; **501** 7-11 Inc.; **502** Photo courtesy of Costco Wholesale; **504** Courtesy of the Tupperware Corporation; **505** AP Wide World Photos; **506** © 2004 Lands' End, Inc., and My Virtual Model™. All rights reserved; **510** © Citigroup. All rights reserved; **511** Courtesy of Lisa Gangadeen; **511** Courtesy of Tom Lacny; **511** Courtesy of Eric Nelson; **511** Courtesy of Professor W. Rocky Newman; **512** © 2004 Hot Topic Inc. All rights reserved; **513** Corbis/Bettmann; **514** Corbis/Bettmann; **518** (Boston Quincy Market) Peter Arnold, Inc.; **518** (Mall of America) Getty Images Inc.-Stone Allstock; **518** D. Young-Wolf/PhotoEdit; **518** Michael Newman/PhotoEdit; **513** (Kids "R" Us and Target) PhotoEdit; **520** Courtesy of Limited Brands. © 2004 Limited Brands. All rights reserved; **520** Courtesy of Limited Brands and Subha Ramesh

INDEX

COMPANY/NAME INDEX

(Page numbers followed by italic "f" indicate illustrations, page numbers followed by italic "t" indicate tables)

SUBJECT INDEX